Lecture Notes in Computer Science   13826

Founding Editors

Gerhard Goos
Juris Hartmanis

Editorial Board Members

The series Lecture Notes in Computer Science (LNCS), including its subseries Lecture Notes in Artificial Intelligence (LNAI) and Lecture Notes in Bioinformatics (LNBI), has established itself as a medium for the publication of new developments in computer science and information technology research, teaching, and education.

LNCS enjoys close cooperation with the computer science R & D community, the series counts many renowned academics among its volume editors and paper authors, and collaborates with prestigious societies. Its mission is to serve this international community by providing an invaluable service, mainly focused on the publication of conference and workshop proceedings and postproceedings. LNCS commenced publication in 1973.

Roman Wyrzykowski · Jack Dongarra ·
Ewa Deelman · Konrad Karczewski
Editors

Parallel Processing and Applied Mathematics

14th International Conference, PPAM 2022
Gdansk, Poland, September 11–14, 2022
Revised Selected Papers, Part I

 Springer

Editors
Roman Wyrzykowski
Czestochowa University of Technology
Czestochowa, Poland

Jack Dongarra
University of Tennessee
Knoxville, TN, USA

Ewa Deelman
University of Southern California
Marina del Rey, CA, USA

Konrad Karczewski
Czestochowa University of Technology
Czestochowa, Poland

ISSN 0302-9743   ISSN 1611-3349 (electronic)
Lecture Notes in Computer Science
ISBN 978-3-031-30441-5   ISBN 978-3-031-30442-2 (eBook)
https://doi.org/10.1007/978-3-031-30442-2

This Springer imprint is published by the registered company Springer Nature Switzerland AG
The registered company address is: Gewerbestrasse 11, 6330 Cham, Switzerland

Preface

This volume comprises the proceedings of the 14th International Conference on Parallel Processing and Applied Mathematics – PPAM 2022, which was held in Gdańsk, Poland, September 11–14, 2022. It was organized by the Department of Computer Science of the Częstochowa University of Technology together with the Gdańsk University of Technology, under the patronage of the Committee of Informatics of the Polish Academy of Sciences, in technical cooperation with the Poznań Supercomputing and Networking Center. Scheduled initially for the year 2021, the fourteenth edition of PPAM was postponed to 2022 because of the COVID-19 pandemic. PPAM 2022 was primarily an in-person event. However, the organizers also made provision for authors and delegates to present, attend, and interact online.

PPAM is a biennial conference. Thirteen previous events have been held in different places in Poland since 1994, when the first conference took place in Częstochowa. The proceedings of the last ten conferences have been published by Springer in the Lecture Notes in Computer Science series (Nałęczów, 2001, vol. 2328; Częstochowa, 2003, vol. 3019; Poznań, 2005, vol. 3911; Gdańsk, 2007, vol. 4967; Wrocław, 2009, vols. 6067 and 6068; Toruń, 2011, vols. 7203 and 7204; Warsaw, 2013, vols. 8384 and 8385; Kraków, 2015, vols. 9573 and 9574; Lublin, 2017, vols. 10777 and 10778; Białystok, 2019, vols. 12043 and 12044.

The PPAM conferences have become an international forum for exchanging ideas between researchers involved in parallel and distributed computing, including theory and applications, as well as applied and computational mathematics. The focus of PPAM 2022 was on models, algorithms, and software tools that facilitate efficient and convenient utilization of modern parallel and distributed computing architectures, as well as on large-scale applications, including artificial intelligence and machine learning problems. Special attention was given to the future of computing beyond Moore's Law.

This meeting gathered about 170 participants from 25 countries, including about 130 in-person participants. One hundred thirty-two articles were submitted for review. Each paper secured at least three single-blind reviews from program committee members. A thorough peer-reviewing process that included discussion and agreement among reviewers whenever necessary resulted in the acceptance of 76 contributed papers for publication in the conference proceedings. For regular conference tracks, 33 papers were selected from 62 submissions, giving an acceptance rate of about 53%.

The regular tracks covered such important fields of parallel/distributed/cloud computing and applied mathematics as:

- Numerical algorithms and parallel scientific computing
- GPU computing
- Parallel non-numerical algorithms
- Performance analysis and prediction in HPC (high performance computing) systems
- Scheduling for parallel computing
- Environments and frameworks for parallel/cloud computing

- Applications of parallel and distributed computing
- Soft computing with applications

The keynote talks were presented by:

- Anima Anandkumar from the California Institute of Technology and Nvidia (USA)
- Hartwig Anzt from the Karlsruhe Institute of Technology (Germany) and University of Tennessee (USA)
- Ivona Brandic from the Vienna University of Technology (Austria)
- Ümit V. Çatalyürek from Georgia Institute of Technology (USA)
- Jack Dongarra from the University of Tennessee and ORNL (USA)
- Torsten Hoefler from ETH Zurich (Switzerland)
- Georg Hager from the University of Erlangen-Nuremberg (Germany)
- Simon Knowles from Graphcore (UK)
- Satoshi Matsuoka from the Tokyo Institute of Technology (Japan)
- Michał Mrozek from Intel (Poland)
- Simon McIntosh-Smith from the University of Bristol (UK)
- Manish Parashar from Rutgers University (USA)
- Voica Radescu from IBM (Germany)
- Enrique S. Quintana-Orti from the Universitat Politècnica de València (Spain)
- John Shalf from the Lawrence Berkeley National Laboratory (USA)
- Michela Taufer from the University of Tennessee (USA)
- Christian Terboven from RWTH Aachen (Germany)
- Manuel Ujaldon from the University of Malaga Nvidia

Important and integral parts of the PPAM 2022 conference were the workshops:

- The 9th Workshop on Language-Based Parallel Programming (WLPP 2022) organized by Ami Marowka from the Bar-Ilan University (Israel).
- The 6th Workshop on Models, Algorithms and Methodologies for Hybrid Parallelism in New HPC Systems (MAMHYP 2022) organized by Marco Lapegna, Giulliano Laccetti and Valeria Mele from the University of Naples Federico II (Italy), Raffaele Montella from the University of Naples "Parthenope" (Italy), and Sokol Kosta from Aalborg University Copenhagen (Denmark).
- The First Workshop on Quantum Computing and Communication organized by Krzysztof Kurowski, Cezary Mazurek, and Piotr Rydlichowski from the Poznań Supercomputing and Networking Center (Poland)
- The First Workshop on Applications of Machine Learning and Artificial Intelligence in High Performance Computing organized by Sergio Iserte from the Universitat Jaume I (Spain) and Krzysztof Rojek from the Częstochowa University of Technology (Poland).
- The 9th Workshop on Scheduling for Parallel Computing organized by Maciej Drozdowski from the Poznań University of Technology (Poland).
- The 4th Workshop on Applied High Performance Numerical Algorithms for PDEs organized by Piotr Krzyżanowski and Leszek Marcinkowski from Warsaw University (Poland), Talal Rahman from Bergen University College (Norway), and Jan Valdman from the University of South Bohemia (Czech Republic).

- The 5th Minisymposium on HPC Applications in Physical Sciences organized by Grzegorz Kamieniarz and Michał Antkowiak from Adam Mickiewicz University in Poznan (Poland).
- The 8th Minisymposium on High Performance Computing Interval Methods organized by Bartłomiej J. Kubica from the Warsaw University of Technology (Poland).
- The 7th Workshop on Complex Collective Systems organized by Jarosław Wąs from the AGH University of Science and Technology (Poland), Tomasz Gwizdałła from the University of Łódz (Poland) and Krzysztof Małecki from the West Pomeranian University of Technology (Poland).

The PPAM 2022 meeting began with four tutorials:

- Introduction to Programming Graphcore IPU, by Graphcore (Pawel Gepner team).
- Fundamentals of Deep Learning using the Nvidia Deep Learning Institute infrastructure, by Manuel Ujaldon from the University of Malaga (Spain) and Nvidia.
- Quantum Computing, by IBM, and Poznań Supercomputing and Networking Center (Poland).
- LUMI European Pre-Exascale Supercomputer Hands-on, by Maciej Szpindler and Marek Magryś from the Academic Computer Centre Cyfronet AGH (Poland).

The PPAM Best Paper Award is given upon recommendation of the PPAM Chairs and Program Committee in recognition of the research paper quality, originality, and significance of the work in high performance computing. For the main track, the PPAM 2022 winners were:

- Rafael Ravedutti Lucio Machado, Jan Eitzinger, Harald Köstler and Gerhard Wellein from the University of Erlangen-Nuremberg and Erlangen Regional Computing Center, who submitted the paper "MD-Bench: A generic proxy-app toolbox for state-of-the-art molecular dynamics algorithms".
- Anna Sasak-Okoń from the Maria Curie-Skłodowska University and Marek Tudruj from the Polish Academy of Sciences and Polish-Japanese Academy of Information Technology, who presented the paper "RDBMS speculative support improvement by the use of the query hypergraph representation".

For workshops, the PPAM 2022 winners were Yu-Hsiang Tsai, Natalie Beams, and Hartwig Anzt from the Karlsruhe Institute of Technology and the University of Tennessee, who submitted the paper "Mixed Precision Algebraic Multigrid on GPUs". To stimulate potential authors' interest in submitting high-quality articles to the PPAM conference, one author of each winning paper will receive a significant reduction in the conference fee for the next PPAM.

New Topic at PPAM 2022: First Workshop on Applications of Machine Learning and Artificial Intelligence in High Performance Computing

Machine learning and artificial intelligence methods have become pervasive in recent years due to numerous algorithmic advances and the accessibility of computational power. In high performance computing, these methods have been used to replace, accelerate, or enhance existing solvers.

Research topics of this workshop focused on: (i) disruptive uses of HPC technologies in the field of AI (artificial intelligence), ML (machine learning), and DL (deep learning);

(ii) integration of predictive models to improve the performance of scientific applications in terms of execution time and/or simulation accuracy; (iii) workflow of applying AI/ML/DL to scientific applications in HPC infrastructures; (iv) characterization and study of how to use HPC techniques with AI/ML/DL; (v) HPC tools and infrastructure to improve the usability of AI/ML/DL for scientific applications; (vi) optimized HPC systems design and setup for efficient AI/ML/DL.

These topics were covered at a session that consisted of five presentations:

- adaptation of AI-accelerated CFD simulations to the IPU platform (by P. Rościszewski, A. Krzywaniak, S. Iserte, K. Rojek, and P. Gepner)
- performance analysis of convolution algorithms for deep learning on edge processors (by P. Alonso-Jorda, H. Martinez, E. S. Quintana-Orti, and C. Ramirez)
- machine learning-based online scheduling in distributed computing (by V. Toporkov, D. Yemelyanov, and A. Bulkhak)
- high performance computing queue time prediction using clustering and regression (by S. Hutchison, D. Andresen, M. Neilsen, W. Hsu, and B. Parsons)
- acceptance rates of invertible neural networks on electron spectra from near-critical laser-plasmas: a comparison (by T. Miethlinger, N. Hoffmann, and T. Kluge).

New Topic at PPAM 2022: First Workshop on Quantum Computing and Communication

The dedicated workshop focused on two relevant quantum technology areas: quantum computation and communication. The main goal of this event was to bring together scientists and practitioners experimenting with different software and hardware in the existing Noisy Intermediate-Scale Quantum (NISQ) era. This workshop was also an excellent opportunity to catch up on taking advantage of quantum computing, particularly Adiabatic Quantum Computing, and communication technologies from theoretical and practical angles. There are many exciting research topics today, from the design of quantum algorithms, experiments on early access quantum devices, and performance analysis of classical-quantum approaches to early experiences with quantum communication applications and distributed quantum testbeds.

Therefore, the workshop consisted of nine presentations on various exciting topics delivered during two sessions:

- An analysis of the potential of quantum computing by examining problems involved with determining the worst-case execution time of a restricted set of programs (by Gabriella Bettonte, Stephane Louise, and Renaud Sirdey)
- A study of LDPC decoding using quantum annealing (by Aditya Das Sarma, Utso Majumder, Vishnu Vaidya, M Girish Chandra, Anil Kumar, and Sayantan Pramanik)
- An overview of ongoing Quantum Key Distribution (QKD) communication technology in operational networks within commercial network operators and national research and education networks in Europe (by Piotr Rydlichowski)
- A new QUBO-based algorithm for the scheduling of heterogeneous tasks on unrelated parallel machines problem solved using quantum annealing (by F. Orts, A. M. Puertas, E. M. Garzon, and G. Ortega)
- An approach to studying specific aspects of quantum entanglement contained in the bipartite pure quantum states (by Roman Gielerak and Marek Sawerwain)

– A study of a set of early experiments with a photonic quantum simulator for solving the job shop scheduling problem (by Mateusz Slysz, Krzysztof Kurowski, and Jan Weglarz)
– A proposal for solving the traveling salesman problem with a hybrid quantum-classical feedforward neural network (by Justyna Zawalska, and Katarzyna Rycerz)
– An analysis of the Eisert-Wilkens-Lewenstein scheme of quantum extension for selected games on the example of Prisoners Dilemma (by Piotr Kotara, Tomasz Zawadzki, and Katarzyna Rycerz)
– A new approach to generative quantum machine learning and description of a proof-of-principle experiment (by Karol Bartkiewicz, Patrycja Tulewicz, Jan Roik, and Karel Lemr).

The organizers are indebted to PPAM 2022's sponsors, whose support was vital to the conference's success. The main sponsors were the Intel Corporation and Graphcore; the others were Hewlett Packard Enterprise, Koma Nord, and Inspur. We thank all the International Program Committee members and additional reviewers for their diligent work in refereeing the submitted papers. Finally, we thank all of the local organizers from the Częstochowa University of Technology and the Gdańsk University of Technology, who helped us to run the event very smoothly. We are especially indebted to Łukasz Kuczyński, Marcin Woźniak, Tomasz Chmiel, Piotr Dzierżak, Anna Woźniak, and Ewa Szymczyk from the Częstochowa University of Technology; and to Paweł Czarnul and Mariusz Matuszek from the Gdańsk University of Technology.

We hope that this volume will be useful to you. We would like everyone who reads it to feel invited to the next conference, PPAM 2024, which will be held on September 8–11, 2024.

January 2023

Roman Wyrzykowski
Jack Dongarra
Ewa Deelman
Konrad Karczewski

Organization

Program Committee

Jan Węglarz (Honorary Chair)	Poznań University of Technology, Poland
Roman Wyrzykowski (Chair of Program Committee)	Częstochowa University of Technology, Poland
Ewa Deelman (Vice-chair of Program Committee)	University of Southern California, USA
Konrad Karczewski (Vice-chair for Publication)	Częstochowa University of Technology, Poland
Marco Lapegna (Vice-chair for Tutorials)	University of Naples Federico II, Italy
Robert Adamski	Intel Corporation, Poland
Francisco Almeida	Universidad de La Laguna, Spain
Pedro Alonso	Universidad Politécnica de Valencia, Spain
Alexander Antonov	Moscov State University, Russian Federation
Hartwig Anzt	Karlsruhe Institute of Technology, Germany, and University of Tennessee, USA
Peter Arbenz	ETH Zurich, Switzerland
Cevdet Aykanat	Bilkent University, Turkey
Marc Baboulin	University of Paris-Sud, France
David A. Bader	New Jersey Institute of Technology, USA
Michael Bader	TU Munchen, Germany
Bartosz Baliś	Institute of Computer Science AGH, Poland
Piotr Bała	ICM, Warsaw University, Poland
Krzysztof Banaś	AGH University of Science and Technology, Poland
Jorge G. Barbosa	Universidade de Porto, Portugal
Olivier Beaumont	Inria Bordeaux, France
Włodzimierz Bielecki	West Pomeranian University of Technology, Poland
Paolo Bientinesi	Umea University, Sweden
Jacek Błażewicz	Poznań University of Technology, Poland
Pascal Bouvry	University of Luxembourg, Luxembourg
Jerzy Brzeziński	Poznań University of Technology, Poland
Marian Bubak	AGH Kraków, Poland, and University of Amsterdam, The Netherlands

Tadeusz Burczyński	Polish Academy of Sciences, Warsaw
Christopher Carothers	Rensselaer Polytechnic Institute, USA
Jesus Carretero	Universidad Carlos III de Madrid, Spain
Andrea Clematis	IMATI-CNR, Italy
Paweł Czarnul	Gdańsk University of Technology, Poland
Zbigniew Czech	Silesia University of Technology, Poland
Davor Davidovic	Ruder Boskovic Institute, Croatia
Jack Dongarra	University of Tennessee and ORNL, USA
Maciej Drozdowski	Poznań University of Technology, Poland
Mariusz Flasiński	Jagiellonian University, Poland
Tomas Fryza	Brno University of Technology, Czech Republic
Lin Gan	Tsinghua University and National Supercomputing Center in Wuxi, China
Jose Daniel Garcia	Universidad Carlos III de Madrid, Spain
Pawel Gepner	Graphcore, Poland
Shamsollah Ghanbari	Iranian Distributed Computing and Systems Society, Iran
Domingo Gimenez	University of Murcia, Spain
Jacek Gondzio	University of Edinburgh, UK
Andrzej Gościński	Deakin University, Australia
Georg Hager	University of Erlangen-Nuremberg, Germany
José R. Herrero	Universitat Politècnica de Catalunya, Spain
Ladislav Hluchy	Slovak Academy of Sciences, Slovakia
Sasha Hunold	Vienna University of Technology, Austria
Roman Iakymchuk	Umea University, Sweden
Aleksandar Ilic	Technical University of Lisbon, Portugal
Krzysztof Jurczuk	Białystok University of Technology, Poland
Grzegorz Kamieniarz	Adam Mickiewicz University, Poland
Eleni Karatza	Aristotle University of Thessaloniki, Greece
Jacek Kitowski	Institute of Computer Science, AGH, Poland
Joanna Kołodziej	NASK and Cracow University of Technology, Poland
Jozef Korbicz	University of Zielona Góra, Poland
Tomas Kozubek	Technical University of Ostrava, Czech Republic
Dieter Kranzlmueller	Ludwig-Maximillian University and Leibniz Supercomputing Centre, Germany
Henryk Krawczyk	Gdańsk University of Technology, Poland
Carola Kruse	CERFACS, France
Piotr Krzyżanowski	University of Warsaw, Poland
Krzysztof Kurowski	PSNC, Poland
Jan Kwiatkowski	Wrocław University of Technology, Poland
Giulliano Laccetti	University of Naples Federico II, Italy

Alexey Lastovetsky	University College Dublin, Ireland
Joao Lourenco	University Nova of Lisbon, Portugal
Tze Meng Low	Carnegie Mellon University, USA
Hatem Ltaief	KAUST, Saudi Arabia
Piotr Luszczek	University of Tennessee, USA
Maciej Malawski	Sano Center for Computational Medicine and Institute of Computer Science AGH, Poland
Allen D. Malony	University of Oregon, USA
Victor E. Malyshkin	Siberian Branch, Russian Academy of Sciences, Russia
Tomas Margalef	Universitat Autònoma de Barcelona, Spain
Svetozar Margenov	Bulgarian Academy of Sciences, Sofia
Ami Marowka	Bar-Ilan University, Israel
Norbert Meyer	PSNC, Poland
Iosif Meyerov	Lobachevsky State University of Nizhni Novgorod, Russian Federation
Marek Michalewicz	ICM, Warsaw University, Poland
Carl Ch. K. Mikkelsen	Umea University, Sweden
Ricardo Morla	INESC Porto, Portugal
Daichi Mukunoki	Riken Center for Computational Science, Japan
Jarek Nabrzyski	University of Notre Dame, USA
Koji Nakano	Hiroshima University, Japan
Raymond Namyst	University of Bordeaux and Inria, France
Edoardo Di Napoli	Forschungszentrum Juelich, Germany
Gabriel Oksa	Slovak Academy of Sciences, Slovakia
Tomasz Olas	Częstochowa University of Technology, Poland
Ariel Oleksiak	PSNC, Poland
Marcin Paprzycki	IBS PAN and SWPS University, Poland
Dana Petcu	West University of Timisoara, Romania
Loic Pottier	University of Southern California, USA
Radu Prodan	University of Innsbruck, Austria
Enrique S. Quintana-Ortí	Universitat Politècnica de València, Spain
Thomas Rauber	University of Bayreuth, Germany
Lubomir Riha	Technical University of Ostrava, Czech Republic
Krzysztof Rojek	Częstochowa University of Technology, Poland
Witold Rudnicki	University of Białystok, Poland
Leszek Rutkowski	Częstochowa University of Technology, Poland
Krzysztof Rzadca	Warsaw University, Poland
Robert Schaefer	Institute of Computer Science, AGH, Poland
Stanislav Sedukhin	University of Aizu, Japan
Franciszek Seredyński	Cardinal Stefan Wyszyński University in Warsaw, Poland

Sebastiano F. Schifano	University of Ferrara, Italy
Jurij Silc	Jozef Stefan Institute, Slovenia
Renata Słota	Institute of Computer Science, AGH, Poland
Masha Sosonkina	Old Dominion University, USA
Leonel Sousa	Technical University of Lisbon, Portugal
Vladimir Stegailov	Joint Institute for High Temperatures of RAS and MIPT/HSE, Russian Federation
Przemysław Stpiczyński	Maria Curie-Skłodowska University, Poland
Robert Strzodka	University of Heidelberg, Germany
Lukasz Szustak	Częstochowa University of Technology, Poland
Boleslaw Szymanski	Rensselaer Polytechnic Institute, USA
Domenico Talia	University of Calabria, Italy
Andrei Tchernykh	CICESE Research Center, Mexico
Christian Terboven	RWTH Aachen, Germany
Parimala Thulasiraman	University of Manitoba, Canada
Sivan Toledo	Tel-Aviv University, Israel
Victor Toporkov	National Research University "MPEI", Russian Federation
Roman Trobec	Jozef Stefan Institute, Slovenia
Giuseppe Trunfio	University of Sassari, Italy
Denis Trystram	Grenoble Institute of Technology, France
Marek Tudruj	Polish Academy of Sciences and Polish-Japanese Academy of Information Technologies, Poland
Bora Ucar	École Normale Supérieure de Lyon, France
Marian Vajtersic	Salzburg University, Austria
Vladimir Voevodin	Moscow State University, Russian Federation
Bogdan Wiszniewski	Gdańsk University of Technology, Poland
Andrzej Wyszogrodzki	Institute of Meteorology and Water Management, Poland
Ramin Yahyapour	University of Göttingen/GWDG, Germany
Krzysztof Zielinski	Institute of Computer Science, AGH, Poland
Julius Žilinskas	Vilnius University, Lithuania
Jarosław Żola	University of Buffalo, USA

Steering Committee

Jack Dongarra	University of Tennessee and ORNL, USA
Leszek Rutkowski	Częstochowa University of Technology, Poland
Boleslaw Szymanski	Rensselaer Polytechnic Institute, USA

Contents – Part I

Soft Computing with Applications

**Special Session on Parallel EVD/SVD and its Application in Matrix
Computations**

Contents – Part II

7th Workshop on Complex Collective Systems

Numerical Algorithms and Parallel Scientific Computing

How Accurate Does Newton Have to Be?

Carl Christian Kjelgaard Mikkelsen[1]([✉]) [iD], Lorién López-Villellas[2] [iD],
and Pablo García-Risueño[3] [iD]

[1] Department of Computing Science, Umeå University, 90187 Umeå, Sweden
spock@cs.umu.se
[2] Barcelona Supercomputing Center, Barcelona, Spain
lorien.lopez@bsc.es
[3] Zaragoza, Spain
risueno@unizar.es

Abstract. We analyze the convergence of quasi-Newton methods in
exact and finite precision arithmetic. In particular, we derive an upper
bound for the stagnation level and we show that any sufficiently exact
quasi-Newton method will converge quadratically until stagnation. In
the absence of sufficient accuracy, we are likely to retain rapid linear
convergence. We confirm our analysis by computing square roots and
solving bond constraint equations in the context of molecular dynamics.
We briefly discuss implications for parallel solvers.

Keywords: Systems of nonlinear equations · Quasi-Newton methods ·
approximation error · rounding error · convergence · stagnation

1 Introduction

Let $\Omega \subseteq \mathbb{R}^n$ be open, let $F \in C^1(\Omega, \mathbb{R}^n)$ and consider the problem of solving

$$F(x) = 0.$$

If the Jacobian F' of F is nonsingular, then Newton's method is given by

$$x_{k+1} = x_k - s_k, \quad F'(x_k)s_k = F(x_k). \tag{1}$$

A quasi-Newton method is any iteration of the form

$$y_{k+1} = y_k - t_k, \quad F'(y_k)t_k \approx F(y_k). \tag{2}$$

In exact arithmetic, we expect local quadractic convergence from Newton's
method [7]. Quasi-Newton methods normally converge locally and at least linearly and some methods, such as the secant method, have superlinear convergence [5,8]. In finite precision arithmetic, we cannot expect convergence in the
strict mathematical sense and we must settle for stagnation near a zero [11]. In

---

P. García-Risueño—Independent scholar.

© The Author(s), under exclusive license to Springer Nature Switzerland AG 2023
R. Wyrzykowski et al. (Eds.): PPAM 2022, LNCS 13826, pp. 3–15, 2023.
https://doi.org/10.1007/978-3-031-30442-2_1

this paper we analyze the convergence of quasi-Newton methods in exact and finite precision arithmetic. In particular, we derive an upper bound for the stagnation level and we show that any sufficiently exact quasi-Newton method will converge quadratically until stagnation. We confirm our analysis by computing square roots and solving bond constraint equations in the context of molecular dynamics.

2 Auxiliary Results

The line segment $l(x, y)$ between x and y is defined as follows:

$$l(x, y) = \{tx + (1 - t)y \,:\, t \in [0, 1]\}.$$

The following lemma is a standard result that bounds the difference between $F(x)$ and $F(y)$ if the line segment $l(x, y)$ is contained in the domain of F.

Lemma 1. *Let $\Omega \subseteq \mathbb{R}^n$ be open and let $F \in C^1(\Omega, \mathbb{R}^n)$. If $l(x, y) \subset \Omega$, then*

$$F(x) - F(y) = \int_0^1 F'(tx + (1 - t)y)(x - y)dt$$

and

$$\|F(x) - F(y)\| \le M\|x - y\|.$$

where

$$M = \sup\{\|F'(tx + (1 - t)y)\| \,:\, t \in [0, 1]\}.$$

It is convenient to phrase Newton's method as the functional iteration:

$$x_{k+1} = g(x_k), \quad g(x) = x - F'(x)^{-1}F(x).$$

and to express the analysis of quasi-Newton methods in terms of the function g. The next lemma can be used to establish local quadratic convergence of Newton's method.

Lemma 2. *Let $\Omega \subseteq \mathbb{R}^n$ be open and let $F \in C^1(\Omega, \mathbb{R}^n)$. Let z denote a zero of F and let $x \in \Omega$. If $F'(x)$ is nonsingular and if $l(x, z) \subset \Omega$, then*

$$g(x) - z = C(x)(x - z)$$

where

$$C(x) = F'(x)^{-1}\left(\int_0^1 [F'(x) - F'(tx + (1 - t)z)]\,dt\right)$$

Moreover, if F' is Lipschitz continuous with Lipschitz constant $L > 0$, then

$$\|g(x) - z\| \le \frac{1}{2}\|F'(x)^{-1}\|L\|x - z\|^2.$$

The following lemma allows us to write any approximation as a very simple function of the target vector.

Lemma 3. *Let $x \in \mathbb{R}^n$ be nonzero, let $y \in \mathbb{R}^n$ be an approximation of x and let $E \in \mathbb{R}^{n \times n}$ be given by*

$$E = \frac{1}{x^T x}(y - x)x^T.$$

Then

$$y = (I + E)x, \quad \|E\| = O\left(\frac{\|x - y\|}{\|x\|}\right), \quad y \to x, \quad y \neq x.$$

In the special case of the 2-norm we have

$$\|E\|_2 = \frac{\|x - y\|_2}{\|x\|_2}.$$

Proof. It is straightforward to verify that

$$(I + E)x = x + \frac{1}{x^T x}(y - x)x^T x = x + (y - x) = y.$$

Moreover, if z is any vector, then

$$\|Ez\| \leq \frac{1}{\|x\|_2^2}\|y - x\|\|x^T z\| = \left(\frac{\|x^T\|\|x\|}{\|x\|_2^2}\right)\left(\frac{\|x - y\|}{\|x\|}\right)\|z\|.$$

In the case of the 2-norm, we have

$$\|Ez\|_2 \leq \frac{\|x - y\|_2}{\|x\|_2}\|z\|_2$$

for all $z \neq 0$ and equality holds for $z = x$. This completes the proof.

3   Main Results

In the presence of rounding errors, *any* quasi-Newton method can written as

$$x_{k+1} = (I + D_k)\left(x_k - (I + E_k)F'(x_k)^{-1}F(x_k)\right). \tag{3}$$

Here $D_k \in \mathbb{R}^{n \times n}$ is a diagonal matrix which represents the rounding error in the subtraction and $E_k \in \mathbb{R}^{n \times n}$ measures the difference between the computed correction and the correction used by Newton's method. We simply treat the update t_k needed for the quasi-Newton method (2) as an approximation of the update $s_k = F'(x_k)^{-1}F(x_k)$ needed for Newton's method (1) and define E_k using Lemma 3. It is practical to restate iteration (3) in terms of the function g, i.e.,

$$x_{k+1} = (I + D_k)\left(g(x_k) - E_k F'(x_k)^{-1}F(x_k)\right). \tag{4}$$

We shall now analyze the behavior of iteration (4). For the sake of simplicity, we will assume that there exist nonnegative numbers K, L, and M such that

$$\forall x \ : \ \|F'(x)^{-1}\| \leq K, \quad \|F'(x) - F'(y)\| \leq L\|x - y\|, \quad \|F'(x)\| \leq M.$$

In reality, we only require that these inequalities are satisfied in a neighborhood of a zero. We have the following generalization of Lemma 2.

Theorem 1. *The functional iteration given by Eq. (4) satisfies*

$$x_{k+1} - z = g(x_k) - z - E_k F'(x_k)^{-1} F(x_k)$$
$$+ D_k\big[g(x_k) - E_k F'(x_k)^{-1} F(x_k)\big] \quad (5)$$

and

$$\|x_{k+1} - z\| \leq \frac{1}{2}LK\|x_k - z\|^2 + \|E_k\|KM\|x_k - z\|$$
$$+ \|D_k\|\left(\|z\| + \frac{1}{2}LK\|x_k - z\|^2 + \|E_k\|KM\|x_k - z\|\right). \quad (6)$$

Proof. It is straightforward to verify that Eq. (5) is correct. Inequality (6) follows from Eq. (5) using the triangle inequality, Lemma 1, and Lemma 2. The second occurrence of the term $\|g(x_k)\|$ can be bounded using the inequality

$$\|g(x_k)\| \leq \|z\| + \|g(x_k) - z\|.$$

This completes the proof.

It is practical to focus on the case of $z \neq 0$ and restate inequality (6) as

$$r_{k+1} \leq \frac{1}{2}LK(1 + \|D_k\|)\|z\|r_k^2 + \|E_k\|KM(1 + \|D_k\|)r_k + \|D_k\| \quad (7)$$

where r_k is the normwise relative forward error given by

$$r_k = \|z - x_k\|/\|z\|.$$

3.1 Stagnation

We assume that the sequences $\{D_k\}$ and $\{E_k\}$ are bounded. Let D and E be nonnegative numbers that satisfy

$$\|D_k\| \leq D, \quad \|E_k\| \leq E. \quad (8)$$

In this case, inequality (7) implies

$$r_{k+1} \leq \frac{1}{2}LK(1 + D)\|z\|r_k^2 + EMK(1 + D)r_k + D.$$

It is certain that the error will be reduced, i.e., $r_{k+1} < r_k$ when

$$D < r_k - \left(\frac{1}{2}LK(1+D)\|z\|r_k^2 + EMK(1+D)r_k^2 \right)$$

$$= (1 - EMK(1+D)) r_k - \frac{1}{2}LK(1+D)\|z\|r_k^2.$$

This condition is equivalent to the following inequality:

$$D - [1 - EMK(1+D)] r_k + \frac{1}{2}LK(1+D)\|z\|r_k^2 < 0.$$

This is an inequality of the second degree. The roots are

$$\lambda_{\pm} = \frac{[1 - EMK(1+D)] \pm \sqrt{[1 - EMK(1+D)]^2 - 2LK(1+D)D\|z\|}}{LK(1+D)\|z\|}.$$

If D and E are sufficiently small then the roots are positive real numbers and the error will certainly be reduced provided

$$\lambda_- < r_k < \lambda_+.$$

It follows that we cannot expect to do better than

$$r_k = \frac{\|z - x_k\|}{\|z\|} \approx \lambda_-.$$

If D and E are sufficiently small, then a Taylor expansion ensures that

$$\lambda_- \approx \frac{D}{(1 - EMK(1+D))^2}$$

is a good approximation. We cannot expect to do better than $r_{k+1} = \lambda_-$, but the threshold of stagnation is not particularly sensitive to the size of E.

3.2 The Decay of the Error

We assume that the sequences $\{D_k\}$ and $\{E_k\}$ are bounded. Let D and E be upper bounds that satisfy (8). Suppose that we are not near the threshold of stagnation in the sense that

$$D \leq Cr_k. \tag{9}$$

for a (modest) constant $C > 0$. In this case, inequality (7) implies

$$r_{k+1} \leq \rho_k r_k, \quad \rho_k = \frac{1}{2}LK(1+D)\|z\|r_k + EKM(1+D) + C. \tag{10}$$

If $C < 1$, then we may have $\rho_k < 1$, when r_k and E are sufficiently small. This explains when and why local linear decay is possible. We now strengthen our assumptions. Suppose that there is a $\lambda \in (0, 1]$ and $C_1 > 0$ such that

$$\|E_k\| \leq C_1 r_k^\lambda \tag{11}$$

and that we are far from the threshold of stagnation in the sense that

$$D \leq C_2 r_k^{1+\lambda} \tag{12}$$

for a (modest) constant $C_2 > 0$. In this case, inequality (7) implies

$$r_{k+1} \leq \left[\frac{1}{2} LK(1+D)\|z\|r_k^{1-\lambda} + C_1 KM(1+D) + C_2 \right] r_k^{1+\lambda}. \tag{13}$$

This explains when and why local superlinear decay is possible.

3.3   Convergence

We cannot expect a quasi-Newton method to converge unless the subtraction $y_{k+1} = y_k - t_k$ is exact. Then $D_k = 0$ and inequality (7) implies

$$r_{k+1} \leq \eta_k r_k, \quad \eta_k = \left(\frac{1}{2} LK\|z\|r_k + \|E_k\|KM \right).$$

We may have $\eta_k < 1$ for all k, provided $E = \sup \|E_k\|$ and r_0 are sufficiently small. This explains when and why local linear convergence is possible. We now strengthen our assumptions. Suppose that there is a $\lambda \in (0,1]$ and a $C > 0$ such that

$$\forall k \in \mathbb{N} : \|E_k\| \leq C r_k^\lambda.$$

In this case, inequality (7) implies

$$r_{k+1} \leq \left(\frac{1}{2} LK\|z\|r_k^{1-\lambda} + CKM \right) r_k^{1+\lambda}.$$

This inequality allows us to establish local convergence of order at least $1 + \lambda$.

3.4   How Accurate Does Newton Have to Be?

We will assume the use of normal IEEE floating point numbers and we will apply the analysis given in Sect. 3.2. If we use the 1-norm, the 2-norm or the ∞-norm, then we may choose $D = u$, where u is the unit roundoff. Suppose that Eqs. (11) and (12) are satisfied with $\lambda = 1$. Then inequality (13) reduces to

$$r_{k+1} \leq \left[\frac{1}{2} LK(1+u)\|z\| + C_1 KM(1+u) + C_2 \right] r_k^2.$$

Due to the basic limitations of IEEE floating point arithmetic we cannot expect to do better than

$$r_{k+1} = O(u), \quad u \to 0, \quad u > 0.$$

It follows that we *never* need to do better than

$$\|E_k\| = O(\sqrt{u}), \quad u \to 0, \quad u > 0.$$

4   Numerical Experiments

4.1   Computing Square Roots

Let $\alpha > 0$ and consider the problem of solving the nonlinear equation

$$f(x) = x^2 - \alpha = 0$$

with respect to $x > 0$ using Newton's method. Let r_k denote the relative error after k Newton steps. A simple calculation based on Lemma 2 yields

$$|r_{k+1}| \leq r_k^2/2, \quad |r_k| \leq 2\,(|r_0|/2)^{2^k}.$$

We see that convergence is certain when $|r_0| < 2$. The general case of $\alpha > 0$ can be reduced to the special case of $\alpha \in [1,4)$ by accessing and manipulating the binary representation directly. Let $x_0 : [1,4] \to \mathbb{R}$ denote the best uniform linear approximation of the square root function on the interval $[1,4]$. Then

$$x_0(\alpha) = \alpha/3 + 17/24, \quad |r_0(\alpha)| \leq 1/24.$$

In order to illustrate Theorem 1 we execute the iteration

$$x_{k+1} = x_k - (1 + e_k)f(x_k)/f'(x_k)$$

where e_k is a randomly generated number. Specifically, given $\epsilon > 0$ we choose e_k such that $|e_k|$ is uniformly distributed in the interval $[\frac{1}{2}\epsilon, \epsilon]$ and the sign of e_k is positive or negative with equal probability. Three choices, namely $\epsilon = 10^{-2}$ (left), $\epsilon = 10^{-8}$ (center) and $\epsilon = 10^{-12}$ (right) are illustrated in Fig. 1.

In each case, eventually the perturbed iteration reproduces either the computer's internal representation of the square root or stagnates with a relative error that is essentially the unit roundoff $u = 2^{-53} \approx 10^{-16}$. When $\epsilon = 10^{-2}$ the quadratic convergence is lost, but the relative error is decreased by a factor of approximately $\epsilon = 10^{-2}$ from one iteration to the next, i.e., extremely rapid linear convergence. Quadratic convergence is restored when ϵ is reduced to $\epsilon = 10^{-8} \approx \sqrt{u}$. Further reductions of ϵ have no effect on the convergence as demonstrated by the case of $\epsilon = 10^{-12}$. We shall now explain exactly how far this experiment supports the theory that is presented in this paper.

Stagnation. By Sect. 3.1 we expect that the level of stagnation is essentially independent of the size of E, the upper bound on the relative error between the computed step and the step needed for Newton's method. This is clearly confirmed by the experiment.

Error Decay. Since we are always very close to the positive zero of $f(x) = x^2 - \alpha$ we may choose

$$L \approx 2, \quad K|z| \approx 1/2, \quad MK \approx 1,$$

In the case of $\epsilon = 10^{-2}$, Fig. 1 (left) shows that we satisfy inequality (9) with $D = u$ and $C = \epsilon < 1$, i.e.,

$$u \le \epsilon r_k, \quad 0 \le k < 5.$$

By Eq. (10) we must have

$$r_{k+1} \le \rho_k r_k, \quad \rho_k \approx 2\epsilon, \quad 0 < k < 5.$$

This is exactly the linear convergence that we have observed. In the case of $\epsilon = 10^{-8}$, Fig. 1 (center) shows that we satisfy inequality (12) with $C_2 = 1$ and $\lambda = 1$, i.e.,

$$u \le r_k^2, \quad k = 0, 1.$$

By inequality (13) we must have quadratic decay in the sense that

$$r_{k+1} \le C r_k^2, \quad C \approx \frac{3}{2}, \quad k = 0, 1.$$

Manual inspection of Fig. 1 reveals that the actual constant is close to 1 and certainly smaller than $C \approx \frac{3}{2}$. By Sect. 3.4 we do not expect any benefits from using an ϵ that is substantially smaller than $\sqrt{u}$. This is also supported by the experiment.

4.2 Constrained Molecular Dynamics

The objective is to solve a system of differential algebraic equations

$$q'(t) = v(t),$$
$$Mv'(t) = f(q(t)) - g'(q(t))^T \lambda(t),$$
$$g(q(t)) = 0.$$

Here q and v are vectors that represent the position and velocity of all atoms, M is a nonsingular diagonal mass matrix, f represents the external forces acting on the atoms and $-g'(q)^T \lambda$ represents the constraint forces. Here g' is the Jacobian of the constraint function g. The standard algorithm for this problem is the SHAKE algorithm [10]. It uses a pair of staggered uniform grids and takes the form

$$v_{n+1/2} = v_{n-1/2} + hM^{-1}\left(f(q_n) - g'(q_n)^T \lambda_n\right),$$
$$q_{n+1} = q_n + hv_{n+1/2},$$
$$g(q_{n+1}) = 0, \tag{14}$$

where $h > 0$ is the fixed time step and $q_n \approx q(t_n)$, $v_{n+\frac{1}{2}} \approx v(t_{n+\frac{1}{2}})$, where $t_n = nh$ and $t_{n+\frac{1}{2}} = (n+1/2)h$. Equation (14) is really a nonlinear equation for the unknown Lagrange multiplier λ_n, specifically

$$g(\phi_n(\lambda)) = 0, \quad \phi_n(\lambda) = q_n + h(v_{n-\frac{1}{2}} + hM^{-1}(f(q_n) - g'(q_n)^T\lambda)).$$

The relevant Jacobian is the matrix

$$A_n(\lambda) = (g(\phi_n(\lambda)))' = g'(\phi_n(\lambda))M^{-1}g'(q_n)^T.$$

The matrix $A_n(\lambda)$ is close to the constant symmetric matrix S_n given by

$$S_n = g'(q_n)M^{-1}g'(q_n)^T$$

simply because $\phi_n(\lambda) = q_n + O(h)$ as $h \to 0$ and $h > 0$. It is therefore natural to investigate if the constant matrix S_n^{-1} is a good approximation of $A_n^{-1}(\lambda)$.

For this experiment, we executed a production molecular dynamics run using the GROMACS [1] package. We replaced the constraint solver used by GRO-MACS's SHAKE function with a quasi-Newton method based on the matrix S_n. Our experiment was based on GROMACS's Lysozyme in Water Tutorial [6]. We simulated a hen egg white lysozyme [9] molecule submerged in water inside a cubic box. Lysozyme is a protein that consists of a single polypeptide chain of 129 amino acid residues cross-lined at 4 places by disulfide bonds between cys-teine side-chains in different parts of the molecule. Lysozyme has 1960 atoms and 1984 bond length constraints. Before executing the production run, we added ions to the system to make it electrically neutral. The energy of the system was minimized using the steepest descent algorithm until the maximum force of the system was below 1000.0 kJ/(mol·nm). Then, we executed 100 ps of a temperature equilibration step using a V-Rescale thermostat in an NVT ensem-ble to stabilize the temperature of the system at 310 K. To finish, we stabilized the pressure of the system at 1 Bar for another 100 ps using a V-Rescale ther-mostat and a Parrinello-Rahman barostat in an NPT ensemble. We executed a 100 ps production run with a 2 fs time step using an NPT ensemble with a V-Rescale thermostat and a Parrinello-Rahman barostat with time constants of 0.1 and 2 ps, respectively. We collected the results of the constraint solver every 5 ps starting at time-step 5 ps, for a total of 20 sample points. Specifically, we recorded the normwise relative error $r_k = \|\lambda_n - x_k\|_2/\|\lambda_n\|_2$ as a function of the number k of quasi-Newton steps using the symmetric matrix S_n instead of the nonsymmetric matrix A_n and we recorded $\|E_k\|_2 = \|s_k - t_k\|_2/\|s_k\|_2$ where t_k is needed for a quasi-Newton step and s_k is needed a Newton step. By (10) we have $r_{k+1} \leq \rho_k r_k$, but we cannot hope for more than $r_{k+1} \approx \rho_k r_k$ where $\rho_k = O(\|E_k\|_2)$ and this is indeed what we find in the Fig. 2c until we hit the level of stagnation where the impact of rounding errors is keenly felt.

5   Related Work

It is well-known that Newton's method has local quadratic convergence sub-ject to certain regularity conditions. The simplest proof known to us is due to Mysovskii [7]. Dembo et al. [2] analyzed the convergence of quasi-Newton methods in terms of the ratio between the norm of linear residual, i.e., $r_k = F(x_k) - F'(x_k)t_k$ and the norm of the nonlinear residual $F(x_k)$. Tisseur [11] studied the impact of rounding errors in terms of the backward error associated

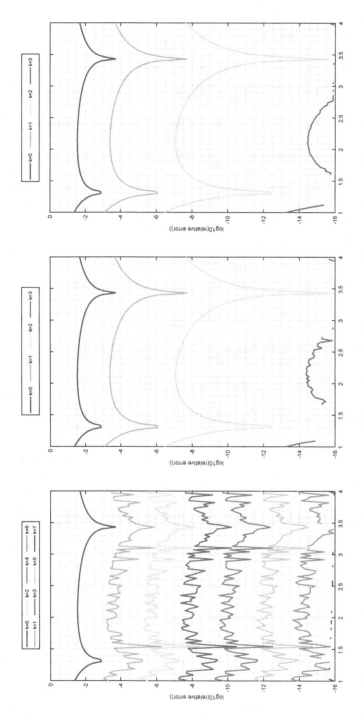

Fig. 1. The impact of inaccuracies on the convergence of Newton's method for a computing square roots. Newton's corrections have been perturbed with random relative errors of size $\epsilon \approx 10^{-2}$ (left), $\epsilon \approx 10^{-8}$ (center) and $\epsilon \approx 10^{-12}$. In each case, the last iteration produces an approximation that matches the computer's value of the square root at many sample points. In such cases, the computed relative error is 0. Therefore, it is not possible to plot a data point and the last curve of each plot are discontinuous.

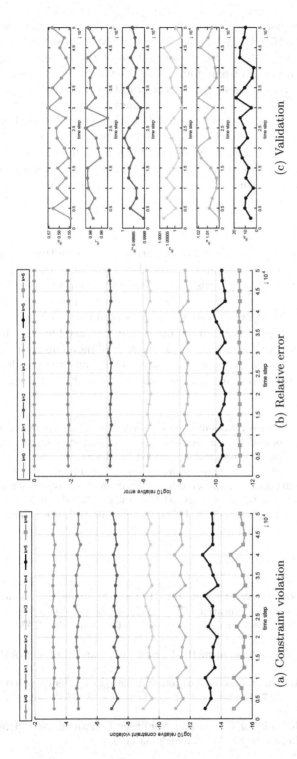

(a) Constraint violation

(b) Relative error

(c) Validation

Fig. 2. Data generated during a simulation of lysozyme in water using GROMACS. The GROMACS solver have been replaced with a quasi-Newton method that uses a fixed symmetric approximation of the Jacobian. Figure 2a is mainly of interest to computational chemists. It shows that the maximum relative constraint violation always stagnates at a level that is essentially the IEEE double precision unit roundoff after 6 quasi-Newton steps. The convergence is always linear and the rate of convergence is $\mu \approx 10^{-2}$. Figure 2b shows the development of the relative error r_k between the relevant zero z, i.e., the Lagrange multiplier for the current time step and the approximations generated by k steps of the quasi-Newton method. The convergence is always linear and the rate of convergence is $\mu \approx 10^{-2}$. Figure 2c provides partial validation of a theoretical result. Specifically, the fractions $\nu_k = r_{k+1}/(r_k \|E_k\|_2)$ are plotted for $k = 0, 1, 2, 3, 4, 5$. When ν_k is modest, we have experimental verification that the rate of convergence is essentially $\|E_k\|$.

with approximating the Jacobians and computing the corrections, as well as the errors associated with computing the residuals. Here we have pursued a third option by viewing the correction t_k as an approximation of the correction s_k needed for an exact Newton step. Tisseur found that Newton's method stagnate at a level that is essentially independent of the stability of the solver and we have confirmed that this is true for quasi-Newton methods in general. It is clear to us from reading Theorem 3.1 of Dennis and Moore's paper [3] that they would instantly recognize Lemma 3, but we cannot find the result stated explicitly anywhere. Forsgren [4] uses a stationary method for solving linear systems to construct a quasi-Newton method that is so exact that the convergence is quadratic. Section 4.1 contains a simple illustration of this phenomenon.

6   Conclusions

Quasi-Newton methods can also be analyzed in terms of the relative error between Newton's correction and the computed correction. We achieve quadratic convergence when this error is $O(\sqrt{u})$. This fact represent an opportunity for improving the time-to-solution for nonlinear equations. General purpose libraries for solving sparse linear systems apply pivoting for the sake of numerical accuracy and stability. In the context of quasi-Newton methods we do not need maximum accuracy. Rather, there is some freedom to pivot for the sake of parallelism. If we fail to achieve quadratic convergence, then we are likely to still converge rapidly. It is therefore worthwhile to develop sparse solvers that pivot mainly for the sake of parallelism.

Acknowledgments. Prof. I. Argyros commented on an early draft of this paper and provided the reference to the work of I. P. Mysovskii. The first author is supported by eSSENCE, a collaborative e-Science programme funded by the Swedish Research Council within the framework of the strategic research areas designated by the Swedish Government. This work has been partially supported by the Spanish Ministry of Science and Innovation (contract PID2019-107255GB-C21/AEI/10.13039/501100011033), by the Generalitat de Catalunya (contract 2017-SGR-1328), and by Lenovo-BSC Contract-Framework Contract (2020).

References

1. Berendsen, H., van der Spoel, D., van Drunen, R.: GROMACS: a message-passing parallel molecular dynamics implementation. CPC **91**(1), 43–56 (1995)
2. Dembo, R.S., Eisenstat, S.C., Steihaug, T.: Inexact Newton methods. SIAM J. Numer. Anal. **19**(2), 400–408 (1982)
3. Dennis, J.E., More, J.J.: Quasi-Newton methods, motivation and theory. SIAM Rev. **19**(1), 46–89 (1977)
4. Forsgren, A.: A sufficiently exact inexact Newton step based on reusing matrix information. TRITA-MAT OS7, Department of Mathematics, KTH, Stockholm, Sweden (2009)
5. Kelley, C.T.: Iterative Methods for Linear and Nonlinear Equations. No. 16 in Frontiers in Applied Mathematics. SIAM, Philadelphia (1995)

6. Lemkul, J.A.: GROMACS Tutorial Lysozyme in Water. https://www.mdtutorials. com/gmx/lysozyme/index.html
7. Mysovskii, I.P.: On the convergence of Newton's method. Trudy Mat. Inst. Steklova **28**, 145–147 (1949). (In Russian)
8. Ortega, J.M., Rheinboldt, W.C.: Iterative Solution of Nonlinear Equations in Several Variables. Computer Science and Applied Mathematics, Academic Press, New York (1970)
9. RSCB: Protein Data Bank. https://www.rcsb.org/structure/1AKI
10. Ryckaert, J.P., Ciccotti, G., Berendsen, H.J.: Numerical integration of the Cartesian equations of motion of a system with constraints: molecular dynamics of n-alkanes. J. Comput. Phys. **23**(3), 327–341 (1977)
11. Tisseur, F.: Newton's method in floating point arithmetic and iterative refinement of generalized eigenvalue problems. SIAM J. Matrix Anal. Appl. **22**(4), 1038–1057 (2001)

General Framework for Deriving Reproducible Krylov Subspace Algorithms: BiCGStab Case

Roman Iakymchuk[1,2(✉)]📵, Stef Graillat[2], and José I. Aliaga[3]

[1] Umeå University, Umeå, Sweden
riakymch@cs.umu.se
[2] Sorbonne Université, CNRS, LIP6, Paris, France
{roman.iakymchuk,stef.graillat}@lip6.fr
[3] Universitat Jaume I, Castellón de la Plana, Spain
aliaga@uji.es

Abstract. Parallel implementations of Krylov subspace algorithms often help to accelerate the procedure to find the solution of a linear system. However, from the other side, such parallelization coupled with asynchronous and out-of-order execution often enlarge the non-associativity of floating-point operations. This results in non-reproducibility on the same or different settings. This paper proposes a general framework for deriving reproducible and accurate variants of a Krylov subspace algorithm. The proposed algorithmic strategies are reinforced by programmability suggestions to assure deterministic and accurate executions. The framework is illustrated on the preconditioned BiCGStab method for the solution of non-symmetric linear systems with message-passing. Finally, we verify the two reproducible variants of PBiCGStab on a set matrices from the SuiteSparse Matrix Collection and a 3D Poisson's equation.

Keywords: Reproducibility · accuracy · floating-point expansion · long accumulator · fused multiply-add · preconditioned BiCGStab

1 Introduction

Solving large and sparse linear systems of equations appears in many scientific applications spanning from circuit and device simulation, quantum physics, large-scale eigenvalue computations, and up to all sorts of applications that include the discretization of partial differential equations (PDEs) [3]. In this case, Krylov subspace methods fulfill the roles of standard linear algebra solvers [15]. The Conjugate Gradient (CG) method can be considered as a pioneer of such iterative solvers operating on symmetric and positive definite (SPD) systems. Other Krylov subspace methods have been proposed to find the solution of more general classes of non-symmetric and indefinite linear systems. These include the Generalized Minimal Residual method (GMRES) [16], the Bi-Conjugate Gradient (BiCG) method [7], the Conjugate Gradient Squared (CGS) method [17],

R. Wyrzykowski et al. (Eds.): PPAM 2022, LNCS 13826, pp. 16–29, 2023.
https://doi.org/10.1007/978-3-031-30442-2_2

and the widely used BiCG stabilized (BiCGStab) method by Van der Vorst [18] as a smoother converging version of the above two. Preconditioning is usually incorporated in real implementations of these methods in order to accelerate the convergence of the methods and improve their numerical features.

One would expect that the results of the sequential and parallel implementations of Krylov subspace methods to be identical, for instance, in the number of iterations, the intermediate and final residuals, as well as the sought-after solution vector. However, in practice, this is not often the case due to different reduction trees – the Message Passing Interface (MPI) libraries offer up to 14 different implementations for reduction –, data alignment, instructions used, etc. Each of these factors impacts the order of floating-point operations, which are commutative but not associative, and, therefore, violates reproducibility. We aim to ensure identical and accurate outputs of computations, including the residuals/errors, as in our view this is a way to ensure *robustness* and *correctness* of iterative methods. The robustness and correctness in this case have a three-fold goal: *reproducibility*[1] of the results with the *accuracy guarantee* as well as *sustainable (energy-efficient)* algorithmic solutions.

In general, Krylov subspace algorithms are built from three components: sparse-matrix vector multiplication Ax (SpMV), DOT product between two vectors (x, y), and scaling a vector by a scalar with the following addition of two vectors $x := \alpha x + y$ (AXPY). If a block data distribution is used, only AXPY is perfomed locally, while SpMV needs to gather the full operand vector, e.g. via the `MPI_Allgatherv()` collective, and DOT product requires communication and computation, e.g. via the `MPI_Allreduce()` collective, among MPI processes.

In this paper, we aim to re-ensure reproducibility of Krylov subspace algorithms in parallel environments. Our contributions are the following:

- we propose a *general framework for deriving reproducible Krylov subspace algorithms*. We follow the bottom-up approach and ensure reproducibility of Krylov subspace algorithms via reproduciblity of their components, including the global communication. We build our reproducible solutions on the ExBLAS [4] approach and its lighter version.
- even when applying our reproducible solutions, we particularly stress the importance of arranging computations carefully, e.g. avoid possibly replacements by compilers of $a * b + c$ in the favor of fused multiply-add (`fma`) operation or postponing divisions in case of data initialization (i.e. divide before use). We refer to the 30-year-old but still up-to-date guide "What every computer scientist should know about floating-point arithmetic" by Goldberg [9].
- we verify the applicability of the proposed method on the preconditioned BiCGStab algorithm. We derive two reproducible variants and test them on a set of SuiteSparse matrices and a 3D Poisson's equation.

This article is structured as follows. Section 2 reviews several aspects of computer arithmetic as well as the ExBLAS approach. Section 3 proposes a general

---

[1] Reproducibility is the ability to obtain a bit-wise identical and accurate result for multiple executions on the same data in various parallel environments.

framework for constructing reproducible Krylov subspace methods. Section 4 introduces the preconditioned BiCGStab algorithms and describes in details its MPI implementation. We evaluate the two reproducible implementations of PBiCGStab in Sect. 5. Finally, Sect. 6 draws conclusions.

2 Background

At first, we will use a floating-point arithmetic that consists in approximating real numbers by numbers that have a finite, fixed-precision representation adhering to the IEEE 754 standard. The IEEE 754 standard requires correctly rounded results for the basic arithmetic operations $(+, -, \times, /, \sqrt{}, \texttt{fma})$. It means that they are performed as if the result was first computed with an infinite precision and then rounded to the floating-point format. The correct rounding criterion guarantees a unique, well-defined answer, ensuring bit-wise reproducibility for a single operation; correct rounding alone is not necessary to achieve reproducibility. Emerging attention to reproducibility strives to draw more careful attention to the problem by the computer arithmetic community. It has led to the inclusion of error-free transformations (EFTs) for addition and multiplication – to return the exact outcome as the result and the error – to assure numerical reproducibility of floating-point operations, into the revised version of the 754 standard in 2019. These mechanisms, once implemented in hardware, will simplify our reproducible algorithms – like the ones used in the ExBLAS [4], ReproBLAS [6], OzBLAS [12] libraries – and boost their performance.

There are two approaches that enable the addition of floating-point numbers without incurring round-off errors or with reducing their impact. The main idea is to keep track of both the result and the error during the course of computations. The first approach uses EFT to compute both the result and the rounding error and stores them in a floating-point expansion (FPE), which is an unevaluated sum of p floating-point numbers, whose components are ordered in magnitude with minimal overlap to cover the whole range of exponents. Typically, FPE relies upon the use of the traditional EFT for addition that is `twosum` [10] and for multiplication that is `twoprod` EFT [13]. The second approach projects the finite range of exponents of floating-point numbers into a long vector so called a long (fixed-point) accumulator and stores every bit there. For instance, Kulisch [11] proposed to use a 4288-bit long accumulator for the exact dot product of two vectors composed of `binary64` numbers; such a large long accumulator is designed to cover all the severe cases without overflows in its highest digit.

The ExBLAS project[2] is an attempt to derive fast, accurate, and reproducible BLAS library by constructing a multi-level approach for these operations that are tailored for various modern architectures with their complex multi-level memory structures. On one side, this approach is aimed to be fast to ensure similar performance compared to the non-deterministic parallel versions. On the other side, the approach is aimed to preserve every bit of information before the final

---

[2] ExBLAS repository: https://github.com/riakymch/exblas.

rounding to the desired format to assure correct-rounding and, therefore, reproducibility. Hence, ExBLAS combines together long accumulator and FPE into algorithmic solutions as well as efficiently tunes and implements them on various architectures, including conventional CPUs, Nvidia and AMD GPUs, and Intel Xeon Phi co-processors (for details we refer to [4]). Thus, ExBLAS assures reproducibility through assuring correct-rounding.

---

while $(\tau > \tau_{\max})$

Step Operation		Kernel	Communication
$S1:$	$d := Ap$	SpMV	Allgatherv
$S2:$	$\rho := \beta/<p, d>$	Dot product	Allreduce
$S3:$	$r := r - \rho d$	Axpy	–
$S4:$	$y := M^{-1}r$	Apply preconditioner	depends
$S5:$	$p := y + \alpha p$	Axpy(-type)	–
$S6:$	$\tau := \sqrt{<r, r>}$	Dot product + sqrt	Allreduce

end while

Fig. 1. Standard preconditioned Krylov subspace method with annotated BLAS kernels and message-passing communication.

Our interest in this article is the dot product of two vectors, which is a crucial fundamental BLAS operation. The ExDOT algorithm is based on the reproducible parallel reduction and the twoprod EFT: the algorithm accumulates the result and the error of twoprod to same FPEs and then follows the reduction scheme. We derive its distributed version with two FPEs underneath (one for the result and the other for the error) that are merged at the end of computations.

3   General Framework for Reproducible Krylov Solvers

This section provides the outline of a general framework for deriving a reproducible version of any traditional Krylov subspace method. The framework is based on two main concepts: 1) identifying the issues caused by parallelization and, hence, the non-associativity of floating-point computations; 2) carefully mitigating these issues primarily with the help of computer arithmetic techniques as well as programming guidelines. The framework was implicitly used for the derivation of the reproducible variants of the Preconditioned Conjugate Gradient (PCG) method [1, 2].

The framework considers the parallel platform to consist of K processes (or MPI ranks), denoted as $P_1, P_2, \ldots, P_K$. In this, the coefficient matrix A is partitioned into K blocks of rows $(A_1, A_2, \ldots, A_k)$, where each P_k stores one row-block with the k-th *distribution block* $A_k \in \mathbb{R}^{p_k \times n}$, and $n = \sum_{k=1}^{K} p_k$. Additionally, vectors are partitioned and distributed in the same way as A. For example, the residual vector r is partitioned as $r_1, r_2, \ldots, r_K$ and r_k is stored in P_k. Besides, scalars are replicated on all K processes.

Identifying Sources of Non-reproducibility. The first step is to identify sources of non-associativy and, thus, non-reproducibility of the Krylov subspace methods in parallel environments. As it can verify in Fig. 1, there are four common operations as well as message-passing communication patterns associated with them: sparse matrix-vector product (SpMV) and Allgatherv for gathering the vector[3], DOT product with the Allreduce collective, scaling a vector with the following addition of two vectors (AXPY(-type)), and the application of the preconditioner. Hence, we investigate each of them.

In general, associativity and reproducibility are not guaranteed when there is perturbation of floating-point operations in parallel execution. For instance, while invoking the `MPI_Allreduce()` collective operation cannot ensure the same result (its execution path) as it depends on the data, the network topology, and the underlying algorithmic implementation. Under these assumptions, AXPY and SpMV are associativity-safe as they are performed locally on local slices of data. The application of preconditioner can also be considered safe, e.g. the Jacobi preconditioner, until all operations are reduction-free; more complex preconditioners will certain raise an issue. Thus, the main issue of non-determinism emerges from parallel reductions (steps S3 and S6 in Fig. 1).

Re-assuring Reproducibility. We construct our approach for reassuring reproducibility by primarily targeting DOT products and parallel reductions. Note that the non-deterministic implementation of the Krylov subspace method utilizes the DOT routine from a BLAS library like Intel MKL followed by `MPI_Allreduce()`. Thus, we propose to refine this procedure into four steps:

- exploit the ExBLAS and its lighter FPE-based versions to build reproducible and correctly-rounded DOT product;
- extend the ExBLAS- and FPE-based DOT products to distributed memory by employing `MPI_Reduce()`. This collective acts on either long accumulators or FPEs. For the ExBLAS approach, since the long accumulator is an array of long integers, we apply regular reduction. Note that we may need to carry an extra intermediate normalization after the reduction of 2^{K-1} long accumulators, where $K = 64 - 52 = 12$ is the number of carry-safe bits per each digit of long accumulator. For the FPE approach, we define the MPI operation that is based on the `twosum` EFT;
- rounding to double: for long accumulators, we use the ExBLAS-native `Round()` routine. To guarantee correctly rounded results of the FPE-based computations, we employ the `NearSum` algorithm from [14] for FPEs;
- distribute the result of DOT product to the other processes by `MPI_Bcast()` as only master performs rounding.

It is evident that the results provided by ExBLAS DOT are both correctly-rounded and reproducible. With the lightweight DOT, we aim also to be generic and, hence, we provide the implementation that relies on FPEs of size eight

---

[3] Certainly, there are better alternatives for banded or similar sparse matrices, but using `MPI_Allgatherv` is the simplified solution for nonstructured sparse matrices.

with the early-exit technique. Additionally, we add a check for both FPE-based implementations for the case when the condition number and/or the dynamic range are too large and we cannot keep every bit of information. Then, the warning is thrown, containing also a suggestion to switch to the ExBLAS-based implementation. But, note that these lightweight implementations are designed for moderately conditioned problems or with moderate dynamic range in order be accurate, reproducible, but also high performing, since the ExBLAS version can be very resource demanding, specially on the small core count. To sum up, if the information about the problem is know in advance, it is worth pursuing the lightweight approach.

Programmability Effort. It is important to note that compiler optimization and especially the usage of the fused-multiply-and-add (`fma`) instruction, which performs $a * b + c$ with single rounding at the end, may lead to some non-deterministic results. For instance, in the SpMV computation, each MPI rank computes its dedicated part d_k of the vector d by multiplying a block of rows A_k by the vector p. Since the computations are carried locally and sequentially, they are deterministic and, thus, reproducible. However, some parts of the code like $a*b+c*d*e$ and $a+ = b*c$ – present in the original implementation of PBiCGStab – may not always provide with the same result [19]. This is due to the fact that for

Compute preconditioner for $A \rightarrow M$
Set starting guess x^0
Initialize $r^0 := b - Ax^0, p^0 := r^0, \tau^0 :=\| r^0 \|_2, j := 0$ (iteration count)

while $(\tau^j > \tau_{\max})$			
Step	Operation	Kernel	Comm
$S1:$	$\tilde{s}^j \quad := M^{-1}p^j$	Apply precond.	–
$S2:$	$s^j \quad := A\tilde{s}^j$	SpMV	Allgatherv
$S3:$	$\alpha^j \quad := <r^0, r^j> / <r^0, s^j>$	DOT product	Allreduce
$S4:$	$q^j \quad := r^j - \alpha^j s^j$	AXPY-like	–
$S5:$	$\tilde{y}^j \quad := M^{-1}q^j$	Apply precond.	–
$S6:$	$y^j \quad := A\tilde{y}^j$	SpMV	Allgatherv
$S7:$	$\omega^j \quad := <q^j, y^j> / <y^j, y^j>$	Two DOT products	Allreduce
$S8:$	$x^{j+1} := x^j + \alpha^j p^j + \omega^j q^j$	Two AXPY	–
$S9:$	$r^{j+1} := q^j - \omega^j y^j$	AXPY-like	–
$S10:$	$\beta^j \quad := \frac{<r^0, r^{j+1}>}{<r^0, r^j>} * \frac{\alpha^j}{\omega^j}$	DOT product	Allreduce
$S11:$	$\tau^{j+1} := \| r^{j+1} \|_2$	DOT product + sqrt	Allreduce
$S12:$	$p^{j+1} := r^{j+1} + \beta^j (p^j - \omega^j s^j)$	Two AXPY-like	–
end while			

Fig. 2. Formulation of the PBiCGStab solver annotated with computational kernels and communication. The threshold $\tau_{\max}$ is an upper bound on the relative residual for the computed approximation to the solution. In the notation, $<\cdot, \cdot>$ computes the DOT (inner) product of its vector arguments.

performance reasons, the C++ language standard allows compilers to change the execution order of this type of operation. It also allows merging multiplications and summations with fused multiply-add (`fma`) instructions. Hence, a compiler might translate $a*b+c*d$ to two multiplications $t1 = a*b$ and $t2 = c*d$, and a subsequent summation $t1+t2$; it might generate a single multiplication $t = c*d$ with a subsequent `fma` (`fma(a,b,t)`), which gives a slightly different result; or it may even compute $t = a*b$ first and then use the `fma` (`fma(c,d,t)`). Thus, we advise to instruct compilers to use `fma` explicitly via `std::fma` in C++ 11, assuming the underlying architecture supports `fma`.

4   BiCGStab

The classic Biconjugate Gradient Stabilized method (BiCGStab) [18] was proposed as a fast and smoothly converging variant of the BiCG [7] and CGS [17] methods. We consider the linear system $Ax = b$, where the coefficient matrix $A \in \mathbb{R}^{n \times n}$ is sparse with n_z nonzero entries; $b \in \mathbb{R}^n$ is the right-hand side vector; and $x \in \mathbb{R}^n$ is the sought-after solution vector. The algorithmic description of the classical iterative PBiCGStab is presented in Fig. 2. For simplicity, we integrate the Jacobi preconditioner [15] in our implementation, which is composed of the diagonal elements of the matrix ($M = diag(A)$), whereas its application is conducted on a vector and requires an element-wise multiplication of two vectors.

As described in Sect. 3, the framework includes a reproducible implementation of the most common operations in a parallel implementation of a Krylov subspace method. Therefore, we next perform a communication and computation analysis of a message-passing implementation of the BiCGStab solver. From there, we derive the reproducible version by following the guide from Sect. 3.

Message-Passing Parallel BiCGStab Implementation. For clarity, hereafter we will drop the superindices that denote the iteration count in the variable names. Thus, for example, $x^{(j)}$ becomes x, where the latter stands for the storage space employed to keep the sequence of approximations $x^{(0)}, x^{(1)}, x^{(2)}, \ldots$ computed during the iterative process. Taking into account these previous considerations, we analyze the different computational kernels (S1–S12) that compose the loop body of a single PBiCGStab iteration in Fig. 2.

Sparse Matrix-Vector Product (S2, S6): This kernel needs as input operands: the coefficient matrix A, which is distributed by blocks of rows, and the corresponding vector ($\tilde{s}$ or $\tilde{y}$), which is partitioned and distributed using the same partitioning as A. For simplicity, we just explain below how S2 is computed.

Prior to computing this kernel, we need to obtain a replicated copy of the distributed vector $\tilde{s}$ in all processes, denoted as $\tilde{s} \rightarrow e$; vector e is the only array that is replicated in all processes. We can recognize here a communication stage, but, after that, each process can then compute its local piece of the output vector v concurrently: $P_k : s_k = A_k e$. This kernel thus requires assembling the distributed pieces of the vector $\tilde{s}$ into a single vector e that is replicated in all processes (in MPI, for example via `MPI_Allgatherv()`). The computation can then proceed in parallel, yielding the vector result s in the expected distributed state with no further communication involved. At the end, each MPI process owns the corresponding piece of the computed vector.

DOT *Products (S3, S7, S10, S11):* The next kernel in the loop body is the DOT product in the step S3 between the distributed vectors r^0 and s. Here, each process can compute concurrently a partial result $P_k : \rho_k = <r_k^0, s_k>$ and when all processes have finished this partial computation, these intermediate values have to be reduced into a globally-replicated scalar $\alpha := \sigma/(\rho_1 + \rho_2 + \cdots + \rho_K)$. We can apply the same idea to the DOT products in the steps S7, S10 and S11, yielding a total of five process synchronizations (in MPI, via `MPI_Allreduce()`) since all scalars are globally-replicated, and communications in S10 and S11 can be merged in a single `MPI_Allreduce()`.

AXPY(-type) *Vector Updates (S4, S8, S9, S12):* The next kernel is the AXPY-like kernel in the step S4, which involves the distributed vectors q, r, s and the globally-replicated scalar α. The operations in the steps S8, S9, and S12 follow the same idea because all scalars are globally-replicated. In these types of kernels, all processes can perform their local parts of the computation to obtain the result without any communication: $P_k : q_k = r_k - \alpha s_k$.

Application of the Preconditioner (S1, S5): The kernel in the step S1 consists of applying the Jacobi preconditioner M, scaling the vector p by the diagonal of the matrix. Therefore, it can be executed in parallel by all processes because each of them stores a different set of the diagonal elements (those related with the piece of the matrix that it stores) and the corresponding set of the vector elements: $P_k : \tilde{s}_k = M_k^{-1} p_k$. The same procedure can be applied on the step S5 to scale the vector q, resulting in $\tilde{y}$.

5   Experimental Results

In this section, we report a variety of numerical experiments to examine the convergence, scalability, accuracy, and reproducibility of the original and two reproducible versions of PBiCGStab. In our experiments, we employed IEEE754 double-precision arithmetic and conducted them on the SkyLake partition at Fraunhofer with a dual Intel Xeon Gold 6132 CPU @2.6 GHz, 28 cores, and 192 GB of memory. Nodes are connected with the 54 Gbit/s FDR Infiniband.

Evaluation on the SuiteSparse Matrices. We carried out tests on a range of different linear systems from the SuiteSparse matrix collection on a single SkyLake node using 1, 2, 4, 8, 16, and 28 (full) cores. Table 1 lists a set of tested matrices with the number of rows/columns N and the number of nonzeros nnz. The right-hand side vector b in the iterative solvers was always initialized to the product $Ad, d = \frac{1}{\sqrt{N}}(1, \ldots, 1)^T$, where N is the number of rows/columns of A. However, in both ExBLAS- and FPE-based versions, marked as ReproPBiCGStab in the table, we computed $b = Ad, d = (1, \dots, 1)^T$ and then scaled b by $\frac{1}{\sqrt{N}}$. The PBiCGStab iterations were started with the initial guess $x_0 = 0$. The parameter that controls the convergence of the iterative process is $\|r^j\|_2 / \|r^0\|_2 \leq 10^{-6}$.

Table 1 also reports the number of required iterations to reach the stopping criterion as well the final true residual for PBiCGStab and ReproPBiCGStab; the latter marks both ExBLAS- and FPE-based variants as they report identical results independently from the number of cores/MPI processes used. For the original version, we display the number of iterations on single and eight cores as they differ. Notably, the two reproducible variants show the tendency to deliver better accuracy of the approximate result (the final true residual) or converge faster, for example for orsreg_1, rdb3200l, and tmt_unsym matrices.

Figure 3 demonstrates the strong scalability results – when the problem is fixed but the number of allocated resources varies – for the original and both ExBLAS- and FPE-based preconditioned BiCGStab variants on the s3dkq4m2 and af_shell10 matrices. The figure reports the mean execution time for the entire loop of the solver among five samples. We select these matrices due to their large number of nonzero elements, i.e. enough work to show scalability. Note that MPI communication is performed within a node, most likely being exposed to intra-node communication via shared memory. All three variants show good scalability

Table 1. Convergence of the PBiCGStab and ReproPBiCGStab on a set of the SuiteSparse matrices. The initial guess is $x^0 = 0$. The number of iterations required to reach the tolerance of 10^{-6} on the scaled residual, i.e. $\|r^j\|_2 / \|r^0\|_2$, is reported along with the corresponding true residual $\|b - Ax^j\|_2$.

Matrix	Prec	N	nnz	$\|r^0\|_2$	BiCGStab			ReproBiCGStab	
					iter1	iter8	$\|b - Ax^j\|_2$	iter	$\|b - Ax^j\|_2$
add32	Jac	4,960	19,848	$6.38e - 05$	36	36	$4.97e - 09$	35	$7.12e - 09$
bcsstk18	Jac	11,948	149,090	$5.29e + 18$	7	7	$7.51e + 02$	7	$7.51e + 02$
bcsstk26	Jac	1,922	30,336	$3.80e + 19$	11	11	$5.62e + 03$	11	$5.62e + 03$
orsreg_1	Jac	2,205	14,133	$2.34e + 01$	225	228	$4.18e - 06$	210	$4.68e - 06$
pde2961	Jac	2,961	14,585	$9.24e - 02$	128	123	$5.28e - 08$	125	$2.67e - 07$
rdb3200l	Jac	3,200	18,880	$9.92e + 01$	641	605	$4.09e - 06$	583	$3.17e - 06$
saylr4	Jac	3,564	22,316	$9.44e + 06$	10	10	$1.95e - 03$	10	$7.26e - 05$
s3dkq4m2	Jac	90,449	4,427,725	$3.70e + 05$	23	23	$7.26e - 05$	23	$7.27e - 05$
af_shell10	Jac	1,508,065	52,259,885	$1.48e + 05$	12	12	$3.44e - 04$	12	$3.44e - 04$
atmosmodd	Jac	1,270,432	8,814,880	$3.75e + 03$	255	272	$3.41e - 05$	257	$2.33e - 05$
atmosmodm	Jac	1,489,752	10,319,760	$3.50e + 05$	117	110	$3.47e - 03$	109	$2.73e - 03$
cage15	Jac	5,154,859	99,199,551	$1.00e + 00$	8	8	$4.56e - 09$	8	$4.56e - 09$
tmt_unsym	Jac	917,825	4,584,801	$6.45e - 06$	6957	7458	$7.44e - 12$	5969	$1.02e - 11$
Hardesty1	Jac	938,905	12,143,314	$9.99e + 00$	24	24	$8.45e - 08$	25	$8.61e - 08$
ecology1	Jac	1,000,000	4,996,000	$1.96e + 01$	11	12	$1.30e - 07$	12	$9.08e - 08$
ecology2	Jac	999,999	4,995,991	$1.96e + 01$	14	13	$1.79e - 08$	13	$5.39e - 08$
CurlCurl_3	Jac	1,219,574	13,544,618	$2.42e + 10$	24	24	$2.00e + 02$	24	$2.00e + 02$

results for s3dkq4m2 with 10.4×, 12.8×, and 13.3× speed up on 16 MPI processes for the original, FPE, and ExBLAS variants, respectively; the corresponding speed up of 8.8×, 12.2×, and 12.8× for af_shell10. The reproducible variants demonstrate higher speedup due to extra floating-point operations. The overhead of the ExBLAS and FPE variants compared to the original variant is reduced to 2.4× and 2× for s3dkq4m2 as well as to 1.9× and 2.2× for af_shell10, accordingly, on 28 MPI processes. The scalability on the other matrices from Table 1 shows the similar pattern and overhead. However, the smaller number of nonzeros leads to the worse scalability. For instance, for the orsreg_1 matrix, the original and ExBLAS/FPE variants are only 4× and 8×, respectively, faster on 16 MPI processes.

Note that the average execution time per loop for many matrices is not sufficient for distributed memory computations. This is due to the fact that the potential performance gain from extra nodes is demolished by communication.

Scalability. We leverage a sparse s.p.d. coefficient matrix arising from the finite-difference method of a 3D Poisson's equation with 27 stencil points. We perturb the matrix with the values $1.0 - 0.0001$ below the central point to create the unsymmetric 27-point stencil aka the e-type model [5]. The fact that the vector involved in the SpMV kernel has to be replicated in all MPI ranks constrains the size of the largest problem that can be solved. Given that the theoretical cost of PBiCGStab is $t_c \approx 4nnz + 26n$ floating-point arithmetic operations, where nnz denotes the number of nonzeros of the original matrix and its size n, the execution time of the method is usually dominated by that of the SpMV kernel. Therefore, in order to analyze the weak scalability of the method, we maintain the number of non-zero entries per node. For this purpose, we modified the

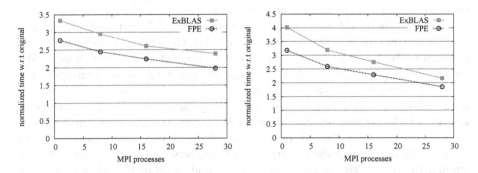

Fig. 3. Strong scaling results of the original and reproducible PBiCGStab variants with the Jacobi preconditioner on one SkyLake node for the s3dkq4m2 (left) and af_shell10 (right) matrices, see Table 1 for details.

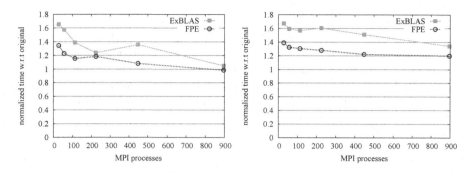

Fig. 4. Strong (left) and weak (right) scalability of the reproducible PBiCGStab variants with the normalized time against the non-deterministic MPI variant.

original matrix, transforming it into a band matrix, where the lower and upper bandwidths (*bandL* and *bandU*, respectively) depend on the number of nodes employed in the experiment as follows:

$$bandL = bandU = 100 \times \#nodes \quad \rightarrow \quad nnz = (bandL + bandU + 1) \times n.$$

With 32 nodes, the bandwidth ranges between 100 and 3200. With this approach we can then maintain the number of rows/columns of the matrix equal to $n = 4M$ (4,019,679), while increasing its bandwidth and, therefore, the computational workload proportionally to the hardware resources, as required in a weak scaling experiment.

The right-hand side vector b in the iterative solvers was always initialized to the product of A with a vector containing ones only; and the PBiCGStab iteration was started with the initial guess $x_0 = 0$. The parameter that controls the convergence of the iterative process was set to 10^{-8}.

Figure 4 reports the results of both strong and weak scaling for the reproducible variants against the original version. For the strong scaling, we fix the problem to 16M non-zeros and varied the number of nodes/cores used, while for the weak scaling the work load per node was fixed to 4M non-zeros and the bandwidth was increased with respect to the number of nodes involved. For both scalability cases, the initial overhead is the same, namely 67% for the version with ExBLAS and 38–40% for FPE. With the strong scaling, the overhead reduces to 8.2% for ExBLAS and 3.0% for FPE as the communication starts to take over and the overhead between the two versions narrows. For the weak scaling, the matrix size is kept constant per node so that there is enough load to hide the impact of communication.

Accuracy and Reproducibility. In addition, we derive a sequential version of the preconditioned BiCGStab as in Fig. 2 that relies on the GNU Multiple Precision Floating-Point Reliably (MPFR) library [8] – a C library for multiple (arbitrary) precision floating-point computations on CPUs – as a highly accurate

Table 2. Accuracy and reproducibility of the intermediate and final residual against MPFR for the orsreg_1 matrix, see Table 1.

Iteration	Residual			
	MPFR	*Original* 1 proc	*Original* 8 procs	*Exblas & FPE*
0	0x1.3566ea57eaf3fp+2	0x1.3566ea57eab49p+2	0x1.3566ea57eab49p+2	0x1.3566ea57eaf3fp+2
1	0x1.146d37f18fbd9p+0	0x1.146d37f18**faaf**p+0	0x1.146d37f18**fab**p+0	0x1.146d37f18fbd9p+0
...	...	...	...	...
99	0x1.cedf0ff322158p-13	**0x1.88008701ba87p-12**	**0x1.04e23203fa6fcp-12**	0x1.cedf0ff322158p-13
100	0x1.be3698f1968cdp-13	**0x1.55418acf1af27p-12**	**0x1.fbf5d3a5d1e49p-13**	0x1.be3698f1968cdp-13
...	...	...	...	...
208	0x1.355b0f18f5ac1p-20	**0x1.19edf2c932ab8p-18**	**0x1.b051edae310c7p-20**	0x1.355b0f18f5ac1p-20
209	0x1.114dc7c9b6d38p-20	**0x1.19b74e383f74ep-18**	**0x1.a18fc929018d4p-20**	0x1.114dc7c9b6d38p-20
210	0x1.03b1920a49a7ap-20	**0x1.19c846848f361p-18**	**0x1.c7eb5bbc198b1p-20**	0x1.03b1920a49a7ap-20

reference implementation. This implementation uses 2,048 bits of accuracy for computing dot product, 192 bits for internal element-wise product, and performs correct rounding of the computed result to double precision.

Table 2 reports the intermediate and final (except from original that takes longer) scaled residual on each iteration of the PBiCGStab solvers for the orsreg_1 matrix, as in Table 1, under the tolerance of 10^{-6} on eight MPI processes. We also add the results of the original code on one core/process to highlight the reproducibility issue. The results are presented with all digits using hexadecimal representation. We report only few iterations, however the difference is present on all iterations. The sequential MPFR version confirms the accuracy and reproducibility of parallel ExBLAS and FPE variants by reporting identical number of iterations, intermediate residuals, and both the final true and initial scaled residuals. However, the MPFR variant of PBiCGStab converges to the approximate solution in 3.39e−01 s, while the ExBLAS and FPE variants take 3.95e−02 and 2.75e−02 s ($8.57\times$ and $12.32\times$ faster), accordingly, on eight MPI processes. The original code shows the discrepancy from few digits on the initial iteration and up to almost the entire number on the final iterations; the count of required iterations also differs from the reproducible and MPFR variants.

6   Conclusions

Parallel Krylov subspace algorithms may exhibit the lack of reproducibility when implemented in parallel environments as the results in Table 2 confirm. Such numerical reliability is needed for debugging and validation & verification. In this work, we proposed a general framework for re-constructing reproducibility and re-assuring accuracy in any Krylov subspace algorithm. Our framework is based on two steps: analysis of the underlying algorithm for the arithmetic abnormalities; addressing them via algorithmic solutions and programmability hints. The algorithmic solutions are build around the ExBLAS project, namely: ExBLAS that effectively combines long accumulator and FPEs; FPEs only for the leightweight version. The programmability effort was focused on: explicitly invoking `fma` instructions to avoid replacements by compilers as well as to postpone the division to the moment where it is required. As a test case, we used the preconditioned BiCGStab algorithm and derived two reproducible algorithmic variants of it. Both reproducible variants deliver identical results of PBiCGStab, which are confirmed by its MPFR version, to ensure reproducibility in the number of iterations, the intermediate and final residuals, as well as the sought-after solution vector. We verified our implementations on the SuiteSparse matrices, showing the performance overhead of 2.5× and 2× for the ExBLAS and FPE-based versions, accordingly; tests with the 27-point stencil on 32 nodes show almost negligible overhead of 8% and 3%, respectively.

Acknowledgment. This research was partially supported by the EU H2020 MSCA-IF Robust project (No. 842528); the French ANR InterFLOP project (No. ANR-20-CE46-0009). The research from Universitat Jaume I was funded by the project PID2020-113656RB-C21 via MCIN/AEI/10.13039/501100011033.

References

1. Iakymchuk, R., et al.: Reproducibility of parallel preconditioned conjugate gradient in hybrid programming environments. IJHPCA **34**(5), 502–518 (2020). https://doi.org/10.1177/1094342020932650
2. Iakymchuk, R., et al.: Reproducibility strategies for parallel preconditioned conjugate gradient. JCAM **371**, 112697 (2020). https://doi.org/10.1016/j.cam.2019.112697
3. Barrett, R., et al.: Templates for the Solution of Linear Systems: Building Blocks for Iterative Methods, 2nd edn. SIAM (1994)
4. Collange, S., et al.: Numerical reproducibility for the parallel reduction on multi- and many-core architectures. Parallel Comput. **49**, 83–97 (2015). https://doi.org/10.1016/j.parco.2015.09.001
5. Cools, S., Vanroose, W.: The communication-hiding pipelined BiCGstab method for the parallel solution of large unsymmetric linear systems. Parallel Comput. **65**, 1–20 (2017). https://doi.org/10.1016/j.parco.2017.04.005
6. Demmel, J., Nguyen, H.D.: Parallel reproducible summation. IEEE Trans. Comput. **64**(7), 2060–2070 (2015). https://doi.org/10.1109/TC.2014.2345391
7. Fletcher, R.: Conjugate gradient methods for indefinite systems. In: Watson, G.A. (ed.) Numerical Analysis. LNM, vol. 506, pp. 73–89. Springer, Heidelberg (1976). https://doi.org/10.1007/BFb0080116
8. Fousse, L., et al.: MPFR: a multiple-precision binary floating-point library with correct rounding. ACM TOMS **33**(2), 13 (2007). https://doi.org/10.1145/1236463.1236468
9. Goldberg, D.: What every computer scientist should know about floating-point arithmetic. ACM Comput. Surv. **23**(1), 5–48 (1991). https://doi.org/10.1145/103162.103163
10. Knuth, D.E.: The Art of Computer Programming: Seminumerical Algorithms, vol. 2. Addison-Wesley (1969)
11. Kulisch, U., Snyder, V.: The exact dot product as basic tool for long interval arithmetic. Computing **91**(3), 307–313 (2011). https://doi.org/10.1007/s00607-010-0127-7

12. Mukunoki, D., Ogita, T., Ozaki, K.: Reproducible BLAS routines with tunable accuracy using Ozaki scheme for many-core architectures. In: Wyrzykowski, R., Deelman, E., Dongarra, J., Karczewski, K. (eds.) PPAM 2019. LNCS, vol. 12043, pp. 516–527. Springer, Cham (2020). https://doi.org/10.1007/978-3-030-43229-4_44

13. Ogita, T., Rump, S.M., Oishi, S.: Accurate sum and dot product. SIAM J. Sci. Comput. **26**, 1955–1988 (2005). https://doi.org/10.1137/030601818

14. Rump, S.M., Ogita, T., Oishi, S.: Accurate floating-point summation part II: sign, K-fold faithful and rounding to nearest. SIAM J. Sci. Comput. **31**(2), 1269–1302 (2008). https://doi.org/10.1137/07068816X

15. Saad, Y.: Iterative Methods for Sparse Linear Systems, 2nd edn. SIAM, Philadelphia (2003). https://doi.org/10.1137/1.9780898718003

16. Saad, Y., Schultz, M.H.: GMRES: a generalized minimal residual algorithm for solving nonsymmetric linear systems. SIAM J. Sci. Stat. Comput. **7**, 856–869 (1986). https://doi.org/10.1137/0907058

17. Sonneveld, P.: CGS, a fast Lanczos-type solver for nonsymmetric linear systems. SIAM J. Sci. Stat. Comput. **10**(1), 36–52 (1989). https://doi.org/10.1137/0910004

18. van der Vorst, H.A.: Bi-CGSTAB: a fast and smoothly converging variant of Bi-CG for the solution of nonsymmetric linear systems. SIAM J. Sci. Stat. Comput. **13**(2), 631–644 (1992). https://doi.org/10.1137/0913035

19. Wiesenberger, M., et al.: Reproducibility, accuracy and performance of the Feltor code and library on parallel computer architectures. CPC **238**, 145–156 (2019). https://doi.org/10.1016/j.cpc.2018.12.006

A Generalized Parallel Prefix Sums Algorithm for Arbitrary Size Arrays

Andrzej Sikorski[1] , Izajasz Wrosz[1,2]([⊠]) , and Michał Lewandowski[1]

[1] Intel, Gdańsk, Poland
[2] Faculty of Electronics, Telecommunications and Informatics,
Gdańsk University of Technology, Gdańsk, Poland
izajasz.p.wrosz@intel.com

Abstract. The prefix sums algorithm is a fundamental parallel programming building block used to solve significant problems in engineering, mathematical software, and big data analytics. In this paper, we present a generalization of the work-efficient prefix sums algorithm introduced by Blelloch, which in its original form is particularly well-performing on highly parallel architectures. However, the algorithm works only with arrays whose size is a power of 2. While various solutions have been developed to alleviate this limitation, we propose a canonical extension of the classical algorithm, which preserves its original form and maintains the performance characteristics of the work-efficient algorithm.

Keywords: parallel prefix sums · scan · parallel algorithms

1 Introduction

Prefix sums, also known as *all partial sums* or *scan*, is one of the fundamental building blocks used for designing parallel applications. As such, the prefix algorithms can be found as primitive operations in many parallel software libraries, languages, and standards, e.g., MPI, ISO C++, and SYCL [15, 22, 25]. The research of parallel kernels contributes to improved processes of designing complex parallel applications, which can leverage the knowledge about intrinsic characteristics of the fundamental kernels, as well as their behavior on different hardware platforms.

The prefix sums problem receives as an input array $X = x_0, x_1, ..., x_{N-1}$ and a binary associative operation $\oplus$. The elements of X belong to a domain $\mathcal{D}$, so that $\oplus$ is defined on the Cartesian product $\mathcal{D} \times \mathcal{D}$. The elements might be integers, floating point numbers, or matrices, and the operation $\oplus$ may represent a min, max, matrix multiply, etc. The goal is to calculate an array $Y = y_0, y_1, ..., y_{N-1}$ that contains all partial sums of X, using the operation $\oplus$ [7]. I.e., for every element $x_i \in X$ we want to calculate the sum of all elements preceding x_i. Typically, two variants of prefix are considered, which differ depending on whether the element x_i should be included in the sum. The *inclusive scan* is such that $y_k = x_0 \oplus x_1 \oplus ... \oplus x_k$, $0 \le k \le N-1$. Otherwise, for the *exclusive scan* we have that $y_0 = I$, and for each $0 < k \le N-1$, $y_k = x_0 \oplus x_1 \oplus ... \oplus x_{k-1}$, where I is

R. Wyrzykowski et al. (Eds.): PPAM 2022, LNCS 13826, pp. 30–39, 2023.
https://doi.org/10.1007/978-3-031-30442-2_3

the identity of operation $\oplus$. Although the problem is stated sequentially, it can be solved in parallel by leveraging the associativity of the operation $\oplus$.

The prefix sums algorithm and its variants are used in a variety of parallel applications from many computational domains such as image processing and computational geometry [5,8], functional programming [11,12,20], sorting and list ranking [10,23], linear algebra [4], graph analytics [19]. For a comprehensive overview of the parallel applications which use prefix sums kernels, refer to [3,7, 18].

The remaining parts of the paper are organized as follows. Sections 2 and 3 summarize, respectively, the prior work related to parallel prefix sums and the approaches to handling inputs whose size is not a power of two. Section 4 describes our algorithmic extension, which is the main result of this work. Section 5 provides an experimental evaluation of the proposed solution. Section 6 concludes the work.

All logarithms in the paper have a base of 2. I.e., $\log n = \log_2 n$, for all n. For an array $x_0, x_1, ..., x_{n-1}$, the partial sum $x_i \oplus x_{x+1}... \oplus x_j$ is denoted by $\sum_{i,j}$.

2   Parallel Prefix

In the context of electronic circuits, a recursion-based method was used to design prefix circuits in a form of binary trees [16]. The method allowed to generate a circuit calculating the prefix for arrays of a given size. The exact depth and size of the circuit were provided in a closed form for power of two array sizes. Subsequently, the obtained solution was used to efficiently simulate a finite-state transducer [16,18]. Thus, the presented approach potentially enables a general method applicable to problems whose parallelization is difficult as opposed to straightforward serial computation.

In the context of parallel programming, a method based on the balanced binary tree was introduced in [6,7]. As shown in Algorithm 1, prefix sums are calculated in two phases called up-sweep and down-sweep. The input size N must be a power of two. The data flow during computation is represented by a balanced binary tree, whose each level corresponds to a parallel step. The algorithm requires linear amount of work and $2 \log N$ parallel steps. The calculations are performed in-place, using a linear representation of the input array. The amount of the parallel work halves with each level of the binary tree. At the same time, the stride of the memory accesses needed for each of the reduced pair doubles.

The classical step-efficient parallel algorithm for prefix sums was introduced in [14]. Although it requires more work than a trivial serial solution (by a multiplicative factor of $\log N$), it requires only $\log N$ parallel steps, and exposes more parallelism than the work-efficient algorithm. A hybrid approach was proposed in [24], where the work-efficient algorithm is applied as long as the amount of the parallel work is sufficient to utilize the processors available. Subsequently, the more parallel step-efficient algorithm is used.

Algorithm 1: The original work-efficient prefix sums algorithm [6]. The array size N must be a power of two.

```
/* up-sweep phase                                                        */
```
1   **for** d from 0 to $\log N - 1$
2   **in parallel for** i from 0 to $N - 1$ **by** 2^{d+1}
3        $a[i + 2^{d+1} - 1] \leftarrow a[i + 2^{d+1} - 1] + a[i + 2^d - 1]$

4

5    $a[N - 1] \leftarrow 0$

6

```
/* down-sweep phase                                                      */
```
7   **for** d from $\log N - 1$ **downto** 0
8   **in parallel for** i from 0 to $N - 1$ **by** 2^{d+1}
9        $t \leftarrow a[i + 2^d - 1]$
10     $a[i + 2^d - 1] \leftarrow a[i + 2^{d+1} - 1]$
11     $a[i + 2^{d+1} - 1] \leftarrow a[i + 2^{d+1} - 1] + t$

---

3 Handling Arbitrary Size Inputs

A general method for handling inputs of arbitrary lengths (e.g., larger than the total number of processors in the system) has been proposed in [6]. In this method, for a given a machine with P processors, the input array is divided into segments. Each segment is of length N/P, where N is the size of the input. In case P does not divide N, the reminding elements are spread across the processors. In particular, $N \bmod P$ segments are of length $N/P + 1$. The method consists of three phases. First, each processor calculates the sum of the assigned segment, which is stored in an auxiliary array. Subsequently, prefix sums are calculated for the values stored in the auxiliary array. As can be seen in Fig. 1, in the third step, each processor calculates prefix sums for the assigned segment, while including the corresponding element from the auxiliary array in its running sum. The per-segment calculations can be efficiently mapped on vector machines [9]. We note that there is freedom in terms of calculating the partial prefixes in either the first or the third phase, which opens a space for a variety of optimization techniques, cf. [13,26,27].

    The general flow of the block-based algorithm from [6,9] has been optimized for a GPU architecture [13]. For instance, to achieve high bandwidth utilization, bank conflicts in the memory system were avoided by modifying the in-memory layout of the array, which allowed for more optimal memory access patterns. Next, the block-based approach was used to overcome an architecture limitation of the maximum array size that could be processed in parallel in the considered device. At the same time, the technique allows for handling arrays whose size is not a power of two. As in [6,9], the proposed algorithm consists of three phases.

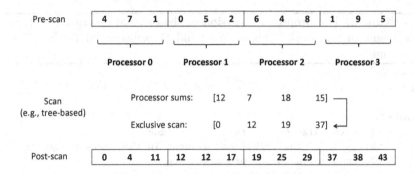

Fig. 1. The original method from [6], which generalizes the tree-based scan to arbitrary sized arrays. Sums of the segments are calculated in the pre-scan. Then, a scan is calculated over the total sums of per-processor segments. During the post-scan, values from the intermediate array are added to the running sums in the corresponding segments, which obtains the final scan of the input array.

The method is different in terms of the operations performed in the first and the last phase. In the first phase, each block is scanned by the assigned processor, so that in the last phase it suffices to just add the values from the auxiliary array to the values in the corresponding segments. The method presented in [13] also differs from the approach in [6,9] in terms of handling array sizes which cannot be evenly distributed among the processors. I.e., after distributing the even blocks, the remaining part of the array is padded with zeros up to the block size and processed separately.

4   The Right-Sweep Phase

We extend the work-efficient algorithm from [6,7] into the domain of arbitrary sized arrays. The original up-sweep reduction applies directly to the input array. As shown in Fig. 2, the reduction is performed independently in segments of the input. The first segment is the largest and has size of the highest power of two that is less or equal than the input size. The following segments are sized to subsequent lower powers of two. Note that simply applying the up-sweep and then the down-sweep operation would result in calculating a segmented scan [6]. To calculate prefix sums for the entire input, we introduce a new phase called *right-sweep* that is executed between the up-sweep and the down-sweep passes. As can be seen in Fig. 3, the right-sweep pass performs an exclusive scan over the right-most elements of the segments. Because there are $\log N$ such elements, the work complexity of the new phase is significantly lower than the linear complexity

---

Algorithm 2: The proposed extension of the original algorithm and the main result of our work. This code should be substituted for line 7 in Algorithm 1.

```
1 t1 ← N
2 t2 ← 0
3 t3 ← 0
4 while t1 > 0 do
       /* t1: total size of the remaining segments              */
       /* t2: index of the right-most element in the current segment */
       /* t3: cumulative sum of processed segments              */
       /* bsr: returns the position of the highest enabled bit  */
5      t2 ← t2 + 1 ≪ bsr(t1)
6      t ← a[t2 − 1]
7      a[t2 − 1] ← t3
8      t3 ← t3 + t
9      t1 ← N − t2
10 end
```

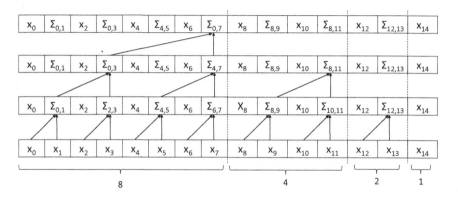

Fig. 2. The up-sweep phase applied to an array whose size is not a power of two. In 3 parallel steps, independent reductions are performed on segments of the array. The size of the largest segment is equal to the largest power of 2 that is less than the array size. After the last parallel step, the right-most element of each segment contains the generalized sum of the corresponding elements.

of the two other phases. E.g., even for an input size close to 2^{64}, the new pass would processes up to 64 elements. Algorithm 2 shows the pseudo code of the right-sweep phase. Note that the *while* loop iterates over the enabled bits in the binary representation of N, the size of the input array.

The right-sweep pass performs an exclusive scan over the right-most values of each array segment. The right-most elements correspond to the roots of the binary trees underlying the reduction the reduction in the up-sweep phase. The values stored at those roots are equal to the sum of elements in the respective segments of the array. After the right-sweep, each root node holds the sum of elements in all segments that lie before the segment corresponding to the root.

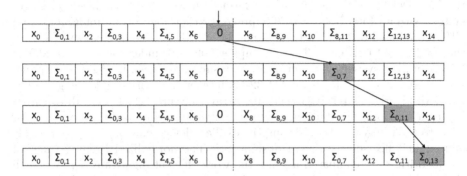

Fig. 3. The right-sweep phase. A scan over the right-most elements of the segments is performed. In the presented example, after 4 sequential steps, each right-most element contains the generalized sum of all preceding segments.

During the down-sweep phase see (Fig. 4), we leverage the property of the down-sweep operator so that the value stored at the root of the binary tree contributes to every element of the output. Because the right-sweep pass assigns roots with the sum of all segments that precede the current segment, the scan of each segment is modified by the constant needed to obtain the scan for the entire sequence.

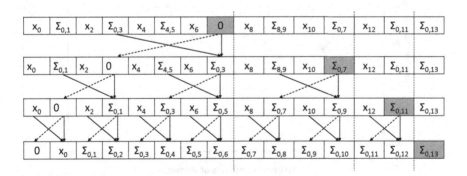

Fig. 4. The down-sweep phase over an array with 15 elements. The pair-wise down-sweep operation is applied to elements of the array in 3 parallel steps, independently in the segments of the array. The down-sweep phase concludes our three-phase algorithm that calculates the scan of the array.

5   Experimental Results

We implemented both the classical algorithm [7] and our extended version in SYCL, by using Data Parallel C++ [21,25] and verified the Data Parallel C++ implementation on heterogeneous hardware and software platforms available in the Intel Developer Cloud [1]. We performed the tests on a single socket server system with an Intel Xeon E-2176G processor that contains an integrated Intel UHD Graphics P630 GPU. The system had 64GB of system memory. We used the Intel oneAPI DPC++/C++ Compiler 2022.1.0 under the Ubuntu 20.04.4 LTS operating system. The performance results are shown in Fig. 5. The prefix sums were calculated for arrays of 32-bit integers and the simple integer addition. All algorithms received the same array contents, which were drawn from a pseudo-random distribution. Prefix calculation was offloaded from the host CPU to the integrated GPU, using the explicit device memory allocation mode and explicit host-device data transfers [21]. The normalized running times of our algorithm are compared against the work-efficient algorithm [7]. We recall that the implementation of the work-efficient and the new generalized algorithm differ only by the right-sweep pass introduced in the generalized algorithm. As can be seen in Fig. 5, for both algorithms, we show results for the power-of-two array sizes, while for the generalized algorithm also the in-between data points are provided. The performance of both algorithms is equivalent for array sizes which are exactly a power of two. While for many in-between array sizes the performance of the generalized algorithm is close to the trend line implied by the

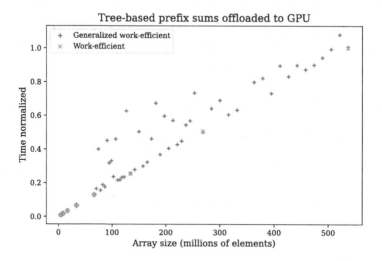

Fig. 5. Normalized execution times of parallel prefix sums algorithms as a function of the array size. Prefix sums are calculated using the standard addition of 32-bit integer values. For the work-efficient algorithm, the results are available for array sizes that are powers-of-two. For the generalized algorithm results are obtained also for the in-between array sizes.

work-efficient algorithm data points, for some array sizes, the processing time of the generalized algorithm is higher. We anticipate that incorporating key aspects of the system architecture (e.g., the memory architecture) into the design of the algorithm is necessary to achieve sustained performance characteristics for a large range of array sizes.

6 Conclusions

In this work we proposed a canonical method for extending the well-known work-efficient parallel prefix sum algorithm [7] into the domain of arrays of arbitrary size. The method is based on adding a new phase, which we call right-sweep, between the existing up-sweep and down-sweep phases. The right-sweep phase performs a scan over specific $\log N$ elements of the input array. Thus, in practical scenarios, a sequential algorithm should be sufficient as requiring only $\log n$ work. In general, a parallel algorithm can be used, reducing the number of steps to $\log(\log N)$. We used SYCL to experimentally evaluate the new algorithm by offloading the prefix kernel to a GPU accelerator.

We observe that processing the binary-tree-based reductions with a linear representation of the input array may not be efficient on typical NUMA systems, primarily due to low data locality. A variety of software-based approaches exist for managing distributed and sparse data. For instance, the optimized heap data layouts enable using of the key characteristics of a compute architecture more efficiently, specifically the tradeoff between optimal arithmetic compute power and memory bandwidth utilization. On the other hand, canonical representations of sparse and irregular workloads are efficiently mapped on domain-specific architectures like the Intel PIUMA [2,17]. The architecture features such as partitioned global address space, power-efficient cores, as well as fast and efficient in-network collective operations, allow for achieving high power efficiency and performance in the domain of sparse computations and graph analytics, especially with datasets, which size exceeds the memory capacity of a single shared-memory system.

References

1. Intel Developer Cloud. https://devcloud.intel.com/. Accessed 30 Oct 2022
2. Aananthakrishnan, S., et al.: Piuma: programmable integrated unified memory architecture. arXiv preprint arXiv:2010.06277 (2020)
3. Akl, S.G.: Parallel Computation: Models and Methods. Prentice-Hall, Inc., Hoboken (1997)
4. Bell, N., Garland, M.: Implementing sparse matrix-vector multiplication on throughput-oriented processors. In: Proceedings of the ACM/IEEE Conference on High Performance Computing, SC 2009, November 14–20, 2009, Portland, Oregon, USA. ACM (2009). https://doi.org/10.1145/1654059.1654078
5. Bilgic, B., Horn, B.K.P., Masaki, I.: Efficient integral image computation on the GPU. In: IEEE Intelligent Vehicles Symposium (IV), 2010, La Jolla, CA, USA, June 21–24, 2010, pp. 528–533. IEEE (2010). https://doi.org/10.1109/IVS.2010.5548142

6. Blelloch, G.E.: Scans as primitive parallel operations. IEEE Trans. Comput. **38**(11), 1526–1538 (1989). https://doi.org/10.1109/12.42122
7. Blelloch, G.E.: Prefix sums and their applications. Technical report. CMU-CS-90-190, School of Computer Science, Carnegie Mellon University, November 1990
8. Blelloch, G.E., Little, J.J.: Parallel solutions to geometric problems in the scan model of computation. J. Comput. Syst. Sci. **48**(1), 90–115 (1994). https://doi.org/10.1016/S0022-0000(05)80023-6
9. Chatterjee, S., Blelloch, G.E., Zagha, M.: Scan primitives for vector computers. In: Martin, J.L., Pryor, D.V., Montry, G.R. (eds.) Proceedings Supercomputing '90, New York, NY, USA, November 12–16, 1990, pp. 666–675. IEEE Computer Society (1990). https://doi.org/10.1109/SUPERC.1990.130084
10. Cole, R., Vishkin, U.: Faster optimal parallel prefix sums and list ranking. Inf. Comput. **81**(3), 334–352 (1989). https://doi.org/10.1016/0890-5401(89)90036-9
11. Elliott, C.: Generic functional parallel algorithms: scan and FFT. Proc. ACM Program. Lang. **1**(ICFP), 7:1–7:25 (2017). https://doi.org/10.1145/3110251
12. Fisher, A.L., Ghuloum, A.M.: Parallelizing complex scans and reductions. In: Sarkar, V., Ryder, B.G., Soffa, M.L. (eds.) Proceedings of the ACM SIGPLAN 1994 Conference on Programming Language Design and Implementation (PLDI), Orlando, Florida, USA, June 20–24, 1994, pp. 135–146. ACM (1994). https://doi.org/10.1145/178243.178255
13. Harris, M., Sengupta, S., Owens, J.D.: Chapter 39. parallel prefix sum (scan) with CUDA (2007). https://developer.nvidia.com/gpugems/gpugems3/part-vi-gpu-computing/chapter-39-parallel-prefix-sum-scan-cuda
14. Hillis, W.D., Jr., G.L.S.: Data parallel algorithms. Commun. ACM. **29**(12), 1170–1183 (1986). https://doi.org/10.1145/7902.7903
15. Iso/iec 14882:2020(en) programming languages - c++. Standard, International Organization for Standardization, Geneva, Switzerland, December 2020
16. Ladner, R.E., Fischer, M.J.: Parallel prefix computation. J. ACM **27**(4), 831–838 (1980). https://doi.org/10.1145/322217.322232
17. Lakhotia, K., Petrini, F., Kannan, R., Prasanna, V.K.: Accelerating all reduce with in-network reduction on intel PIUMA. IEEE Micro **42**(2), 44–52 (2022)
18. Lakshmivarahan, S., Dhall, S.K.: Parallel Computing Using the Prefix Problem. Oxford University Press, Oxford (1994)
19. Merrill, D., Garland, M., Grimshaw, A.S.: High-performance and scalable GPU graph traversal. ACM Trans. Parallel Comput. **1**(2), 14:1–14:30 (2015). https://doi.org/10.1145/2717511
20. Morihata, A.: Lambda calculus with algebraic simplification for reduction parallelisation: extended study. J. Funct. Program. **31**, e7 (2021). https://doi.org/10.1017/S0956796821000058
21. Reinders, J., Ashbaugh, B., Brodman, J., Kinsner, M., Pennycook, J., Tian, X.: Data Parallel C++: Mastering DPC++ for Programming of Heterogeneous Systems Using C++ and SYCL. Springer Nature, CA (2021). https://doi.org/10.1007/978-1-4842-5574-2
22. Sanders, P., Träff, J.L.: Parallel prefix (scan) algorithms for MPI. In: Mohr, B., Träff, J.L., Worringen, J., Dongarra, J.J. (eds.) Recent Advances in Parallel Virtual Machine and Message Passing Interface, 13th European PVM/MPI User's Group Meeting, Bonn, Germany, September 17–20, 2006, Proceedings. LNCS, vol. 4192, pp. 49–57. Springer, Cham (2006). https://doi.org/10.1007/11846802_15
23. Satish, N., Harris, M.J., Garland, M.: Designing efficient sorting algorithms for manycore GPUs. In: 23rd IEEE International Symposium on Parallel and Dis-

tributed Processing, IPDPS 2009, Rome, Italy, May 23–29, 2009, pp. 1–10. IEEE (2009). https://doi.org/10.1109/IPDPS.2009.5161005

24. Sengupta, S., Lefohn, A., Owens, J.D.: A work-efficient step-efficient prefix sum algorithm (2006)

25. Sycl 2020 specification (revision 5). Standard, Khronos Group, Beaverton, OR, USA, May 2022

26. Zhang, N.: A novel parallel prefix sum algorithm and its implementation on multi-core platforms. In: 2010 2nd International Conference on Computer Engineering and Technology, vol. 2, pp. V2–66–V2-70. IEEE (2010). https://doi.org/10.1109/ICCET.2010.5485315

27. Zhang, W., Wang, Y., Ross, K.A.: Parallel prefix sum with SIMD. In: Bordawekar, R., Lahiri, T. (eds.) International Workshop on Accelerating Analytics and Data Management Systems Using Modern Processor and Storage Architectures, ADMS@VLDB 2020, Tokyo, Japan, August 31, 2020. pp. 1–11 (2020)

Infinite-Precision Inner Product and Sparse Matrix-Vector Multiplication Using Ozaki Scheme with Dot2 on Manycore Processors

Daichi Mukunoki[1](✉)(iD), Katsuhisa Ozaki[2](iD), Takeshi Ogita[3](iD), and Toshiyuki Imamura[1](iD)

[1] RIKEN Center for Computational Science, Kobe, Hyogo, Japan
daichi.mukunoki@riken.jp
[2] Shibaura Institute of Technology, Saitama, Japan
[3] Tokyo Woman's Christian University, Tokyo, Japan

Abstract. Infinite-precision operations do not incur rounding errors except when rounding the computed result to a finite-precision value. This can be an effective solution for the accuracy and reproducibility concerns associated with floating-point operations. This research presents an infinite-precision inner product (IP-DOT) and sparse matrix-vector multiplication (IP-SpMV) on FP64 data for manycore processors. We propose using a 106-bit computation using Dot2 in the Ozaki scheme, which is an existing IP-DOT method. First, we discuss the theoretical performance of our method using the roofline model. Then, we demonstrate the actual performance as IP-DOT and reproducible conjugate gradient (CG) solvers, with IP-SpMV as their primary operation, using an Ice Lake CPU and an Ampere GPU. Although the benefits and performance are dependent on the input data, our experiments on IP-DOT demonstrated a speedup of approximately 1.9–3.4 times compared to the previous method, and an execution time overhead of approximately 10–25 times compared to the standard FP64 operation. On reproducible CG, a speedup of 1.1–1.7 times was achieved compared to the existing method, and an execution time overhead of approximately 3–19 times was observed compared to the non-reproducible standard solvers.

Keywords: Infinite-precision · Accurate · Reproducible · Inner product · Sparse matrix-vector multiplication (SpMV) · Conjugate gradient (CG)

1 Introduction

Floating-point operations are susceptible to rounding errors, which might lead to inaccurate computational result. Additionally, since a change in the order of operation causes different errors, the output may vary even when the same

R. Wyrzykowski et al. (Eds.): PPAM 2022, LNCS 13826, pp. 40–54, 2023.
https://doi.org/10.1007/978-3-031-30442-2_4

input is used on parallel computations where the order of operations is non-deterministic for each execution or in different hardware (e.g., CPUs and GPUs). This can be troublesome when debugging or porting codes to multiple environments [1]. Thus, computing methods that are both accurate and reproducible are being developed.

Infinite-precision operations do not incur rounding errors except when rounding the computed result to a finite-precision value, such as in FP64. This can be an effective solution for the accuracy and reproducibility concerns associated with floating-point operations[1]. Furthermore, infinite-precision operations can be utilized as a tool to analyze the mathematical behavior of numerical algorithms [27]. However, one of the major drawbacks of infinite-precision operations is their high runtime and program development costs, especially on modern manycore processors.

This research focuses on the infinite-precision inner product (IP-DOT) and sparse matrix-vector multiplication (IP-SpMV) for FP64 data on manycore processors. It proposes a fast computation method by combining an existing infinite-precision method with a 106-bit precision operation algorithm. IP-DOT and IP-SpMV are then implemented on an Ice Lake CPU and an Ampere GPU. The advantage of the proposed method is not only justified theoretically but also demonstrated as a speedup of IP-DOT separately and a speedup of reproducible sparse iterative solvers based on IP-DOT and IP-SpMV on matrices selected from a database collecting real-world problems.

2   Related Work

Several arithmetic tools, including iRRAM [20], RealLib [13], and Briggs's work [3], have been developed to enable infinite-precision computation. Its efficient implementation for vector and matrix operations (i.e., Basic Linear Algebra Subprograms (BLAS) operations) on parallel architectures can be investigated; for example, RARE-BLAS [4], ExBLAS [5], and OzBLAS [17] have been developed. OzBLAS adopts the same methodology that is referenced as an existing method in this paper.

Reproducible computation[2] does not necessarily require infinite-precision. The simplest way to ensure reproducibility is to fix the order of computation, although this is often inefficient in parallel computing. The Intel Math Kernel Library (MKL) supports conditional numerical reproducibility [26], but this is restricted to limited environments (with MKL on certain Intel processors) and execution conditions. ReproBLAS [7] is a reproducible BLAS implementation that uses a high-precision accumulator and pre-rounding technique but is not parallelized on manycore processors.

---

[1] Be aware, however, that infinite-precision operations do not necessarily improve the stability or accuracy of numerical algorithms.

[2] The concept of reproducibility is independent of accuracy. It is simply intended to be able to reproduce the same result.

Algorithm 1 Ozaki scheme with Dot2

1: **function** ($r = $ IP_DOT_Dot2$(\boldsymbol{x}, \boldsymbol{y})$)
2:    $\underline{\boldsymbol{x}}[1 : s_x] = $ Split2$(\boldsymbol{x})$
3:    $\underline{\boldsymbol{y}}[1 : s_y] = $ Split2$(\boldsymbol{y})$
4:    $i = 1$
5:    **for** $q = 1 : s_y$ **do**
6:       **for** $p = 1 : s_x$ **do**
7:          $(u, v)[i] = $ Dot2$(\underline{\boldsymbol{x}}[p], \underline{\boldsymbol{y}}[q])$
8:          $i = i + 1$
9:       **end for**
10:    **end for**
11:    $r = $ NearSum$((u, v))$
12: **end function**

Algorithm 2 Dot2

1: **function** $((u, v) = $ Dot2$(\boldsymbol{x}, \boldsymbol{y}))$
2:    $(u, v) = $ TwoProdFMA$(\boldsymbol{x}_1, \boldsymbol{y}_1)$
3:    **for** $i = 2$ to n **do**
4:       $(h, r) = $ TwoProdFMA$(\boldsymbol{x}_i, \boldsymbol{y}_i)$
5:       $(u, q) = $ TwoSum(u, h)
6:       $v = $ fl$(v + (q + r))$
7:    **end for**
8: **end function**

Algorithm 3 Splitting for Ozaki scheme with Dot2. Lines 9–10 are computations for $1 \leq i \leq n$.

1: **function** $(\underline{\boldsymbol{x}}[1 : s_x] = $ Split2$(\boldsymbol{x}))$
2:    $\rho = $ ceil$(\log 2(n)/2)$
3:    $\mu = \max_{1 \leq i \leq n}(|\boldsymbol{x}_i|)$
4:    $j = 0$
5:    **while** $\mu \neq 0$ **do**
6:       $j = j + 1$
7:       $\tau = $ ceil$(\log 2(\mu))$
8:       $\sigma = 0.75 \times 2^{(\rho + \tau)}$
9:       $\underline{\boldsymbol{x}}[j]_i = $ fl$((\boldsymbol{x}_i + \sigma) - \sigma)$
10:      $\boldsymbol{x}_i = $ fl$(\boldsymbol{x}_i - \underline{\boldsymbol{x}}[j]_i)$
11:      $\mu = \max_{1 \leq i \leq n}(|\boldsymbol{x}_i|)$
12:    **end while**
13:    $s_x = j$
14: **end function**

The use of high-precision arithmetic (in lower than infinite but better than FP64 precision) can be a lightweight solution for improving accuracy (without reproducibility). MPLAPACK [21] is an example of a linear algebra library that supports various high-precision operations with a backend of several high-precision arithmetic libraries such as the GNU Multiple Precision Floating-Point Reliable Library [9]. However, it is often difficult to determine the required level of precision for a specific objective.

3   Method

Hereafter, $\mathbb{F}_{\mathsf{FP64}}$ will denote a set of FP64 floating-point numbers, and fl$(\cdot)$ will denote the FP64 floating-point operations. The objective is to compute $r = \boldsymbol{x}^T \boldsymbol{y}$ for $\boldsymbol{x}, \boldsymbol{y} \in \mathbb{F}_{\mathsf{FP64}}{}^n$ with infinite precision.

Originally proposed as an accurate matrix multiplication technique, the Ozaki scheme [23] is employed in this research as an IP-DOT method. This scheme computes an IP-DOT as the sum of multiple inner products that can be calculated with some precision and without rounding errors using floating-point operations. Algorithm 1 shows the entire IP-DOT process. It consists of the following three steps:

Algorithm 4 TwoSum	**Algorithm 5** TwoProdFMA
1: **function** $((s, e) = \texttt{TwoSum}(a, b))$	1: **function** $((p, e) = \texttt{TwoProdFMA}(a, b))$
2: $s = \mathrm{fl}(a + b)$	2: $p = \mathrm{fl}(a \times b)$
3: $t = \mathrm{fl}(s - a)$	3: $e = \texttt{FMA}(a \times b - p)$
4: $e = \mathrm{fl}((a - (s - t)) + (b - t))$	4: **end function**
5: **end function**	

1. **Splitting**: In lines 2–3 of Algorithm 1, Split2 (Algorithm 3) performs the element-wise splitting of the input vectors x and y into $\underline{x}$ and $\underline{y}$ (FP64 vectors). Split2 divides the input vectors so that the inner products of the split vectors ($\underline{x}$ and $\underline{y}$) can be computed with 106-bit precision without rounding errors. In line 8 of Algorithm 3, the constant 0.75 was introduced by [15]. Due to the possibility of overflow in this splitting technique, the inner product using the Ozaki scheme accepts a narrower input range than the standard inner product using FP64 arithmetic.

2. **Computation**: In line 7 of Algorithm 1, Dot2 [22] (Algorithm 2) computes the inner products of the split vectors with at least 106-bit precision and returns the result in 106-bit as a pair of FP64 values[3]. Dot2 is built utilizing TwoSum [12] (Algorithm 4) and TwoProdFMA [11] (Algorithm 5). $\texttt{FMA}(a \times b - p)$ denotes the calculation of $a \times b - p$ using the fused multiply-add (FMA) operation. Note that although Dot2 is composed of FP64 arithmetic, the term "FP64" will henceforth refer to the absence of Dot2 usage. In lines 5–10 of Algorithm 1, several inner inner products can be computed using general matrix multiplication (GEMM) by combining multiple split vectors into a matrix. This is a key aspect of the implementation process. The use of GEMM is beneficial from a performance perspective because it permits data reuse.

3. **Summation**: In Algorithm 1, the infinite-precision result of IP-DOT is first obtained as an array of a pair of FP64 values ($[u, v]$) with a length of $s_x \times s_y$. Then, in line 11, the IP-DOT result in the FP64 format is obtained with NearSum [25], which is a correctly-rounded summation algorithm.

This scheme applies naturally to other inner-product-based operations, including SpMV. There are two observations in SpMV. First, in Algorithm 3, the number of non-zero elements in each row can be used instead of n. Second, just as GEMM was used for DOT, the computation can be performed using sparse-matrix dense-matrix multiplication (SpMM) by combining the split vectors into a matrix.

---

[3] The original Dot2 algorithm is designed to obtain the output as an FP64 value with $\mathrm{fl}(u + v)$ at the end.

The performance of this scheme is input-dependent; it is determined by the numbers of split vectors (s_x and s_y)[4]. Each of them depends on the absolute range, the number of significant digits of the elements in the input vector (lines 3 and 11 of Algorithm 3), and the vector length n (line 2 of Algorithm 3). As demonstrated in Sect. 5, it is often expected to be around 2 to 3 for real problems. Thus, the GEMM utilized in the computation is usually very skinny. Additionally, the summation cost using NearSum is expected to be relatively small in terms of overall execution time, as the summed elements are $s_x \times s_y \times 2$ (2 is the pair of FP64 values), which is typically small enough compared to n.

Existing studies, such as [17], use FP64 (or lower precision [18]) for computation, but our proposal in this research is to use 106-bit operations using Dot2 for the computation (i.e., GEMM in DOT and SpMM in SpMV) and the corresponding modification at line 2 in Algorithm 3. This permits the packing of more bits into the split vectors ($\boldsymbol{x}$, $\boldsymbol{y}$), thereby reducing the number of split vectors. In contrast, there are concerns regarding the increase in execution time due to the additional computational cost required by Dot2. In practice, however, the cost of Dot2 can be ignored in memory-intensive operations, as discussed in [16]. Our method yields skinny-shaped GEMM and SpMM that are sufficiently memory-intensive, and operate in Dot2 with memory-bound performance. As a result, the throughput is unaffected when using Dot2 instead of FP64. We provide a theoretical explanation of this in the next section.

4   Performance Estimation

4.1   Throughput of GEMM and SpMM Using Dot2

To demonstrate that the use of Dot2 does not reduce the throughput of GEMM and SpMM relative to FP64, we first estimate the throughput of them computed using Dot2 and FP64. We intend to use Xeon Platinum 8360Y (Ice Lake, 36 cores) later in the evaluation. Note that this discussion almost reaches the same conclusion also for the GPU (A100-SXM4-40) used in this research. The SpMV uses the compressed sparse row (CSR) format with 32-bit indices.

The roofline model [28] estimates the achievable throughput of the target kernel in bytes/s (B)

$$B = \min(B_{\mathrm{CPU}}, O_{\mathrm{CPU}} \times Q/W) \tag{1}$$

using the following parameters:

- B_{CPU}: the memory throughput of the CPU in bytes/s
- O_{CPU}: the computation throughput of the CPU in Ops/s
- Q: the target kernel's memory traffic in bytes
- W: the number of operations of the target kernel in Ops.

---

[4] In fact, it is even possible to adjust the accuracy of the result by varying the number of split vectors. The result will no longer be infinite precision, but reproducibility can still be preserved. See [17] for details.

Note that we use "Ops" as the number of operations per second to represent the throughput of Dot2 and FP64 on the same scale (i.e., an inner product for $x, y \in \mathbb{F}_{\text{FP64}}{}^n$ performs $2n$ (Ops) in both Dot2 and FP64).

For Q and W in the GEMM and SpMM, we assume the following parameters:

- d: number of split vectors/matrices
- n: dimensions of vectors/matrices ($n \times n$)
- n_{nz}: number of non-zero elements of the sparse matrix in SpMM.

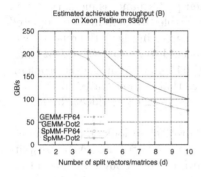
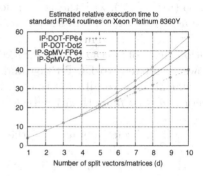

Fig. 1. Estimated achievable throughput (B) of GEMM and SpMM.

Fig. 2. Estimated relative execution times compared to the standard FP64 routines.

The GEMM computes $C_{d \times d} = A_{n \times d}{}^T B_{n \times d}$ and the SpMM computes $C_{n \times d} = A_{n \times n} B_{n \times d}$. Thus, assuming that data reusability is fully considered, the Q and W are as follows:

- GEMM: $Q = 16dn$ (bytes), $W = 2d^2n$ (Ops)
- SpMM: $Q = 12n_{nz}$ (bytes), $W = 2dn_{nz}$ (Ops) (assuming $n_{nz} \gg n$).

For B_{CPU} and O_{CPU}, the target CPU has the following theoretical peak hardware performance parameters:

- $B_{\text{CPU}} = 204.8$ GB/s
- FP64: $O_{\text{CPU}} = 1382.4$ GOps/s
- Dot2: $O_{\text{CPU}} = 125.7$ GOps/s (1/11 of the case in FP64 as it requires 11 times the number of floating-point instructions).

Using the above parameters with Eq. (1), the throughput of GEMM and SpMM in bytes/s (B) is estimated, as shown in Fig. 1. In this figure, we denote "-FP64" and "-Dot2" for operations computed by FP64 and Dot2, respectively (the same hereinafter). When d is small, both FP64 and Dot2 can be executed in the same amount of time as they are memory-bound. However, when d is large, Dot2 becomes computational-bound, and the memory throughput decreases. Here, d serves as a parameter that controls the arithmetic intensity for the roofline model.

4.2   Performance of IP-DOT and IP-SpMV

Next, we discuss the total execution time of IP-DOT and IP-SpMV. We first estimate the relative execution time compared with the standard DOT and SpMV
using FP64 arithmetic (DOT-FP64 and SpMV-FP64, respectively). As discussed
in [17], based on the number of memory read/written to vectors and matrices,
the relative execution time is estimated to increase by a factor of $4d$, depending on d. The splitting process accounts for $3d$ of the $4d$, and the remaining d
is attributable to the computation utilizing GEMM-FP64 (for DOT) or SpMM-
FP64 (for SpMV), with the assumption that their performance is memory-bound
and achieves B_{CPU}. However, the estimated achievable throughput B is depicted
in Fig. 1 as discussed in Sect. 4.1. Accordingly, as shown in Fig. 2, the relative execution times of IP-DOT and IP-SpMV are projected to be $(3 + B_{\text{CPU}}/B)d$ times
slower compared to DOT-FP64 and SpMV-FP64. The required d is problem-
dependent; however, if the situation is similar to that demonstrated in the next
section, d is no more than 7 with FP64, and using Dot2 can reduce d by half or
less.

We then discuss a practical rather than a theoretical outlook on performance.
Although up to three-quarters of the execution time is attributable to the splitting process (Algorithm 3), it is a straightforward memory-bound operation that
poses no implementation challenges for manycore processors. The remaining
one-fourth, which results from matrix multiplications (GEMM or SpMM), can
be problematic. There are two issues present. First, since the highly-optimized
implementation of GEMM-Dot2 and SpMM-Dot2 are not readily available, one
must create it themselves. Second, which concerns not only in Dot2 but also in
FP64, is that GEMM for very skinny matrices, performed in our scheme, may
require a different optimization strategy than GEMM for square matrices to
achieve adequate performance. This problem is discussed in [8][5]. The aforementioned issues are certainly challenges in software development. However, GEMM
for skinny matrices with FP64 and Dot2 have their independent uses and should
be discussed independently from our method[6].

5   Demonstration on CPU and GPU

We demonstrate our method on DOT and conjugate gradient (CG) solvers,
where SpMV is the primary operation, using a CPU and GPU of a node
(Wisteria-A node) of the Wisteria/BDEC-01 system at the University of Tokyo.
The specifics of the CPU and GPU environments are as follows:

- **CPU**: Intel Xeon Platinum 8360Y (Ice Lake, 36 cores, 1382.4 GFlops in FP64,
  204.8 GB/s), Intel oneAPI 2022.1.2 (with ICC 2021.5.0 and MKL 2022.0.0),
  compiled with `-O3 -fma -fp-model source -fprotect-parens -qopenmp
  -march=icelake-server`, executed with `numactl --localalloc` using the
  same number of threads as the number of physical cores.

---

[5] This problem is not encountered in SpMM.
[6] For example, XBLAS [14] supports 106-bit operations.

- **GPU**: NVIDIA A100-SXM4-40GB (Ampere, 9.7 TFlops in FP64[7], 1555 GB/s), CUDA 11.4 (driver: 470.57.02), nvcc V11.4.152, compiled with "-O3 -gencode arch= compute_60, code=sm_80".

The codes are implemented in C++ with OpenMP and CUDA. They extend the existing implementations (the Ozaki scheme with FP64 operations) for CPUs and GPUs in [19]; however, there have been some improvements.

Table 1. Results of DOT ($n = 2^{25}$). Overhead is the relative execution time compared to the standard DOT with FP64 arithmetic (DOT-FP64).

	Abs. range of input	d	Theor. overhead	CPU		GPU	
				GB/s	Overhead	GB/s	Overhead
DOT-FP64	–	–	–	142.7	1	1314.0	1
IP-DOT-FP64	[1e0,1e1]	4	16	67.7	33.7	1105.3	19.0
	[1e0,1e4]	5	20	65.2	43.8	1022.6	25.7
	[1e0,1e8]	6	24	61.4	55.8	1126.8	28.0
	[1e0,1e16]	7	28	59.1	67.7	993.4	37.0
IP-DOT-Dot2	[1e0,1e1]	2	8	68.6	16.6	1043.2	10.1
	[1e0,1e4]	2	8	76.1	15.0	1039.2	10.1
	[1e0,1e8]	2	8	69.9	16.3	1038.4	10.1
	[1e0,1e16]	3	12	69.3	24.7	1055.8	14.9

5.1 DOT

As discussed in Sect. 4.2, the skinny GEMM employed in the computation represents a potential challenge in DOT. We developed not only GEMM-Dot2 but also GEMM-FP64 ourselves for comparison, which outperformed GEMM-FP64 of MKL and cuBLAS in the Ozaki scheme. They are implemented using the Advanced Vector Extensions 2 (AVX2) intrinsic and are parallelized along the long axis of the matrix; this can be described as an extension of the typical parallel implementation of DOT to compute multiple vectors.

Table 1 illustrates the performance for $n = 2^{25}$, which is sufficient to exceed the cache size. Since the performance depends on the absolute range of the elements of the input vectors, we demonstrate the performance for different inputs using a random number within the specified absolute value range. The number of split vectors (d) increases proportionally, and the theoretical overhead (relative execution time) multiplies by a factor of $4d$ compared with DOT-FP64, which is performed using the DOT routines of MKL and cuBLAS. In these cases, Dot2 decreased d by half or less compared to IP-DOT-FP64. On the

---

[7] 9.7 TFlops is the performance without Tensor Cores. 19.5 TFlops with Tensor Cores but cannot be used for Dot2.

CPU, the observed overhead is larger than the theoretical overhead because IP-DOT-FP64/Dot2 has a lower throughput (GB/s) than DOT-FP64 because of the insufficient performance optimization of GEMM-FP64/Dot2.

Table 2. Test matrices ($n \times n$ with n_{nz} non-zeros, sorted by n_{nz}/n).

#	name	n	n_{nz}	n_{nz}/n	kind
1	tmt_sym	726,713	5,080,961	7.0	electromagnetics problem
2	gridgena	48,962	512,084	10.5	optimization problem
3	cfd1	70,656	1,825,580	25.8	computational fluid dynamics problem
4	cbuckle	13,681	676,515	49.4	structural problem
5	BenElechi1	245,874	13,150,496	53.5	2D/3D problem
6	gyro_k	17,361	1,021,159	58.8	duplicate model reduction problem
7	pdb1HYS	36,417	4,344,765	119.3	weighted undirected graph
8	nd24k	72,000	28,715,634	398.8	2D/3D problem

5.2   Reproducible CG Solvers

IP-DOT and IP-SpMV are used to ensure reproducibility in CG solvers [10] [19]. These are simply intended to ensure reproducibility but not to improve the numerical stability or accuracy of the solution. We demonstrate the proposed method on existing reproducible CG solvers based on the Ozaki scheme [19]. Our implementations used in this evaluation are based on the codes of previous studies, with a few improvements[8]. The implementation overview of the reproducible CG solvers can be summarized as follows.

- The unpreconditioned CG algorithm is implemented. All data are stored in the FP64 format.
- All inner-product-based operations, including DOT, NRM2, and SpMV, are performed with infinite precision using the Ozaki scheme with NearSum. The implementations in Sect. 5.1 are used for DOT. NRM2 is implemented using DOT.
- For SpMV, the CSR format is used, and the symmetry of the matrix is not considered. The computation of SpMV was performed using SpMM. The GPU implementation of SpMM extends the vector-CSR [2] SpMV implementation to compute multiple vectors. The CPU implementation computes the output vector in parallel in threads, and the inner product computed in each thread is parallelized with AVX2.
- AXPY is implemented by explicitly using FMA.

---

[8] Major improvements: (1) use of [15], (2) use of in-house GEMM and SpMM with asymmetric splitting on CPUs, (3) use of more recent vendor libraries.

- The matrix splitting is required and performed only once before the iterations begin.
- The number of split matrices is reduced by using the asymmetric splitting technique [24], which shifts ρ at line 2 in Algorithm 3 for the matrix and vector (it contributes to reducing the number of SpMM computed, see [19] for details).

Eight matrices from [6] are used (Table 2) (those are the same ones used in [19]). For $Ax = b$, b and the initial solution x_0 are $b = x_0 = (1, 1, ..., 1)^T$. The iteration is terminated when $||r_i||/||b|| \leq 10^{-16}$. Since the focus of this research is the speedup with Dot2, we do not present the numerical behavior (it is available in [19]), but the use of Dot2 does not affect the numerical behavior at the bit level. Hereafter, the reproducible CG solvers will be referred to as ReproCG-FP64 (existing method using FP64) and ReproCG-Dot2 (proposed method using Dot2), and the standard non-reproducible solvers implemented

Table 3. Execution time in seconds and the relative execution time compared to the standard CG (CG-FP64) (in parentheses).

	CPU				GPU				
#	CG-FP64	ReproCG -FP64		ReproCG -Dot2		CG-FP64	ReproCG -FP64		ReproCG -Dot2	
1	2.3e+0	7.5e+1	(32.5)	4.5e+1	(19.4)	1.6e+0	2.0e+1	(12.6)	1.8e+1	(11.2)
2	4.3e-1	3.9e+0	(9.1)	2.9e+0	(6.6)	3.3e-1	2.2e+0	(6.6)	1.8e+0	(5.3)
3	9.4e-1	7.8e+0	(8.3)	5.2e+0	(5.5)	4.7e-1	3.2e+0	(6.8)	2.5e+0	(5.4)
4	2.9e+0	3.7e+1	(12.7)	2.4e+1	(8.3)	2.9e+0	2.2e+1	(7.7)	1.5e+1	(5.4)
5	3.5e+1	3.9e+2	(10.9)	2.3e+2	(6.5)	1.8e+1	1.1e+2	(6.1)	9.4e+1	(5.2)
6	7.5e+0	8.3e+1	(11.0)	5.2e+1	(6.9)	7.2e+0	4.4e+1	(6.0)	3.1e+1	(4.2)
7	2.3e+0	1.8e+1	(7.6)	1.3e+1	(5.5)	1.7e+0	8.9e+0	(5.1)	6.0e+0	(3.5)
8	2.4e+1	8.9e+1	(3.7)	7.0e+1	(2.9)	5.4e+0	2.5e+1	(4.5)	1.7e+1	(3.2)

Table 4. Number of split matrices/vectors.

	ReproCG-FP64					ReproCG-Dot2				
#	matrix	vectors				matrix	vectors			
		min	max	med	avg		min	max	med	avg
1	3	3	7	5	4.9	2	2	3	2	2.0
2	2	3	5	4	4.0	2	2	2	2	2.0
3	3	3	6	4	4.1	3	2	3	2	2.0
4	5	4	7	4	4.0	3	2	3	2	2.0
5	3	4	6	5	4.8	2	2	3	2	2.0
6	5	4	7	4	4.0	3	2	3	2	2.0
7	3	3	5	4	4.0	2	2	2	2	2.0
8	3	3	5	4	4.2	2	2	3	2	2.0

50   D. Mukunoki et al.

using the BLAS routines in MKL and cuBLAS/cuSparse will be referred to as CG-FP64.

Table 3 illustrates the execution and relative execution times compared to CG-FP64. First, when compared to ReproCG-FP64, ReproCG-Dot2 achieved a speedup of 1.3–1.7 times on the CPU and a speedup of 1.1–1.5 times on the GPU. This range of performance improvement is supported by the reduction in the number of split matrices/vectors used in the computation, as depicted in Table 4. Dot2 reduced the number of split vectors, which varies during iterations, by about half, while the number of split matrices remained the same or decreased by no more than three-fifths. Next, ReproCG-Dot2 requires 2.9–19.4 times more execution time on the CPU and 3.2–11.2 times more execution time on the GPU than CG-FP64. These overheads are, in most cases, lower than those reported in [19] for reproducible CG performed using ExBLAS [10] for identical problems and conditions. As discussed in Sect. 4, in DOT, the Ozaki scheme incurs a $4d$-fold relative execution time overhead compared to the standard operation with

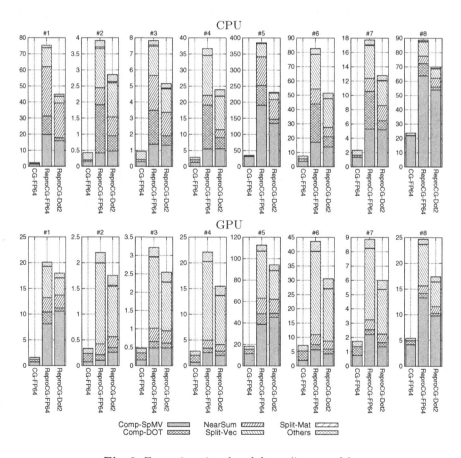

Fig. 3. Execution time breakdown (in seconds).

FP64 arithmetic, whereas in the CG method, the matrix is split only once before iterations. Thus, if SpMV is dominant in execution time, the optimum overhead would be d-fold. However, SpMV's influence on execution time diminishes as the matrix becomes more sparse (matrices are numbered in ascending order starting with the most sparse in Table 2). This explains why the overhead for highly sparse matrices is significant.

Figure 3 illustrates the execution time breakdowns to elaborate on the preceding results. Examining the computational cost for SpMV (Comp-SpMV, which is computed by SpMM), there are cases where the execution time has increased despite the decrease in the number of split matrices by Dot2. ReproCG-FP64 employs SpMM in MKL/cuSparse, while ReproCG-Dot2 uses in-house implementations. Since the kernel design has a large impact on the performance of SpMM, factors other than the Dot2 overhead may also be affected. Also, the observed NearSum overhead, particularly on the CPU, maybe a future concern.

6   Conclusion

This study presents an IP-DOT and IP-SpMV on FP64 data on CPU and GPU. We propose using 106-bit precision arithmetic (Dot2) rather than working precision (FP64) to compute the Ozaki scheme, which is an existing infinite-precision method. Although the performance depends on various conditions, including the input data, we demonstrate a theoretical and practical performance improvement of more than twofold in IP-DOT compared with the existing method using the Ozaki scheme with FP64 arithmetic, and the effectiveness of our approach increases as the input range increases. As a result, our IP-DOT requires approximately 10–25 times more execution time in reality (8–12 times in theory) than the standard DOT with FP64 arithmetic in MKL and cuBLAS. On CG solvers, a speedup of approximately 1.1–1.7 times is achieved compared to the existing method, and the overhead required to ensure reproducibility is approximately 3–19 times compared to the standard non-reproducible solvers.

Although this research successfully improves the performance of IP-DOT and IP-SpMV using the Ozaki scheme, the relative execution time compared to the standard FP64 operations is still significant. Furthermore, the Ozaki scheme is somewhat vulnerable to overflow. The superiority of this method, based on the Ozaki scheme, over other methods (ExBLAS and RARE-BLAS) is debatable. They have claimed lower overhead than our IP-DOT (e.g., RARE-BLAS [4] reported an overhead of 1–2 times at most on CPUs). However, our method offers the advantage of low development cost. It can be built upon matrix multiplication, enabling hierarchical software development and easy implementation on manycore processors, and it can be easily extended from DOT to other BLAS routines or tunable-accuracy operations with reproducible results, as demonstrated in [17]. We expect that, as a means to rapidly developing infinite-precision (accurate and reproducible) BLAS, our method is still an attractive option along with other faster methods. Also, it is a practical achievement to realize the lowest level of overhead for reproducible CG on both CPU and GPU.

This research utilized Dot2 as a swift quadruple-precision operation. However, a better alternative would be a hardware-implemented fast FP128 (with 113-bit mantissa), which would be capable of accelerating the infinite-precision operation of computationally intensive operations on FP64 data, such as matrix multiplication. Our research demonstrates that quadruple-precision arithmetic, such as FP128 and Dot2, is beneficial not only for accurate computations but also for reproducible computations in FP64 through infinite-precision operations.

Acknowledgment. This research was supported by the Japan Society for the Promotion of Science (JSPS) KAKENHI Grant #19K20286. This research was conducted using the FUJITSU Server PRIMERGY GX2570 (Wisteria/BDEC-01) at the Information Technology Center, The University of Tokyo (project #jh220022).

References

1. Arteaga, A., Fuhrer, O., Hoefler, T.: Designing bit-reproducible portable high-performance applications. In: Proceedings of IEEE 28th International Parallel and Distributed Processing Symposium (IPDPS 2014), pp. 1235–1244 (2014). https://doi.org/10.1109/IPDPS.2014.127
2. Bell, N., Garland, M.: Implementing sparse matrix-vector multiplication on throughput-oriented processors. In: Proceedings of International Conference for High Performance Computing, Networking, Storage and Analysis (SC 2009), pp. 1–11. No. 18 (2009). https://doi.org/10.1145/1654059.1654078
3. Briggs, K.: Implementing exact real arithmetic in python, c++ and c. Theoret. Comput. Sci. **351**(1), 74–81 (2006). https://doi.org/10.1016/j.tcs.2005.09.058
4. Chohra, C., Langlois, P., Parello, D.: Reproducible, accurately rounded and efficient BLAS. In: 22nd International European Conference on Parallel and Distributed Computing (Euro-Par 2016), pp. 609–620 (2016). https://doi.org/10.1007/978-3-319-58943-5_49
5. Collange, S., Defour, D., Graillat, S., Iakymchuk, R.: Numerical reproducibility for the parallel reduction on multi- and many-core architectures. Parallel Comput. **49**, 83–97 (2015). https://doi.org/10.1016/j.parco.2015.09.001
6. Davis, T.A., Hu, Y.: The university of Florida sparse matrix collection. ACM Trans. Math. Softw. **38**(1), 1:1–1:25 (2011). https://doi.org/10.1145/2049662.2049663
7. Demmel, J., Ahrens, P., Nguyen, H.D.: Efficient Reproducible Floating Point Summation and BLAS. Technical report. UCB/EECS-2016-121, EECS Department, University of California, Berkeley (2016)
8. Demmel, J., Eliahu, D., Fox, A., Kamil, S., Lipshitz, B., Schwartz, O., Spillinger, O.: Communication-optimal parallel recursive rectangular matrix multiplication. In: 2013 IEEE 27th International Symposium on Parallel and Distributed Processing, pp. 261–272 (2013). https://doi.org/10.1109/IPDPS.2013.80
9. Fousse, L., Hanrot, G., Lefèvre, V., Pélissier, P., Zimmermann, P.: MPFR: a multiple-precision binary floating-point library with correct rounding. ACM Trans. Math. Softw. **33**(2), 13:1–13:15 (2007). https://doi.org/10.1145/1236463.1236468

10. Iakymchuk, R., Barreda, M., Graillat, S., Aliaga, J.I., Quintana-Ortí, E.S.: Reproducibility of parallel preconditioned conjugate gradient in hybrid programming environments. IJHPCA (2020). https://doi.org/10.1177/1094342020932650
11. Karp, A.H., Markstein, P.: High-precision division and square root. ACM Trans. Math. Softw. **23**, 561–589 (1997). https://doi.org/10.1145/279232.279237
12. Knuth, D.E.: The Art of Computer Programming. Seminumerical Algorithms, vol. 2. Addison-Wesley, Boston (1969)
13. Lambov, B.: Reallib: an efficient implementation of exact real arithmetic. Math. Struct. Comp. Sci. **17**(1), 81–98 (2007). https://doi.org/10.1017/S0960129506005822
14. Li, X.S., et al.: Design, implementation and testing of extended and mixed precision BLAS. ACM Trans. Math. Softw. **28**(2), 152–205 (2000). https://doi.org/10.1145/567806.567808
15. Minamihata, A., Ozaki, K., Ogita, T., Oishi, S.: Preconditioner for ill-conditioned tall and skinny matrices. In: The 40th JSST Annual International Conference on Simulation Technology (JSST2016) (2016)
16. Mukunoki, D., Ogita, T.: Performance and energy consumption of accurate and mixed-precision linear algebra kernels on GPUs. J. Comput. Appl. Math. **372**, 112701 (2020). https://doi.org/10.1016/j.cam.2019.112701
17. Mukunoki, D., Ogita, T., Ozaki, K.: Reproducible BLAS routines with tunable accuracy using Ozaki scheme for many-core architectures. In: Wyrzykowski, R., Deelman, E., Dongarra, J., Karczewski, K. (eds.) PPAM 2019. LNCS, vol. 12043, pp. 516–527. Springer, Cham (2020). https://doi.org/10.1007/978-3-030-43229-4_44
18. Mukunoki, D., Ozaki, K., Ogita, T., Imamura, T.: DGEMM using tensor cores, and its accurate and reproducible versions. In: Sadayappan, P., Chamberlain, B.L., Juckeland, G., Ltaief, H. (eds.) ISC High Performance 2020. LNCS, vol. 12151, pp. 230–248. Springer, Cham (2020). https://doi.org/10.1007/978-3-030-50743-5_12
19. Mukunoki, D., Ozaki, K., Ogita, T., Iakymchuk, R.: Conjugate gradient solvers with high accuracy and bit-wise reproducibility between CPU and GPU using Ozaki scheme. In: Proceedings of The International Conference on High Performance Computing in Asia-Pacific Region (HPC Asia 2021), pp. 100–109 (2021). https://doi.org/10.1145/3432261.3432270
20. Müller, N.T.: The irram: Exact arithmetic in c++. In: Computability and Complexity in Analysis. pp. 222–252. Springer, Berlin Heidelberg (2001). DOI: 10.1007/3-540-45335-0_14
21. Nakata, M.: Mplapack version 1.0.0 user manual (2021)
22. Ogita, T., Rump, S.M., Oishi, S.: Accurate sum and dot product. SIAM J. Sci. Comput. **26**, 1955–1988 (2005). https://doi.org/10.1137/030601818
23. Ozaki, K., Ogita, T., Oishi, S., Rump, S.M.: Error-free transformations of matrix multiplication by using fast routines of matrix multiplication and its applications. Numer. Algorithms **59**(1), 95–118 (2012). https://doi.org/10.1007/s11075-011-9478-1
24. Ozaki, K., Ogita, T., Oishi, S., Rump, S.M.: Generalization of error-free transformation for matrix multiplication and its application. Nonlinear Theory Appl. IEICE **4**, 2–11 (2013). https://doi.org/10.1587/nolta.4.2
25. Rump, S.M., Ogita, T., Oishi, S.: Accurate floating-point summation Part II: sign, K-Fold faithful and rounding to nearest. SIAM J. Sci. Comput. **31**(2), 1269–1302 (2009). https://doi.org/10.1137/07068816X

26. Todd, R.: Introduction to Conditional Numerical Reproducibility (CNR) (2012). https://software.intel.com/en-us/articles/introduction-to-the-conditional-numerical-reproducibility-cnr

27. Wei, S., Tang, E., Liu, T., Müller, N.T., Chen, Z.: Automatic numerical analysis based on infinite-precision arithmetic. In: 2014 Eighth International Conference on Software Security and Reliability (SERE), pp. 216–224 (2014). https://doi.org/10.1109/SERE.2014.35

28. Williams, S., Waterman, A., Patterson, D.: Roofline: an insightful visual performance model for multicore architectures. Commun. ACM **52**(4), 65–76 (2009). https://doi.org/10.1145/1498765.1498785

Advanced Stochastic Approaches for Applied Computing in Environmental Modeling

Venelin Todorov[1,2]($\boxtimes$) (iD), Ivan Dimov[2], Maria Ganzha[3], and Marcin Paprzycki[3]

[1] Department of Information Modeling, Institute of Mathematics and Informatics, Bulgarian Academy of Sciences, Acad. Georgi Bonchev Street, Block 8, 1113 Sofia, Bulgaria
vtodorov@math.bas.bg
[2] Department of Parallel Algorithms, Institute of Information and Communication Technologies, Bulgarian Academy of Sciences, Acad. G. Bonchev Street, Block 25 A, 1113 Sofia, Bulgaria
venelin@parallel.bas.bg, ivdimov@bas.bg
[3] Polish Academy of Sciences, Warszawa, Poland
{maria.ganzha,marcin.paprzycki}@ibspan.waw.pl

Abstract. Mathematical models are used to study and predict the behavior of a variety of complex systems - engineering, physical, economic, social, environmental. Sensitivity studies are nowadays applied to some of the most complicated mathematical models from various intensively developing areas of applications. Sensitivity analysis is a modern promising technique for studying large-scale systems such as ecological systems. The uncertainty in the model input in our case, as in many others, can be due to various reasons: inaccurate measurements or calculation, approximation, data compression, etc. Two kinds of sensitivity analysis have been discussed in the literature: local and global. In the current paper the subject of our study is the global sensitivity analysis performed via the Sobol' variance-based approach, applied to a specific large-scale air pollution model. The mathematical treatment of the problem of providing global sensitivity analysis consists in evaluating total sensitivity indices which leads to computing multidimensional integrals. We propose a new specific stochastic approach which significantly improves the results by the standard stochastic approaches.

Keywords: Monte Carlo methods · Sensitivity Analysis · Air pollution modelling

Venelin Todorov is supported by the Bulgarian National Science Fund under Project KP-06-N52/5 "Efficient methods for modeling, optimization and decision making" and KP-06-M32/2 - 17.12.2019 "Advanced Stochastic and Deterministic Approaches for Large-Scale Problems of Computational Mathematics". The work is also supported by the BNSF under Projects KP-06-N52/5 "Efficient methods for modeling, optimization and decision making" and Bilateral Project KP-06-Russia/17 "New Highly Efficient Stochastic Simulation Methods and Applications".

R. Wyrzykowski et al. (Eds.): PPAM 2022, LNCS 13826, pp. 55–67, 2023.
https://doi.org/10.1007/978-3-031-30442-2_5

1   Introduction

An important issue when large-scale mathematical models are used to support decision makers is their reliability [10]. Sensitivity analysis (SA) has a crucial role during the process of validating computational models to ensure their accuracy and reliability [15]. In a popular definition SA is the study of how uncertainty in the output of a model can be apportioned to different sources of uncertainty in the model input [20]. The focus of the present work is to perform global SA [16] of a large-scale mathematical model describing remote transport of air pollutants. The Unified Danish Eulerian Model (UNI-DEM) [24] is in the focus of our study as one of the most advanced large-scale mathematical models that describes adequately all physical and chemical processes during remote transport of air pollutants. The **U**nified **D**anish **E**ulerian **M**odel (UNI-DEM) has been developed at the Danish National Environmental Research Institute (http://www2.dmu.dk/ AtmosphericEnvironment/DEM/, [23–25]). The model is described mathematically [23,24] by the following system of partial differential equations:

$$\frac{\partial c_s}{\partial t} = -\frac{\partial(uc_s)}{\partial x} - \frac{\partial(vc_s)}{\partial y} - \frac{\partial(wc_s)}{\partial z} +$$
$$+\frac{\partial}{\partial x}\left(K_x\frac{\partial c_s}{\partial x}\right) + \frac{\partial}{\partial y}\left(K_y\frac{\partial c_s}{\partial y}\right) + \frac{\partial}{\partial z}\left(K_z\frac{\partial c_s}{\partial z}\right) +$$
$$+E_s + Q_s(c_1, c_2, \ldots, c_q) - (k_{1s} + k_{2s})c_s, \quad s = 1, 2, \ldots, q.$$

The number of q equations in this system is equal to the number of pollutants studied by the model. The other dimensions included in the model are described below:

c_s - pollutant concentrations,
u, v, w - wind components along the coordinate axes,
K_x, K_y, K_z - diffusion coefficients,
E_s - space emissions,
k_{1s}, k_{2s} - dry and wet deposit coefficients, respectively ($s = 1, \ldots, q$),
$Q_s(c_1, c_2, \ldots, c_q)$ - nonlinear functions describing chemical reactions between pollutants.

If the model results are sensitive to a given process, one can describe it mathematically more precisely in a more adequate way. Therefore, the goal of our work is to increase the reliability of the results produced by the large-scale air pollution model, and to identify processes that must be studied more carefully, as well as to find input parameters that need to be measured with a higher precision. A careful SA is needed in order to decide where and how simplifications of the model can be made. That is why it is important to develop and study more adequate and reliable stochastic methods for SA.

The paper is organised as follows. Some basic aspects of the used large-scale air pollution model are given in the Introduction. Some basic definitions for global SA are given in Sect. 2. The stochastic methods and the new proposed

method are given in Sect. 3. We introduce the simplest possible Monte Carlo approach - crude approach and also the simplest possible quasi-random sequence -
the van der Corput sequence and its modification. We also introduce different
lattice rules and the proposed method. The monographs of Sloan and Kachoyan
[13], Niederreiter [11], Hua and Wang [5] and Sloan and Joe [14] provide comprehensive expositions on the theory of integration lattices. Applications of the
methods for multidimensional numerical integration are studied in Paskov [12],
Wang and Hickernell [22], F.Y. Kuo and D. Nuyens [9]. The numerical experiments are given in Sect. 4. Some final remarks are given in the Conclusion.

2 Sensitivity Analysis - Definitions

Consider a scalar model output u $= f(\mathbf{x})$ corresponding to a number of
non-correlated model parameters x $= (x_1, x_2, \ldots, x_d)$ with a joint probability density function (p.d.f.) $p(\mathbf{x}) = p(x_1, \ldots, x_d)$. In Sobol' approach
[16] the parameter importance is studied via numerical integration in the
terms of analysis of variance (ANOVA) model representation $f(\mathbf{x}) = f_0 +$
$\sum_{\nu=1}^{d} \sum_{l_1 < \ldots < l_\nu} f_{l_1 \ldots l_\nu}(x_{l_1}, x_{l_2}, \ldots, x_{l_\nu})$, $f_0 = const$, $f(\mathbf{x})$ is a square integrable
model function, $\int_0^1 f_{l_1 \ldots l_\nu}(x_{l_1}, \ldots, x_{l_\nu}) dx_{l_k} = 0$, $1 \le k \le \nu$, $\nu = 1, \ldots, d$, and
$f_0 = \int_{E^d} f(\mathbf{x}) d\mathbf{x}$. The following quantities $S_{l_1 \ldots l_\nu} = \dfrac{\mathbf{D}_{l_1 \ldots l_\nu}}{\mathbf{D}}$, $\nu \in \{1, \ldots, d\}$.
are called Sobol' global sensitivity indices [16] of the corresponding order (first
or higher), where $\mathbf{D}_{l_1 \ldots l_\nu}$ and $\mathbf{D}$ are the partial and the total variance of the
model function, respectively.
  According to definition [20] the total and the partial variances are defined by
the following formulas:

$$\mathbf{D} = \int_{U^d} f^2(\mathbf{x}) d\mathbf{x} - f_0^2, \quad \mathbf{D}_{l_1 \ldots l_\nu} = \int f_{l_1 \ldots l_\nu}^2 dx_{l_1} \ldots dx_{l_\nu}. \tag{1}$$

The total variance that is represented by the corresponding partial variances:
$\mathbf{D} = \sum_{\nu=1}^{d} \sum_{l_1 < \ldots < l_\nu} \mathbf{D}_{l_1 \ldots l_\nu}$. The main sensitivity measures following the Sobol
approach are the so-called Sobol global sensitivity indices [19,20] defined by

$$S_{l_1 \ldots l_\nu} = \frac{\mathbf{D}_{l_1 \ldots l_\nu}}{\mathbf{D}}, \quad \nu \in \{1, \ldots, d\}. \tag{2}$$

and the total sensitivity index (TSI) of an input parameter $x_i, i \in \{1, \ldots, d\}$
defined by [19,20]:

$$S_i^{tot} = S_i + \sum_{l_1 \ne i} S_{i l_1} + \sum_{l_1, l_2 \ne i, l_1 < l_2} S_{i l_1 l_2} + \ldots + S_{i l_1 \ldots l_{d-1}}, \tag{3}$$

where S_i is called *the main effect (first-order sensitivity index)* of x_i and $S_{i l_1 \ldots l_{j-1}}$
is the j-th order sensitivity index. The higher-order terms describe the interac-
tion effects between the unknown input parameters $x_{i_1}, \ldots, x_{i_\nu}, \nu \in \{2, \ldots, d\}$

on the output variance. It is clear that the mathematical treatment of the problem of providing global SA consists in evaluating total sensitivity indices (3) of corresponding order that, based on the formula (1)–(3), leads to computing multidimensional integrals.

For evaluating *small* sensitivity indices and to avoid loss of accuracy because the analyzed database comes under this case we will use a combined approach between approach of reducing of the mean value and correlated sampling suggested in [17]. We will replace the original model function with the function $\varphi(\mathbf{x}) = f(\mathbf{x}) - c$ where the constant $c \sim f_0$. Thus the partial and total variance estimations are presented in such a way:

$$D_y = \int \varphi(\mathbf{x}) \left[\varphi(\mathbf{y}, \mathbf{z}') \mathrm{d}\mathbf{x}\mathrm{d}\mathbf{z}' - \varphi(\mathbf{x}')\right] \mathrm{d}\mathbf{x}\mathrm{d}\mathbf{x}', \ D = \int \varphi(\mathbf{x})[\varphi(\mathbf{x}) - \varphi(\mathbf{x}')] \ \mathrm{d}\mathbf{x}\mathrm{d}\mathbf{x}'.$$

Homma and Saltelli discussed in [4] which is the better estimation of

$$f_0^2 = \left(\int_{U^s} f(\mathbf{x})\mathrm{d}\mathbf{x}\right)^2 \tag{4}$$

for evaluating the total variance and Sobol global sensitivity measures. The first formula is

$$f_0^2 \approx \frac{1}{n}\sum_{i=1}^{n} f(\mathbf{x}_{i,1}, \ldots, \mathbf{x}_{i,s}) \ f(\mathbf{x}'_{i,1}, \ldots, \mathbf{x}'_{i,d}) \tag{5}$$

and the second one is

$$f_0^2 \approx \left\{\frac{1}{n}\sum_{i=1}^{n} f(\mathbf{x}_{i,1}, \ldots, \mathbf{x}_{i,s})\right\}^2 \tag{6}$$

where $\mathbf{x}$ and $\mathbf{x}'$ are two independent sample vectors. In case of estimating sensitivity indices of a fixed order, formula (5) is better [4] and therefore we will use it.

3   Stochastic Approaches

Crude Monte Carlo (CRU) is the simplest possible stochastic approach for solving multidimensional integrals [2,6]. Let $I = \int_{\Omega} g(\mathbf{x})p(\mathbf{x})\mathrm{d}\mathbf{x}$. Let ξ be a random point with a p.d.f. $p(\mathbf{x})$. We introduce random variable $\theta = f(\xi)$ such that $\mathbf{E}\theta = \int_{\Omega} g(\mathbf{x})p(\mathbf{x})\mathrm{d}\mathbf{x}$. Let the random points $\xi_1, \xi_2, \ldots, \xi_N$ be independent realizations of the random point ξ with p.d.f. $p(\mathbf{x})$ and $\theta_1 = f(\xi_1), \ldots, \theta_N = f(\xi_N)$. Then an approximate value of I is $\bar{\theta}_N = \frac{1}{N}\sum_{i=1}^{N} \theta_i$.

The well-known **van der Corput** (VDC) sequence [3,21] is the simplest example of quasirandom number (or low-discrepancy) sequences. The generation is quite simple. Let $n = \ldots a_3(n), a_2(n), a_1(n)$ is the representation of an integer n in base b, then the expansion of n in base b is generated: $n = \sum_{i=0}^{\infty} a_{i+1}(n)b^i$. The radical inverse sequence is generated by writing a decimal point followed by the digits of the expansion of n, in reverse order: $\phi_b(n) = \sum_{i=0}^{\infty} a_{i+1}(n)b^{-(i+1)}$. This decimal value is actually still in base b, so it must be properly interpreted to generate a usable value. **van der Corput** sequence VDC2 is obtained when $b = 2$. The modified **van der Corput** VDC3 is obtained when $b = 3$.

To introduce lattice rules, firstly consider the quadrature formula $I_N(f) = \frac{1}{N} \sum_{i=1}^{N} f(x_i)$, where $P_N = \{x_1, x_2, \ldots, x_N\}, x_i \in [0,1)^s$ are the integration nodes of the formula. The choice of the nodes is essential, because it determines the discrepancy of the sequence and the accuracy of the quadrature. The integration nodes, of the lattice rules proposed by Korobov [7,8], are defined by the following formula:

$$x_k = \left(\left\{ \frac{kz_1}{N} \right\}, \left\{ \frac{kz_2}{N} \right\}, \ldots, \left\{ \frac{kz_s}{N} \right\} \right), \quad k = 1, 2, \ldots, N, \qquad (7)$$

where N is the number of the nodes, z is an s-dimensional generating vector of the lattice set and $\{a\} = a - [a]$ is the fractional part of a. The lattice rules with nodes (7) and generators z are called "rank 1" rules [1]. We will use some of the most famous lattice rules for computing multidimensional integrals.

For $s = 2$ optimal construction exists based on generalized Fibonacci numbers. Based on [5] we have the following definition for the generalized Fibonacci numbers for any dimension: $F_{l+s}^{(s)} = F_l^{(s)} + F_{l+1}^{(s)} + \ldots + F_{l+s-1}^{(s)}, l = 0, 1, \ldots$ with initial conditions: $F_0^{(s)} = F_1^{(s)} = \ldots = F_{s-2}^{(s)} = 0, F_{s-1}^{(s)} = 1$. The generating vector is constructed based on the generalized Fibonacci numbers of the corresponding dimension.

$$z = \left(1, F_{l+1}^{(s)}, \ldots, F_{l+s-1}^{(s)} \right), \quad n_l = F_l^{(s)}, \qquad (8)$$

where $F_j^{(s)}$ is the generalized Fibonacci number of dimension s. The lattice method with this generating vector (8) is **Fibonacci based lattice rule** (FIBO).

Now consider second lattice rule applying the polynomial transformation function $\varphi(t) = 3t^2 - 2t^3$ to a nonperiodic integrand to make it suitable for applying a lattice rule. The transformation satisfy $\varphi(0) = 0$, $\varphi(1) = 1$, $\varphi'(t) > 0$. Thus φ is a continuous bijection from $[0,1]$ to $[0,1]$. This is a special type of **bijectional lattice rule** BIJ.

Now we proposed a new lattice rule which is a modification of a lattice rule, suitable for periodic integrand functions, for use with a non-periodic function F, by applying the lattice rule to the function

$$G(x_1, \ldots, x_s) =$$

$$2^{-s} \sum_{\varepsilon \in \{0,1\}^s} F\left(\varepsilon_1 x_1 + (1 - \varepsilon_1)(1 - x_1), \ldots, \varepsilon_s x_s + (1 - \varepsilon_s)(1 - x_s) \right). \qquad (9)$$

The arguments over which summation is being done could be considered as vertices of parallelotope whose diagonals intersected at the point $(1/2, 1/2, \ldots, 1/2) \in [0,1]^s$. At the first step of the proposed **special lattice** rule NEWL the s-dimensional optimal generating vector $\mathbf{z} = (z_1, z_2, \ldots z_s)$ is generated [9]. The second step of the algorithm include generating the points of lattice rule by formula $\mathbf{x}_k = \left\{\frac{k}{N}\mathbf{z}\right\}$, $k = 1, \ldots, N$. And at the third and last step of the algorithm an approximate value I_N of the multidimensional integral is evaluated by the formula: $I_N = \frac{1}{N} \sum_{k=1}^{N} f\left(\left\{\frac{k}{N}\mathbf{z}\right\}\right)$.

4   Sensitivity Studies with Respect to Emission Levels

In this section we will present the results for the sensitivity of UNI-DEM output (in particular, the ammonia mean monthly concentrations) with respect to the anthropogenic emissions input data variation. The anthropogenic emissions input consists of 4 different components
$\mathbf{E} = (\mathbf{E^A}, \mathbf{E^N}, \mathbf{E^S}, \mathbf{E^C})$:

$\mathbf{E^A}$ – ammonia (NH_3); $\mathbf{E^S}$ – sulphur dioxide (SO_2);
$\mathbf{E^N}$ – nitrogen oxides $(NO + NO_2)$; $\mathbf{E^C}$ – anthropogenic hydrocarbons.

The domain under consideration is the 4-dimensional hypercube $[0.5, 1]^4$). In the experiments the relative error is equal to the absolute value of the difference between the computed value and the exact value of the integral, divided by the exact value. Results of the relative error estimation for the quantities f_0, the total variance $\mathbf{D}$, first-order (S_i) and total (S_i^{tot}) sensitivity indices are given in Tables 1, 2, 3, 4, 5, respectively. f_0 is presented by a 4-dimensional integral, while the rest of the above quantities are presented by 8-dimensional integrals, following the ideas of *correlated sampling* technique to compute sensitivity measures in a reliable way (see [4, 18]). The four different stochastic approaches used for numerical integration are presented in separate columns of the tables.

For $n = 2^{20}$ for the model function f_0 the best algorithm is the NEWL, followed by FIBO and BIJ - see the results in Tables 1 for the maximum number of samples. A big improvement over the other algorithms is obtained - FIBO gives $4.21e - 07$ while NEWL gives $5.64e - 12$.

For number of samples $n = 2^{20}$ for the total variance D the best algorithm is the NEWL, followed again by FIBO and BIJ - see the results in Tables 2 for the maximum number of samples. A big improvement over the other algorithms is obtained - FIBO gives $1.19e - 04$ while NEWL gives $1.09e - 07$. However for small number of samples VDC and BIJ gives better results by at least 1 order.

For the total and first order sensitivity indices in the Table 4 it can be seen that the new lattice rule significantly improves the results produced by the other algorithms.

Generally the increased number of samples to 2^{20} improved the results produced by the new algorithm versus the other algorithms - see the results for the relative error in Table 5 versus the results in Table 3 and Table 4.

For number of samples $n = 2^{10}$ in Table 3 the proposed algorithm NEWL gives the best relative errors for S_2, S_3, S_4, S_1^{tot}, S_2^{tot}, S_4^{tot}, while BIJ gives the best result for S_1 and S_3^{tot}.

Table 1. Relative error for the evaluation of $f_0 \approx 0.048$.

# of samples n	CRU Relative error	VDC2 Relative error	VDC3 Relative error	FIBO Relative error	BIJ Relative error	NEWL Relative error
2^{10}	8.82e–03	2.80e–04	9.25e–04	2.09e–04	8.46e–04	**5.95e–06**
2^{12}	3.50e–03	7.73e–05	8.22e–04	4.32e–05	1.79e–04	**3.72e–07**
2^{14}	4.83e–04	1.37e–05	6.01e–05	2.25e–05	2.62e–06	**2.32e–08**
2^{16}	2.25e–03	3.11e–04	6.04e–04	8.70e–06	4.14e–07	**1.45e–09**
2^{18}	5.14e–04	7.66e–05	6.72e–04	1.79e–06	1.17e–06	**9.07e–11**
2^{20}	3.20e–05	1.48e–04	3.69e–04	4.21e–07	1.15e–06	**5.64e–12**

For number of samples $n = 2^{16}$ in Table 4 the developed algorithm NEWL gives the best relative errors for S_1, S_2, S_3, S_4, S_1^{tot}, S_2^{tot}, S_3^{tot}, S_4^{tot}, and the difference with BIJ and FIBO is at least 1 order.

For number of samples $n = 2^{20}$ in Table 4 the new algorithm NEWL gives the best relative errors for all sensitivity indices S_1, S_2, S_3, S_4, S_1^{tot}, S_2^{tot}, S_3^{tot}, S_4^{tot}, and one can see that increasing the number of samples gives essential difference versus the other stochastic approaches - the difference is at least 4 or even 5 orders versus the worst algorithms CRU and VDC. The most important small in value sensitivity indices which are essential for reliable interpretation of the results, are S_2, S_2^{tot} and S_4^{tot} and for them only the proposed algorithm NEWL give high accuracy.

The performance of the algorithms can be summarized as follows: the best algorithm is NEWL, followed by lattice rules FIBO and BIJ, and after that the basic algorithm VDC2 and the modified VDC3, and the simplest possible stochastic approach CRU is the worst.

Table 2. Relative error for the evaluation of the total variance $\mathbf{D} \approx 0.0002$.

# of samples n	CRU Relative error	VDC2 Relative error	VDC3 Relative error	FIBO Relative error	BIJ Relative error	NEWL Relative error
2^{10}	1.09e–01	**6.86e–03**	5.50e–02	1.63e–01	1.54e–02	1.25e–01
2^{12}	8.93e–02	3.75e–03	8.61e–03	2.39e–02	**3.67e–03**	7.98e–03
2^{14}	3.04e–03	**2.64e–04**	5.57e–03	2.90e–03	1.49e–03	6.64e–04
2^{16}	3.48e–03	2.22e–03	1.64e–02	2.65e–04	1.61e–03	**1.31e–05**
2^{18}	1.93e–02	2.22e–03	7.24e–03	3.01e–04	1.48e–03	**1.39e–06**
2^{20}	3.26e–03	7.58e–03	2.04e–03	1.19e–04	1.46e–03	**1.09e–07**

62   V. Todorov et al.

Table 3. Relative error for estimation of sensitivity indices of input parameters using various stochastic approaches ($n \approx 2^{10}$).

EQ	RV	CRU	VDC2	VDC3	FIBO	BIJ	NEWL
S_1	9e–01	3.21e–01	2.20e–02	3.49e–02	2.91e–02	**1.04e–03**	1.54e–03
S_2	2e–04	1.25e+00	4.47e–02	2.85e+00	1.29e+01	3.44e+00	**3.10e–02**
S_3	1e–01	7.10e–03	6.91e–01	3.14e–01	6.59e–02	8.05e–03	**3.47e–04**
S_4	4e–05	6.27e+00	8.88e–01	2.30e+01	2.19e+01	1.76e+00	**1.58e–02**
S_1^{tot}	9e–01	7.65e–02	1.07e–02	2.18e–02	3.49e–03	1.78e–03	**3.38e–05**
S_2^{tot}	2e–04	1.23e+02	4.95e+02	1.97e+02	2.25e+01	3.32e+00	**1.40e–01**
S_3^{tot}	1e–01	2.25e+00	3.12e+00	9.69e–01	1.98e–01	**4.37e–03**	1.21e–02
S_4^{tot}	5e–05	8.94e+03	3.22e+03	3.00e+03	1.84e+01	1.06e+01	**1.98e–01**

Table 4. Relative error for estimation of sensitivity indices of input parameters using various stochastic approaches ($n \approx 2^{16}$).

EQ	RV	CRU	VDC2	VDC3	FIBO	BIJ	NEWL
S_1	9e–01	2.04e–02	3.13e–02	7.08e–02	3.62e–04	7.27e–04	**7.22e–06**
S_2	2e–04	2.32e–01	1.28e+00	9.89e–01	1.74e–01	2.76e–02	**1.94e–02**
S_3	1e–01	2.72e–02	9.13e–02	1.96e–02	3.22e–03	4.24e–03	**1.53e–05**
S_4	4e–05	3.40e+00	8.30e–01	3.62e–01	4.87e–01	1.65e–02	**2.19e–03**
S_1^{tot}	9e–01	1.52e–03	7.54e–03	8.68e–03	4.61e–04	5.14e–04	**2.77e–06**
S_2^{tot}	2e–04	5.90e+01	4.69e+01	1.36e+01	3.45e–01	2.21e–01	**1.24e–02**
S_3^{tot}	1e–01	1.19e–01	4.14e–02	1.54e–01	1.96e–03	6.41e–03	**8.63e–05**
S_4^{tot}	5e–05	6.42e+02	5.54e+02	1.05e+02	5.06e–01	1.60e–01	**1.52e–03**

5   Sensitivity Studies with Respect to Chemical Reactions Rates

In this section we will study the sensitivity of the ozone concentration values in the air over Genova with respect to the rate variation of some chemical reactions of the condensed CBM-IV scheme ([23]), namely: # 1, 3, 7, 22 (time-dependent) and # 27, 28 (time independent). The simplified chemical equations of those reactions are:

[#1] $NO_2 + h\nu \Longrightarrow NO + O$;   [#22] $HO_2 + NO \Longrightarrow OH + NO_2$;
[#3] $O_3 + NO \Longrightarrow NO_2$;   [#27] $HO_2 + HO_2 \Longrightarrow H_2O_2$;
[#7] $NO_2 + O_3 \Longrightarrow NO_3$;   [#28] $OH + CO \Longrightarrow HO_2$.

The domain under consideration is the 6-dimensional hypercube $[0.6, 1.4]^6$.

The relative error estimation for the quantities f_0, the total variance **D** and some sensitivity indices are given in Tables 6, 7, 8, 9 and 10 respectively.

The quantity f_0 is presented by 6-dimensional integral, while the rest are presented by 12-dimensional integrals, following the ideas of *correlated sampling*.

For $n = 2^{20}$ for the model function f_0 the best algorithm is the NEWL, followed by FIBO and BIJ - see the results in Tables 6 for the maximum number

Table 5. Relative error for estimation of sensitivity indices of input parameters using various stochastic approaches ($n \approx 2^{20}$).

EQ	RV	CRU	VDC2	VDC3	FIBO	BIJ	NEWL
S_1	9e-01	8.54e–03	2.92e–03	5.44e–03	5.29e–08	2.78e–03	**1.16e–08**
S_2	2e-04	2.73e–01	1.58e–01	5.83e–01	3.17e–03	2.32e–02	**8.81e–06**
S_3	1e-01	1.40e–02	3.14e–02	1.33e+00	6.88e–05	4.28e–03	**1.09e–08**
S_4	4e-05	5.87e–01	3.08e–01	3.17e–01	1.88e–01	3.46e–02	**4.58e–07**
S_1^{tot}	9e-01	1.43e–03	2.99e–03	2.65e–03	2.14e–05	5.20e–04	**5.86e–10**
S_2^{tot}	2e-04	1.42e+00	9.96e+00	3.32e+01	4.56e–03	2.19e–01	**6.39e–06**
S_3^{tot}	1e-01	9.31e–03	8.13e–02	4.80e–02	4.69e–05	6.41e–03	**1.08e–07**
S_4^{tot}	5e-05	5.92e+01	4.08e+01	6.61e+01	6.08e–02	1.66e–01	**2.06e–06**

of samples. A big improvement over the other algorithms is obtained - FIBO gives $4.57e - 07$ while NEWL gives $1.07e - 10$.

For number of samples $n = 2^{20}$ for the total variance D the best algorithm is the proposed algorithm NEWL, followed again by FIBO and BIJ - see the results in Tables 7 for the maximum number of samples. An essential improvement over the other algorithms is obtained - BIJ gives $2.22e-03$ while NEWL gives $6.58e-05$. However for small number of samples the other stochastic algorithms and especially BIJ, VDC2 and VDC3 give better results by at least 1 order.

Generally the increased number of samples to 2^{20} improved the results produced by the new algorithm versus the other algorithms - see the results for the relative error in Table 10 versus the results in Table 8 and Table 9.

For number of samples $n = 2^{10}$ in Table 8 the proposed algorithm NEWL gives the best relative errors for S_1, S_3, S_4, S_5, S_6, S_1^{tot}, S_2^{tot}, S_3^{tot}, S_4^{tot}, S_5^{tot}, S_6^{tot}, S_{14} and S_{45}, while BIJ gives the best result for S_2 and CRU the best results for S_{24} and S_{12}. However for this small number of samples the relative error for small in value sensitivity indices is insufficient.

For number of samples $n = 2^{16}$ in Table 9 the new algorithm NEWL gives the best relative errors for S_1, S_2, S_3, S_4, S_5, S_1^{tot}, S_2^{tot}, S_3^{tot}, S_4^{tot}, S_5^{tot}, S_6^{tot} and S_{24}, while BIJ gives the best result for S_{12} and S_6, CRU the best results for S_{14} and VDC2 gives the best relative error for S_{45}.

For number of samples $n = 2^{20}$ in Table 10 the algorithm under consideration NEWL gives the best relative errors for S_1, S_2, S_3, S_4, S_5, S_6, S_1^{tot}, S_2^{tot}, S_3^{tot}, S_4^{tot}, S_5^{tot}, S_6^{tot}, S_{12}, S_{14} and S_{24}, and VDC2 gives the best relative error only for S_{45}. It can be seen that for the small in value sensitivity index S_{45} VDC gives also reliable results. However the most important and smallest in value sensitivity index S_5 only the proposed approach NEWL gives reliable relative errors.

The performance of the algorithms can be summarized as follows: the best algorithm is NEWL, followed by VDC2 (for one of the small in value sensitivity indices it gives better results), and after that follows BIJ and VDC3. Sometimes the simplest possible stochastic approach CRU is even better than FIBO which shows that the latter is not appropriate for higher dimensions.

Table 6. Relative error for the evaluation of $f_0 \approx 0.27$.

# of samples n	CRU Relative error	VDC2 Relative error	VDC3 Relative error	FIBO Relative error	BIJ Relative error	NEWL Relative error
2^{10}	1.36e–03	1.35e–04	**1.05e–04**	2.08e–03	7.12e–03	1.13e–04
2^{12}	3.37e–03	1.56e–05	2.17e–04	1.40e–04	1.80e–03	**7.03e–06**
2^{14}	4.85e–04	9.23e–06	2.70e–05	3.98e–04	4.04e–05	**4.40e–07**
2^{16}	5.51e–04	8.66e–04	1.40e–04	2.61e–04	9.91e–06	**2.75e–08**
2^{18}	2.49e–04	4.63e–04	4.75e–04	7.29e–06	7.24e–06	**1.72e–09**
2^{20}	5.95e–05	7.85e–05	1.14e–04	4.57e–07	7.04e–06	**1.07e–10**

Table 7. Relative error for the evaluation of the total variance $\mathbf{D} \approx 0.0025$.

# of samples n	CRU Relative error	VDC2 Relative error	VDC3 Relative error	FIBO Relative error	BIJ Relative error	NEWL Relative Relative
2^{10}	1.37e–01	5.63e–02	6.16e–02	6.73e + 00	**3.11e–02**	1.00e + 00
2^{12}	7.97e–02	1.01e–01	**3.15e–03**	5.27e–01	8.76e–02	2.07e + 00
2^{14}	1.23e–01	2.07e–02	4.56e–03	1.02e–01	**7.54e–04**	1.37e–01
2^{16}	1.81e–03	4.21e–02	3.78e–02	1.97e–03	**9.13e–04**	6.64e–03
2^{18}	1.59e–02	1.06e–02	2.45e–02	4.53e–03	2.22e–03	**1.13e–03**
2^{20}	1.11e–02	6.51e–03	1.04e–02	9.33e–03	2.22e–03	**6.58e–05**

Table 8. Relative error for estimation of sensitivity indices of input parameters using various stochastic approaches($n \approx 2^{10}$).

EQ	RV	**CRU**	VDC2	VDC3	FIBO	BIJ	NEWL
S_1	4e-01	1.82e–01	2.18e–01	1.58e–01	7.19e–01	3.32e–01	**2.49e–02**
S_2	3e-01	1.05e + 00	6.47e–01	4.73e–01	2.11e + 00	**6.25e–03**	4.37e–02
S_3	5e-02	1.27e + 00	5.01e–01	1.36e + 00	9.29e–01	1.76e–01	**4.22e–02**
S_4	3e-01	4.35e–01	3.52e–01	5.30e–02	5.50e–01	2.27e–01	**2.66e–02**
S_5	4e-07	9.72e + 03	1.82e + 03	8.37e + 03	7.87e + 03	1.93e + 04	**2.93e–02**
S_6	2e-02	1.78e + 00	7.82e–01	1.39e + 00	6.38e + 00	1.20e + 00	**4.52e–02**
S_1^{tot}	4e-01	7.07e–01	1.16e + 00	1.13e + 00	7.89e–01	2.65e–01	**3.60e–02**
S_2^{tot}	3e-01	4.79e–01	4.97e–01	1.59e–01	1.98e + 00	1.42e–01	**1.84e–02**
S_3^{tot}	5e-02	3.71e + 00	4.40e + 01	4.22e + 00	8.38e–01	1.15e + 00	**1.87e–02**
S_4^{tot}	3e-01	1.14e + 00	3.05e + 00	8.65e–01	6.99e–01	4.82e–01	**3.99e–02**
S_5^{tot}	2e-04	9.16e + 02	2.96e + 03	7.52e + 02	2.19e + 01	4.09e + 01	**1.22e + 00**
S_6^{tot}	2e-02	1.86e + 01	2.32e + 01	4.37e + 00	7.06e + 00	1.16e + 00	**3.30e–02**
S_{12}	6e-03	**5.07e–01**	2.73e + 00	5.27e + 00	4.22e + 00	2.81e + 00	1.93e + 00
S_{14}	5e-03	8.79e + 00	2.89e + 00	1.85e + 00	6.17e + 00	5.51e + 00	**1.93e + 00**
S_{24}	3e-03	**8.53e–03**	4.89e + 00	1.00e + 01	1.79e + 00	9.97e + 00	1.23e + 00
S_{45}	1e-05	1.32e + 01	1.12e + 02	8.40e + 01	2.21e + 02	1.82e + 02	**1.23e + 00**

Table 9. Relative error for estimation of sensitivity indices of input parameters using various stochastic approaches ($n \approx 2^{16}$).

EQ	RV	CRU	VDC2	VDC3	FIBO	BIJ	NEWL
S_1	4e-01	2.90e–02	1.07e–01	1.85e–02	3.82e–02	1.50e–02	**4.80e–03**
S_2	3e-01	6.00e–02	5.08e–02	1.19e–01	1.03e–02	2.14e–02	**9.01e–03**
S_3	5e-02	6.21e–02	4.05e–02	2.63e–01	5.48e–01	8.28e–02	**1.90e–02**
S_4	3e-01	1.84e–02	7.39e–02	7.51e–03	1.07e–02	6.81e–03	**5.24e–03**
S_5	4e-07	7.75e+02	7.26e+02	7.15e+02	3.40e+03	2.07e+03	**5.79e–03**
S_6	2e-02	6.09e–02	4.10e–01	8.59e–02	1.32e+00	**1.19e–02**	2.21e–02
S_1^{tot}	4e-01	7.98e–02	8.89e–02	2.30e–02	7.92e–02	1.07e–02	**1.06e–02**
S_2^{tot}	3e-01	1.55e–01	1.06e–02	2.33e–02	3.06e–02	2.28e–02	**8.76e–03**
S_3^{tot}	5e-02	5.93e–01	1.25e–01	3.94e–01	1.31e+00	4.92e–02	**4.52e–03**
S_4^{tot}	3e-01	1.38e–01	1.51e–01	1.32e–01	3.84e–01	1.93e–02	**2.30e–03**
S_5^{tot}	2e-04	4.70e+02	3.45e+02	2.69e+02	8.85e+01	6.78e+00	**5.51e–01**
S_6^{tot}	2e-02	2.33e+00	1.63e+00	3.73e–01	2.15e+00	7.63e–02	**1.36e–03**
S_{12}	6e-03	8.88e–01	9.16e–01	1.01e+00	3.21e+00	**2.21e–01**	8.35e–01
S_{14}	5e-03	**8.09e–02**	1.91e–01	1.90e–01	8.64e+00	1.31e+00	1.71e–01
S_{24}	3e-03	7.96e–01	3.25e–01	1.30e+00	1.37e+01	5.63e–01	**1.71e–01**
S_{45}	1e-05	5.21e+00	**1.41e–01**	1.53e+01	4.25e+01	3.87e+01	8.35e–01

Table 10. Relative error for estimation of sensitivity indices of input parameters using various stochastic approaches ($n \approx 2^{20}$).

EQ	RV	CRU	VDC2	VDC3	FIBO	BIJ	NEWL
S_1	4e-01	7.43e–03	1.57e–02	1.17e–02	9.21e–03	1.49e–02	**4.26e–04**
S_2	3e-01	3.90e–02	1.39e–02	3.55e–03	1.47e–02	2.11e–02	**4.34e–04**
S_3	5e-02	4.42e–03	7.04e–03	3.78e–02	6.50e–01	8.25e–02	**6.74e–05**
S_4	3e-01	1.30e–02	7.13e–04	3.73e–02	1.53e–01	5.68e–03	**4.66e–05**
S_5	4e-07	2.08e+02	8.03e+02	3.11e+02	2.68e+03	2.08e+03	**5.79e–03**
S_6	2e-02	3.48e–02	2.09e–02	7.06e–02	1.13e+00	1.55e–02	**3.66e–03**
S_1^{tot}	4e-01	6.61e–03	1.44e–03	9.23e–03	9.69e–03	1.08e–02	**4.42e–04**
S_2^{tot}	3e-01	9.65e–03	5.82e–03	1.58e–03	3.01e–02	2.19e–02	**5.28e–04**
S_3^{tot}	5e-02	2.30e–01	1.29e–01	2.64e–01	1.37e+00	4.96e–02	**6.43e–05**
S_4^{tot}	3e-01	2.22e–02	1.75e–02	6.95e–03	3.67e–01	1.91e–02	**1.39e–04**
S_5^{tot}	2e-04	1.72e+01	6.31e+01	1.33e+01	3.90e+01	1.45e+01	**9.73e–02**
S_6^{tot}	2e-02	4.26e–01	7.22e–02	7.34e–02	1.76e+00	7.68e–02	**2.06e–03**
S_{12}	6e-03	1.49e–01	3.69e–01	2.05e–01	8.40e–02	2.14e–01	**5.04e–02**
S_{14}	5e-03	3.55e–02	2.36e–01	3.84e–02	1.85e–01	1.30e+00	**1.01e–03**
S_{24}	3e-03	1.50e–01	2.04e–01	3.03e–02	1.41e+01	6.63e+00	**2.00e–03**
S_{45}	1e-05	3.69e+00	**9.62e–02**	7.22e–01	2.60e+01	3.85e+01	8.00e–01

6   Conclusion

The present study is in the area of environmental protection. In this paper we proposed a new highly efficient stochastic methods based on lattice rule with special function. We make a performance computing with the simplest possible crude Monte Carlo approach, the van der Corput sequence and its modification and two lattice rules based on generalized Fibonacci numbers and a bijectional transformation function which are among the most famous before the developing of the new algorithm. In our numerical experiments the stochastic methods has been applied for multidimensional integration to provide sensitivity studies under consideration. Sensitivity studies of the model output were performed with two aspects in mind: the sensitivity of the ammonia mean monthly concentrations with respect to the anthropogenic emissions variation, and the sensitivity of the ozone concentration values with respect to the rate variation of several chemical reactions. The numerical results show that the proposed method based on a special function leads to higher accuracy of the estimated quantities in almost all of the case studies, and there is a significant improvement for the model function and the total variance, as well as for some small in value sensitivity indices. Further investigations are necessary to examine if this approach is optimal for the corresponding class of multidimensional integrals. In the future we will developed also some Sobol based polynomial lattice rules which are expected to receive even better accuracy. The results obtained here can be used for increasing the reliability of the mathematical model results, and identifying input parameters that should be measured more precisely. The developed Sobol based approach is also general enough to be applied for sensitivity analysis for other environmental large-scale models. The obtained results will improve mathematical models and more importantly will help to reliably interpret the numerical results by relevant specialists.

Acknowledgements. Venelin Todorov is supported by the Bulgarian National Science Fund (BNSF) under Project KP-06-N52/5 "Efficient methods for modeling, optimization and decision making" and BNSF under Project KP-06-N62/6 "Machine learning through physics-informed neural networks". The work is also supported by BNSF under Project KP-06-M32/2âĂŞ17.12.2019 "Advanced Stochastic and Deterministic Approaches for Large-Scale Problems of Computational Mathematics" and Bilateral Project KP-06-Russia/17 "New Highly Efficient Stochastic Simulation Methods and Applications".

References

1. Bahvalov. N.: On the approximate computation of multiple integrals. In: Vestnik Moscow State University, Ser. Mat., Mech. vol. 4, pp. 3–18 (1959)
2. Dimov, I.: Monte Carlo Methods for Applied Scientists. World Scientific, Singapore (2008)
3. Faure, H., Kritzer, P., Pillichshammer, F.: From van der Corput to modern constructions of sequences for quasi-monte carlo rules. Indagationes Mathematicae **26**(5), 760–822 (2015)

4. Homma, T., Saltelli, A.: Importance measures in global sensitivity analysis of non-linear models. Reliab. Eng. Syst. Saf. **52**, 1–17 (1996)
5. Hua L. K., Wang, Y.: Applications of number theory to numerical analysis (1981)
6. Karaivanova, A., Atanassov, E., Ivanovska, S., Gurov, T., Durchova, M.: Parallel Quasi-Monte Carlo Integration with Application in Environmental Studies, pp. 67–71. SEE-GRID-SCIUserForum, Istanbul (2009)
7. Korobov, N.M.: Properties and calculation of optimal coefficients. Soviet Math. Doklady **1**, 696–700 (1960)
8. Korobov, N.M.: Number-theoretical methods in approximate analysis, Fizmatgiz (1963)
9. Kuo, F.Y., Nuyens, D.: Application of quasi-monte Carlo methods to elliptic PDEs with random diffusion coefficients - a survey of analysis and implementation. Found. Comput. Math. **16**(6), 1631–1696 (2016)
10. Marchuk, G.I.: Mathematical modeling for the problem of the environment, Studies in Mathematics and Applications, No. 16, North-Holland, Amsterdam (1985)
11. Niederreiter, H., Talay, D.: Monte Carlo and Quasi-Monte Carlo Methods, Springer (2002)
12. Paskov, S.H.: Computing high dimensional integrals with applications to finance. Technical report CUCS-023-94, Columbia University (1994)
13. Sloan, I.H., Kachoyan, P.J.: Lattice methods for multiple integration: theory, error analysis and examples. S I A M J. Numer. Anal. **24**, 116–128 (1987)
14. Sloan, I.H., Joe, S.: Lattice Methods for Multiple Integration. Oxford University Press, Oxford (1994)
15. Saltelli, A., et al.: Global sensitivity analysis. Wiley, The Primer (2008)
16. Sobol', I.M.: Global sensitivity indices for nonlinear mathematical models and their monte carlo estimates. Math. Comput. Simul. **55**(1–3), 271–280 (2001)
17. Sobol', I., Myshetskaya, E.: Monte carlo estimators for small sensitivity indices. Monte Carlo Methods Appl. **13**(5–6), 455–465 (2007)
18. Sobol, I.M., Tarantola, S., Gatelli, D., Kucherenko, S., Mauntz, W.: Estimating the approximation error when fixing unessential factors in global sensitivity analysis. Reliab. Eng. Syst. Saf. **92**, 957–960 (2007)
19. Sobol, I.M.: Sensitivity estimates for nonlinear mathematical models. Math. Model. Comput. Experiment. **4**, 407–414 (1993)
20. Saltelli, A., Tarantola, S., Campolongo, F., Ratto, M.: Sensitivity Analysis in Practice: A Guide to Assessing Scientific Models. Halsted Press, New York (2004)
21. Van der Corput, J.G.: Verteilungsfunktionen (Erste Mitteilung) (PDF). In: Proceedings of the Koninklijke Akademie van Wetenschappen te Amsterdam (in German), vol. 38, pp. 813–821, Zbl 0012.34705 (1935)
22. Wang, Y., Hickernell, F.J.: An historical overview of lattice point sets, in monte carlo and quasi-monte carlo methods. In: Proceedings of a Conference held at Hong Kong Baptist University, China (2000)
23. Zlatev, Z.: Comput. Treat. Large Air Pollut. Models. KLUWER Academic Publishers, Dorsrecht-Boston-London (1995)
24. Z. Zlatev, Z., Dimov, I.: Computational and Numerical Challengies in Environmental Modelling, Amsterdam, Elsevier (2006)
25. Zlatev, Z., Dimov, I.T., Georgiev, K.: Three-dimensional version of the Danish Eulerian model. Z. Angew. Math. Mech. **76**(S4), 473–476 (1996)

Parallel Non-numerical Algorithms

Parallel Suffix Sorting for Large String Analytics

Zhihui Du$^{1(\boxtimes)}$ ⓘ, Sen Zhang^2 ⓘ, and David A. Bader^1 ⓘ

^{1} New Jersey Institute of Technology, Newark, NJ, USA
{zhihui.du,bader}@njit.edu
^{2} State University of New York, College at Oneonta, Oneonta, NY, USA
zhangs@oneonta.edu

Abstract. The suffix array is a fundamental data structure to support string analysis efficiently. It took about 26 years for the sequential suffix array construction algorithm to achieve $\mathcal{O}(n)$ time complexity and in-place sorting. In this paper, we develop the D-Limited Parallel Induce ($DLPI$) algorithm, the first $\mathcal{O}(\frac{n}{p})$ time parallel suffix array construction algorithm. The basic idea of $DLPI$ includes two aspects: dividing the $\mathcal{O}(n)$ size problem into p reduced sub-problems with size $\mathcal{O}(\frac{n}{p})$ so we can handle them on p processors in parallel; developing an efficient parallel induce sorting method to achieve correct order for all the reduced sub-problems. The complete algorithm description is given to show the implementation method of the proposed idea. The time and space complexity analysis and proof are also given to show the correctness and efficiency of the proposed algorithm. The proposed $DLPI$ algorithm can handle large strings with scalable performance.

Keywords: Suffix Array · String Algorithm · Parallel Sorting · String Analysis · Optimal Algorithm

1 Introduction

Suffix arrays were initially introduced by Manber and Myers [18] as a space efficient alternative to suffix trees [21]. Suffix arrays can be widely used in string processing, data compression, text indexing, information retrieval and computational biology. Since the volume of string data is increasing constantly, high performance suffix array construction algorithms (SACAs) have been a challenging problem. Thirteen years after the suffix array was proposed, the first linear time algorithm for suffix sorting over integer alphabets was achieved by three research groups, Ko and Aluru [12] , Kärkkäinen and Sanders [9] and Kim *et al.* [11] at almost the same time. They reduced the time complexity of suffix array construction algorithms from original $\mathcal{O}(nlog(n))$ to $\mathcal{O}(n)$. These sequential algorithms are optimal in terms of asymptotic time complexity. Furthermore, many lightweight algorithms [1,8,19,20] with small working space were developed. Especially, Nong *et al.* [22] can achieve $\mathcal{O}(1)$ space complexity for constant

© The Author(s), under exclusive license to Springer Nature Switzerland AG 2023
R. Wyrzykowski et al. (Eds.): PPAM 2022, LNCS 13826, pp. 71–82, 2023.
https://doi.org/10.1007/978-3-031-30442-2_6

alphabets and Li *et al.* [17] can achieve $\mathcal{O}(1)$ in-place sorting for read-only integer alphabets. This also took about thirteen years to reduce the working space complexity from $\mathcal{O}(n)$ to $\mathcal{O}(1)$.

Many parallel SACAs have also been developed. For examples, Futamura *et al.* [4] gave a very early effort to implement a parallel SACA based on the sequential prefix-doubling method. Shun's problem-based benchmark suite (PBBS) [26] leveraged the task-parallel Cilk Plus programming model in its parallel multicore skew algorithm implementation. Osipov [23] and Deo and Keely [2] implemented the parallel Difference Cover 3 [10] or skewed algorithm on GPU. Homann *et al.* [6] introduced the mkESA tool on multithreaded CPUs that could parallelize the sequential induce copy method. Lao *et al.* [14,15] implemented their parallel recursive algorithm on multicore computers. All the parallel methods can significantly improve the practical performance compared with the corresponding sequential methods. Yet, none of them can handle very large string on many (p) processors in $\mathcal{O}(\frac{n}{p})$ time. To achieve scalable performance, we need a parallel SACA with $\mathcal{O}(\frac{n}{p})$ time complexity. The major contributions of this paper are as follows.

- A high level parallel suffix sorting framework is proposed. This framework aims to divide a large string's suffix sorting problem ($T(n, p)$) into many even size reduced sub-problems ($T(\frac{n}{p}, 1)$) and the large problem can be solved by handling the many reduced sub-problems on p processors in parallel. In other words, $T(n, p) = T(\frac{n}{p}, 1)$.
- The first parallel suffix array construction algorithm $DLPI$ with $\mathcal{O}(\frac{n}{p})$ time is presented. $DLPI$ is optimal in terms of asymptotic time complexity.

2   Problem Description

We first give some basic definitions and notations to present the problem clearly.

Definition 1. *Suffix Array: Given a string $S = S[0..n-1]$ with n characters, the string's suffix array (SA) is an array of integers providing the indices of suffixes of S in lexicographical order. This means that $\forall i < j$, we have $suf(i') < suf(j')$, where $i' = SA[i]$, $j' = SA[j]$ and $suf(k)$ is the suffix $S[k..n-1]$.*

Definition 2. *Read-only integer alphabets: The alphabets Σ is a set of characters ($\Sigma \subseteq \mathbb{Z}$) that can be used to build a string. Given a string $S = S[0..n-1]$ with n characters, $\forall S[i], 0 \leq i < n$, we have $S[i] \in \Sigma$. At the same time, the given string S cannot be changed during the procedure of building its suffix array. Since different characters can be encoded as different integers, we assume $\forall S[i]$, we have $S[i] \in \{x | 1 \leq x \leq |\Sigma|\}$.*

In this paper, our problem is based on read-only integer alphabets instead of constant alphabets, which have only constant characters, or integer alphabets, whose input strings can be updated during the sorting procedure. The constant or integer alphabets is a special case of our problem.

The proposed problem is as follows. Given a very large string S built from a read-only integer alphabets Σ with length n and a parallel random access machine (PRAM) with p processors, can we have a parallel algorithm to build the suffix array of S in $\mathcal{O}(\frac{n}{p})$ time?

3 Algorithm Design

Unlike the existing parallel SACAs, we do not try to explore the parallelism in the framework of sequential SACAs. Instead, we first build a parallel framework that aims to divide the whole problem into many reduced sub-problems; and then develop a parallel induce method to solve all the reduced sub-problems.

Definition 3. *Order of Suffix Sets: Given two non-empty suffix sets Set_1 and Set_2 of a string S, if $\forall x \in Set_1, \forall y \in Set_2$, their lexicographical order meets $x < y$ (or $x > y$), then we define $Set_1 < Set_2$ (or $Set_1 > Set_2$).*

In this section, we propose an idea to sort the suffixes of a long string in two steps. First, we construct many (p) suffix subsets to cover all the suffixes. The suffix subsets are ordered, but suffixes in each suffix subset are not sorted. Then, we sort each suffix subset in parallel into its own sub-suffix array and achieve the complete suffix array by combining the different sub-suffix arrays corresponding to different suffix subsets together.

Algorithm 1: *DLPI* Algorithm

---

1 **Function** DLPI(*String*, p)
2   Step (1) Build parallel reduced subproblems
3   1.1 Divide all suffixes of S into p suffix subsets
     $SubSet_1, ..., SubSet_p, \forall 1 \le i \le p, |SubSet_i| = \mathcal{O}(\frac{n}{p})$
4   1.2 Call Parallel Suffix SubSets Sorting function $SA = PSSS(SubSet_1, ..., SubSet_p)$
5   1.3 Evenly select $(p-1)$ splitters from each processor p_i's returned suffix array $SA[i]$
6   1.4 Add the $(p-1) \times p$ splitters into each subset to get $SpSubSet_i, 1 \le i \le p$
7   1.5 Call Parallel Suffix SubSets Sorting function
     $SA = PSSS(SpSubSet_1, ..., SpSubSet_p)$
8   1.6 According to the returned SA, divide all suffixes into p ordered subsets that meet
     $OSubSet_1 < ... < OSubSet_p$
9   Step (2) Sort reduced subproblems in parallel
10   2.1 Call Parallel Suffix SubSets Sorting function $SA = PSSS(OSubSet_1, ..., OSubSet_p)$
11   2.2 **return** SA
12 **end**

3.1 Algorithm Framework

In Algorithm 1, we present the framework of our parallel suffix array construction algorithm D-Limited Parallel Induce (*DLPI*). This framework transforms a large $T(n, p)$ problem, where n represents the problem size and p represents the number processors of the PRAM, into p parallel $T(\frac{n}{p}, 1)$ problems, which means that each single problem is of size $\mathcal{O}(\frac{n}{p})$ and can be handled in one processor.

In line 3 of Algorithm 1, for all the n suffixes of a given string S, we assign them into p subsets evenly. The *PSSS* function will generate different sub-suffix arrays corresponding to different subsets and we can select $(p-1)$ different splitters [5] that divide each subset evenly (line 5). Then we augment each subset by adding $(p-1) \times (p-1)$ splitters from the rest of the subsets and call PSSS again on the augmented subsets. Afterwards, we utilize the ordered $p \times (p-1)$ splitters as guides to assign all the suffixes (in a round-robin order) into p ordered subsets, $OSubSet_1, ..., OSubSet_p$ (lines 6–8). Here, all suffixes are assigned into p ordered subsets with the size of $\mathcal{O}(\frac{n}{p})$.

The second step is straightforward, where we just call *PSSS* again to generate the order of suffixes in different subsets and then combine them together to obtain the complete suffix array SA (lines 10–11).

3.2   Parallel Induce Method

In Algorithm 2, we describe the essential function *PSSS* that can support parallel induce on all reduced sub-problems. The basic idea of this function is that we first construct p much smaller strings to express the different sub-problems. The suffixes with different short prefixes can be sorted easily and the novel parallel induce method is used to derive the order of suffixes with long and the same prefixes.

Algorithm 2: Parallel Suffix SubSets Sorting Algorithm

---

1 **Function** PSSS($SubSet_1, ..., SubSet_p$)
2   Step (1) Sort suffixes of each subsets and distinguish Fixed and Changeable suffixes
3   Build D-limited shrunk strings $DS\_S_1, ..., DS\_S_p$ according to different subsets
4   **forall** *(i in 1..p)* **do**
5          $ESA[i][] = SeqOptSA(DS\_S_i)$
6   Remove all indices $ESA[i][\bar{j}]$ that are not in Set_i and get $SA[i][]$ corresponding to $SubSet_i$
7   var mg=-1
8   **for** *(j in 0..|$SubSet_i$|-1)* **do**
9   **if** *($Suf(SA[i][j])$) and its closest suffix in SA have the same D prefix)* **then**
10   Flag[i][j]=Changeable
11   **if** *($Suf(SA[i][j])$) is the first Changeable suffix of a new group)* **then**
12   mg++
13   ChgGrp[i][mg].head=j;ChgGrp[i][mg].num=1
14   **end**
15   ChgGrp[i][mg].num++
16   **end**
17   **else**
18   Flag[i][j]=Fixed
19   **end**
20   **end**
21   **end**
22   Step (2) Induce the order of Changeable suffixes in each Changeable suffix group
23   2.1 Build aligned subsets $AliSubSet_1, ..., AliSubSet_p$ for Changeable suffix groups
24   2.2 Generate the new suffix array $AliSA$ of the suffixes just like the previous step (1)
25   2.3 Generate the distinguishable tail suffix array DTA for suffixes in the Changeable suffix groups
26   2.4 Induce the correct order of all Changeable suffixes in SA based on DTA and $AliSA$
27   **return** SA
28 **end**

We introduce the first step of *PSSS* function at first.

Definition 4. *D-limited substring and D-limited shrunk string: Given a constant D, a string S with length n and one of its suffix subset $SubSet$, if two suffixes $suf(i) \in SubSet$ and $suf(j) \in SubSet$, where $i < j$ and no other suffix sits between i and j in $SubSet$(we will let $j = n$ if no such $suf(j)$ in $SubSet$), then the D-limited substring of $suf(i)$ is the substring $S[i..j-1]$ if $j-i \leq D$ or $S[i..i+D-1]$ if $j-i > D$. The D-limited shrunk string DS of S is the string by concatenating all D-limited substrings from $SubSet$ together according to their original order in S.*

Definition 5. *D-prefix substring: Given a constant D, a string S with length n, and an index i, the D-prefix substring of $suf(i)$ is the substring $S[i..i+D-1]$ if $i < n - D$ or $S[i..n]$ otherwise.*

Building Reduced Strings. The first step of this function is building p much smaller D-limited shrunk strings $DS_1, ..., DS_p$ so each processor can handle one smaller string in parallel (line 3). We use D-prefix substrings to replace the original suffixes.

We will call the existing optimal sequential SACA *SeqOptSA* [17] to generate the extended suffix array for the given shrunk string. Since we do not need to compare the suffixes not included in the given subset, we remove the indices of such suffixes in the extended suffix array and get the exact suffix array SA (lines 5–6). We use a two-dimension array to express the partitioned data in different processors. The cardinality of the first dimension stands for the number of processors and that of the second dimension stands for the maximum number of suffixes assigned to different processors.

For the suffix whose order can be decided based on its D-prefix substring, its rank in the suffix array is correct. If there are two or more suffixes whose D-prefix substrings are exactly the same, their ranks in SA should be induced based on their complete suffixes. We use a two-dimension array $Flag$ to mark the correct rank as Fixed and the rank to be induced as Changeable. At the same time, we use a two-dimension array $ChgGrp$ to manage the clustered Changeable suffixes by their D-prefix substrings. $ChgGrp[i][mg]$ keeps the current group of Changeable suffixes on processor i. $ChgGrp[i][mg].head$ is the rank of the first suffix in the corresponding suffix array and $ChgGrp[i][mg].num$ is the total number of suffixes in the current group (lines from 7 to 20).

Based on the $ChgGrp$ data structure, the induce sorting method works as follows. When we know the smallest suffix within the group mg, we just need to switch the rank of the smallest suffix with that of the head suffix, advance $ChgGrp[i][mg].head$ by one, and reduce $ChgGrp[i][mg].num$ by 1. If a suffix can split the suffixes into two ordered subsets, we will put the suffix at the correct position in its SA and split its Changeable suffix group into two smaller groups. This way, we can induce one suffix at its correct position. When $ChgGrp[i][mg].num$ is one, all suffixes in the Changeable group mg have been correctly ranked. The suffixes in different groups can be induced in parallel.

The second step is to induce the correct ranks of Changeable suffixes (line 22). The basic idea is building induce chain for all the Changeable suffixes; then identifying the tail suffix that can distinguish the Changeable suffix from other suffixes; inducing the order for each Changeable suffix based on the tail suffixes. It includes four substeps and we will present the detailed descriptions as follows.

Definition 6. *Aligned suffix set: Given a Changeable suffix group CG and a non negative integer k, the set $\{suf(x)|\forall e \in CG, e = suf(y) \land x = y + D \times k \land x < n\}$ is the k aligned suffix set of CG.*

Building Aligned Suffix Sets. In the first substep (line 23) we build p completely new suffix subsets $AliSubSet_1$, ..., $AliSubSet_p$ that are used to induce the correct order of all the Changeable suffixes. Suffixes in an aligned suffix set will be assigned to the same processor so we can get their order based on each processor's suffix array.

For all the Changeable suffix groups, we can generate all of their k aligned suffix set. We will merge some overlapping aligned suffix sets and assign these sets into p processors and form p suffix subsets $AliSubSet_1$, ..., $AliSubSet_p$.

Generating SA for Aligned Suffix Sets. In the second substep, we may employ the similar method as before (lines from 2 to 21) to generate the suffix array of each aligned suffix subset. Here we use $AliSA$ to express the new suffix array corresponding to the aligned suffixes. $AliFlag$ has the similar meaning as before to mark the Fixed and Changeable suffixes.

Now we have obtained two sets of Fixed and Changeables, we will use the later set of Fixed suffixes to induce the previous set of Changeable suffixes by using a data structure called DTA (to be further defined next).

Building the Distinguishable Tail Suffix Array. In the third substep, we will build an array DTA to store the suffixes that can be used to distinguish one Changeable suffix from other suffixes in the same Changeable group.

Definition 7. *Distinguishable Tail Suffix: For any Changeable suffix $suf(x)$ in a Changeable suffix group $ChgGrp$, its distinguishable tail suffix $suf(DTA(x))$ is the suffix that can distinguish the order of $suf(x)$ from the other Changeable suffixes according to $suf(DTA(x))$'s D-prefix substring.*

We will transfer the index t of suffix $suf(t)$ whose flag is Fixed to its left suffix $suf(t - D)$ and let $DTA[t - D] = t$ if $suf(t - D)$ exists and it is a changeable suffix. This procedure will continue to the head of the string along the induce chain of $suf(t)$. The challenge here is that we should do it in parallel. The basic idea is as follows.

We first assign all suffixes to different processors based on the indices of different suffixes evenly and each processor only checks about $\frac{n}{p}$ suffixes. For suffixes assigned to the current processor i, we will cluster them into D classes based on their indices' modulo D values. Each processor will scan every class from its end suffix to its start suffix, in parallel. The index of the Fixed suffix $suf(f)$ will be passed to its left suffix $suf(f - D)$ one by one until the new Fixed suffix is met. Then the index of the new Fixed suffix will replace the old one and be passed to the left suffix. In order to pass the distinguishable indices across processors, we use a 2-D temporary array $tmp[D][p]$ consisting of $(D \times p)$ elements. If an ending suffix $suf(e)$ (there are D of them) is changeable, we let $tmp[e\%D][i] = -1$ and $DTA[e] = -(i)$, where i refers to the id of the processor (ranged from 0 to $(p - 1)$) that means that $suf(e)$'s DTA value $DTA(e)$ is unknown and it will get its value from $tmp[e\%D][i]$. Each Changable $suf(j)$ on the processor i that cannot get its distinguishable tail suffix from upto its last D-prefix suffix on the same processor will point to the same element $tmp[j\%D][i]$.

After this, we will scan the temporary array from end to start for different modulo values. For current temporary element $tmp[d][i]$ that corresponds to the (i) processor and d^{th} class, if $suf(r)$ is the first suffix of its right processor, $r\%D = d$, and $DTA[r] > 0$, we will let $tmp[d][i] = DTA[r]$. If not, we will let $tmp[d][i] = tmp[d][i+1]$. This means that the temporary array update will start from $tmp[d][p-2]$ and end with $tmp[d][0]$ (for all d in $[0..D-1]$), sequentially. Finally, each processor will check its suffixes whose DTA values are still negative and update them with their respective corresponding temporary values. This way, we can propagate the distinguishable tail suffixes from end to start in parallel.

Inducing the Order of Changeable Suffixes. In the fourth substep, we know the distinguishable tail suffix of each Changeable suffix. We can use such information to induce the order of suffixes in each Changeable suffix group. For each Changeable suffix group, first we will use its closest distinguishable tail suffixes to distinguish the corresponding Changeable suffixes from others. Then, we will induce the correct order of all Changeable suffixes based on their distinguishable tail suffixes' indices from small to large. The order of different Changeable suffix groups can be induced in parallel.

4 Complexity Analysis

In this section, we adopt the widely used Parallel Random Access Machine (PRAM) model [7] to analyze our parallel algorithm. The time complexity of the proposed algorithm is $\mathcal{O}(\frac{n}{p})$ and the space complexity is $\mathcal{O}(n)$. We will prove that every step of our algorithm can be done in $\mathcal{O}(\frac{n}{p})$ time and at most $\mathcal{O}(n)$ working space (the space except the input string S and the returned suffix array) is needed to generate the complete suffix array.

The $DLPI$ function gives the framework of our algorithm. For substep 1.1 of step 1, we can assign the suffixes of the given string S with length n into p parts and each has $\mathcal{O}(\frac{n}{p})$ elements in $\mathcal{O}(\frac{n}{p})$ time. The p D-limited shrunk strings will need $\mathcal{O}(p \times D \times \frac{n}{p}) = \mathcal{O}(D \times n) = \mathcal{O}(n)$ space. For substep 1.2, we will give the time and space complexity of the parallel induce function $PSSS$ later. Selecting $(p-1)$ splitters for each processor based on its returned suffix array and adding them into different subsets are straightforward and can also be done in $\mathcal{O}(\frac{n}{p})$ time. Here we assume $p^3 < n$, when we add $(p-1)^2$ new elements to each subset, each subset will have $\mathcal{O}(\frac{n}{p}) + \mathcal{O}((p-1)^2) \leq \mathcal{O}(\frac{n}{p}) + \mathcal{O}(\frac{n}{p}) = \mathcal{O}(\frac{n}{p})$ elements. So, the total working space will also be $\mathcal{O}(p \times \frac{n}{p}) = \mathcal{O}(n)$.

For substep 1.5, just like before, we will discuss the time complexity of $PSSS$ later. From substeps 1.3 to 1.6, we know that the total number of elements between two closest splitters cannot be larger than $\mathcal{O}(\frac{n}{p^2})$. So, when we combine p parts of elements divided by the same splitters together into one subset, its size cannot be larger than $\mathcal{O}(\frac{n}{p})$. At the same time, the elements of each subset will be no larger than $\mathcal{O}(\frac{n}{p})$. Based on this conclusion, it is feasible for us to build p ordered subsets according to the $p \times (p-1)$ splitters.

Hence, we can claim that $DLPI$ function can generate the complete suffix array of a given string S with length n in $\mathcal{O}(\frac{n}{p})$ time on p processors using $\mathcal{O}(n)$ space if the parallel induce function $PSSS$ can return the suffix array for each suffix subset in $\mathcal{O}(\frac{n}{p})$ time on p processors using $\mathcal{O}(n)$ working space.

Theorem 1. *For a string S with length n, if its suffixes are assigned to p given subsets with size $\mathcal{O}(\frac{n}{p})$, then the corresponding D-prefix substrings of each subset can be sorted in $\mathcal{O}(\frac{n}{p})$ time on p processors with $\mathcal{O}(n)$ space.*

Proof. We can build D-limited shrunk strings based on given p suffix subsets of the string S in parallel. The shrunk stings can be done by directly concatenating all the D-limited substrings corresponding to the suffixes in each subset directly. This work will take $\mathcal{O}(\frac{n}{p})$ time with $\mathcal{O}(n)$ space. Then, we may employ the existing in-place sequential linear suffix array algorithm $SeqOptSA$ to directly return their corresponding extended suffix arrays in $\mathcal{O}(\frac{n}{p})$ time. The extended suffix arrays will contain more indices than each subset's elements. So, we need to remove the additional indices. This can also be done in at most $\mathcal{O}(\frac{n}{p})$ time. Totally, $\mathcal{O}(\frac{n}{p})$ time and $\mathcal{O}(n)$ space will be needed to sort the D-prefix substrings of suffixes in all the given subsets.

Lemma 1. *All suffixes can be marked as Fixed or Changeable suffixes and clustered into groups in $\mathcal{O}(\frac{n}{p})$ time and $\mathcal{O}(n)$ space.*

Proof. To mark all suffixes as Fixed or Changeable, a $Flag[1..p][]$ array with $\mathcal{O}(n)$ space will be needed. To store the Changeable group information, at most $\mathcal{O}(\frac{n}{2})$ space for a Changeable suffix array $ChgGrp[1..p][]$ will be needed because the suffixes can be divided into at most $(\frac{n}{2})$ groups. Based on the returned suffix array, each processor can compare any suffix's D-prefix substring with its neighbor to check if they are the same. The different D-prefix substrings mean that the corresponding suffixes can be marked as Fixed; otherwise, they will be marked as Changeable. The entire character comparison operations for any processor should be $\mathcal{O}(D \times \frac{n}{p}) = \mathcal{O}(\frac{n}{p})$. Clustering the Changeable suffixes based on their D-prefix substrings and storing the group information into $ChgGrp$ are similar. So, the marking and clustering operations can be done in $\mathcal{O}(\frac{n}{p})$ time and $\mathcal{O}(n)$ space.

Lemma 2. *The aligned subsets $AliSubSet_1, ..., AliSubSet_p$ that each is no more than $\mathcal{O}(\frac{n}{p})$ elements can be built in $\mathcal{O}(\frac{n}{p})$ time and $\mathcal{O}(n)$ space.*

Proof. The total number of aligned suffixes cannot be larger than $\mathcal{O}(n)$. Since we combine some overlapping aligned suffix sets and assign them to different processors evenly, the total number of suffixes assigned to one processor cannot be larger than $\mathcal{O}(\frac{n}{p})$. The total number of suffixes in the Changeable suffix groups cannot be larger than $\mathcal{O}(n)$, and the total number of suffixes in all aligned suffix sets cannot be larger than $\mathcal{O}(n)$ either. So, for the first substep, totally at most $\mathcal{O}(n)$ space will be needed to store all the suffixes. Generating at most $\mathcal{O}(\frac{n}{p})$ suffixes $AliSubSet_1, ..., AliSubSet_p$ for each processor from the Changeable suffix groups is straightforward and can be done at most in $\mathcal{O}(\frac{n}{p})$ time.

Corollary 1. *The D-prefix substrings of subsets $AliSubSet_1, ..., AliSubSet_p$ can be sorted in $\mathcal{O}(\frac{n}{p})$ time on p processors with $\mathcal{O}(n)$ space.*

Proof. $AliSubSet_1, ..., AliSubSet_p$ are p suffix subsets and each of them have at most $\mathcal{O}(\frac{n}{p})$ suffixes. Based on theorem 1, we can get the corollary and the third substep can be done in $\mathcal{O}(\frac{n}{p})$ time and $\mathcal{O}(n)$ space.

Subsequently, again all suffixes of AliSubSets can be marked as Fixed or Changeable suffixes and clustered into groups in $\mathcal{O}(\frac{n}{p})$ time and $\mathcal{O}(n)$ space, a direct application of Lemma 1 on the new subsets i.e. AliSubsets.

Lemma 3. *The distinguishable tail suffix array DTA can be generated in $\mathcal{O}(\frac{n}{p})$ time and $\mathcal{O}(n)$ space.*

Proof. We can allocate the DTA array with size n to cover all suffixes. So, $\mathcal{O}(n)$ space is sufficient. The basic idea of distinguishable tail suffix generation is passing the closest Fixed suffix to the current Changeable suffix and storing the Fixed suffix's index in DTA. The short passing path will be easy to implement. In order to reduce the passing time for a very long passing path, our implementation method divides the long passing path into multiple parallel subpaths. The suffix passing can be done on different subpaths in parallel. We allocate at most p temporary memory space to transfer the index across different processors. Since all the suffixes assigned to one processor cannot be larger than $\mathcal{O}(\frac{n}{p})$, the first scan procedure can be done in $\mathcal{O}(\frac{n}{p})$ time for all the processors. Then we let one processor pass the value in the temporary memory one by one from end to start. So, at most $\mathcal{O}(p)$ time is needed. Finally, during the last scan, every processor will assign the suffixes with the value of the temporary memory space if they point to this memory space. The third substep will need at most $\mathcal{O}(\frac{n}{p})$ time. So, totally, $\mathcal{O}(\frac{n}{p})$ time and $\mathcal{O}(n)$ space are needed to generate DTA.

Lemma 4. *Inducing the order of all Changeable suffixes based on DTA and AliSA can be done in $\mathcal{O}(\frac{n}{p})$ time and $\mathcal{O}(n)$ space.*

Proof. Generating the relative order of suffixes in each Changeable group based on its DTA can be done in $\mathcal{O}(\frac{n}{p})$ time on each processor because the length of each suffix to be sorted will be no more than D (D or $<D$ at the end of the string), and we have at most $\mathcal{O}(\frac{n}{p})$ such suffixes for each processor. It will need to scan all the corresponding distinguishable tail suffixes to induce the order of Changeable suffixes. The total number of distinguishable tail suffixes is the same as the total number of Changeable suffixes that is no more than $\mathcal{O}(\frac{n}{p})$ on each processor. So, the induce procedure also can be done in $\mathcal{O}(\frac{n}{p})$ time. The total space to keep the $AliSA$ and the temporary string is no more than $\mathcal{O}(n)$. So the fourth substep can also be done in $\mathcal{O}(\frac{n}{p})$ time and $\mathcal{O}(n)$ space.

Theorem 2. *For a string S with length n, its suffix array can be generated in $\mathcal{O}(\frac{n}{p})$ time on p processors with $\mathcal{O}(n)$ space in parallel.*

Proof. Based on the above theorem and the lemmas, every algorithm step can be done in $\mathcal{O}(\frac{n}{p})$ time and $\mathcal{O}(n)$ space. So, after adding them together, we will get the conclusion.

5   Related Work

There have been many works on the suffix array construction algorithm since suffix array was invented in 1990 by Manber and Myers [18]. "Induce" is an essential technique in suffix sorting. Although prefix-doubling [24] adopts the induce technique, it cannot reduce the problem size step by step. This is why it cannot achieve $\mathcal{O}(n)$ time complexity. The following works [9,11,12] recursively solve the problem by constructing a reduced problem and employing the induce technique to sort the suffixes.

All existing parallel suffix array construction algorithms were trying to parallelize one or combined sequential algorithms. Futamura *et al.* [4] gave the early effort to parallel the prefix-doubling method. Larsson *et al.* [16] implemented optimized methods based on the previous prefix-doubling technology and improved its performance in parallel. Osipov *et al.* [23] implemented prefix-doubling algorithm on GPUs. Flick and Aluru [3]'s parallel MPI-based implementation of the prefix-doubling method can achieve very high practical performance on human genome datasets. Kulla *et al.* [13] parallelized the sequential DC3 method, which regularly samples the string to build a smaller $\frac{2}{3}n$ problem. Deo *et al.* [2] further implement the DC3 method on GPUs. Shun [25]'s parallel skew (DC3) algorithm could achieve good performance on shared-memory multi-core computers. Wang *et al.* [27] implemented a hybrid prefix-doubling and DC3 method on GPUs to improve the existing GPU methods significantly. Lao *et al.* [14,15] employed pipeline technology to parallelize their previous sequential linear algorithms on multicore computers.

The existing sequential algorithm framework is the barrier to the existing parallel methods of achieving scalable performance. We develop a parallel framework and propose a parallel induce method to achieve $\mathcal{O}(\frac{n}{p})$ time complexity.

6   Conclusion

The novel idea provided in this paper is the concept of D-limited shrunk substrings that divides the complete problem with size n into p reduced subproblems with size $\mathcal{O}(\frac{n}{p})$. An optimal parallel suffix array construction algorithm to handle the problem in $\mathcal{O}(\frac{n}{p})$ time complexity (p is the number of parallel processors and we assume $p^3 < n$) is critical for us to handle large strings (built on an integer alphabet) with scalable performance. The critical technology is parallel induce. The suffixes with long repeat prefixes can induce their order based on their distinguishable tail suffixes in parallel. We take advantage of the existing optimal sequential suffix array construction algorithm as an independent execution unit to generate the order of all D-prefix substrings that can be used to separate suffixes with long repeat prefixes from those with short unique prefixes. The simplicity and the $\mathcal{O}(\frac{n}{p})$ time complexity make the proposed D-Limited Parallel Induce ($DLPI$) algorithm very promising to handle huge strings with scalable performance. $DLPI$ is the first parallel suffix array construction algorithm with $\mathcal{O}(\frac{n}{p})$ time complexity. We will focus on further reducing the total working space $\mathcal{O}(n)$ in the future work.

Acknowledgement. This research was funded in part by NSF grant number CCF-2109988.

References

1. Burkhardt, S., Kärkkäinen, J.: Fast lightweight suffix array construction and checking. In: Baeza-Yates, R., Chávez, E., Crochemore, M. (eds.) CPM 2003. LNCS, vol. 2676, pp. 55–69. Springer, Heidelberg (2003). https://doi.org/10.1007/3-540-44888-8_5
2. Deo, M., Keely, S.: Parallel suffix array and least common prefix for the GPU. In: Proceedings of the 18th ACM SIGPLAN Symposium on Principles and Practice of Parallel Programming, pp. 197–206 (2013). https://doi.org/10.1145/2442516.2442536
3. Flick, P., Aluru, S.: Parallel distributed memory construction of suffix and longest common prefix arrays. In: Proceedings of the International Conference for High Performance Computing, Networking, Storage and Analysis, pp. 1–10 (2015)
4. Futamura, N., Aluru, S., Kurtz, S.: Parallel suffix sorting. Electrical Engineering and Computer Science - All Scholarship 64 (2001). https://surface.syr.edu/eecs/64
5. Helman, D.R., JáJá, J., Bader, D.A.: A new deterministic parallel sorting algorithm with an experimental evaluation. J. Exp. Algorithmics (JEA) **3**, 4-es (1998). https://doi.org/10.1145/297096.297128
6. Homann, R., Fleer, D., Giegerich, R., Rehmsmeier, M.: mkESA: enhanced suffix array construction tool. Bioinformatics **25**(8), 1084–1085 (2009). https://doi.org/10.1093/bioinformatics/btp112
7. JáJá, J.: An Introduction to Parallel Algorithms, vol. 10, p. 133889. Addison-Wesley, Reading (1992)
8. Kärkkäinen, J.: Fast BWT in small space by blockwise suffix sorting. Theoret. Comput. Sci. **387**(3), 249–257 (2007). https://doi.org/10.1016/j.tcs.2007.07.018
9. Kärkkäinen, J., Sanders, P.: Simple linear work suffix array construction. In: Baeten, J.C.M., Lenstra, J.K., Parrow, J., Woeginger, G.J. (eds.) ICALP 2003. LNCS, vol. 2719, pp. 943–955. Springer, Heidelberg (2003). https://doi.org/10.1007/3-540-45061-0_73
10. Kärkkäinen, J., Sanders, P., Burkhardt, S.: Linear work suffix array construction. J. ACM (JACM) **53**(6), 918–936 (2006). https://doi.org/10.1145/1217856.1217858
11. Kim, D.K., Sim, J.S., Park, H., Park, K.: Linear-time construction of suffix arrays. In: Baeza-Yates, R., Chávez, E., Crochemore, M. (eds.) CPM 2003. LNCS, vol. 2676, pp. 186–199. Springer, Heidelberg (2003). https://doi.org/10.1007/3-540-44888-8_14

12. Ko, P., Aluru, S.: Space efficient linear time construction of suffix arrays. J. Discret. Algorithms **3**(2–4), 143–156 (2005). https://doi.org/10.1016/j.jda.2004.08.002
13. Kulla, F., Sanders, P.: Scalable parallel suffix array construction. Parallel Comput. **33**(9), 605–612 (2007)
14. Lao, B., Nong, G., Chan, W.H., Pan, Y.: Fast induced sorting suffixes on a multicore machine. J. Supercomput. **74**(7), 3468–3485 (2018). https://doi.org/10.1007/s11227-018-2395-5
15. Lao, B., Nong, G., Chan, W.H., Xie, J.Y.: Fast in-place suffix sorting on a multicore computer. IEEE Trans. Comput. **67**(12), 1737–1749 (2018). https://doi.org/10.1109/TC.2018.2842050
16. Larsson, N.J., Sadakane, K.: Faster suffix sorting. Theoret. Comput. Sci. **387**(3), 258–272 (2007). https://doi.org/10.1016/j.tcs.2007.07.017
17. Li, Z., Li, J., Huo, H.: Optimal in-place suffix sorting. Inf. Comput. **285**, 104818 (2022)
18. Manber, U., Myers, G.: Suffix arrays: a new method for on-line string searches. SIAM J. Comput. **22**(5), 935–948 (1993). https://doi.org/10.1137/0222058
19. Maniscalco, M.A., Puglisi, S.J.: Faster lightweight suffix array construction. In: Proceedings of International Workshop on Combinatorial Algorithms (IWOCA), pp. 16–29 (2006)
20. Manzini, G., Ferragina, P.: Engineering a lightweight suffix array construction algorithm. Algorithmica **40**(1), 33–50 (2004). https://doi.org/10.1007/s00453-004-1094-1
21. McCreight, E.M.: A space-economical suffix tree construction algorithm. J. ACM (JACM) **23**(2), 262–272 (1976). https://doi.org/10.1145/321941.321946
22. Nong, G.: Practical linear-time O(1)-workspace suffix sorting for constant alphabets. ACM Trans. Inf. Syst. (TOIS) **31**(3), 1–15 (2013). https://doi.org/10.1145/2493175.2493180
23. Osipov, V.: Parallel suffix array construction for shared memory architectures. In: Calderón-Benavides, L., González-Caro, C., Chávez, E., Ziviani, N. (eds.) SPIRE 2012. LNCS, vol. 7608, pp. 379–384. Springer, Heidelberg (2012). https://doi.org/10.1007/978-3-642-34109-0_40
24. Puglisi, S.J., Smyth, W.F., Turpin, A.H.: A taxonomy of suffix array construction algorithms. ACM Comput. Surv. (CSUR) **39**(2), 4-es (2007). https://doi.org/10.1145/1242471.1242472
25. Shun, J.: Fast parallel computation of longest common prefixes. In: SC 2014: Proceedings of the International Conference for High Performance Computing, Networking, Storage and Analysis, pp. 387–398. IEEE (2014). https://doi.org/10.1109/SC.2014.37
26. Shun, J., et al.: Brief announcement: the problem based benchmark suite. In: Proceedings of the Twenty-Fourth Annual ACM Symposium on Parallelism in Algorithms and Architectures, pp. 68–70 (2012). https://doi.org/10.1145/2312005.2312018
27. Wang, L., Baxter, S., Owens, J.D.: Fast parallel skew and prefix-doubling suffix array construction on the GPU. Concurr. Comput. Pract. Exp. **28**(12), 3466–3484 (2016). https://doi.org/10.1002/cpe.3867

Parallel Extremely Randomized Decision Forests on Graphics Processors for Text Classification

Julio Cesar Batista Pires[1] and Wellington Santos Martins[2(✉)] ⓘ

[1] Federal University of Mato Grosso do Sul, Campo Grande, MS 79070-900, Brazil
juliopires@discente.ufg.br
[2] Federal University of Goiás, Goiânia, GO 74690-900, Brazil
wellington@inf.ufg.br

Abstract. The amount of readily available on-line text has grown exponentially, requiring efficient methods to automatically manage and sort data. Automatic text classification provides means to organize this data by associating documents with classes. However, the use of more data and sophisticated machine learning algorithms has demanded an increasingly computing power. In this work we accelerate a novel Random Forest-based classifier that has been shown to outperform state-of-art classifiers for textual data. The classifier is obtained by applying the boosting technique in bags of extremely randomized trees (forests) that are built in parallel to improve performance. Experimental results using standard textual datasets show that the GPU-based implementation is able to reduce the execution time by up to 20 times compared to an equivalent sequential implementation.

Keywords: Extremely Randomized Trees · GPUs · Text

1 Introduction

The amount of readily available on-line text has grown unprecedentedly since the advent of the Web. This brings new challenges as to automatically manage and sort vast volumes of data. Fortunately, progress in computer technology and algorithms has produced innovative solutions in this direction. On one hand, the computer industry has shifted from single core to multicore (CPU) and manycore (GPU) processors, making it possible to achieve superior performance through parallel computing. On the other hand, advances in machine learning algorithms have improved solutions that learn from this large amount of data. These two factors have contributed to a revolution in the way we generate knowledge and organize data.

This study was financed in part by the Coordenação de Aperfeiçoamento de Pessoal de Nível Superior - Brazil (CAPES) - Finance Code 001, Goiano Federal Institute - IF Goiano/MEC - Brazil and Federal University of Mato Grosso do Sul - UFMS/MEC - Brazil. Supported by Federal University of Goiás - UFG/MEC - Brazil.

R. Wyrzykowski et al. (Eds.): PPAM 2022, LNCS 13826, pp. 83–94, 2023.
https://doi.org/10.1007/978-3-031-30442-2_7

Machine learning (ML) applied to text data requires a special approach since text can have hundreds of thousands of dimensions (size of the vocabulary) where only a few have nonzero values, i.e. high dimensionality and high sparsity. Nonetheless, advances in natural language processing (NLP) continue to evolve with outstanding results. For instance, GPT-3 [4], a language model consisting of a deep learning (DL) neural network with 175 billion parameters, was trained using powerful parallel machines and with large text datasets, showing amazing performance in various NLP tasks, such as language translation, text summarization, question-answering, among others.

Deep Learning really shines when there is some hierarchical structure in the data, of a compositional nature, like syllable, word, phrase and other groupings of a text. However, this structure is not decisive for the text classification task which is at the heart of important applications such as recommender systems, spam filtering, sentiment analysis, among others. In this case, traditional ML approaches can do the job much faster and with a comparable or superior result [6]. In particular, ensembles of classifiers have been shown to excel in this task, with Random Forest (RF) standing out. However, RF may suffer from overfitting issues in the presence of many irrelevant or noisy attributes - a characteristic of text datasets. Recently, a RF-based classifier was shown to achieve state-of-the-art results by exploiting distinct strategies to mitigate these problems [5]. The Boosted Extremely Randomized Trees (Boosted ERT) introduced another source of randomization in the boosted strategy, i.e. it applies the boosting technique in bags of extremely randomized trees. This makes the method rather computationally expensive, thus limiting its use. This situation motivated us to propose an accelerated (parallel) version of this RF-based classifier.

Although GPUs have been successfully applied to accelerate many machine learning algorithms, it is not a trivial task to fully exploit them for training RF-based text classifiers. Besides the high dimensionality and sparsity of text data, the nature of tree structures adds challenges like tree traversals, irregular memory accesses, varying parallel granularity, among others. In this work we focus on GPU acceleration of the most demanding parts for extremely randomized tree bags, namely sampling for bagging, document class counting, Min/Max calculation, finding the best split, and splitting the database. The CPU gathers and processes this information, at each boosting step, to produce the final classification model. Experiments performed with standard textual datasets showed significant performance gains when compared with the non-accelerated implementation.

The main contributions of the paper are:

(i) A parallel algorithm to support extremely randomized tree bags.
(ii) A scalable GPU-based implementation of the parallel algorithm.
(iii) An extensive experimental work with standard real-world textual datasets.

This paper is organized as follows. In Sect. 2, the literature on GPU tree induction is presented. In Sect. 3 we describe the proposed parallel algorithm to support extremely randomized tree bags. The experiments are described and discussed in Sect. 4. Finally, in Sect. 5 we present our conclusions and highlight future work.

2   Trees and Ensembles

Some approaches to accelerate decision trees on the GPU can be found in the literature. Most of the works deal with the construction of classifiers using the CUDA programming model. One of the first implementations found consisted of mapping a forest onto a texture vector from the graphics memory [21]. This section presents the main GPU tree work of the last decade.

2.1   Decision Trees

Decision trees (DT) are one of the most powerful and popular approaches in exploring large amounts of data to find useful patterns [19]. The tree structure consists of internal nodes representing tests (decisions) and terminal nodes (leaves) representing class labels [23]. Induction algorithms such as CART (Classification and Regression Trees) [1] use metrics to select the best attributes and recursively partition the dataset while creating the tree. Different types of parallel strategies are described in the literature, each with a different objective. They range from parallelizing the steps that require more processing, such as node splitting [15], to accelerating the construction of a decision tree in two levels, node by node, and with node data sorting [18]. Some of these strategies divide the construction tasks, with the heavier tasks performed in the GPU exploiting parallelism at node level, attribute level or splitting level [22]. A more recent work uses evolutionary tree induction, which evaluates individuals on the GPU and stores previously constructed trees [13].

2.2   Bagging

The bagging (bootstrap aggregating) procedure replicates the original dataset many times. Each tree is built with a different replica [2]. Approximately two-thirds of the samples are used in training. The remaining one-third (out-of-bag) is used as the test suite [11]. Combining multiple trees can mitigate errors made by a single tree [19]. A popular example is random forests (RF) [3], which grows several trees by bagging, randomly selecting and evaluating a small group of attributes. After construction, the responses from the trees are combined into a voting scheme [23]. A variation of the RF is the extremely randomized trees (ERT) [8]. The difference is that the trees are generated from the original dataset using random cutpoints on attribute values.

In the multiple parallel tree approaches, the first choice was building a tree per thread (CudaRF). Each tree is created sequentially by the corresponding thread. Using a greater number of trees can result in greater performance gains [9]. There is also the hybrid construction of the decision tree (CudaTree), which starts with a depth strategy switching to a breadth strategy later on. In the depth strategy, each thread block is responsible for a subset of examples of a single attribute. In the breadth strategy, the thread group is responsible for one node and the whole level is processed simultaneously [14]. There is yet another breadth strategy to generate ERTs and RFs, independently and in parallel (gpuRF and gpuERT). The approach adopted works at the node level, that is, the entire forest level is processed by the block grid and the threads slide over the node examples. More parallelization potential is gained as trees grow [12].

2.3 Boosting

Boosting is an ensemble method that combines weak models in an iterative process [7]. In each pass it samples using weights from the training set and builds a new submodel, which is evaluated. If a sample is classified incorrectly, its weight is increased. Each new model depends on the previous one. At the end of all steps, all classifiers built form the new classifier. Boosting is one of the most powerful learning ideas and seems to dominate bagging in many problems [10]. Some boosting algorithms build histograms for the attributes in order to find the best split (Light-GBM GPU) on the GPU [25]. In [17] - XGBoost GPU - all nodes of a tree level are processed concurrently on the GPU, with the training data being able to be partitioned in different GPUs [16]. One of the most recent strategies (ThunderGBM) parallelizes the trees using some sophisticated techniques like compression and dynamic workload between thread and block. Parallelization takes place at the node, attribute and data split level [24].

2.4 Ensembles of Ensembles

Systems that combine a series of forests in boosting [5,20] correspond to an efficient strategy to deal with overfitting problems caused by irrelevant attributes present in large text datasets. The randomness provided by the trees allows to decrease the variance, which makes the algorithm more robust to the presence of noise in the data. The idea is to produce a model with high generalization capability. Our proposal, Parallel Extremely Randomized Trees with teXt (X-PERT), is meant to contribute on this front. The core of the system is shown in Algorithm 1, and its comparison with the others proposals is shown in Table 1. As can be seen, our proposal is not directly comparable to any other proposal.

3   Parallel Approach

It is highly desirable to build computationally efficient algorithms to handle large amounts of data. However, efficient algorithms must be thought of carefully taking into account various aspects of the hardware and the partition and mapping of the problem [25]. One way of decomposing and mapping the problem of building trees using large volumes of data is to consider each level of the forest as being processed at once. Thus, each block of threads is responsible for a tree node, taking care of the terms (words) and documents. Our hybrid (CPU-GPU) heterogeneous solution is detailed below.

The proposed solution builds a forest from top to bottom, in a breadthwise way, i.e. level by level. The assembly of the trees takes place on the CPU

---

input : a training set S.
output: a tree ensemble $T = t_1, ..., t_M$.

```
1  for i ← 1 to M do
2  │   for j ← 1 to N do
3  │   │   if |S| < min or candidates are constant or output is constant then
4  │   │   │   build a leaf labeled by class frequencies in S
5  │   │   end
6  │   │   else
7  │   │   │   1. Select randomly a attributes among all non constant;
8  │   │   │   2. Compute the maximal a_max^S and minimal a_min^S value of a in S;
9  │   │   │   3. Draw a cut-point in a [a_min^S, a_max^S];
10 │   │   │   4. Select a split with best Score;
11 │   │   │   5. Split S into subsets l and r according to selected;
12 │   │   │   6. Build nodes from these subsets;
13 │   │   end
14 │   end
15 end
```

Algorithm 1: Extremely Randomized Trees Algorithm adapted from [8].

Table 1. GPU tree induction comparison.

Author	Tree	Height	Split	Growth	Bagging	Boosting	Parallelism
Grahn [9]	Forest	Max	Best	Depth	Yes	No	Thread/Tree
Liao [14]	Single	Max	Best	Depth/Breadth	Yes	No	Block/Node
Nasridinov [18]	Single	Max	Best	Depth	No	No	Thread/Node
Jansson [12]	Forest	100	Best/Random	Breadth	Yes	No	Block/Node
Strnad [22]	Forest	Max	Best	Depth	No	No	Block/Feature
Zhang [25]	Single	8	Best	Depth	No	Yes	Thread/Features
Mitchel [16]	Single	12	Best	Depth	No	Yes	Block/Feature
Wen [24]	Forest	6	Best	Depth	Yes	Yes	Thread/Gain
Jurczuk [13]	Forest	Max	Best	Depth	No	No	Block/Subset
Pires [this]	Forest	Max	Random	Breadth	Yes	Yes	Block/Node

side while the GPU is in charge of processing the construction steps, which demand greater computational power. The first step is to allocate the necessary resources and load the text file into the GPU memory. The textual collection consists of a matrix, where the rows represent documents and the columns the terms, being that each column has word frequency values within the document. The next steps are sampling, the root construction, and dataset splitting as the tree grows. The entire process is repeated until some constraint is reached. The following subsections explain the steps performed on the GPU.

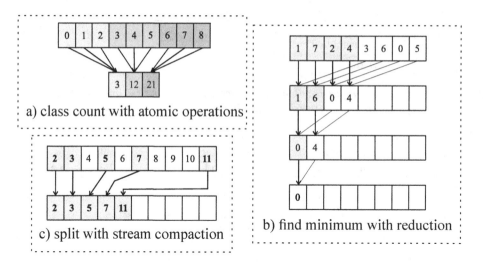

Fig. 1. Illustration of the procedures performed on the GPU.

3.1   Sampling

Once the data is moved to the GPU, the sampling can take place, initializing the weight vector of the dataset using a number of threads equal to the number of documents. Thus, the bagging procedure chooses random documents based on the weights. For this to occur, the weight values are accumulated using an inclusive prefix sum. Then each thread generates a random number and does a binary search on the vector to choose the document. In this way, each tree is given a list of new instances to use. The construction of the trees happens from top to bottom, level by level, by dividing the vector of documents at each level until reaching the leaves. The entire tree level is built in parallel.

3.2   Class Count

The first step in building the trees is to count the class frequency of the documents in each node, as shown in Fig. 1a. Each block of threads is associated with a tree-level node. Block threads go through the documents counting class labels with atomic operations on shared memory[1], a sort of programmable cache in that access is almost 100 times faster than in global memory. After being counted and returned to the CPU, the node is defined as a leaf if all documents have the same class or the number of documents is insufficient to create new nodes.

---

[1] https://developer.nvidia.com/blog/using-shared-memory-cuda-cc.

3.3   Min/Max and Candidates

The step to find minimum and maximum values (Fig. 1b) consists of a block of threads for each term of the dataset. To find the values of each term, a reduction takes place inside the warp with shuffle instructions, in which the threads exchange data with each other using registers. The described step finds the values of each group of 32 threads, whereas to find the values between the groups the shared memory is used. The minimum and maximum values also guarantee whether a term is a candidate, that is, it has different values, meaning that division of documents can be used.

3.4   Find Best and Split

To evaluate the best split, a subset of candidate terms is randomly chosen. Each thread in the block chooses a cut-point between the maximum and minimum values and evaluates the purity of the split using the chosen term and random values. The calculation is done using the Gini index. Once the best split is found, the document vector is split into left and right for the child nodes. This partition uses stream compaction operations, as shown in Fig. 1c. The example shown aggregates the prime values of the vector but, in our case, we join the values that go to the left and those that go to the right. After the split, each part of the vector is considered as possible internal nodes and is added to the queue of the next node to be processed. All these steps are repeated until there are no more nodes.

3.5   The Complete Solution

The steps described in the subsections above correspond to the tasks performed by the proposed parallel algorithm. To implement these tasks on the GPU, kernel functions were develop in order to exploit the fine-grained parallelism of GPUs. The execution flow of the implementation on the CPU-GPU platform can be seen in Fig. 2. The sampling operation follows the bagging strategy, while the count labels, find min max, find best split and split dataset operations are in agreement with Algorithm 1. On the left side of the figure (CPU) is the assembly of the tree, while the operations that demand the highest processing load are shown on the right side (GPU) of the figure. These operations use different kernel launching configurations. In sampling, there are as many threads as there are documents, 100,000 for the largest dataset. In count labels, each thread block is in charge of a tree node, and the entire tree level is processed at once. For the find min max, one block is used for each term of the dataset, approximately 50,000 blocks for the dataset with the largest vocabulary. The find best and split operations use the same thread configuration per document, a value that corresponds to the number of documents that the node has. All these steps are repeated at least 200x within the iterative algorithm of boosting, as described in [5].

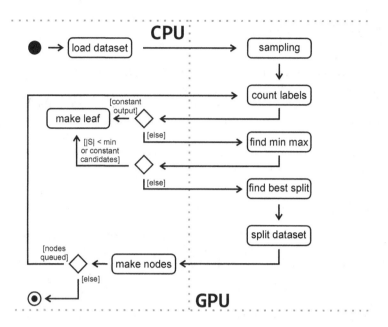

Fig. 2. Algorithm execution flow.

4   Experimental Results

In this section, we report the results of the experiments conducted. A comparison is made between the sequential solution and our parallel approach. The main objective of the experiments is to identify when it is worthwhile to employ a parallel strategy on the GPU.

4.1   System

All experimentation was carried out on a mid-range desktop machine equipped with a quad-core Intel i7-7700 CPU (Kaby Lake) running at 3.60 GHz and 16 GB of DDR4 RAM. An NVIDIA GeForce 1070 (Pascal) GPU with 8 GB of memory and 1920 CUDA cores at 1.77 GHz was used. The programs were written in C/C++, CUDA[2] 11.6 and OpenMP 2.0. The tests were conducted in a Windows 11 environment. To ensure standardized experimentation, all algorithms were run with the same parameters, at least 5 times to obtain the averages. For each dataset, we built 8 trees, which grew to maximum depth. The subset of terms used was the square root of the total terms and we set the minimum number of documents to perform a split at 2. All these hyperparameters are in agreement with the literature.

---

[2] https://docs.nvidia.com/cuda/cuda-c-programming-guide.

4.2   Datasets

The tests considered 5 real-world text datasets: Spambase (email), 4Uni (web pages), Reuters (news articles), 20NG (news groups), and ACM (computing papers). All sets were pre-processed with the removal of stopwords and low-frequency attributes [5]. In addition, we have increased the number of documents in larger datasets to the limit of available memory. Datasets are composed of documents represented by vectors of terms TF-IDF (Term Frequency-Inverse Document Frequency). A detailed description can be found in Table 2. Most of these sets can be found in the UCI Machine Learning Repository[3].

Table 3. Average runtime and speedup.

Table 2. Dataset descriptions.

Names	Docs	Terms	Classes
spam	4,601	57	2
4uni	8,199	22,581	7
reuters	13,327	17,029	90
20ng	18,846	49,025	20
acm	24,897	23,110	11

Names	Seq. (s)	Par. 1 (s)	Par. 2 (s)	Speedup
spam	0.25	0.08	2.97	0.08
4uni	417.16	100.88	487.66	0.86
reuters	440.42	97.74	255.04	1.73
20ng	5,255.40	1,678.58	1,045.31	5.03
acm	5,533.41	1,551.11	1,388.98	3.98
2x20ng	12,526.26	5,270.50	1,951.94	6.42
2xacm	13,849.34	4,882.27	1,385.27	10.00
4xacm	31,591.14	12,301.54	1,520.24	20.78

4.3   Analysis

In evaluating the performance of the algorithms, the sequential version was compared with the proposed parallel version. The speedup metric (sequential time divided by parallel time) was used in the comparison. Accuracy results were not included, since the focus of the article is the analysis of runtime efficiency in relation to the size of the sets. However, we observed that there is no loss of quality when comparing the two algorithms. Execution time is measured in seconds and considers all data movement between CPU and GPU over the PCIe bus. Memory requirements of the algorithm is proportional to the dataset size.

It can be seen in Table 3, that from the third dataset onwards, the use of parallel computing becomes worthwhile. For 100,000 documents, the GPU parallel version (Par. 2) takes approximately 28 min, while its sequential counterpart takes almost 9 h, meaning the parallel version is 20x faster. A multicore (OpenMP) CPU parallel version version (Par. 1) is included for comparison reasons. Acceleration is proportional to the size of the dataset, which suggests that our strategy is highly scalable.

As can be seen from the graphs in Fig. 3, the greater the amount of data, the greater the sequential computational effort, and the greater the speedup factor,

---

[3] https://archive.ics.uci.edu/ml/datasets/.

that is, the parallel algorithm gets an even greater advantage when the dataset grows. As expected, very small sets are not feasible, the sequential algorithm is faster enough. All this indicates that using a strategy with different granularities of parallelism in large datasets, a good performance can be obtained.

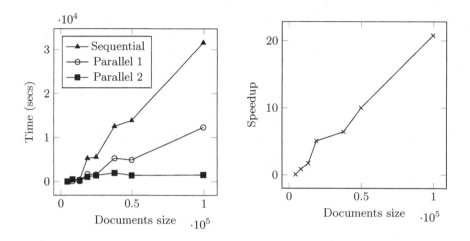

Fig. 3. Execution and speedup according to the amount of documents.

5   Conclusions

Many important applications, such as sentiment analysis, spam filtering, topic categorization, recommender systems, among others, can be solved by automatic textual classifiers. However, text classification has to deal with noisy and high-dimensional data, which makes the construction of classifiers a costly task. The boosted extremely randomized trees with bagging have proved to be a great alternative for automatic text classification, but with significant additional computational costs. In this work we proposed an accelerated (parallel) version of this RF-based classifier and implemented it on a heterogeneous platform (CPU-GPU). Promising results showed that it was possible to decrease the execution time many times, up to 20x, for the largest dataset, showing that the approach scales well. Results suggest that even more gains can be made with larger sets, especially with a greater number of documents.

A natural direction of the work is running on dedicated servers with multiple GPUs, assigning each tree to a separate GPU. Another direction would be to increase the number of trees used in each pass of boosting, and experiment with larger datasets.

References

1. Breiman, L., Friedman, J.H., Olshen, R.A., Stone, C.J.: Classification and Regression Trees. Wadsworth and Brooks, Monterey (1984)
2. Breiman, L.: Bagging predictors. Mach. Learn. **24**(2), 123–140 (1996). https://doi. org/10.1023/A:1018054314350
3. Breiman, L.: Random forests. Mach. Learn. **45**(1), 5–32 (2001). https://doi.org/ 10.1023/A:1010933404324
4. Brown, T., et al.: Language models are few-shot learners. Adv. Neural. Inf. Process. Syst. **33**, 1877–1901 (2020)
5. Campos, R., Canuto, S., Salles, T., de Sá, C.C., Gonçalves, M.A.: Stacking bagged and boosted forests for effective automated classification. In: Proceedings of the 40th International ACM SIGIR Conference on Research and Development in Information Retrieval, SIGIR 2017, pp. 105–114. ACM, New York (2017). https://doi. org/10.1145/3077136.3080815. http://doi.acm.org/10.1145/3077136.3080815
6. Cunha, W., et al.: On the cost-effectiveness of neural and non-neural approaches and representations for text classification: a comprehensive comparative study. Inf. Process. Manag. **58**(3), 102481 (2021)
7. Freund, Y., Schapire, R.E.: A decision-theoretic generalization of on-line learning and an application to boosting. J. Comput. Syst. Sci. **55**(1), 119–139 (1997). https://doi.org/10.1006/jcss.1997.1504. http://www.sciencedirect. com/science/article/pii/S002200009791504X
8. Geurts, P., Ernst, D., Wehenkel, L.: Extremely randomized trees. Mach. Learn. **63**(1), 3–42 (2006). https://doi.org/10.1007/s10994-006-6226-1
9. Grahn, H., Lavesson, N., Lapajne, M.H., Slat, D.: CudaRF: a Cuda-based implementation of random forests. In: 2011 9th IEEE/ACS International Conference on Computer Systems and Applications (AICCSA), pp. 95–101 (2011). https://doi. org/10.1109/AICCSA.2011.6126612
10. Hastie, T., Tibshirani, R., Friedman, J.: The Elements of Statistical Learning: Data Mining, Inference and Prediction, 2 edn. Springer, Heidelberg (2009). http://www-stat.stanford.edu/tibs/ElemStatLearn/
11. James, G., Witten, D., Hastie, T., Tibshirani, R.: An Introduction to Statistical Learning - with Applications in R. Springer Texts in Statistics, vol. 103. Springer, New York (2013). https://doi.org/10.1007/DOI
12. Jansson, K., Sundell, H., Boström, H.: gpuRF and gpuERT: efficient and scalable GPU algorithms for decision tree ensembles. In: 2014 IEEE International Parallel Distributed Processing Symposium Workshops, pp. 1612–1621 (2014). https://doi. org/10.1109/IPDPSW.2014.180
13. Jurczuk, K., Czajkowski, M., Kretowski, M.: Accelerating GPU-based evolutionary induction of decision trees - fitness evaluation reuse. In: Wyrzykowski, R., Deelman, E., Dongarra, J., Karczewski, K. (eds.) PPAM 2019. LNCS, vol. 12043, pp. 421–431. Springer, Cham (2020). https://doi.org/10.1007/978-3-030-43229-4_36
14. Liao, Y., Rubinsteyn, A., Power, R., Li, J.: Learning random forests on the GPU. In: Big Learning 2013: Advances in Algorithms and Data Management. Lake Tahoe (2013)
15. Lo, W.T., Chang, Y.S., Sheu, R.K., Chiu, C.C., Yuan, S.M.: CUDT: a CUDA based decision tree algorithm. Sci. World J. **2014** (2014)
16. Mitchell, R., Adinets, A., Rao, T., Frank, E.: Xgboost: scalable GPU accelerated learning. CoRR abs/1806.11248 (2018)

17. Mitchell, R., Frank, E.: Accelerating the xgboost algorithm using GPU computing. PeerJ Comput. Sci. **3**, e127 (2017). https://doi.org/10.7717/peerj-cs.127
18. Nasridinov, A., Lee, Y., Park, Y.-H.: Decision tree construction on GPU: ubiquitous parallel computing approach. Computing **96**(5), 403–413 (2013). https://doi.org/10.1007/s00607-013-0343-z
19. Rokach, L.: Decision forest: twenty years of research. Inf. Fusion **27**, 111–125 (2016). https://doi.org/10.1016/j.inffus.2015.06.005. http://www.sciencedirect.com/science/article/pii/S1566253515000561
20. Salles, T., Gonçalves, M., Rodrigues, V., Rocha, L.: Broof: exploiting out-of-bag errors, boosting and random forests for effective automated classification. In: Proceedings of the 38th International ACM SIGIR Conference on Research and Development in Information Retrieval, SIGIR 2015, pp. 353–362. ACM, New York (2015). https://doi.org/10.1145/2766462.2767747. http://doi.acm.org/10.1145/2766462.2767747
21. Sharp, T.: Implementing decision trees and forests on a GPU. In: Forsyth, D., Torr, P., Zisserman, A. (eds.) ECCV 2008. LNCS, vol. 5305, pp. 595–608. Springer, Heidelberg (2008). https://doi.org/10.1007/978-3-540-88693-8_44
22. Strnad, D., Nerat, A.: Parallel construction of classification trees on a GPU. Concurr. Comput. Pract. Exper. **28**(5), 1417–1436 (2016). https://doi.org/10.1002/cpe.3660
23. Tan, P.N., Steinbach, M., Kumar, V.: Introduction to Data Mining: Pearson New International Edition, English Pearson Education Limited, Harlow (2013)
24. Wen, Z., Liu, H., Shi, J., Li, Q., He, B., Chen, J.: ThunderGBM: fast GBDTS and random forests on GPUs. J. Mach. Learn. Res. **21**(108), 1–5 (2020). http://jmlr.org/papers/v21/19-095.html
25. Zhang, H., Si, S., Hsieh, C.J.: GPU-acceleration for large-scale tree boosting. CoRR abs/1706.08359 (2017). https://doi.org/10.48550/arXiv.1706.08359. http://dblp.uni-trier.de/db/journals/corr/corr1706.html#ZhangSH17

RDBMS Speculative Support Improvement by the Use of the Query Hypergraph Representation

Anna Sasak-Okoń[1]([⊠]) [iD] and Marek Tudruj[2,3] [iD]

[1] University of Maria Curie Skłodowska in Lublin,
Pl. Marii-Curie Skłodowskiej 5, 20-031 Lublin, Poland
`anna.sasak@umcs.pl`
[2] Institute of Computer Science Polish Academy of Sciences,
ul. Jana Kazimierza 5, 01-248 Warsaw, Poland
[3] Polish-Japanese Academy od Information Technology,
ul. Koszykowa 83, 02-008 Warsaw, Poland
`tudruj@ipipan.waw.pl`

Abstract. The paper concerns the methodology for speculative support for query execution in Relational Database Management Systems (RDBMSs). It discusses and develops our proposal of supporting the RDBMS query execution based on a graph-based analytic approach. This approach assumes using the results of speculative queries defined by analyzing a multigraph representation of a stream of input queries arriving to a RDBMS. The queries from the RDBMS input stream are permanently analysed using a Speculation Window moving on the query stream to define the optimized speculative queries for execution. More specifically, the current paper develops the basic idea of the speculative query support and shows how the use of the speculative query results by the awaiting input user queries can be improved by the analysis of a query hypergraph representation. The analysis of a joint hypergraph representation of the speculative and user input queries has been employed to better organize the use of the speculative query results in the stream of input user queries of a RDBMS. The advantages of the proposed approach are positively assessed based on the experiments with the simulated execution of the testbed sets of queries.

Keywords: speculative computations · speculative database queries · hypergraph modelling

1 Introduction

If data dependencies in a program code make its parallel execution impossible then a speculative instruction execution can be a method to obtain parallel execution but at the cost of using extra processing resources which are additional processor cores. The cores can execute the fragments of code whose execution

R. Wyrzykowski et al. (Eds.): PPAM 2022, LNCS 13826, pp. 95–109, 2023.
https://doi.org/10.1007/978-3-031-30442-2_8

is conditioned by the results of an earlier code. Speculative processing can be applied in Relational Databases Management Systems (RDBMSs) to produce query partial speculative results in advance to the query standard execution order to be later used to speed-up query processing [7]. Storing the partial query results can be a side-effect of execution of standard queries arriving to the RDBMS (known as Query Caching [14]) or can concern Speculative Queries specially generated based on the analysis of queries meant for execution in the nearest future which is the method assumed in our approach [15,22].

The essence of our approach is the systematic parallel analysis of the input query stream in a RDBMS. Multiple query optimization has been studied [11] but without the speculative query concept nor an idea of using the streaming processing. To implement our approach we have designed a multi-threaded middleware called the Speculative Layer which works between user applications and the RDBMS. The motivation for our approach are RDBMSs which respond to streams of queries of similar structures such as product browsing queries in the Internet stores. Such databases feature a static behaviour where data modifying queries occur rarely and predictably. The proposed speculative support for query execution is based on a sliding Speculation Window (SW) on the input query stream. The set of all SW queries is represented by a common multigraph. The SW multigraph is analysed to define the possibly best Speculative Queries to support fast execution of awaiting input queries. For this analysis, the queries are represented by their extended graphs showing the features relevant for the query execution speculative support. The Speculative Queries are determined and executed for each SW position. They produce the speculative results which are stored in the Speculative Database (SDB), located in the system Main Memory, to be used in execution of awaiting input queries. During execution of standard input queries the speculative results can be quickly accessed in SDB avoiding time consuming transmissions from the secondary storage.

In this paper, we propose an improved method for the use of speculative query results based on an analysis of an extended query hypergraph representation. A query hypergraph is a graph representation of queries in which the hyperedges represent relations determined on the multi-sets of nodes, instead of two nodes as in the ordinary graphs. The set-oriented hypergraph structures can easily show relations between the already executed speculative queries and user queries awaiting execution. Due to the limited size of the Speculative DB, the results of the executed Speculative Queries are frequently deleted to provide space for newly generated speculative results. We propose in advance assignment of speculative query results to a number of input queries nearest to SW i.e. placed in the input query stream next to SW. This extension will reduce the situations when just deleted speculative query results will be generated again in a short time to support soon upcoming user input queries. The proposed method can strongly improve the overall strategy of using the query speculative results by extension of their life period. The idea of analyzing hypergraph joint representation of speculative queries and input user queries has been described in the paper. It has been positively assessed by simulation experiments.

The paper text which follows contains 5 Sections. Section 2 discusses the related works. Section 3 presents basics of the Speculative Layer concept i.e. the rules of query graphs creation and the process of speculative analysis resulting in optimized generation of speculative queries. Section 4 describes a new strategy of in advance assignment of speculative query results to input queries. Section 5 presents experimental results obtained for user query test sets. Section 6 includes the concluding remarks.

2   Related Work

The model of speculative execution was developed as a new method of program parallelization the most often associated with thread level parallelism [1]. Speculative parallelization assumes parallel execution of the code fragments which in the initial program would be run sequentially being imposed by some mutual instruction dependences. For speculative parallelization usually some extra executive resources are used. Three main concepts of thread level speculations have been distinguished in the literature: control, data value and data dependence speculations. Since speculative parallel execution is done with violation (neglecting) of the respective sequential program limitations, the corectness speculative execution results must be validated against the "unspeculative" execution. As a means for the sequential program restructuring for the speculative execution, the program code splitting is introduced as a result of some analysis of the control structure of the speculatively parallelized program. The speculative results which have not been validated are rejected. However, if the speculative assumptions are correct, the considerable efficiency improvement is obtained [2–4]. Important research results on the speculative parallelization support for the complex branch execution control in programs executed on processor clusters are reported in [5]. The paper, containing an adequate references, proposes to use a synergie of an improved code splitting technique based on conditional branch unfolding (separate paths executed by threads for true and false branch results) with the statistically supported speculative branch handling in the environment of a cluster of the single processor systems.

The speculative support for relational database query execution has been a subject of research. Most of the known optimization methods belong to a general concept of query folding [6]. Query folding is the process of query execution support trying to determine whether a query can be answered using an additional given set of resources. The considered additional resources can consist of materialized views, some cached results of previous queries, or query results coming from other supporting databases. In [7] authors implement a speculative execution support to integrate the reception of data asynchronously coming from different databases which can show some non-neglectable delays. The speculative support for alleviating the influence of the delays was based on annotations included into the data gathering plans. The implied operations performed speculatively, ahead of their normal schedule, provide significant plan implementation speedups. The database system idle time is used for asynchronous anticipated database data transformations so as in [8]. If the results of these operations were correct, the target query would be executed in a shorter time.

Papers [9,10] present speculative execution used as a support technique for transaction protocols in databases. An idea of the speculative locking protocol for sequences of transactions was described which is based on two executions: for previous and next transaction images when using some extra executive resources. With this approach one of the speculative results is validated depending on the obtained real result of the blocking (previous) transaction. The techniques to support multiple query optimization, though without using the exact speculation concept, are proposed in [11,12]. If some common sub-expressions are shared in a group of queries, they can be used to generate a more appropriate execution plan or as candidates for potential materialized views. This approach tries to have a single execution of the shared sub-expressions. A popular method of query optimization is cashing the results of previously executed queries [13,14,16]. The concept is based on the assumption that the same query can be requested again. In such case, instead of evaluating the query, the cached results can be reused. Three cache variants are considered: tuple, page and semantic cache which are used to decompose query is such way that only data not available in cache must be loaded from database server, which speedups query execution.

Query hypergraph representation employed in this paper provides some natural modelling means for relations and interactions between query nodes of different types and have been often used in query optimization [17–19]. The hypergraph representation to support query processing with the speculative approach has several advantages: the considered optimization items can be relations which are easily represented as hyperedges, the operations on hypergraph elements can be set oriented and query optimization can be simplified by a systematic separation of operations on query elements from their semantics.

It should be noted that in the speculative parallelization there is always some in advance processing, often based on the speculatively assumed computing states. In our case, the speculative approach is based on two components. The first relates to the speculatively generated data - the Speculative Query results. The second component concerns the speculatively assumed query processing states in which the speculatively generated data will be used. According to our best knowledge none of the methods known in the literature was based on performing speculative actions that would be defined by a systematic analysis of a database input query stream to cover needs of many future queries at a time. Instead of caching the results of past queries, we analyse the stream of queries which wait for execution in the nearest future and we generate speculative query results prepared in advance as a result of specially defined Speculative Queries. The above features together with the query modelling approach based on multigraphs and hypergraphs are the essential originality features of our methods.

3   The Speculative Layer

The Speculative Layer is located between user database applications and the RDBMS. The cooperation between the Speculatie Layer and the RDBMS is based on permanent analysis of arriving user queries which form a linear queue waiting for the RDBMS's answer. This analysis is performed based on a sliding window of user queries called a Speculation Window (SW) organized in the input query stream. The analysis is called the Speculative Analysis (SA) and it determines the Speculative Queries to be executed for the current contents of SW. For SA, each SW query is first represented by a query graph created with a set of defined rules. The single query representations are next used to create a joint representation of the SW query contents in the form of a Query Multigraph QM. The QM is then converted into its extended version called the Speculative Query Multigraph (SQM) used in further steps of SA. SQM contains an additional type of edges, not appearing in QM, called the Speculative Edges. These edges represent some important SW query features which are taken into account in the optimized speculative query generation. As a result of selection performed by SA on the Speculative Edges in SQM, a set of Speculative Queries is generated for the current contents of SW which should be executed to produce partial results useful for particular queries from the input stream.

For each contents of SW, two types of actions are performed concurrently. First of them is the execution of the top query from SW - the non-speculative query - adapted to use the speculative query results. The second type of action involves execution of speculative queries (selected for execution by some defined usefulness metrics). After the non-speculative input query is executed, the Speculation Window moves on the stream of input queries. As a result, the representation of the executed user query in the Q_M is replaced by the representation of next user query from the input query queue. This process is repeated until there are user queries waiting for execution. In each step of SA, from the group of generated potential speculative queries, the top rated queries are selected for execution. The speculative query rating and selection is done based on some validation metrics. The Horizontal and Vertical Selectivities are the most important here - representing the horizontal and vertical reduction of the original data base relation size as we want to avoid full copies of db relations. The selection algorithm also takes into account the numbers of potential input queries in SW which will use results of the analysed potential speculative queries. The results of the executed speculative queries are stored in the RAM memory called the Speculative DB which co-operates a particular RDBMS distributed worker process housing an RDBMS engine executed inside the executive distributed system. The results from the Speculative DB constitute ready-to-use working data, and when used, eliminate full scans of the RDB relations thus shortening the query processing and the user waiting time. The implemented model of the Speculative Layer accepts Conjunctive Queries With Arithmetic Comparisons (CQAC) with AND as a logical operator allowed in WHERE clause. An extended functionality of queries is obtained by allowing two more operators, which are IN for value sets and LIKE for strings.

Each user query is represented by its Query Graph $G_Q(V_Q, E_Q)$ with design inspired by [20]. We use three types of vertices representing **Relations Attributes** and **Values** from the modelled queries joined with edges representing functions of adjacent vertices in the query. Thus there are: **Membership edges** (μ) for SELECT clause, **Predicate** (θ) and **Selection** (σ) edges for WHERE clause. The process of the Speculative Analysis is executed for each QM to determine and insert a set of Speculative Edges. These edges indicate which graph elements should be used for speculative queries generation. Depending on the use of speculation results we introduce three types of Speculative Edges corresponding to equivalent Speculative Queries:

- **Speculative Parameter Edges** - these edges identify nested queries which, if obtained speculatively, can be used as a parameter value in its parent query
- **Speculative Data Edges** - this type of Speculative Queries aims at obtaining and storing in the Speculative DB a subset of records or/and attributes of the relation so as it could be used in execution of many user queries
- **Speculative State Edges** - concerning a modifying query presence in the Speculation Window.

Figure 1 presents the QM representing a set of three following component queries created for a Speculation Window:

1. SELECT $A_{4,2}, A_{4,3}$ FROM R_3, R_4 WHERE $A_{3,1} = A_{4,3}$ AND $A_{4,2} < C_1$
2. SELECT $A_{2,1}, A_{2,2}$ FROM R_2, R_3 WHERE $A_{2,1} = A_{3,3}$ AND $A_{2,2} < C_5$
3. SELECT $A_{2,1}, A_{2,2}$ FROM R_2 WHERE $A_{2,2} > C_6$

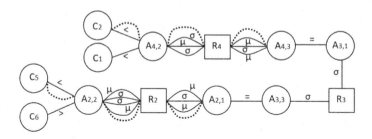

Fig. 1. Speculative Query Multigraph SQM with speculative edges representing two speculative queries

The QM contains additional speculative edges (dotted lines) representing two speculative queries which could be generated for different relation vertices from the analysed QM: (1) SELECT $A_{4,1}, A_{4,2}, A_{4,3}$ FROM R_4 WHERE $A_{4,2} < C_2$ (assuming $C_1 < C_2$ it would be useful for two user queries), (2) SELECT $A_{2,1}, A_{2,2}$ FROM R_2 WHERE $A_{2,2} < C_5$ (assuming there are fewer records having $A_{2,2} < C_5$ then $A_{2,2} > C_6$ the result size of such query would use less space in the Speculative DB). For each analysed attribute vertex there would be considered also another speculative queries which are not represented in the figure for better readability. More precise description of the query graph creation process and the speculative algorithm is included in [22–24].

4 A New Strategy for Speculative Query Assignment to Input Queries

In this paper, we propose an optimized procedure of speculative query results assignment to awaiting input queries. We execute the Speculative Analysis as it was assumed in the previous papers but we want to verify the expected usefulness of speculative query results for the input queries waiting for execution just behind the current Speculation Window by the assignment in advance. With this early assignment rule we want to maintain the speculative query results for the use for consecutive Speculative Windows. On the other hand, with the old assignment strategy it frequently happened that the speculative query results were removed from the Speculative DB (its size limit was exceeded) and the identical speculative query was executed again in a nearby future. The speculative query assignment in advance should prevent such situations.

So far the Speculative Analysis took under consideration only user queries from the current Speculation Window (SW). For these queries a set of awaiting speculative queries was generated. Then, a number of speculative queries were chosen for parallel execution (two - for the use of a single SQLite engine). The results of executed speculative queries were stored in the Speculative DB and assigned to user queries from SW. After SW moved on, we updated query multigraph and a new set of awaiting speculative queries was generated from which again the top rated queries were chosen for execution if not identical to such whose results already resided in the Speculative DB. We next assigned the selected queries to appropriate user queries in SW for fast use of the speculative results. Such strategy aimed at keeping the Speculative DB as small and stable as possible.

In this paper, we propose an optimized procedure of executed speculative query assignment to the awaiting input queries. We execute the Speculative Analysis as it was assumed in the previous papers but we want to extend the use of existing speculative results by input user queries for the use at a number of consecutive next positions of SW. It will be done by their "in advance" assignment to user queries in the input stream just behind the current SW. The motivation is that with the old assignment only to queries from SW it frequently happened that the speculative query results were removed from the Speculative DB when its size limit was exceeded and the identical speculative query was executed again in a nearby future. The speculative query assignment in advance should prevent such situations and keep speculative results usable as many times as possible.

5 A Hypergraph for Speculative Query Assignment

As a support for the in advance speculative query assignment we introduce a new hypergraph structure called the Assignment Hypergraph (AHg). It is used to jointly represent the executed speculative queries from the Speculative DB with N user queries situated in the input queue just behind SW.

The Assignment Hypergraphs are created according to the rules given below. There are three types of allowed vertices:

– Query Ids Vertices (marked with a big dot) - these vertices represent unique ids of executed speculative queries (pointing the specific relation in the Speculative DB) and user queries. The Query Ids Vertices of speculative and user queries are distinguishable.
– Attribute Vertices A_i (marked with a square)- single attribute vertex for each attribute appearing either in the executed speculative query or the user query
– Condition Vertices C_i (marked with a star)- one for each condition (operator and value) appearing in the executed speculative query or the user query

Each node in the hypergraph can be adjacent to more than one hyperedge. The AHg includes three obligatory types of hyperedges for each represented query:

– Speculative Query Hyperedge (labelled SQ_h) which encloses one id vertex, all attributes appearing in the SELECT and WHERE clauses and all condition vertices from the WHERE clause of the represented speculative query;
– Select Hyperedge (labelled S_h) which encloses one id vertex and all attribute vertices appearing in the SELECT clause of the query;
– Where Hyperedge (labelled W_h) which encloses one id vertex and all attribute vertices appearing in the WHERE clause of the query.

In addition, we introduce optional Condition Hyperedges to model diferrent types of conditions appearing in the WHERE clauses:

– Nested Query Hyperedge (labelled NQ_h) which encloses an attribute vertex and a condition vertex including a nested query;
– Value Condition Hyperedge (labelled VC_h) which encloses an attribute vertex and a condition vertex containing value and one of allowed arithmetical operators: $<, \leqslant, >, \geqslant, =$
– IN Condition Hyperedge (labelled IN_h) - encloses an attribute vertex and a condition vertex including IN operator and a value set
– LIKE Condition Hyperedge (labelled $LIKE_h$) - encloses an attribute vertex and a condition vertex including LIKE operator and a string

Notice, that the hypergraph structure does not include hyperedges for join conditions as joins between relations are not important in the speculative queries assignment process. We also do not include vertices for database relations as it is clear which attribute relates to which relation.

Figure 2 presents the hypergraphs created for the following two executed speculative queries (sq_1, sq_2) and three user queries (Q_1, Q_2, Q_3):

sq_1: SELECT $A_{1,1}, A_{1,2}$ FROM R_1 WHERE $A_{1,3} < 8$
sq_2: SELECT $A_{2,2}, A_{2,3}$ FROM R_2 WHERE $A_{2,4} > 1$
Q_1: SELECT $A_{1,1}$ FROM R_1 WHERE $A_{1,3} < 6$
Q_2: SELECT $A_{1,1}, A_{1,2}, A_{3,1}$ FROM R_1, R_3 WHERE $A_{1,2} = A_{3,1}$ AND $A_{1,3} < 7$
    AND $A_{3,2}$ IN (a, b)

Q_3: SELECT $A_{1,1}, A_{1,2}, A_{2,3}$ FROM R_1, R_2 WHERE $A_{1,1} = A_{2,1}$ AND $A_{1,3} > 3$
    AND $A_{2,4} = 2$

Since a full hypergraph structure contains a lot of hyperedges, first (Fig. 2a), we present only a part of an Assignment Hypergraph created for two speculative queries sq_1 and sq_2. We can see how particular hyperedges group certain vertices according to their functions. We can also see that a particular vertex (for example sq_2 or $A_{1,3}$) can be adjacent to a few hyperedges.

Figure 2 presents a full AH_g structure which includes also three user queries.

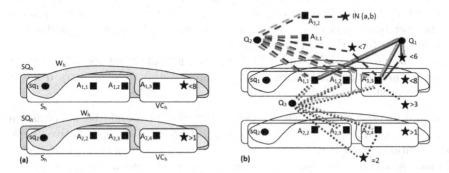

Fig. 2. A part of the hypergraph representing two speculaive queries (a). Full AHg representing two speculaive queries and three user queries (b).

For better picture readability, we skip all hyperedge labels. For user queries, we also mark hyperedges with colored lines instead of shapes. We use blue color for Speculative Query Hyperedges, green for Select Hyperedges, yellow for Where Hyperedge and violet for different types of Condition Hyperedges.

6   In Advance Speculative Query Matching Algorithm

The in advance Speculative Query Matching Algorithm covers the executed speculative query assignment for the current SW and runs according to the following strategy plan:

- add representation of an executed Speculative Query/Queries to the AH_g
- get the set of Condition Hyperedges (CH set) $(NQ_h, VC_h, IN_h, LIKE_h)$
- for each attribute edge in CH set, get a set of Condition Vertices from adjacent Condition Hyperedges (CV set). Depending on the adjacent Condition Hyperedge type do :
  - for each vertex (CV_Q) in CV set incident with IN_h hyperedge and adjacent with Q_n vertex (linked with it by the Where Hyperedge W_h) check if other vertices (CV_sq) in the CV set adjacent with sq_n vertex contains all elements of the CV_Q set. If so, check if the appropriate Select Hyperedge contains enough attributes. Then, assign the Speculative Query represented by the sq_n vertex to the user query represented by the Q_n vertex.

- for each vertex (CV_Q) in CV set incident with VC_h hyperedge and adjacent with Q_n vertex (linked with it by the Where Hyperedge W_h) check other vertices (CV_sq) in the CV set adjacent with sq_n vertex. If the ranges of values included in CV_sq vertex are wider that range values in (CV_Q), check if the appropriate Select hyperedge contains enough attributes. Then, assign the speculative query represented by the sq_n vertex to the user query represented by the Q_n vertex.
  - for the $LIKE_h$ and NQ_h hyperedges the compared values of CV_Q and CV_sq must be identical to conform to the assignment process.
- when the Speculation Window moves after the nonspeculative query is executed, update the hypergraph representation - remove the representation of the user query which now enters the Speculation Window and add a next user query from the user query queue.
- if in the process of Speculative DB cleanup any executed speculative query results are removed, then remove the representation of such query from the hypergraph.

The implementation of the new in advance strategy of speculative query assignment does not influence (so far) the original strategy of the speculative queries for execution selection in the Speculative Layer. Our aim is to verify if such in advance speculative queries assignment influences the execution process of the Speculative Layer. For the AH_g hypergraph shown in Fig. 2 we would have three speculative query assignments: sq_1 to Q_1 and Q_2 (based on attribute $A_{1,3}$) and q_2 to Q_3 (based on $A_{2,4}$).

7   Experimental Results

The Speculative Layer is implemented in C++ with multithreaded execution supported by the Pthread library and SQLite as a database engine. The database used for the experiments contained the structure and data (8 relations, 1GB data) taken from the well known TPC-H benchmark [21]. A set of 6 query templates was prepared to generate 3 sets of 1000 user queries each with random values for the attributes in WHERE clauses and similar densities of each query type in the set. The structures of the T1-T6 templates are described below, including the relations they refer to and the attributes appearing in their WHERE clauses (in brackets). Each listed attribute appears in at least one condition in WHERE clause of such query which also contains one of the allowed operators and a randomly generated value appropriate for this attribute. A more detailed description of a similar testbed query set can be found in our paper [15].
T1: LINEITEM(L_ORDERKEY nested query from ORDERS)
T2: LINEITEM (L_DISCOUNT, L_QUANTITY), PART (P_BRAND, P_CO NTAINER)
T3: PART(P_BRAND, P_TYPE, P_SIZE), PARTSUPP(PS_AVAILQTY)
T4: LINEITEM(L_EXTENDEDPRICE,L_QUANTITY), ORDERS(O_TOTA LPRICE, O_ORDERPRIORITY), CUSTOMER(C_MKTSEGMENT)
T5: LINEITEM(L_DISCOUNT, L_QUANTITY), PART(P_BRAND,P_ TYPE,

P_SIZE), PARTSUPP(PS_AVAILQTY)
T6: LINEITEM (L_EXTENDEDPRICE, L_QUANTITY), ORDERS (O_OR
DER PRIORITY), CUSTOMER (C_MKTSEGMENT), PART (P_TYPE,
P_SIZE)

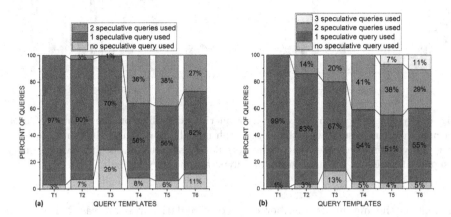

Fig. 3. Percentage of each template user queries supported by 0 to 2 speculative results
- execution without the in advance speculative query assignment (a). Percentage of
each template user queries supported by 0 to 3 speculative results - execution with the
hypergraph-based in advance speculative query assignment (b).

In Fig. 3, we show a percentage comparison of the numbers of 6 query templates as described above, executed with the use of different numbers of speculative results with and without the hypergraph-based in advance speculative
query assignments, respectively. We can see that from 3% (T1) up to 29% (T3)
of user queries were executed without the speculative support when we used
only the multigraph query representation. When we have used the hypergraph-
based speculative assignment, the number of speculatively un-supported user
queries decreased to the maximal 13% (for T3). What's more, the number of
user queries supported by 2 speculative query results increased and new query
groups appeared (for T5 and T6) supported by the use of 3 speculative query
results.

Figure 4a presents average execution times for each query template depending on the number of speculative query results we managed to prepare and use
when we have added the hypergraph modelling for the in advance speculative
query assignment. We can see that each used speculative result provided further
reduction in the user query execution time. For each template, the maximal number of used speculative results equals to the number of relations in its WHERE
clause. Thus, for templates T1, T2, T3, T5 we have managed to execute some
user queries with the maximum possible number of used speculative results (1,
2 and 3 speculative queries used, respectively), while for the multigraph only

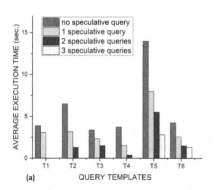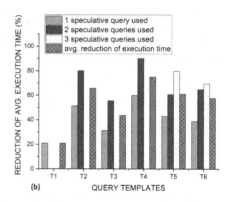

Fig. 4. Average execution times for user queries depending on the number of used speculative query results with the hypergraph modelling a). The reduction of average user query execution time due to the speculative support of the in advance query assignment based on the multigraph and hypergraph query modelling (b).

modelling, the maximum number of used speculative results was 2. Figure 4b presents the percentage reduction of user query execution times obtained with each additional speculative result used. We can see that we can obtain up to 85% reduction in a user query execution time (plain green, blue and yellow bars), with average reduction between 20% and 73% for all query templates (orange patterned bar).

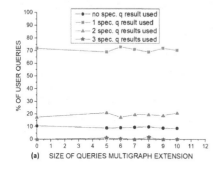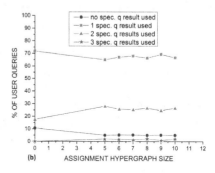

Fig. 5. User queries executed with 0–2 spec. results used for different sizes of the extended QM representation (a). User queries executed with 0, 1 or 2 speculative results used for different sizes of the Assignment Hypergraph (b).

Figure 5 shows the positive influence of the proposed algorithm of in advance speculative query assignment based on the hypergraph structures on the execution of user queries. We run comparative experiments which measured the numbers of user queries executed without and with the in advance speculative query assignment and the use of different numbers of speculative results. First, we did not use the hypergraph query representation but we extended the number of user queries analysed inside the SW multigraph. As we can see in Fig. 5(a), there is almost no visible change in the number of user queries executed without the use of speculative results. What's more, there are only single user queries executed with the use of 3 speculative results and the number of user queries executed with 2 speculative results is decreasing in favour of user queries executed with only 1 speculative result which is not a favourable effect. In Fig. 5(b), we present the average percentage of queries executed with the support of 0 to 3 speculative query results where instead of extending the size of SW we used the algorithm of in advance speculative query assignment based on hypergraphs. As we can see in Fig. 5(b) - the line with blue circles, the number of user queries executed without speculative query results decreased 2 times (from 10% to 5%). We can also see that input user queries were observed which used 3 speculative query results (bottom line with red stars). The stabilization of the algorithm for bigger numbers of user queries assigned in advance is dependent on the size limit of the Speculative DB and the strategy of the speculative results removal when this limit is exceeded. The speculative results assigned to the user queries from the current SW are always the last to be deleted. Thus, the speculative results assigned to future user queries based on the hypergraph analysis may be deleted if it is immediately required to provide space in the Speculative DB.

8 Conclusions

This paper has presented an optimized method for using speculative query results in RDBMS systems. It was implemented inside the multithreaded middleware called the Speculative Layer. The Speculative Layer, based on joint graph modelling of the speculative and input user queries, controls execution of the speculative queries which are assigned and used to speedup execution of input user queries. In this paper, we have introduced the use of a hypergraph query representation, which due to its set-oriented characteristics, can easily be used to analyze relations between executed speculative and not yet examined input user queries. The experimental results have confirmed the advantages from using this representation for the new proposed mechanism of the in advance speculative query assignment. The proposed methods have reduced the number of user queries executed without the use of the speculative query results. They have also increased the use of the speculative query results, comparing the execution based only on the multigraph query modelling, thus speeding up execution of input user queries in RDBMS. Our further research will focus on development of the query speculative support algorithms exclusively based on the hypergraph modelling.

References

1. Kejariwal, A., et al.: On the performance potential of different types of speculative thread-level parallelism. In: ICS Proceedings, pp. 1–24, Cairns (2006)

2. Silc, J., Ungerer, T., Robic, B.: Dynamic branch prediction and control speculation. Int. J High Perform. Sys. Arch. **1**(1), 2–13 (2007)
3. Pan, S., So, K., Rahmeh, J.T.: Improving the accuracy of dynamic branch prediction using branch correlation, in International Conference on Architectural Support for Programming Languages and Operating Systems, Boston, pp. 76–84 (1992)
4. Moshovos, A., Breach, S.E., Vijaykumar, T.N., Sohi G.S.: dynamic speculation and synchronization of data dependence. In: 24th ISCA, ACM SIGARCH Computer Architecture News, vol. 25 (202)
5. Puiggali, J., Szymański, B.K., Jove, T., Marzo, J.L.: Dynamic branch speculation in a speculative parallelization architecture for computer clusters. Concurr. Comput Pract. Exp. **25**, 932–960 (2013)
6. Gryz, J.: Query folding with inclusion dependencies. In: Proceedings 14th International Conference on Data Engineering, pp. 126–133 (1998)
7. Barish, G., Knoblock, C.A.: Speculative plan execution for information gathering. Artif. Intell. **172**(4–5), 413–453 (2008)
8. Polyzotis, N., Ioannidis, Y.: Speculative query processing. In: CIDR Conference Proceedings, pp. 1–12, Asilomar (2003)
9. Reddy, P.K., Kitsuregawa, M.: Speculative locking Protocols to Improve Performance for Distributed Database Systems. IEEE Trans. Knowl. Data Eng. **16**(2), 54–169 (2004)
10. Ragunathan, T., Reddy, P.K.: Improving the performance of Readonly transactions through Asynchronous Speculation. In: SPRINGSIM, pp. 467–474, Ottawa (2008)
11. Ge, X., et al.: LSShare: an efficient multiple query optimization system in the cloud. Distrib. Parallel Databases **32**(4), 593–605 (2014)
12. Chaudhari, M.B., Dietrich, S.W.: Detecting common sub-expressions for multiple query optimization over loosely-coupled heterogeneous data sources. Distrib. Parallel Databases **34**, 119–143 (2016)
13. Faisal, H.M., et al.: A Query Matching approach for object relational databases over semantic cache. In: Chapter 13 in Application of Decision Science in Business and Management (2019)
14. Ahmad, M., Qadir, M.A., Sanaullah, M.: Query processing over relational databases with semantic cache: a survey. In: IEEE International Multitopic Conference, pp. 558–564, Karachi (2008)
15. Sasak-Okoń, A.: Tudruj, M. Graph-based speculative query execution in relational databases. In: ISPDC, IEEE Explore, Innsbruck (2017)
16. Cybula, P., Subieta, K.: Query optimization by result caching in the stack-based approach. In: Dearle, A., Zicari, R.V. (eds.) ICOODB 2010. LNCS, vol. 6348, pp. 40–54. Springer, Heidelberg (2010). https://doi.org/10.1007/978-3-642-16092-9_7
17. Han, J.L.: Optimizing relational queries in connection hypergraphs: nested queries, views, and binding propagations. VLDB J. **7**, 1–11 (1998)
18. Sen, S., Ghosh, M., Dutta, A., Dutta B.: Hypergraph Based Query Optimization. In: ICCI-2015, pp. 1–8, Combinatore (2015)
19. Qian, X.: Query folding. In: ICDE, pp. 48–55 (1996)
20. Koutrika, G., Simitsis, A., Ioannidis, Y.E.: Explaining structured queries in natural language. In: ICDE Proceedings, pp. 333–344, Long Beach (2010)
21. TPC benchmarks (2015). http://www.tpc.org/tpch/default.asp
22. Sasak-Okoń, A., Tudruj, M.: Graph-based speculative query execution for RDBMS. In: Wyrzykowski, R., Dongarra, J., Deelman, E., Karczewski, K. (eds.) PPAM 2017. LNCS, vol. 10777, pp. 303–313. Springer, Cham (2018). https://doi.org/10.1007/978-3-319-78024-5_27

23. Sasak-Okoń, A.: Modifying queries strategy for graph-based speculative query execution for RDBMS. In: Wyrzykowski, R., Deelman, E., Dongarra, J., Karczewski, K. (eds.) PPAM 2019. LNCS, vol. 12043, pp. 408–418. Springer, Cham (2020). https://doi.org/10.1007/978-3-030-43229-4_35
24. Sasak-Okoń, A., Tudruj, M.: Speculative query execution in RDBMS based on analysis of query stream multigraphs. In: IDEAS, pp. 192–201, Seoul (2020)

GPU Computing

Mixed Precision Algebraic Multigrid on GPUs

Yu-Hsiang Mike Tsai[1], Natalie Beams[2], and Hartwig Anzt[1,2](✉)

[1] Karlsruhe Institute of Technology, Karlsruhe, Germany
[2] University of Tennessee, Knoxville, USA
hanzt@icl.utk.edu

Abstract. In this paper, we present the first GPU-native platform-portable algebraic multigrid (AMG) implementation that allows the user to use different precision formats for the distinct multigrid levels. The AMG we present uses an aggregation size 2 parallel graph match as the AMG coarsening strategy. The implementation provides a high level of flexibility in terms of configuring the bottom-level solver and the precision format for the distinct levels. We present convergence and performance results on the GPUs from AMD, Intel, and NVIDIA, and compare against corresponding functionality available in other libraries.

Keywords: Algebraic multigrid · Mixed precision · Portability · GPUs

1 Introduction

Multigrid methods approximate the solution of a linear system aided by a solution computed for a smaller system of equations arising from a coarser mesh. The coarser and finer mesh are related through operators that *restrict* the fine grid solution to the coarse grid and *prolongate* the coarse grid solution to the fine grid. This idea of approximating solutions on a coarser grid can be applied recursively, resulting in a hierarchy of successively coarser grids which can efficiently target different frequencies in the error on the fine grid. Traditionally, one distinguishes two classes of multigrid methods: those that use the geometric mesh information from a spatial discretization to derive the hierarchy of grids are called "geometric multigrid methods" (GMG); those that generate the hierarchy of grids exclusively from the large sparse matrix are called "algebraic multigrid methods" (AMG). Thus, in AMG, the coarse grids no longer directly correspond to coarser discretizations of the original problem, making AMG methods effective for unstructured grids or problems of unknown origin, and particularly attractive for black-box usage.

With the widespread use of GPU accelerators in scientific computing, much effort is focused on effective and efficient multigrid methods targeting GPUs or amenable to GPU porting (see, e.g., [8–10]). Increased use of GPUs also motivates further development and analysis of mixed-precision multigrid methods for accelerators that can exploit high performance available in low precision computations [11].

R. Wyrzykowski et al. (Eds.): PPAM 2022, LNCS 13826, pp. 113–125, 2023.
https://doi.org/10.1007/978-3-031-30442-2_9

In this paper, we present an AMG, implemented in and available through the open-source GINKGO library, that

1. allows for mixed-precision AMG execution;
2. is platform portable and can execute on AMD, Intel, and NVIDIA GPUs;
3. allows independent configuration of components for each level in the grid hierarchy, as well as the bottom-level solver;
4. is competitive with AmgX [13] for real-world applications and benchmarks.

2   Background on AMG and Related Work

Algebra multigrid (AMG) is a popular choice for solving or preconditioning linear problems originating from finite element discretizations. Unlike geometric multigrid (GMG), which relies on using information about the underlying geometric mesh, an AMG solver is constructed directly from the sparse system matrix. Similarly to GMG, AMG builds a hierarchy of consecutively-coarser grids and computes error correction terms on the coarser grids to improve the solution on finer grids. Specifically, it restricts the residual on a fine grid to a coarser grid, then uses the coarser grid to obtain an error correction that is prolongated back to the finer grid to update the solution approximation. These correction computations generally entail a few iterations of an iterative method, called a "smoother" because it acts to smooth the high-frequency errors on the scale of that grid, while the coarsest grid may opt for a direct solve of the restricted problem, which is much smaller than the original matrix.

Parallel Graph Match. Strategies for creating the successively coarser grids are generally more complicated in AMG than GMG, due to the lack of a physical grid or mesh in the AMG initialization process (or entirely). The AMG implementation in GINKGO uses parallel graph match (PGM), which was introduced by Naumov et al. [13] as a GPU-based algorithm for deriving a coarse approximation through exploration of the graph representation of a matrix. It is a type of *aggregation* method, in which nodes in the fine grid are combined to form a single coarse grid node.

AmgX [13] is a library developed by NVIDIA that allows for single-GPU and multi-GPU use and provides several coarsening methods, including parallel maximal independent set (PMIS) and parallel graph match (PGM). The library only supports execution on NVIDIA GPUs. **HYPRE** [7] is a powerful library for distributed computing with its popular BoomerAMG [15] a central component. Its different interfaces allows HYPRE to customize integration into specific applications, often permitting users to avoid conversions to a generic matrix format. Currently, HYPRE supports execution on both NVIDIA and AMD GPUs, with work in progress for Intel GPUs. We will compare the performance of GINKGO to both of these popular libraries in Sect. 4. Other open-source GPU-enabled AMG implementations can be found in **rocALUTION** [1], an iterative sparse solver library developed by AMD, and **MueLu** [4], a multigrid package inside the Trilinos [14] ecosystem.

To the best of our knowledge, there exists no AMG implementation that can execute on Intel GPUs. We also did not find any AMG implementation that allows the use of different precision formats for the distinct multigrid levels. NVIDIA AmgX can use `AMGX_mode` to choose the matrix and vector precisions of the top-level linear system, but not the precision of each level in the multigrid. Hence, our AMG implementation is leading the community in platform portability (AMD, Intel and NVIDIA GPUs) and flexibility (level components and mixed precision mode).

3   Design of the Flexible and Platform-Portable AMG

The design of the GINKGO AMG is driven by three main goals: flexibility, performance, and platform portability.

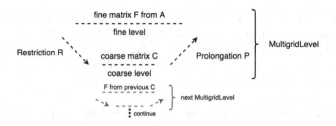

Fig. 1. The `MultigridLevel` class with its components.

MultigridLevel. In GINKGO, we define a `MultigridLevel` class, visualized in Fig. 1, that contains a fine grid matrix from which it constructs the coarse grid matrix (C) via the coarsening algorithm, as well as the restriction (R) and prolongation (P) operators. The fine matrix (F) is merely the input matrix A, but with the storage precision or format potentially altered by the `MultigridLevel` according to the algorithm requirement or settings.

Using GINKGO's factory design pattern [3], a `MultigridLevelFactory` stores the configuration and allows a top-level `Multigrid` object to use it repeatedly to generate `MultigridLevel` objects for different levels in the multigrid hierarchy. The parameters for the factory are order-free and optional where the factory has sensible default values.

Multigrid Cycle. Multiple `MultigridLevel` objects combine with smoothing operations at the interfaces to form a full AMG cycle in a `Multigrid` object. The `Multigrid` class is highly flexible in configuring its components, with a long list of parameters defining pre-/mid-/post-smoother options, coarse grid solvers, the maximum number of levels in the multigrid hierarchy, the minimum number of rows in the coarsest matrix, and mixed-precision use options, among others.

Supporting Mixed Precision in AMG. GINKGO's AMG implementation allows the use of different precision formats on different levels of the multigrid hierarchy, resulting in a mixed-precision AMG. The precision conversion happens on-the-fly in the restriction and prolongation operations.

```
1  multigrid::build()
2      .with_max_levels(10u) // equal to NVIDIA/AMGX 11 max levels
3      .with_min_coarse_row(64u)
4 DP   .with_pre_smoother(sm)
5 |    .with_mg_level(pgm)
6 DP   .with_coarest_solver(coarest_solver)
7 MP   .with_pre_smoother(sm, sm_f)
8 ||   .with_mg_level(pgm, pgm_f)
9 ||   .with_coarest_solver(coarest_solver_f)
10 ||  .with_level_selector(
11 ||      [](const size_type level, const LinOp*) -> size_type {
12 ||          // Only the first level is generated by MultigridLevel(double).
13 ||          // The subsequent levels are generated by MultigridLevel(float)
14 ||          return level >= 1 ? 1 : 0;
15 MP      })
```

Listing 1.1. Configuration of a GINKGO `Multigrid` object. Lines with a red background are used when configuring for double precision (DP), while the green background indicates configuration for mixed precision (MP).

The gray and red portions of Listing 1.1 show a standard AMG V-cycle with a max level depth of 10 (equivalent to 11 in NVIDIA/AmgX), a smoother `sm` that is used for all smoothing operations, a `MultigridLevel` `pgm`, and a coarse level solver, `coarest_solver`. (Note that the number of smoothing sweeps is a parameter of the smoother object `sm`.)

In the configuration shown in the gray and green parts of Listing 1.1, we enable mixed precision by adding two `MultigridLevel`s and two smoothers in the corresponding configuration list, with `_f` indicating "float" or single precision. We also need to configure the `level_selector` to describe the desired scheme. Here, when the level is larger than or equal to 1 (that is, all levels except the finest grid), we use the second pair (`pgm_f`, `sm_f`). When the level is less than 1, we use the first pair (`pgm`, `sm`). Taken together, this configuration generates a mixed-precision `Multigrid` where only the finest level is using double precision, and all other levels use single precision. We note that this mixed-precision `Multigrid` configuration allows for smooth integration as a preconditioner into an iterative solver using double precision, as the input and output vectors, as well as the original matrix, remain in double precision.

Performance and Platform Portability. To enable both platform and performance portability, we implement the GINKGO AMG using a backend model as described in [3,5], where we complement an algorithm skeleton invoking a sequence of subroutines with backends containing the corresponding subroutines as heavily optimized GPU kernels in the vendor-native programming languages. Specifically, we implement CUDA kernels for NVIDIA GPUs, DPC++ kernels for Intel GPUs, and HIP kernels for AMD GPUs. Instead of having three complete stand-alone AMG implementations for the distinct GPU architectures with the corresponding kernel sets, we use C++ runtime polymorphism for automatically selecting and invoking the suitable kernels when executing the AMG algorithm. This allows the deployment of the AMG solver in an application or a software library without having to maintain different variants for different hardware architectures. By doing so, we keep the cutting-edge features from vendors' official compilers without waiting for another compiler to adopt the new features. In [3], the basic idea and the library design of GINKGO are outlined, and [5] describes more details about how to prepare different backends and how to reduce the maintenance efforts.

Reusing temporary storage and avoiding redundant residual computation were found to be key performance features required by GINKGO's AMG. Unlike GINKGO's Krylov solvers (CG, BiCG, or GMRES) which solve the linear system in one application, AMG requires several pieces of GINKGO solvers in each level. Each call to a solver for smoothing will likely only do a few iterations at a time, so if we generate a temporary workspace and free the memory after application, it creates large overhead; the full AMG cycle contains many smoothing steps, so the overhead is noticeable. In fact, before improving GINKGO's temporary storage allocation to alleviate this overhead in AMG, profiling for a sample V-cycle showed that only 6% of the total time was spent in GPU activities, versus 27% for AmgX. We mark these temporary storage allocations with the mutable keyword in order to avoid reallocation. We also avoid unnecessary residual computations, e.g. when the input is zero and thus the residual can be copied directly from right hand side.

4 Experiments

To evaluate performance of our mixed-precision AMG implementation, we use both simulations of real-world problems within the MFEM finite element framework and a set of benchmark problems taken from the Suite Sparse Matrix Collection [6]; see Table 1 for the list of test problems and their key characteristics.

Table 1. Matrix characteristics for the selected MFEM discretizations and Suite Sparse Matrix Collection matrices. The MFEM matrices marked with (*) were exported from MFEM and also used in the platform-independent tests.

	Problem	Size	Nonzero elements
Matrices in MFEM integration test	Beam (−o2 −l3)	37, 281	21, 67, 425
	Beam (−o3 −l3)*	120, 625	14, 070, 001
	Beam (−o4 −l3)	279, 873	57, 251, 713
	Beam (−o3 −l4)	924, 385	111, 573, 601
	L-shape (−o3 −l7)*	443, 905	11, 066, 881
	L-shape (−o3 −l8)	1, 772, 545	44, 252, 161
	L-shape (−o4 −l7)	788, 481	28, 323, 841
	L-shape (−o4 −l8)	3, 149, 825	113, 270, 785
	2cubes_sphere	101, 492	1, 647, 264
	Thermal2	1, 228, 045	8, 580, 313
SuiteSparse matrices	cage14	1, 505, 785	27, 130, 349
for platform-independent	cage13	445, 315	7, 479, 343
Tests	offshore	259, 789	4, 242, 673
	tmt_sym	726, 713	5, 080, 961

To demonstrate platform portability, we evaluate GINKGO's AMG implementation on GPU architectures from AMD, Intel, and NVIDIA. The GPUs and corresponding compilers are listed along with some key characteristics in Table 2. We compare the performance of GINKGO's AMG against two well-established AMG libraries: HYPRE [7][1] for NVIDIA and AMD GPUs, and NVIDIA's AmgX[2] for NVIDIA GPUs. For GINKGO's AMG, we have two execution modes: **Ginkgo's AMG (DP):** The AMG executes the full algebraic multigrid cycle in IEEE double precision (DP); **Ginkgo's AMG (MP):** The mixed-precision AMG executes the first level in DP and the rest of levels in IEEE single precision.

Table 2. GPU characteristics.

GPU	Peak Perf. (DP)	Peak Perf. (SP)	Mem. size	Bandwidth	Compiler	Type
AMD MI100	11.54 TFLOP/s	23.1 TFLOP/s	32 GB	1,229 GB/s	HIP 4.3	Discrete
Intel UHD P630	0.12 TFLOP/s	0.46 TFLOPS	RAM	42 GB/s	DPC++ 2021.4	Integrated
NVIDIA V100	7.79 TFLOP/s	15.7 TFLOP/s	16 GB	900 GB/s	CUDA 11.4	Discrete

Experiments on Real-World Test Problems in MFEM. First, we compare GINKGO's AMG and NVIDIA's AmgX when used as a preconditioner for the solution of finite element problems in MFEM. MFEM [2,12] is a popular open-source finite element library with support for high-order meshes and basis functions, among many other features. We consider a modification of MFEM's "example 1", solving a standard diffusion problem $-\nabla \cdot (c\nabla u) = 1$, where c is a given coefficient. We use homogeneous Dirichlet boundary conditions. Two of MFEM's provided meshes are tested; they are shown in Fig. 2. For the "L-shape" mesh, a constant coefficient of $c = 1$ is used, while the "beam" mesh uses a piecewise constant coefficient with a jump from 1 to 0.1 at the midpoint of the length of the beam. All tests use standard tensor-product basis functions on the Legendre-Gauss-Lobatto nodes and MFEM's default choices for quadrature points based on the order of basis functions.

Fig. 2. Meshes used for MFEM diffusion experiments. Left: L-shape mesh with 7 levels of uniform refinement (49,152 elements); Right: Beam mesh with 3 levels of uniform refinement (4,096 elements).

---

[1] HYPRE using commit 84fa589.
[2] NVIDIA AmgX using commit 77f91a9.

We use AMG as a preconditioner within MFEM's CG solver, with one V-cycle application for each iteration of CG. Intending to provide a fair comparison, we have matched parameter settings as closely as possible for AmgX and GINKGO; as comparison is our main goal, we have not attempted to determine an optimal set of parameters for either library individually. We use the parallel graph match with deterministic aggregation of size 2 for coarsening. The maximum number of levels is 11 (which corresponds to a parameter value of 10 in GINKGO, but 11 in AmgX), with a minimum of 64 rows in the coarsest matrix. The pre-/post-smoothing is weighted Jacobi with a weight of 0.9, i.e., $x_{i+1} = x_i + 0.9 * D^{-1}(b - Ax_i)$ where x_i is the solution at iteration i, D is the diagonal matrix of A, and b is the right-hand side of the linear system being solved. The same relaxation is used on the coarse grid problem, but with four relaxation sweeps instead of one. We built on MFEM's existing GINKGO wrappers to use GINKGO AMG within MFEM, and AmgX preconditioning support is provided through MFEM's AmgXSolver class. In the following tests, we consider several *orders* of basis functions (-o) and *levels* of mesh refinement (-l), which define the problem names in Table 1. Increasing the order of basis functions increases both the problem size and the number of non-zeros per row; increasing the refinement of the mesh increases the problem size while retaining sparsity. We set the stopping criterion as implicit relative residual norm reduction of 10^{-12} or maximum 300 iterations.

Table 3. MFEM **Beam** (top) and **L-shape** (bottom) examples using MFEM's AMG-preconditiond CG solver. GINKGO's AMG is executed in IEEE double precision (DP) and mixed precision mode (MP) using IEEE single precision on the subsequent levels. Target architecture is the NVIDIA V100 GPU.

Geometry	Problem	NVIDIA AmgX (DP)		GINKGO AMG (DP)		GINKGO AMG (MP)	
		Runtime [ms]	#iter	runtime [ms]	#iter	runtime [ms]	#iter
Beam	−o 2 −l 3	20.71	15	20.27	15	19.96	15
	−o 3 −l 3	52.94	20	39.93	21	39.56	21
	−o 4 −l 3	155.47	26	128.69	27	120.41	27
	−o 3 −l 4	329.68	29	294.68	29	270.39	29
L-shape	−o 3 −l 7	242.27	93	178.02	93	170.08	94
	−o 3 −l 8	1211.38	180	1033.96	173	943.27	177
	−o 4 −l 8	3452.91	251	3044.24	236	2722.63	237
	−o 4 −l 7	551.99	129	407.27	122	366.99	120

In Table 3, we list the iteration counts and runtime performance for different CG/preconditioner configurations on the NVIDIA V100 GPU. We first focus on four discretizations for the **Beam** geometry. The iteration counts of the AMG-preconditioned CG solver are generally consistent, and using GINKGO's AMG in mixed-precision mode does not, in this case, increase the CG iteration count above the double precision setting. The CG preconditioned with NVIDIA's

AmgX preconditioner sometimes converges one iteration sooner, but the AmgX preconditioner application is more expensive per iteration than GINKGO's AMG preconditioner: see Fig. 3 (top), which shows the average execution time per one CG iteration, with GINKGO's AMG being approximately 20–40% faster than NVIDIA's AmgX for the three larger problems. This performance combined with nearly-identical iteration counts results in GINKGO's AMG consistently outperforming NVIDIA's AmgX for this test case – with the mixed-precision configuration increasing the performance advantages.

Compared to the **Beam** geometry, the **L-shape** geometry is numerically more challenging due to its re-entrant corner. We use the same experiment settings and report the results in the bottom part of Table 3. Here, the trend of the AmgX-preconditioned CG requiring fewer iterations is reversed, as in this case GINKGO's AMG enables faster convergence. Combined with the faster preconditioner application per iteration, which holds for this test case as well (see bottom of Fig. 3), GINKGO's AMG offers attractive runtime savings over AmgX for all discretizations of the **L-shape** geometry. The runtime savings increase when using GINKGO's AMG in mixed-precision mode. For example, for the "-o 4 -l 7" discretization, preconditioning CG with GINKGO's mixed-precision AMG allows us to solve the problem 1.5× faster than when using NVIDIA's AmgX; see Table 3 (bottom).

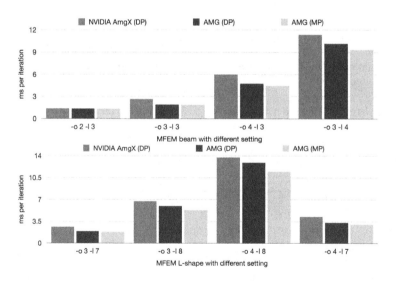

Fig. 3. Runtime of one AMG-preconditioned CG iteration on the V100 GPU for MFEM's example 1 for the beam mesh (top) and the L-shape mesh (bottom).

Platform Portability Experiments. For demonstrating the full platform portability of GINKGO's AMG, we can no longer rely on simulations within MFEM, as MFEM does not yet support execution on Intel GPUs (though this feature is in development as of this writing). Furthermore, while MFEM does support AMD GPU use, AmgX—and thus the use of MFEM's `AmgXSolver` class—is limited to NVIDIA GPUs. Instead, for evaluating platform portability, we consider AMG as a stand-alone solver and use one discretization of the beam mesh and one discretization of the L-shape mesh in conjunction with benchmark problems from the Suite Sparse Matrix Collection [6], as summarized in Table 1. The MFEM-exported matrices are accompanied with their corresponding MFEM-generated right-hand sides for the linear systems solved in the previous experiments. For the Suite Sparse test matrices, we use a right-hand side of all-ones. The initial guess is in all experiments set to all-zeros. We use a residual stopping criterion of 10^{-9} and allow for at most 100 AMG iterations. In the standalone solver performance tests, we compare NVIDIA AmgX and HYPRE against GINKGO DP AMG and GINKGO MP AMG where allowed by current library support, meaning HYPRE on AMD and NVIDIA GPUs, and AmgX for NVIDIA GPUs. We configure HYPRE to use a similar multigrid configuration as the one used by NVIDIA's AmgX and GINKGO's AMG from the previous section: we use 1 pre-/post-sweep, 4 coarse sweeps, HYPRE's weighted Jacobi smoother, 11 total levels, and set the minimum coarse system size to 64. However, as HYPRE BoomerAMG only fully supports the parallel maximal independent set (PMIS) coarsening on GPUs, coarsening, the interpolation, and the level sizes differ from the other libraries. While HYPRE supports multi-GPU usage, we restrict the comparison to single-GPU runs.

Table 4. Comparison of performance, convergence, and accuracy of different AMG solvers on the NVIDIA V100 GPU. For HYPRE, we mark * on iteration when HYPRE does not generate any level for the problem.

Problem	NVIDIA AmgX (DP)			GINKGO's AMG (DP)			GINKGO's AMG (MP)			HYPRE AMG (DP)		
	[ms]	#it	res.norm	[ms]	#it	res.norm	[ms]	#it	res.norm	[ms]	#it	res.norm
beam(o313)	199.44	87	9.03e-10	152.87	84	9.75e-10	142.49	83	8.94e-10	82.394	30	9.68e-10
L-shp.(o317)	251.01	100	7.43e-04	236.43	100	6.89e-04	226.15	100	6.91e-04	67.892	33	9.99e-10
2cubes.	130.14	88	7.94e-10	160.63	91	8.88e-10	114.90	91	8.88e-10	187.48	100	1.33e-8
thermal2	284.73	100	1062.42	304.79	100	1062.74	286.56	100	1062.73	327.42	100	5.7206
cage14	79.30	15	4.28e-10	84.01	14	6.73e-10	76.08	14	6.67e-10	119.67	*86	8.46e-10
cage13	40.99	17	7.29e-10	42.61	18	5.37e-10	40.26	18	5.40e-10	44.87	*87	8.68e-10
offshore	180.92	100	1.76e33	172.48	100	1.95e33	172.10	100	1.95e33	236.34	100	inf
tmt_sym	211.65	100	858.151	197.63	100	858.84	188.58	100	858.83	265.46	100	1.45e6

We first consider the stand-alone AMG solver experiments for an NVIDIA V100 GPU, summarized in Table 4. The per-iteration runtimes in Fig. 4 (top) reveal that AmgX and GINKGO's double precision AMG have similar per-iteration runtimes. GINKGO's mixed-precision AMG benefits from the higher performance in single precision. In the time-to-solution metric, NVIDIA's AmgX outperforms GINKGO's double precision AMG for the SuiteSparse test problems, but GINKGO's AMG outperforms NVIDIA's AmgX for the MFEM test problems. However, in both cases, the differences are small, and the faster iteration execution makes GINKGO's mixed-precision AMG superior or similar to

NVIDIA's AmgX for all test problems. HYPRE's AMG[3] is significantly faster than NVIDIA's AmgX and GINKGO's AMG for the MFEM test problems. For the SuiteSparse problems, HYPRE's AMG is slower and/or converging more slowly than the competitors. For cage14 and cage13 in Table 4, the settings we choose result in HYPRE not generating any grid hierarchy.

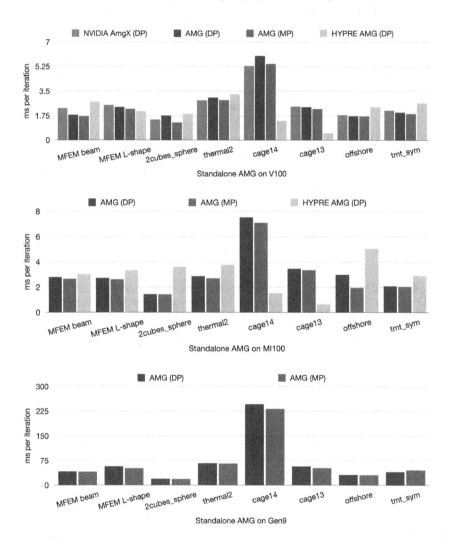

Fig. 4. AMG per-iteration runtime on the NVIDIA V100 GPU (top), the AMD MI100 GPU (center) and the Intel Gen9 GPU (bottom).

We now turn to AMD's MI100 GPU and run both HYPRE's AMG and GINKGO's AMG on the same test matrices. The results in Table 5 reveal that

---

[3] The coarsening method is different from others' settings.

Table 5. Comparison of performance, convergence, and accuracy of HYPRE's AMG solver and GINKGO's AMG solver on the AMD MI100 GPU. In HYPRE, we mark * on iterations where HYPRE does not generate any level for the problem, and # when HYPRE terminates early due to a nan result.

Problem	GINKGO's AMG (DP)			GINKGO's AMG (MP)			HYPRE AMG (DP)		
	[ms]	#it	res.norm	[ms]	#it	res.norm	[ms]	#it	res.norm
beam (−o3 −l3)	235.23	84	9.80e−10	220.30	83	9.30e−10	93.79	31	6.56e−10
L-shape (−o3 −l7)	272.28	100	6.88e−04	261.14	100	6.88e−04	109.95	33	9.25e−10
2cubes_sphere	130.63	91	8.88e−10	130.08	91	8.88e−10	360.54	100	1.38e−07
thermal2	287.12	100	1062.74	270.79	100	1062.73	376.19	100	5.4256
cage14	105.50	14	6.75e−10	99.61	14	6.68e−10	130.68	*86	8.46e−10
cage13	62.27	18	5.37e−10	60.24	18	5.40e−10	55.71	*87	8.68e−10
offshore	207.69	100	1.95e33	195.82	100	1.95e33	247.89	#49	nan
tmt_sym	208.72	100	858.843	205.13	100	858.854	289.58	100	3.18e9

the convergence and accuracy results are consistent with those obtained for the V100 results. Running GINKGO's AMG in mixed-precision mode renders small performance advantages on the MI100 GPU; see center row in Fig. 4. The advantages are, however, smaller than on the V100 GPU. Again, HYPRE is faster for the MFEM problems, but GINKGO is faster for the selected SuiteSparse benchmark problems. Although the theoretical bandwidth of the MI100 is higher than the V100's, we can not achieve the same usage ratio of the bandwidth, rendering the performance of the MI100 slightly slower. [5] shows the GINKGO SpMV achieves similar performance to hipSPARSE, but both of them attain a smaller fraction of peak bandwidth than corresponding routines on NVIDIA GPUs.

We now run the same experiments on an Intel Gen9 UHD P630 GPU, which is an integrated GPU with Intel E-2146G CPU. Table 6 demonstrates that convergence and accuracy of GINKGO's AMG solvers carry over to Intel GPUs. We visualize the per-iteration runtime in the bottom of Fig. 4.[4] On the P630 GPU, we see a small runtime advantage for the mixed-precision AMG over double precision except for the tmt_sym problem.

Comparing in Fig. 4 the performance of GINKGO's AMG on the three GPUs, we note that the NVIDIA V100 GPU allows for the fastest AMG execution, closely followed by the AMD MI100 GPU. The execution on the Intel P630 GPU being more than an order of magnitude slower is expected from the hardware characteristics in Table 2.

---

[4] At the time of writing, the integrated P630 GPU is the only widely-available GPU from Intel supporting double precision.

Table 6. GINKGO's AMG characteristics on the Intel P630 GPU.

problem	GINKGO's AMG (DP)			GINKGO's AMG (MP)		
	[ms]	#iter	res. norm	[ms]	#iter	res. norm
beam (−o3 −13)	3535.40	85	8.53e−10	3403.34	83	9.57e−10
L-shape (−o3 −17)	5756.48	100	6.89e−04	5206.85	100	6.94e−04
2cubes_sphere	1806.15	91	8.88e−10	1746.48	91	8.88e−10
thermal2	6715.82	100	1062.7	6641.03	100	1062.7
cage14	3449.86	14	6.77e−10	3247.38	14	6.67e−10
cage13	1031.46	18	5.37e−10	949.23	18	5.40e−10
offshore	3155.41	100	1.95e33	3085.29	100	1.95e33
tmt_sym	4043.05	100	857.767	4656.52	100	858.304

5 Conclusion

We describe the design, usage, portability, and performance of a new algebraic multigrid (AMG) implementation for GPUs. The new AMG implemented in the GINKGO library allows for more flexibility in terms of choosing multigrid components and precision formats: we can configure the AMG to use different precision formats for the distinct multigrid levels, resulting in a mixed-precision AMG. The AMG is performance portable via a backend model that features kernels written in the vendor-native programming language for GPUs from AMD, Intel, and NVIDIA. We demonstrate that the new AMG implementation is competitive to NVIDIA's AmgX implementation, and the mixed-precision configuration is outperforming AmgX. On AMD and NVIDIA GPUs, we compare also with HYPRE's GPU-capable AMG implementation that is based on PMIS aggregation. We conclude with performance results for AMG execution on Intel GPUs.

References

1. AMD: rocALUTION. https://dgithub.com/ROCmSoftwarePlatform/rocALUTION
2. Anderson, R., et al.: Ginkgo: a Modern linear operator algebra framework for high performance Comput. ACM Trans. Math. Softw. **48**(1), 2:1–2:33 (2022). https://doi.org/10.1016/j.camwa.2020.06.009
3. Anzt, H., et al.: Ginkgo: a modern linear operator algebra framework for high performance. Comput. ACM Trans. Math. Softw. **48**(1), 2:1–2:33 (2022). https://doi.org/10.1145/3480935
4. Berger-Vergiat, L., et al.: MueLu multigrid framework 2019). https://trilinos.org/packages/muelu
5. Cojean, T., Tsai, Y.H.M., Anzt, H.: Ginkgo-a math library designed for platform portability. Parallel Comput. **111**, 102902 (2022)
6. Davis, T.A., Hu, Y.: The university of Florida sparse matrix collection. ACM Trans. Math. Softw. (TOMS) **38**(1), 1–25 (2011)

7. Falgout, R.D., Yang, U.M.: *hypre*: a library of high performance preconditioners. In: Sloot, P.M.A., Hoekstra, A.G., Tan, C.J.K., Dongarra, J.J. (eds.) ICCS 2002. LNCS, vol. 2331, pp. 632–641. Springer, Heidelberg (2002). https://doi.org/10. 1007/3-540-47789-6_66

8. Ganesan, S., Shah, M.: SParSH-AMG: a library for hybrid CPU-GPU algebraic multigrid and preconditioned iterative methods. arXiv preprint arXiv:2007.00056 (2020)

9. Li, R., Sjögreen, B., Yang, U.M.: A new class of AMG interpolation methods based on matrix-matrix multiplications. SIAM J. Sci. Comput. **43**(5), S540–S564 (2021)

10. Liu, H., Yang, B., Chen, Z.: Accelerating algebraic multigrid solvers on NVIDIA GPUs. Comput. Math. Appl. **70**(5), 1162–1181 (2015)

11. McCormick, S.F., Benzaken, J., Tamstorf, R.: Algebraic error analysis for mixed-precision multigrid solvers. SIAM J. Sci. Comput. **43**(5), S392–S419 (2021)

12. MFEM: Modular finite element methods [Software]. https://mfem.org/. https:// doi.org/10.11578/dc.20171025.1248

13. Naumov, M., et al.: AmgX: a library for GPU accelerated algebraic multigrid and preconditioned iterative methods. SIAM J. Sci. Comput. **37**(5), S602–S626 (2015)

14. Trilinos Project Team, T.: The Trilinos Project Website

15. Yang, U.M., et al.: BoomerAMG: a parallel algebraic multigrid solver and preconditioner. Appl. Numer. Math. **41**(1), 155–177 (2002)

Compact In-Memory Representation of Decision Trees in GPU-Accelerated Evolutionary Induction

Krzysztof Jurczuk$^{(\boxtimes)}$ (ID), Marcin Czajkowski (ID), and Marek Kretowski (ID)

Faculty of Computer Science, Bialystok University of Technology, Wiejska 45a,
15-351 Bialystok, Poland
{k.jurczuk,m.czajkowski,m.kretowski}@pb.edu.pl

Abstract. Decision trees (DTs) are popular techniques in the field of explainable machine learning. Traditionally, DTs are induced using a top-down greedy search that is usually fast; however, it may lead to sub-optimal solutions. Here, we deal with an alternative approach which is an evolutionary induction. It provides global exploration that results in less complex DTs but it is much more time-demanding. Various parallel computing approaches were considered, where GPU-based one seems to be the most efficient. To speed up the induction further, different GPU memory organization/layouts could be dealt with.

In this paper, we introduce a compact in-memory representation of DTs. It is a one-dimensional array representation where links between parent and children tree nodes are explicitly stored next to the node data (testes in internal nodes, classes in leaves, etc.). On the other side, when the complete representation is applied, children positions are calculated based on the parent place. However, it needs a spacious one-dimensional array as if all DT levels would be completely filled, no matter if all nodes actually exist. Experimental validation is performed on real-life and artificial datasets with various sizes and dimensions. Results show that by using the compact representation not only the memory requirements are reduced but also the time of induction is decreased.

Keywords: Evolutionary data mining · Decision trees · Compact in-memory representation · Graphics processing unit (GPU) · CUDA

1 Introduction

Explainable Machine Learning (XML) [2] is a new subfield of Machine Learning (ML) that aims to explain how ML models make predictions. Until recently, most research has focused on the predictive power of algorithms rather than on understanding rationale behind these predictions. The revival in this field reflects, as it were, an interest in and demand for understandable and interpretable methods for real-world applications. A learning model, to qualify as an XML algorithm, should be understandable using concepts related to human intelligence.

Decision trees (DTs) form a class of models that generally fall into the XML category. They are usually induced by top-down greedy methods. Such an induction is usually fast; however, it can lead to sub-optimal solutions [1]. One of the

R. Wyrzykowski et al. (Eds.): PPAM 2022, LNCS 13826, pp. 126–138, 2023.
https://doi.org/10.1007/978-3-031-30442-2_10

alternative approaches is the use of evolutionary algorithms (EAs). The incorporation of EAs into the DT induction allows for global solution-space exploration, leading to better solutions, that is, generated trees are much simpler and at least as accurate as those induced with traditional methods. Moreover, evolutionary induced DTs are less prone to overfitting, instability to changes in training data and attribute-selection bias [14]. At the same time, EA approach in the DT induction brings new challenges. Population-based and iterative calculations may be time-demanding, or even unachievable for big data [1,7,10].

To speed up the evolutionary induction of DTs, different parallel computing approaches were studied [10]. In this paper, we focus on the GPU-supported one that appeared to be the most efficient [6,7]. To boost the induction calculations we investigated different GPU memory layouts and representations, and we would like to propose a compact in-memory representation of DTs. It uses a one-dimensional array where links (corresponding to tree branches) between parent and children nodes are explicitly stored. In comparison to (previous) complete representation, it only holds the nodes that actually exist. There is no need to store all nodes as if all DT levels would be completely filled, no matter if a node really exists. We experimentally show that the compact representation not only saves memory resources but also speeds up the induction further.

The next section gives a brief overview of DTs, the ways of their induction as well as describes the Global Decision Tree (GDT) system that serves as the framework for our solution. Section 3 describes the GPU-boosted solution using the compact in-memory representation. Section 4 provides the evaluation, while Sect. 5 includes the conclusion and possible future works.

2   Background

2.1   Decision Trees

Despite more than 50 years of research [11], DTs are still being developed to address the various challenges they continue to face. They can be used as stand-alone single-tree solutions or as part of larger models such as random forests and gradient boosted DTs. In the latter case, however, it is not possible to speak of XML models, because in the pursuit of greater accuracy, the ease of interpreting and understanding ensemble models has been lost.

A typical DT consists of nodes and branches (see Fig. 1), where: each internal node is associated with a test on one or more attributes; each branch represents a test result, and each leaf (terminal node) contains a prediction [9]. Most tree-inducing algorithms partition the feature space using axis-parallel hyperplanes. Trees of this type are often called univariate because the test at each non-terminal node usually involves a single attribute that is selected according to the given goodness of split. Multivariate tests, which are generally based on linear combinations of many dependent qualities, are also used in some algorithms. The oblique split causes a non-orthogonal hyperplane to partition the feature space in a linear manner. DTs that enable multiple features to be tested

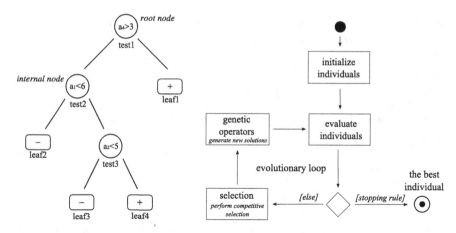

Fig. 1. An example of univariate decision tree.

Fig. 2. Flowchart of the typical evolutionary algorithm.

at a node may be smaller than those confined to single univariate splits, but they have a substantially higher computing cost and are often difficult to interpret.

To make a prediction forecast, the new instance is followed down from a root node to a leaf, with the attribute values of each internal node being used to determine which branch to choose. The terminal node reflects the problem to which the DT is applied. In the case of classification trees, we are concerned with assigning a decision (class label) to each leaf. Typically, this is the class of the majority of all training instances that go into a given leaf. For the regression problem, DT models are used to approximate real-valued functions, so each leaf contains either a constant value or some linear (or nonlinear) regression model.

2.2 Decision Tree Induction

The complexity of inducing an optimal DT is NP-complete [5]. Therefore, heuristic improvements to practical DT learning algorithms are needed [9,11]. One of the major changes proposed in recent years for DTs concerns the induction process which has traditionally relied on a greedy partitioning strategy. Originally, the algorithm starts with a root node where a locally optimal split (test) is searched for based on a given criterion. The training instances are then redirected to the newly constructed nodes, and the procedure is repeated until a stopping condition is satisfied for each node. Furthermore, post-pruning is often used after induction to avoid the problem of over-fitting the training data and to improve the generalization ability of the predictive model. CART and C4.5/5.0 are the two most commonly applied top-down DT inducers.

To limit the impact of local, sub-optimal splits, alternative approaches based on metaheuristics, such as evolutionary algorithms (EAs), have been introduced to the tree induction process [1]. EAs belong to a family of meta-heuristic methods and represent techniques for solving a wide range of difficult optimization problems [12]. The general framework (see Fig. 2) is based on biological evolution mechanisms. The typical EA works on the individuals, gathered in a population, that represent potential solutions to the target problem. In each evolutionary iteration, individuals are:

- transformed with genetic operators such as mutation and crossover that produce new offspring;
- evaluated according to a measure named the fitness function which determines its score;
- selected for reproduction - individuals with better fitness individuals being reproduced more frequently.

When the convergence criteria are met, the evolutionary loop is terminated.

The strength of the evolutionary approach lies in the global search in which tree structure and tests in internal nodes are searched simultaneously. It has been shown that evolutionary induced decision trees offer better suited, more stable, and simpler prediction models [1,10]. Of course, such a global induction is clearly more computationally demanding, but it can reveal underlying patterns that greedy approaches generally miss.

2.3   Global Decision Tree System

The proposed solution has been integrated into a system called the Global Decision Tree (GDT) [10]. The family of algorithms based on the GDT framework is very diverse and addresses almost every aspect related to evolutionary induced DTs like problem domain (classification, regression), tree representation (univariate, oblique, mixed), search (cost-sensitive, Pareto, memetic), real-world application (finance, medicine), parallelization and more [3,8].

GDT's overall structure is based on a typical EA schema [12] with an unstructured population and generational selection. The individuals are represented in their actual form as potential solutions using a tree-encoding schema. Initialization is performed in a simple greedy top-down manner with randomly selected samples of the training data. This way the population is fed with average solutions that should keep an initial balance between exploration and exploitation.

The selection mechanism is based on a ranking linear selection [12] with the elitist strategy, which copies the best individual found so far to the next population. Evolution terminates when a maximum number of generations is reached (default: 10 000) or the fitness of the best individual in the population does not improve during a fixed number of generations (default: 1 000).

To preserve genetic diversity, the GDT system applies two specialized meta-operators corresponding to the classical mutation and crossover. Both operators may have a two-level influence on the individuals as either the decision tree structure or a test in the splitting node can be modified. The type of node (internal, leaf), position in the tree (upper or lower parts), and node prediction error is taken into account to determine the crossover/mutation point. This way low quality nodes (or leaves) in the bottom parts of the tree are modified more

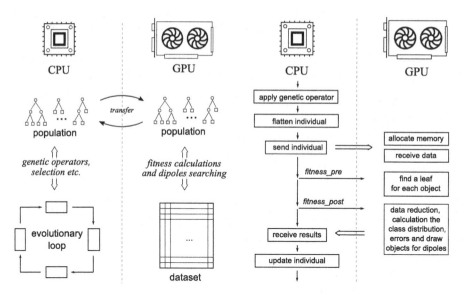

Fig. 3. General idea of the GPU-accelerated evolutionary induction. On the GPU, side the training dataset calculations are performed, while the CPU controls the evolution.

Fig. 4. Flow chart of updating an individual when a genetic operator is applied, including CPU-GPU communication, memory allocation and kernels' execution.

often. GDT offers dozens of specialized variants of crossover/mutations [10], often specific to the DT representation and problem domain, but the generic ones cover: (i) pruning nodes and expanding leaves; (ii) replacing, modifying or exchanging subtrees, branches, nodes, tests. New tests are created according to the dipolar strategy. A dipole is a pair of objects used to find the effective test.

The fitness function controls the accuracy and complexity of each individual. GDT offers various multi-objective optimization strategies [10]. Among them a weighted formula is the most universal one as it maximalizes the following fitness function: $Fitness(T) = Q(T) - \alpha * Complexity(T)$, where: Q(T) is the accuracy calculated on the training set, Complexity(T) is the tree complexity calculated as the sum of leaves and α is the relative importance of the complexity term (default: 0.001) and it is a user-supplied parameter.

3   GPU-Supported Evolution Using Compact In-Memory Representation of Decision Trees

The general idea of the GPU-supported solution (called cuGDT) is illustrated in Fig. 3. The most time-consuming operations (like fitness calculations or searching objects for dipoles, which are directly related to the training dataset) are isolated and delegated to the device [6]. The evolutionary induction is controlled by a CPU. Such a construction of cuGDT ensures that the parallelization does not affect the behavior of the original EA.

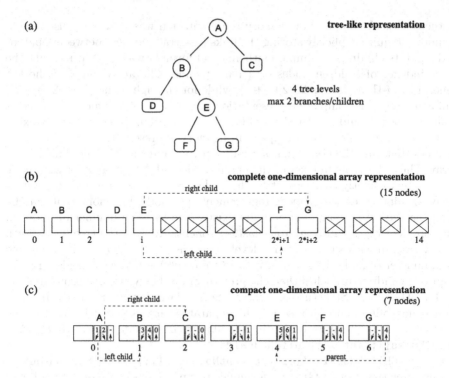

Fig. 5. Complete vs. compact one-dimensional array in-memory representation of a decision tree. Dotted lines indicate sample links between parent and children nodes. In the compact representation, each tree node contains three additional elements: array indexes of the left child, right child and parent nodes. In the complete representation, a parent node and its descendants can be found using the mathematical formula.

The dataset is transferred to the device before the evolution starts and it is kept till the evolutionary induction stops. This transfer time is negligible in relation to the evolution time. It was a conscious design decision to reduce the bottleneck of host/device memory transfers. However, this forced us to perform most of the dataset-related operations on the device, not only related to fitness calculations but also to searching for optimal splits. The CPU does not have direct access to the training dataset, it only receives sample objects to construct dipoles. During the evolution, the transfer between host and device includes sending the individuals to the GPU and sending back the results (class distribution, errors and objects for dipoles) to the CPU.

3.1 In-Memory Representation of Decision Trees

In the evolutionary loop, each time the genetic operator is successfully applied, the GPU is asked to help the CPU (see Fig. 4). Before transferring the modified individual, its flat representation is created based on its tree-like (using pointers) host representation (see Fig. 5). A one-dimensional array is built and then sent to the device. A complete in-memory representation was previously used [6–8]. It did not require explicitly storing the links (as array indexes) between a parent node and its children. A simple mathematical formula was used to indicate the array indexes of children nodes or a parent node. The array index of the left child of the i-th node equals $(2 * i + 1)$, while for the right child, it is $(2 * i + 2)$. Unfortunately, the complete representation imposed to reserve memory space as if all DT levels would be completely filled, no matter if all the nodes really exist.

On the other side, the compact in-memory representation (see Fig. 5(c)) assumes that only the nodes that actually exist are put into the one-dimensional array. Thus, the array indexes of the parent node and descendants for each node have to be explicitly saved (next to the node data, like tests or classes). Obviously, this increases the memory requirements per node, but globally it may be compensated by keeping only actually existing nodes. The number of nodes in the complete representation grows fast, exponentially with the tree level. For a binary tree, in each successive tree level, it equals: $2\hat{}(tree\_level - 1)$, while the total number of nodes is: $2\hat{}(number\_of\_tree\_levels) - 1$. If we considered more than two children/branches then the growth would be even more prominent.

For DTs, the Structure-of-Arrays (SoA) data layout is used. In SoA [16], multi-value data are stored in separated arrays and the arrays are grouped in a structure. In our case, it is `struct DT{float thresholds[];int attributes[]; int leftChildNodesIdx[];` `int rightChildNodesIdx[];int parentNodesIdx[];}`. The SoA layout is usually preferred from a GPU performance perspective because one thread may copy data to cache for other threads (coalesced memory access).

3.2   GPU Kernels Implementation

GPU computations are organized into two kernel functions: $fitness_{pre}$ and $fitness_{post}$ (see Fig. 4). The first kernel calculates the number of objects of each class located in each tree leaf. In addition, two randomly selected objects of each class are provided in each tree leaf. They may be later used to construct dipoles and finally effective tests. However, the results are scattered over separated copies of the individual created for each GPU block.

The $fitness_{post}$ function reduces the partial results collected by each GPU block. When the information about the class distribution is reduced, prediction errors in all leaves are found. Then, the class distribution, estimated errors and selected objects for dipoles are propagated from the leaves towards the tree root. Finally, all the results, in all tree nodes, are sent to the host.

The use of compact representation forced us to modify the way of traversing through DTs, among others. Considering the kernel $fitness_{pre}$, when objects are propagated from the tree root towards the leaves, children nodes are found based on stored indexes in the arrays `int leftChildNodesIdx[]` and `int rightChildNodesIdx[]`. For the $fitness_{post}$ kernel, when the results are propagated from the leaves towards the tree root, parent nodes are found based on

Table 1. Characteristics of the real-life and artificial datasets.

Dataset	No. samples	No. attributes	No. classes
Chess10K	10 000	2	2
Chess100K	100 000	2	2
Chess1M	1 000 000	2	2
Chess10M	10 000 000	2	2
*SDD_2C**	10 639	49	2
*SDD_4C**	21 277	49	4
*SDD_6C**	31 915	49	6
*SDD_8C**	42 553	49	8
*SDD_10C**	53 191	49	10
SDD	58 509	49	11

* Note: A subset of the *SDD* dataset containing objects of first 2, 4, 6, 8 and 10 classes.

the indexes in the array `int parentNodesIdx[]`. The reduction is similar but is performed on less (compact) array elements.

4 Experimental Validation

Validation was performed on both real-life and artificial datasets. The details of each one are presented in Table 1. The artificial dataset, called *Chess*, represents a classification problem with two classes, two real-values attributes and objects arranged on a 3 × 3 chessboard [10]. We used the synthetic dataset to scale it freely (from 10 000 to 10 000 000 objects). Concerning the real-life dataset, *Sensorless Drive Diagnosis (SDD)* from UCI Machine Learning Repository [4] was used. It contains 48 features extracted from the motor current signal and 11 different class labels. To check the solution behavior when the number of classes increases, we extracted from the *SDD* dataset five subsets, containing successively objects of the first 2, 4, 6, 8 and 10 classes. We called them *SDD_2C*, *SDD_4C*, *SDD_6C*, *SDD_8C* and *SDD_10C*.

Experiments were performed using two NVIDIA GPU cards installed on:

- server with two 8-core processors Intel Xeon E5-2620 v4 (20 MB Cache, 2.10 GHz), 256 GB RAM, NVIDIA Tesla P100 GPU card (3 584 CUDA cores and 12 GB of memory);
- server with two 24-Core processors AMD EPYC 7402 (128 MB Cache, 2.80 GHz), 1 TB RAM, NVIDIA Tesla A100 GPU card (13 824 CUDA cores and 40 GB of memory).

Servers run 64-bit Ubuntu Linux 18.04.6 LTS. The original GDT system was implemented in C++ and compiled with the use of gcc version 7.5.0. The GPU-based parallelization was implemented in CUDA-C [15] and compiled by nvcc

Table 2. Mean execution times of sequential, OpenMP and GPU-supported implementations (in seconds). Concerning GPU-supported ones, time for complete and compact in-memory representations of DTs is shown.

Dataset	Sequential	OpenMP	GPU			
			P100		A100	
			Complete	Compact	Complete	Compact
Chess10K	61	14.5	19.2	8.1	14.3	7.3
Chess100K	692	145.3	21.5	10.7	15.2	8.2
Chess1M	23 536	3 605.7	55.9	51.2	25.3	23.8
Chess10M	324 000	47 600.4	641.1	621.7	143.9	142.5
SDD_2C	38	10.7	10.1	8.53	8.9	8.1
SDD_4C	87	27.2	24.7	10.35	12.5	9.5
SDD_6C	411	128.8	119.9	19.74	51.7	12.1
SDD_8C	945	286.4	195.2	33.91	75.8	14.9
SDD_10C	1 984	548.4	420.4	57.64	301.1	27.2
SDD	2 858	766.8	561.2	75.76	447.5	36.1

CUDA 11.6 [13] (single-precision arithmetic was applied). All presented results correspond to averages of 5-10 runs and were obtained with a default set of parameters from the original GDT system [6,10]. As we are focused in this paper only on time and memory resources, results for the classification accuracy are not included (they can be found in [6,10]).

4.1 Results

Table 2 presents the preliminary results for all tested datasets. The mean execution times of cuGDT (using two different GPUs) as well as OpenMP-accelerated and sequential GDT versions (using the Intel CPU server) are shown. It is clearly visible that the use of compact representation gives an additional reduction in the evolution time. Concerning *Chess* dataset, the acceleration is more relevant for smaller datasets. When the number of objects grows, the difference between compact and complete representations becomes less important. The reason can be found when the run-time breakdown is analyzed (see Fig. 6(a,b)). We see that for 10M of objects, the $fitness_{pre}$ kernel dominates (more than 97% of time in both cases). The applied DT in-memory representation has no significant impact on the workload in this kernel. On the other side, for 10K of objects, the $fitness_{post}$ kernel is the most important, and here the representation makes a real difference. The reduction and propagation of results (towards the root node) are done through all elements of the one-dimensional array (representing DT) without any control decision. Thus, in the complete representation, many more operations have to be done.

As regards the *SDD* dataset, the compact representation also reduces the evolution time. However, the improvement grows when the number of classes

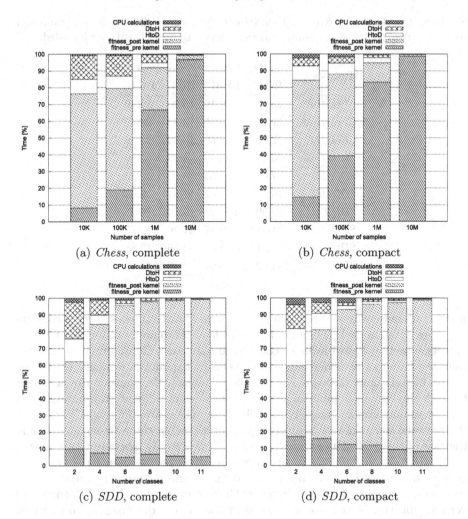

Fig. 6. The run-time breakdown of the GPU-accelerated algorithm using complete and compact in-memory representations of decision trees for NVIDIA Tesla P100 GPU card. The average time (as a percentage of total run-time) of the most relevant parts is shown, both communication between host and device (HtoD, DtoH) and GPU/CPU computations are included.

(and objects) increases. Similarly, the run-time breakdown in Fig. 6(c,d) can be used to explain the solution behavior. The kernel $fitness_{post}$ dominates and the compact representation is more efficient in it (as the reduction is performed on a smaller (compact) array). Another reason can be deduced from the results in Table 3 where the transfer size between the host and device is presented. We see that when the number of classes increases also the size of transfer grows. At the same time, the difference in the size of sent data becomes more important, particularly, for the transfer from the device to the host (transfer of the results).

Table 3. Transfer size in MB for Tesla P100 GPU card. Decision trees sent from host to device (HtoD) as well as results sent from device to host (DtoH) are included.

Dataset	Complete		Compact	
	HtoD	DtoH	HtoD	DtoH
Chess10K	18.05	72.19	15.36	24.49
Chess100K	17.71	70.85	14.83	23.62
Chess1M	17.17	68.68	15.64	24.99
Chess10M	20.07	80.29	14.39	22.99
SDD_2C	7.01	28.05	8.02	12.83
SDD_4C	16.57	115.61	11.81	33.05
SDD_6C	59.99	597.21	19.24	76.95
SDD_8C	71.71	929.37	27.46	142.77
SDD_10C	84.91	1 358.57	34.36	219.88
SDD	134.02	2 338.61	41.16	288.12

If there are more classes, there is a need to send back to the host results containing more data (in each DT node, for each class, the number of located training objects as well as two objects for constructing dipoles). Considering the transfer from the host to the device, the increase can be explained by bigger DTs when the problem is more difficult. For the *Chess* dataset, the transfer size is similar through the various number of objects as it does not influence the problem and DTs of similar size are transferred. Obviously, there are differences in transfer size between compact and complete representations but there are smaller than in the case of the *SDD* dataset as objects in *Chess* are only labeled by two classes.

NVIDIA Tesla A100 GPU card provides better results than P100 GPU one as it is more powerful, both from computational and memory (bandwidth) perspectives. If compared to the sequential GDT or even to its OpenMP-supported version [10], the GPU-boosted GDT is at least one order faster in most cases. cuGDT with the compact representation is always at least a little faster than using the complete one. Moreover, in some cases (8 and more classes), we had to limit the maximum size of DTs able to be processed by a GPU when the complete representation was used. It was the case when very deep DTs with sparsely filled nodes were verified. The memory size needed to store the structure of DTs was quite small, but the results (sent to the host) required too much GPU memory.

5   Conclusion

In this paper, we introduce a compact in-memory representation of DTs into the GPU-supported evolutionary induction. This representation stores explicitly links between parent and children nodes. It required allocating additional memory space for each tree node to save these links. However, in comparison to the (previously used) complete representation, the compact one allowed us to globally decrease both the memory and time resources. It is only a preliminary investigation, and we are conscious that more research is needed, e.g. processing other datasets with different characteristics, checking kernel call settings and deeper profiling. Moreover, our plans include more research on other memory layouts and representations both for training data and DTs.

Acknowledgements. This work was supported by Bialystok University of Technology, Poland under the Grant WZ/WI-IIT/4/2023 founded by Ministry of Science and Higher Education.

References

1. Barros, R.C., Basgalupp, M.P., De Carvalho, A.C., Freitas, A.A.: A survey of evolutionary algorithms for decision-tree induction. IEEE Trans. SMC, Part C **42**(3), 291–312 (2012)
2. Belle, V., Papantonis, I.: Principles and practice of explainable machine learning. Front. Big Data. **4**, 39 (2021)
3. Czajkowski, M., Kretowski, M.: Decision tree underfitting in mining of gene expression data. An evolutionary multi-test tree approach. Expert Syst. Appl. **137**, 392–404 (2019)
4. Dua, D., Karra Taniskidou, E.: UCI machine learning repository (2022). https://archive.ics.uci.edu/ml
5. Hyafil, L., Rivest, R.L.: Constructing optimal binary decision trees is NP-complete. Inf. Process. Lett. **5**(1), 15–17 (1976)
6. Jurczuk, K., Czajkowski, M., Kretowski, M.: Evolutionary induction of a decision tree for large-scale data: a GPU-based approach. Soft. Comput. **21**(24), 7363–7379 (2017)
7. Jurczuk, K., Czajkowski, M., Kretowski, M.: Multi-GPU approach to global induction of classification trees for large-scale data mining. Appl. Intell. **51**(8), 5683–5700 (2021). https://doi.org/10.1007/s10489-020-01952-5
8. Jurczuk, K., Czajkowski, M., Kretowski, M.: GPU-based acceleration of evolutionary induction of model trees. Appl. Soft Comput. **119**, 108503 (2022)
9. Kotsiantis, S.B.: Decision trees: a recent overview. Artif. Intell. Rev. **39**(4), 261–283 (2013)
10. Kretowski, M.: Evolutionary Decision Trees in Large-Scale Data Mining. Springer, Cham (2019). https://doi.org/10.1007/978-3-030-21851-5
11. Loh, W.Y.: Fifty years of classification and regression trees. Int. Stat. Rev. **82**(3), 329–348 (2014)
12. Michalewicz, Z.: Genetic Algorithms + Data Structures = Evolution Programs, 3rd edn. Springer-Verlag, Berlin, Heidelberg (1996). https://doi.org/10.1007/978-3-662-03315-9
13. NVIDIA: NVIDIA Developer Zone - CUDA Toolkit Documentation (2022). https://docs.nvidia.com/cuda/
14. Rivera-Lopez, R., Canul-Reich, J., Mezura-Montes, E., Cruz-Chávez, M.A.: Induction of decision trees as classification models through metaheuristics. Swarm Evol. Comput. **69**, 101006 (2022)

15. Storti, D., Yurtoglu, M.: CUDA for Engineers: An Introduction to High-Performance Parallel Computing. Addison-Wesley, New York (2016)
16. Strzodka, R.: Abstraction for AoS and SoA layout in C++. In: Hwu, W.W. (ed.) GPU Computing Gems Jade Edition, pp. 429–441. Morgan Kaufmann (2012)

Neural Nets with a Newton Conjugate Gradient Method on Multiple GPUs

Severin Reiz[(⊠)][iD], Tobias Neckel[iD], and Hans-Joachim Bungartz[iD]

School of Computation, Information and Technology, Technical University
of Munich (TUM), Munich, Germany
`s.reiz@tum.de`

Abstract. Training deep neural networks consumes increasing computational resource shares in many compute centers. Often, a brute force approach to obtain hyperparameter values is employed. Our goal is (1) to enhance this by enabling second-order optimization methods with fewer hyperparameters for large-scale neural networks and (2) to compare optimizers for specific tasks to suggest users the best one for their problem. We introduce a novel second-order optimization method that requires the effect of the Hessian on a vector only and avoids the huge cost of explicitly setting up the Hessian for large-scale networks.

We compare the proposed second-order method with two state-of-the-art optimizers on five representative neural network problems, including regression and very deep networks from computer vision or variational autoencoders. For the largest setup, we efficiently parallelized the optimizers with Horovod and applied it to a 8 GPU NVIDIA A100 (DGX-1) machine with 80% parallel efficiency.

Keywords: Numerical methods · Machine learning · Deep learning · Second-order optimization · Data parallelism

1 Introduction

Machine Learning (ML) is widely used in todays software world: regression or classification problems are solved to obtain efficient models of input-output relationships learning from measured or simulated data. In the context of scientific computing, the goal of ML frequently is to create surrogate models of similar accuracy than existing models but with evaluation runtimes of much cheaper computational costs. Applying an ML technique typically results in an online vs. an offline phase. While the offline phase comprises all computational steps to create the ML model from given data (the so-called training data), the online phase is associated to obtaining desired answers for new data points (typically called validation points). Different types of ML techniques exist: Neural networks in various forms, Gaussian processes which incorporate uncertainty, etc. [1].

For almost all methods, numerical optimization is necessary to tune parameters or hyperparameters of the corresponding method in the offline phase such

© The Author(s) 2023
R. Wyrzykowski et al. (Eds.): PPAM 2022, LNCS 13826, pp. 139–152, 2023.
https://doi.org/10.1007/978-3-031-30442-2_11

that good/accurate results can be obtained in the online phase. Even though numerical optimization is a comparably mature field that offers many solution approaches, the optimization problem associated with real-world large-scale ML scenarios is non-trivial and computationally very demanding: The dimensionality of the underlying spaces is high, the amount of parameters to be optimized is large to enormous, and the cost function (the loss) is typically mathematically complicated being non-convex and possessing many local optima and saddle points in general. Additionally, the performance of a method typically depends not only on the ML approach but also on the scenario of application.

Of the zoo of different optimization techniques, certain first-order methods such as the stochastic gradient descent (SGD) have been very popular and represent the de-facto fallback in many cases. Higher-order methods provide generally nice convergence features since they include more derivative information of the loss function. These methods, however, come at the price of evaluating the Hessian of the problem, which typically is way too costly for real-world large-scale ML scenarios, both w.r.t. setting up and storing the matrix and w.r.t. evaluating the matrix-vector product with standard implementations (e.g., the ResNet50 scenario discussed below has about 16 million degrees of freedom in form of corresponding weights).

In this paper, we analyze a second-order Newton-based optimization method w.r.t. accuracy and computational performance in the context of large-scale neural networks of different type. To cope with challenging costs in such scenarios, we implemented a special variant of a regularized Newton method using the Pearlmutter scheme together with a matrix-free conjugate gradient method to evaluate the effect of the Hessian on a given vector with about twice the costs of a backpropagation itself. All implementations are publicly available and easy to integrate since they rely on TensorFlow Keras code[1]. We compare our proposed solution with existing TensorFlow implementations of the prominent SGD and Adam method for five representative ML scenarios of different categories. In particular, we exploit parallelisation in the optimization process on two different levels: a parallel execution of runs the as well as data parallelism by treating several chunks of data (the so-called batches or mini batches) in parallel. The latter results in a quasi-Newton method where the effect of the Hessian is kept constant for a couple of data points before the next update is computed. Our approach, thus, represents a combination of usability, accuracy and efficiency.

The remainder of this paper is organized as follows. Section 2 lists work in the community that is related to our approach. In Sect. 3, basic aspects of deep neural networks are briefly stated to fix the nomenclature for the algorithmic building blocks we combine for our method. The detailed neural network structures and architectures for the five scenarios to be discussed are discussed in Sect. 4. We briefly describe aspects of the implementation in Sect. 5 and show results for the five neural network scenarios in Sect. 6. Section 7 finally concludes the discussion.

---

[1] https://github.com/severin617/Newton-CG.

2 Related Work

Hessian multiplication for neural networks without forming the matrix was introduced very early [2]; while there are multiple optimization techniques around [3], it gained importance again with *Deep Learning via Hessian-free optimization* [4]. Later, the Kronecker-factored approximate curvature (KFAC) of the Fisher matrix(similar to Gauss-Newton Hessian) was introduced [5]; for *high performance computing*, chainerkfac was introduced [6]. AdaHessian uses the Hutchinson method for adapting learning rate [7], other work involves inexact newton methods for neural networks [8] or a comparison of optimizers [9]. With GOFMM, we performed initial studies on Hessian matrices [10], where later we looked at the fast approximation for a multilayer perceptron [11].

3 Methods

In this section, we first briefly describe the basics of deep neural networks[2] and the peculiarities of the variants we are going to use in the five different scenarios in Sect. 6. Afterwards, we highlight the basic algorithmic ingredients of the reference implementations (SGD and Adam) [1]. Finally, we explain the building blocks of our approach: The Pearlmutter trick and the Newton-CG step.

3.1 Scientific Computing for Deep Learning

Consider a feed-forward deep neural network defined as the parameterized function $f(X, \mathbf{W})$. The function f is composed by vector-valued functions $f^{(i)}$, $i = 1, \ldots, D$, which represent each one layer in the network of depth D, in the following way: $f(x) = f^{(D)}(\ldots f^{(2)}(f^{(1)}(x)))$

The function corresponding to a network layer (d) and the output of the j-th neuron are computed via

$$
f^{(d)} = \begin{bmatrix} z_1^{(d)} \\ z_2^{(d)} \\ \vdots \\ z_{M^{(d)}}^{(d)} \end{bmatrix} \text{ and } z_j^{(d)} = \phi\left(\sum_{i=1}^{M^{(d-1)}} (w_{ji}^{(d)} f_i^{(d-1)}) + w_j^0 \right)
$$

with activation function ϕ and weights w. All weights w are comprised in a large vector $\mathbf{W} \in \mathbb{R}^n$ which represents a parameter for f. The optimization problem consists now of finding weights $\mathbf{W}$ a given loss function l will be minimized for given training samples X, Y: $\min_{\mathbf{W}} l(X, Y, \mathbf{W})$.

A prominent example of a loss function is the categorical cross-entropy:

$$
l_{entr}(X, Y, \mathbf{W}) := - \sum_{l=1}^{N} y_i \log(f^{(D)}(X, \mathbf{W})) .
$$

---

[2] For a brief introduction on deep NN, cf. [12].

Note that only the last layer function $f^{(D)}$ of the network directly shows up in the loss, but all layers are indirectly relevant due to the optimization for all weights in all layers.

Optimizers look at stochastic *mini batches* of data, i.e. disjoint collections of data points. The union of all mini batches will represent the whole training data set. The reason for considering data in chunks of mini batches and not in total is that the backpropagation in larger neural networks will face severe issues w.r.t. memory. Hence, the mini batch loss function, where the mini batch is varied in each optimization step in a round-robin manner, is now defined by

$$L(x, y, \mathbf{W}) := - \sum_{i=1}^{\text{batch-size}} y_i \log(f^{(D)}(X, \mathbf{W})) \ .$$

3.2 State-of-the-Art Optimization Approaches

In order to solve the optimization problem (3.1), different first-order methods exist (for a survey, see [1], e.g.). The pure *gradient descent* without momentum computes weights $\mathbf{W}_k$ in iteration k via $\mathbf{W}_k = \mathbf{W}_{k-1} - a_{k-1}\nabla l(\mathbf{W}_{k-1})$ where $\nabla l(\mathbf{W}_{k-1})$ denotes the gradient of the total loss l w.r.t. the weights $\mathbf{W}$.

The *stochastic gradient descent* method (SGD) includes stochasticity by changing the loss function to the input of a specific mini batch of data, i.e. using L instead of l. Each mini batch of data provides a noisy estimator of the average gradient over all data points, hence the term stochastic. Technically, this is realised by switching the mini batches in a round-robin manner to reach over the full dataset (one full sweep is called an epoch; frequently, more than one epoch of iterations is necessary to achieve quality in the optimization).

The family of *Adam* methods updates weight values by enhancing averages of the gradient s_k with estimates of the 1st moment (the mean) and the 2nd raw moment (the uncentered variance). The approach called *AdaGrad* is directly using these estimators:

$$W_{k+1} = W_k - \alpha_k \frac{s_k}{\delta + \sqrt{r_k}} \tag{1}$$

The Adam method corrects for the biases in the estimators by using the estimators $\hat{s_k} = \frac{s_k}{1-\beta_1^k}$ and $\hat{r_k} = \frac{r_k}{1-\beta_2^k}$ instead of s_k and r_k. Good default settings for the tested machine learning problems described in this paper are $a_0 = 0.001$, $\beta_1 = 0.9$, $\beta_2 = 0.999$, and $\delta = 10^{-8}$.

3.3 Proposed 2nd-Order Optimizer

The second-order optimizer implemented and used for the results of this work consists of a Newton scheme with a matrix-free conjugate gradient (CG) solver for the linear systems of equations arising in each Newton step. The effect of the Hessian on a given vector (i.e. a matrix-vector multiplication result) is realised via the so-called Pearlmutter approach and avoids setting up the Hessian explicitly.

Pearlmutter Approach. The explicit setup of the Hessian is memory-expensive due to the quadratic dendence on the problem size; e.g., a 16M×16M matrix requires about 1 TB of memory. We can obtain "cheap" access to the problems curvature information by computing the Hessian-vector product. This method is called Fast Exact Multiplication by the Hessian H (see [2], e.g.). Specifically, it computes the Hessian vector product Hs for any s in just **two** (instead of the number of weights n) backpropagations (i.e. automatic differentiations for 1st derivative components). For our formulation of the problem this is defined as:

$$H_L(\mathbf{W})s = \begin{pmatrix} \sum_{i=1}^{n} s_i \frac{\delta^2}{\delta w_1 \delta w_i} L(\mathbf{W}) \\ \sum_{i=1}^{n} s_i \frac{\delta^2}{\delta w_2 \delta w_i} L(\mathbf{W}) \\ \vdots \\ \sum_{i=1}^{n} s_i \frac{\delta^2}{\delta w_n \delta w_i} L(\mathbf{W}) \end{pmatrix} = \begin{pmatrix} \frac{\delta}{\delta w_1} \sum_{i=1}^{n} s_i \frac{\delta}{\delta w_i} L(\mathbf{W}) \\ \frac{\delta}{\delta w_2} \sum_{i=1}^{n} s_i \frac{\delta}{\delta w_i} L(\mathbf{W}) \\ \vdots \\ \frac{\delta}{\delta w_n} \sum_{i=1}^{n} s_i \frac{\delta}{\delta w_i} L(\mathbf{W}) \end{pmatrix} = \nabla_w (\nabla_w L(\mathbf{W}) \cdot s)$$

The resulting formula is both efficient and numerically stable [2]. This results in the Algorithm 1, denoted **Pearlmutter** in the implementation.

Newton's Method. Recall the Newton equation

$$H_L(\mathbf{W}^k)d^k = -\nabla L(\mathbf{W}^k)$$

for the network loss function $L : \mathbb{R}^n \to \mathbb{R}$, where $\mathbf{W}$ is the vector of network weights and $\mathbf{W}^k$ the current iterate of Newton's method to solve for the update vector d^k. The size of the Hessian is $\mathbb{R}^{n \times n}$ which becomes infeasible to store with state-of-the-art weight parameter ranges of ResNets (or similar).

Since frequently the Hessian has a high condition number, which implies near-singularity and provokes imprecision, one would apply regularization techniques to counteract a bad condition. A common choice is Tikhonov regularization. To this end, a multiple of the unit matrix is added to the Hessian of the loss function such that the regularized system is given by

$$(H(\mathbf{W}^k) + \tau I)d^k = H(\mathbf{W}^k)d^k + \tau I d^k = -\nabla L(\mathbf{W}^k) \qquad (2)$$

Note that for large τ the solution will converge to a fraction of the negative gradient $\nabla L(\mathbf{W}^k)$, similar to a stochastic gradient descent method. The regularized Newton method is summarized in Algorithm 2.

Algorithm 1. Pearlmutter

Require: $X, Y, \mathbf{W}, s$:   Compute $H_L s = \nabla_w (\nabla_w L(\mathbf{W}) \cdot s)$
Require: W_0:   Initial estimate for $\mathbf{W}$.
1: $g_0 \leftarrow$ gradient$(L(\mathbf{W}))$ ▷ Back-Prop
2: intermediate $\leftarrow$ matmul(g_0, s) ▷ Matrix-Multiplication
3: $Hs \leftarrow$ gradient(intermediate)   ▷ Back-Prop
4: **return** Hs

Algorithm 2. Newton Step

Require: $\mathbf{W}_0$:   Starting point
Require: τ: Tikhonov regularization/damping factor
 1: $k \leftarrow 0$
 2: **while** $\mathbf{W}_k$ not converged **do**
 3:     $k \leftarrow k + 1$
 4:     $p_k \leftarrow \mathtt{CG}((H + \tau I), -\nabla L(\mathbf{W}_k))$ # Approx $(H + \tau I) p_k = -\nabla L(\mathbf{W}_k)$
 5:     **if** $\nabla L(\mathbf{W}_k)^\top p_k > \tau$ **then** $p_k \leftarrow -\nabla L(\mathbf{W}_k)$ # Feasibility check.
 6:     **end if**
 7:     $\alpha_k \leftarrow \alpha$ # Compute with lr-scheduler or use a given step size.
 8:     $\mathbf{W}_k \leftarrow \mathbf{W}_{k-1} + \alpha_k p_k$
 9: **end while**

Conjugate Gradient Step. Since **Pearlmutter** realises a matrix-vector product without setting up the full matrix, we employ an iterative solver that requires matrix products only. We therefore employ a few (inaccurate) $\mathtt{CG}$-iterations to solve Newton's regularized Eq. (2), resulting in an approximated Newton method. The standard $\mathtt{CG}$-algorithm is e.g. described in [13]; note that no direct matrix-access is required since $\mathtt{CG}$ relies only on products of vectors.

Complexity: The method described above requires $O(bn)$ operations for the evaluation of the gradient, where n is the number of network weights and b is the size of the mini batch. In addition, for the evaluation of the Hessian product and the solution of the Newton-like equation $O(2mbn)$ is needed, where m is the number of iterations conducted by the $\mathtt{CG}$ solver until a sufficient approximation to the solution is reached. Although the second-order optimizer requires more work than ordinary gradient descent, it may still be beneficial since, under the conditions that it promises local q-superlinear convergence, where $\mathbf{W}^\star$ is a local minimizer (see [14]), i.e. $\exists\, \gamma \in (0,1), l \geq 0$, such that

$$||\mathbf{W}^{k+1} - \mathbf{W}^*|| \leq \gamma ||\mathbf{W}^k - \mathbf{W}^*|| \quad \forall k > l .$$

4   Scenarios and Neural Network Architectures

In this section, we briefly outline the different neural network structures for the five different ML scenarios used in Sect. 6. Those networks share the general structure outlined in Sect. 3.1 but differ in details considerably.

Regressional Analysis: Most regression models connect the input X with some parametric function f to the output Y, including some error ϵ, i.e. $Y = f(X, \beta) + \epsilon$. The goal is find $\mathbf{W}$ to minimize the loss function which here is the sum of the squared error for all samples i in the training data set

$$l = \sum_{i=1}^{N} (y_i - f(x_i, \mathbf{W}))^2 .$$

Variational Autoencoder: A variational autoencoder (VAE) consists of two coupled but independently parametrized components: The encoder compresses the sampled input X into the latent space. The decoder receives as input the information sampled from the latent space and produces x' as close as possible to X. In a variational autoencoder, encoder and decoder are trained simultaneously such that output X' minimizes a reconstruction error to X by the Kullback-Leibler divergence. For details on VAEs, see [15], e.g.

Bayesian Neural Network: One of the biggest challenges in all areas of machine learning is deciding on an appropriate model complexity. Models with too low complexity will not fit the data well, while models possessing high complexity will generalize poorly and provide bad prediction results on unseen data, a phenomenon widely known as overfitting. Two commonly deployed strategies to counteract this problem are hold-out or cross-validation on one hand, where part of the data is kept from training in order to optimize hyperparameters of the respective model that correspond to model complexity, and controlling the effective complexity of the model by inducing a penalty term on the loss function on the other hand. The latter approach is known as regularization and can be implemented by applying Bayesian techniques on neural networks [16].

Let $\theta, \epsilon \sim N(0,1)$ be random variables, $w = t(\theta, \epsilon)$, where t is a deterministic function. Moreover, let $w \sim q(w|\theta)$ be normally distributed. Then our optimization task where the loss function l is the log-likelihood reads [17]

$$l(w, \theta) = \log q(w|\theta) - \log P(D|w) - \log P(w) .$$

Convolutional Neural Network (CNN): In general, the convolution is an operation on two functions I, K, defined by

$$S(t) = (I * K)(t) = \int I(a)K(t-a)da .$$

If we use a 2D image I as input with a 2D kernel K, we obtain a two-dimensional discrete convolution $S(i,j) = (I * K)(i,j) = \sum_x \sum_y I(x,y)K(i-x, j-y)$.

Color images additionally have at least a channel for red, blue and green intensity at each pixel position. Assume that each image is a 3D-tensor and $V_{i,j,k}$ describes the value of channel i at row j and column k. Then let our kernel be a 4D-tensor with $K_{l,i,j,k}$ denoting the connection strength (weight) between a unit in input channel i and output channel l at an offset of k rows and l columns between input and output. CNNs apply, besides other incredients, convolution kernels of different size in different layers in a sliding window approach to extract features. For a brief introduction to CNN, see [12], e.g. As an example, the prominent ResNet 50 network structure consists of 50 layers of convolutions or other layers, with *skip connections* to avoid the problem of diminishing gradients.

Transfer Learning: Transfer learning (TL) deals with applying already gained knowledge for generalization to a different, but related domain [18]. Creating a separate, labeled dataset of sufficient size for a specific task of interest in the context of image classification is a time-consuming and resource-intensive process. Consequently, we find ourselves working with sets of training data that are significantly smaller than other renowned datasets, such as CIFAR and Ima-geNet [19]. Moreover, the training process itself is time-consuming too and relies on dedicated hardware. Since modern CNNs take around 2–3 weeks to train on ImageNet in a professional environment, starting this process from scratch for every single model is hardly efficient. Therefore, general pretrained networks are typically used which are then tailored to specific inputs.

5   Implementation

5.1   Automatic Differentiation Framework

The `Newton-CG` optimization strategy is independent of the implementation, and of course, is suitable in any setting where second-order is beneficial **(1)** and stor-ing Hessians is infeasible w.r.t. memory consumption **(2)**. However, one needs a *differentiation* framework. During the course of the work, a custom auto-encoder (and similar) implementation with optimized matrix operations [10] became dif-ficult w.r.t. the automatic differentiation (especially with convolutions), so we decided to move to a prominent framework, *TensorFlow*. The TensorFlow pro-gramming model consists of two main steps: (1) Define computations in form of a "stateful dataflow graph" and (2) execute this graph. At the heart of model training in TensorFlow lies the optimizer; like `Adam` or `SGD`, `newton-cg` uses inheritance from the class `tf.python.keras.optimizer_v2.Optimizer_v2`. The base class handles the two main steps of optimization: `compute_gradients()` and `apply_gradients()`. When applying the gradients, for each variable that is optimized, the method `resource_compute_dense(grad, var)` is called with the variable and its (earlier computed) gradient. In this method, the algorithm update step for this variable is computed. It has to be overwritten by any sub-classing optimizer. We implemented two versions of our optimizer: one inheriting from the optimizer in tf.train and one inheriting from the Keras Optimizer_v2. The constructor accepts the learning rate as well as the `Newton-CG` hyperparam-eters: regularization factor τ, the `CG`-convergence-tolerance and the maximum number of CG iterations. Internally, the parameters are converted to tensors and stored as python object attributes. The main logic happens in the above men-tioned `resource_compute_dense(grad, var)` method[3]. Table 1 lists the five ML scenarios and their implementation used to generate the results below.

5.2   Data Parallelism

In order to show the applicability of the proposed second-order optimizer for real-world large-scale networks, it was necessary to parallelize optimization com-putations to obtain suitable runtimes. We decided to use the comparably simple and prominent strategy of data parallelism. Data-parallel strategies t distribute data across different compute units, and each unit operates on the data in par-allel. So in our setting, we compute different Newton-CG steps on i different

---

[3] See the implementation in https://github.com/severin617/Newton-CG/blob/main/newton_cg/newton_cg.py#L127.

Table 1. Five ML scenarios with different neural network structures.

Scenario	Description
reg-lif	one-layer life expectancy prediction[a]
reg-bos	two-layer boston housing price projection with keras [b]
vae-mnist	variational autoencoder from Keras [c]
bnn-mnist	Bayesian neural network with tensorflow-probability[d] [20]
resnet	ResNet architecture from Keras [e]

[a]https://valueml.com/predicting-the-life-expectancy-using-tensorflow/.
[b]https://www.kaggle.com/code/prasadperera/the-boston-housing-dataset.
[c]https://keras.io/examples/generative/vae/.
[d]https://www.tensorflow.org/probability/.
[e]https://www.tensorflow.org/api_docs/python/tf/keras/applications/resnet50/ResNet50.

mini-batches in parallel, and the resulting update vectors are accumulated using an Allreduce. Note that this is different to e.g. a i-times as big batch or i-times as many steps since this would use an updated weight when computing gradient information via backpropagations. In a smoothly defined function, this could converge to a similar minimum, however due to stochasticity this may not.

Horovod is a data-parallel distributed training framework (open source) for TensorFlow, Keras, PyTorch, and Apache MXNet, that scales a training script up to many GPUs using MPI [21]. We apply Horovod for the data parallelisation of the second-order Newton-CG approach. In a second step the whole algorithms could be parallelized, this would then be model parallelism. The following matrix summarizes the data and model parallelism in the context of neural network optimization.

Data parallelism	Model parallelism
Operations performed on different batches of data	Parallel operations performed on same data (in identical batch)

5.3 Software and Hardware Setup

Training with Keras and Horovod was used to show applicability and scalability of the proposed second order optimization. The ResNets for computer vision were pretrained for 200 epochs to improve second-order convergence, see Fig. 1 (f), with training data from the Imagenet Large Scale Visual Recognition Challenge 2012 (ILSVRC2012)[4]. Test runs were performed on the *Leibniz Rechenzentrum (LRZ)* AI System DGX-1 A100 Architecture with 8 NVIDIA Tesla A100 and 80 GB per GPU.

[4] Following parameters were utilized in the pretraining: training/val-batch-size: 64, learning-rate: 0.001, momentum: 0.9, weight-decay: 0.00005. After each step, ten validation steps were used to calculate the top_5 accuracy, resulting in a final loss of 4.5332 and a final top_5 accuracy of 0.6800 after 2e5 steps.

6 Results

6.1 Accuracy Results for Different Scenarios

In this study, we applied the Newton-CG method as well as the two state-of-the-art methods SGD and Adam for the five different network architectures and specific scenarios described in Sect. 4 and Table 1 to evaluate the performance for each case and obtain insight into potential patterns. We show the detailed optimization behavior in Fig. 1 while the final validation loss optimum is summarized in Fig. 2. A similar comparison figure was used in [9] highlighting a similar insight that it is hard to predict the performance of different optimizers for considerably different scenarios.

One can observe significant benefits of the 2nd-order Newton-CG in regression models, be it the life expectancy prediction or the boston housing data regression. We believe this is mostly due to the continuity in loss/optimization, whereas in the other scenarios this could jump, due to mini batches and classification.

The variatonal autoencoder seems to work better with the conventional optimizers. Our hope was that due to the continuous behaviour we may see some benefits. However, this is also very hyper-parameter dependent, and the conventional methods have to be considerably tuned for that. In the Bayesian Neural Network we see benefits of Newton-CG especially against Adam.

We observe hardly any benefits of 2nd-order optimization for the ResNet50 model. While at first we follow the near-optimal training curve, Newton-CG moves away from the minimum. One problem could be that we work with a fixed learning rate. This could be tuned with a *learning-rate-scheduler*, which we currently work on.

6.2 Parallel Runs

Exploiting parallelism allows for distributing work in case of failures (e.g. resilience), usage of modern compute architectures with accelerators, and ultimately, lower *time-to-solution*. All network architectures shown before can be run in parallel, in the data parallel approach explained in Sect. 5.2.

For the following measurements, we ran the ResNet50 model on the DGX-1 partition of the *LRZ*, since it is our biggest network model and therefore, allows for the biggest parallelism gains (see Table 2).[5] Note that the batch size is reduced with *GPUs*, in order to account for a similar problem to be solved when increasing the amount of *workers*. However, it cannot be fully related to *strong scaling*, since the algorithm changes as explained in Sect. 5. In a parallel setup, the loss is calculated for a smaller *mini-batch* and then the *update* is accumulated. This is different to looking at a bigger *batch*, since the loss function is a different one (computed for *mini-batch* per *GPU* only).

---

[5] On the LRZ cluster, we had to reduce to 20% training images for lower memory disk usage and 60% of the optimization layers, 30 layers for ResNet-50.

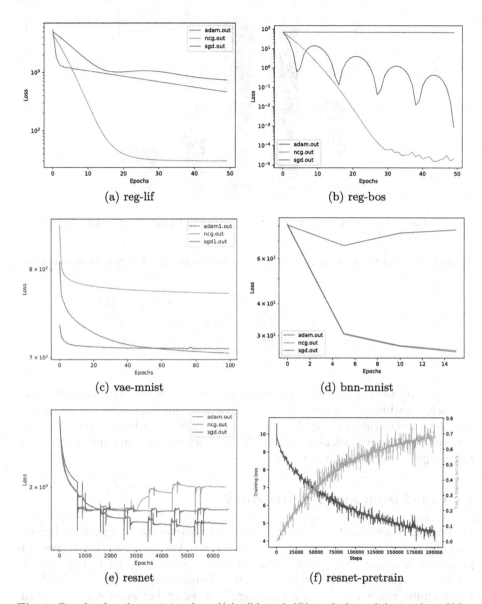

Fig. 1. Results for the training loss ((a), (b) and (f)) and the validation loss ((c)–(e)) for the three compared methods: SGD in green, Adam in blue and Newton-CG in orange. The methods have been applied to the five different ML scenarios with corresponding different neural network structure: (a) regression case for life expectancy prediction, (b) regression for boston housing dataset, (c) Variational Auto Encoder with MNIST, (d) Bayesian Neural Network with MNIST, (e) ResNet50 with ImageNet, and (f) the corresponding sgd pretraining run ("steps" corresponds to epochs). (Color figure online)

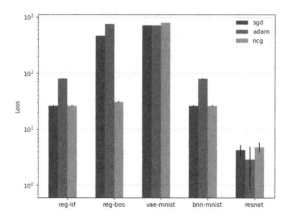

Fig. 2. Final loss value of each optimizer for the five different neural network architectures and scenarios.

Table 2. Newton-CG runtimes per epoch with batch-size 512, ResNet-50 on ImageNet

	1 GPU	2 GPUs	4 GPUs	8 GPUs
A100 runtime	238 s	121 s	65 s	37 s
A100 parallel efficiency	100%	98.3%	91.5%	80.4%

Similarly, we conducted the performance study on a single GPU for the two other optimizers. *SGD* and *Adam* take 238 s and 242 s per epoch, resp., showing similar runtimes as *Newton-CG* with 238 s. We believe that for this big scenario the runtime is dominated by memory transfer and the one vs. two backpropagations hardly makes a difference.

7   Conclusion and Future Work

In conclusion, we found benefits of second-order curvature information plugged into the optimization of the neural network weights especially for regression cases, but not much benefits in classification scenarios. In order to improve for classification, we experimented with a cyclical learning rate scheduler for ResNets for computer vision and Natural Language Processing, but more studies need to be investigated. The data-parallel approach seems to work well in performance numbers, since we reach about 80% parallel efficiency for 8 A100 GPUs.

For showcasing purposes, you may also try the frontend android application TUM-lens[6], where some models have been trained with Newton-CG.

---

[6] https://play.google.com/store/apps/details?id=com.maxjokel.lens.

References

1. Goodfellow, I., Bengio, Y., Courville, A.: Deep Learning. MIT Press, Cambridge (2016). http://www.deeplearningbook.org
2. Pearlmutter, B.A.: Fast exact multiplication by the Hessian. Neural Comput. **6**(1), 147–160 (1994)
3. Nocedal, J., Wright, S.J.: Numerical Optimization. Springer, Heidelberg (1999)
4. Martens, J., et al.: Deep learning via Hessian-free optimization. In: ICML, vol. 27, pp. 735–742 (2010)
5. Martens, J.: Second-order optimization for neural networks. University of Toronto (Canada) (2016)
6. Osawa, K., Tsuji, Y., Ueno, Y., Naruse, A., Yokota, R., Matsuoka, S.: Large-scale distributed second-order optimization using kronecker-factored approximate curvature for deep convolutional neural networks. In: Proceedings of the IEEE/CVF Conference on Computer Vision and Pattern Recognition, pp. 12359–12367 (2019)
7. Yao, Z., Gholami, A., Shen, S., Mustafa, M., Keutzer, K., Mahoney, M.W.: Adahessian: an adaptive second order optimizer for machine learning. arXiv preprint arXiv:2006.00719 (2020)
8. O'Leary-Roseberry, T., Alger, N., Ghattas, O.: Inexact newton methods for stochastic nonconvex optimization with applications to neural network training. arXiv preprint arXiv:1905.06738 (2019)
9. Schmidt, R.M., Schneider, F., Hennig, P.: Descending through a crowded valley-benchmarking deep learning optimizers. In: International Conference on Machine Learning, pp. 9367–9376. PMLR (2021)
10. Chenhan, D.Y., Reiz, S., Biros, G.: Distributed-memory hierarchical compression of dense SPD matrices. In: SC 2018: International Conference for High Performance Computing, Networking, Storage and Analysis, pp. 183–197. IEEE (2018)
11. Chen, C., Reiz, S., Yu, C.D., Bungartz, H.-J., Biros, G.: Fast approximation of the Gauss-Newton Hessian matrix for the multilayer perceptron. SIAM J. Matrix Anal. Appl. **42**(1), 165–184 (2021)
12. Lecun, Y., Bengio, Y., Hinton, G.: Deep learning. Nature **521**(7553), 436 (2015)
13. Shewchuk, J.R., et al.: An introduction to the conjugate gradient method without the agonizing pain (1994)
14. Suk, J.: Application of second-order optimisation for large-scale deep learning. Masterarbeit, TUM (2020)
15. Kingma, D.P., Welling, M.: An introduction to variational autoencoders. Found. Trends® Mach. Learn. **12**(4), 307–392 (2019)
16. Bishop, C.M., et al.: Neural Networks for Pattern Recognition. Oxford University Press, Oxford (1995)
17. Blundell, C., Cornebise, J., Kavukcuoglu, K., Wierstra, D.: Weight uncertainty in neural network. In: International Conference on Machine Learning, pp. 1613–1622. PMLR (2015)
18. Yosinski, J., Clune, J., Bengio, Y., Lipson, H.: How transferable are features in deep neural networks? In: Advances in Neural Information Processing Systems, vol. 27 (2014)
19. Krizhevsky, A., Hinton, G., et al.: Learning multiple layers of features from tiny images. Master's thesis, University of Tront (2009)
20. Weigold, H.: Second-order optimization methods for Bayesian neural networks. Masterarbeit, Technical University of Munich (2021)
21. Sergeev, A., Del Balso, M.: Horovod: fast and easy distributed deep learning in TensorFlow. arXiv preprint arXiv:1802.05799 (2018)

Performance Analysis and Prediction in HPC Systems

Exploring Techniques for the Analysis of Spontaneous Asynchronicity in MPI-Parallel Applications

Ayesha Afzal[1]([✉]) [iD], Georg Hager[1] [iD], Gerhard Wellein[1,2] [iD],
and Stefano Markidis[3] [iD]

[1] Erlangen National High Performance Computing Center (NHR@FAU),
91058 Erlangen, Germany
{ayesha.afzal,georg.hager,gerhard.wellein}@fau.de
[2] Department of Computer Science, University of Erlangen-Nürnberg,
91058 Erlangen, Germany
[3] Department of Computer Science, KTH Royal Institute of Technology,
11428 Stockholm, Sweden
markidis@kth.se

Abstract. This paper studies the utility of using data analytics and machine learning techniques for identifying, classifying, and characterizing the dynamics of large-scale parallel (MPI) programs. To this end, we run microbenchmarks and realistic proxy applications with the regular compute-communicate structure on two different supercomputing platforms and choose the per-process performance and MPI time per time step as relevant observables. Using principal component analysis, clustering techniques, correlation functions, and a new "phase space plot," we show how desynchronization patterns (or lack thereof) can be readily identified from a data set that is much smaller than a full MPI trace. Our methods also lead the way towards a more general classification of parallel program dynamics.

Keywords: Parallel distributed computing · Data analytic techniques · Machine learning techniques · Asynchronous MPI execution · Scalability and bottleneck

1 Introduction and Related Work

Highly parallel MPI programs with no or weak global synchronization points show interesting dynamics that go beyond what is expected from their usually regular compute-communicate structure. Initiated by what is typically called "noise," a plethora of patterns can emerge: Propagating delays emanating from strong one-off disturbances, so-called *idle waves* [10], can interact [1] and eventually decay [1–3] via various mechanisms. Caused by idle waves, but also under

R. Wyrzykowski et al. (Eds.): PPAM 2022, LNCS 13826, pp. 155–170, 2023.
https://doi.org/10.1007/978-3-031-30442-2_12

the natural, fine-grained system noise, some applications are unstable and leave their initial lock-step mode (Fig. 2 (left)) where all processes either compute or communicate. It was shown [2,5] that a hardware bottleneck such as main memory bandwidth is a prerequisite for this *bottleneck evasion* to occur. As a consequence, such programs settle in a metastable state, a *computational wavefront*, where neighboring processes are shifted in time with respect to each other (Fig. 2 (right)). It was also shown [4] that this *desynchronization* can lead to substantial speedups via automatic overlap of communication and code execution.

Investigating these dynamics typically requires the analysis of MPI traces taken by tools such as Intel Trace Analyzer/Collector or VAMPIR. Apart from the often prohibitive amount of data contained in such traces, the relevant patterns are often hidden in the data and not readily visible to the human eye. Furthermore, it is hard, if not impossible, to obtain this data in a production environment without adverse effects on the performance of applications. For applications that have natural regular compute-communicate cycles, we propose to use the MPI waiting time per process and time step (i.e., the time spent in the MPI library, regardless of whether communication takes place or not) as a starting point and input metric for data analysis methods that can identify the structural processes described above. The performance per process and time step can serve as a supplemental metric to track the impact of automatic communication overlap.

This paper makes the following relevant contributions:

- We demonstrate how to automatically characterize different flavors of synchronous versus non-synchronous execution of MPI-parallel codes without taking full MPI traces or in-depth application analysis.
- We show that the MPI waiting time per process and time step provides a powerful input metric for principal component analysis (PCA) and clustering methods in order to spot these patterns.
- We introduce the *MPI phase space plot* as a tool to visualize the long-term evolution and peculiar patterns of MPI waiting time in a parallel program.

This paper is organized as follows: We first provide details about our experimental environment and methodology in Sect. 2. To investigate the dynamics of large-scale parallel programs, simple metrics such as the histogram and timelines for all or individual MPI processes are studied in Sect. 3, while Sect. 4 covers advanced methods like correlation coefficient matrices and phase space plots. Sect. 5 addresses machine learning techniques such as Principal Component analysis and k-means clustering. Finally, Sect. 6 concludes the paper and gives an outlook to future work.

2   Case Studies, Testbed and Experimental Methods

Table 1. Key hardware and software properties of systems.

	Systems	Meggie	Fritz
Micro-architecture	Processor	Intel Xeon Broadwell EP	Intel Xeon Ice Lake
	Processor Model	E5-2630 v4	Platinum 8360Y
	Base clock speed	2.2 GHz	2.4 GHz
	Physical cores per node	20	72
	Numa domains per node	2	4
	Last-level cache (LLC) size	25 MB (L3)	54MB (L3)
	Memory per node (type)	64 GB (DDR4)	256 GB (DDR4)
	Theor. memory bandwidth	68.3 GB/s	102.4 GB/s
Network	Node interconnect	Omni-Path	Infiniband
	Interconnect topology	Fat-tree	Fat-tree
	Raw bandwidth p. lnk n. dir	100 Gbit s^{-1}	100 Gbit s^{-1}
Software	Compiler	Intel C++ v2019.5.281	intel C++ v2021.4.0
	Message passing library	Intel MPI v2019u5	intelmpi/2021.4.0
	Operating system	CentOS Linux v7.7.1908	AlmaLinux v8.5 rhel centos fedora

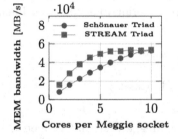

Fig. 1. Saturation attributes

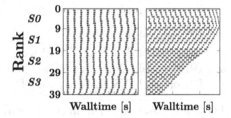

Fig. 2. Timeline traces of synchronized (left) and desynchronized (right) MPI processes on sockets (Si).

2.1   Test Systems and Methodology

The details of the hardware and software environments on the "Meggie"[1] and "Fritz"[2] clusters can be found in Table 1. By default, hyper-threading (SMT) is disabled on both systems and Sub-NUMA Clustering (SNC) is enabled on the Fritz system. The optimization flag -O3 was utilized with the Intel compiler. Process-core affinity was enforced using the I_MPI_PIN_PROCESSOR_LIST environment variable. The clock frequency was always fixed to the base value

---

[1] https://hpc.fau.de/systems-services/systems-documentation-instructions/clusters/meggie-cluster/.

[2] https://hpc.fau.de/systems-services/systems-documentation-instructions/clusters/fritz-cluster/.

of the respective CPUs. Working sets were chosen large enough to not fit into any cache, i.e., at least ten times the last-level cache size on both systems. All floating-point computations were done in double precision. All experiments were performed for 500 k iterations (compute-communicate cycles), except for LBM where we used 100 k iterations. Each experiment was repeated at least five times to ensure that the runtime analysis is stable. The scripts, which are used to generate plots for all data analytic and machine learning techniques, are available online at https://github.com/RRZE-HPC/PPAM22-AA.

2.2   Synthetic Microbenchmarks

We ran pure-MPI versions of the McCalpin STREAM Triad [11] (A(:)=B(:)+ s*C(:))) and a "slow" Schönauer vector Triad (A(:)=B(:)+cos(C(:)/D(:)))[3] with bidirectional next-neighbor communication. The saturation characteristics of these streaming kernels on one socket (ccNUMA domain) of Meggie are shown in Fig. 1. Each MPI rank i sends and receives messages to and from each of its direct neighbors $i + 1$ and $i - 1$ after each full loop traversal. Each array had 400 M elements, which yields a 9.6 GB working set for the STREAM Triad and a 12.8 GB working set for the Schönauer Triad. To mimic scalable applications, we set up a PISOLVER code which calculates the value of π by evaluating $\int_0^1 4/(1 + x^2)\,\mathrm{d}x$ using the mid-point rule with 500 M steps. Overall, four microbenchmark variants were employed:

1. MPI-parallel STREAM Triad with 5 MB messages
2. MPI-parallel STREAM Triad with 8 B messages
3. MPI-parallel "slow" Schönauer Triad with 8 B messages
4. MPI-parallel PISOLVER with 8 B messages

These four cases were run in two scenarios on the Meggie system: (A) open-chain process topology with 40 MPI processes on four ccNUMA domains (sockets), and (B) closed-ring process topology with 400 MPI processes on 40 sockets. Later these scenarios will be denoted *"Bench iA"* and *"Bench iB"*, respectively, where i is the label in the enumeration list above.

2.3   Proxy Memory-Bound Parallel Applications

We experiment with the following two MPI-parallel proxy applications and run them with 1440 MPI processes on 40 sockets of the Fritz system.

MPI-Parallel LBM Solver. This is a prototype application based on a Lattice Boltzmann Method (LBM) from computational fluid dynamics using the Bhatnagar-Gross-Krook collision operator [6] and implementing a 3D lid-driven cavity scenario. It is purely memory bound on a single ccNUMA domain, but

---

[3] The low-throughput cosine and floating-point division shifts the bandwidth saturation point to a higher number of cores.

the halo exchange makes it communication dominated in strong scaling scenarios. The double-precision implementation employs a three-dimensional D3Q19 space discretization [12]. The domain decomposition is performed by cutting slices in the z direction. For halo exchange, five PDFs per boundary cell must be communicated. The MPI communication is done with non-blocking point-to-point calls, but no explicit overlapping of communication with useful work is implemented. We use an overall problem size of $n_x \times n_y \times n_z = 1440^3$ lattice cells, which amounts to a working set of 908 GB plus halo layers. Due to the one-dimensional domain decomposition, the communication volume per halo depends on n_x and n_y only and is independent of the number of processes.

MPI-Parallel spMVM Solver. The sparse matrix-vector multiplication (SpMVM) $\vec{b} = A\vec{x}$ is a most relevant, time-consuming building block of numerous applications in science and engineering. Here, A is an $n \times n$ sparse matrix, and $\vec{b}$, $\vec{x}$ are n-dimensional vectors. SpMVM plays a central role in the iterative solution of sparse linear systems, eigenvalue problems and Krylov subspace solvers. Due to its low computational intensity, the SpMVM kernel is mostly limited by the main memory bandwidth if the matrix does not fit into a cache. Our implementation uses non-blocking point-to-point communication calls, where the communication requests for reading the remote parts of $\vec{x}$ are issued and then collectively finished via `MPI_Waitall`. After that, the whole SpMVM kernel is executed. The communication volume is crucially dependent on the structure of the matrix; the distribution of the nonzero entries plays a decisive role. In this paper, we use a matrix that arises from strongly correlated electron-phonon systems in solid state physics. It describes a Holstein-Hubbard model [7] comprising 3 electrons on 8 lattice sites coupled to 10 phonons. The sparse matrix A has $60,988,928$ rows and columns and $889,816,368$ non-zero entries, respectively, which leads to an average of 13 nonzeros per row and an overall data set size of 10.9 GB using four-byte indices in the Compressed Row Storage format (one-dimensional arrays for values, column indices, and row pointers).

2.4   Observables for Analysis

We instrument all codes to collect the time stamps of entering and leaving MPI calls (MPI waiting time per process) at each iteration of each MPI process across the full run. From this data we construct a non-square matrix of size $N_p \times N_{it}$, where N_p is the number of MPI processes and N_{it} is the number of iterations. Each row (column) of the observable matrix represents the observable value, i.e., the time spent in MPI, for each process (iteration). There is a choice as to how this data can be used in analysis: One can either use the full timeline per process, which takes the end-to-end evolution of execution characteristics (such as desynchronization) into account, or cut out a number of consecutive iterations from different execution phases, which allows to investigate the development of interesting patterns in more detail. In addition, for some experiments we collect performance per MPI process averaged over the 1000 time steps.

3   Simple Timeline Metrics for Analysis

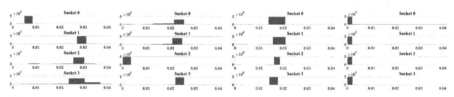

(a) Bench1A-500k it   (b) Bench2A-500k it   (c) Bench3A-500k it   (d) Bench4A-500k it

Fig. 3. Histograms sorting MPI times [sec] into bins for all benchmarks on the first process of each Meggie socket used in the run. The x-axes show the MPI times and the y-axes indicate the number of MPI time values in each bin.

3.1   Rank/ccNUMA-wise Timelines and Histogram of MPI Time and Performance

The histograms in Fig. 3 sort the MPI time values of end-to-end (500 k iterations) runs of Bench[1–4]A into 35 bins. For memory-bound code, idle times are lower for desynchronized processes if the bandwidth saturation on a ccNUMA domain is weaker [2] (see Fig. 3(c)). In the compute-bound PISOLVER case (Fig. 3(d)), all processes are synchronized because of the absence of any contention on the memory interface or on the network. Open-chain boundary conditions and strong memory contention ((a) and (b)) lead to a single synchronized socket. In the other cases, all sockets desynchronize gradually over 500 k iterations, which causes a spread in the histogram because processes evolve from lower to higher idle times. We have observed that this spread is more prominent for codes with stronger saturation and higher communication (*Bench1B*, LBM, and spMVM; data not shown for brevity).

We first investigate the open chain high communication overhead benchmark mode (*Bench1A*). Figure 4(a) shows the histograms at the different stages of evolution of a single MPI process (i.e., rank 20 on third ccNUMA domain) through the whole execution. Each histogram encompasses 1000 iterations. Initially (e.g., till 50 k iterations), the distributions are multimodal, which indicates different phases. On closer inspection it can be observed that the peak snaps from left to right as the process goes out of sync with its neighbors. This corroborates that the MPI waiting time is a good observable in our context. Since desynchronization cannot yield significant speedup if communication is insignificant, we show plots of performance vs. time step for significant communication cases only (*Bench1A* in Fig. 4(b) and *Bench1B* in Fig. 4(c)). These plots show the initial 1 k iterations. With open boundary conditions (b), one observes fluctuating performance as processes get desynchronized on all but one socket. However, this slow synchronized socket does not permit a global performance increase as desynchronized processes on other sockets cannot lag behind indefinitely. With closed boundary conditions (c), as the simulation progresses, performance (along

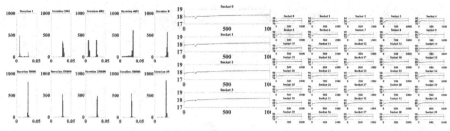

(a) Bench1A-500k it-Rank 20   (b) Bench1A-1k it   (c) Bench1B-1k it of 500k it run

Fig. 4. (a) Snippet view of histograms for MPI times [sec] (x-axes) of rank 20 only and (b-c) performance [iterations/sec] (y-axes) on every first MPI process of each Meggie socket for the initial-zoomed 1 k iterations (x-axes) snapshot of Bench1A and Bench1B. Since the performance remains constant afterwards, we don't show the whole run of 500 k iterations.

with MPI waiting times) increases by about 15% and stays constant at the higher level till the end of the run.

3.2 Timeline in Compact Representation

MPI waiting times facilitate a compact representation of the timeline of a parallel program. Figure 5 show ranks on the x-axis and time steps on the y-axis, with the normalized MPI waiting time for each rank and time step color coded. For this representation, the mean value of MPI times across all processes and time steps is shown in white while red (positive value) and blue (negative value) represent values above and below the mean, respectively. This makes it possible to distinguish between synchronized and desynchronized groups of processes: Strongly desynchronized processes spend more time in MPI (red), while white color marks synchronized processes (Ranks 1–10 and 20–30 in Fig. 5(b) and (c), respectively). This visualization is similar to what tracing tools like ITAC or Vampir display; however, these tools often encompass too much information, and depending on the chosen resolution one can easily get lost in the data. In contrast, compact timelines of the waiting time per time step deliver a condensed view on this information and help to better visualize certain phenomena. For instance, the weaker saturation cases collect lower idle times which can be seen when comparing Figs. 5(c)–(e) and (h)–(j)). Asymptotic behavior in longer runs can be observed at the top part of the plot in all cases. Idle waves are prominently visible as dark-blue stripes in the LBM benchmark (Fig. 5(a)).

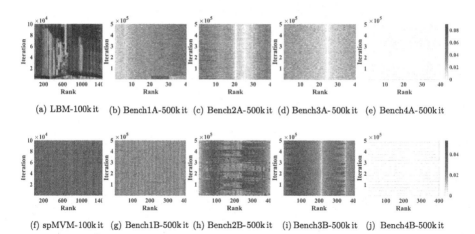

(a) LBM-100kit   (b) Bench1A-500kit   (c) Bench2A-500kit   (d) Bench3A-500kit   (e) Bench4A-500kit

(f) spMVM-100kit   (g) Bench1B-500kit   (h) Bench2B-500kit   (i) Bench3B-500kit   (j) Bench4B-500kit

Fig. 5. Compact rank(x-axis)-iteration(y-axis) timelines of MPI waiting times [sec] for all benchmarks and full end-to-end runs.

4   Advanced Metrics for Analysis

Beyond timeline visualization and statistics, a plethora of advanced data analysis methods exist which can lead to deeper insights into the desynchronization process. Here we pick the *correlation coefficient* and the *phase space plot*.

4.1   Correlation Coefficient

The correlation coefficient function [14] provides a simple way to uncover correlations between the timelines of two MPI processes. Figure 6 shows the color-coded correlation coefficients of rank pairs for all benchmarks, using the full end-to-end timelines. The matrices are obviously symmetric, and the diagonal entries (dark red) are set to one by convention. The correlation coefficients range from −1 to 1, with −1 representing a direct, negative correlation, 0 representing no correlation, and 1 representing a direct, positive correlation. For the memory-bound applications, the ccNUMA domain structure is clearly visible in Figs. 6(a–c, f–h). This implies that processes within ccNUMA domains are strongly correlated, while they are less (or not) correlated across sockets. The data shows strong correlations within desynchronized sockets with a bi-modal distribution of MPI times since the socket already started to lose the sync pattern. In the open chain scenarios, processes on the last socket show a weaker correlation. In the SpMVM application, the sparse matrix structure is reflected in the correlation coefficients since the desynchronization process is strongly influenced by the communication structure (Fig. 6(f)). In weakly or non-saturated applications (Figs. 6(d–e, i–j)), correlations are generally weaker, as expected.

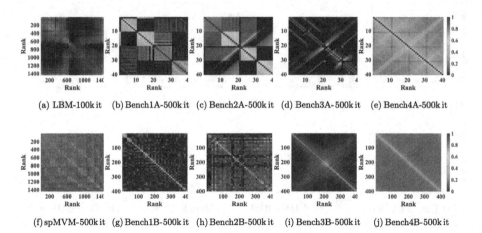

(a) LBM-100k it (b) Bench1A-500k it (c) Bench2A-500k it (d) Bench3A-500k it (e) Bench4A-500k it

(f) spMVM-500k it (g) Bench1B-500k it (h) Bench2B-500k it (i) Bench3B-500k it (j) Bench4B-500k it

Fig. 6. Correlation coefficients of MPI times [sec] between process pairs for all benchmarks.

4.2 Phase Space Plots

In order to capture the temporal evolution of MPI waiting time, we set up a scatter plot where each data point has coordinates (MPItime(t_i, r), MPItime($t_i + 1, r$)). For each process, a fixed point in this "phase space" is a point on the slope-1 line through the origin. If the waiting time evolves, a process will move through the first quadrant; if waiting time increases over time (e.g., due to desynchronization), the path of a process will rise above the axis and move further up and to the right. Color coding in the point cloud, from early (blue) to late (yellow), helps to visualize how processes move. We choose two different types of analysis.

In the *snippet view*, only a small part (e.g., 1000 iterations) of the data is visualized per plot; separate plots are used to show the long-term temporal evolution (*initial-mid-end* in Fig. 7). In Figs. 7(a)–(c), after the initial in-sync phase, the cloud gets spread out. Asymptotically, we identify multiple weak and strong clusters (smaller and bigger attractors basin for observable). Stronger or weaker clustering along the diagonal line expresses how much the observable fluctuates around a "steady-state" value. In the example shown, all but one (blue points) sockets get desynchronized. This separation of sockets should go away as time progresses for the close chain scenario (see Figs. 7(f)–(h)), but obviously the progression is too slow to be discernible in this visualization. For PISOLVER (Figs. 7(d)–(e)), the point cloud starts around the origin and remains there since this scalable code is self-synchronizing.

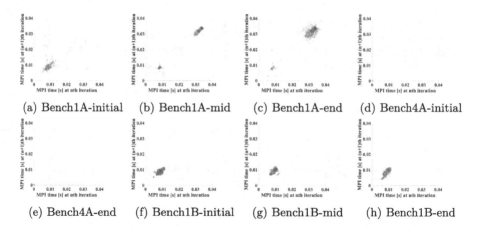

Fig. 7. (a, c, f, h) *Snippets view* of phase space of all MPI processes for 100 iterations at the beginning. (b) Snapshot of 1 K iterations (9.9–10 K iterations) for LBM in the middle state. (d, e, g, i, j) Snapshot of 1 K iterations in the middle (1.9–2 k iterations) and at the end evolved state (499.9–500 k iterations).

In the *overall view* (see Fig. 8), the full timeline is shown for one process in one plot (plotting all processes would not allow useful conclusions)). Here the gradual evolution of waiting time is hard to see since it is drowned in fluctuations. However, especially in the open-chain scenarios (Figs. 8(b)–(d)) we observe structures parallel to the axes, indicating singular long delays of a few preferred lengths. These are signatures of traveling idle waves, which for a single process manifest themselves as singular high waiting time in one time step.

5   Machine Learning Techniques for Analysis

In order to prepare the timeline data for machine learning techniques, we subtract the mean values of MPI times across all time steps and processes of each experiment from the value at each step. This is one of many possible options for data normalization; better ones might exist. We then apply PCA [8] to the timelines of each run, using the MPI times of each process as feature vectors, and then classify the projections of the feature vectors on the first two principal component vectors using clustering techniques. Finally, we validate the quality of the clustering for an accurate evaluation. To do that, we look at the reconstruction error that is generated using an essential number of Principal Components only.

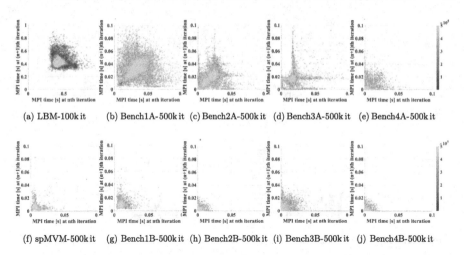

(a) LBM-100k it   (b) Bench1A-500k it   (c) Bench2A-500k it   (d) Bench3A-500k it   (e) Bench4A-500k it

(f) spMVM-500k it   (g) Bench1B-500k it   (h) Bench2B-500k it   (i) Bench3B-500k it   (j) Bench4B-500k it

Fig. 8. *Overall view* of phase space for one MPI process (rank 32) of all benchmarks. The axes show the time spent in the MPI library at the n-th and $(n+1)$-th iteration, respectively.

5.1   Principal Component Analysis (PCA)

Principal Component analysis projects the directions of high-dimensional data onto a lower-dimensional subspace while retaining most of the information. Ideally, the low-dimensional manifolds still retain almost all variance of the data set needed to identify and interpret generic behavior. Coarse features are captured by the first principal components while the highest-frequency features are captured by highest principal components. PCA centers the data and uses the *singular value decomposition* algorithm on the non-square observable matrix. Rows and columns of the input matrix correspond to observations and variables, respectively. Each row vector is the timeline of MPI times in a process; the observable values in different iterations are the coordinates in a high-dimensional space.

Projection Plot on the Reduced Principal Components. The points in Fig. 9(a, e) indicate the score of each observation for the first three principal components in the Bench1B experiment. They show the PCA analysis on the full run and on the last 1000 iterations, respectively. For the compute-bound PISOLVER (Bench4), all processes cluster around one point because of absence of contention on the sockets (data not shown). In contrast, for the memory-bound Triad variants, four or 40 clusters emerge at the start due to the presence of four or 40 ccNUMA domains, respectively. As time progresses, all desynchronized sockets form weak clusters by collecting larger scores for PC1 and nonzero scores for PC2, while the in-sync domain forms a compact cluster due to lower scores for PC1 and zero scores for PC2. Desynchronization is strongest for the processes on the top right of the plot. The negative values for projections on eigenvectors indicate an

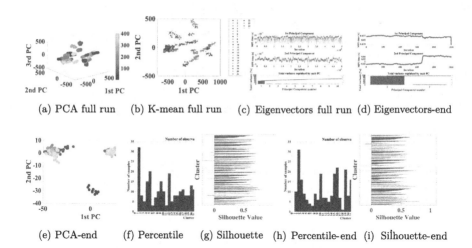

(a) PCA full run   (b) K-mean full run   (c) Eigenvectors full run (d) Eigenvectors-end

(e) PCA-end   (f) Percentile   (g) Silhouette   (h) Percentile-end   (i) Silhouette-end

Fig. 9. Principal Component analysis, k-mean clustering, eigenvectors, percentile and Silhouette analyses of Bench1B (a–c, f–g) for the whole run time of 500k iterations and (d–e, h–i) for snapshot of last 1 k iterations only.

inverse relationship, but large (either positive or negative) values indicate that a vector has a strong overlap with that principal component. If all ccNUMA domains are eventually desynchronized, all processes cluster on the top right as shown in Fig. 9(e) for the last 1000 iterations.

Principal Components (Eigenvectors). In order to get better insight into the governing characteristics of desynchronized execution, We analyze the essential eigenvectors. Figures 9(c, d) show the eigenvectors and how ranks contribute to the reduced number of principal components for the full run and the last 1000 iterations. In the full-run case (Fig. 9(c)), the PC1 eigenvector characterizes desynchronizing processes and thus indicates a lot of waiting times with in-between downward spikes. The PC2 eigenvector characterizes in-sync processes and shows almost no waiting time, but upward spikes (idle periods) in between. It must be noted that the PCs for end-to-end runs encompass the entire evolution of the program, including initial in-sync phases, transient states, and final, stable states. Looking at the final 1000 iterations (Fig. 9dc)), the signatures are much clearer; PC1 characterizes stable desynchronization while PC2 maps transient behavior where a noise-induced event between iteration 600 and 700 causes processes to change from a state with small waiting times to a state with large waiting times. One can interpret this as processes within a ccNUMA domain "snapping" out of sync.

Total Variance Explained by Each Principal Component. The percentage of the total variance explained by each principal component (Pareto plots in Figs. 9(c-bottom, d-bottom)) indicates for Bench1B how many PCs are required to reconstruct the original data sets using only the projections. In this particular case, one component is sufficient near the end of the run but many are required (with the first one still dominating) over the full run. Overall, the results show that more PCs are needed to explain the data variance for a more pronounced memory-bandwidth saturation on the ccNUMA domain. In contrast, the compute-bound PISOLVER has much less variance as no typical structure exists except natural, noise-induced fluctuations. Further, the more revealing socket behavior in short-runs is captured by the higher number of PCs compared to the asymptotic behavior in long runs.

5.2   K-means Clustering

While PCA delivers insight into typical patterns, it does not allow for automatic grouping (clustering) of processes. This can be accomplished by partitioning the projection of observations on the principal components into k clusters by using k-means. Rows of PC scores correspond to points and columns correspond to variables. We use the k-means++ algorithm [13] for the cluster center initialization; it is strongly dependent on the distance metric used.

Distance Types. Clustering quality was studied for four metrics. In the cluster, each centroid c is either the mean $((x - c)(x - c)')$ or component-wise median $((\sum_{j=1}^{p} |x_j - c_j|)$ of the points in *squared Euclidean* and *city-block* metrics, respectively. Here, x is a row of PC scores. For the *cosine* and *correlation* metrics, each centroid c is either the mean of the points which are already normalized to unit Euclidean length $(1 - \dfrac{xc'}{\sqrt{(xx')(cc')}})$ or component-wise mean of the points which are already centered and normalized to zero mean and unit standard deviation $(1 - \dfrac{(x - \bar{x})(c - \bar{c})'}{\sqrt{(x - \bar{x})(x - \bar{x})'}\sqrt{(c - \bar{c})(c - \bar{c})'}})$, with $\bar{x} = \dfrac{1}{p}(\sum_{j=1}^{p} x_j)1_p$ and $\bar{c} = \dfrac{1}{p}(\sum_{j=1}^{p} c_j)1_p$.

The result is a matrix containing the k cluster centroid locations and a vector containing cluster indices. Figure 9(b) shows a scatter plot of essential PC scores grouped by the cluster indices of each observation in the *Bench1B* case. K-means uses the squared Euclidean distance here. We expect one cluster if all processes are in a fully evolved desynchronized state.

Number of Observables per Cluster. The number of clusters k is chosen in a way that it assigns all unalike clusters, while the number of observables belonging to each cluster could be significantly different. Figures 9(f, h) show the histogram bar chart of the cluster indices in the vector, which are sorted into k bins. We choose k equal to the number of ccNUMA domains. The x-axis indicates the cluster IDs and the y-axis shows the number of samples.

Validation of Clustering Quality. A potential application of Principal Component analysis is its evaluation by calculating the error between original and reconstructed signal from fewer PCs. To this end, one can reconstruct the signal by multiplying the scores with the first two PCs and then sum them up. This should be very close to the original signal if the reconstruction error (using the Euclidean norm) is less than some threshold value. In Figs. 9(g, i), we performed a Silhouette analysis [9] to quantify the quality of the clustering. A highly representative clustering is associated with a large positive coefficient value close to one and indicates that the point is well matched to other points in its own cluster, and poorly matched to other clusters. On the other hand, a negative coefficient value represents a disqualified clustering. We get higher reconstruction error for the high-frequency signal of the PISOLVER case as expected. While exploring the influence of distance metrics, it turned out that *cosine* is the best-suited and *city-block* is the worst-suited distance metric.

6   Summary and Future Work

Key Takeaways. We have presented expressive data analytics techniques for investigating the dynamics of MPI-parallel programs with regular compute-communicate cycles. We consider MPI waiting time per time step and process as a good observable metric since it encompasses much of the relevant dynamics in a very condensed format. Our new "phase space" analysis based on this data provides an efficient, visual way to observe the evolution of a program from its initial, synchronized state into a desynchronized state. However, it is not strictly a data analytics technique since it involves manual inspection of the data (moving dot clouds). PCA and subsequent k-means clustering allow for a more automated analysis, providing feature extraction, i.e., typical timeline behavior, as well as grouping of MPI processes into clusters with similar features. Hence, these methods could pave the way towards advanced job-specific monitoring of production jobs on clusters. We have also found that the analysis is more expressive when applied to snippets of the timeline in order to avoid mixing different characteristics. If one is interested in an evolved state only, the final iterations of a run are most relevant.

Since the dynamics of MPI asynchronicity are often concealed in overwhelmed data, our methods facilitate two fundamental benefits; First, they offer a trade-off between the detailed data-intensive tracing analyses and the high-level integrated time and performance metrics. Second, by enabling the investigation of *unknown* applications from condensed traces without in-depth analysis, they can pave the way for a more general classification of the dynamics of parallel programs.

Future Work. We are convinced that PCA applied to MPI waiting time data allows the investigation of unknown applications by mapping their temporal evolution to principal components found in prototypical benchmark runs. It is still an open question how to choose these benchmarks to extract relevant, distinguishable patterns that real application can be tested against. It will also be necessary to investigate how the waiting time metric should be normalized to be as generic as possible. Furthermore, we plan to apply the demonstrated techniques to a wider spectrum of real applications in order to fathom their true scope of applicability. We will additionally investigate the potential of adopting the performance modeling techniques towards these dynamics of MPI synchronicity. This can be achieved by keeping track of the practical limits of potential optimization in parallel program performance. The article [4] discusses a pioneering work along these lines.

Acknowledgments. This research work is supported by KONWIHR, the Bavarian Competence Network for Scientific High Performance Computing in Bavaria, under project name "OMI4papps." The authors gratefully acknowledge the scientific support and HPC resources provided by the Erlangen National High Performance Computing Center (NHR@FAU) of the Friedrich-Alexander-Universität Erlangen-Nürnberg (FAU). The hardware is funded by the German Research Foundation (DFG).

References

1. Afzal, A., Hager, G., Wellein, G.: Propagation and decay of injected one-off delays on clusters: a case study. In: 2019 IEEE International Conference on Cluster Computing, CLUSTER 2019, Albuquerque, NM, USA, 23–26 September 2019, pp. 1–10 (2019). https://doi.org/10.1109/CLUSTER.2019.8890995
2. Afzal, A., Hager, G., Wellein, G.: Desynchronization and wave pattern formation in MPI-parallel and hybrid memory-bound programs. In: Sadayappan, P., Chamberlain, B.L., Juckeland, G., Ltaief, H. (eds.) ISC High Performance 2020. LNCS, vol. 12151, pp. 391–411. Springer, Cham (2020). https://doi.org/10.1007/978-3-030-50743-5_20
3. Afzal, A., Hager, G., Wellein, G.: Analytic modeling of idle waves in parallel programs: communication, cluster topology, and noise impact. In: Chamberlain, B.L., Varbanescu, A.-L., Ltaief, H., Luszczek, P. (eds.) ISC High Performance 2021. LNCS, vol. 12728, pp. 351–371. Springer, Cham (2021). https://doi.org/10.1007/978-3-030-78713-4_19
4. Afzal, A., Hager, G., Wellein, G.: The role of idle waves, desynchronization, and bottleneck evasion in the performance of parallel programs. IEEE Trans. Parallel Distrib. Syst. TPDS (2022). https://doi.org/10.1109/TPDS.2022.3221085
5. Afzal, A., Wellein, G., Hager, G.: Addressing white-box modeling and simulation challenges in parallel computing. In: Proceedings of the 2022 ACM SIGSIM Conference on Principles of Advanced Discrete Simulation, SIGSIM-PADS 2022, pp. 25–26. Association for Computing Machinery, New York (2022). https://doi.org/10.1145/3518997.3534986
6. Bhatnagar, P.L., Gross, E.P., Krook, M.: A model for collision processes in gases. I. Small amplitude processes in charged and neutral one-component systems. Phys. Rev. **94**(3), 511–525 (1954). https://doi.org/10.1103/PhysRev.94.511
7. Fehske, H., Wellein, G., Hager, G., Weiße, A., Bishop, A.: Quantum lattice dynamical effects on single-particle excitations in one-dimensional Mott and Peierls insulators. Phys. Rev. B **69**(16), 165115 (2004). https://doi.org/10.1103/PhysRevB.69.165115
8. Jolliffe, I.T., Cadima, J.: Principal component analysis: a review and recent developments. Philos. Trans. Roy. Soc. A Math. Phys. Eng. Sci. **374**(2065), 20150202 (2016). https://doi.org/10.1098/rsta.2015.0202

9. Kaufman, L., Rousseeuw, P.J.: Finding Groups in Data: An Introduction to Cluster Analysis. Wiley, Hoboken (2009). https://doi.org/10.1002/9780470316801
10. Markidis, S., Vencels, J., Peng, I.B., Akhmetova, D., Laure, E., Henri, P.: Idle waves in high-performance computing. Phys. Rev. E **91**(1), 013306 (2015). https://doi.org/10.1103/PhysRevE.91.013306
11. McCalpin, J.D., et al.: Memory bandwidth and machine balance in current high performance computers. IEEE Comput. Soc. Tech. Committee Comput. Archit. (TCCA) Newsl. **2**(19–25) (1995)
12. Qian, Y.H., d'Humières, D., Lallemand, P.: Lattice BGK models for Navier-Stokes equation. Europhys. Lett. (EPL) **17**(6), 479–484 (1992)
13. Vassilvitskii, S., Arthur, D.: k-means++: the advantages of careful seeding. In: Proceedings of the Eighteenth Annual ACM-SIAM Symposium on Discrete Algorithms, pp. 1027–1035 (2006). https://dl.acm.org/doi/10.5555/1283383.1283494
14. Vetterling, W.T., et al.: Numerical Recipes: Example book C. Cambridge University Press, Cambridge (1992)

Cost and Performance Analysis of MPI-Based SaaS on the Private Cloud Infrastructure

Oleg Bystrov$^{(\boxtimes)}$ (ID), Arnas Kačeniauskas (ID), and Ruslan Pacevič (ID)

Vilnius Gediminas Technical University, 10223 Vilnius, Lithuania
oleg.bystrov@vilniustech.lt

Abstract. The paper presents the cost and performance analysis of parallel MPI-based software as a service (SaaS) deployed on the OpenStack cloud infrastructure. The parallel SaaS was developed by using C++ programming language and MPI library for the scientific discrete element method (DEM) computations of granular flows. The performance measured on KVM-based virtual machines was slightly higher than that on Docker containers of the OpenStack cloud. Round up and proportional pricing schemes were examined and compared from the user's perspective. The difference in cost computed by using alternative pricing schemes varied from 0.6% to 15.4%. However, this difference can be reduced to 1.0%, increasing execution time of considered tasks. The investigation of a trade-off between the execution time and cost was performed by using Pareto front analysis and a linear scalarization method. Bi-objective decision making revealed the preferable configurations of virtual machines specific to memory bound DEM computations, exploiting higher bandwidth.

Keywords: Cost and Performance Trade-off · Pareto Front · MPI · OpenStack

1 Introduction

In recent years, cloud computing has gained great popularity and transformed the IT industry [1]. Cloud computing infrastructures can provide the scalable resources on-demand to deploy performance and cost effective services. The NIST SPI model [2] represents a layered, high-level abstraction of cloud services classified into three main categories: Infrastructure as a Service (IaaS), Platform as a Service (PaaS) and Software as a Service (SaaS). Organizations can use different implementations of cloud software for deploying their own private clouds. OpenStack [3] is an open source cloud management platform that delivers an integrated foundation to create, deploy and scale a secure and reliable public or private cloud. Another open source local cloud framework is Eucalyptus [4], provided by Eucalyptus Systems, Inc.

Cloud computing makes extensive use of virtual machines (VMs) because they allow workloads to be isolated and resource usage to be controlled. Kernel

R. Wyrzykowski et al. (Eds.): PPAM 2022, LNCS 13826, pp. 171–182, 2023.
https://doi.org/10.1007/978-3-031-30442-2_13

Virtual Machine (KVM) [5] is a feature of Linux that allows Linux to act as a type 1 hypervisor, running an unmodified guest operating system inside a Linux process. Containers present an emerging technology for improving the productivity and code portability in cloud infrastructures. Due to the layered file system, Docker [6] container images require less disk space and I/O than the equivalent VM disk images. Thus, Docker has emerged as a standard runtime, image format and build system for Linux containers. IBM has added Docker container integration to Platform LSF to run the containers on an HPC cluster [7]. EDEM software has been deployed on Rescale's cloud simulation platform for high-performance computations [8]. However, it is difficult to provide precise guidelines regarding the optimal cloud platform and virtualization technology for each type of research and application [9].

Deployment of scientific codes as software services for data preparation, high-performance computation and visualization on the cloud infrastructure increases the mobility of users and achieves better exploitation. Thus, flexible cloud infrastructures and software services are perceived as a promising avenue for future advances in the multidisciplinary area of discrete element method (DEM) applications [8]. However, the cloud SaaS might suffer from severe performance degradation due to higher latencies of networks, virtualization overheads and other issues [1]. Cloud computing still lacks cost and performance analyses in the case of specific MPI-based applications, such as granular materials. Most evaluations of the virtualization overhead and performance of cloud services are based on standard benchmarks or theoretical unrealistic load models [9], therefore, the impact of the cloud infrastructure on the performance and cost of parallel MPI-based DEM computations remains unclear. Moreover, cost and performance are critical factors in deciding whether cloud infrastructures are viable for scientific DEM software.

The performance of virtual machines and lightweight containers has already received some attention in the academic literature [10–13]. However, few studies include the performance analysis of the virtualized distributed memory architectures for parallel MPI-based applications [14–16]. Bag-of-gangs applications [17] consist of parallel jobs that are in very frequent communication and must execute simultaneously and concurrently. Moschakis and Karatza [18] evaluated gang scheduling performance in the Amazon EC2 cloud. Sood [19] compared gang scheduling algorithms to other scheduling mechanisms in cloud computing. Hao et al. [20] proposed a 0–1 integer programming for the gang scheduling. Their proposed method tried its best finishing more jobs and minimizing the average waiting time. Bystrov et al. [21] investigated a trade-off between the computing speed and the consumed energy of a real-life hemodynamic application on a heterogeneous cloud. Beloglazov et al. [22] have proposed a modified best-fit algorithm for energy-aware resource provisioning in data centers while continuing to deliver the negotiated service level agreement. The survey [23] concludes that there exists no predictive model today truly and comprehensively capturing performance and energy consumption of the highly heterogeneous and hierarchi-

cal architecture of the modern HPC node. Moreover, the cost analysis of the
MPI-based computations was not performed in the above overviewed research.

The resource allocation problem in cloud computing has received a lot of
attention mainly in terms of cost optimization. Malawski et al. [24] presented
a model, which assumed multiple cloud providers offering computational and
storage services. The considered optimization objective was to reduce the total
cost under deadline constraints. Liu et al. [25] focused on cost minimization and
guarantee of performance, proposing the least cost per connection algorithm,
which chose the most cost-effective VMs from the available public clouds. Zhou
et al. [26] developed two evolutionary algorithms to optimize cost and execution time of scheduling workflows. Genez et al. [27] proposed an integer linear
programming-based VM scheduler to produce low-cost scheduling for workflows
execution in multiple cloud providers. Entrialgo et al. [28] designed a state-of-
the-art cost optimization tool for the optimal allocation of VMs in hybrid clouds.
Rosa et al. [29] developed the computational resource and cost prediction service,
which measured user resources and reported the runtime financial cost before
starting the workflow execution. A comprehensive review of workload scheduling and resource provisioning in cloud environments can be found in Wang et
al. [30]. The most authors considered the total cost as the objective and solved
the optimization problem with deadline constraint, which did not minimize the
execution time, reducing its importance. Moreover, parallel MPI-based scientific
applications were rarely examined because of their intensive communications
between VMs and complex non-monotonous performance profiles.

The remaining paper is organized as follows: Sect. 2 outlines the governing
relations of the discrete element method, Sect. 3 describes parallel MPI-based
SaaS deployed on the OpenStack cloud infrastructure, Sect. 4 presents the cost
and performance analysis and the conclusions are given in Sect. 5.

2   The Governing Relations of the Discrete Element Method

The discrete element method is a class of numerical techniques to simulate granular materials [31]. The frictional visco-elastic particle system consists of the finite
number of deformable spherical particles with the specified size distribution and
material properties. Any particle i in the system of N spherical particles undergoes the translational and rotational motion, involving the forces and torques
originated in the process of their interaction. Finally, the motion of the i-th
contacting spherical particle in time t is described as follows:

$$m_i \frac{d^2 \boldsymbol{x}_i}{dt^2} = \boldsymbol{F}_i, I_i \frac{d\boldsymbol{\omega}_i}{dt} = \boldsymbol{T}_i, \tag{1}$$

where m_i and I_i are the mass and the moment of inertia of the particle, respec-
tively, while the vectors $\boldsymbol{x}_i$ and $\boldsymbol{\omega}_i$ initiate the position of the centre of particle
i and the rotational velocity around the particle centre of mass. The vectors $\boldsymbol{F}_i$
and $\boldsymbol{T}_i$ present the resultant force and the resultant torque, acting in the centre

of the particle i. The vector $\boldsymbol{F}_i$ can be expressed by the external force and the sum of the contact forces between the interacting particles:

$$\boldsymbol{F}_i = \boldsymbol{F}_{i,cont} + \boldsymbol{F}_{i,ext} = \sum_{j=1,j\neq i}^{N} \boldsymbol{F}_{ij,cont} + m_i, \boldsymbol{g}, \tag{2}$$

where $\boldsymbol{F}_{i,ext}$ and $\boldsymbol{F}_{i,cont}$ are the external force and the resultant contact force of particle i, respectively, $\boldsymbol{g}$ is the acceleration due to gravity, $\boldsymbol{F}_{ij,cont}$ is the interparticle contact force vector, describing the contact between the particles i and j. Thus, in the present work, the electromagnetic force [32], the aerodynamic force [33] and other external forces [34,35], except for the gravity force are not considered. The rotational motion is governed by particle torques $\boldsymbol{T}_i$ that can be expressed by torques $\boldsymbol{T}_{ij}$ of the neighbouring particles:

$$\boldsymbol{T}_i = \sum_{j=1,j\neq i}^{N} \boldsymbol{T}_{ij} = \sum_{j=1,j\neq i}^{N} \boldsymbol{d}_{cij} \times \boldsymbol{F}_{i,cont}, \tag{3}$$

where $\boldsymbol{d}_{cij}$ is the vector pointing from the particle centre to the contact centre. The interparticle contact force vector $\boldsymbol{F}_{i,cont}$ may be expressed in terms of normal and tangential components. The normal component of the contact force comprises the elastic counterpart according to Hertz theory and the viscous counterpart that can be represented by the spring-dashpot model [36] as follows:

$$\boldsymbol{F}_{ij,n} = \frac{4}{3} \cdot \frac{E_i E_j}{E_i(1-\nu_j^2) + E_j(1-\nu_i^2)} R_{ij}^{1/2} \delta_{ij,n}^{3/2} \boldsymbol{n}_{ij} - \gamma_n m_{ij} \boldsymbol{v}_{ij,n}, \tag{4}$$

where $\boldsymbol{n}_{ij}$ is the normal vector, R_{ij} is the reduced radius of the contacting particles, γ_n is the constant normal damping coefficient, m_{ij} is the reduced mass of the contacting particles and $\boldsymbol{v}_{ij,n}$ is the normal component of the relative velocity of the contact point. E_i and E_j are elastic moduli, ν_i and ν_j are Poison's ratios of contacting particles i and j, respectively. In the normal direction, the depth of the overlap between particles i and j is defined by $\delta_{ij,n}$.

The evolution of the tangential contact force can be divided into the parts of static friction prior to sliding $\boldsymbol{F}_{ij,stat,t}$ and dynamic slip friction $\boldsymbol{F}_{ij,dyn,t}$ [36]:

$$\boldsymbol{F}_{ij,t} = -\boldsymbol{t}_{ij} \begin{cases} |\boldsymbol{F}_{ij,stat,t}|, & |\boldsymbol{F}_{ij,stat,t}| < \mu|\boldsymbol{F}_{ij,n}| \\ |\boldsymbol{F}_{ij,dyn,t}|, & |\boldsymbol{F}_{ij,stat,t}| \geq \mu|\boldsymbol{F}_{ij,n}| \end{cases}, \tag{5}$$

where $\boldsymbol{t}_{ij}$ is the unit vector of the tangential contact direction. The model of static friction force is implemented, when the tangential force is smaller than the Coulomb-type cut-off limit. In the opposite case, the dynamic friction expressed by the normal contact force and the Coulomb friction coefficient μ is considered:

$$\boldsymbol{F}_{ij,dyn,t} = -\mu|\boldsymbol{F}_{ij,n}|\boldsymbol{t}_{ij}, \tag{6}$$

The static friction force is calculated by summing up the elastic and viscous damping components [37]:

$$\boldsymbol{F}_{ij,stat,t} = -\frac{16}{3} \cdot \frac{G_i G_j \sqrt{R_{ij} \delta_{ij,n}}}{G_i(2 - \nu_j) + G_j(2 - \nu_i)} |\delta_{ij,t}| \boldsymbol{t}_{ij} - \gamma_t m_{ij} \boldsymbol{v}_{ij,t}, \qquad (7)$$

where $|\delta_{ij,t}|$ is the length of tangential displacement, $\boldsymbol{v}_{ij,t}$ is the tangential component of the relative velocity of the contact point, γ_t is the constant tangential damping coefficient, while G_i and G_j are shear moduli of the particles i and j, respectively.

The main CPU-time-consuming computational procedures of the DEM are contact detection, contact force computation and time integration. Contact detection was based on the simple and fast implementation of a cell-based algorithm [38]. The explicit velocity Verlet algorithm [38] was used for time integration employing small time steps. The details of outlined DEM model (1–7) and its implementation can be found in [36,39].

3   DEM SaaS Deployed on OpenStack Cloud

The parallel DEM software was developed and deployed as SaaS on the cloud infrastructure to perform time-consuming computations of granular materials.

3.1   Parallel DEM SaaS

The simulation of systems at the particle level of detail has the disadvantage of making DEM computationally very expensive. The selection of an efficient parallel solution algorithm depends on the specific characteristics of the considered problem and the numerical method used [39–41]. The parallel DEM algorithms differ from the analogous parallel processing in the continuum approach. Moving particles dynamically change the workload configuration, making parallelization of DEM software much more difficult and challenging. Domain decomposition is considered one of the most efficient coarse grain strategies for scientific and engineering computations, therefore, it was implemented in the developed DEM code. The recursive coordinate bisection (RCB) method from the Zoltan library [42] was used for domain partitioning because it is highly effective for particle simulations. The RCB method recursively divides the computational domain into nearly equal subdomains by cutting planes orthogonal to the coordinate axes, according to particle coordinates and workload weights. This method is attractive as a dynamic load-balancing algorithm because it implicitly produces incremental partitions and reduces data transfer between processors caused by repartitioning.

The employed DEM software was developed using C++ programming language. Interprocessor communication was implemented in the DEM code by subroutines of the message passing library MPI. Each processor computes the forces and updates the positions of particles only in its subdomain. To perform their computations, the processors need to share information about particles that are near the division boundaries in ghost layers. The main portion of communications is performed prior to performing contact detection and contact force computation. In the present implementation, particle data from the ghost layers are exchanged between neighboring subdomains. The exchange of positions and velocities of particles between MPI processes is a common strategy often used in DEM codes [43]. Despite its local character, interprocessor particle data transfer requires a significant amount of time and reduces the parallel efficiency of computations. The parallel DEM software was deployed on the cloud infrastructure by developing the environment launchers designed for users to configure the SaaS and define custom settings. After successful authorization, the user can define configuration parameters and run the parallel SaaS on ordered virtual resources.

3.2   OpenStack Cloud Infrastructure

The university private cloud infrastructure based on OpenStack Train 2019 version [3] is hosted in the Vilnius Gediminas Technical University. The deployed capabilities of the OpenStack cloud infrastructure include compute service Nova, compute service Zun for containers, networking service Neutron, container network plugin Kuryr, image service Glance, identity service Keystone, object storage service Swift and block storage service Cinder. Nova automatically deploys the provisioned virtual compute instances (VMs), Zun launches and manages containers, Swift provides redundant storage of static objects, Neutron manages virtual network resources, Kuryr connects containers to Neutron, Keystone is responsible for authentication and authorization, while Glance provides service discovery, registration and delivery for virtual disk images.

The cloud infrastructure is managed by the OpenStack API, which provides access to infrastructure services. The OpenStack cloud IaaS provides platforms (PaaS) to develop and deploy software services called SaaS. The PaaS layer supplies engineering application developers with programming-language-level environments and compilers, such as GNU compiler collection. Parallel software for distributed memory systems is developed using the Open MPI platform, which includes the open source implementation of the MPI standard for message passing. The development platform as a service for domain decomposition and dynamic load balancing is provided based on the Zoltan library [42]. It simplifies the load-balancing and data movement difficulties that arise in dynamic simulations. The DEM SaaS was deployed on top of the provided platforms, such as GNU compiler collection, the message passing library Open MPI and the Zoltan library. Computational results are visualized using the cloud visualization service VisLT [44].

The cloud infrastructure is composed of OpenStack service nodes and compute nodes (Intel®Core i7-6700 3.40 GHz CPU, 32 GB DDR4 2133 MHz MHz RAM and 1 TB HDD) connected to 1 Gbps Ethernet LAN. Two alternatives of the virtualization layer are implemented to gain more flexibility and efficiency in resource configuration. Version 2.11.1 of QEMU-KVM is used for virtual machines (VMs) deployed and managed by Nova. Alternatively, Docker version

Table 1. Characteristics of virtual machines and containers.

	Cores	CPU type	RAM, GB	HDD, TB	Price, $/h
VM.small	1	i7-6700	8	0.5	0.0455
VM.small	1	i7-6700	8	0.5	0.0455
VM.small	1	i7-6700	8	0.5	0.0455

19.03.6 containers (CNs) launched and managed by Zun create an abstraction layer between computing resources and the services using them. Ubuntu 18.04 LTS (Bionic Beaver) is installed in the VMs and CNs. Characteristics and prices of VMs and CNs are provided in Table 1. Monetary costs of allocated VMs/CNs are described by price per hour according to Amazon EC2 VM type C5. Two pay-per-use pricing schemes are considered for all VM/CN types. In the case of the traditional cloud pricing scheme named round up, VM instances are billed per hour of usage, but each partial instance-hour is billed as a full hour. In the case of the pricing scheme named proportional, the cost is directly proportional to the time the VMs are allocated, which corresponds to price per second scheme.

4   The Cost and Performance Analysis

The cost and performance of the developed DEM SaaS for parallel computations of granular flows is investigated. The gravity packing problem of granular material, falling under the influence of gravity into a container, was considered because it often served as a benchmark for performance measurements [16]. The solution domain was assumed to be a cubic container with the 1.0m-long edges.

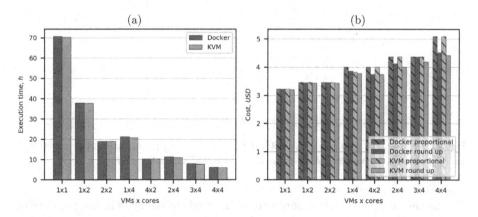

Fig. 1. Execution time and cost: (a) the execution time on KVM virtual machines and Docker containers, (b) the cost computed by using round up and proportional pricing schemes.

Half of the domain was filled with 1000188 monosized particles, using a cubic structure. Performing the benchmark on VMs and CNs of OpenStack cloud, the computation time of 200000 time steps equal to 1.0×10^{-6} was measured.

Figure 1 presents the SaaS execution time and cost on KVM VMs and Docker CNs measured for different numbers of VMs/CNs and cores used. Higher computational performance of DEM SaaS was observed on KVM virtual machines, but the measured difference did not exceed 3.9% of execution time on Docker CNs. Speedup of parallel computations equal to 11.6 was measured on 4x4 configuration of KVM VMs (16 cores), which gave parallel efficiency equal to 0.73. The measured speedup values are close to those obtained for relevant numbers of cores in other parallel performance studies of DEM software [16,43]. The obvious difference in cost computed by using alternative pricing schemes can be observed. This difference varied from 0.6% to 15.4%, depending on the number of VMs or CNs used.

Figure 2 shows the relative difference in cost calculated by using two pricing schemes for various software execution times. The execution time of the numerical DEM software almost linearly depends on the number of time steps used for time integration of Eq. (1). Thus, the number of computed time steps provides the length of the simulated physical time interval, which represents the amount of computations. It can be observed that the difference decreased when longer tasks were executed. The difference diminished to 1.0% in the case of 1600000 computed time steps. Moreover, larger differences caused by multi-node and multi-core execution of MPI-based SaaS can be observed for larger number of VMs/CNs and cores in spite of scattered results.

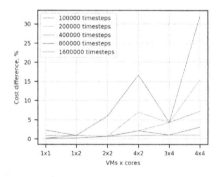

Fig. 2. The relative difference in cost calculated by using round up and proportional pricing schemes for various execution times on KVM virtual machines.

The choice of the optimal hardware setup needs to be taken in the presence of two conflicting objectives or criteria: the execution time T and the computation cost C. This bi-objective optimization problem can be formulated as follows:

$$\min_{p_i \in X}(T(p_i), C(p_i)), \tag{8}$$

where $X = \{1x1,\ 1x2,\ 2x2,\ 1x4,\ 4x2,\ 2x4,\ 3x4,\ 4x4\}$ is the set of feasible solutions. The alternative VMs/CNs configurations 2x2 and 1x4 mean 2 VM.medium instances with 2 cores on 2 nodes and 1 VM.large instance with 4 cores on 1 node, respectively.

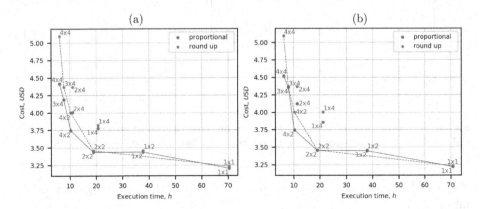

Fig. 3. Pareto fronts for alternative pricing schemes: (a) KVM VMs, (b) Docker CNs.

There are many different approaches to deal with multi-objective optimization problems. A common approach is to find the Pareto optimal solutions, i.e., the solutions that cannot be improved in any of the objectives without degrading at least one of the other objectives. For the formulated bi-objective optimization problem (8), the Pareto optimal solutions are presented in Fig. 3. It was expected that the proportional pricing scheme dominated over the round up pricing scheme and was preferable for users. Solutions based on KVM VMs were better than that based on Docker CNs, but the difference was not large in most cases. The VMs configuration 1x2 belonged to Pareto front in the case of the proportional pricing scheme, but it was excluded from the Pareto front in the case of the round up pricing scheme. It is worth noting that the VMs configurations 2x2 and 4x2 were always preferable over 1x4 and 2x4, which was specific to memory bound DEM computations exploiting higher bandwidth.

Scalarization is as a popular approach to solve a multi-objective optimization problem, considering subjective preferences of a decision maker. The original problem (8) is converted to a single-objective optimization problem by using user defined weights w_T and w_C for normalized execution time objective and normalized cost objective, respectively. Figure 4 shows dependency of scalarized objective function on VMs/CNs configuration for equal (Fig. 4a) and execution time oriented (Fig. 4b) weights. The difference between pricing schemes can be clearly observed only for VMs/CNs configurations with the total number of cores larger than 4. The equal weights resulted in optimal VMs/CNs configuration 2x2, while execution time-oriented weights gave the optimal configuration 4x2. DEM SaaS computations on VMs/CNs configurations 2x2 and 4x2 were so fast

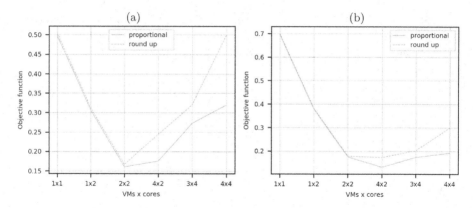

Fig. 4. The application of linear scalarization method: (a) the equal weights ($w_T = 0.5$ and $w_C = 0.5$), (b) the execution time oriented weights ($w_T = 0.7$ and $w_C = 0.3$).

(Fig. 1a) that they dominated over other solutions in the wide range of weights values.

5 Conclusions

In this article, cost and performance analysis of MPI-based computations performed by the discrete element method SaaS on KVM virtual machines and Docker containers of the OpenStack cloud is presented. The SaaS execution time measured on KVM virtual machines was shorter by 0.3–3.9% than that on Docker containers. The difference in cost computed by using alternative pricing schemes varied from 0.6% to 15.4%, depending on the number of virtual machines or containers used. However, the difference decreased to 1.0% for 8 times longer tasks. Pareto front and linear scalarization revealed the preferable VMs/CNs configurations specific to memory bound DEM computations exploiting higher bandwidth.

References

1. Khan, A.A., Zakarya, M.: Energy, performance and cost efficient cloud datacentres: a survey. Comput. Sci. Rev. **40**, 100390 (2021)
2. Mell, P.M., Grance, T.: The NIST definition of cloud computing. Technical report (2011)
3. Openstack. https://www.openstack.org. Accessed 9 Apr 2022
4. Nurmi, D., et al.: The Eucalyptus open-source cloud-computing system. In: 2009 9th IEEE/ACM International Symposium on Cluster Computing and the Grid, pp. 124–131. IEEE (2009)
5. Chierici, A., Veraldi, R.: A quantitative comparison between XEN and KVM. J. Phys: Conf. Ser. **219**(4), 1–10 (2010)
6. Docker. https://www.docker.com. Accessed 9 Apr 2022

7. McMillan, B., Chen, C.: High performance docking. Technical report (2014)
8. Edem now available on rescale's cloud simulation platform. https://www.edemsimulation.com/blog-and-news/news/edem-now-available-rescales-cloud-simulation-platform/. Accessed 9 Apr 2022
9. Sakellari, G., Loukas, G.: A survey of mathematical models, simulation approaches and testbeds used for research in cloud computing. Simul. Model. Pract. Theory **39**, 92–103 (2013)
10. Kačeniauskas, A., et al.: Private cloud infrastructure for applications of mechanical and medical engineering. Inf. Technol. Control **44**(3), 254–261 (2015)
11. Kozhirbayev, Z., Sinnott, R.O.: A performance comparison of container-based technologies for the cloud. Futur. Gener. Comput. Syst. **68**, 175–182 (2017)
12. Chae, M., Lee, H., Lee, K.: A performance comparison of linux containers and virtual machines using docker and KVM. Clust. Comput. **22**(S1), 1765–1775 (2017)
13. Potdar, A.M., Narayan, G.D., Kengond, S., Mulla, M.M.: Performance evaluation of docker container and virtual machine. Procedia Comput. Sci. **171**, 1419–1428 (2020)
14. Hale, J.S., Li, L., Richardson, C.N., Wells, G.N.: Containers for portable, productive, and performant scientific computing. Comput. Sci. Eng. **19**(6), 40–50 (2017)
15. Mohammadi, M., Bazhirov, T.: Comparative benchmarking of cloud computing vendors with high performance Linpack. In: Proceedings of the 2nd International Conference on High Performance Compilation, Computing and Communications - HP3C. ACM Press (2018)
16. Bystrov, O., Pacevič, R., Kačeniauskas, A.: Performance of communication- and computation-intensive SaaS on the OpenStack cloud. Appl. Sci. **11**(16), 7379 (2021)
17. Papazachos, Z.C., Karatza, H.D.: Performance evaluation of bag of gangs scheduling in a heterogeneous distributed system. J. Syst. Softw. **83**(8), 1346–1354 (2010)
18. Moschakis, I.A., Karatza, H.D.: Evaluation of gang scheduling performance and cost in a cloud computing system. J. Supercomput. **59**(2), 975–992 (2010)
19. Sood, K.: Comparative study of scheduling mechanisms in cloud computing. IOSR J. Eng. **4**(5), 30–33 (2014)
20. Hao, Y., Liu, G., Hou, R., Zhu, Y., Lu, J.: Performance analysis of gang scheduling in a grid. J. Netw. Syst. Manage. **23**(3), 650–672 (2014)
21. Bystrov, O., et al.: Performance evaluation of parallel haemodynamic computations on heterogeneous clouds. Comput. Inform. **39**(4), 695–723 (2020)
22. Beloglazov, A., Abawajy, J., Buyya, R.: Energy-aware resource allocation heuristics for efficient management of data centers for cloud computing. Futur. Gener. Comput. Syst. **28**(5), 755–768 (2012)
23. O'Brien, K., Pietri, I., Reddy, R., Lastovetsky, A., Sakellariou, R.: A survey of power and energy predictive models in HPC systems and applications. ACM Comput. Surv. **50**(3), 1–38 (2017)
24. Malawski, M., Figiela, K., Nabrzyski, J.: Cost minimization for computational applications on hybrid cloud infrastructures. Futur. Gener. Comput. Syst. **29**(7), 1786–1794 (2013)
25. Luo, B., Niu, Y., Liu, F.: Cost-effective service provisioning for hybrid cloud applications. In: Guo, S., Liao, X., Liu, F., Zhu, Y. (eds.) CollaborateCom 2015. LNICST, vol. 163, pp. 47–56. Springer, Cham (2016). https://doi.org/10.1007/978-3-319-28910-6_5
26. Zhou, J., Wang, T., Cong, P., Lu, P., Wei, T., Chen, M.: Cost and makespan-aware workflow scheduling in hybrid clouds. J. Syst. Architect. **100**, 101631 (2019)

27. Genez, T.A., Bittencourt, L.F., Madeira, E.R.: Time-discretization for speeding-up scheduling of deadline-constrained workflows in clouds. Futur. Gener. Comput. Syst. **107**, 1116–1129 (2020)
28. Entrialgo, J., García, M., Díaz, J.L., García, J., García, D.F.: Modelling and simulation for cost optimization and performance analysis of transactional applications in hybrid clouds. Simul. Model. Pract. Theory **109**, 102311 (2021)
29. Rosa, M.J., Ralha, C.G., Holanda, M., Araujo, A.P.: Computational resource and cost prediction service for scientific workflows in federated clouds. Futur. Gener. Comput. Syst. **125**, 844–858 (2021)
30. Wang, B., Wang, C., Song, Y., Cao, J., Cui, X., Zhang, L.: A survey and taxonomy on workload scheduling and resource provisioning in hybrid clouds. Clust. Comput. **23**(4), 2809–2834 (2020). https://doi.org/10.1007/s10586-020-03048-8
31. Cundall, P.A., Strack, O.D.L.: A discrete numerical model for granular assemblies. Géotechnique **29**(1), 47–65 (1979)
32. Tumonis, L., Schneider, M., Kačianauskas, R., Kačeniauskas, A.: Comparison of dynamic behaviour of EMA-3 railgun under differently induced loadings. Mechanika **78**(4), 31–37 (2009)
33. Kačeniauskas, A., Rutschmann, P.: Parallel FEM software for CFD problems. Informatica **15**(3), 363–378 (2004)
34. Liu, G., Marshall, J.S., Li, S.Q., Yao, Q.: Discrete-element method for particle capture by a body in an electrostatic field. Int. J. Numer. Meth. Eng. **84**(13), 1589–1612 (2010)
35. Tumonis, L., Kačianauskas, R., Kačeniauskas, A., Schneider, M.: The transient behavior of rails used in electromagnetic railguns: numerical investigations at constant loading velocities. J. Vibroeng. **9**, 15–17 (2007)
36. Džiugys, A., Peters, B.: An approach to simulate the motion of spherical and non-spherical fuel particles in combustion chambers. Granul. Matter **3**(4), 231–266 (2001)
37. Kohring, G.A.: Studies of diffusional mixing in rotating drums via computer simulations. J. Phys. I **5**(12), 1551–1561 (1995)
38. Norouzi, H.R., Zarghami, R., Sotudeh-Gharebagh, R., Mostoufi, N.: Coupled CFD-DEM Modeling. Wiley, Chichester (2016)
39. Kačeniauskas, A., Kačianauskas, R., Maknickas, A., Markauskas, D.: Computation and visualization of discrete particle systems on gLite-based grid. Adv. Eng. Softw. **42**(5), 237–246 (2011)
40. Šešok, D., Belevičius, R., Kačeniauskas, A., Mockus, J.: Application of GRID computing for optimization of grillages. Mechanika **82**(2), 63–69 (2010)
41. Stupak, E., et al.: The geometric model-based patient-specific simulations of turbulent aortic valve flows. Arch. Mech. **69**(4–5), 317–345 (2017)
42. Devine, K., Boman, E., Heaphy, R., Hendrickson, B., Vaughan, C.: Zoltan data management services for parallel dynamic applications. Comput. Sci. Eng. **4**(2), 90–96 (2002)
43. Berger, R., Kloss, C., Kohlmeyer, A., Pirker, S.: Hybrid parallelization of the LIGGGHTS open-source DEM code. Powder Technol. **278**, 234–247 (2015)
44. Pacevič, R., Kačeniauskas, A.: The development of VisLT visualization service in Openstack cloud infrastructure. Adv. Eng. Softw. **103**, 46–56 (2017)

Building a Fine-Grained Analytical Performance Model for Complex Scientific Simulations

Jelle van Dijk$^{(\boxtimes)}$ ⓘ, Gabor Zavodszky ⓘ, Ana-Lucia Varbanescu ⓘ,
Andy D. Pimentel ⓘ, and Alfons Hoekstra ⓘ

Institute for Informatics, Faculty of Science, University of Amsterdam,
Amsterdam, The Netherlands
jelle.van.dijk@uva.nl

Abstract. Analytical performance models are powerful for understanding and predicting the performance of large-scale simulations. As such, they can help identify performance bottlenecks, assess the effect of load imbalance, or indicate performance behavior expectations when migrating to larger systems. Existing automated methods either focus on broad metrics and/or problems - e.g., application scalability behavior on large scale systems and inputs - or use black-box models that are more difficult to interpret e.g., machine-learning models.

In this work we propose a methodology for building per-process analytical performance models relying on code analysis to derive a simple, high-level symbolic application model, and using empirical data to further calibrate and validate the model for accurate predictions.

We demonstrate our model-building methodology on HemoCell, a high-performance framework for cell-based bloodflow simulations. We calibrate the model for two large-scale systems, with different architectures. Our results show good prediction accuracy for four different scenarios, including load-balanced configurations (average error of 3.6%, and a maximum error below 13%), and load-imbalanced ones (with an average prediction error of 10% and a maximum error below 16%).

Keywords: Performance modeling · workload imbalance ·
performance prediction · coupled simulations

1 Introduction

Analytical performance models are powerful for understanding and predicting the performance of large-scale simulations. An *analytical performance model* is a closed-form expression that describes application performance, expressed in a metric of choice, as a combination of *application components*, *application specific parameters* and *hardware parameters*. Analytical models are human-readable and cost little to no resources to use. Furthermore, they can provide many insights that are otherwise expensive to obtain, e.g., locating the performance bottlenecks [10], or are not obtainable at all, e.g., predicting how an application will perform on a next generation of supercomputers [7].

© The Author(s), under exclusive license to Springer Nature Switzerland AG 2023
R. Wyrzykowski et al. (Eds.): PPAM 2022, LNCS 13826, pp. 183–196, 2023.
https://doi.org/10.1007/978-3-031-30442-2_14

Analytical performance models are also useful in determining the impact of load-imbalance in large-scale parallel applications running on current parallel (distributed) systems. Load-imbalance occurs when the parallel processes of an application are not assigned an equal amount of work. This can cause significant inefficiency during the parallel execution of applications on large-scale systems. Several large-scale applications and libraries [5,9,15,21] already use different simple analytical performance models to predict load imbalance. Some of these analytical models have a per-process view of the application, thus allowing for detailed load imbalance predictions [9].

Despite its advantages, analytical modeling remains challenging, as it requires both performance-modeling and application-specific expertise. Furthermore, because the resulting models are application-specific, most of the work needs to be redone when modeling a different application, or even the next version of the same application. While work on generalizing the *process* of building analytical performance models already exists [10,14], most of these approaches aim to provide performance models that predict scalability and extrapolate to new, larger systems, and/or lack the fine granularity needed to support a better understanding of application inefficiency.

To address such limitations, we propose in this work a detailed methodology for building fine-grained, per-process analytical performance models for scientific simulations. By design, the per-process modeling gives us more detailed insights into the performance and load-balance of the modeled application. Our four-step modeling process is as follows: (1) we identify the code-sections and input parameters with a relevant performance impact (2) we build a symbolic analytical performance model that describes the application performance at process level, (3) we calibrate the models for a specific machine with the help of empirical performance data, and we aggregate the per-process models for an application-wide performance prediction. (4) We validate the model performance. The resulting model is outlined in Fig. 1. We note that the symbolic model remains constant for the target application - that is, migrating the model to a different system only requires re-calibration, i.e., collecting empirical performance data.

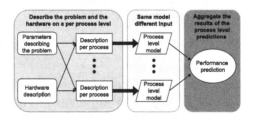

Fig. 1. Overview of the per-process analytical model.

We demonstrate the feasibility of our approach on HemoCell, a high-performance framework for dense cellular suspension flows [19,20]. Previous work, starting from L. Axner, et al. [2], developed a model to predict runtime performance from fractional overheads and showed that, when accurate estimation of these overheads is available, the model is an accurate tool (at most 5% error) for analyzing code execution, even in load-imbalanced scenarios. S. Allowayyad, et al. [1] applied this model for HemoCell, where the fractional overhead caused by load imbalance was estimated under the assumption that it is entirely dependent on local red blood cell count. In this work, we propose a novel methodology to build a model for the function level performance, which, after calibration, provides *an estimation* for the main sources of computational load (i.e., for the fractional loads). This method is demonstrated using HemoCell, similarly to [1]. However, the calibrated performance functions are defined using natural units of the simulation (red blood cell count and fluid node count). Specifically, we build a per-process function-level symbolic model for HemoCell, and calibrate it for two different HPC platforms: Snellius (SURF, Netherlands) and DAS6 (ASCI, Netherlands) [3]. The model accuracy is evaluated on balanced and non-balanced simulations, using three scenarios that showcase different types of execution imbalance[1]. Our results demonstrate good *prediction accuracy* for our models, indicating they can be useful tools for assessing load-imbalance impact in scientific simulations.

The remainder of this paper is structured as follows. We present our modeling approach in Sect. 2 and further show, in Sect. 3, how it is applied to build and calibrate an analytical performance model for HemoCell. We further evaluate the accuracy of the model in Sect. 4 on four different scenarios with different degrees and types of load-imbalance. Finally, we provide a brief overview of related work in Sect. 5, and conclude the paper in Sect. 6.

2   Performance Modeling Methodology

In this section we present our methodology for building per-process analytical performance models for large-scale simulations. We assume a Single-Program, Multiple-Data model, where processes with different ranks and are executed concurrently on different processing units (e.g., cores or nodes). Throughout the modeling process we also assume that at least function level performance measurements of the application are available. The collected data depends on the desired model output, e.g., time (s), execution rate (Mflop/s), or energy (J).

Our methodology has four steps: (1) identifying relevant code sections and parameters, (2) building the model, (3) calibrating the model, and (4) validating the model. In this section we elaborate on each of these steps.

(1) **Identify performance relevant code sections and parameters.** A code section can be any part of the application code which is monitored individually. Usually, in practice, such code sections are *functions*. The *relevant code sections* are those code sections that are significant in the performance breakdown. The performance of a code section will change based on external

---

[1] The code for data processing and the raw data used in this paper are available at DOI:10.5281/zenodo.6570501.

parameters, e.g., size of the simulated domain. For each code section, we identify the relevant parameters, which are then selected as inputs for the model.

(2) Build the symbolic model: The model is built in a top-down manner: we start from a coarse symbolic model, and refine parts as needed, which allows for control over the level of detail incorporated into the model. The results, is a symbolic analytical performance model that describes the performance of a singe process in terms of the code-sections and parameters selected in step (1).

The output of the per-process model is aggregated into a final prediction using operators that are application- and metric-specific (see Fig. 1). For example, when predicting execution time for fully concurrent applications, the performance is dominated by the longest process; however, when processes run sequentially, the aggregated execution time is the sum of the execution time of all processes.

(3) Calibrate the model: To calibrate the model we replace the symbolic terms describing code section performance with predictive functions. Firstly, empirical data of code section performance is collected. This data is used to fit a function for each individual code section, the degree of the function depends on the relationship between the code section and the input parameters e.g., the output can scale linearly or exponentially in relation to the parameters.

(4) Validate the model: To validate the model, we measure performance on relevant (unseen) datasets, and report prediction error, calculated as $e = \text{abs}(\text{predicted} - \text{measured}) * 100/\text{measured}$. If needed, to increase prediction accuracy, the model can be further refined (i.e., functions can be further split into smaller units). This, however, also increases the model complexity.

3   Modeling Hemocell

In this section, we build an analytical performance model describing the execution time of Hemocell. This model is calibrated on two different machines, Snellius (SURF, Netherlands) and DAS6 (ASCI, Netherlands) [3].

3.1   Hemocell

Hemocell is a coupled multi-scale simulation code used for modeling blood flow. The application simulates blood as a dense cellular suspension flow, modeling the evolution of particles, i.e., red blood cells (RBCs) and platelets, suspended in a solvent, i.e., the blood plasma, over multiple discrete time steps [19,20]. The solvent is modeled as a fluid using the lattice Boltzman method (LBM). LBM calculations are handled by the Palabos library [12]. The movement, deformation, and interaction of particles is modeled separately from the LBM calculation. Both models are coupled together intermittently to simulate the full blood flow system.

For parallelization, Hemocell uses multi-processing: each process receives a section of the *simulated domain*, i.e., a *subdomain*, and is responsible for computing the fluid and particles within that subdomain. During the simulation, the processes communicate with each other using MPI. The edges of the fluid field, as well as parts of the particles which may span multiple subdomains, must be communicated to ensure correct results.

Previous research focused on improving Hemocell's overall performance [16], as well as improving the scaling performance through better load balancing [1].

3.2   Performance-Relevant Functions and Parameters

A Hemocell simulation consists of three phases: (1) setup, (2) computation, and (3) data output. Our work focuses on the most expensive of these phases, the computation. In turn, the Hemocell computation phase has three components: (i) fluid computation, (ii) particle computation, and (iii) model coupling.

We define *performance-relevant functions* as those functions that have a non-negligible performance impact. Similarly, we define *performance-relevant parameters* as function parameters that have a non-negligible performance impact. The process of identifying the performance-relevant functions and parameters is based on both expert application knowledge, code inspection, and investigation of any available fine-grained performance measurements. Table 1 shows the performance-relevant functions and parameters for Hemocell.

Table 1. Performance-relevant functions and parameters for Hemocell.

Name	Component	Description	Parameters
CollideAndStream	Fluid field	Lattice-Boltzmann calculations	(xs, ys, zs)
CollideAndStream_comm	Fluid field	Lattice-Boltzmann communication	(xs, ys, zs)
spreadParticleForce	Model coupling	Apply particle forces to the fluid field	RBCs
interpolateFluidVelocity	Model coupling	Apply fluid forces to the particles	RBCs
syncEnvelopes	Particle field	Setup for particle communication.	RBCs
syncEnvelopes_comm	Particle field	Communicate particle vertices.	RBCs, (xs, ys, zs)
AdvanceParticles	Particle field	Calculate new particle position.	RBCs
applyConstitutiveModel	Particle field	Compute and apply internal particle forces.	RBCs
deleteNonLocalParticles	Particle field	Remove non-local particle information.	RBCs
setExternalVector	Fluid field	Apply external forces to the fluid.	(xs, ys, zs)

3.3   Model-Building

For building the model, we start with the highest-level description of the application: the components.

$$T = \text{Iters} \times [\ \text{FluidField}(\text{xs}, \text{ys}, \text{zs}) \tag{1}$$
$$+ \text{ParticleField}(\text{xs}, \text{ys}, \text{zs}, \text{RBCs})$$
$$+ \text{ModelCoupling}(\text{RBCs})\ ]$$

In Eq. (1), *Iters* is the number of iterations, (xs, ys, zs) are the dimensions of the domain, RBCs is the number of red blood cells within the domain, and *FluidField*, *ParticleField* and *ModelCoupling* are the functions that describe the execution time per iteration for each component[2]. We improve on this initial model by expanding the component terms. Each component term is made up of the summation of the time spent in the respective relevant functions, see Table 1.

To simplify the calibration step we derive two new parameters: V and SA, representing the subdomain volume and surface area, respectively. For rectangular domains they are defined as $V = xs \times xy \times xz$ and $SA = 2 \times (xs \times ys + xs \times zs + ys \times zs)$. Expanding on the initial model, replacing xs, ys, zs with either V or SA, gives us the following analytical model:

$$T = \text{Iters} \times [\ \text{FluidField}(V, SA) \tag{2}$$
$$+ \text{ParticleField}(SA, \text{RBCs})$$
$$+ \text{ModelCoupling}(\text{RBCs})\ ]$$
$$\text{FluidField}(V, SA) = \text{CollideAndStream}(V) \tag{3}$$
$$+ \text{CollideAndStream\_comm}(SA)$$
$$+ \text{setExternalVector}(V)$$

$$\text{ParticleField}(SA, RBCs) = \text{syncEnvelopes}(RBCs) \tag{4}$$
$$+ \text{syncEnvelopes\_comm}(RBCs, SA)$$
$$+ \text{AdvanceParticles}(RBCs)$$
$$+ \text{applyConstitutiveModel}(RBCs)$$
$$+ \text{deleteNonLocalParticle}(RBCs)$$
$$\text{ModelCoupling}(RBCs) = \text{spreadParticleForce}(RBCs) \tag{5}$$
$$+ \text{interpolateFluidVelocity}(RBCs)$$

3.4   Model Calibration

In the calibration step the terms in the model are replaced with *predictors*. The predictors are fitted, using empirical data collected from the two machines, Snellius and DAS6, the machine details are presented in Table 2.

Table 2. Machine Descriptions

Machine	CPU	Cores	Frequency	Memory
Snellius	AMD Rome 7H12 (x2)	128	3.2 GHz	256 GiB
DAS6	AMD EPYC-2 7402P	24	2.8 GHz	128 GB

To collect the data, we simulate a cuboid-shaped domain of blood for 500 iterations. The size of the domain ranges from $(12.5, 12.5, 12.5)\mu m$ to $(75, 75, 50)\mu m$.

---

[2] Please note: for readability purposes, when using the name of a function in a model, we denote its performance, in most cases, execution time. In other words, we use **ParticleField** instead of $T_{ParticleField}$.

Every domain size is run with 7 different volume fractions of RBCs (hematocrit): 0%, 9%, 10%, 12%, 14%, 16%, and 18%. The workload in these experiments is fully balanced, i.e., every process performs the same amount of work. Throughout the modeling and analysis process, we use the Scalasca toolchain for automatic code instrumentation and performance measurements of Hemocell [8,11].

The predictors are all fitted functions over the respective performance data. The degree of the fit function is dependent on the relationship between the parameters and the output metric. For this model we have chosen the parameters such that all relationships are linear. The calibrated predictors are presented in Table 3.

Table 3. Calibrated performance predictors for Snellius and DAS6.

Name	Predictors Snellius [S]	Predictors DAS6 [S]
collideAndStream	$0.0062 + V \times 3.5 \times 10^{-7}$	$0.008 + V \times 2.5 \times 10^{-7}$
setExternalVector	$2.6 \times 10^{-5} + V \times 4.3 \times 10-8$	$-0.00022 + V \times 2.1 \times 10-8$
collideAndStream_comm	$-0.00047 + SA \times 9.1 \times 10^{-7}$	$0.00094 + SA \times 2.2 \times 10^{-7}$
syncEnvelopes_comm	$0.00048 + SA \times 1.3 \times 10^{-7}$ $+RBCs \times 3.5 \times 10^{-5}$	$0.00046 + SA \times 1.3 \times 10-8$ $+RBCs \times 9.5 \times 10-6$
syncEnvelopes	$-1.4 \times 10^{-5} + RBCs \times 8.3 \times 10^{-5}$	$9.2 \times 10^{-5} + RBCs \times 3.6 \times 10^{-5}$
advanceParticles	$0.00049 + RBCs \times 0.00014$	$0.00059 + RBCs \times 8.2 \times 10^{-5}$
applyConstitutiveModel	$-1.3 \times 10^{-5} + RBCs \times 4.4 \times 10^{-5}$	$-4.4 \times 10^{-5} + RBCs \times 2.8 \times 10^{-5}$
deleteNonLocalParticles	$5.1 \times 10^{-5} + RBCs \times 1.5 \times 10^{-5}$	$2.1 \times 10^{-5} + RBCs \times 7.5 \times 10^{-5}$
spreadParticleForce	$0.00081 + RBCs \times 0.0004$	$0.0012 + RBCs \times 0.00025$
interpolateFluidVelocity	$0.00013 + RBCs \times 7.7 \times 10^{-5}$	$0.00031 + RBCs \times 4.2 \times 10^{-5}$

4   Scenario Analysis

The fine granularity of the model allows for accurate performance predictions in scenarios that differ from the configuration used for calibration. In this section we evaluate the model, as presented in Sect. 3, and use it to analyze the performance of Hemocell in four different scenarios, (1) balanced workload, (2) imbalanced subdomains, (3) imbalanced hematocrit, and (4) imbalanced communication.

4.1   Scenario: Balanced Workload

In the balanced scenario each process receives the same amount of work. The setup is identical to the simulation configurations used for model calibration, however the domain sizes are of course different. Empirical and predicted results are shown for Snellius and DAS6 in Fig. 2a and 2b. The results show that the model can accurately predict the performance in this scenario a maximum error of 12.87% and an average error of 3.6%.

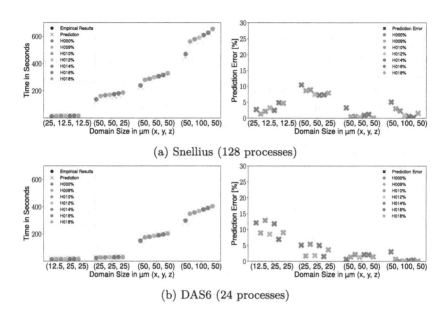

(a) Snellius (128 processes)

(b) DAS6 (24 processes)

Fig. 2. Observed and predicted execution time and prediction error for the load balanced scenario, on DAS6 and Snellius. The standard deviation of the observed results is within 1.5%

4.2 Scenario: Imbalanced Subdomains

In an ideal scenario each process is assigned a subdomain of the same size. However, due to complex simulation domains this is not always achievable. An imbalanced distribution of the domain leads to a loss of performance.

The imbalance in this scenario is generated by assigning half of the processes to 75% of the full domain, and the other half of the process to 25% of the full domain, see Fig. 3. This means that half of the process are assigned three times more work than the other half.

Fig. 3. Imbalanced domain distribution. Both the red and blue parts are assigned to half of the processes. (Color figure online)

For each configuration, the results for the imbalanced and balanced configurations are measured and predicted. By comparing the balanced and imbalanced predictions we estimate the overhead introduced by the load imbalance. The results are presented in Fig. 4.

We observe good accuracy for the imbalanced scenario predictions, with a maximum error of 15.83% and an average of 10.26%. The prediction accuracy on Snellius is lower than on DAS6. This is most likely caused by the difference in memory layout. A node on Snellius is dual-socket, meaning that the L3 cache is not shared between all threads. By assigning most of the domain to half of the processes we are moving most of the data onto a single socket, significantly increasing the amount of data that is accessed by that socket. This combined with the larger overall domain on Snellius, which results in the subdomains of one process being further apart. The result is that the cost of memory operations increases more on Snellius, which is not captured by the model.

We also observe that the load-imbalance overhead is higher for the 18% hematocrit configurations, compared to the equivalent 0% runs. This increase is due to the RBC computation, which worsens the already-present workload imbalance. This increase is correctly captured by the model.

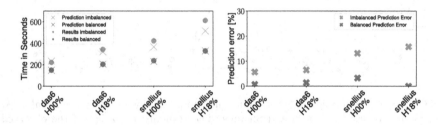

Fig. 4. Observed and predicted execution time and prediction error for the imbalanced domain scenario, on DAS6 and Snellius. The standard deviation of the observed results is within 1.5%

4.3   Scenarios: Imbalanced Hematocrit

The hematocrit value has a significant impact on performance, as can be seen in Fig. 2. A higher hematocrit means more of the volume is occupied by RBCs, resulting in more computation and communication. In the configurations up till now, we assumed a homogeneous hematocrit throughout the domain. However, in more realistic scenarios the hematocrit varies throughout the domain.

The imbalanced hematocrit scenario shows the performance overhead of having a non-homogeneous hematocrit. To create an imbalanced hematocrit each domain is initialized such that part of the domain has a hematocrit of 18%, the other part is either initialized at 9% or 0%. On DAS6 both parts are evenly sized, on Snellius they are either evenly sized, see Fig. 5a, or the first 16 threads are assigned the higher hematocrit subdomains, see Fig. 5b.

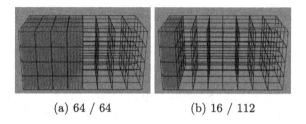

(a) 64 / 64   (b) 16 / 112

Fig. 5. Snellius imbalanced hematocrit (18% and 0%) across 128 processes.

Because the fluid computation is not affected by the hematocrit for the results in this scenario we only show the time spend on the particle and coupling components. The results are presented in Fig. 6.

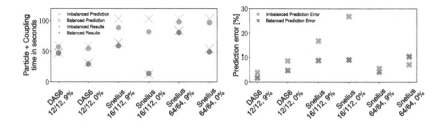

Fig. 6. Observed and predicted execution time and prediction error for the imbalanced hematocrit scenario, on DAS6 and Snellius. The standard deviation of the observed results is within 1.5%

For the imbalanced configurations where the domain is split in half, the highest observed prediction error is acceptable, at 8.61%. However, for the (16/112) configurations, the predictions are less accurate, with errors above 16.8%. The large error is caused by a change in the number of communication neighbors, which is *not captured* in the current model. We address this limitation in Sect. 4.4.

4.4 Scenario: Imbalanced Communication

In the imbalanced hematocrit results, we observe a lower prediction accuracy on the (16 / 112) distribution configurations. This is partially caused by a change in the communication costs. The processes that are assigned more work, in the (16/112) configuration, as shown in Fig. 5b, are located at the edge of the non-periodic domain. This means that the number of neighbors that need to be communicated with is less than if the subdomain computed by the process is located in the middle of the domain. However, during calibration it is assumed that the processes are fully surrounded by neighbors. To address this we expand the original model to include a term to express how many direct neighbors a process needs to communicate with.

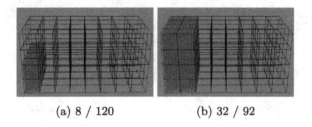

(a) 8 / 120   (b) 32 / 92

Fig. 7. Snellius imbalanced hematocrit (18% and 0%) across 128 processes.

The model is expanded by adding CR_x, which denotes the communication ratio of the fluid or particle component, $CR_x = \frac{\#\text{Neighbors}}{\text{Max Neighbors}}$. This ratio is defined separately for the fluid and particle communication because for fluid communication the maximal number of neighbors that need to be communicated with is 18, as opposed to 26 possible neighbors for the particle communication[3]. In Eqs. (3) and (4) the functions describing the fluid and particle communications are replaced with Eqs. (6) and (7). The functions in Eqs. (6) and 7 multiply the original communication term with the newly introduced $CR_{component}$ ratio.

$$\text{syncEnvelopes\_comm}(RBCs, SA, CR_{particle}) = \tag{6}$$
$$CR_{particle} \times \text{syncEnvelopes\_comm}(RBCs, SA)$$
$$\text{collideAndStream\_comm}(SA, CR_{fluid}) = \tag{7}$$
$$CR_{fluid} \times \text{collideAndStream\_comm}(SA)$$

To verify that the model expansion improves the accuracy the updated model is applied to the (16/112) configuration, as well as a (8/120) configuration, shown in Fig. 7a, and a (32/92) configuration, shown in Fig. 7b. These experiments are run on Snellius for 500 iterations with a subdomain size of (50, 50, 50) μm. The results are presented in Fig. 8.

The results show a clear improvement in the prediction accuracy, compared to the previous version without the added imbalance term. The highest prediction error is reduced from 24.53% to 16.19% when using the updated model. The results in all experiments performed before this did not change, because in those configurations the processes that dominate performance need to communicate with the maximum number of neighbors. Not only is the accuracy better, but the results also provide more detailed information about the different configurations. With the old model, the prediction for each configuration is identical. However, in the results we see that the different configurations do not perform the same. The updated model is capable of better highlighting this difference in performance.

---

[3] For CR_{fluid} neighbors with no RBCs are not counted, because the communication is overlapped by computation. For $CR_{particle}$ the value of each neighbor is scaled with the relative number of RBCs, i.e., if the neighboring hematocrit is half the neighbors value is 0.5.

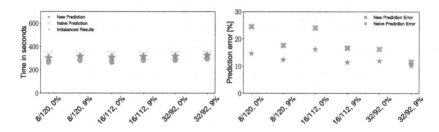

Fig. 8. Observed and predicted results and prediction error for the imbalanced communication scenario, on DAS6 and Snellius. Standard deviation of the observed results is within 1.5%

5   Related Work

This section provides a brief overview of alternative performance models, and how they differ from our own approach.

Analytical performance models for modeling the performance of large-scale applications have been proposed for many years [14]. However, such models are application-specific, and not generalizable to a wider range of applications. To address this, Hoefler et al. [10] propose a multistep approach for building analytical performance models. Their metric of interest is application scaling behavior; therefore, these models do not capture per-process performance.

Other tools to automate parts of the modeling process, such as *EXTRA-P* [6, 7], target on finding scalability bugs in large-scale applications. EXTRA-P builds a statistical model based on empirical performance results of the application. However, the resulting model is non-trivial to understand and tweak, and cannot predict scalability bugs at process-level.

Beyond analytical models, other types of performance models, such as simulators and machine-learning based models, are typically more accurate, but have interpretability issues. For example, models based on machine-learning require significant training data and resources, and the resulting black-box models provide a lot less insight into the application performance characteristics [13,17]. Functional and cycle-accurate simulations provide accurate information on how an application behaves, and why, but they take a very long time to build and calibrate, which renders them difficult to use for large-scale applications [4,18].

6   Conclusion

In this paper we proposed a methodology for building per-process performance models for large-scale, multi-processing simulations. The per-process modeling approach gives portable, fine-grained, accurate, analytical performance models.

We further used the proposed methodology to build an accurate predictive model for Hemocell, a coupled simulation for blood flow. We demonstrated that the resulting model is capable of accurate performance prediction for both balanced workloads, where we see a maximum error of 12.9%, and an average of 3.6% error, and imbalanced scenarios, with a maximum of 16.2% error, and an average of 10.2% error. These results indicate that, although the model-building and calibration steps are based on simple balanced workloads, the model is able to analyze and predict simulation performance in load-imbalanced scenarios. This is a significant advantage for our per-process approach. Finally, we have shown how to refine the model to address potential inaccuracies, thus showing the advantage of a white-box, analytical approach.

In future work we aim to reduce the amount of manual work required to build the model, by for example incorporating statistical methods for determining performance behavior of code sections. In the near future, we aim to extend the model to work for multi-node computations and both apply our model to more simulations and increasingly dynamic scenarios. Specifically, at runtime, the workload could be dynamically shifting between processes as a result of the simulated phenomena, thus showing different load-imbalance patterns during execution. Thus, we plan to use the model to predict the performance degradation due to such changes in load balancing.

References

1. Alowayyed, S., et al.: Load balancing of parallel cell-based blood flow simulations. J. Comput. Sci. **24**, 1–7 (2018). https://doi.org/10.1016/j.jocs.2017.11.008
2. Axner, L., et al.: Performance evaluation of a parallel sparse lattice Boltzmann solver. J. Comput. Phys. **227**(10), 4895–4911 (2008). https://doi.org/10.1016/j.jcp.2008.01.013
3. Bal, H., et al.: A medium-scale distributed system for computer science research: infrastructure for the long term. Computer **49**(5), 54–63 (2016). https://doi.org/10.1109/MC.2016.127
4. Bohrer, P., et al.: Mambo: a full system simulator for the PowerPC architecture. SIGMETRICS Perform. Eval. Rev. **31**(4), 8–12 (2004). https://doi.org/10.1145/1054907.1054910
5. Borgdorff, J., et al.: Performance of distributed multiscale simulations. Philos. Trans. A Math. Phys. Eng. Sci. **372**(2021), 20130407 (2014). https://doi.org/10.1098/rsta.2013.0407
6. Calotoiu, A., et al.: Using automated performance modeling to find scalability bugs in complex codes. In: SC 2013, pp. 1–12. ACM (2013). https://doi.org/10.1145/2503210.2503277
7. Calotoiu, A., et al.: Lightweight requirements engineering for exascale co-design. In: IEEE Cluster 2018, pp. 201–211 (2018). https://doi.org/10.1109/CLUSTER.2018.00038
8. Geimer, M., et al.: The Scalasca performance toolset architecture. Concurr. Computat. Pract. Exper. (2010). https://doi.org/10.1002/cpe.1556
9. Germaschewski, K., et al.: The plasma simulation code: a modern particle-in-cell code with patch-based load-balancing. J. Comput. Phys. **318**, 305–326 (2016). https://doi.org/10.1016/j.jcp.2016.05.013
10. Hoefler, T., et al.: Performance modeling for systematic performance tuning. In: SC 2011, pp. 1–12 (2011). https://doi.org/10.1145/2063348.2063356

11. Knüpfer, A., et al.: Score-P: a joint performance measurement run-time infrastructure for periscope, Scalasca, TAU, and Vampir. In: Brunst, H., et al. (eds.) Tools for High Performance Computing, pp. 79–91. Springer, Heidelberg (2012). https://doi.org/10.1007/978-3-642-31476-6_7

12. Latt, J., et al.: Palabos: parallel lattice Boltzmann solver. Comput. Math. Appl. (2020). https://doi.org/10.1016/j.camwa.2020.03.022

13. Lee, B.C., et al.: Methods of inference and learning for performance modeling of parallel applications. In: Ppopp 2007, pp. 249–258. Association for Computing Machinery (2007). https://doi.org/10.1145/1229428.1229479

14. Mathis, M.M., Amato, N.M., Adams, M.L.: A general performance model for parallel sweeps on orthogonal grids for particle transport calculations. In: ISC 2000, pp. 255–263. Association for Computing Machinery (2000). https://doi.org/10.1145/335231.335256

15. Murtaza, S., Hoekstra, A.G., Sloot, P.M.A.: Compute bound and I/O bound cellular automata simulations on FPGA logic. ACM Trans. Reconfigurable Technol. Syst. **1**(4), 23:1–23:21 (2009). https://doi.org/10.1145/1462586.1462592

16. Tarksalooyeh, V.A., Závodszky, G., Hoekstra, A.G.: Optimizing parallel performance of the cell based blood flow simulation software HemoCell. In: Rodrigues, J.M.F., et al. (eds.) Computational Science. LNCS, vol. 11538, pp. 537–547. Springer, Cham (2019). https://doi.org/10.1007/978-3-030-22744-9_42

17. Witt, C., et al.: Predictive performance modeling for distributed batch processing using black box monitoring and machine learning. Inf. Syst. **82**, 33–52 (2019). https://doi.org/10.1016/j.is.2019.01.006

18. Xu, G., et al.: Simulation-based performance prediction of HPC applications: a case study of HPL. In: 2020 IEEEACM International Workshop HPC User Support Tools HUST Workshop on Programming and Performance Visualization Tools Pro-Tools, pp. 81–88 (2020). https://doi.org/10.1109/HUSTProtools51951.2020.00016

19. Závodszky, G., et al.: Cellular level in-silico modeling of blood rheology with an improved material model for red blood cells. Front. Physiol. **8** (2017). https://doi.org/10.3389/fphys.2017.00563

20. Zavodszky, G., et al.: Hemocell: a high-performance microscopic cellular library. Procedia Comput. Sci. **108**, 159–165 (2017)

21. Zhu, X., et al.: Gemini: a computation-centric distributed graph processing system. In: 12th USENIX Symposium on Operating Systems Design and Implementation, OSDI 2016, pp. 301–316 (2016)

Evaluation of Machine Learning Techniques for Predicting Run Times of Scientific Workflow Jobs

Bartosz Balis[✉] and Michal Grabowski

AGH University of Science and Technology, Krakow, Poland
balis@agh.edu.pl

Abstract. Predicting execution time of computational jobs helps improve resource management, reduce execution cost, and optimize energy consumption. In this paper, we evaluate machine learning techniques for the purpose of predicting execution times of scientific workflow jobs. Various aspects of applying these techniques are evaluated in terms of their impact on prediction performance. These include (1) Comparison of performance of different regressors; (2) using a single-stage prediction pipeline vs. two-stage one; (3) impact of categorization granularity in the first stage of the two-stage pipeline; (4) training one global model for all jobs vs. using separate models for individual job types. We also propose a novel prediction model based on symbolic regression and evaluate its performance. Interpretability of prediction models and usage of proper performance metrics are also discussed. Experimental evaluation has led to a number of interesting findings that provide valuable insight on how to apply machine learning techniques to prediction of execution time of computational jobs.

Keywords: scientific workflows · performance prediction · machine learning · symbolic regression

1 Introduction

Learning and predicting characteristics of computational workloads is crucial for efficient resource management [7,13], optimization of energy consumption [11], or reduction of execution cost [8]. Scientific workflows are an example of computational workloads which are graphs of tasks, typically large and diverse in terms of such characteristics as resource utilization, data footprint and execution times. Unsurprisingly, machine learning techniques are increasingly used to learn characteristics of scientific workflows in order to improve various aspects of their management [4].

In this paper, we present experimental evaluation of different machine learning methods for prediction of the execution time of computational jobs that are part of scientific workflows. We investigate several aspects that affect the prediction performance:

- We compare performance of a single-stage vs. two-stage prediction pipeline. In this approach, selected job properties are estimated in the first stage and then added to the input vector for the second stage. In addition, we investigate the impact of categorization granularity (from two-class to continuous) in the first stage on the overall performance of prediction.
- In addition to evaluating several widely-used regression techniques (KNN, MLP, SVR), we propose and evaluate a novel approach to job execution time prediction based on symbolic regression.
- We evaluate the performance of one global model (all jobs) vs. multiple specialized models (one model per job type).
- We discuss interpretability of prediction models and usage of proper model performance metrics.

The paper is organized as follows. Section 2 reviews related work. Section 3 describes the data set used for model training. Section 4 presents details of the model training process. Section 5 presents the experiments and their results. Finally, Sect. 6 concludes the paper.

2   Related Work

ML-based prediction for Spark jobs, presented in [10], focuses on the benefits achieved by improving job execution time prediction. The paper presents a broad comparison of models, metrics, and features used for vectorization. In [5], a method for predicting job durations of HPC jobs is presented. However, it is based on simple heuristics, not machine learning. In [3], various machine learning methods are used to predict power consumption of HPC jobs. These papers neither contain analysis of the impact of different factors on prediction performance, nor discuss model interpretability, which might be considered as flaws for a modern machine learning-based paper.

Some methods combine the foundations laid by machine learning-agnostic research, for example, Pemogen [2]. In this paper, researchers present an approach that combines machine learning and analytic methods described in detail in the previous section. By leveraging the static analysis of the properties of the jobs, which authors named *kernels*, they simplify the prediction process and improve significantly the models' accuracy. They also focus on the speed of predictive model generation, making their research applicable in an ad hoc way for newly created jobs. Their approach is also easily interpretable, as they use LASSO as their predictive model.

Pham and others [12] explore how the properties of computational jobs can be reasoned about, describe their vectorizable parameters, and establish important definitions of runtime and pre-runtime job parameters. They introduce a two-stage prediction pipelines, a novel method that involves predicting some runtime metadata in the first stage and including it in the final process of prediction of the execution time. However, since they do not provide results with commonly used error metrics, their work can be improved upon via extensive model validation and error metrics discussion. Moreover, the paper lacks discussion on model interpretability.

3   Data Set Characterization

The data set used in this study comes from execution logs of the HyperFlow workflow management system [1]. It consists of over 186k job execution traces from 263 runs of Montage[1], Montage2[2] and Soykb[3] workflows on Kubernetes clusters deployed in Amazon AWS and Google Cloud. Analysis of the data set reveals that most jobs are short-lived, with execution times of between 1000 ms and 10 min, as visualized in Fig. 1.

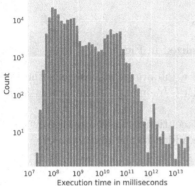
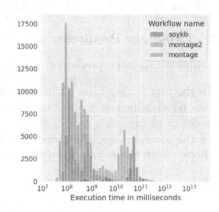

Fig. 1. Distribution of jobs' execution times.

Fig. 2. Distribution of job's execution times by workflow type.

Moreover, there is an additional disproportion between the distributions of execution times of jobs originating from different workflows. **Montage** contains substantially more shorter jobs, **Montage2** has a slightly more balanced distribution and **Soykb** contains more long-running jobs. The distributions among workflow types is shown in Fig. 2. In addition, the short analysis provided above is related exclusively to the predicted value – job's execution time and does not include various factors included in the feature vectors. This illustrates the need for partitioning of the dataset, to avoid producing predictors biased towards specific types of jobs, which would harm the predictor's overall quality and reliability. Consequently, we have decided to partition data into the following (overlapping) subsets:

– Jobs shorter than 1200 ms – these are very short jobs, compared to the average time of spawning a Kubernetes' pod which hosts the execution [9]. Such jobs are typically agglomerated into batches by HyperFlow to avoid the overhead introduced by the aforementioned mechanism.

---

[1] https://github.com/hyperflow-wms/montage-workflow.
[2] https://github.com/hyperflow-wms/montage2-workflow.
[3] https://github.com/hyperflow-wms/soykb-workflow.

- Jobs with execution time between 2 and 25 s.
- Jobs executed more than 3000 times – isolating this set is an attempt to extract information from the jobs that impact the overall workflow execution the most.
- All jobs – this is an obvious 'partition', however, analyzing it might prove to be costly in terms of training the models and will certainly be biased towards the jobs executed most frequently.

4   Models for Execution Time Prediction

4.1   Two-Stage Prediction Architecture

We employ two-stage prediction which is visualized in Fig. 3:

1. In the first stage, some useful properties of a job are estimated, e.g. the job can be classified according to its overall CPU/memory utilization as *high*, *medium* or *low*, etc.
2. In the second stage, the target property (execution time in our case) is predicted, with the results from the first stage added to the input vector.

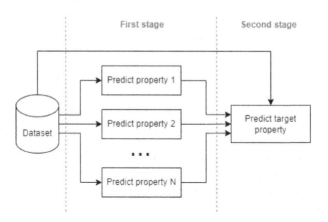

Fig. 3. Two-step prediction process.

This approach has been shown to perform better than a single-stage one in [12]. In this paper, we investigate *how the prediction granularity (the number of categories) used in the first stage affects the performance of the prediction in the second stage.*

4.2 Model Training and Building Pipeline

Building efficient and reliable ML models typically involves several steps. Firstly, the data set must be prepared and a proper vectorization must be applied. Then, the models need to be trained and tested, often repeatedly, with different evaluation metrics. Below we summarize ML techniques used in this work. The ML pipeline is automated using *Scikit-learn*[4].

Feature Extraction. Vectorization or feature extraction is a process of translating data into vectors or scalars, which one suspects are meaningful in the process attempted to capture with the predictive model. This is often the most important step in the whole process and requires the most human supervision and expertise. In this paper, we use Principal Component Analysis *(PCA)* for feature selection.

Model Training and Tuning. Model training involves partitioning of the data set, repeated evaluation, and improving the predictive models. To avoid overfitting, we employ the *k-fold cross-validation*. In addition, grid search is used to select best possible hyperparameters of models.

For the classification step, we have tested several algorithms: MLP Classifier, KNN Classifier and Support-Vector (SVC) classifier. We have evaluated the following regressors: K-Nearest Neighbor (KNN), Lasso, Multi-Layer Perceptron (MLP), Support-Vector Regression (SVR).

Evaluation Metrics. We use the following metrics to measure model performance:

- Coefficient of determination R^2 – it denotes how much of the variance in the observed data is explained by the predictions. The bigger R^2, the better the predictive model.
- Adjusted coefficient of determination R^2_{adj} – it denotes how well the predictor uses additional input variables. When the variables used in the model enhance its predictions to be better than the values expected by chance, R^2_{adj} increases.
- Mean Absolute Percentage Error (MAPE) – it is the mean of relative errors expressed as a percentage. The smaller the MAPE, the better the predictive model. As MAPE represents a relative value, it is easily interpretable and does not require any additional statistical information about the target values.

4.3 Symbolic Regression Model

Symbolic regression is a type of regression that combines symbolic manipulation with genetic programming. The population used as part of genetic manipulation is based on algebraically correct and calculable expressions. These expressions are modified and mutated using the principles of Genetic Programming to find the one that fits the data with the least error score. Expression complexity can be constrained in terms of the depth of the expression tree combined with penalties for using nontrivial nodes, such as trigonometric or logarithmic functions.

---

[4] https://scikit-learn.org.

In this study, we have used the DataRobot's Eureqa tool to build the model. This experiment involved choosing several parameters of the symbolic regression search:

- The R^2 metric was chosen for model selection. For additional comparisons for each model, MAE, $MAPE$ and RAE were also calculated, as they are easily interpretable.
- The train/test set split ratio was set to 3:1. It is important to point out that the train and test subsets were the product of partitioning the train test used for training classic regression models.
- For the set of operations available for use in expressions, we decided to use simple algebraic expressions extended with basic trigonometrical and exponential functions.
- As an implicit assumption on the maximal model's complexity – to avoid overfitting by producing overly complex expressions – we chose to discard any model with complexity higher than 15.

5   Evaluation

5.1   Prediction Architecture Evaluation

The first experiment aims at establishing the better performing prediction architecture. For this purpose, all data sets were used to train various models using both the single stage and the two-stage approach. The results are provided in Table 1. The results of the best models for each dataset in terms of R^2 are in bold and among those, the one with the smallest $MAPE$ is underlined.

It is clear that the two-step prediction architecture, in the best case of the least erroneous first-step prediction, outperforms single-step architecture. In almost all cases the two-step architecture yielded results better both in terms of R^2 and $MAPE$ which means it not only did predict more accurately but also explained the underlying variance more precisely. The only case where single-step architecture performs better is the case of prediction on **"All"** dataset where it achieved smaller $MAPE$. However, compared to the best two-step model on this dataset, it yielded worse R^2, with the difference between their R^2 being very small. Permutation tests [6] can provide the answer to whether the difference does come from the data.

In summary, there are a few takeaways from this experiment:

- two-step prediction architecture appears to give better results in terms of both R^2 and $MAPE$ on smaller datasets,
- to ensure the validity of comparisons, further research should employ a type of statistical significance tests, such as permutation tests.

Table 1. Performance of best single-stage and two-stage prediction architectures.

Dataset	Pipeline	Regressor	R^2	$MAPE$
ShorterThan1.2Kms	Single step	MLP	0.68	0.37
		KNN	0.67	0.36
		DTR	0.6	0.51
	Two steps	**MLP**	**0.85**	**0.22**
		KNN	0.82	0.23
		DTR	0.79	0.28
Between2KmsAnd25Kms	Single step	KNN	0.77	0.24
		MLP	0.73	0.3
		DTR	0.69	0.32
	Two steps	textubMLP	**0.95**	**0.12**
		KNN	0.93	0.13
		DTR	0.89	0.15
ExecutedMoreThan3Ktimes	Single step	KNN	0.96	0.4
		MLP	0.95	0.97
		DTR	0.94	1.47
	Two steps	**MLP**	**0.99**	**0.47**
		KNN	0.98	0.22
		DTR	0.97	0.55
All	Single step	DTR	0.97	0.4
		MLP	0.78	11.56
		KNN	0.56	1.16
	Two steps	**DTR**	**0.99**	**0.45**
		KNN	0.93	0.43
		MLP	0.92	3.04

5.2 Impact of Granularity of the First-Stage Prediction

The goal of the second experiment was to find the best granularity for resource utilization prediction in the two-stage prediction architecture. A detailed comparison of results is provided in Table 2. The best performing model for each dataset is marked in bold.

It is apparent that among the few top-performing granularity schemes, there is no significant difference in terms of R^2, for the reasons stated before. However, in terms of $MAPE$ and the "All" dataset, the continuous granularity scheme appears to be substantially better while maintaining almost the same R^2.

In summary, we can conclude that **continuous granularity appears to give the best results in terms of** $MAPE$.

5.3 Increasing Specialization of Predictors

The second experiment aimed to explore whether choosing predictors that are more specialized and easier to interpret does increase the prediction accuracy. Thus, this experiment consisted of preparing the more specialised, i.e. per-job-type models, and comparing their performance with the best-performing regressor discovered in the previous experiment. The results are presented in Table 3.

Table 2. Summary of performance of models using various categorisation granularities for the first-step prediction in two-step prediction model.

Dataset	Number of categories	Regressor	R^2	$MAPE$
ShorterThan1.2Kms	4	MLP	0.84	23.0
	5	MLP	0.83	23.0
	6	MLP	0.82	24.0
	7	MLP	0.84	22.0
	8	MLP	0.84	23.0
	9	MLP	0.84	23.0
	10	**MLP**	**0.85**	**22.0**
	continuous	**MLP**	**0.85**	**22.0**
Between2KmsAnd25Kms	4	MLP	0.92	16.0
	5	MLP	0.92	16.0
	6	MLP	0.93	13.0
	7	MLP	0.94	13.0
	8	MLP	0.94	12.0
	9	MLP	0.94	12.0
	10	**MLP**	**0.95**	**12.0**
	continuous	MLP	0.93	14.00
ExecutedMoreThan3Ktimes	4	MLP	0.96	60.0
	5	MLP	0.96	48.0
	6	MLP	0.96	52.0
	7	MLP	0.97	41.0
	8	MLP	0.97	42.0
	9	MLP	0.97	35.0
	10	MLP	0.97	39.0
	continuous	**MLP**	**0.99**	**45.0**
All	4	DTR	0.98	119.0
	5	DTR	0.93	155.0
	6	**DTR**	**0.98**	**91.0**
	7	DTR	0.97	139.0
	8	DTR	0.97	57.99
	9	MLP	0.91	728.0
	10	DTR	0.96	140.0
	continuous	DTR	0.97	23.0

Each row contains the R^2 and $MAPE$ scores achieved by the globally-trained regressor (R_G^2, $MAPE_G$) and specialized (R_S^2, $MAPE_S$) one.

Specialization of prediction models proved to be beneficial for 50% (14 out of 28) of the job types. Interestingly, more specialized predictors achieved better performance in several cases worth mentioning:

- For jobs like **combine_variants** where global regressor had already satisfactory score (0.88 R^2), specialization increased both R^2 and $MAPE$.
- For jobs like **seq_dict** or **bwa-index** specialization apparently led to the discovery of job's execution model properties, as it yielded results with $R^2 > 0.9$ and $MAPE$ decreased even up to 4 times.

What is more, specialized predictors were far less complex in terms of length of the input vector – PCA of the global model used 71 components, while specialized models, on average, used 26 components of PCA. Such downsizing of PCA translates to shorter training and prediction times.

There were also cases where specialization failed to improve beyond the global regressor. Such failures occurred both for jobs with large (e.g., mDiffFit, mBack-

Table 3. Comparison of performance for both types of regressors – globally and locally trained ones. Rows marked with gray represent cases where specialized predictors performed better.

Job	Dataset size	R_G^2	$MAPE_G$	R_S^2	$MAPE_S$
add_replace	427	0.98	0.21	0.35	0.14
alignment_to_reference	427	0.82	0.22	0.89	0.19
bwa-index	63	0.31	0.16	0.94	0.04
combine_variants	62	0.88	0.19	0.9	0.04
dedup	427	0.99	0.17	0.9	0.06
faidx	63	0.92	0.21	0.81	0.17
filtering_indel	62	0.02	0.15	0.75	0.06
filtering_snp	62	0.95	0.12	0.87	0.05
genotype_gvcfs	1259	0.96	0.15	0.97	0.11
haplotype_caller	8539	0.98	0.13	0.92	0.03
indel_realign	427	0.65	0.13	0.83	0.05
mAdd	160	0.97	0.48	0.63	26.63
mBackground	15340	1.0	0.2	0.95	0.66
mBgModel	160	0.48	0.56	0.93	2.21
mConcatFit	160	0.87	0.65	0.81	1.17
mDiffFit	65323	1.0	0.28	0.88	0.41
mImgtbl	157	-23.02	1.9	0.02	1.49
mJPEG	43	0.21	0.16	0.14	0.08
mProject	11316	0.86	0.14	0.98	0.04
mProjectPP	5551	0.99	0.14	0.79	0.1
mShrink	43	1.0	0.23	0.92	0.66
mViewer	156	0.79	0.4	0.95	0.16
merge_gcvf	61	0.9	0.18	0.96	0.19
realign_target_creator	427	0.97	0.11	0.92	0.07
select_variants_indel	62	-96.12	2.12	-0.02	0.14
select_variants_snp	62	-161.86	2.12	0.02	0.18
seq_dict	63	0.34	0.25	0.82	0.09
sort_sam	427	0.76	0.24	0.32	0.16

ground) and small (e.g., mShrink, realign_target_creator) number of executions. However, only in 35% (5 out of 14) of such cases specialized predictors achieved worse $MAPE$ and in 65% (9 out of 14) of the cases they outperformed the global regressor in this metric. The question why the more specialized predictors achieve worse performance might be answered at least in two ways.

Firstly, the advantage of the global model could come from the amount of data that was used for its training in comparison to the smaller models. This might influence the model's susceptibility to the influence of outliers, which often introduce bias into the underlying model.

Secondly, a single global regressor might have the advantage of learning about various jobs produced by the same workflow and uncovering the relationships inherent to the workflow which fade out when jobs are considered separately. The same conclusion might be drawn in the context of the execution environment – a larger model might infer more about the job's execution time when it has more information about its computational environment. These two conclusions, however, are yet to be proved or disproved as conducting such a proof is beyond the scope of this paper.

To summarize, this experiment proves that **specialized predictors are a good way to improve on** $MAPE$ **in the prediction**. However, reasoning and inferring about workflow-related properties and their embedding in the cloud environment should be explored more as it might extend our knowledge about the workflows we predict about and about the cloud environments.

5.4   Employing Symbolic Regression to Prediction Tasks

The aim of the final experiment is to assess whether employing symbolic regression to a specialized prediction task can provide better performance than the previous models. The results are presented in Table 4. The table includes results from the previous experiment for increased interpretability where results for global and specialized regressors were marked with respective G and S subscripts. Results for models generated via symbolic regression are marked with subscript λ.

Table 4. Performance of three types of regressors – global, classical-specialized and one originating from symbolic regression. Rows marked with gray represent cases where symbolic regression models outperformed other types of models.

Job	R_G^2	$MAPE_G$	R_S^2	$MAPE_S$	R_λ^2	$MAPE_\lambda$
add_replace	0.98	0.21	0.35	0.14	0.34	0.15
alignment_to_reference	0.82	0.22	0.89	0.19	0.94	0.3
bwa-index	0.31	0.16	0.94	0.04	0.94	0.03
combine_variants	0.88	0.19	0.9	0.04	0.58	0.09
dedup	0.99	0.17	0.9	0.06	0.85	0.11
faidx	0.92	0.21	0.81	0.17	0.3	0.2
filtering_indel	0.02	0.15	0.75	0.06	0.57	0.08
filtering_snp	0.95	0.12	0.87	0.05	0.84	0.05
genotype_gvcfs	0.96	0.15	0.97	0.11	0.99	0.12
haplotype_caller	0.98	0.13	0.92	0.03	0.82	0.06
indel_realign	0.65	0.13	0.83	0.05	0.73	0.08
mAdd	0.97	0.48	0.63	26.63	0.02	1.18
mBackground	1.0	0.2	0.95	0.66	0.51	1.19
mBgModel	0.48	0.56	0.93	2.21	0.98	1.73
mConcatFit	0.87	0.65	0.81	1.17	0.99	0.33
mDiffFit	1.0	0.28	0.88	0.41	0.59	3.43
mImgtbl	-23.02	1.9	0.02	1.49	-1.33	3.31
mJPEG	0.21	0.16	0.14	0.08	0.73	0.06
mProject	0.86	0.14	0.98	0.04	0.95	0.07
mProjectPP	0.99	0.14	0.79	0.1	0.61	0.13
mShrink	1.0	0.23	0.92	0.66	0.97	0.3
mViewer	0.79	0.4	0.95	0.16	0.81	0.55
merge_gcvf	0.9	0.18	0.96	0.19	0.98	0.08
realign_target_creator	0.97	0.11	0.92	0.07	0.78	0.05
select_variants_indel	-96.12	2.12	-0.02	0.14	-0.02	0.16
select_variants_snp	-161.86	2.12	0.02	0.18	-0.02	0.13
seq_dict	0.34	0.25	0.82	0.09	0.76	0.13
sort_sam	0.76	0.24	0.32	0.16	0.15	0.18

As presented in Table 4, models acquired from symbolic regression did not perform outstandingly better than other types of models presented earlier. There are, however, interesting exceptions – the **mConcatFit** and **mJPEG** jobs. In these cases we can observe a significant increase in terms of R^2 and also a significant decrease in terms of $MAPE$. This means that symbolic-regression-generated models not only managed to capture the underlying model but also did it effectively in terms of robustness and reliability in future predictions, as they maintained a high R^2.

In other cases where symbolic-regression-generated models performed better than other types of models in terms of R^2 they often failed to improve $MAPE$. An example of such case is **genotype_gvcfs** job, where we can observe slight increase in both R^2 and $MAPE$ for symbolic regression. This case raises again the question about the statistical significance of differences so small as the one described. There were also cases where models differed more in terms of R^2 and symbolic regression still worsened the $MAPE$. In those cases (e.g. **alignment_to_reference** or **select_variants_indel**), apparently the expressions generated via symbolic regression were less prone to bias introduced by outliers at the cost of larger errors.

In 20 out of 28 cases, the symbolic-regression-based models performed worse than other predictors, however, they usually maintained comparable performance to the worse models. This might indicate that either the assumed maximal expression complexity was too low, or that the available expression set used in the expression search was too narrow. However, allowing for more complex models would most probably take away their simplicity, which could be invaluable for understanding the job's execution model. For example, symbolic regression produced a model that was several times more robust in terms of R^2 and more accurate in terms of $MAPE$ for the **mJPEG** job, while maintaining extreme simplicity, as shown below in Eq. 1:

$$executionTimeMs = 733 - 34 \cdot cpuSpeed^2 \tag{1}$$

Such a model is not only lightweight and fast in prediction and thus perfect for applications in job scheduling but also clearly shows the implementor directions of possible future optimizations.

To summarize, this experiment shows that while symbolic regression does not always provide good results, **in some cases it generates models outstanding in terms of performance and simple in terms of interpretability.**

6   Conclusion

In this paper, we evaluated various aspects of machine learning techniques applied to prediction of execution times of scientific workflow jobs. A number of experiments have led to several interesting conclusions. The two-stage prediction method proved to perform better in almost all cases. We also found that continuous granularity of categorization used in the first stage of this method gives the best results. Specialized (per-job-type) models perform better in only 50% of cases for the tested data sets. This is a surprising and hard to interpret finding which requires further investigation. Finally, symbolic regression can perform exceptionally well in selected cases, so it proved to be a useful tool to consider in future research and applications.

Acknowledgment. The research presented in this paper was partially supported by the funds of Polish Ministry of Education and Science assigned to AGH University of Science and Technology.

References

1. Balis, B.: Hyperflow: a model of computation, programming approach and enactment engine for complex distributed workflows. Futur. Gener. Comput. Syst. **55**, 147–162 (2016)
2. Bhattacharyya, A., Hoefler, T.: Pemogen: automatic adaptive performance modeling during program runtime. In: Parallel Architectures and Compilation Techniques - Conference Proceedings, PACT (2014). https://doi.org/10.1145/2628071. 2628100
3. Borghesi, A., Bartolini, A., Lombardi, M., Milano, M., Benini, L.: Predictive modeling for job power consumption in HPC systems (2016). https://doi.org/10.1007/978-3-319-41321-1_10
4. Deelman, E., Mandal, A., Jiang, M., Sakellariou, R.: The role of machine learning in scientific workflows. Int. J. High Perform. Comput. Appl. **33**(6), 1128–1139 (2019)
5. Galleguillos, C., Sîrbu, A., Kiziltan, Z., Babaoglu, O., Borghesi, A., Bridi, T.: Data-driven job dispatching in HPC systems (2018). https://doi.org/10.1007/978-3-319-72926-8_37
6. Good, P.: Permutation Tests: A Practical Guide to Resampling Methods for Testing Hypotheses. Springer, Heidelberg (2013)
7. Kim, I.K., Wang, W., Qi, Y., Humphrey, M.: Forecasting cloud application workloads with cloudinsight for predictive resource management. IEEE Trans. Cloud Comput. **10**(3), 1848–1863 (2020)
8. Li, W., Xia, Y., Zhou, M., Sun, X., Zhu, Q.: Fluctuation-aware and predictive workflow scheduling in cost-effective infrastructure-as-a-service clouds. IEEE Access **6**, 61488–61502 (2018)
9. Medel, V., Rana, O., Bañares, J.Á., Arronategui, U.: Modelling performance & resource management in kubernetes. In: Proceedings of the 9th International Conference on Utility and Cloud Computing, pp. 257–262 (2016)
10. Mustafa, S., Elghandour, I., Ismail, M.: A machine learning approach for predicting execution time of spark jobs. Alex. Eng. J. **57**, 3767–3778 (2018). https://doi.org/10.1016/j.aej.2018.03.006
11. Nawrocki, P., Sniezynski, B.: Adaptive context-aware energy optimization for services on mobile devices with use of machine learning. Wireless Pers. Commun. **115**(3), 1839–1867 (2020)
12. Pham, T.P., Durillo, J.J., Fahringer, T.: Predicting workflow task execution time in the cloud using a two-stage machine learning approach. IEEE Trans. Cloud Comput. **8**(1), 256–268 (2020). https://doi.org/10.1109/TCC.2017.2732344
13. Pietri, I., Juve, G., Deelman, E., Sakellariou, R.: A performance model to estimate execution time of scientific workflows on the cloud. In: 2014 9th Workshop on Workflows in Support of Large-Scale Science, pp. 11–19. IEEE (2014)

Smart Clustering of HPC Applications Using Similar Job Detection Methods

Denis Shaikhislamov$^{(\boxtimes)}$ (iD) and Vadim Voevodin (iD)

Lomonosov Moscow State University, Moscow, Russia
sdenis1995@gmail.com, vadim@parallel.ru

Abstract. In order for supercomputer resources to be effectively used, it is necessary to constantly analyze various aspects of the operation of modern HPC systems. One of the most significant aspects is the efficiency of execution of parallel applications running on a supercomputer. To study this, system administrators need to constantly monitor and analyze the entire flow of running jobs. This is a very difficult task, and there are several reasons for this - a large number and a significant variety of executed applications; the extreme complexity of the structure of modern HPC systems, and, as a result, a huge number of characteristics that need to be evaluated for each job. One way to make this analysis easier is to cluster similar jobs. Such clustering allows you to infer the behavior and performance issues of all jobs in the cluster by examining only one of these jobs, and it also helps to better understand the structure of the supercomputer job flow as a whole. In this paper, we propose a new method that allows solving this clustering task with high accuracy. This smart clustering method analyzes both static information on the executable files and dynamic data about the behavior of applications during their execution. Using the Lomonosov-2 supercomputer as an example, we demonstrate how this method can help in practice to facilitate the analysis of the execution efficiency of supercomputing applications.

Keywords: Supercomputer · Similar applications · Application performance · Data analysis · Clustering · Machine learning

1 Introduction

Many scientists in various subject areas use supercomputers for the modeling which they need to solve their scientific tasks. And every such scientist, being a supercomputer user, wants to conduct as detailed and full-scale experiments as possible, while minimizing the time waiting for his experiments to perform. To help users with that, the HPC field is constantly evolving - more large-scale and powerful supercomputers appear each year, more and more advanced software is being developed, and huge human and financial resources are spent all over the world for these purposes [1,9].

Much attention is also paid to the thorough analysis of the performance of individual supercomputer applications. At the moment, many tools have been

© The Author(s), under exclusive license to Springer Nature Switzerland AG 2023
R. Wyrzykowski et al. (Eds.): PPAM 2022, LNCS 13826, pp. 209–221, 2023.
https://doi.org/10.1007/978-3-031-30442-2_16

developed for profiling, debugging, and optimizing parallel applications (like Scalasca, Vampir, ARM MAP, Valgrind, and many others). However, in order for the user to be able to properly use these tools, it is necessary that: 1) the user is aware that his application is underperforming; 2) the user has sufficient skills to correctly select and use such software tools to analyze the performance of his application. Our experience shows that these points are often not fulfilled. For example, a survey we conducted in 2020 [12] showed that 2/3 of the users of our Supercomputing center in the Moscow State University admit that they either do not know about the presence of performance issues in their applications (i.e. they haven't investigated this, which in most cases means there are actually some issues), or they know about issues but haven't tried (or failed) to eliminate them. At the same time, half of those users who admitted that their applications have performance issues do not know what exactly this issue is. And, in our experience, such situation is basically the same in many other modern supercomputer centers as well.

To solve this problem, it is necessary for administrators and/or analysts of supercomputing centers to constantly analyze the efficiency of the entire flow of jobs running on a supercomputer, which makes it possible to identify the very fact of performance issues in applications, as well as to get a first idea of what could be causing these issues. And this topic, which is an urgent problem that needs to be addressed, is given much less attention, in contrast to those mentioned above.

One of the challenges of this problem – it is considered that a general modern supercomputer usually runs a huge variety of applications that can differ in almost everything: the intensity and profile of the usage of different computational resources, the duration and the number of processes, the use of certain compilers, system libraries or application packages, and so on. In this case, it is very difficult to individually study all the jobs running on a supercomputer.

While this is basically true, our experience shows that often some supercomputer jobs are very similar to each other in terms of their behavior and performance. This happens, for example, when one user runs a series of similar or even the same experiments, or when different users solve similar problems, using, for example, the same functionality implemented in an application package (like GROMACS, NAMD or VASP). And the ability to cluster such similar jobs would greatly facilitate the aforementioned task of studying the efficiency of the job flow, since in order to study the behavior of one entire cluster, it will, in fact, be generally enough to analyze and optimize only one application from this cluster. Then, the knowledge gained and the optimization strategy obtained for the studied application can be similarly applied to other applications in the cluster. Such a grouping can be useful, in particular, for identifying clusters of failed or very inefficient job launches, as well as for determining the most common groups of jobs, further detailed study and optimization of which can significantly increase the overall efficiency of the supercomputer functioning after analyzing only one application from each cluster. In current practice, supercomputer administrators usually can use only quite straightforward methods for grouping jobs, using basic job launch and performance data only, which does not allow fully addressing the problem.

This work is aimed at solving the task of such clustering. The main contribution of this paper is the development of a machine learning based method for smart clustering of HPC applications, using both static and dynamic information about launches of each application. This method, based on the methods we developed earlier for searching for similar applications [15], works automatically and, after the initial setup, allows constantly analyzing the entire flow of jobs running on a supercomputer. This solution is implemented on the Lomonosov-2 supercomputer [20] installed in the Lomonosov Moscow State University, but it can be adapted for usage on other HPC systems as well.

The rest of the paper is organized as follows. Section 2 is devoted to our background on this topic as well the review of related works. Section 3 is focused on the description of the proposed clustering method, its evaluation and parameter tuning processes. Section 4 shows real-life noteworthy examples obtained in practice. Section 5 draws conclusions and describes our future plans.

2   Background and Related Work

As stated before, the main objective of this work is to develop a method for clustering user applications using static and dynamic information. The clustering is a widely popular technique for analysis because it's results are easily interpreted and it provides information on natural grouping in the data set. It also can be used as additional information for other types of analysis, for example, anomaly detection.

There are basically two types of information describing an application that can be used for its analysis – static and dynamic data. Static data specifies the information available before the application's execution. Primary sources of information for this type of clustering are source code and executable files. There are other data, like scheduling information or list of linked libraries, but during research we haven't found any papers using this data for clustering. In [21] authors present source code clustering algorithm used for plagiarism detection in student assignment submissions. Clustering is based on feature extraction of abstract syntax trees, that are obtained by analyzing the source code. Another work [10] tries to cluster source codes in a very different manner – by analyzing not the code structure and algorithms, but the comments, names of variables and functions. Authors believe that resulting clusters form linguistic groups and show the intention of the code. In our case, we have no access to the source codes of the applications, and we need different approach.

Dynamic data refers to the information available only after the application launch. This data is mainly obtained by a monitoring system that regularly collects the information about the application behavior during it's execution, for example by collecting real-time data from different sensors. The examples of such information are CPU or GPU load, network usage intensity, amount of L1 or LLC cache misses per second, etc., which we will further refer to as dynamic characteristics. From this point of view, every job can be described as multivariate time series of dynamic data.

The task of multivariate time series analysis was always difficult due to the large amount of data needed to process and the length of time series not being constant. That's why multivariate time series are usually converted into a feature vector of fixed length. These features are obtained by extracting statistical features of each time series. That approach is used, for example, in [7]. Authors of this paper extracted so called KPIs describing the behavior of the applications, and then further calculated statistical features of each time series like mean, max, deviation, etc. Then they used Agglomerative Clustering algorithm to cluster obtained features. Similar approach was used in [16], where authors used PCA to reduce dimensionality and avoid data sparsity problem, and then applied K-Means clustering to further analyze the performance of selected applications. They used Silhouette score to obtain optimal number of clusters for K-means algorithm.

In [3] the same approach with feature extraction is used, but for different purpose – to classify applications. Using ensemble classification model and labeled data, they were able to identify whether a new job is one of the known applications. In [19] authors also used features of dynamic characteristics for classification, but instead of classifying applications themselves, they tried to find anomalous events on the compute nodes.

Previously we tried to use similar feature based methods (used in all papers described above) for job similarity detection, but the accuracy was not high enough. Also we want to pay more attention to the behavior of the application, in what chronological order the phases of execution occurred, etc, because some of this crucial information is lost when statistical features are used. Therefore, in our proposed method we analyze time series themselves. We have recently developed metrics for measuring job similarity, which appear to be suitable to help us solve the task of job clustering. In [15] we developed methods for similar application detection based on static and dynamic data. The static method for assessing the similarity of supercomputer jobs is based on the analysis of executable files. We extract the names of the used functions and variables using the UNIX nm utility, which we then feed into the trained Doc2vec [11] model. Doc2vec model converts a set of words into a fixed-length vector. The resulting vectors can be compared using the cosine similarity function, which calculates the cosine of the angle between the vectors, and the closer the value to 1, the closer the vectors are to each other. The Doc2vec model was trained on the function names of over 7000 different executable files running on the Lomonosov-2 supercomputer. We used this method in practice to detect launches of application packages, and it showed the accuracy of ∼95% on this task.

The dynamic method for similar application detection is based on the analysis of performance dynamic characteristics of each job execution. Lomonosov-2 has DiMMon monitoring system [17] that provides the data on aforementioned dynamic characteristics of each job during its execution. We use Dynamic Time Warping (DTW) algorithm [4] for time series comparison and distance estimation. DTW is a method that calculates an optimal match between two given time series, allowing to get distance metric for time series of different lengths. During the evaluation of this method, it showed the accuracy of $\sim$90% on the task of application package detection.

It should be mentioned that these two methods differ in used input data and working algorithms, and therefore are most suitable in different cases, complementing each other. For example, by using static method we can distinguish different application package usages, but the use cases of some packages are vast and can greatly differ in terms of behavior, and only dynamic approach can detect those nuances during application's execution.

3   Solving the Problem of Smart Job Clustering

3.1   Proposed Method

The proposed method for smart job clustering consists of the following major steps:

1. *Coarse-grain static clustering.* We assume that behavior of any HPC job is similar predominantly to the jobs with similar executable files. We understand that there are exceptions to this assumption, but in our experience such exceptions are very rare in practice. Thus we can first use the aforementioned static method to get the distance estimate between jobs and group them (based on data on their executables) using clustering algorithms. After this step, jobs are compared only within these clusters, which significantly speeds up the operation of the method as a whole.
2. *Fine-grain dynamic clustering.* After obtaining the static clusters, we use DTW-based method described in Sect. 2 to estimate the distances between jobs inside each cluster using dynamic data, and then group jobs into fine-grain clusters using yet another clustering algorithm, thus concluding smart grouping of user jobs.

We will refer to this algorithm as an offline method, as it is suited not to constantly analyze the job flow in near real-time, but to process big batches of jobs. Also it should be noted that for the proposed method to work, we need both static and dynamic data on the analyzed jobs, which is not always available: static information sometimes cannot be accessed due to not having read permissions on user files, or executable files have been modified or deleted prior to our analysis thus invalidating further analysis; dynamic data can be absent due to monitoring system malfunction, or if the job is too short for accurate analysis. For example, since the beginning of year 2022, 45% of CPU hours on Lomonosov-2 were consumed by jobs that have both static and dynamic data. We plan to increase this share in future by improving reliability of the monitoring system as well as tuning the proposed method configuration.

Choosing Clustering Algorithm. One of the main tasks that has to be solved in order for the proposed method to work is to choose appropriate clustering algorithms for both static and dynamic steps. The main requirements for the algorithms were the following:

- no predefined number of clusters, because it is not known beforehand how many groups of jobs there are;
- is able to use custom distance metric (e.g. Birch method relies on Euclidean distance for operation);
- do not construct additional points for clustering, as we cannot introduce new points of comparison (like centroids in K-means clustering method).

The most popular groups of clustering algorithms meeting that requirements are hierarchical and density-based clustering algorithms. One of the most used in each category are Agglomerative Clustering [18] and DBSCAN [5], correspondingly. We used scikit-learn package's implementation of those algorithms [13]. Agglomerative Clustering uses bottom-up approach to clustering, meaning that initially each cluster consists of one job, and then iteratively clusters are merged based on the chosen principle. DBSCAN operates in the similar manner: it finds core samples of high density and expands clusters from them. During the experiments we found out that DBSCAN performs worse than Agglomerative Clustering by ~5%, that's why we chose the latter (all further results are shown only for this algorithm). Also it is important to mention that using DBSCAN in static phase and Agglomerative Clustering in dynamic didn't change the results that much, and if we use them vice versa we observed less accurate results. That's why we chose the Agglomerative clustering for both static and dynamic steps.

Selecting Metric for Assessing Clustering Accuracy. To compare and evaluate results of the clustering algorithms, we need to choose a suitable metric. There are a lot of available options, and they could be divided into 2 groups, depending on whether there is available ground truth labels or not. First group include such functions as Rand index, Mutual Information based scores, MojoFM, etc. The most popular of them is Rand index [8] due to its interpretability: the score is proportional to the number of sample pairs which were assigned to the correct clusters. It ranges from 0 to 1, 1 being perfect match, and 0 usually specifies random labelling. Second group includes scoring functions like Silhouette Coefficient, Calinski-Harabasz Index, Davies-Bouldin Index. They all produce higher scores if the resulting clusters are dense and well separated, but Silhouette Coefficient [14] also provides additional semantic information: score is ranged from -1 to 1, where 1 means highly dense clustering, and if score is closer to zero, it means that clusters are overlapping. Negative values generally indicate that a sample has been assigned to the wrong cluster, meaning that there is another cluster which is closer to the sample than the selected one. Manually labeled data is hard to obtain in our case, that's why for the first iteration of parameter tuning we used Silhouette Coefficient, and for more precise testing we manually clustered a part of jobs and used Rand Index (see next subsections for details).

3.2 Tuning of Proposed Solution

As mentioned before, there are two major steps in the proposed method, and we can change their parameters to improve the overall accuracy. We consider tuning of the following parameters:

- a threshold needed in static and dynamic clustering stages for considering jobs similar,
- a window parameter in DTW that controls how much time series can differ in terms of time shifts.

Clustering algorithm has a lot more parameters, but we found out that these thresholds were the most important to the evaluation score, so we focused on them. Next, other DTW parameters and time series preprocessing steps were fine tuned in the previous work and therefore should not be changed, but the DTW window can change the results significantly, so we need to consider changing it as well.

The process of searching for the optimal parameter values is arranged as follows. We can fix the value ranges for each parameter based on the empirical observations during initial testing, which gives us the ability to carry out a brute-force search for the best parameter values based on the Silhouette coefficient. This gives us a first estimate of possible parameters, and in order to get more precise results (i.e. verify and tune results obtained based on Silhouette coefficient), we need to manually label user jobs and calculate Rand Index. To do so, we can find the best parameters according to the Silhouette coefficient, and then use these parameters to cluster user jobs. This greatly reduce the efforts needed to manually cluster user jobs – most of the work is almost done, we generally just need to split or merge formed clusters. Using such approach, we selected top 4 users (by the number of job launches on Lomonosov-2 from January to April 2022) and labelled their jobs. We emitted obviously anomalous jobs that were showing almost no activity within a significant part of execution time, as well as too short jobs and jobs without needed static or dynamic data. This resulted in ~300 labelled jobs, that we used for tuning.

During the tuning process, it became clear that we need to solve one important issue – is it possible to find the unified set of parameter values suitable for all jobs and all users? The jobs of different users may behave in completely different ways, therefore they may need different clustering configurations. So it was unclear whether it is possible to select a unified set of parameters. But doing this is of great interest, since it allows clustering supercomputer jobs not only within a particular user or a series of jobs, but within the entire job flow or any its subset (like launches of a particular application package, jobs with specified performance property, etc.). To test that, we took 4 top users as a train set and calculated Rand Index for every possible parameter variation. Then we were able to calculate adjusted average score for every parameter variation, which gave us an estimation on how suitable parameters are for all users. A parameter set that resulted in the highest adjusted average score was then selected, further referred as best unified parameters set, or BUP.

$$adjusted\ average\ score = \frac{\sum_{users} user\ Rand\ Index\ score * user\ job\ count}{total\ job\ count}$$

After determining BUP on a train set, we needed to check whether it was suitable to use BUP in our case; this means that for each user we needed to make sure that the difference between the best possible score and the score using BUP was not significant. The best possible score for a user was the highest Rand Index score specifically for this user on all available parameter sets. We considered the difference significant if it exceeds 0.1, which in terms of Rand Index means that there is a difference of about 10% of pairs whose labels are not the same. This value was chosen empirically during the testing on real-life jobs.

The Rand Index values (both best possible scores and scores using BUP) for 4 users from a train set are shown in Table 1. We found that there was no difference between two scores, which meant that there was no need to adjust parameters separately for each user, and we could test found BUP on other users.

Table 1. Rand Index scores obtained during parameter tuning

	User 1	User 2	User 3	User 4
Best possible score	0.953	0.957	0.986	0.989
Score using BUP	0.953	0.957	0.986	0.989

3.3   Evaluation of Proposed Method

Clustering Accuracy. After selecting the best unified parameters set in the previous subsection, we needed to verify if it was suitable for other users as well. To do so, we selected next top 7 users from the same time period and manually labeled their jobs. This as well resulted in ~300 jobs in a test set. Table 2 shows the Rand Index scores using BUP for these users. As we can see, scores are very high for all users, except User 10. A more detailed study of his jobs showed that there was an issue with DTW not being able to distinguish particular behaviour differences; we might need to change the proposed approach for these kinds of jobs in the future. Overall, the total Rand Index score is equal to 0.95, which means that the overall clustering accuracy is very high. This also means that we can use a unified set of parameter values in practice, which significantly increases the applicability of the proposed method, as stated above.

Table 2. Rand Index scores for 7 users from the test set

	User 5	User 6	User 7	User 8	User 9	User 10	User 11
BUP Rand Index	1.0	1.0	1.0	1.0	1.0	0.78	0.978

Online Clustering Evaluation. The proposed smart clustering method is intended to be used for on-the-fly analysis of supercomputer jobs, but to do so we need to study on a regular basis a constantly changing flow of supercomputer jobs. The described offline method has to do the clustering for both static and dynamic phases for every new job, which is not feasible. There are incremental hierarchical algorithms [6] that allow you not to recompute all the clusters, but we have selected a computationally easier approach. During the parameter tuning, one of the clustering parameters is the threshold of when to consider jobs similar, and we can use this threshold to perform 1NN search (i.e. search for one nearest neighbor). In this case, another way of cluster detection for a new job (further referred as online method) can be the following:

- Look for the most similar job in the knowledge base (i.e. manually clustered jobs) based on static data. If the distance to that job is less than the static threshold – go to the next step, as it means that executable files are similar. If the distance is bigger – we consider that this new job forms a new static cluster, and add it to the knowledge base.
- Look for the most similar job in the found static cluster based on dynamic data. If the distance to the found job is less than dynamic threshold – new job belongs to this cluster. If the distance is greater – we create new dynamic cluster for the new job.

We can update the knowledge base using the original offline method once a selected period (once a month, for example).

To test the accuracy of this approach, we need to compare results obtained using offline and online methods. In this case, we can think of offline method's clustering result as the ground truth, and use Rand Index to evaluate online method's clustering results.

For this purpose, we selected all Lomonosov-2 jobs from January to April of 2022 to conduct the tests. We built the knowledge base for the online method using jobs from January to March, and used jobs running in April to conduct 1NN clustering. Comparing the results of 1NN clustering to the clustering obtained using offline method on all jobs from that period, we obtained Rand Index score of 0.9948, which indicates that two clustering results are practically identical. That means that we can use a little less accurate but much faster online method for constant on-the-fly clustering, and we can periodically rerun offline method to update and fine-tune its knowledge base.

4 Using Proposed Solution in Practice

In this section we describe several examples of useful results achieved using the proposed method. We clustered and studied all jobs launched from Jan to April 2022 on the Lomonosov-2 supercomputer, which resulted in the total of 6000 jobs that we were able to analyze. As stated before, our method doesn't take into account short jobs as well as jobs for which no static or dynamic data was available.

At first we wanted to study the size of the clusters – how big clusters can be found in real-life data using the proposed method. It turned out that there are definitely big groups of jobs – $\sim$25% of all job launches belong to only 10 clusters. It becomes even more noticeable if we look at jobs that use specific packages: 50% out of $\sim$1500 LAMMPS job launches are from 7 clusters, 25% out of $\sim$1500 Gromacs launches are from 3 clusters, and 60% out of $\sim$350 CP2K jobs are from only 1 cluster! This means that not only we are able to locate big groups of interest, but it also makes the task of analyzing most impactful applications a lot easier. The same situation can be observed with incorrectly finished jobs (that have "FAILED" finish state): only 4 clusters are responsible for 25% of such jobs, and supercomputer administrators definitely should pay special attention to them in order to find the reason why these applications are failing.

Another interesting field for research – finding performance issues in user jobs. And there are several ways we can use clustering results to find anomalous job launches. First option was described before: we can locate most impactful clusters in terms of failed or most inefficient jobs and analyze them. Second option is to match user jobs to their corresponding clusters, for example:

$$\{Job_1, Job_2, ...\} \rightarrow \{Cluster_{Job_1}, Cluster_{Job_2}, ...\}$$

and then analyze clusters of subsequent job launches to determine whether there are anomalous ones among such launch series. If this series consists of mostly non-similar jobs, then it is difficult to draw any conclusion. But if there is a significant number of launches belonging to the same cluster, among which there is one job from another cluster, we can assume that this job might be anomalous. Consider following sequence of job launches (jobs are colored based on the cluster):

$Job1, Job2, Job3, Job4, Job5, Job6, Job7, Job8, Job9, Job10, Job11, \textbf{\textit{Job}12}$

We can see that there are plenty of consecutive launches of green labeled jobs, but there is unexpected red labeled job, which may indicate two things: either a user wanted to launch some different application, and everything is fine, or the launch was anomalous in terms of unexpected behavior. We can check, whether it is supposed to be the same application or not by using static analysis. And if the binary files are similar, we can assume that Job7 in this case is suspicious, and the user should be notified. Note that yellow and blue labeled jobs might be anomalous as well, but we need to study all jobs before and after them in order to find that out. We can't be 100% sure that jobs are really anomalous, but signaling users of potential issues is crucial to further decrease their number. For example, with this method we were able to locate anomalous job launches of at least 5 users during the selected time period. Some cases could be detected using less sophisticated methods, but we can identify others using the proposed approach only.

During the results analysis we found one more peculiar benefit of clustering algorithm. As mentioned earlier, we use application package detection system, which are based on XALT [2] and our previously developed static method. They work together and supplement each other, showing very high overall accuracy. But sometimes they miss some jobs due to malfunctions in XALT or static method, incomplete knowledge base used in static method, etc. And that is when proposed clustering might fill in these missed jobs. During our testing we found out that XALT+static missed 143 jobs, which accounts to ~2% of total found application package usages.

5 Conclusions

In this paper, we have proposed a new method for smart clustering of supercomputer jobs. This method uses both static and dynamic analysis techniques: static information on terms found in the binary file is used for first-level coarse clustering, and after that dynamic data describing performance characteristics during job execution is used for subsequent subclustering. This method works on a constant basis, analyzing all jobs running on a supercomputer, and can be used, as shown in our examples, to simplify the process of job flow efficiency analysis or to detect anomalies in a series of job launches.

Our future plans include providing an open-source software package, which will make it easy to try this solution on other HPC systems as well.

Acknowledgements. The results described in this paper were achieved at Lomonosov Moscow State University with the financial support of the Russian Science Foundation, agreement No. 21-71-30003.

References

1. High performance computing market size to surpass USD 64.65. https://www.globenewswire.com/news-release/2022/04/04/2415844/0/en/High-Performance-Computing-Market-Size-to-Surpass-USD-64-65-Bn-by-2030.html
2. Agrawal, K., Fahey, M., Mclay, R., James, D.: User environment tracking and problem detection with xalt, pp. 32–40, November 2014. https://doi.org/10.1109/HUST.2014.6
3. Ates, E., et al.: Taxonomist: application detection through rich monitoring data. In: Aldinucci, M., Padovani, L., Torquati, M. (eds.) Euro-Par 2018. LNCS, vol. 11014, pp. 92–105. Springer, Cham (2018). https://doi.org/10.1007/978-3-319-96983-1_7
4. Berndt, D.J., Clifford, J.: Using dynamic time warping to find patterns in time series. In: Proceedings of the 3rd International Conference on Knowledge Discovery and Data Mining, AAAIWS 1994, pp. 359–370. AAAI Press (1994). http://dl.acm.org/citation.cfm?id=3000850.3000887

5. Ester, M., Kriegel, H.P., Sander, J., Xu, X.: A density-based algorithm for discovering clusters in large spatial databases with noise. In: Proceedings of the Second International Conference on Knowledge Discovery and Data Mining, KDD 1996, pp. 226–231. AAAI Press (1996)
6. Gurrutxaga, I., Arbelaitz, O., Martín, J., Muguerza, J., Pérez, J., Perona, I.: Sihc: a stable incremental hierachical clustering algorithm, pp. 300–304, January 2009
7. Halawa, M., Díaz Redondo, R., Vilas, A.: Unsupervised kpis-based clustering of jobs in HPC data centers. Sensors **20**, 4111 (2020). https://doi.org/10.3390/s20154111
8. Hubert, L.J., Arabie, P.: Comparing partitions. J. Classif. **2**, 193–218 (1985)
9. Joseph, E., Conway, S.: Major trends in the worldwide HPC market. Technical Report (2017). https://hpcuserforum.com/presentations/stuttgart2017/IDC-update-HLRS.pdf
10. Kuhn, A., Ducasse, S., Gîrba, T.: Semantic clustering: identifying topics in source code. Inf. Softw. Technol. **49**(3), 230–243 (2007). https://doi.org/10.1016/j.infsof.2006.10.017, https://www.sciencedirect.com/science/article/pii/S0950584906001820, 12th Working Conference on Reverse Engineering
11. Le, Q.V., Mikolov, T.: Distributed representations of sentences and documents. CoRR abs/1405.4053 (2014)
12. Nikitenko, D.A., Shvets, P.A., Voevodin, V.V.: Why do users need to take care of their HPC applications efficiency? Lobachevskii J. Math. **41**(8), 1521–1532 (2020). https://doi.org/10.1134/s1995080220080132
13. Pedregosa, F., et al.: Scikit-learn: machine learning in python. J. Mach. Learn. Res. **12**, 2825–2830 (2011)
14. Rousseeuw, P.J.: Silhouettes: a graphical aid to the interpretation and validation of cluster analysis. J. Comput. Appl. Math. **20**, 53–65 (1987). https://doi.org/10.1016/0377-0427(87)90125-7, https://www.sciencedirect.com/science/article/pii/0377042787901257
15. Shaikhislamov, D., Voevodin, V.: Solving the problem of detecting similar supercomputer applications using machine learning methods. In: Sokolinsky, L., Zymbler, M. (eds.) PCT 2020. CCIS, vol. 1263, pp. 46–57. Springer, Cham (2020). https://doi.org/10.1007/978-3-030-55326-5_4
16. Shin, M., Park, G., Park, C.Y., Lee, J., Kim, M.: Application-specific feature selection and clustering approach with HPC system profiling data. J. Supercomput. **77**(7), 6817–6831 (2021). https://doi.org/10.1007/s11227-020-03533-2
17. Stefanov, K., Voevodin, V., Zhumatiy, S., Voevodin, V.: Dynamically reconfigurable distributed modular monitoring system for supercomputers (dimmon). In: 4th International Young Scientist Conference on Computational Science. Procedia Computer Science, vol. 66, pp. 625–634. Elsevier B.V Netherlands (2015). https://doi.org/10.1016/j.procs.2015.11.071
18. Steinbach, M., Karypis, G., Kumar, V.: A comparison of document clustering techniques. In: KDD Workshop on Text Mining (2000)
19. Tuncer, O., et al.: Diagnosing performance variations in HPC applications using machine learning. In: Kunkel, J.M., Yokota, R., Balaji, P., Keyes, D. (eds.) ISC High Performance 2017. LNCS, vol. 10266, pp. 355–373. Springer, Cham (2017). https://doi.org/10.1007/978-3-319-58667-0_19
20. Voevodin, V.V., et al.: supercomputer lomonosov-2: large scale, deep monitoring and fine analytics for the user community. Supercomput. Front. Innov. **6**(2), 4–11 (2019). https://doi.org/10.14529/jsfi190201

21. Duračík, M., Krsak, E., Hrkút, P.: Scalable source code plagiarism detection using source code vectors clustering, pp. 499–502, November 2018. https://doi.org/10.1109/ICSESS.2018.8663708

Scheduling for Parallel Computing

Distributed Work Stealing
in a Task-Based Dataflow Runtime

Joseph John[1]([⊠])[iD], Josh Milthorpe[1,2][iD], and Peter Strazdins[1][iD]

[1] Australian National University, Canberra, Australia
{joseph.john,josh.milthorpe,peter.strazdins}@anu.edu.au
[2] Oak Ridge National Laboratory, Oak Ridge, TN, USA

Abstract. The task-based dataflow programming model has emerged as an alternative to the process-centric programming model for extreme-scale applications. However, load balancing is still a challenge in task-based dataflow runtimes. In this paper, we present extensions to the PaR-SEC runtime to demonstrate that distributed work stealing is an effective load-balancing method for task-based dataflow runtimes. In contrast to shared-memory work stealing, we find that each process should consider future tasks and the expected waiting time for execution when determining whether to steal. We demonstrate the effectiveness of the proposed work-stealing policies for a sparse Cholesky factorization, which shows a speedup of up to 35% compared to a static division of work.

Keywords: Tasks · Runtime · Distributed Work Stealing · PaRSEC

1 Introduction

The task-based dataflow programming model has emerged as an alternative to the process-centric model of computation in distributed memory. In this model, an application is a collection of tasks with dependencies derived from the data flow among the tasks. Tasks can be executed in any order that maintains the dependency relations between them. When compared to a process-centric model, the task-based dataflow programming model has shown more scalability as it exposes more asynchronicity within the application [6]. Also, the programmer has a global view of tasks and data, while low-level problems such as scheduling and data transfer are taken care of by the runtime.

At present, most implementations of the task-based dataflow programming model are limited to a static work division between nodes. This paper addresses this limitation by exploring whether distributed work stealing can be used as an automatic load balancing method in a task-based dataflow runtime. We use Parallel Runtime Scheduling and Execution Controller (PaRSEC) [6,7] as the base framework. To the best of our knowledge, this is the first work in a task-based dataflow runtime in distributed memory to use distributed work stealing as a load balancing technique.

R. Wyrzykowski et al. (Eds.): PPAM 2022, LNCS 13826, pp. 225–236, 2023.
https://doi.org/10.1007/978-3-031-30442-2_17

1.1 Contributions

The contributions of this paper are as follows: We add distributed work stealing to PaRSEC runtime for automatic load balancing and we extend the Template Task Graph (TTG) to allow the programmer to decide if a particular task can be stolen. We introduce new victim policies based on waiting time and show that this is more efficient than the existing victim policies. We also introduce a new thief policy based on future tasks and show that this is more efficient than the existing thief policies.

2 Related Work

Work sharing and work stealing are two primary approaches to load balancing in task-based programming models. In work sharing, an overloaded compute node shares its work with the underloaded nodes, while in work stealing, an underloaded node steals work from the overloaded nodes. Work sharing requires information collection about the load in a set of nodes and coordination between the nodes in this set to balance the load between them. The main disadvantages of work sharing are that collecting load information may pose scalability issues, and due to the asynchronous nature of task execution there is no guarantee that the information received reflects the actual load status. On the other hand, in work stealing, a thief node initiates a steal request based on its load and the victim node chooses whether to allow the steal based on its load. Both victim and thief make independent decisions without any coordination between them. While load-balancing in task-based runtimes was first introduced in shared memory through work stealing in Cilk [4,9], shared memory load-balancing is not discussed here as we are only interested in load-balancing across nodes in partitioned global address space (PGAS) and distributed memory.

The PGAS model presents a unified global memory, logically partitioned among different nodes. This global address space makes it possible to use global data structures, shared between nodes, to implement load-balancing strategies. In Habanero-UPC++ [13], each node publishes the current count of stealable tasks in a shared variable in global address space and the work stealing decisions are made based on this. In X10, each node maintains a shared queue to hold stealable tasks and a local queue to hold non-stealable tasks [2,10,15,20]. A starving node can directly steal from the shared queue of another node. X10 also enforces work sharing if work stealing fails [16]. Chapel [8] allows dynamic task mapping i.e. a task can be mapped to any node in the system but once the tasks are mapped to a node they cannot be stolen.

In the distributed-memory model, each node is a separate memory and execution domain. Unlike PGAS models, there are no shared global data structures that can be leveraged for cooperation between the different nodes. Perarnau et al. [17] study work stealing performance in MPI, but here the work stealing is a property not of the runtime but of the benchmark itself. In Chameleon [11,12], work sharing is possible but it can happen only at global MPI synchronization points. Samfass et al. [18] implement work sharing in partial differential equation workloads but the work sharing is possible only between time steps. In CnC [19] and Legion [3], similar to Chapel, dynamic task mapping is possible, but once mapped to a node the tasks cannot be stolen. CnC also uses a broadcast operation to locate data items and this operation is not scalable either.

Task-based dataflow programming model is a subset of a task-based programming model where the execution progression is controlled by the flow of data from one task to the next. Charm++ is a task-based dataflow runtime that supports work sharing [1] and it is especially well suited for iterative applications. At present, there is no dataflow task-based programming model that offers work stealing in distributed memory.

3 Adding Work Stealing to PaRSEC

PaRSEC is a heterogeneous task-based dataflow runtime, where the execution of tasks is fully distributed, with no centralized components. Each task in PaRSEC is an instance of a task class and all tasks that belong to a particular task class have the same properties except the data it operates on and its unique id. PaRSEC supports multiple domain-specific languages (DSL) and these DSLs help the user define the different task classes in a program, as well the dependency relations between the tasks. In this paper, we focus on the Templated Task Graph (TTG) DSL [5] as it can better handle irregular applications. An application can be called irregular if it has unpredictable memory access, data flow or control flow. To study whether work stealing is effective in a task-based dataflow runtime, we added an extra module *migrate* to PaRSEC to do all operations related to work stealing. We also changed how tasks are described in TTG, to support work stealing.

The migrate module uses a dedicated *migrate* thread for all stealing related activities. The thread is created when the PaRSEC communication module is initialized and destroyed when the termination detection module in PaRSEC detects distributed termination. All communication to and from the migrate module is carried out using the PaRSEC communication module. The migrate thread constantly checks the state of the node and transitions the node to a *thief* if it detects starvation. On detecting starvation, the thief node sends a steal request to a *victim* node. The victim's migrate thread processes the steal request and selects tasks to be migrated to the thief node. When a task is selected as a victim of a steal request, the input data of the victim task are copied to the thief node and the victim task is recreated in the thief node. To implement this functionality, we added a new function `migrate` to the task class. The migrate thread invokes this function to copy the input data to the thief node. Once all data have arrived, the thief recreates the victim task, with the same unique id, and it is treated like any other task by the thief node.

New Task Description. To give the user control over which tasks can be stolen, we introduced another wrapper function in TTG (Listing 1.1), which takes a function `is_stealable` as an additional argument (The details about the wrapping function are available in   [5]). For instance, in a sparse linear algebra computation, tasks of the same type may operate on a dense or sparse tile. So the programmer may decide that tasks that operate on a sparse tile cannot be stolen.

Listing 1.1. New TTG wrapping function

```
ttg::wrapG(task_body, is_stealable, input_edges,
  output_edges, task_name, input_edge_names, output_edge_names);
```

The function **is_stealable** has the same signature as the task body, and it has access to the same data as the task body.

Thief Policy. The thief policy dictates two aspects of stealing: 1) How is a victim node selected? and 2) What qualifies as starvation in a node? Perarnau et al. [17] demonstrated that randomised victim node selection is best suited for distributed work stealing, so we use the same in this paper. A naive approach to work stealing only consider the ready tasks waiting for a worker thread as the indicator for available load in a node and if the **available** ready task is zero, starvation is assumed. We show that this is not the correct way to predict starvation as stealing takes non-zero time, and in that time new tasks can be activated in a starving node. So, we propose that along with ready tasks we should also consider the tasks that will be scheduled in the near future to measure starvation. We take the successors of the tasks in execution as the future tasks. Based on these we tested two starvation policies:

1. Ready tasks only: a steal request is initiated if there are no currently ready tasks.
2. Ready tasks + Successor tasks: a steal request is initiated if there are no currently ready tasks and no local successors of tasks currently in execution.

Victim Policy. Victim policies impose an upper bound on the number of tasks allowed to be stolen by a thief node. We test three victim policies:

1. Half: Half the stealable tasks are allowed to be stolen per steal request.
2. Chunk: An arbitrary number of stealable tasks is allowed to be stolen per steal request (we went with a chunk size of 20 as it is half of the total worker threads available).
3. Single: Only one stealable task is allowed to be stolen per steal request (this is a special case *chunk*, where the chunk size is 1).

The victim policy does not guarantee work stealing. For instance, if there are 40 stealable tasks available, the victim policy *Half* requests the scheduler to return as many tasks as possible up to a maximum of 20. This is not guaranteed to yield a task, as the migrate thread competes with worker threads, and the worker threads may end up getting all the available tasks. So the victim policy makes the best effort to migrate a permissible number of stealable tasks, with an upper bound on the number of tasks migrated.

At present, the waiting time of the task is not considered when permitting a steal. In this paper, the victim policies have an additional condition: work stealing is allowed only if the time required to migrate the task to the thief node is less than the time the task has to wait for a worker thread. The waiting time is calculated as follows:

$$average\ task\ execution\ time = \frac{execution\ time\ elapsed}{tasks\ executed\ till\ now}$$

$$waiting\ time = (\frac{\#ready\ tasks}{\#worker\ threads} + 1) * average\ task\ execution\ time$$

4 Experiments

The experiments were conducted on the Gadi supercomputer in the National Computing Infrastructure, Australia. Each node on Gadi has two 24-core Intel Xeon Scalable Cascade Lake processors with 3.2 GHz clock speed and 192 GiB of memory. All the experiments were run using openmpi (v4.0.2), intel-mkl (v2020.2.254) and intel-compiler (v2020.2.254). As there is only one MPI process per node, *node* and *process* are used interchangeably in this section. All the experiments are conducted using 40 worker threads per node.

4.1 Benchmarks

We use Cholesky factorization on a tiled sparse matrix as the benchmark to measure the different aspects of work stealing. In this benchmark, the matrix is divided into tiles and each tile is either sparse (filled with zeroes) or dense. In our runs, exactly half of the tiles are dense and tiles are cyclically distributed across nodes. We chose Cholesky factorization as the benchmark because it is a good representative of linear algebra benchmarks, and it has been used extensively to study various aspects of distributed computing including work-stealing. Also, there are 4 types of tasks in Cholesky factorization – POTRF, GEMM, TRSM and SYRK. The different task types have different execution times for the same tile size, presenting a challenge for distributed work-stealing.

We also used the Unbalanced Tree Search (UTS) benchmark [14] to study the victim policies. In the UTS benchmark, different trees can be created by configuring the different features of the benchmarks.

4.2 Potential for Work Stealing

Intuitively, task stealing is most effective when there is a workload imbalance and when there are active thief nodes. To quantify the potential for work stealing as the computation progresses, we divided the execution time of the benchmarks without work stealing into intervals of equal duration. Within each interval, whenever a worker thread successfully executed a *select* operation, the number of ready tasks were polled. Using these polled ready tasks, the potential for work stealing E^b in the interval b for P processes is calculated as:

$$E^b = I^b * P \qquad (1)$$

where I^b is the workload imbalance in the interval b, calculated as:

$$I^b = max(w_1^b, w_2^b, ..., w_P^b) - \frac{\sum_{i=1}^{P} w_i^b}{P} \qquad (2)$$

where w_i^b is the workload of process i in the interval b, calculated as:

$$w_i^b = \frac{\frac{\sum_{j=1}^{N} o_j^b}{N_b}}{max(o_1^b, o_2^b, ..., o_{N_b}^b)} \qquad (3)$$

where o_j^b is the jth polled value in interval b and N_b is the total number of polled values in interval b. Figure 1 gives the potential for work stealing obtained experimentally for the different intervals for the different number of nodes. From Fig. 1, we see that the work stealing has the most potential at the beginning of the execution for all numbers of nodes, remaining highest for 8 nodes as the execution progresses.

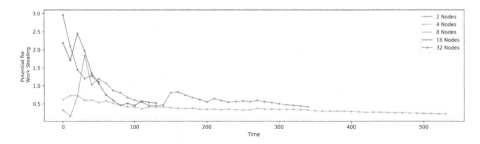

Fig. 1. Potential for work stealing when using an interval size of 10 s. (Global matrix of 10000^2 64-bit elements, organized as 200^2 tiles of 50^2 elements)

4.3   Thief Policy

The experiments on thief policy show that performance of work stealing is better when future tasks are taken into consideration to determine starvation. Figure 2 shows the performance of a thief policy that uses only ready tasks to determine starvation, against a thief policy that use ready tasks as well as future tasks ('No-Steal' in the experiments refer to the experimental runs without using work stealing). Here, the successor tasks of tasks currently in execution are taken as

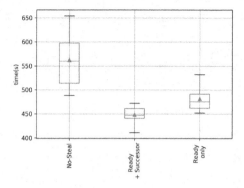

Fig. 2. Thief policies that counts only ready tasks versus policy that counts ready and successor tasks. (Global matrix of 10000^2 64-bit elements, organized as 200^2 tiles of 50^2 elements. Four nodes, *Single* victim policy)

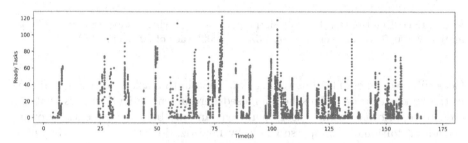

Fig. 3. Ready tasks in a thief node when a stolen task arrives. Only ready tasks were considered to determine starvation. (Global matrix of 10000^2 64-bit elements, organized as 100^2 tiles of 100^2 elements; two nodes)

future tasks. From the figure, we observe that the performance of work stealing is better if future tasks are taken into consideration when determining starvation.

To understand why work stealing underperforms while using only ready tasks to determine starvation, we counted the ready tasks in a thief node when a stolen task arrives. Figure 3 shows the result of this experiment and we can see that when the task arrives the number of ready tasks in the thief node is quite high. This means that the stolen task will have to wait a substantial amount of time before it is selected for execution. This happens because even when there are no ready tasks in a thief node, there may still be tasks in execution, each of which can have multiple successor tasks. So by the time a stolen task arrives, the tasks in execution may have added their successors to the ready queue.

4.4 Victim Policy

The previous experiments showed that work stealing reduces the variation in execution across multiple runs. We postulated that variation occurs because all threads are competing to extract tasks from the scheduling queues. Thus, if the number of threads is large, the queues will be under significant stress, and all the

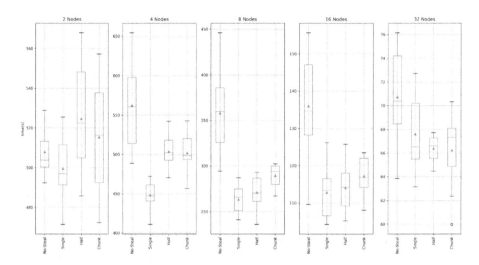

Fig. 4. Execution time for different victim policies on varying number of nodes. (Global matrix of 10000^2 64-bit elements organized as 200^2 tiles of 50^2 elements.)

locks will be conflicted leading to large variation in the task acquisition, and thus in the task execution. The scheduler used here use node level queues that are ordered by priority, so the *select* operation can only be done sequentially on all threads. Additionally, in sparse Cholesky factorization, there are a substantial number of tasks that do not do any useful computation, as they are operating on a sparse tile. In such cases, the threads will be spending more time waiting to extract the work, when compared to actual task execution. Figure 4 shows the execution time for different victim policies across different numbers of nodes for multiple runs and it shows that work stealing reduces the variation in the execution time.

The speedup from work stealing (against 'No-Steal' as the baseline is not uniform across different numbers of nodes as shown in Fig. 5. For each victim policy, speedup is highest (35%) for 8 nodes, as the potential for work stealing is high (see Fig. 1). The speedup decreases for larger number of nodes as the potential for work stealing decreases.

Waiting Time. In all the above experiments, victim policies permit a steal only if the waiting time to execute a task is more than the time taken to steal the task. Figure 6 shows the comparison in performance when waiting time is taken into consideration and when it is not. Waiting time does not seem to affect *Chunk*, as the mean execution times with and without considering waiting time are similar. Conversely, waiting time has a significant effect on *Half* and *Single*.

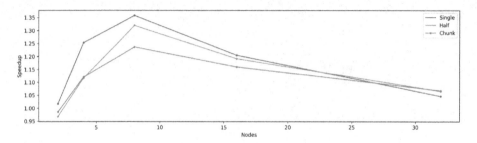

Fig. 5. Speedup for different victim policies on varying number of nodes. (Global matrix of 10000^2 64-bit elements, organized as 200^2 tiles of 50^2 elements)

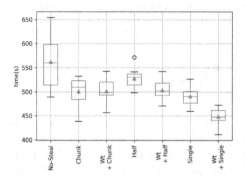

Fig. 6. Execution time for different victim policies, with and without waiting time taken into consideration. (Global matrix of 10000^2 64-bit elements, organized as 200^2 tiles of 50^2 elements)

In previous work, Perarnau et al. [17] found that *Half* gives three times the performance of *Chunk* for the Unbalanced Tree Search (UTS) benchmark when waiting time is not considered. UTS has the property that a child task is always mapped to the same node as its parent task unless stolen by a thief. Due to this mapping property, *Half* makes sense in UTS as no new task will be generated on a starving node. At the same time, there can be an exponential increase in tasks in a busy node. Also, UTS will not suffer from the same problems demonstrated in Fig. 3, as no new tasks are generated in a starving node. We were able to achieve similar results for UTS (Fig. 7) but the performance of *Half* was not transferred Cholesky factorization (Fig. 6). We also found that *Single* has comparable performance to *Half* when using UTS.

Experiments we conducted using sparse Cholesky factorization (Fig. 6) show that when waiting time is not considered *Half* performs worse than *Chunk*. When waiting time is taken into consideration, *Half* performs better than *Chunk*, but not by a huge margin. These experiments suggest that when using workloads that have child tasks with multiple parents located on different nodes, it is better to consider waiting time in victim policies. The experiments also demonstrate that

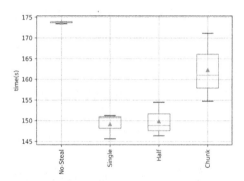

Fig. 7. Execution time for different victim policies when using UTS benchmark (b=120, m=5, q= 0.200014, g=12 ∗ 10^6).

if a victim policy gives good performance on one workload, it is not guaranteed that it will deliver similar performance on another.

Granularity. Granularity is the time taken to execute a single task. The granularity of different task types may be different but in sparse Cholesky factorization, the granularity of all task types is proportional to the tile size. So we tested the performance of different victim policies against different tile sizes. Table 1 show that work stealing is more effective with increasing granularity. Also, for smaller granularity, *Chunk* outperforms *Half*. Additionally, for small granularity, work stealing using *Half* actually degrades performance.

Steal Success Percentage. *Steal success percentage* is the percentage of steal requests that have yielded at least one task. Figure 8 shows the steal success percentage for different victim policy. When imbalance is high, steal success is the highest for *Chunk*. At the same time, Fig. 5 shows that the speedup is highest for *Single* when imbalance is high. From both these experiments, we can conclude that stealing more tasks does not guarantee better speedup, even when there is a high imbalance.

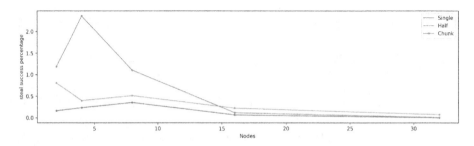

Fig. 8. Steal success percentage of different victim policies on varying numbers of nodes. (Global matrix of 10000^2 64-bit elements, organized as 200^2 tiles of 50^2 elements)

Table 1. Speedup for different victim policies for different tile sizes. (tiled matrix, 10000^2 tiles, four nodes)

Tile size	Execution Time				Speedup		
	No-Steal	Chunk	Half	Single	Chunk	Half	Single
10×10	230	214	244	221	1.077	0.94	1.03
20×20	237	235	246	228	1.006	0.96	1.03
30×30	255	246	253	238	1.03	1.008	1.07
40×40	400	370	388	370	1.08	1.032	1.08
50×50	562	501	503	448	1.12	1.11	1.25

5   Conclusion

In this paper, we showed that work stealing is an effective load balancing strategy in task-based dataflow runtime, delivering a speedup of up to 35% and reducing variability in execution time. We also demonstrate that stealing more tasks does not guarantee better speedup, even when there is a high imbalance. *When* the task is stolen is more important than *how many* tasks are stolen and counting future tasks is critical in determining starvation in a thief policy. These experiments suggest that when using workloads that have child tasks with multiple parents located on different nodes, it is better to consider waiting time in victim policies. As an extension of this work, we will be exploring work stealing between accelerator devices in the same node.

Acknowledgement. This research is undertaken with the assistance of resources and services from the National Computational Infrastructure (NCI), which is supported by the Australian Government. We thank George Bosilca and Thomas Herault (Innovative Computing Laboratory, UTK) for the detailed design discussions.

References

1. Acun, B., et al.: Parallel Programming with Migratable Objects: Charm++ in Practice, SC 2014, pp. 647–658 (2014). https://doi.org/10.1109/SC.2014.58
2. Agarwal, S., Barik, R., Bonachea, D., Sarkar, V., Shyamasundar, R.K., Yelick, K.: Deadlock-Free scheduling of X10 computations with bounded resources. In: SPAA (2007). https://doi.org/10.1145/1248377.1248416
3. Bauer, M., Treichler, S., Slaughter, E., Aiken, A.: Legion: expressing locality and independence with logical regions. SC 2012. https://doi.org/10.1109/SC.2012.71
4. Blumofe, R.D., Joerg, C.F., Kuszmaul, B.C., Leiserson, C.E., Randall, K.H., Zhou, Y.: Cilk: an efficient multithreaded runtime System. J. Parallel Distrib. Comput. **37**(1), 55–69 (1996). https://doi.org/10.1006/jpdc.1996.0107
5. Bosilca, G., Harrison, R., Hérault, T., Javanmard, M., Nookala, P., Valeev, E.F.: The template task graph (TTG) - an emerging practical dataflow programming paradigm for scientific simulation at extreme scale. SC 2021 (2021). https://doi.org/10.1109/ESPM251964.2020.00011

6. Bosilca, G., Bouteiller, A., Danalis, A., Herault, T., Lemarinier, P., Dongarra, J.: DAGuE: a generic distributed DAG engine for high performance computing. Parallel Comput. (2012). https://doi.org/10.1109/IPDPS.2011.281

7. Cao, Q., et al.: Extreme-scale task-based cholesky factorization toward climate and weather prediction applications. PASC 2020 (2020). https://doi.org/10.1145/3394277.3401846

8. Chamberlain, B.L., Callahan, D., Zima, H.P.: Parallel programmability and the chapel language. Int. J. High Perform. Comput. Appl. (2007). https://doi.org/10.1177/1094342007078

9. Frigo, M., Leiserson, C.E., Randall, K.H.: The implementation of the Cilk-5 multi-threaded language. In: PLDI 1998. ACM (1998). https://doi.org/10.1145/277650.277725

10. Guo, Y., Barik, R., Raman, R., Sarkar, V.: Work-first and help-first scheduling policies for async-finish task parallelism. In: IPDPS 2009 (2009). https://doi.org/10.1109/IPDPS.2009.5161079

11. Klinkenberg, J., Samfass, P., Bader, M., Terboven, C., Müller, M.S.: Reactive task migration for hybrid MPI+OpenMP applications. In: PPAM 2019 (2019). https://doi.org/10.1007/978-3-030-43222-5_6

12. Klinkenberg, J., Samfass, P., Bader, M., Terboven, C., Müller, M.S.: CHAMELEON: reactive load balancing for hybrid MPI+OpenMP task-parallel applications. J. Parallel Distrib. Comput. (2020). https://doi.org/10.1016/j.jpdc.2019.12.005

13. Kumar, V., Murthy, K., Sarkar, V., Zheng, Y.: Optimized distributed work-stealing. SC 2016 (2016). https://doi.org/10.1109/ia3.2016.019

14. Olivier, S.L., et al.: UTS: an unbalanced tree search benchmark. In: LCPC (2006). https://doi.org/10.1007/978-3-540-72521-3_18

15. Paudel, J., Tardieu, O., Amaral, J.N.: On the merits of distributed work-stealing on selective locality-aware tasks. In: ICPP 2013 (2013). https://doi.org/10.1109/ICPP.2013.19

16. Paudel, J., Amaral, J.N.: Hybrid parallel task placement in irregular applications. J. Parallel Distrib. Comput. (2015). https://doi.org/10.1016/j.jpdc.2014.09.014

17. Perarnau, S., Sato, M.: Victim selection and distributed work stealing performance: a case study. IPDPS 2014 (2014). https://doi.org/10.1109/IPDPS.2014.74

18. Samfass, P., Klinkenberg, J., Bader, M.: Hybrid MPI+OpenMP reactive work stealing in distributed memory in the PDE framework sam(oa)^2. In: IEEE International Conference on Cluster Computing (2018). https://doi.org/10.1109/CLUSTER.2018.00051

19. Schlimbach, F., Brodman, J.C., Knobe, K.: Concurrent collections on distributed memory theory put into practice. In: Euromicro PDP 2013 (2013). https://doi.org/10.1109/PDP.2013.40

20. Tardieu, O., Wang, H., Lin, H.: A work-stealing scheduler for X10's task parallelism with suspension. SIGPLAN 2012 (2021). https://doi.org/10.1145/2145816.2145850

Task Scheduler for Heterogeneous Data Centres Based on Deep Reinforcement Learning

Jaime Fomperosa, Mario Ibañez, Esteban Stafford[(✉)], and Jose Luis Bosque

Dpto. de Ingeniería Informática y Electrónica, Universidad de Cantabria,
Santander, Spain
{jaime.fomperosa,mario.ibanez,esteban.stafford,
joseluis.bosque}@unican.es

Abstract. This article advocates for the leveraging of machine learning to develop a workload manager that will improve the efficiency of modern data centres. The proposals stem from an existing tool that allows training deep reinforcement agents for this purpose. However, it incorporates several major improvements. It confers the ability to model heterogeneous data centres and then it proposes a novel learning agent that can not only choose the most adequate job for scheduling, but also determines the best compute resources for its execution. The evaluation experiments compare the performance of this learning agent against well known heuristic algorithms, revealing that the former is capable of improving the scheduling.

Keywords: Deep Reinforcement Learning · Task scheduling ·
Heterogeneous data centres · Machine Learning

1 Introduction

Modern Information Technology (IT) relies heavily on *data centres* which host massive amounts of interconnected computers. A subset of these data centres support the scientific and engineering communities with high performance computing services. The computers that integrate these combine their processing capabilities to accelerate the execution of complex problems [4].

To harness the power of computer clusters, data centres rely on a Workload Manager. It is in charge of job scheduling, or choosing jobs awaiting execution and assigning them to computing resources of the data centre. But this is an NP-Complete problem that cannot be solved in polynomial time. This is exacerbated by the huge growth of data centres [1], the wide variety and heterogeneity of architectures and configurations they host [13,14]. This means that the decision space of the workload manager has increased substantially, and consequently so has the difficulty of finding optimal solutions to the problem. It is possible to find *near-optimal* solutions using *approximation* methods [17] or *heuristic* [11] algorithms. The latter are commonly found at the core of modern resource managers, like Slurm [18]. They are characterised by sacrificing optimality for speed, which is a necessary compromise.

R. Wyrzykowski et al. (Eds.): PPAM 2022, LNCS 13826, pp. 237–248, 2023.
https://doi.org/10.1007/978-3-031-30442-2_18

These heuristic algorithms are fairly simple. Three algorithms are usually implemented nowadays: First In, First Out (FIFO), Shortest Job First (SJF) [12] and BackFill [7]. There are more complex algorithms that consider several attributes of each job in order to compute a score, which is then used to sort and prioritize them, such as WFP3 or UNICEP [16] or F1 [2]. However, these have difficulties in adapting to changes in the resources, the type of job or the objectives. Recently, machine learning has shown its adaptability to different scenarios, contrasting with the static approach of heuristic algorithms [9, 10].

Reinforcement Learning (RL) is a branch of machine learning that can autonomously improve its behaviour through trial and error. A key advantage of this approach is that it can consider many more parameters than heuristic algorithms and learn which are the most important. In this context *IRMaSim* [6], emerges as a tool to develop and test reinforcement learning algorithms on a simulator of heterogeneous data centres. A further development of this idea is *RLScheduler* [19]. Its results are fairly good despite its coarse simulator, where only homogeneous data centers with identical compute devices can be modeled.

The main *hypothesis* of this article is that the Deep Reinforcement Learning (DRL) techniques used in [19] can be adapted to schedule jobs in a heterogeneous data centre and with better performance than state-of-the-art heuristic algorithms. The pursuit of this hypothesis requires the completion of three steps. First, the definition of an environment that adequately represents heterogeneous data centres. To this end the cores of the cluster are grouped into nodes with possibly differing properties. Second, is the development of the agent itself, deciding its internal structure, how is the information from the environment fed to it, and how is the action selected. And third, an evaluation procedure must be devised where the performance of the agent is compared to that of well known heuristic algorithms.

The experimental results presented in the evaluation section show two important conclusions. First, that heterogeneity poses new challenges to the scheduling problem, even for classic algorithms that are optimal in homogeneous systems. Secondly, the proposed agent is able to obtain better results in all the studied objectives than heuristic algorithms, which confirms that machine learning-based scheduling is an important new field of study.

The remainder of this article is organised as follows. Section 2 gives an overview of reinforcement learning resource managers. Section 3 describes the main proposals of the article. Section 4 presents the evaluation methodology and discusses its results. Finally, a summary with the most important conclusions of the article is in Sect. 5.

2   Background

Reinforcement learning systems usually revolve around the concept of an *agent* that must drive the behaviour of the *environment* in order to reach a given *objective*. The agent is in charge of making decisions that affect the environment in some manner, and its aim is to learn how to satisfy the objective. Internally the agent is implemented with a *Deep Neural Network (DNN)* that, before going into production, must be trained. This is done by exposing the environment to stimuli, the agent considers the consequences of the *actions* it takes and it progressively learns which ones are better than others.

The training process is divided in *epochs*, or iterations of sets of stimuli. In turn, epochs consist of a series of *steps*, representing the processing of a given stimulus [15]. In each step the agent performs an *action* that has an impact in the environment. This is measured through *observations* and qualified by a *reward* value that indicates whether the impact was positive or negative. At the end of each epoch, the agent evaluates these and encourages those actions that helped in reaching the objective. After experiencing a number of epochs, the agent converges to using a particular set of actions that maximise the rewards it obtains, and therefore, satisfies the objective.

In the context of resource managers, the environment represents the compute resources of a data centre and the set of jobs, or workload, to be executed. The agent must observe the incoming jobs and the state of the data centre, and decide which job is allocated to which resource in order to achieve an optimization objective, e.g. slowdown or average waiting time. The jobs are usually stored in a *workload queue*, which can potentially be very long and become unmanageable. Modern resource managers, use an *eligible job queue*, which is a fixed length queue that holds the oldest jobs pending execution. The scheduler only considers jobs in this queue for execution, and when one gets chosen, it vacates the queue leaving space for another from the workload queue.

RLScheduler combines a reinforcement learning resource manager with a simplistic data centre simulator to accelerate the training process [19]. The simulated environment defines a number of computational resources, all with the same characteristics. Then it is only necessary to keep a number of free resources to represent the status of the data centre. And knowing to which processors in particular the job is assigned does not really matter. In RLScheduler, an observation represents the state of the environment by means of a vector that contains the attributes of all the eligible jobs.

The simplicity of RLScheduler is also its major drawback, as it considers the resources to be identical and unrelated. On contrast, modern data centres are heterogeneous and structured, as they host compute nodes with a number of processors or cores. These can have different architectures and compute capacities, which can have a great impact on scheduling. In addition, some applications must execute on processors belonging to the same node. Rising to these challenges is the main objective of this paper. Thus, a redesign of RLScheduler is proposed that will allow the modeling of heterogeneous systems. As a consequence, it will train agents to decide on which job to schedule and to which resource it will be assigned.

3   DRL for Scheduling in Heterogeneous Data Centres

This section details the improvements made to RLScheduler allowing its use in heterogeneous and structured data centres, and also proposes a scheduler agent that is able to select the best possible combinations of job and node. In order to adequately model these systems, the simulated environment must keep track of the jobs assigned to each node and their attributes to properly predict the execution time of the jobs. This also increases the amount of information that must be taken into account by the agent to make the best possible scheduling decisions. As a consequence, the observation and actions spaces must be redefined.

3.1 Observation and Action Spaces

The observation space must be able to represent the state of the environment that the agent will use to decide its next action. Similarly, the action space contains all the possible actions an agent can take over the environment. As mentioned in the previous section, RLScheduler considers all the computational resources of the data centre to have the same properties, making it unnecessary to identify which resources are allocated to each job. However, in heterogeneous data centres it is imperative that the compute resources are represented as a set of nodes with different number of processors. This information must be included in the observation space. Therefore, it is divided in two sets of attributes, the *Node Observation* representing the state of the data centre nodes, and the *Job Observation* containing the job information.

The proposed representation of the computational resources is based on the concept of *node*. Each one can have a different *size* and *speed*, regarding the number of processors it contains and its clock frequency. As for the jobs, they are considered memory-sharing embarrassingly parallel applications requesting a number of *processors*. Meaning that a job cannot be assigned to more than one node, that the node must have enough free processors to host the complete job, and that there is no communication overhead. The reason behind this decision is to streamline the simulator model. The proposed set of attributes for the observation space is shown in Table 1. The number of attributes is lower than in real resource managers, but since the model is expandable, it is fairly simple to add new attributes for the agent to consider.

Table 1. List of attributes of the Job and Node Observations.

Field Name	Notation	Description
Job Observation Space		
Requested Processors	n_j	Number of processors requested for the job
Requested Time	r_j	Amount of time requested for the job
Wait Time	w_j	Amount of time spent by the job in the job queue
Node Observation Space		
Total Processors	tp_n	Number of processors in the node
Free Processors	fp_n	Free processors in the node
Frequency	f_n	CPU clock rate of the node processors

The action space has also been improved to accommodate the node concept. The agent must not only decide which is the next job to be scheduled, but also to which resource it is allocated. This translates into a new bidimensional action space, where one dimension covers the jobs in the eligible job queue and the other represents the nodes in the data centre.

3.2 Agent Architecture

The proposed agent adheres to the actor-critic architecture, which is common in DRL systems. It combines the use of two similar networks, the actor decides on the next action, while the critic evaluates the performance of the actor. This structure tends to improve training times. Compared to the agent in [19], there are changes in the observation and action spaces that have a significant impact on its design. A diagram describing the new agent, as well as its relationship with said spaces is shown in Fig. 1.

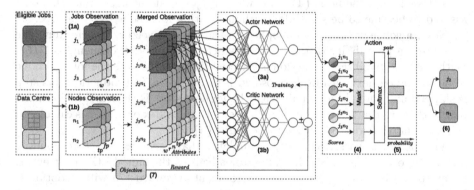

Fig. 1. Proposed agent with observation and actions spaces for three jobs and two nodes.

Since the input to the DNN has to have a fixed size and the number of jobs in the queue varies over time, an eligible job queue is used with the first 128 pending jobs. This value is the same as in RLScheduler and is also common practice in workload managers such as Slurm. The agent considers the jobs in the eligible job queue and their three corresponding attributes, composing the Job Observation, an array of size 128×3 **(1a)**. Simultaneously it obtains information about the nodes through the Node Observation array. It has as many rows as nodes in the data centre and three columns, one for each node attribute **(1b)**.

Next, the agent prepares the observation by merging the Job Observation and the Node Observation attributes of each combination of job and node, and adds an extra value called *Can Be Scheduled* **(2)**, which is defined as $c_{j,n} = n_j \leq fp_n$ resulting in true if the node n has room for the job j and false otherwise. This combined observation is a matrix with $128 \times NumNodes$ rows and $JobAttributes + NodeAttributes + 1$. Here, the rows represent all the possible pairings of jobs and nodes, and the columns are the total number of attributes that define each of these pairs, which in this instance it is equal to seven. The fact that the Node and Job Observations are combined serves the purposes of presenting the agent all the possible pairings of nodes and jobs, and allow it to make a decision with sufficient information.

The next step is to let the agent select from the observation the job-node pair to be scheduled. This decision is reached with the aid of the actor network of the agent (3a), which has seven inputs, one for each attribute in the observation. Then it has three fully-connected hidden layers of 32, 16 and 8 neurons each, with ReLU as their activation function. Finally, the output layer is of size 1, as purpose of this network is to provide a single score value for each jobs-node pairs. The actor is fed the whole observation matrix, therefore, the output is also not a single score but a column vector of $128 \times NumNodes$ scores. Then, a mask is applied to the score vector to remove the values corresponding to padding jobs added to complete the observation, or those that request more processors than those free in the node (4). This way, any job that the agent may choose is assured to be able to be scheduled without waiting for resources to get free.

Next, a softmax function is applied to the masked vector, transforming the scores into a probability distribution in which the sum of all elements is 1 (5). With these probabilities, an action is selected that will indicate the job and node to be scheduled next, favouring those with higher score. In production this step is skipped and the job-node pair with the highest score is chosen. The job-node pair is an integer $a_i \in [0, 128 \times NumNodes-1]$, the index of the job is calculated as $\lfloor \frac{i}{128} \rfloor$ and the node as $i \bmod NumNodes$ (6).

This action is passed on to the simulator that executes the corresponding scheduling operation. After the simulator advances the time to the next event, which results in a new state of the environment, a reward (7) will be obtained based on the chosen objective, together with a new observation representing the new state of the environment. These are used by the critic network in the agent (3b) to evaluate the performance of the actor network. It guides the training process of both networks toward a state where the agent consistently schedules the jobs to the right computing resources, such that the objective is satisfied. The goal of the critic network is to predict the reward that a set of jobs would produce with the given objective.

Three reward functions have been implemented, each corresponding to a different scheduling metric to be minimised. If e_i and w_i are the execution and wait times of job i, the metrics are

– *Slowdown (SLD)*: is the average slowdown, defined as $\frac{w_i+e_i}{e_i}$, for all the jobs. This metric can give very high values when jobs are short.
– *Average bounded slowdown (BSLD)*: variation of the slowdown that is less sensitive to very short execution times. The bounded slowdown of a job is defined as $max((w_i + e_i)/max(e_i, 10), 1)$.
– *Average waiting time (AVGW)*: simply averages w_i of all jobs.

It is worth noting that all the objectives are related, since they strive to reduce the delay in the execution of the jobs. However, the average the bounded slowdown metric is better suited to agent training than the other two. First, it conveys more information than the average waiting time because it includes the execution time of the jobs, and second, it is more stable than the average slowdown, since it eludes giving very high values due to short execution times.

3.3 Size Reduction Through Clustering

A drawback of this agent is the large size of the input. For instance, in a data centre with 16 nodes, the total number of elements of both observations would be $128 \times 16 \times 7 = 14336$. Doubling the number of nodes in the data centre results in 28672 elements, which has a clear impact in the performance and the scalability. Since the size of the queue is fixed to 128, reducing the size of the observation can only be done by limiting the size of the node observation. This section describes how this can be accomplished with clustering techniques.

In a data centre, it is common that many nodes have a similar situation, either due to their equivalent architectural properties or similar load. Then, it is not necessary to identify exactly which node is going to receive a job, and it suffices to indicate what kind of node is the target. Taking this into account, the n nodes of the data centre can be grouped in k *clusters* of similar attributes using the k-*means* algorithm [5]. The attributes of each cluster are calculated as their mean value for all the nodes in each one. This is applied to the node observation **(1b)** before it is merged to the job observation (Fig. 1), which now carries job-cluster pairs instead of job-node pairs. Like before an attribute c is calculated, indicating if the job fits in at least one node in the cluster.

The final step after the job-cluster selection has been made is to choose a specific node for scheduling the job, which is done by simply finding the first node of the cluster that can execute the job. This selection does not need any further considerations, as the assumption is that nodes in the same cluster are similar enough. By grouping the nodes in a fixed number of clusters, the size of the node observation becomes constant. Thus, it is possible to increase the number of nodes in the platform without complicating the agent.

4 Evaluation

The proposed agent is evaluated through four instances. The *SqSLD agent, SqB-SDL agent* and *SqAVGW agent* aim to minimise the slowdown, average bounded slowdown and waiting time, respectively. The *ClBSLD agent* uses clustering of the compute resources to minimize the average bounded slowdown, although any of the other two objectives could have been employed.

The target system is a heterogeneous data centre with 20 nodes. Each can have between 4 and 64 processors, running at 2, 2.5, 3 or 3.5 GHz. The workload used is generated from models defined in the Parallel Workloads Archive, *Lublin, 1999/2003*, commonly used in HPC [3,8]. This workload is composed of 10 000 jobs with varying required processors and execution times.

Also, a set of heuristic algorithms were used for comparison. They are able to select jobs and the nodes to execute them. These result by combining two algorithms, one to choose the job and another for the resource. These are summarised in Table 2, then algorithm xy combines job selection x with node selection y.

The hyper-parameters used to control the training process of the agents are mostly the same as in RLScheduler. The most relevant ones are the learning rate α, with values of 0.0003 and 0.001 for the actor and the critic networks, respectively, and gamma γ is equal to 0.99.

Table 2. Heuristic job and node selection algorithms.

Name	Symbol	Description
Job Selection		
Random	r	Random job from the job queue is selected
First	f	Job with lowest submit time is selected
Shortest	s	Job with lowest requested run time is selected
Smallest	l	Chooses job with lowest requested number of processors
Node Selection		
Random	r	Random node is selected
Biggest node	b	Node with highest number of processors is selected
Fastest node	f	Node with highest frequency is selected

To explore the training phase, each instance of the agent is subjected to 100 epochs and the evolution of the process is observed to ensure that it converges. To lighten this process, the workload trace is not used in its full length. One training epoch consists of 20 *trajectories*, which are sets of 256 consecutive jobs, taken at a random time from the original trace. The experimental results show that 100 epochs are more that enough because convergence was observed after 60 epochs, since the behaviour did not improve in the following epochs.

Once the training phase concludes, the inference stage is evaluated. The trained agents must schedule trajectories of 1024 jobs extracted from the same workload. Note that the presented results consider 20 repetitions to avoid obtaining wrong conclusions due to outliers. The scheduling results are evaluated by comparing the behaviour of the trained instances to that of the heuristic algorithms. These are shown in graphs where the horizontal axis represents the values of the metrics used, and the vertical axis shows the different schedulers, sorted by the median. To avoid clutter, only the results for the best heuristic algorithms are shown. The graphs combine box-and-whisker and violin representations of the results. The box shows the 25 and 75 percentile, the line in the box indicates the median, and the whiskers represent extreme values. The violin plots show result distribution, where fatter parts indicate a higher data density.

Figures 2, 3 and 4 show the promising results of the four agents. In general, the results prove that intelligent schedulers can perform better than the state-of-the-art algorithms in a heterogeneous data centre, at least for the objectives considered in this article.

Note how the algorithms that select the random or first jobs, the first six in the graphs, give very bad results. In some cases, more than tripling the results

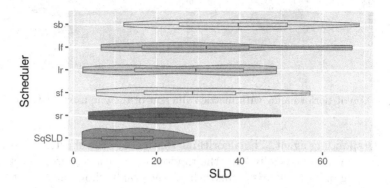

Fig. 2. Average slowdown results for heuristic algorithms and SqSLD Agent.

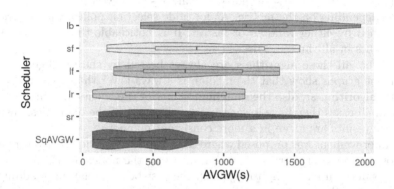

Fig. 3. Average waiting time results for heuristic algorithms and SqAVGW Agent.

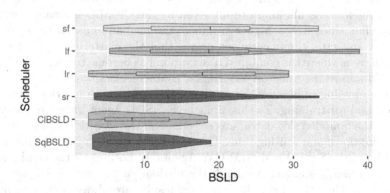

Fig. 4. Average bounded slowdown results for heuristic algorithms, SqBSLD and ClB-SLD Agents.

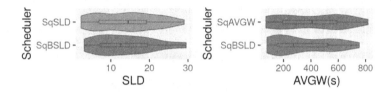

Fig. 5. Agent performance with metrics different of the one used for training.

of the corresponding agent. The algorithms that choose the shortest or smallest jobs perform better, especially with the random or fastest resource selections.

Considering only the heuristic algorithms, the graphs show the importance of choosing the right node for a job in the context of a heterogeneous data centre. Note that only the algorithms that choose the shortest or smallest jobs first appear in the graphs. The rest had significantly worse results and were excluded to avoid clutter. It can be seen that sr has always the lowest median, followed by sf or lr, depending on the metric. As for node selection policy, the best results are obtained by either random or fastest. It is noticeable that lr presents the lowest values in all three metrics.

However, all these algorithms are always bested by the intelligent agents. Indeed, the graphs show that the median is always lower than that of the best heuristic algorithm sr, also the minimum values of the agents are similar to the lr. But in all cases they have lower variance than any of the heuristics, ensuring that good results are given in a more consistent manner.

An improvement was proposed where the complexity of the agent was reduced by incorporating a clustering algorithm to group the nodes of the data centre. As this evaluation aims only to establish the cost-benefit relation of adding the clustering vs. reducing the complexity of the agent, only one objective has been tested, the average bounded slowdown. The 20 nodes of the system were grouped into 10 clusters, so the complexity of the DNN was reduced in half.

The results of the ClBSLD Agent (Fig. 4) are comparable to those of the SqBSDL Agent. The minimum result given by the ClBSLD is smaller than the SqBSDL, but since it has higher variance, the median ends up being slightly higher. At any rate, the experiment proves that the clustering method can be applied in cases where the combined observation has become too large, and many of the nodes have the same or very similar characteristics.

It is interesting to observe the results of the agents with metrics different to the ones used for training. To this aim, the SqBSDL Agent instance, trained to minimise the bounded slowdown, was selected and tested with the other metrics, average slowdown and waiting time. The results are shown in Fig. 5, compared to the results of the SqSLD and SqAVGW Agents. In both cases the results of the agents are roughly similar. Although the median values of SqBSDL are lower than those of the other two, the best case results are always obtained by the other instances. This is explained by the fact that bounded slowdown is better suited to agent training, and therefore, it is able to give a better scheduling.

The above evaluation proves that an intelligent agent is able to learn how to take scheduling actions and obtain better results than classic scheduling algorithms. And this can be done not for a single goal but for different ones, only constrained by the capabilities of the simulator in which it is working. All this suggests that using a machine learning agent to schedule a real data centre is an idea worth considering. Provided that it is possible to obtain a trace of the jobs typically executed in the system to perform the training of the agent.

5   Conclusions

The fact that data centres are more and more heterogeneous, combined with the variety of the applications and their requirements, complicates scheduling significantly. With homogeneous clusters, heuristic algorithms are used to schedule jobs, but in heterogeneous ones it is crucial to decide also to which compute resource they scheduled. This problem is no longer possible to solve with such algorithms and there has been advances in employing machine learning instead.

This article presents a first approach to solving the scheduling problem in heterogeneous clusters with deep reinforcement learning. To this aim, it was necessary to redefine the observation space of the agent, allowing it to perceive more data from the environment. As well as to broaden the action space to accommodate the fact that not only jobs but also nodes had to be selected.

Also, two different agents were developed capable of successfully processing the state of a small heterogeneous data centre and learning to choose adequate scheduling actions. The second agent is a refinement of the first that through the use of clustering techniques is capable of giving the similar performance using a fraction of the memory requirements. The successful training of the agents was possible thanks to the development of a simulation infrastructure with a simplistic model of a heterogeneous data centre, that can simulate nodes with a different number of processors and frequencies.

The evaluation included in this article suggests that it is possible to replace heuristic schedulers with ones that leverage machine learning techniques. The experiments show that the behaviour of the machine learning agent gives very promising results, compared to well known heuristic algorithms.

Next developments could see larger clusters simulated with more detail, in which contention could be modeled, like that appearing in memory or network access. Furthermore, the set of objectives to optimise by the scheduler could be increased by considering energy related metrics.

Acknowledgment. This work has been supported by the Spanish Science and Technology Commission under contract PID2019-105660RB-C22 and the European HiPEAC Network of Excellence.

References

1. Bosque, J.L., Perez, L.P.: Theoretical scalability analysis for heterogeneous clusters. In: 4th IEEE/ACM International Symposium on Cluster Computing and the Grid (CCGrid 2004), Chicago, USA, pp. 285–292. IEEE Computer Society (2004)

2. Carastan-Santos, D., De Camargo, R.Y.: Obtaining dynamic scheduling policies with simulation and machine learning. In: Proceedings of the International Conference for High Performance Computing, Networking, Storage and Analysis, pp. 1–13 (2017)
3. Feitelson, D.G., Tsafrir, D., Krakov, D.: Experience with using the parallel workloads archive. J. Parallel Distrib. Comput. **74**(10), 2967–2982 (2014)
4. García-Saiz, D., Zorrilla, M.E., Bosque, J.L.: A clustering-based knowledge discovery process for data Centre infrastructure management. J. Supercomput. **73**(1), 215–226 (2017)
5. Hartigan, J.A., Wong, M.A.: Algorithm AS 136: a K-means clustering algorithm. J. Roy. Stat. Soc. ser. C **28**(1), 100–108 (1979)
6. Herrera, A., Ibáñez, M., Stafford, E., Bosque, J.: A simulator for intelligent workload managers in heterogeneous clusters. In: 2021 IEEE/ACM 21st International Symposium on Cluster, Cloud and Internet Computing (CCGrid), pp. 196–205 (2021)
7. Leonenkov, S., Zhumatiy, S.: Introducing new backfill-based scheduler for SLURM resource manager. In: Procedia Computer Science, 4th International Young Scientist Conference on Computational Science, vol. 66, pp. 661–669 (2015)
8. Lublin, U., Feitelson, D.G.: The workload on parallel supercomputers: modeling the characteristics of rigid jobs. J. Parallel Distrib. Comput. **63**(11), 1105–1122 (2003)
9. Mao, H., Alizadeh, M., Menache, I., Kandula, S.: Resource management with deep reinforcement learning. In: Proceedings of the 15th ACM Workshop on Hot Topics in Networks, pp. 50–56 (2016)
10. Mao, H., Schwarzkopf, M., Venkatakrishnan, S.B., Meng, Z., Alizadeh, M.: Learning scheduling algorithms for data processing clusters. In: Proceedings of the ACM Special Interest Group on Data Communication, p. 270–288. SIGCOMM 2019 (2019)
11. Pearl, J.: Heuristics: Intelligent Search Strategies for Computer Problem Solving. Addison-Wesley Longman Publishing Co., Inc, Boston (1984)
12. Pinedo, M.: Scheduling, vol. 29. Springer, Berlin (2012)
13. Stafford, E., Bosque, J.L.: Improving utilization of heterogeneous clusters. J. Supercomput. **76**(11), 8787–8800 (2020). https://doi.org/10.1007/s11227-020-03175-4
14. Stafford, E., Bosque, J.L.: Performance and energy task migration model for heterogeneous clusters. J. Supercomput. **77**(9), 10053–10064 (2021). https://doi.org/10.1007/s11227-021-03663-1
15. Sutton, R.S., Barto, A.G.: Reinforcement Learning: An Introduction. MIT press, Cambridge (2018)
16. Tang, W., Lan, Z., Desai, N., Buettner, D.: Fault-aware, utility-based job scheduling on blue, gene/p systems. In: IEEE International Conference on Cluster Computing and Workshops, pp. 1–10 (2009)
17. Vazirani, V.V.: Approximation Algorithms. Springer Science & Business Media, Berlin (2013)
18. Yoo, A.B., Jette, M.A., Grondona, M.: SLURM: simple Linux utility for resource management. In: Feitelson, D., Rudolph, L., Schwiegelshohn, U. (eds.) JSSPP 2003. LNCS, vol. 2862, pp. 44–60. Springer, Heidelberg (2003). https://doi.org/10.1007/10968987_3
19. Zhang, D., Dai, D., He, Y., Bao, F.S., Xie, B.: RLScheduler: an automated HPC batch job scheduler using reinforcement learning. In: SC20: International Conference for High Performance Computing, Networking, Storage and Analysis, pp. 1–15. IEEE (2020)

Shisha: Online Scheduling of CNN Pipelines on Heterogeneous Architectures

Pirah Noor Soomro[1(✉)], Mustafa Abduljabbar[2], Jeronimo Castrillon[3], and Miquel Pericàs[1]

[1] Department Computer Science and Engineering, Chalmers University of Technology, Gothenburg, Sweden
{pirah,miquelp}@chalmers.se
[2] Ohio State University, Columbus, USA
abduljabbar.1@osu.edu
[3] Chair for Compiler Construction, Technische Universität Dresden, Dresden, Germany
jeronimo.castrillon@tu-dresden.de

Abstract. Many modern multicore processors integrate asymmetric core clusters. With the trend towards Multi-Chip-Modules (MCMs) and interposer-based packaging technologies, platforms will feature heterogeneity at the level of cores, memory subsystem and the interconnect. Due to their potential high memory throughput and energy efficient core modules, these platforms are prominent targets for emerging machine learning applications, such as Convolutional Neural Networks (CNNs). To exploit and adapt to the diversity of modern heterogeneous chips, CNNs need to be quickly optimized in terms of scheduling and workload distribution among computing resources. To address this we propose Shisha, an online approach to generate and schedule parallel CNN pipelines on heterogeneous MCM-based architectures. Shisha targets heterogeneity in compute performance and memory bandwidth and tunes the pipeline schedule through a fast online exploration technique. We compare Shisha with Simulated Annealing, Hill Climbing and Pipe-Search. On average, the convergence time is improved by $\sim 35\times$ in Shisha compared to other exploration algorithms. Despite the quick exploration, Shisha's solution is often better than that of other heuristic exploration algorithms.

Keywords: CNN parallel pipelines · Online tuning · Design space exploration · Processing on heterogeneous computing units · Processing on chiplets

1 Introduction

Multicore processors are becoming more and more heterogeneous. Intel's Meteor Lake [2] features asymmetric multicore design containing high performance and power saving cores. Similarly, Apple's A14 Bionic [1] integrates high performance cores called Firestorm and power saving cores called Icestorm. The trend towards heterogeneity is complemented with the trend towards Multi-Chip-Module (MCM) integration, which enables lower cost during design and improves

R. Wyrzykowski et al. (Eds.): PPAM 2022, LNCS 13826, pp. 249–262, 2023.
https://doi.org/10.1007/978-3-031-30442-2_19

yield by reducing chip area (chiplets) [13]. When combined with interposer-based packaging technology, it enables lower latency and high bandwidth transmission to memory devices such as High Bandwidth Memory (HBM) [8]. Chip manufacturers are adopting a mix of these technologies in order to design high performance processors, resulting in heterogeneity at the level of the cores, memory subsystem and the Network on Chip (NoC). In order to effectively exploit such architectures, applications must be optimized considering the impact of different levels of heterogeneity. Furthermore, to address the diversity of hardware platforms, the optimization process must be fast and preferably online.

Convolutional Neural Networks (CNNs) have high computational, bandwidth and memory capacity requirements owing to the large amount of weights and the increasing size of intermediate results that need to be transferred between layers. Parallel pipelining has the potential to address these requirements by partitioning the whole network across devices, and requiring only the inputs to be exchanged among stages. In chiplet architectures, CNNs could be efficiently pipelined by distributing layers across chiplets so as to reduce the amount of weights that need to be copied. Furthermore, pipelining makes the task of load balancing manageable among heterogeneous computing units.

In order to partition and schedule pipelines, current approaches rely on designing cost models to steer design space exploration [3,5]. For instance, the auto-scheduler in [3] explores over ten thousand schedules for a single CNN-layer pipeline using Halide [22]. The effectiveness of these approaches depends on the accuracy of the cost model and the scalability of the exploration algorithm. Sophisticated cost models, some of them using ML-models themselves, have been proposed and used in [3,4,14,18,32–34]. These models, however, require extensive training for near-optimal solutions [5], are sensitive to changes in the execution environment (e.g., DVFS) and architectural parameters, need in-depth architectural knowledge for model updates, and do not consider the impact of heterogeneous multicore or chiplet architectures. As heterogeneity at different levels of processing (e.g. core performance, memory bandwidth and/or MCM organization) is expected to increase in future HPC platforms, static pipeline partitioning and scheduling become inflexible. Online auto-tuning of the pipeline schedule would help to ensure performance portability to future architectures. However, to make it practical, it is critical that online pipeline partitioning and scheduling finds an acceptable configuration with low overhead.

Pipe-Search [29] adopts an online exploration approach for finding a pipeline configuration. It generates a database of pipeline configurations which is space-intensive and prohibitively slow for larger systems and deeper CNNs. In this paper, we propose a quick method to determine a meaningful starting point, or seed, for the exploration coupled with a simple navigation heuristic for efficient runtime auto-tuning. In Shisha, we leverage statically available information from the CNN and from the target platform to reduce the number of exploration points and find a near-optimal solution within reasonable time. A *configuration* explored by Shisha suggests grouping CNN layers into pipeline stages and mapping of pipeline stages onto available sets of processing units referred to as

Execution Places (EPs). When generating initial configurations, `Shisha` aims at balancing the load among pipeline stages while considering the allocation of stages to EPs. `Shisha` improves upon related work in two ways:

- `Shisha` achieves faster convergence by introducing two novel schemes: (i) the seed generation and (ii) the online tuning. We demonstrate that `Shisha` is able to converge faster than existing algorithms (Simulated Annealing, Hill Climbing and Pipe-Search) and that it is able to find a solution within practical time limits.
- We show that `Shisha` scales better with deeper CNNs and with larger amount of EPs per processing unit which is one of the limitations of prior online tuning approaches such as Pipe-Search [29].

`Shisha` maps pipeline stages to EPs, which could be of any type and number of processing units, such as multicores or manycores. To measure the quality of schedules explored by `Shisha` we compare our results to conventional search exploration algorithms such as Simulated Annealing (also used by TVM [34]), Hill Climbing, Exhaustive Search and Random Walk (executed for a longer period of time), and to Pipe-search, an earlier online tuning approach. We test `Shisha` on state of the art CNNs such as ResNet50 [11] and YOLOv3 [24]. The results show that, despite exploring only a tiny portion of the design space ($\sim 0.1\%$ of design space for ResNet50 and YOLOv3), `Shisha` finds a solution that is equivalent to exhaustive search. Moreover, due to the guided exploration, the convergence time is improved by $\sim 35\times$ in `Shisha` compared to the other representative exploration algorithms.

2   Motivation and Problem Definition

In a computing platform with different types of memories, the assignment of workload and data objects becomes crucial for better performance. To investigate the impact of different thread and data assignment strategies, we tested the STREAM Triad benchmark [16] with two data sizes, 19 GB and 31 GB on Intel's Knights Landing (KNL) [28]. KNL has two types of memories, 16 GB of high bandwidth memory(HBM), also called MCDRAM, and 90 GB of DDR4 DRAM. The bandwidth of HBM is $4\times$ higher than that of DRAM [26]. This suggests that most of the application data should be placed in HBM. It also means that HBM should be able to handle more parallelism until the bandwidth is saturated. For each data size, 15 GB of data are placed in MCDRAM and the remainder of the data are placed in DRAM. In Fig. 1, we show three cases, namely, 1) when all data are placed in DRAM (DDR only), 2) when MCDRAM is used as a cache (cache mode), and 3) when data is distributed across the two memories. As can be seen, with a sensible thread assignment, the case 3 yields the best performance. This shows that a clever data partitioning and thread assignment are key to achieve high performance in the presence of memory heterogeneity. Further analyzing case 3, Fig. 2 shows the heatmap of the execution time of STREAM Triad with different thread assignments to MCDRAM [16, 32, 64, 128] and DRAM [2, 4, 8, 16]. The optimal number of threads is determined by a) the memory bandwidth of each memory type, b) the

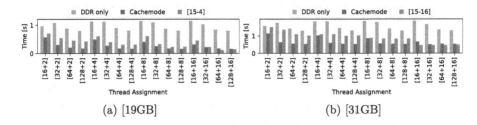

Fig. 1. Comparison of cases 1, 2 and 3. X-axis [X + Y] shows X = threads assigned to MCDRAM and Y = threads assigned to DRAM

additional bandwidth consumed by each extra thread, and c) the amount of data to be processed. Results from the experiment show that for each data partitioning between HBM and DRAM there is a different optimal thread partitioning. An important observation from Figs. 2 is that better performance can be achieved by assigning fewer number of threads per memory type, rather than opting for assigning maximum number of threads.

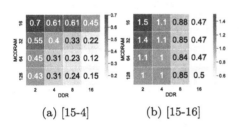   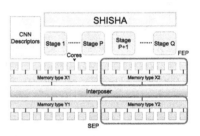

Fig. 2. (a) & (b) Execution time [s] of STREAM Triad with data distribution [X-Y], where X = GBs placed in MCDRAM and Y = GBs placed in DRAM

Fig. 3. System targeted in this paper. Memory type X and Y represent different memory bandwidths.

Problem Definition and General Approach of the Solution:
This work considers a computing platform which is composed of a set of nodes consisting of high performance cores attached to a high-bandwidth memory (referred to as Fast Execution Place – FEP) and clusters of relatively slower cores attached to a low-bandwidth memory (referred to as Slow Execution Place – SEP). This MCM based scenario is expected for chiplet architectures with heterogeneous integration and is shown in Fig. 3. Our goal is to run throughput maximizing CNN inference pipelines on such an architecture.

3   Background and Related Work

There are various schemes for parallelizing CNNs. In data parallelism the work of a minibatch (a set of inputs) is partitioned among multiple computational resources. In model parallelism the work is divided according to neurons in each layer which corresponds to the tensor dimensions in each layer. In layer pipelining [6] the work is partitioned by distributing network layers among computational resources. Model parallelism within the layer is combined with layer pipelining by arranging computational resources into multiple teams of workers. This hybrid parallelism has following benefits: 1) there is no need to replicate weight and input tensors on all devices, 2) the communication volume and points are reduced, and 3) the weights can remain cached, thus decreasing memory round-trips. In the rest of the paper we will refer to CNN pipelines in which network layers are grouped into pipeline stages. Each pipeline stage is assigned a unique set of computational resources, referred to as EPs.

Finding out the right schedule and mapping of CNN pipelines on mentioned architectures is a design space exploration problem, where we are interested in the configuration that achieves the highest throughput. The configuration consists of the number of pipeline stages, CNN layers per pipeline stage and a mapping of pipeline stages to EPs. In the literature, various meta heuristic and machine learning algorithms have been used such as Simulated Annealing [34], evolutionary algorithms [3,29], reinforcement learning [4,21] and deep neural network techniques [5]. The design space under consideration is large and complex, requiring tens of thousands of trials in order to reach a near optimum with current search schemes.Exploring in such a complex space is NP-hard. Parallel pipelines for CNN training have been applied in practice [9,12,19,20]. Recently, Chimera [14] generates a schedule for bi-directional pipelines by using complex cost models that represent the execution time of one network pass and calculate the depth and parallelism per pipeline stage. In Halide, [3] the pipeline scheduling approach uses a cost model that considers 66 platform and application specific features. For the cost model, 26 out of 66 feature values are predicted by a neural network trained on random representative programs. According to the specifications, one training point takes at most 320 min to train the neural network using different schedule configurations. To predict a schedule for Halide pipelines of a single CNN layer, the scheduler considers 10k configurations. In comparison, we show that for a large YOLOv3 network of 52 layer, Shisha considers only 18 configurations.

4   Shisha Exploration Approach

A pipeline configuration consists of two components: 1) the number of CNN layers assigned to each pipeline stage, and 2) the assignment of each pipeline stage to an EP. An EP can be a single or multiple cores attached to a memory module. Therefore, we classify the EPs according to the type of memory. For example, in Fig. 3 EPs are colored in green or red. We use this classification in Shisha to provide hints about the characteristics of the computing platforms with heterogeneous modules.

Shisha is a two-step approach. The first step is the "seed generation", in which we use a simplified cost-model to come up with an initial solution. This initial solution is used in the second step, "online tuning" for faster convergence.

4.1   Seed Generation

The goal of the seed generation is to determine a sensible starting configuration using only static information.

Algorithm 1. Seed Generation	**Algorithm 2.** Online Tuning
Require: W_l, H_e, N, L, C	**Require:** $seed, E, H_e, \alpha$
1: $seed[N]$	1: $conf \leftarrow seed$
2: $E[N]$	2: $throughput = execute(conf)$
3: **for** $passes$ in $[0..|L-N|]$ **do**	3: $\gamma \leftarrow 0$
4: $min_w \leftarrow min(W_l)$	4: **while** $\gamma < \alpha$ **do**
5: $n \leftarrow min(min_w - 1, min_w + 1)$	5: $stage \leftarrow slowest\_stage(conf)$
6: $W_l \leftarrow merge(min_w, n)$	6: $t\_stage \leftarrow nearestFEP(E)$
7: $seed \leftarrow merge\_layers(min_w, n)$	7: $conf \leftarrow move(conf, t\_stage)$
8: **end for**	8: $Tp = execute(conf)$
9: $Rank \leftarrow rank(seed, W_l, C)$	9: **if** $Tp \leq throughput$ **then**
10: **for** i in $[0...N]$ **do**	10: $\gamma ++$
11: $E[Rank_i] \leftarrow assign(Rank_i, H_{ei})$	11: **else**
12: **end for**	12: $\gamma \leftarrow 0$
13: **return** $seed, E$	13: $throughput \leftarrow Tp$
	14: **end if**
	15: **end while**
	16: **return** $conf$

Firstly, Eq. 1 is used to calculate the weights of the CNN layers [15,17,31,32]. For each layer, H, W, C denote the height, width and depth of the input tensor. R, S represent the height and width of the underlying convolutional kernel and K is the number of filters of the convolutional kernel. Note that, we are considering conventional CNNs in this paper, other type of layers can be incorporated in the context of this work by replacing Eq. 1 with a model for the estimation of computational intensity of the layers.

$$W = H \times W \times C \times R \times S \times K \tag{1}$$

Secondly, we capture the heterogeneity of the system to support the seed generation. This is used to guide the mapping of pipeline stages to EPs together with the total weight of each pipeline stage. We rank the EPs in a decreasing order of performance, for example, from Fig. 3 green EPs have rank 1 (FEP) and red ones have rank 2 (SEP). This is a hint to Shisha to balance the workload considering static knowledge about the heterogeneity of the system.

The seed generation process is described in Algorithm 1. $W_l = [w_{l1}, w_{l2}, ...w_{lL}]$ is the weight list, where a layer weight w_{li} is calculated using Eq. 1. $H_e = [e_1, e_2, ...e_N]$ is a list of EPs sorted in descending order w.r.t. performance. For example, for Fig. 3 $H_e = [G_1, G_2, ..G_p, R_1, R_2, ..R_q]$ represents the p EPs that belong to memory types X (green) and q Y (red) EPs. L is the total number of layers in a given CNN. N is the total number of pipeline stages in final pipeline ($N \leq L$) and C is assignment choice which is discussed later in this section. The output of Algorithm 1 is a pipeline configuration

$Seed = [PS_1, PS_2, ...PS_N]$, where PS_i represents the number of CNN layers assigned to i_{th} pipeline stage. Output $E = [e_1, e_2, ...e_N]$ is a list of EPs from H_e and the corresponding assignment to pipeline stages. Algorithm 1 comprises two phases. In phase 1 (Lines from 3–8) we generate pipeline stages by combining CNN layers. The goal of this phase is to merge layers into groups in order to balance out the cumulative weight of groups. These groups eventually become pipeline stages. The idea is to look for the layer with lowest weight (Line 4) and merge it with the immediate neighbour with the smallest weight (Line 5,6). Typically, the weight distribution in CNN layers does not follow any order, i.e. a light weight layer can be found between two layers with heavy weights. The second phase of Algorithm 1 (Lines 9–11) assigns the pipeline stages output by phase 1 to EPs. In principle, heavy pipeline stages should be assigned to high performance EPs, however, the assignment is not trivial in practice and requires to examine the impact of a few heuristics. Eventually, this will help in balancing execution time per pipeline stage, thus achieving a balanced pipeline.

Stage-to-EP Assignment Heuristics: Once CNN layers are grouped into pipeline stages, we then assign an EP to each pipeline stage. Since we have information about performance heterogeneity among EPs, we can make different choices, such as; 1) Rank pipeline stages w.r.t. number of *layers* assigned to each pipeline stage ($Rank_l$). While merging layers into stages, it is sometimes inevitable to have pipeline stages which are heavy in terms of aggregated weight with many light weight layers as opposed to a pipeline stage with one heavy layer. The highest rank corresponds to the pipeline stage with highest number of layers. We assign higher ranks to SEPs. This facilitates the online tuning phase later to greedily move the layers among pipeline stages to reach a solution. 2) Rank pipeline stages w.r.t. aggregated *weight* of each pipeline stage ($Rank_w$) Here, we assign the pipeline stages with heavy weights to fast EPs to balance the load. Line 9 controls this choice in Algorithm 1.

4.2   Online Tuning

For the exploration phase, we strive to reduce the exploration time so that it is still practical to carry out an online exploration without causing a significant overhead on execution time. This is particularly challenging given the size of the multidimensional pipeline configuration space, which often includes an overwhelming majority of slow configurations. We avoid visiting such configurations by starting from the seed configuration and incrementally adjusting load distribution by moving layers from one pipeline stage to an adjacent lighter stage. In Algorithm 2, we describe the auto-tuning scheme of ShishaThe required input is a pipeline configuration generated as a seed. A list of EPs E which represent a mapping of pipeline stages to the computing platform. The α parameter controls how many configurations are attempted after a configuration that outperforms the seed and recently found solution has been detected. The rationale behind Algorithm 2 is to gradually reduce the load of the slowest pipeline stage in order to improve the overall throughput of the pipeline. Hence, Shisha finds the slowest stage (Line 5) and remaps one layer at a time to the nearest faster

EPs (Line 6–7). The layer could be popped from front or back end of the stage depending on the location of new EP. Once a better configuration is found than any previous one, we try α more times to search for a better configuration. In Line 6 we balance the workload by moving layers to a nearest fast EP ($nFEP$) in pipeline i.e a closer stage which is running on an FEP. However, this is not the only choice that can be made. The nearest lightest fast EP ($nlFEP$) is also a good target to move layers as well. Therefore we keep both options open for the user to select. The complexity of Shisha is negligible therefore it does not cause much work to test different choices for a given CNN and computing platform.

5   Experimental Setup

Shisha targets systems that are heterogeneous in core performance and memory bandwidth. As discussed in Sect. 2, the system under consideration consists of different types of cores attached to different memory modules. Chiplets such as Nvidia's Simba [27] and Intel Meteor Lake [2] resemble such types of architectures. We used the gem5 simulator [7] to simulate heterogeneous cores and memory bandwidth. The simulator provides flexibility in modeling different architectures. To simulate different core performances, we used ARM's bigLittle cores [10] models in gem5 and to simulate different memory types, we tried different memory bandwidth values using a simple memory model connected to core cluster in gem5. Inter-EP latency is set to $20\,ns$ [27]. However, the execution time of pipeline stages is orders of magnitude higher than inter-EP latency, thus it does not impact the performance of pipeline.

A GEMM-based implementation [23] consists of two operators; 1) Im2Col and 2) GEneralized Matrix Multiplication (GEMM). We include both operators to simulate execution time for CNN layers of ResNet50, YOLOv3 and AlexNet.

6   Evaluation

As highlighted previously, Shisha includes a seed generation component and an online tuning heuristic. In this section, we evaluate the quality of the seed and the final solution generated by Shisha and analyze the convergence of the online auto-tuning phase.

Pipe-Search [29] is an online approach that uses a database of pipeline configurations sorted w.r.t. the distribution of workload among pipeline stages. It tests pipeline configurations of various depths and converges to a solution when no better solution is found by a time limit set by the user. This approach incurs a high overhead when generating the database of pipeline configurations which also limits its scalability. We compare Shisha's auto-tuning module with a set of exploration algorithms commonly used in literature, such as Hill Climbing (HC) with proximity equal to the number of layers in the network, Simulated Annealing (SA) with cooling factor values ranging from $0.9^{-5} - 0.01$, Random walk (RW) and in selected cases, Exhaustive Search (ES). For a fair comparison we test SA and HC with seeds produced by Shisha referred to as SA_s and HC_s. For randomized algorithms, we run 200 times and picked the solution which is closer to near optimal value

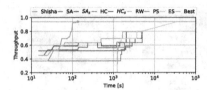 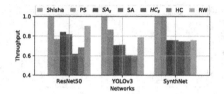

Fig. 4. Convergence of exploration algorithms for SynthNet on 8 EPs. Xaxis is time in log scale

Fig. 5. Throughput of search schemes normalized to ES

We use three CNNs in our experiments. ResNet50 [11] and YOLOv3 [24] are widely used image classification CNNs. There are 50 compute intensive layers in ResNet50 and 52 compute intensive layers in YOLOv3. The generation of sorted configurations, as required by Pipe-Search and ES, incurs an impractical time overhead when running ResNet50 and YOLOv3 for more than 4-stage pipelines. Therefore, we extend our benchmark set with a synthetic network (SynthNet) consisting of 18 convolutional layers. These layers are taken from the AlexNet architecture as AlexNet has only five convolutional layers and our testing platform consists of 8 EPs. This is to analyze CNNs that can be run on a higher number of EPs (i.e. $EP > 8$) and have a compute complexity matching widely used CNNs.

6.1   Comparison of Shisha with Exploration Algorithms

Figure 4 shows the convergence behavior of all exploration algorithms. The solution found by Shisha is equal to the best solution found by ES. For a fair comparison we run SA and HC using the same seed (SA_s, HC_s) generated by Shisha as a starting configuration. HC tries configurations in close proximity; both versions of HC and SA managed to find a better solution (*throughput* $= 0.80$) compared to the best solution (*throughput* $= 0.94$). However, the time of convergence of representative exploration approaches is high, this is because of using many configurations out of which some are very slow. ES and PS, on the other hand, incur the overhead of generating a database of configuration. As shown in Fig. 4, it took 1200 s, after that ES and PS started exploring. Shisha explores 0.12% of the total design space as compared to Pipe-search which explores 2.03% of the design space. this is because Shisha attempts configurations which leads towards the solution faster On average, the convergence time is improved by $\sim 35\times$ in Shisha compared to other search algorithms. In our approach, the stopping condition is controlled by α as mentioned in Sect. 4.2. We used $\alpha = 10$ in our experiments.

6.2   Analysis of Optimality

To quantify the confidence on Shisha solutions, we compared against ES using larger CNNs. In this experiment we configured a system of four EPs as it takes a lot of time for ResNet50 and YOLOv3 to run ES for higher number of EPs.

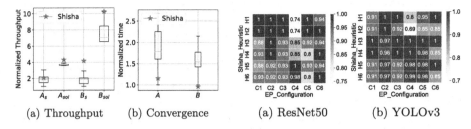

(a) Throughput   (b) Convergence   (a) ResNet50   (b) YOLOv3

Fig. 6. Comparison of Shisha seed against a set of 100 random seeds. $s =$ seed, $sol =$ solution, $A =$ YOLOv3 and $B =$ ResNet50.

Fig. 7. Throughput using different heuristics 1 and configurations of EPs 2

Figure 5 shows the throughput $(= 1/(ExecutionTime\ of\ slowest\ stage))$ of the solution found by Shisha and other algorithms normalized to best solution found by ES. In case of ResNet50 and YOLOv3, Shisha found the best solution by exploring 0.1% of the design space. In case of SynthNet, Shisha explored 2.5% of the design space to find the best solution. This is due to the fact that design space of SynthNet (18 layers) is smaller than ResNet50 (50 layers) and Shisha on average tries 25–35 exploration points with $\alpha = 10$.

6.3 Importance of Seed in the Auto-tuning Phase of Shisha

The seed generated by Shisha contains the mapping of pipeline stages to EPs. Figure 6 represents the throughput and convergence time of Shisha when initiated with the seed generated by Algorithm 1, represented as Shisha mark(red), compared to a set of 100 random seeds and solutions obtained with random seeds. In case of ResNet50, the solution quality in both cases is similar but convergence time is increased by 35% when started with a random seed. In case of YOLOv3, the throughput of the solution found using Shisha seed is 16% better and the convergence time is always better than a solution found using a set of 100 random seeds.

6.4 Assignment and Balancing Schemes in Shisha

Section 4.1 and 4.2 discuss various choices that Shisha makes while assigning EPs and balancing workload among pipeline stages. We investigate the impact of each of these choices, with results shown in Fig. 7. Table 1 lists the heuristics to be configured in Shisha. Assignment of EPs in H5 and H6 is random, in order to study the impact on convergence when no heuristic is used. Table 2 lists various configurations of the computing platform used to run this sensitivity analysis. The balancing scheme *lightest FEP* is effective in all cases as Shisha tries to move workload to an FEP which takes least time to execute assigned pipeline stage. This helps in balancing the pipeline as well as maximizing the throughput of the pipeline. In 80% of the cases, H1 and H3 yield better results. We investigated the convergence time of both schemes in order to determine the effectiveness of H1

Table 1. Heuristics of `Shisha`

Heuristic #	Assignment of EPs	Balancing
H1	$Rank_l$	$nlFEP$
H2	$Rank_l$	$nFEP$
H3	$Rank_w$	$nlFEP$
H4	$Rank_w$	$nFEP$
H5	random	$nlFEP$
H6	random	$nFEP$

Table 2. EPs

Conf.	FEPs	SEPs
C1	1 8-core	1 8-core
C2	2 8-core	2 8-core
C3	4 4-core	2 8-core
C4	2 8-core	4 4-core
C5	4 4-core	4 4-core
C6	8 4-core	NULL

and H3. Figure 8 Shows that the convergence time of H3 is less than H1 in 90% of the cases. This is due to the fact that in H3 assignment is done w.r.t. weights which means the configurations tested during exploration take reasonably less time than in H1. We recommend to use H3 because it converges faster and yields a near optimal solution.

6.5 Sensitivity Analysis of α

The extent of exploration of `Shisha` is controlled by α. The value of α should be chosen such that it allows tuning according to the performance heterogeneity among FEPs and SEPs while keeping a sensible convergence time. A higher value of α also means a longer tuning phase. Figure 9 shows the quality of solution (normalized to throughput obtained when $\alpha = 100$) for the YOLOv3 pipeline tested on three platform configurations with the SEPs $[3\times, 6\times, 12\times]$ slower than the FEPs. In our experiments, the performance difference between ARM's Big and Little cores is three folds on average, which is the first case in the figure. It is shown that with the higher heterogeneity between EPs, higher α yields a better solution. We use the same starting seed for the same CNN in all cases, therefore, for lower values of α, throughput behavior is similar, irrespective to the performance difference between EPs, but in the case of a higher performance difference, throughput is improved with a higher value of α.

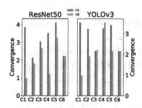

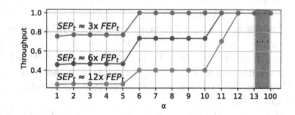

Fig. 8. Convergence time normalized to minimum value in each group for H1 and H3.

Fig. 9. Impact of α on the quality of solution in presence of heterogeneity

7 Conclusion

In this work we demonstrate a fast approach to scheduling CNN pipelines on heterogeneous computing platforms consisting of fast and slow cores. The proposed approach is generic and can be used on platforms featuring GPUs or FPGAs, in addition to asymmetric multicores and chiplets. We utilize compile time information in combination with a brief and guided online search for auto-tuning the CNN layers into parallel pipelines. Our experimental evaluation shows that the solution found by `Shisha` is as good as one produced by an exhaustive search of the design space. The results also show that `Shisha` scales well with larger networks and computing platforms. In future work, we will look at more generic tensor expressions [25] and the effect on seed parameters of high-level algebraic transformations [30].

Acknowledgment. This work has received funding from the EU Horizon 2020 Programme under grant agreement No 957269 (EVEREST), from the AI competence center ScaDS.AI Dresden/Leipzig (01IS18026A-D), PRIDE from Swedish Foundation for Strategic Research with reference number CHI19-0048 and eProcessor from the European High-Performance Computing Joint Undertaking (JU) under grant agreement No 956702. Some of the computations were enabled by resources provided by the Swedish National Infrastructure for Computing (SNIC) at Chalmers Centre for Computational Science and Engineering (C3SE) partially funded by Swedish Research Council https://www.vr.se/ under grant agreement No 2018-05973.

References

1. Apple a14 bionic: Specs and benchmarks. https://nanoreview.net/en/soc/apple-a14-bionic
2. Intel technology roadmaps and milestones, February 2022. https://www.intel.com/content/www/us/en/newsroom/news/intel-technology-roadmaps-milestones.html#gs.z47liy
3. Adams, A., et al.: Learning to optimize halide with tree search and random programs. ACM Trans. Graph. (TOG) **38**(4), 1–12 (2019)
4. Ahn, B.H., et al.: Chameleon: adaptive code optimization for expedited deep neural network compilation. In: 8th International Conference on Learning Representations, ICLR 2020 (2020)
5. Anderson, l., et al.: Efficient automatic scheduling of imaging and vision pipelines for the GPU. Proc. ACM on Program. Lang. **5**(OOPSLA) (2021)
6. Ben-Nun, T., Hoefler, T.: Demystifying parallel and distributed deep learning: an in-depth concurrency analysis. ACM Comput. Surv. (CSUR) **52**(4) (2019)
7. Binkert, N., et al.: The gem5 simulator. ACM SIGARCH Comput. Architect. News **39**(2), 1–7 (2011)
8. Cho, K., et al.: Design optimization of high bandwidth memory (HBM) interposer considering signal integrity. In: 2015 IEEE EDAPS, pp. 15–18 (2015)
9. Fan, S., et al.: DAPPLE: a pipelined data parallel approach for training large models. In: Proceedings of the 26th ACM SIGPLAN Symposium on Principles and Practice of Parallel Programming, pp. 431–445 (2021)

10. Greenhalgh, P.: Big. little processing with arm cortex-a15 & cortex-a7. ARM White paper **17** (2011)
11. He, K., et al.: Deep residual learning for image recognition. In: Proceedings of the IEEE Conference on Computer Vision and Pattern Recognition, pp. 770–778 (2016)
12. Huang, Y., et al.: GPipe: efficient training of giant neural networks using pipeline parallelism. In: Advances in Neural Information Processing Systems, vol. 32, pp. 103–112 (2019)
13. Kannan, A., et al.: Enabling interposer-based disintegration of multi-core processors. In: 2015 48th Annual IEEE/ACM MICRO, pp. 546–558. IEEE (2015)
14. Li, S., Hoefler, T.: Chimera: efficiently training large-scale neural networks with bidirectional pipelines. In: Proceedings of the International Conference for High Performance Computing, Networking, Storage and Analysis, pp. 1–14 (2021)
15. Lu, Z., et al.: Modeling the resource requirements of convolutional neural networks on mobile devices. In: Proceedings of the 25th ACM International Conference on Multimedia, pp. 1663–1671 (2017)
16. McCalpin, J.D.: Stream benchmark. https://www.cs.virginia.edu/stream/ref.html
17. Minakova, S., Tang, E., Stefanov, T.: Combining task- and data-level parallelism for high-throughput CNN inference on embedded CPUs-GPUs MPSoCs. In: Orailoglu, A., Jung, M., Reichenbach, M. (eds.) SAMOS 2020. LNCS, vol. 12471, pp. 18–35. Springer, Cham (2020). https://doi.org/10.1007/978-3-030-60939-9_2
18. Mullapudi, R.T., et al.: Automatically scheduling halide image processing pipelines. ACM Trans. Graph. (TOG) **35**(4), 1–11 (2016)
19. Narayanan, D., et al.: PipeDream: generalized pipeline parallelism for DNN training. In: Proceedings of the 27th ACM SOSP, pp. 1–15 (2019)
20. Narayanan, D., et al.: Memory-efficient pipeline-parallel DNN training. In: International Conference on Machine Learning, pp. 7937–7947. PMLR (2021)
21. Oren, J., et al.: SOLO: search online, learn offline for combinatorial optimization problems. In: Proceedings of the International Symposium on Combinatorial Search, vol. 12, pp. 97–105 (2021)
22. Ragan-Kelley, J., et al.: Halide: a language and compiler for optimizing parallelism, locality, and recomputation in image processing pipelines. Acm Sigplan Noti. **48**(6), 519–530 (2013)
23. Redmon, J.: Darknet: open source neural networks in C (2013–2016). http://pjreddie.com/darknet/
24. Redmon, J., Farhadi, A.: Yolov3: an incremental improvement. arXiv preprint: arXiv:1804.02767 (2018)
25. Rink, N.A., Castrillon, J.: TeIL: a type-safe imperative tensor intermediate language. In: Proceedings of the 6th ACM SIGPLAN International Workshop on Libraries, Languages, and Compilers for Array Programming (ARRAY), ARRAY 2019, pp. 57–68. ACM, New York, June 2019. https://doi.org/10.1145/3315454.3329959
26. Salehian, S., Yan, Y.: Evaluation of knight landing high bandwidth memory for HPC workloads. In: Proceedings of the Seventh Workshop on Irregular Applications: Architectures and Algorithms, pp. 1–4 (2017)
27. Shao, Y.S., et al.: Simba: scaling deep-learning inference with multi-chip-module-based architecture. In: Proceedings of the 52nd Annual IEEE/ACM International Symposium on Microarchitecture, pp. 14–27 (2019)
28. Sodani, A.: Knights landing (KNL): 2nd generation intel® xeon phi processor. In: 2015 IEEE HCS'27, pp. 1–24. IEEE (2015)

29. Soomro, P.N., et al.: An online guided tuning approach to run CNN pipelines on edge devices. In: Proceedings of the 18th ACM International Conference on Computing Frontiers, pp. 45–53 (2021)
30. Susungi, A., Rink, N.A., Cohen, A., Castrillon, J., Tadonki, C.: Meta-programming for cross-domain tensor optimizations. In: Proceedings of 17th ACM SIGPLAN International Conference on Generative Programming: Concepts and Experiences (GPCE2018), GPCE 2018, pp. 79–92. ACM, New York, November 2018. https://doi.org/10.1145/3278122.3278131
31. Tang, L., et al.: Scheduling computation graphs of deep learning models on many-core CPUs. arXiv preprint: arXiv:1807.09667 (2018)
32. Wan, S., et al.: High-throughput CNN inference on embedded arm big. little multi-core processors. IEEE TCAD (2019)
33. Wu, H.I., et al.: A pipeline-based scheduler for optimizing latency of convolution neural network inference over heterogeneous multicore systems. In: 2020 2nd IEEE International Conference on AICAS, pp. 46–49. IEEE (2020)
34. Zheng, L., et al.: Ansor: generating high-performance tensor programs for deep learning. In: 14th {USENIX} Symposium on {OSDI} 20, pp. 863–879 (2020)

Proactive Task Offloading for Load Balancing in Iterative Applications

Minh Thanh Chung[1]([⊠])[ID], Josef Weidendorfer[2][ID], Karl Fürlinger[1][ID], and Dieter Kranzlmüller[1,2][ID]

[1] MNM-Team, Ludwig-Maximilians-Universitaet (LMU), Munich, Germany
{minh.thanh.chung,karl.fuerlinger,kranzlmueller}@ifi.lmu.de
[2] Leibniz Supercomputing Centre (LRZ), Garching, Germany
{josef.weidendorfer,kranzlmueller}@lrz.de

Abstract. Load imbalance is often a challenge for applications in parallel systems. Static cost models and pre-partitioning algorithms distribute the load at the beginning. Nevertheless, dynamic changes during execution or inaccurate cost indicators may lead to imbalance at runtime. Reactive work-stealing strategies can help monitor the execution and perform task migration to balance the load. However, the benefits depend on migration overhead and assumption about future execution.

Our proactive approach further improves existing solutions by applying machine learning to online load prediction. Following that, we propose a fully distributed algorithm for adapting the prediction result to guide task offloading. The experiments are performed with an artificial test case and a realistic application named $Sam(oa)^2$ on three systems with different communication overhead. Our results confirm improvements for important use cases compared to previous solutions. Furthermore, this approach can support co-scheduling tasks across multiple applications.

Keywords: HPC · Task-based Parallel Models · MPI+OpenMP · Machine Learning · Online Prediction · Dynamic Load Balancing

1 Introduction

Load balancing refers to the distribution of tasks over a set of computing resources in parallel systems. We simplify load as execution time, where the load difference between processes results in imbalance. A process is an abstract entity performing its tasks on a processor. For example, the imbalance can happen when a process waits for the others in bulk-synchronous parallel programs. The primary use case in our paper is represented by iterative applications such as adaptive mesh refinement (AMR) solving partial differential equations (PDEs) [22]. Traditional methods distribute the load at the beginning by using cost indicators. However, an unexpected performance slowdown can lead to a new imbalance. Therefore, dynamic load balancing strategies are more practical to help, such as work-stealing [9]. Work-stealing principally waits until the queue of underloaded processes is empty, then overloaded processes will steal tasks within

© The Author(s) 2023
R. Wyrzykowski et al. (Eds.): PPAM 2022, LNCS 13826, pp. 263–275, 2023.
https://doi.org/10.1007/978-3-031-30442-2_20

an agreement. In contrast, the reactive approach monitors execution repeatedly to estimate the load status, and offloads[1] tasks if the imbalance ratio reaches a given condition [13]. The monitored information is the most recent number of waiting tasks on each queue that implicitly represents computing speed per process. Following that, the imbalance ratio is estimated; tasks at an overloaded process can be reactively offloaded to a corresponding underloaded process [23]. Without prior load information, this idea safely fixes a consistent number of offloaded tasks once. Nevertheless, a very high imbalance case is the challenge that can limit reactive load balancing.

We propose a proactive approach for offloading tasks to improve the performance further. The scheme is based on task characterization and online load prediction. Instead of monitoring only queue information, we characterize task features and execution time on-the-fly. Then, we apply this data to train an adaptive prediction model. The prediction knowledge is learned from dynamic change during execution. After that, our proactive algorithm will use the prediction result to guide task offloading. The idea is implemented in a task-based programming framework for shared and distributed memory called Chameleon [13]. We evaluate this work with an artificial benchmark (matrix multiplication) and an adaptive mesh refinement (AMR) named Sam(oa)^2 [18]. Sam(oa)^2 is a hybrid framework PDE systems on dynamically adaptive tree-structured triangular meshes. Variations in computation cost per element are caused by the limiting procedure, space-time predictor, and numerical inundation treatment at coastlines [21]. Our example and implementation can be found in more detail at (See footnote 5). The main contributions are:

- We discuss what limits the existing reactive approaches and define a proactive solution based on load prediction.
- Our approach shows when it is possible to apply machine learning on-the-fly to predict task execution time.
- Then, a fully distributed algorithm for offloading task is proposed to improve load balancing further.

Finally, the rest of paper begins with related work in Sect. 2. Section 3 describes the terminologies of task-based load balancing and problem motivation. Online prediction scheme and proactive algorithm for offloading tasks are addressed in Sect. 4. Finally, Sect. 5 reveals the evaluation and Sect. 6 highlights conclusion with future work.

2   Related Work

Assuming that system performance is stable, load balancing has been studied in terms of static cost models and partitioning algorithms [12] [4]. The balance is achieved by accurately mapping tasks to processors. Our paper focuses on issues after the work has been already partitioned. As mentioned, performance slowdown is a reason for imbalance during execution [27]. There are three classes of

---

[1] "*Offload*" and "*migrate*" are used interchangeably to denote the migration of tasks.

dynamic load balancing algorithms, centralized [5], distributed, and hierarchical [7]. Work stealing is a traditional approach employed in shared memory systems [2]. For distributed memory, work-stealing is risky because of communication overhead. Researchers attempted to improve communication by using RDMA in PGAS programming models [9,15]. Lifflander et al. introduced a hierarchical technique that applies the persistence principle to refine the load of task-based applications [17]. Focus on scientific applications where computational tasks tend to be persistent, Menon et al. proposed using partial information about the global system state to balance load by randomized work-stealing [19]. To improve stealing decisions, Freitas et al. analyzed workload information to combine with distributed scheduling algorithms [10]. The authors reduced migration overhead by packing similar tasks to minimize messages. Instead of enhancing migration, reactive solutions rely on monitoring execution speed to offload tasks from an overloaded process to underloaded targets[2] [13,23]. The following idea is replication that aims at tackling unexpected performance variability [24]. However, this is difficult to know exactly how many tasks should be offloaded or which processes are truly underloaded in high imbalance cases. Without prior load knowledge, replication strategies need to fix the target process for replicas, such as neighbor ranks. The decision is not easy to make and may get high cost. Using machine learning-based prediction to guide task scheduling is not new. However, the difference comes from the problem feature and applied context. Almost all studies have been proposed in terms of cloud [1] or cluster management [8] using historic logs or traces [3,25] in profilers, i.e., TAU [26], Extrae [20]. Li et al. introduced an online prediction model to optimize task scheduling as a master-worker model in R language [16]. Our context is a given distribution of tasks, and the imbalance is caused by online performance slowdown. Therefore, offline prediction from historical data is insufficient.

3   Preliminaries and Motivation

The many-task runtimes have been studied in shared memory architectures [28]. A task is defined by an entry function and its data (e.g., input arguments). An iterative application has a decomposition into distinct parallel phases of executing tasks. Barriers synchronize each parallel execution phase (so-called time step in numerical simulation). Figure 1(A) illustrates an execution phase, where x-axis represents the time progress, y-axis lists four processes (MPI ranks[3] from 0 to 3), and the green boxes indicate tasks. Each rank has 16 tasks, running by two threads per rank. In general, we define n_t independent tasks per phase, where $T = \{0, ..., n_t - 1\}$ denotes a set of tasks. One task has an associated execution wallclock time ($w \geq 0$) and runs on a specific core until termination. All tasks in T are distributed on n_p processes, where $P = \{0, ..., n_p - 1\}$ denotes a set of processes. The real value of w depends on task's input, CPU frequency,

---

[2] Underloaded targets/processes indicate victims with an under-average load.
[3] Process/rank refers interchangeably to an entity where tasks are assigned.

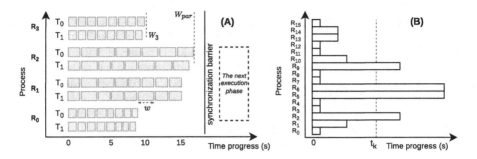

Fig. 1. The illustration of (A) an iterative task-based execution with 4 ranks, 2 threads per rank, and (B) a real load imbalance case with $Sam(oa)^2$.

or memory bandwidth. Therefore, it can only be measured at runtime. Below, we address some definitions and illustrate their symbols in Fig. 1(A).

- W_i: denotes the wallclock execution time of Rank i. Besides, L_i is a total load of Rank i being the sum of load values of all tasks assigned to Rank i.
- W_{par}: indicates the longest wallclock execution time (the so-called parallel wallclock execution time), where $W_{par} = \max_{\forall i \in P} W_i$.

Thereby, the maximum wallclock execution time (W_{max}) is considered as W_{par}, $W_{min} = \min_{\forall i \in P} W_i$, and the average value is $W_{avg} = avg_{\forall i \in P} W_i$. Load balancing strategies need to minimize the W_{par} value. To evaluate the balance, we use a ratio of the maximum and average W values called R_{imb} in Eq. 1, where $R_{imb} \geq 0$ and a high R_{imb} means a high imbalance.

$$R_{imb} = \frac{W_{max}}{W_{avg}} - 1 \tag{1}$$

In work-stealing, underloaded ranks exchange information with overloaded ranks when the task queues are empty, and tasks can be stolen if reaching an agreement. However, this might be too late in distributed memory because of communication overhead. In contrast, the reactive balancing approach uses a dedicated thread[4]. Based on the most current status, tasks are offloaded by speculative balancing operations early instead of waiting for empty queues [23]. This approach has two strategies: reactive task offloading [14] and reactive task replication [24]. Without prior knowledge, the balancing operation of reactive decisions must be safe at runtime about the number of offloaded tasks and potential victims. In the cases of high imbalance ratio, such as Fig. 1(B) shows, the uncertainty of balancing decision at a time t_k can affect the overall efficiency after execution. This leads to motivation for this work such the following points:

(1) For permanently task offloading, how can we know the appropriate number of tasks to offload?

---

[4] In hybrid MPI+OpenMP, we can spawn multiple threads per rank. One thread can be dedicated to repeatedly monitoring execution speed and communication.

(2) For victim selection from phase to phase, how can we know the potential victims to offload tasks proactively?

(3) For a long-term vision, it is necessary to learn the variability of communication overhead along with given topology information at runtime.

4 Online Load Prediction and Proactive Task Offloading

4.1 Online Load Prediction

This work exploits a task-based framework of hybrid MPI+OpenMP and a dedicated thread to perform online prediction by machine learning regression model. The results are then adapted to balance load before a new iteration begins.

Where is dataset from? The inputs (IN) are from two sides: application (IN_{app}) and system (IN_{sys}), where IN_{app} is task-related features and IN_{sys} is related to processor frequencies or performance counters. The output is defined by OUT, which can be the wallclock execution time of a task or the total load of a rank in the next execution phases. IN and OUT are normalized from the characterized information at runtime, being used to create a training dataset. Due to domain-specific applications, users should pre-define influence characteristics or parameters. Therefore, we design this scheme as a user-defined tool outside the main library [6].

When is a prediction model trained? Iterative applications can have many execution phases (iterations) relying on computation scenarios. In hybrid MPI+OpenMP model, our dedicated thread runs asynchronously with other threads, which will characterize and collect runtime data in the first iterations on each rank. We simplify in-out features as configuration parameters in the tool. Users can flexibly tune the parameters before running applications. This issue also raises some related questions below.

- Which input features and how much data are effective?
- Why is machine learning needed?
- In which ways do the learned parameters change during runtime?

First, in-out features are based on observing application characteristics. Depending on each use case, it is difficult to confirm how much data are generally adequate. Therefore, an external user-defined tool is relevant for this issue. Second, the hypothesis is a correlation between application and system characteristics that can map to a prediction target over iterations. Also, the repetition of iterative applications facilitates machine learning to learn the behavior. Third, learning models can be adaptive by re-training in the scope of performance variability. However, how many levels of variability make the model ineffective has not been addressed in the paper; this will be extended in future work.

For our experiments, we describe the input and output parameters of online prediction in Table 1. There are two use cases: synthetic matrix multiplication (denoted by MxM) and Sam(oa)^2. In MxM, the matrix size argument of a task mainly impacts its execution time. Thereby, we configure the training inputs

Table 1. The input-output features for training the prediction models.

No.	App.	Task	IN_{app}	IN_{sys}	OUT
1	MxM	MxM kernel	matrix sizes	core freq (Hz)	load/task (w)
2	Sam(oa)^2	grid traversal	previous L_i	$\emptyset$	next L_i

being matrix sizes and core frequency. For Sam(oa)^2, it uses the concept of grid sections where each section is processed by a single thread [18]. A traversed section is an independent computation unit which is defined as a task. Following the canonical approach of cutting the grid into parts of uniform load, tasks per rank are uniform and a set of tasks on different ranks might not have the same load. By characterizing Sam(oa)^2, we predict the total load of a rank in an iteration (L_i^I) instead of the wall clock time of each task (w), where L denotes the total load value of Rank i in Iteration I. To estimate w, we can divide L by the number of assigned tasks per rank. Furthermore, our observation shows that L_i^I can be predicted by the correlation between the current iteration and the previous iterations. For example, suppose Rank 0 has finished Iteration I, and we take the total load values of four previous iterations. In that case, our training features will be the load values from Iteration $I - 4$ to $I - 1$, such as the following samples $I = 8, 9$.

$$\cdots$$

$$L_0^4, L_0^5, L_0^6, L_0^7 \rightarrow L_0^8 \qquad (2)$$
$$L_0^5, L_0^6, L_0^7, L_0^8 \rightarrow L_0^9$$

Concretely, the left part of the arrow is training inputs, and the right part is training labels. Other ranks also use this format for generating their dataset.

4.2 Proactive Algorithm and Offloading Strategies

As Algorithm 1 shows, our proactive algorithm uses the prediction results as inputs, where Array L contains the total predicted load, Array N denotes the given number of tasks per rank. The number of ranks (n_p mentioned in Sect. 3) is the size of L, N. First, L is sorted by the load values and stored in a new array $\hat{L}$. Second, L_{avg} indicates the average load, which is considered an optimal balanced value. To estimate how many tasks should be offloaded, Algorithm 1 uses Array R to record the total load of offloaded tasks (so-called remote tasks). Also, Array TB is used to track the number of local tasks (remaining tasks in a local rank) and remote tasks. TB is a tracking table with the same number of rows and columns ($= n_p$), where its diagonal represents the local task number, and the others indicate the remote task number. For example, if the value of $TB[i,j] > 0$ ($i \neq j$), Rank i should offload $TB[i,j]$ tasks to Rank j.

In detail, the outer loop goes forward each victim ($\hat{L}[i] < L_{avg}$). The underloaded value between Rank i and L_{avg} is then calculated, named δ_{under}, which means that Rank i needs a load of δ_{under} to be balanced. The inner loop goes backward each offloader ($\hat{L}[j] > L_{avg}$). The overloaded load (δ_{over}) between

---

Algorithm 1: Proactive Task Offloading

Input : Array L, N, where each has n_p elements; $L[i]$ is the predicted load, $N[i]$ is the number of assigned tasks on Rank i.

1 New Array $\hat{L} \leftarrow$ Sort L by the load values
2 $L_{avg} \leftarrow \sum_{i=0}^{n_p-1} \frac{L[i]}{n_p}$
3 New Array R; TB /* R has n_p elements denoting the total load of remote tasks per
      rank, TB has $n_p \times n_p$ elements which record the number of local and remote tasks */
4 **for** $i \leftarrow 0$ to $n_p - 1$ **do**
5 $\quad$ **if** $\hat{L}[i] < L_{avg}$ **then**
6 $\quad\quad$ $\delta_{under} \leftarrow L_{avg} - \hat{L}[i]$ /* the load value under average */
7 $\quad\quad$ **for** $j \leftarrow n_p - 1$ to 0 **do**
8 $\quad\quad\quad$ **if** $\hat{L}[j] > L_{avg}$ **then**
9 $\quad\quad\quad\quad$ $\delta_{over} \leftarrow \hat{L}[j] - L_{avg}$ /* the load value over average */
10 $\quad\quad\quad\quad$ $\hat{w} \leftarrow$ Estimate the load per task and **assert** $\delta_{over} \geq \hat{w}$
11 $\quad\quad\quad\quad$ **if** $\delta_{over} \geq \delta_{under}$ **then**
12 $\quad\quad\quad\quad\quad$ $N_{\text{off}}, L_{\text{off}} \leftarrow$ Calculate the number of tasks to offload and the total
                load of remote tasks by $\hat{w}, \delta_{under}$
13 $\quad\quad\quad\quad$ **else**
14 $\quad\quad\quad\quad\quad$ $N_{\text{off}}, L_{\text{off}} \leftarrow$ Calculate the number of tasks to offload and the total
                load of remote tasks by $\hat{w}, \delta_{over}$
15 $\quad\quad\quad\quad$ **end if**
16 $\quad\quad\quad\quad$ Update δ_{under}, $\hat{L}$ at the index i and j based on $N_{\text{off}}, L_{\text{off}}$
17 $\quad\quad\quad\quad$ Update $N[j]$, $R[j]$; TB at the index (i,j), (j,i), (j,j)
18 $\quad\quad\quad\quad$ *Break* **if abs** $(\delta_{under}, L_{avg}) < \hat{w}$
19 $\quad\quad\quad$ **end if**
20 $\quad\quad$ **end for**
21 $\quad$ **end if**
22 **end for**
23 **return** TB

Rank j and L_{avg} is then calculated and distributed around. To compute the number of tasks for offloading, we need to know the load per task (w) except in the cases we predict w directly, i.e., in MxM. Otherwise, the load per task can be estimated by the total predicted load over the number of assigned tasks per rank, named $\hat{w}$ at line 10. Afterward, the number of offloaded tasks (N_{off}) and the total offloaded load (L_{off}) are calculated. The following values of δ_{under}, $\hat{L}$, N, R, TB will be updated at the corresponding indices. In line 18, the absolute value between δ_{under} and L_{avg} is compared with $\hat{w}$ to check whether or not the current offloader has enough tasks to fill up a load of δ_{under}. If not, we will go through another offloader. Regarding complexity, if we have n_p ranks in total, where K is the number of victims, $n_p - K$ will be offloaders; then the algorithm takes $O(K(n_p - K))$. As mentioned, our implementation is described in more detail at[5]. For offloading tasks, we use two strategies: round-robin and packed-tasks offloading. Round-robin sends task by task, e.g., Algorithm 1 says that R_0 needs to offload 3 tasks to R_1 and 5 tasks to R_2. It will send the 1st task to R_1, the 2nd one to R_2, and repeat the progress until all tasks are sent. In contrast, packed-tasks offloading encodes the three tasks for R_1 as a package and send it once before proceeding R_2.

---

[5] https://github.com/chameleon-hpc/chameleon-apps/tree/master/tools/tool_load_prediction.

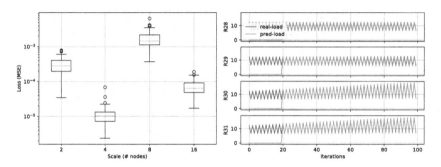

Fig. 2. An evalution of online load prediction for Sam(oa)^2 in simulating the oscillating lake scenario.

Table 2. The overview of compared load balancing methods.

No.	Method	Description
1	baseline	Applications run with default task pre-partition.
2	random_ws	Randomized work-stealing.
3	react_mig	With Chameleon, only reactive migration.
4	react_rep	With Chameleon, only a-priori speculative replication.
5	react_mig_rep	With Chameleon, both reactive migration and replication.
6	proact_off1	With Chameleon, proactive task offloading, round-robind.
7	proact_off2	With Chameleon, proactive task offloading, packed-tasks

5   Evaluation

5.1   Environment and Online Prediction Evaluation

All tests are run on three clusters with different communication infrastructures at Leibniz Supercomputing Centre, CoolMUC2[6], SuperMUC-NG[7] and BEAST[8]. The CoolMUC2 system has 28-way Haswell-based nodes and FDR14 Infiniband interconnect. SuperMUC-NG features Intel Skylake compute nodes with 48 cores per dual-socket, using Intel OmniPath interconnection. In BEAST-system, we use AMD Rome EPYC 7742 nodes with a higher interconnect bandwidth, HDR 200Gb/s InfiniBand.

The first evaluation shows the results of load prediction with Sam(oa)^2. We run 100 time-steps to simulate oscillating lake scenario. Sam(oa)^2 has several configuration parameters that can be found at [18], such as the number of grid sections, grid size, etc. This paper use a default configuration to reproduce the experiments. As mentioned in Subsect. 4.1, the training input features are the total load of the first finished iterations (the dataset from the first 20 iterations). To evaluate accuracy, we use MSE loss [11] between real and predicted values as

---

[6] https://doku.lrz.de/display/PUBLIC/CoolMUC-2.

[7] https://doku.lrz.de/display/PUBLIC/SuperMUC-NG.

[8] https://www.lrz.de/presse/ereignisse/2020-11-06_BEAST/.

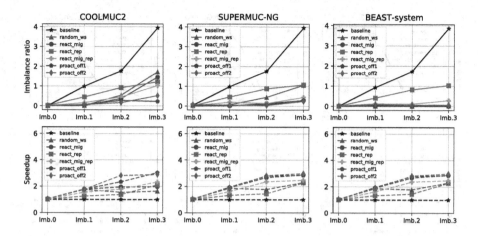

Fig. 3. The comparison of MxM testcases with 8 ranks in total, 2 ranks per node.

the boxplot in Fig. 2 (left). It shows feasibility when using this prediction scheme for load balancing, where x-axis points to the scale of machines, and y-axis is the loss values. Besides, Fig. 2 (right) highlights the comparision between real and predicted load from R_{28} to R_{31} in 16 nodes from Iteration 20 to 99, because we collect data in Iteration 0–19 to generate the training dataset.

5.2   Artificial Imbalance Benchmark

We use the synthetic MxM test cases to ease reproducibility, where tasks are independent and uniform load. The number of tasks per rank is varied to cause different imbalance scenarios. In detail, we generate 4 cases from no imbalance to a high imbalance ratio (Imb.0 - Imb.3). Compared to the baseline and other methods, we name the proposed methods *proact_off1* and *proact_off2* that apply the same prediction scheme and proactive algorithm but different offloading strategies. All compared methods are addressed in Table 2. In Fig. 3, the smaller ratio is the better. It indicates that the W_{par} and waiting-time values between ranks are low. For reactive solutions, *react_mig* and *react_rep_mig* are competitive. However, the case of Imb.3 shows the ratio of ≈ 1.7 with *random_ws*, 1.5–1.1 with *react_mig* and *react_mig_rep* on CoolMUC2. *proact_off1* and *proact_off2* reduce this under 0.6. On SuperMUC-NG and the BEAST system, the communication overhead is mitigated by higher bandwidth interconnection, showing that the reactive methods are still useful. Corresponding to the *Imb.* values, the second row of charts highlights the speedup values calculated by execution time of each method over the baseline.

5.3   Realistic PDE Use Case with Sam(oa)^2

In this experiment, we vary the number of ranks on each system, where two ranks per node and each rank uses full cores of a CPU socket, e.g., 14 threads per rank on CoolMUC2. For different communication overheads, the tests can show

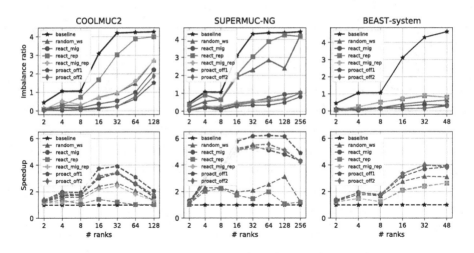

Fig. 4. The comparison of imbalance ratios and speedup in various methods by the usecase of oscillating lake simulation.

scalability and adaptation in various methods. In Fig. 4, reactive or proactive methods obtain higher performance than the baseline. Compared to *react_mig*, speculative replication (*react_rep*) usually comes to some cost. However, their combination *react_mig_rep* could help in the cases from 16 ranks on CoolMUC2 and BEAST. The replication strategy is difficult to deal with the imbalance case of consecutive underloaded ranks. In contrast, our proactive approach uses online prediction to provide information about potential victims. As we can see, *proact_off*1 and *proact_off*2 can improve load balancing in the high imbalance cases (≥ 8 ranks). In two offloading strategies, *proact_off*2 has some delay for encoding a set of tasks when the data is large. Therefore, if an overloaded rank has multiple victims, the second victim must wait long for proceeding the first one. Without any objection, the proactive algorithm must depend on the accuracy of prediction models. However, the features characterized by an online scheme at runtime can reflect the execution behavior flexibly. Therefore, it is feasible to generate a reasonable runtime cost model. Furthermore, we can combine reactive and proactive approaches to improve each other.

6   Conclusion

We have introduced a proactive approach for task-based load balancing in distributed memory systems, which mainly supports the use cases of iterative applications. This approach is enabled by combining online load prediction and proactive task offloading. We proposed a fully distributed algorithm that utilizes prediction results to guide task offloading. The paper shows that existing reactive approaches can be limited in high imbalance use cases by lacking load information to select victims and wisely decide the number of offloaded tasks. Our proactive approach can provide prediction knowledge to make better decisions, e.g., potential victims and how many tasks should be offloaded. We implemented this approach in a task-based parallel library and evaluated it with synthetic and real use cases. The results confirm the benefits in important use cases on three different systems. For a long-term vision, this work can be considered as a potential scheme to co-schedule tasks across multiple applications in future parallel systems. Our solution could work as a plugin on top of a task-based programming framework for load balancing improvement.

Acknowledgment. The authors would like to thank the Chameleon (http://www. chameleon-hpc.org/) and MNM team (http://www.mnm-team.org/) for their support and feedback. Part of the performance results have been obtained on systems in the test environment BEAST (Bavarian Energy Architecture & Software Testbed) at the Leibniz Supercomputing Centre.

References

1. Amiri, M., et al.: Survey on prediction models of applications for resources provisioning in cloud. J. Netw. Comput. Appl. **82**, 93–113 (2017). https://doi.org/10.1016/j.jnca.2017.01.016
2. Blumofe, R.D., Joerg, C.F., et al.: Cilk: an efficient multithreaded runtime system. SIGPLAN Not. **30**(8), 207–216 (1995). https://doi.org/10.1145/209937.209958
3. Carrington, L.C., Laurenzano, M., et al.: How well can simple metrics represent the performance of HPC applications? In: Proceedings of the ACM/IEEE Conference on Supercomputing (2015). https://doi.org/10.1109/SC.2005.33
4. Catalyurek, U.V., Boman, E.G., et al.: Hypergraph-based dynamic load balancing for adaptive scientific computations. In: International Parallel and Distributed Processing Symposium, pp. 1–11 (2007). https://doi.org/10.1109/IPDPS.2007.370258
5. Chow, Y.C., et al.: Models for dynamic load balancing in a heterogeneous multiple processor system. IEEE Trans. Comput. C-**28**(5), 354–361 (1979)
6. Chung, M.T., Kranzlmüller, D.: User-defined tools for characterizing task-parallel applications and predicting load imbalance. In: 15th International Conference on Advanced Computing and Applications (ACOMP), pp. 98–105 (2021). https://doi.org/10.1109/ACOMP53746.2021.00020
7. Corradi, A., Leonardi, L., Zambonelli, F.: Diffusive load-balancing policies for dynamic applications. IEEE Concurrency **7**(1), 22–31 (1999). https://doi.org/10.1109/4434.749133
8. Delimitrou, C., Kozyrakis, C.: Quasar: resource-efficient and GOS-aware cluster management. SIGPLAN Not. **49**(4), 127–144 (2014). https://doi.org/10.1145/2644865.2541941
9. Dinan, J., Larkins, D.B., et al.: Scalable work stealing. In: Proceedings of the Conference on High Performance Computing Networking, Storage and Analysis (2009). https://doi.org/10.1145/1654059.1654113
10. Freitas, V., Pilla, L.L., et al.: Packsteallb: a scalable distributed load balancer based on work stealing and workload discretization. J. Parallel Distrib. Comput. **150**, 34–45 (2021)
11. Goodfellow, I., Bengio, Y., Courville, A.: Deep Learning. MIT Press, Cambridge (2016). http://www.deeplearningbook.org

12. Karypis, G., Kumar, V.: A coarse-grain parallel formulation of multilevel k-way graph partitioning algorithm. In: PPSC (1997)

13. Klinkenberg, J., Samfass, P., et al.: Chameleon: reactive load balancing for hybrid MPI+OpenMP task-parallel applications. J. Parallel Distrib. Comput. **138**, 55–64 (2020). https://doi.org/10.1016/j.jpdc.2019.12.005

14. Klinkenberg, J., Samfass, P., et al.: Reactive task migration for hybrid MPI+OpenMP applications. In: Parallel Processing and Applied Mathematics, pp. 59–71 (2020). https://doi.org/10.1007/978-3-030-43222-5_6

15. Larkins, D.B., Snyder, J., Dinan, J.: Accelerated work stealing. In: Proceedings of the 48th International Conference on Parallel Processing (2019)

16. Li, J., Ma, X., et al.: Machine learning based online performance prediction for runtime parallelization and task scheduling. In: IEEE International Symposium on Performance Analysis of Systems and Software, pp. 89–100 (2009)

17. Lifflander, J., et al.: Work stealing and persistence-based load balancers for iterative overdecomposed applications. In: Proceedings of the 21st International Symposium on High-Performance Parallel and Distributed Computing, pp. 137–148 (2012)

18. Meister, O., Rahnema, K., Bader, M.: Parallel memory-efficient adaptive mesh refinement on structured triangular meshes with billions of grid cells. ACM Trans. Math. Softw. (TOMS) **43**(3), 1–27 (2016)

19. Menon, H., Kalé, L.: A distributed dynamic load balancer for iterative applications. In: Proceedings of the International Conference on High Performance Computing, Networking, Storage and Analysis, pp. 1–11 (2013). https://doi.org/10.1145/2503210.2503284

20. Munera, A., Royuela, S., et al.: Experiences on the characterization of parallel applications in embedded systems with Extrae/Paraver. In: 49th International Conference on Parallel Processing (2020)

21. Rannabauer, L., Dumbser, M., Bader, M.: ADER-DG with a-posteriori finite-volume limiting to simulate tsunamis in a parallel adaptive mesh refinement framework. Comput. Fluids **173**, 299–306 (2018)

22. Renardy, M., Rogers, R.C.: An introduction to partial differential equations, vol. 13. Springer, New York (2006). https://doi.org/10.1007/b97427

23. Samfass, P., Klinkenberg, J., Bader, M.: Hybrid MPI+OpenMP reactive work stealing in distributed memory in the PDE framework Sam(oa)^2. In: IEEE International Conference on Cluster Computing, pp. 337–347 (2018)

24. Samfass, P., Klinkenberg, J., et al.: Predictive, reactive and replication-based load balancing of tasks in chameleon and Sam(oa)^2. In: Proceedings of the Platform for Advanced Scientific Computing Conference (2021)

25. Sharkawi, S., Desota, D., et al.: Performance projection of HPC applications using SPEC CFP2006 benchmarks. In: International Symposium on Parallel & Distributed Processing, pp. 1–12 (2009)

26. Shende, S., Malony, A.D., et al.: Portable profiling and tracing for parallel, scientific applications using C++. In: Proceedings of the SIGMETRICS Symposium on Parallel and Distributed Tools, pp. 134–145

27. Skinner, D., Kramer, W.: Understanding the causes of performance variability in HPC workloads. In: Proceedings of the IEEE Workload Characterization Symposium, pp. 137–149 (2005). https://doi.org/10.1109/IISWC.2005.1526010

28. Thoman, P., et al.: A taxonomy of task-based parallel programming technologies for high-performance computing. J. Supercomput. **74**(4), 1422–1434 (2018). https://doi.org/10.1007/s11227-018-2238-4

Environments and Frameworks for Parallel/Cloud Computing

Language Agnostic Approach for Unification of Implementation Variants for Different Computing Devices

Anshu Dubey[1,2（✉）] and Tom Klosterman[1]

[1] Mathematics and Computer Science Division, Argonne National Laboratory,
Lemont, IL 60439, USA
{adubey,tklosterman}@anl.gov
[2] Department of Computer Science, University of Chicago, Chicago, IL 60637, USA

Abstract. Scientific software used on high performance computing platforms is in a phase of transformation because of combined increase in the heterogeneity and complexity of models and hardware platforms. Having separate implementations for different platforms can easily lead to combinatorial explosion, therefore, computational science community has been looking for mechanisms to express code through abstractions that can be specialized for different platforms. Some approaches have met success through the use of template meta-programming in C++. However, their reliance upon C++ makes these approaches inaccessible to non C++ codes. In this paper, we describe a language agnostic methodology using macros that not only mimics the behavior of templates as applied in the abstractions, but also allows the use of code components as building blocks to explore implementation variants. We have successfully applied this methodology to Flash-X, a new multiphysics multicomponent code with many Fortran legacy components.

Keywords: Performance Portability · Implementation Variants · Program assembly

1 Introduction

Scientific software used on high performance computing (HPC) platforms is undergoing a seismic shift in its development approach because of a confluence of circumstances. On the one side greater understanding of the phenomena of interest is causing the models to become more complex and heterogeneous, and on the other side computing platforms are growing in heterogeneity. Two schools of thoughts have existed for almost the entire history of the field regarding how to deal with these axes of complexity. One school is represented by the ninja programmers who like to "program to metal" to squeeze the last little bit of performance out of a platform, while the other school is represented by the abstraction and tool developers that seek to make the platform complexity transparent to the scientific programmers. Neither approach is viable on its own in this era of complex workflows and widely varying platform specifications. Some approaches

© The Author(s), under exclusive license to Springer Nature Switzerland AG 2023
R. Wyrzykowski et al. (Eds.): PPAM 2022, LNCS 13826, pp. 279–290, 2023.
https://doi.org/10.1007/978-3-031-30442-2_21

that have met with a good amount of success rely upon C++ and its template meta-programming to achieve something in-between the two extremes outlined above, e.g. Kokkos [1], Raja [2], and GridTools [3]. However, their reliance upon C++ makes these approaches inaccessible to non C++ codes. And they too have a bias towards making the tools transparent to the users. Here, we describe a language agnostic methodology that embraces a human-in-the-loop paradigm to provide a way to unify implementation variants needed by different devices.

Our approach has evolved out of a need to adapt FLASH [4], a multiphysics multicomponent software largely written in Fortran, for the new HPC reality of heterogeneous architecture. FLASH has traditionally used program synthesis through component assembly to generate different application instances. Components can have multiple alternative implementations, and each of the implementation is self-describing in the sense that metadata about how it fits into an application configuration is included with it. Alternative implementations have traditionally been at most 2 or 3 for a code component to accommodate situations such as: (1) a different physical regime needing a different algorithm; (2) difference in fidelity of solution to permit cost-benefit trade-off in computation time; (3) difference in parallelization approach for different scales. The lowest granularity of such components has been at the subroutine level, though a typical code component with alternative implementations includes several subroutines.

With the advent of accelerators we were faced with the need to have many more alternative implementations just to accommodate differences in hardware characteristics. Combined with the already existing alternatives, in many situations we would have had a combinatorial explosion of maintained alternatives to continue to have the same level of flexibility in application configurability on different platforms. Often, the alternatives for different devices need either a different data layout or a different control flow while the arithmetic of the algorithm remains the same. Hence, without some form of unification of the code base there would be rampant duplication of arithmetic code leading to maintenance difficulties. This is the primary challenge that template meta-programming in C++ addresses, which is not available in C or Fortran. Another obvious solution is to use macros to encode the invariant arithmetic code. We have taken this approach, but instead of using pre-processor macros, we built a more capable and versatile macroprocessor that lets us exploit the already existing program assembly features of FLASH for more flexibility is applying abstractions.

We are using this approach in the new incarnation of FLASH, called Flash-X [5], which is fundamentally rearchitected with modernization of several key physics solvers. We highlight the efficacy of our approach in the context of Spark [6], a new hydrodynamics (hydro) and magnetohydrodynamics (MHD) solver, which can have many algorithmic variants specialized from a single source expression.

The paper is organized as follows. Section 2 discusses the literature and insights from the literature that guided our design. Section 3 describes the program synthesis process of FLASH, and the enhancements to the process for Flash-X. Section 4 describes our custom macroprocessor and its features designed

for the unification of implementation variants. Section 5 details an example of
how macros are used to unify variants of Spark. Section 6 presents our conclusions.

2   Background and Insights

Separation of Concerns has been the key ingredient of complex HPC software
throughout its history. With a distributed memory model a good design principal was to keep communication primitives to remain largely isolated from the
core computations in the software. Then one could develop and optimize computational sections of the software as though they were sequential, while scaling
optimizations were localized to the communication sections. The biggest challenge was to achieve a good decomposition of work so that such separation was
possible without incurring too much communication overhead.

Ever since GPUs became a part of the HPC landscape, scientific software
developers have been looking for ways to utilize them effectively. The HPC community has been looking for ways to mitigate the challenge of developing and
maintaining code that may need to be different for different devices (i.e. [7,8]).
The solutions have taken several forms, that can be broadly categorized into
two types. The first take the approach of using domain-specific languages such
as [9–11], or abstractions based on C++ template metaprogramming such as
[1,2] where a single expression of the computation can be specialized to the
target device as needed. Some solutions such as Legion [12] also provide asyn-
chronization of data movement along with abstractions. The second set consists
of new HPC languages such as chapel and julia [13,14]. These languages are well
designed, and could become the best option in future, however, they have not
yet reached wide enough adoption for guaranteed future availability.

While many of the solutions described above have been quite useful to HPC
scientific software, none of them is a truly viable option for an already existing
large complex Fortran code such as FLASH because of the extent of rewriting
needed. At the same time, we needed a solution because it is impossible to
refactor the code to suit a divergent set of platform architectures individually.
The outcome of our efforts is a set of tools, one of which is the focus of this
article.

Three key insights have guided the design of our tools. One is that the
more complex portion of abstraction tools is typically the "inferencing", that
is analysis of the code. A compiler based tool must be conservative in making
transformation choices and it must account for exceptional or corner cases. The
execution engines are relatively easy once the analysis is done. If a code can
make its semantics more explicit, the tool that is doing the translation can be
simplified. This is also the key insight behind domain specific languages. In the
first iteration of our tools' design we are treating a human-in-the-loop as the
inferencing engine, who is provided with the executor tools to avoid having to
code-to-metal as has been needed in the past.

The second insight is that decomposition of the code into macro like arbitrarily sized code-snippets allows separating out arithmetic of the computation

from the logic of the control flow, and that turns the code components into building blocks that can be configured in many different ways. The third insight is that different aspects of performance portability need different treatment that are orthogonal to one another. For example, how to unify different variants of a code component into a single source is completely orthogonal to the challenge of composing code components into an application instance. And both of those in turn are orthogonal to the mechanics of orchestrating data movement between devices as needed. Because of these insights we have developed three sets of tools where each set addresses itself to only one aspect of portability. The tools that address the latter two aspects (composing an application instance and orchestrating data movement) are described elsewhere [15,16]. In this paper we focus on the tool that is used to turn code components into building blocks for generating different variants of the same computation.

3   Program Synthesis

Some understanding of program synthesis features in FLASH is a prerequisite for understanding how it is applied in Flash-X. Therefore, we briefly describe the relevant features here (see [4] for more details).

3.1   In FLASH

From the outset FLASH was designed to be a component based software system where different components and their alternative implementations could be composed into different application instances. This was achieved through a very limited configuration domain-specific language (DSL) to encode metadata about code components. Metadata for a component "C1" includes information such as other components that must be included with C1, the components that cannot be included with C1, the state variables, the datafiles, and the runtime parameters that C1 needs. This metadata is encapsulated with the components, making them self-describing for configuration. In FLASH parlance, the highest level code component for a specific type of functionality is called a *unit*, which can have sub-units at various granularities. For example *Grid* is the unit for managing the discretized mesh. It has several sub-units such as *GridMain*, which implements the bookkeeping for finite-difference or finite-volume discretization of the physical domain, *GridSolvers*, which implements generic numerical solvers such as multigrid, multipole etc. that operate on the grid, but are called by physics units with some specialization, *GridParticles*, which handles data movement of Lagrangian entities on the mesh if they are included in the simulation, and a few others. Each of these sub-units can have their own sub-components with arbitrary degree of granularity as long as a sub-component is at least a subroutine and exists in a separate source file. The general rule of thumb is to keep them as coarse-grained as feasible for ease of maintenance.

Figure 1 shows an example of the highest level config file for the code unit that computes gravitational potential and acceleration. The lines with # are

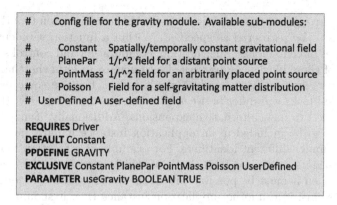

```
#      Config file for the gravity module.  Available sub-modules:

#      Constant    Spatially/temporally constant gravitational field
#      PlanePar    1/r^2 field for a distant point source
#      PointMass   1/r^2 field for an arbitrarily placed point source
#      Poisson     Field for a self-gravitating matter distribution
# UserDefined A user-defined field


REQUIRES Driver
DEFAULT Constant
PPDEFINE GRAVITY
EXCLUSIVE Constant PlanePar PointMass Poisson UserDefined
PARAMETER useGravity BOOLEAN TRUE
```

Fig. 1. Snapshot of a Config file for the Gravity unit.

comments. All boldface words are the keywords of the configuration DSL with specific meaning. For example, this config file indicates that in order to run, the *Gravity* unit requires the *Driver* unit, and that by default it will pick up the *Constant Gravity*. The keywords used in this file represent a large fraction of the DSL syntax. The tool that parses and interprets this DSL has a built in inheritance mechanism that lets it arbitrate on which code components, and within them which specific implementation of the code components, to include. Simultaneously, it can assemble the build system and the necessary runtime parameters for the application instance.

3.2   Modifications in Flash-X

As discussed in Sect. 2 code components in Flash-X needed to be finer-grained than at the level of subroutines and functions for unifying source from different variants of the code components. We refer to the subroutine level components as functions, and the finer-grained components as sub-functions without any loss of generality. Also, we wish to differentiate between fundamentally different numerical methods for a component, which are viewed as alternative implementations of the Unit API, and variants of the same method which differ from one another in implementation details. For example, Flash-X supports two methods for computing shock hydro; *Unsplit*, and *Spark* that we do not attempt to unify. They remain alternative implementations of the hydro unit. However, within these there are variations in implementation details that relate to performance on different devices. These implementation details have been unified into a single high level source for Spark, described later in Sect. 5.

A function in a physics unit typically has some arithmetic interspersed with some control flow logic. Often the features of the implementation that need to be modified for optimization are data structures (i.e. array-of-structs versus structs-of-arrays) and control flow. The fundamental arithmetic operations remain essentially the same. The first of these, the data structure rearrangement can be done through an existing feature in FLASH configuration tool that allows array indices to be reordered as specified. Within a function we identify three different types of code-blocks – declaration, computation and control structures. Any, or all, of these blocks can be turned into macros to form shorthand for the code. However, macros by themselves won't suffice, because some of the sub-function code-blocks will differ between variants. For a unified code, the macros must be allowed to have alternative expansions. Additionally, if more than one variant needs to be included in an application instance it must be possible to invoke them under different identifiers. For example, if a function foo can generate two variants, var1 and var2, both of which need to be included in the application, then it must be possible to call them as foo_var1 and foo_var2, but if they are exclusive in another application instance then it should be possible to simply call foo. Furthermore, with multiple alternative definitions existing for macros, a mechanism is needed to arbitrate on which variants are to be built with which definitions.

To achieve these objectives we added a few more keywords to the configuration DSL, and implemented another inheritance mechanism more suitable for the needs of sub-function level code-blocks. The fundamental difference between unit and function-level code inheritance and subfunction-level code inheritance is that the former need only one pass through the source tree, while latter need as many passes as the number of variants to be included. Some differences also exist in assembling the build system to account for different names of the variants. In Flash-X maintained code in the repository is the version with embedded macros, while the expanded code is used for building the executable, but is never added to the "main" branch of the repository. Preferred mode is to discard the expanded code once the computation is over.

4   Macros and Macroprocessor

The macros supported in Flash-X are similar to C preprocessor macros in how they are defined. They permit arguments, are allowed to be inlined in a regular programming language statement, and one macro name can be embedded in another macro's definition as long as self-reference is avoided. Where our tool differs from the preprocessor is in permitting alternative definitions, including null definitions for macros, and an arbitration mechanism to select a specific definition. The macroprocessor is written in python and the definitions are stored in ".ini" files, according to the Python ConfigParser format. The source files with embedded macros that need translation are given the extension ".F90-mc" to differentiate them from the source files that do not need expansion. For Flash-X the translation is into Fortran, but the tool can be applied to other languages by adding "-mc" extension to files with embedded macros. The tool does not interpret any part of the macro definition, and therefore is completely language agnostic. The tool operates by parsing through the source tree following the inheritance path described in Fig. 2 and accumulates all the definitions.

The tool operates by building a list of files to be linked into the object directory as it traverses the tree. The general rule of inheritance of files is that a

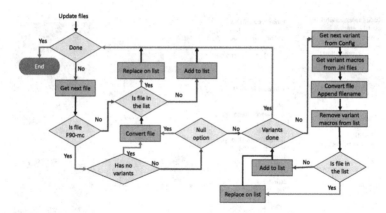

Fig. 2. Algorithm for generating variants and arbitration on which definition of a macro to include where.

source file is added to the list when it is first encountered. However, a file with the same name in a subdirectory replaces previously added files recursively. Files with ".F90-mc" extension are not linked, instead, the expanded files are placed directly into the object directory with a ".F90" extension. As mentioned earlier, this is because we maintain files with embedded macros only, the expanded files are temporary. When the tool encounters a file to be expanded it checks to see if it has variants. A file *foo.F90-mc* with no variants will be expanded into *foo.F90*. However, if it were to have variants for say CPU and GPU, two different files will be generated named foo_CPU.F90 and *foo_GPU.F90*, and in the corresponding Makefile any occurence of *foo.o* will be replaced by *foo_CPU.o foo_GPU.o*. The alternative definitions of the macros reside in different subdirectories named identically to the variant names specified in the Config file of the directory where *foo.F90-mc* lives.

Figure 3 shows a highly simplified example of code with embedded macros. All the macros are preceded with phrase @M to let the tool know that a macro follows. In all the figures macros are encoded in different colors to indicate their different purposes. The red macros are predefined for convenience and available to use anywhere in the code. Macros that are local to the code section and have only one definition are blue, while those that have multiple alternative definitions are purple. The rightmost boxes in the figure show the code emitted for different devices through the use of different definitions of the macros.

5   Spark Variants

We now discuss how the macros are applied in Spark, the solver for the equations of ideal MHD using finite-volume discretization and explicit time integration. The code performance characteristics on CPU and GPU have been documented elsewhere (see [6]), and are not relevant for this discussion. Here our objective is to demonstrate unification of versions of code that are quite different from one

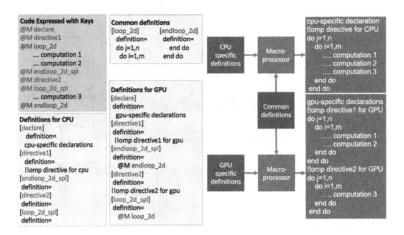

Fig. 3. A highly simplified example of the macros for unifying CPU and GPU variants of the same computation.

another in terms of data access and communication patterns. All the versions can be regenerated from the same maintained source. First we describe the variants, and then explain how they were unified into a compact unified code.

5.1 Variants

Flash-X uses adaptive mesh refinement (AMR) [17] for domain decomposition where each block of cells is typically 16^3 in 3D with surrounding halo cells (called guardcells in Flash-X). The primary computational motif in Spark is stencils. Because stencils tend to be rather large in these calculations, making blocks smaller is not a good option because then guardcells start to dominate the memory footprint. Additionally, guardcells need to be updated after every sweep of stencils update. In AMR this communication step can become expensive at large scales because of irregular communication pattern. A simulation of supernova with Flash-X can have thousands of blocks, but they cannot be coalesced into larger blocks because adjacent blocks may have different resolution. One way to reduce communication overhead is to use communication avoidance techniques, make the halo thicker than is strictly necessary so that every other round of guardcells update can be avoided. This comes at the cost of extra computation of the inner layers of guardcells. We call this the *telescoping* version. This is particularly useful with GPUs because guardcell fill involves communication. However, depending upon the size of the stencil, this extra computation can become quite expensive, and when not operating at the largest scales, may not be a good option. In a *non-telescoping* version, guardcells are filled before each stage of sweeping through the stencils update. A second type of variant comes from the order of traversal of cells during stencil update. For CPUs with their deep cache hierarchy the more suitable approach is *pencil-wise* – a row at a time, While on the GPU even one a whole block may not expose enough parallelism, and it may be necessary to bundle multiple blocks into one data object for one kernel launch.

5.2   Unifying with Macros

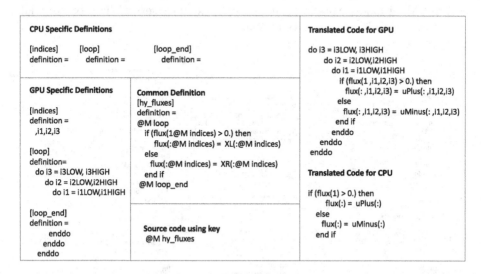

Fig. 4. Example of use of macros with inlining and recursion to unify fine-grain code blocks that need different data layouts.

Figure 4 shows a code snippet from Spark which covers steps in unification at the finest granularity. The code computes fluxes from left and right states, represented in uPlus and uMinus in the example. The first difference is that the CPU version is written with one spatial dimension while the GPU version uses three spatial dimensions. Use of inlined macro *indices* with one of its definitions being null solves this problem. The second difference is that the GPU code has explicit loop nest, while the CPU version uses vector notation. This is also countered with null implementations for *loop* and *loop_end* macros for the CPU. The definition of *hy_fluxes* can be common to both devices through recursion by using already defined macros that have different definitions for different devices. The rightmost box displays the generated code for both CPU and GPU versions.

This method of unification of small code blocks is repeated where possible until we have a collection of building blocks of reasonable granularity. Next we build coarser code-blocks that combine fine code-blocks with control logic as needed. This process is repeated until we arrive at a situation where high level algorithmic variants can be expressed compactly. Figure 5 shows this process with an example of two variants, one in telescoping mode and one in non-telescoping mode. The leftmost box shows the overall structure of the variants at the highest level. The middle top box expands one of the coarser building blocks while the middle bottom box shows one of the subroutines called from that building block. The two rightmost boxes show how some of the definitions used in the middle boxes differ for different devices at the level of finer building blocks. The CPU code has an outer 2D loop with all the routines called one after another for the vectors consisting of leading dimension of the arrays. The GPU code has separate 3D loops for each of the subroutine calls to enable maximum parallelization over the whole data block. Note that the example excludes several lines of essential code at every level of granularity for clarity.

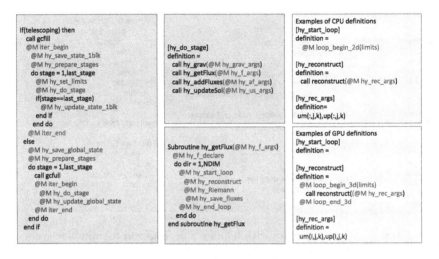

Fig. 5. Use of building blocks where finer blocks are used to create increasingly coarser blocks, that ultimately permit expression of algorithmic variants compactly.

6   Conclusions

We have presented a new approach in using macros to enable data locality on different devices with a single code base for all the arithmetic involved in the computation. Our approach obtains performance portability to different architectures through alternative definitions of macros in macro-value pairs. In terms of functionality this technique resembles template meta-programming of C++ that is used in several abstraction layers being used by various scientific codes. Our approach provides additional flexibility in turning subfunction level code snippets into building blocks that can help make the maintained code more compact. Our approach is unique in that its fundamental design is language agnostic. Additionally, our program synthesis tools are uncomplicated, the macroprocessor took roughly 2–3 person-week to write initially. We have been adding features to it as we think of better ways of using the methodologies. In every instance, updating the tool never takes more than a couple of person days. The initial unification of telescoping versions only of CPU and GPU codes took 2–3 person weeks for a developer who had not written the original code. Since then generating other variants has taken much less time. An added advantage is that the macroprocessor can be applied to any code component as a stand alone tool to generate the corresponding Fortran file that can be inspected by the developers and can be debugged like any other Fortran source. This approach can provide a viable performance portability solution for non C++ scientific codes without a complete rewrite. And the transformation can be applied incrementally which permits continuous verification during development.

Acknowledgements. This work was supported by supported by the Exascale Computing Project (17-SC-20-SC), a collaborative effort of the U.S. Department of Energy Office of Science and the National Nuclear Security Administration.

References

1. Edwards, H.C., Sunderland, D.: Kokkos array performance-portable manycore programming model. In: Proceedings of the 2012 International Workshop on Programming Models and Applications for Multicores and Manycores. PMAM 2012, pp. 1–10. Association for Computing Machinery, New York (2012). https://doi.org/10.1145/2141702.2141703

2. Beckingsale, D.A., et al.: Raja: portable performance for large-scale scientific applications. In: 2019 IEEE/ACM International Workshop on Performance, Portability and Productivity in HPC (P3HPC), pp. 71–81 (2019). https://doi.org/10.1109/P3HPC49587.2019.00012

3. Bianco, M., Benedicic, L., et al.: GridTools (2020). https://github.com/GridTools/gridtools

4. Dubey, A., et al.: Extensible component based architecture for FLASH, a massively parallel, multiphysics simulation code. Parallel Comput. **35**, 512–522 (2009). https://doi.org/10.1016/j.parco.2009.08.001

5. Dubey, A., et al.: Flash-x: a multiphysics simulation software instrument. SoftwareX **19**, 101168 (2022). https://doi.org/10.1016/j.softx.2022.101168

6. Couch, S.M., Carlson, J., Pajkos, M., O'Shea, B.W., Dubey, A., Klosterman, T.: Towards performance portability in the spark astrophysical magnetohydrodynamics solver in the flash-x simulation framework. Parallel Comput. **108**, 102830 (2021). https://doi.org/10.1016/j.parco.2021.102830

7. Unat, D., et al.: Trends in data locality abstractions for HPC systems. IEEE Trans. Parallel Distrib. Syst. **28**(10), 3007–3020 (2017). https://doi.org/10.1109/TPDS.2017.2703149

8. Mittal, S., Vetter, J.S.: A survey of CPU-GPU heterogeneous computing techniques. ACM Comput. Surv. **47**(4) (2015). https://doi.org/10.1145/2788396

9. Ragan-Kelley, J., Barnes, C., Adams, A., Paris, S., Durand, F., Amarasinghe, S.: Halide: a language and compiler for optimizing parallelism, locality, and recomputation in image processing pipelines. SIGPLAN Not. **48**(6), 519–530 (2013). https://doi.org/10.1145/2499370.2462176

10. Gysi, T., Osuna, C., Fuhrer, O., Bianco, M., Schulthess, T.C.: Stella: a domain-specific tool for structured grid methods in weather and climate models. In: Proceedings of the International Conference for High Performance Computing, Networking, Storage and Analysis, SC 2015. Association for Computing Machinery, New York (2015). https://doi.org/10.1145/2807591.2807627

11. Earl, C., Might, M., Bagusetty, A., Sutherland, J.C.: Nebo: an efficient, parallel, and portable domain-specific language for numerically solving partial differential equations. J. Syst. Softw. **125**, 389–400 (2017). https://doi.org/10.1016/j.jss.2016.01.023

12. Bauer, M., Treichler, S., Slaughter, E., Aiken, A.: Legion: expressing locality and independence with logical regions. In: SC 2012: Proceedings of the International Conference on High Performance Computing, Networking, Storage and Analysis, pp. 1–11 (2012). https://doi.org/10.1109/SC.2012.71

13. Chamberlain, B.L., Callahan, D., Zima, H.P.: Parallel programmability and the chapel language. Int. J.High Perform. Comput. Appl. **21**(3), 291–312 (2007). https://doi.org/10.1177/1094342007078442

14. Bezanson, J., Karpinski, S., Shah, V.B., Edelman, A.: Julia: a fast dynamic language for technical computing. CoRR abs/1209.5145 (2012)

15. O'Neal, J., Wahib, M., Dubey, A., Weide, K., Klosterman, T., Rudi, J.: Domain-specific runtime to orchestrate computation on heterogeneous platforms. In: Chaves, R., et al. (eds.) Euro-Par 2021: Parallel Processing Workshops, pp. 154–165. Springer, Cham (2022). https://doi.org/10.1007/978-3-031-06156-1_13

16. Rudi, J., O'Neal, J., Wahib, M., Dubey, A., Weide, K.: CodeFlow for FLASH: code generation system for FLASH-X orchestration runtime. Technical Report ANL-21/17, Argonne National Laboratory, Lemont, IL (2021)

17. MacNeice, P., Olson, K.M., Mobarry, C., de Fainchtein, R., Packer, C.: Paramesh: a parallel adaptive mesh refinement community toolkit. Comput. Phys. Commun. **126**(3), 330–354 (2000). https://doi.org/10.1016/S0010-4655(99)00501-9

High Performance Dataframes
from Parallel Processing Patterns

Niranda Perera[1]([✉])(iD), Supun Kamburugamuve[2], Chathura Widanage[2],
Vibhatha Abeykoon[2], Ahmet Uyar[2], Kaiying Shan[3], Hasara Maithree[4],
Damitha Lenadora[5], Thejaka Amila Kanewala[2], and Geoffrey Fox[6]

[1] Luddy School of Informatics, Computing, and Engineering, Indiana University,
Bloomington, IN 47408, USA
dnperera@iu.edu
[2] Indiana University Alumni, Bloomington, IN 47405, USA
[3] University of Virginia, Charlottesville, VA 22904, USA
[4] University of Moratuwa, Bandaranayake Mawatha, Moratuwa 10400, Sri Lanka
[5] University of Illinois Urbana-Champaign, Urbana, IL 61801, USA
[6] Biocomplexity Institute and Initiative, University of Virginia, Charlottesville,
VA 22904, USA

Abstract. The data science community today has embraced the concept of *Dataframes* as the de facto standard for data representation and manipulation. Ease of use, massive operator coverage, and popularization of R and Python languages have heavily influenced this transformation. However, most widely used serial Dataframes today (R, **pandas**) experience performance limitations even while working on even moderately large data sets. We believe that there is plenty of room for improvement by investigating the generic distributed patterns of dataframe operators.

In this paper, we propose a framework that lays the foundation for building high performance distributed-memory parallel dataframe systems based on these parallel processing patterns. We also present *Cylon*, as a reference runtime implementation. We demonstrate how this framework has enabled *Cylon* achieving scalable high performance. We also underline the flexibility of the proposed API and the extensibility of the framework on different hardware. To the best of our knowledge, *Cylon* is the first and only distributed-memory parallel dataframe system available today.

Keywords: Dataframes · High performance computing · Data engineering · Relational algebra · MPI · Distributed Memory Parallel

1 Introduction

The Data Science domain has expanded monumentally in both research and industry communities over the past few decades, predominantly owing to the *Big Data* revolution. Artificial Intelligence (AI) and Machine Learning (ML) offer even more complexities to data engineering applications, which are now required to process terabytes of data. Typically, a significant amount of *developer time* is spent on data exploration, preprocessing, and prototyping while developing AI/ML pipelines. Therefore, improving its efficiency directly impacts the overall pipeline performance.

With the wide adoption of R and Python languages, the data science community is increasingly moving away from established SQL-based abstractions. *Dataframes* play a pivotal role in this transformation [14] by providing a functional interface and interactive development environment for exploratory data analytics. **pandas** is undoubtedly the most popular dataframe library available today. Its open source community has grown significantly, and the API has expanded up to 200+ operators. Despite this popularity, both R-dataframe and pandas encounter performance limitations even on moderately large data sets. In our view, dataframes have now exhausted the capabilities of a single computer, which paves way for distributed dataframe systems.

There are several significant engineering challenges related to developing a scalable and high performance distributed dataframe system (Sect. 2.1). In this paper, we analyze dataframe operators to establish a set of generic distributed operator patterns and present an open-source high performance distributed dataframe system framework based on them, *Cylon*. We take inspiration from Mattson et al's *Patterns for Parallel Programming* [13]. Our main focus is to present a mechanism that promotes an existing serial/ local operator into a distributed operator (Sect. 2.2, 3). The proposed framework is aimed at a distributed memory system executing in a Bulk Synchronous Parallel (BSP) [8,20] environment. This combination has been widely employed by the high performance computing (HPC) community for exascale computing applications with admirable success.

2   Dataframe Systems

A *dataframe* is a heterogeneous data structure containing a set of arrays that are individually homogeneous. In contrast, deep learning or machine learning use *tensors* which are homogeneously typed multidimensional arrays. These two data structures are integrated to support end-to-end data engineering workloads. Dataframes were first introduced by the S language in 1990, and their popularity grew exponentially with R and Python languages [14]. These libraries contain a large number of SQL-like statistical, linear algebra and, relational algebra operators and are sequential in execution. With the increasing size of data, there have been some attempts to scale dataframe execution both in the cloud and high performance computing environments such as, Dask [19], Modin [18], and Koalas.

2.1   Engineering Challenges

While there is a compelling need for a distributed dataframe system, there are several engineering challenges.

- **Lack of Specification**: Despite the popularity, there is very little consensus on a specification/standard for dataframes and their operators amongst the systems available today. Rapid expansion in applications and the increasing demand for features may have contributed to this divergence. The current trend is to use **pandas** as the reference API specification [18], and we also follow this approach for the work described in this paper.

– **Massive API**: pandas API consists of 240 operators [3,18]. There is also significant redundancy amongst the operators. It would be a mammoth undertaking to parallelize each of these operators individually. Petersohn et al. [18], have taken a more practical approach by identifying a core set of operators (*Dataframe Algebra*) listed in Table 1. In this paper, we have taken a different approach by identifying distributed patterns in dataframe operators, and devise a framework that can best scale them in a distributed memory parallel environment.

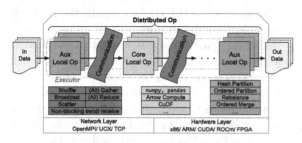

Fig. 1. Distributed Memory Dataframe Abstraction

Table 1. Modin DataFrame Algebra [18]

Selection	Window
Projection	Transpose
Union	Map
Difference	Aggregation*
Join	ToLabels
Unique	FromLabels
GroupBy	Rename
Sort	

*Not categorized in Modin

– **Efficient Parallel Execution**: Distributed data engineering systems generally vary in their execution model. Dask, Modin, and Koalas dataframes are built on top of a fully asynchronous execution environment. Conversely, Bulk-Synchronous-Parallel (BSP) model is used in data parallel deep learning. This mismatch poses a challenge in creating a fully integrated scalable data engineering pipeline. Our framework attempts to bridge this gap by taking an HPC approach to parallelizing Dataframe operators.

2.2   System Considerations

There are multiple aspects that need to be considered when developing a distributed data processing framework [11]. Our distributed dataframe model is designed based on the following considerations.

– **BSP Execution**: The most widely used **execution models** are, 1) *Bulk Synchronous Parallel* [8,20] and 2) *Fully Asynchronous*. The former assumes all the tasks are executing in parallel, and the executors synchronize with each other by exchanging messages at certain points. The sections of code between communication synchronizations execute independently. In the latter, tasks would be executed independently. Input and output messages will be delivered using queues, and often this requires a central scheduler to orchestrate the tasks. Many recent data engineering frameworks (e.g. Apache Spark, Dask, etc.) have adopted fully asynchronous execution. Our framework is based on BSP execution in a distributed memory environment. Gao et al. [9] recently published a similar concept for scaling joins over thousands of GPUs. We intend to show that this approach generalizes to all operators and achieves commendable scalability and high performance.

- **Distributed Memory**: Most often the parallel **memory model** of a system is a choice between, 1) *Shared*: multiple CPU cores in a single machine via threads/ processes (e.g. OpenMP), 2) *Distributed*: every instance of the program is executed on an isolated memory, and data is communicated via message passing (e.g. MPI), and 3) *Hybrid*: combines shared and distributed models. Our framework is developed based on Distributed memory.
- **Columnar Data Format**: Most of dataframe operators access data along columns, and using a columnar format allows operators to be vectorized using SIMD and hardware accelerators (e.g. GPUs). As a result, the patterns described in this paper focus on columnar dataframes.
- **Row-based Partitioning**: Dataframe partitioning is semantically different from traditional matrix/tensor partitioning. Due to the homogeneously typed data storage, when a matrix/ tensor is partitioned, the effective computation reduces for each individual partition. By comparison, dataframe operator patterns (Sect. 3.3) show that not all columns of a dataframe contribute equally to the computation, e.g. join is performed on *key* columns, while the rest of the columns move alongside the keys. Both Apache Spark [23] and Dask [19] follow a row-based partitioning scheme, while Modin [18] uses block-based partitioning with dynamic partition ID allocation. Our framework employs BSP execution on a distributed memory parallel environment. We would like to distribute the computation among all available executors to maximize the scalability. We also use row-based partitioning because it allows us to hand over the data partitions with identical schema to each executor.

3   Distributed Memory Dataframe Framework

The lack of a specification presents a challenge in properly defining a *dataframe* data structure. It is not quite a relation in an SQL sense, nor a matrix/multidimensional array. For our distributed memory model, we borrow definitions from Petersohn et al. [18]. Dataframes contain heterogeneously typed data originating from a known set of *domains*, $Dom = \{dom_1, dom_2, ...\}$. For dataframes, these *domains* represent all the data types they support.

Definition 1. *A **Schema** of a Dataframe, S_M is a tuple (D_M, C_M), where D_M is a vector of M domains and C_M is a vector of M corresponding column labels. Column labels usually belong to String/ Object domain.*

Definition 2. *A **Dataframe** is a tuple (S_M, A_{NM}, R_N), where S_M is the Schema with M domains, A_{NM} is a 2-D array of entries where actual data is stored, and R_N is a vector of N row labels belonging to some domain. Length of the Dataframe is N, i.e. the number of rows.*

3.1   Distributed Memory Dataframe

"How to develop a high performance scalable dataframe runtime?" is the main problem we aim to address in our framework. We attempt to promote an already available *serial (local) operator* into a distributed-memory parallel execution environment (Fig. 1). For this purpose, we extend the definition of a dataframe for a distributed memory parallel execution environment with row-based partitioning (Fig. 2).

Definition 3. *A **Distributed-Memory Dataframe** (DMDF) is a virtual collection of P Dataframes (named Partitions) of lengths $\{N_0, ..., N_{P-1}\}$ and a common Schema S_M. Total length of the DMDF is $\Sigma N_i = N$, and the row labels vector is the concatenation of individual row labels, $R_N = \{R_0 R_1 ... R_{P-1}\}$.*

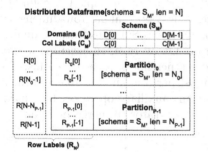

Table 2. Communication semantics in Dataframe Operators and the frequency of occurrence

Operation	Data Structure		
	Dataframe	Array	Scalar
Shuffle (AllToAll)	Common	Rare	N/A
Scatter	Common	Rare	N/A
Gather/AllGather	Common	Common	Common
Broadcast	Common	Common	Common
Reduce/AllReduce	N/A	Common	Common

Fig. 2. Distributed Memory Dataframe

3.2   Building Blocks

As shown in Fig. 1, a distributed operator is comprised of multiple components/building blocks, such as,

1. **Data Structures**: The distributed memory framework we employ uses three main data structures: dataframes, arrays, and scalars. While most of the operators are defined on dataframes, arrays and scalars are also important because they present different communication semantics.
2. **Serial/Local Operators**: These refer to single-threaded implementations of core operators (Table 1). There could be one or more libraries that provide this functionality (e.g. numpy, pandas, RAPIDS CuDF, Apache Arrow Compute, etc). Choice of the library depends on the language runtime, the underlying memory format, and the hardware architecture.
3. **Communication Routines**: A BSP execution allows the program to continue independently until the next communication boundary is reached (Sect. 2.2). HPC message passing libraries such as MPI (OpenMPI, MPICH, MSMPI) and UCX provide communication routines for memory buffers (works for homogeneously typed arrays). The most primitive routines are tag-based *async send* and *async receive*. Complex patterns (generally termed

collectives) can be derived on top of these two primitive routines (e.g. MPI-Collectives, UCX-UCC). The columnar data format represents a column by a tuple of buffers and a dataframe is a collection of such columns. Therefore, a communication routine would have to be called on each of these buffers. We identified a set of communication routines required to implement distributed memory dataframe operators. These are listed in Table 2.

4. **Auxiliary Operators**: *Partition* operators are essential for distributed memory applications. Partitioning determines how a local data partition is split into subsets so that they can be sent across the network. This operator is closely tied with *Shuffle* communication routine. The goal of *hash partitioning* is to assign a partition ID to each row of the dataframe so that at the end of the communication routine, all the equal/key-equal rows end up in the same partition. *Ordered Partitioning* is used when the operators (e.g. *Sort*) need to be arranged based on sorted order. Parallel sorting on multiple key-columns further complicates the operation by accessing values along row-dimension (cache-unfriendly). *Rebalance* repartitions data across the executors equally or based on a sequence of rows per partition. On average, an executor would only have to exchange data with its closest neighbors to achieve this. To determine the boundaries, the executors must perform an *AllGather* on their partition lengths. *Merge* is another important auxiliary operator. It is used to build the final ordered dataframe in *Sort* operator to merge individually ordered sub-partitions (~merge-sort).

3.3 Generic Operator Patterns

Table 3. Generic Dataframe Operator Patterns

Pattern	Operators	Result Semantic	Communication
Embarrassingly parallel	Select, Project, Map, Row-Aggregation	Partitioned	-
Loosely Synchronous			
– Shuffle Compute	Union, Difference, Join, Transpose	Partitioned	Shuffle
– Combine Shuffle Reduce	Unique, GroupBy	Partitioned	Shuffle
– Broadcast Compute	Broadcast-Join*	Partitioned	Bcast
– Globally Reduce	Column-Aggregation	Replicated	AllReduce
– Globally Ordered	Sort	Partitioned	Gather, Bcast, Shuffle, AllReduce
– Halo Exchange	Window	Partitioned	Send-recv
Partitioned I/O	Read/Write	Partitioned	Send-recv, Scatter, Gather

*Specialized join algorithm

Our key observation is that dataframe operators can be categorized into several generic parallel execution patterns. We believe a distributed framework based on these patterns would make the parallelization of the massive API more tractable. These generic patterns (Table 3) have distinct distributed execution semantics, and individually analyzing the semantics allowed us to recognize opportunities for improvement. Rather than optimizing each operator individually, we can focus more on improving bottlenecks of the pattern, and thereby benefiting all operators derived from it.

Result Semantic: A local dataframe operator may produce dataframes, arrays, or scalars as results. When we promote a local operator to distributed memory, these result semantics could be nuanced (a global-viewed dataframe). Distributed memory dataframes (and arrays) are partitioned, and therefore a dataframe/array result (e.g. `select, join, etc.`) should also be partitioned. By contrast, scalars cannot be partitioned, so when an operator produces a scalar, it needs to be *replicated* to preserve the overall operator semantic.

Embarrassingly Parallel (EP). EP operators are the most trivial class of operators. They do not require any communication to parallelize the computation. *Select, Project, Map*, and *Row-Aggregation* fall under this pattern. While *Select* and *Map* apply to rows, *Project* works by selecting a subset of columns. These operations are expected to show linear scaling. Arithmetic operations (e.g. `add`, `mul`, etc.) are good examples of this pattern.

Loosely Synchronous

1. **Shuffle-Compute**: This is a common pattern that can be used for operators that depend on *Equality/Key Equality of rows*. Of the core dataframe operators, `join`, `union` and `difference` directly fall under this pattern, while `transpose` follows a more nuanced approach.

   Hash partitioning and shuffle communication rearrange data in such a way that equal/key-equal rows are on the same partition. Corresponding local operation can then be called trivially. *Join, Union* and *Difference* operators follow this pattern:

   | HashPartition | → | Shuffle | → | LocalOp |

   The local operator may access memory randomly, and allowing it to work on in-cache data improves the efficiency of the computation. We could also simply attach a *local hash partition* block at the end of the shuffle to achieve this since hash-partitioning can stream along the columnar data and is fairly inexpensive.

   | HashPartition | → | Shuffle | → | LocalHashPartition | → | LocalOp |

   A more complex scheme would be to hash-partition data into much smaller sub-partitions from the start. Possible gains on each of these schemes depend heavily on runtime characteristics.

   Transpose is important for dataframe *Pivot* operations. It can be implemented without communication in a block partitioned environment [18]. In a row partitioned setup, a *shuffle* is required at the end of block-wise local transpose to rearrange the blocks.

2. **Combine-Shuffle-Reduce**: An extension of the *Shuffle-Compute* pattern, Combine-Shuffle-Reduce is semantically similar to the famous MapReduce paradigm. The operations that reduce the resultant dataframe length such as *Groupby* and *Unique*, could benefit from this pattern. The initial local operation would reduce data into a set of intermediate results (similar to the combine step in *MapReduce*) e.g. `groupby.std`, creating sum_x^2, sum_x, and

`count_x`, which would then be shuffled. Upon their receipt, a local operation is performed to finalize the results. Perera et al. [17] also discuss a similar approach for dataframe reductions. The effectiveness of *combine-shuffle-reduce* over *shuffle-compute* depends on the *Cardinality* (**C**) (Sect. 3.4).

| LocalOp (interm. res.) | → | HashPartition | → | Shuffle | → | LocalOp (final res.) |

3. **Broadcast-Compute**: This requires a *broadcast* routine rather than *shuffle*. `broadcast_join`, a special algorithm for join, is a good example of this pattern. Broadcasting the smaller length relation to all other partitions and performing a local join is potentially much more efficient than shuffling both relations.

4. **Globally-Reduce**: This is most commonly seen in dataframe *Column Aggregation* operators. It is similar to EP, but requires communication to arrive at the final result. For example, calculating the column-wise `mean` requires a local summation, a global reduction, and a final value calculation. Some utility methods such as *distributed length* and *equality* also follow this pattern. For large data sets, the complexity of this operator is usually governed by the computation rather than the communication.

| LocalOp | → | Allreduce | → | Finalize |

5. **Halo Exchange**: This is closely related to window operations. `pandas` API supports rolling and expanding windows. For row-partitions, the windows at the boundaries would have to communicate with their neighboring partitions and exchange partially computed results. The amount of data sent/received is based on the window type and individual length of partitions.

6. **Globally Ordered**: Ascending order of rows ($row_i \leq row_j$) holds if all elements in row_i are less than or equal to the corresponding element in row_j. *Ordered partitioning* preserves this order along the partition indices. For a single numerical key-column, the data can be range-partitioned based on a key-data histogram.

| Sample | → | Allreduce range | → | Range part. | → | Shuffle | → | Local sort |

For multiple key-columns, we use *sample sort* with regular sampling [12]. It sorts data locally and sends out a sample to a central entity that determines pivot points for data. Based on these points, sorted data will be split and shuffled, and finally all executors merge the received sub-partitions locally.

Partitioned I/O. *Partitioned Input* parallelizes the input data (CSV, JSON, Parquet) by distributing the files to each executor. It may distribute a list of input files to each worker evenly. Alternatively, it receives a custom one-to-many mapping from worker to input file(s) and reads the input files according to the custom assignment. In *Partitioned Output*, each executor writes its own partition dataframe to one file.

3.4 Runtime Aspects

- **Cardinality**: Hash-shuffle in *Shuffle-Compute* pattern roughly takes $O(n) + O(\log P * n)$, where n is average length of a partition. In the *Combine-Shuffle-Reduce* pattern, the initial local operation has the potential to reduce communication order to $n' < n$. This gain depends on the *Cardinality* (**C**) of the dataframe $\mathbf{C} \in [\frac{1}{N}, 1]$, which is the number of unique rows relative to the length. $\mathbf{C} \sim \frac{1}{N} \implies n' \lll n$, making the combine-shuffle-reduce much more efficient than a shuffle-compute. Consequently, when $\mathbf{C} \sim 1 \implies n' \sim n$ may in fact worsen the combine-shuffle-reduce complexity. In such cases, shuffle-compute pattern is more efficient (5).
- **Data Distribution**: This heavily impacts the partitioning operators. When there are unbalanced partitions, some executors may be underutilized, thereby affecting the overall distributed performance. *Work-stealing* scheduling is a possible solution to this problem. In a BSP environment, pseudo-work-stealing execution can be achieved by storing partition data in a shared object store. Some operations could employ different operator patterns based on the data distribution. (e.g. When one relation is very small, *Join* could use a `broadcast_join`).
- **Logical Plan Optimizations**: An application consists of multiple Dataframe operator. Semantically, they are arranged in a DAG (directed acyclic graph), i.e. *logical plan*. An *optimized logical plan* can be generated based on rules (e.g. predicate push-down) or cost metrics. While these optimizations produce significant gains in real-life applications, this is an orthogonal detail to the individual operator patterns we focus on in this paper.

4   Cylon

Cylon is a reference distributed memory parallel dataframe runtime based on Sect. 3. We extended concept to implement a similar GPU Dataframe system, *GCylon*. The source code is openly available in GitHub [6] under Apache License.

4.1 Architecture

- **Arrow Format & Local Operators**: *Cylon* was developed in C++ using Apache Arrow Columnar format, which allows zero-copy data transfer between language runtimes. Arrow C++ Compute library is used for the local operators where applicable. Some operators were developed in-house. Additionally, we use `pandas` and `numpy` in Python for EP operators.
- **Communication**: *Cylon* currently supports MPI (OpenMPI, MPICH, MSMPI), UCX, and Gloo communication frameworks. The communication routines (Table 2) are implemented using a collection of non-blocking routines on internal dataframe buffers. For the user, it would be a blocking routine on dataframes. For example, *Dataframe Gather* is implemented via a series of `NB_Igatherv` calls on each buffer.

- **Auxiliary Operators**: *Cylon* supports all auxiliary operators discussed in Sect. 3. These operators are implemented with utilities developed in-house and from Arrow Compute, and for *GCylon*, we use CuDF utilities where applicable.
- **Distributed Operators** Except for *Window* and *Transpose*, *Cylon* implements the rest of the operators identified in Table 1. As shown in Fig. 1, all of them are implemented as a composition of local, auxiliary and communication operators based on the aforementioned patterns. Currently the `pandas` operator coverage is at a moderate 25%, and we are working on improving the coverage.

4.2 Features

- **Scalability and High Performance**: *Cylon* achieves above-average scalability and higher performance than the commonly used distributed dataframe systems. In Sect. 5, we compare strong scaling of *Cylon*, Modin, and Dask.
- **Flexible Dataframe API**: *Cylon* API clearly distinguishes between local and distributed operators with minimal changes to the `pandas` API semantics. This allows complex data manipulations for advanced users. As an example, a `join` (shuffle) can be easily transformed into a `broadcast_join` just by changing a few lines of code.

```
df1 = read_csv_dist(..., env) # large df
df2 = read_csv(...) if env.rank == 0 else None # read small df at rank 0
df2_b = env.broadcast(df2, root=0) # broadcast
df3 = df1.merge(df2_b, ...) # local join
```

- **Extensibility**: With the proposed model, *Cylon* was able to switch between multiple communication frameworks. Additionally, we extended this model to develop an experimental distributed memory dataframe for GPUs, *GCylon* with minimum development effort.

5 Experiments

Our experiments were carried out in a 15-node Intel® Xeon® Platinum 8160 cluster. Each node has a total RAM of 255 GB, uses SSD for storage and are connected via Infiniband with 40 Gbps bandwidth. A maximum of 40 (of 48) cores were used from each node. The software used: Python v3.8 & Pandas v1.4; *Cylon* (GCC v9.4, OpenMPI v4.1, & Apache Arrow v5.0); Modin v0.12 (Ray v1.9); Dask v2022.1. Uniformly random distributed data was used with two `int64` columns, 10^9 rows (~16 GB), and $\mathbf{C} = 0.9$. This constitutes a worse-case scenario for key-based operators. The scripts to run these experiments are available in Github [7].

The main goal of these operator benchmarks was to show how such generic patterns helped *Cylon* achieve scalable high performance. Dask and Modin operators are compared here only as a baseline. We tried our best to refer to publicly available documentation, user guides and forums while carrying out these tests to get the optimal configurations.

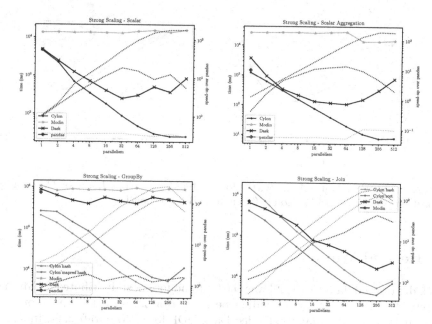

Fig. 3. Strong Scaling (1B rows, Log-Log) with speed-up over `pandas`

- **Scalability**: Figure 3 depicts strong scaling for the patterns. Dotted lines represent the speed-up over `pandas` (*pandas_time/time*). Compared to Dask, Modin, and `pandas`, *Cylon* shows consistent performance and superior scalability. When the parallelism is increased from 1 to 256, the wall-clock time is reduced, and it takes longer to complete at 512 parallelism. Per executor work is at its lowest in this instance, therefore the communication cost dominates over computation. For EP, a *Barrier* is called at the end and it might carry some communication overhead. *Cylon*'s local operators also perform on par or better than *pandas*, which validates our decision to develop in a C++ backend. Unfortunately, Modin `join` for 1B rows failed, therefore we ran a smaller 100 million row test case (Fig. 4(a)). It only uses `broadcast-join` [15], which explains the lack of scalability. However, we encountered similar problems for the rest of the operators (Fig. 3). Compared to Modin, Dask showed comparable scaling to *Cylon* for `join`s. However, the other operations lacked scalability, especially the scalar operations.

- **Cardinality Impact**: Figure 4(b) illustrates the impact of Cardinality (**C**) on the `groupby` performance. When **C** = 0.9, hash-groupby (shuffle-compute) consistently outperforms the mapred-groupby (combine-shuffle-reduce), because the local combining step does not reduce the shuffle workload sufficiently. Whereas when **C** = 10^{-5}, shuffled intermediate result size is significantly lesser, and therefore the latter is much faster. This shows that the same operator might need to implement several patterns and choose an implementation based on runtime characteristics.

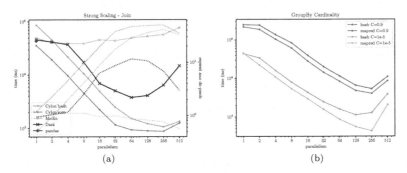

Fig. 4. a: Strong Scaling Joins with Modin (100M rows, Log-Log), b: Cardinality Impact on Combine-Shuffle-Reduce (**groupby**, 1B rows, Log-Log)

6   Related Work

Dask distributed dataframe [19] was the first and foremost distributed dataframe system. It was targeted at providing better performance in personal workstations. RAPIDS CuDF, later extended Dask DDF for GPU dataframes. In large-scale supercomputing environments, HPC-based systems like MPI (Message Passing Interface) [1], PGAS (partitioned global address space) [24], OpenMP, etc. performed better compared to Apache Spark [23] and Dask [2,10,21]). Modin [18], Dask [19], and Koalas (Apache Spark) are some of the emerging distributed dataframe solutions, but the domain shows a lot more room for improvement. HPC-based distributed data engineering systems show promising support for workloads running in supercomputing environments [3,4,17,22], and this is the main motivation for this paper.

7   Limitations and Future Work

Cylon Sort and *Window* operators are still under development. Additionally, larger scale experiments have been planned to provide more finer-grained analysis on communication and computation performance. *Cylon* execution currently requires dedicated resource allocation, which may be a bottleneck in a multi-tenant cloud environment. Furthermore, fault tolerance is another feature that is yet to be added. We believe that both BSP and asynchronous executions are important for complex data engineering pipelines and are currently working on integrating *Cylon* with Parsl [5] and Ray [16]. This would enable the creation of individual workflows that run on BSP, each of which can be scheduled asynchronously, that would optimize resource allocation without hindering the overall performance.

8   Conclusion

We recognize that today's data science community requires scalable solutions to meet their ever-growing data demand. Dataframes are at the heart of such applications, and in this paper we proposed a framework based on a set of generic operator patterns that lays the foundation for building scalable high performance dataframe systems. We discussed how this framework complements the existing literature available. We also presented *Cylon*, a reference runtime developed based on these concepts and showcased the scalability of its operators against leading dataframe solutions available today. We believe that there is far more room for development in domain, and we hope our work contributes to the next generation of distributed dataframe systems.

References

1. MPI: A Message-Passing Interface Standard Version 3.0 (2012). http://mpi-forum. org/docs/mpi-3.0/mpi30-report.pdf. Technical Report
2. Abeykoon, V., et al.: Streaming machine learning algorithms with big data systems. In: 2019 IEEE International Conference on Big Data (Big Data), pp. 5661–5666. IEEE (2019)
3. Abeykoon, V., et al.: Hptmt parallel operators for high performance data science & data engineering. arXiv preprint arXiv:2108.06001 (2021)
4. Abeykoon, V., et al.: Data engineering for HPC with python. In: 2020 IEEE/ACM 9th Workshop on Python for High-Performance and Scientific Computing (PyHPC), pp. 13–21. IEEE (2020)
5. Babuji, Y.N., et al.: Parsl: scalable parallel scripting in python. In: IWSG (2018)
6. CylonData: cylon (2021). https://github.com/cylondata/cylon
7. CylonData: cylon experiments (2021). https://github.com/cylondata/cylon_experiments
8. Fox, G., et al.: Solving problems on concurrent processors, vol. 1: general techniques and regular problems. Comput. Phys. **3**(1), 83–84 (1989)
9. Gao, H., Sakharnykh, N.: Scaling joins to a thousand GPUs. In: 12th International Workshop on Accelerating Analytics and Data Management Systems Using Modern Processor and Storage Architectures, ADMS@ VLDB (2021)
10. Kamburugamuve, S., Wickramasinghe, P., Ekanayake, S., Fox, G.C.: Anatomy of machine learning algorithm implementations in MPI, Spark, and Flink. Int. J. High Perform. Comput. Appl. **32**(1), 61–73 (2018)
11. Kamburugamuve, S., et al.: Hptmt: operator-based architecture for scalable high-performance data-intensive frameworks. In: 2021 IEEE 14th International Conference on Cloud Computing (CLOUD), pp. 228–239. IEEE (2021)
12. Li, X., Lu, P., Schaeffer, J., Shillington, J., Wong, P.S., Shi, H.: On the versatility of parallel sorting by regular sampling. Parallel Comput. **19**(10), 1079–1103 (1993)
13. Mattson, T., Sanders, B., Massingill, B.: Patterns for parallel programming (2004)
14. McKinney, W., et al.: pandas: a foundational python library for data analysis and statistics. Python High Perform. Sci. Comput. **14**(9), 1–9 (2011)
15. Modin: modin scalability issues (2021). https://github.com/modin-project/modin/issues

16. Moritz, P., et al.: Ray: a distributed framework for emerging {AI} applications. In: 13th {USENIX} Symposium on Operating Systems Design and Implementation ({OSDI} 18), pp. 561–577 (2018)
17. Perera, N., et al.: A fast, scalable, universal approach for distributed data reductions. In: International Workshop on Big Data Reduction, IEEE Big Data (2020)
18. Petersohn, D., et al.: Towards scalable dataframe systems. arXiv preprint arXiv:2001.00888 (2020)
19. Rocklin, M.: Dask: parallel computation with blocked algorithms and task scheduling. In: Proceedings of the 14th Python in Science Conference, 130–136. Citeseer (2015)
20. Valiant, L.G.: A bridging model for parallel computation. Commun. ACM **33**(8), 103–111 (1990)
21. Wickramasinghe, P., et al.: Twister2: tset high-performance iterative dataflow. In: 2019 International Conference on High Performance Big Data and Intelligent Systems (HPBD&IS), pp. 55–60. IEEE (2019)
22. Widanage, C., et al.: High performance data engineering everywhere. In: 2020 IEEE International Conference on Smart Data Services (SMDS), pp. 122–132. IEEE (2020)
23. Zaharia, M., et al.: apache spark: a unified engine for big data processing. Commun. ACM **59**(11), 56–65 (2016)
24. Zheng, Y., Kamil, A., Driscoll, M.B., Shan, H., Yelick, K.: UPC++: a PGAS extension for c++. In: 2014 IEEE 28th International Parallel and Distributed Processing Symposium, pp. 1105–1114. IEEE (2014)

Global Access to Legacy Data-Sets
in Multi-cloud Applications with Onedata

Michał Orzechowski[1]($\boxtimes$) , Michał Wrzeszcz[1] , Bartosz Kryza[1] ,
Łukasz Dutka[1] , Renata G. Słota[2] , and Jacek Kitowski[1,2]

[1] Academic Computer Centre CYFRONET AGH, Krakow, Poland
{morzech,kito}@agh.edu.pl, lukasz.dutka@cyfronet.pl
[2] Institute of Computer Science, AGH University of Science and Technology,
Krakow, Poland
rena@agh.edu.pl

Abstract. Data access and management for multi-cloud applications
proves challenging where there is a need for efficient access to large
pre-existing, legacy data-sets. To address this problem, we created an
indexing subsystem incorporated into Onedata data management system achieving a global multi-cloud integration of legacy storage systems
containing large data-sets. The solution is based on metadata management, organization and periodic monitoring of legacy data-sets, what
makes possible scheme-less co-existence a legacy storage system and Onedata for managing the same data collections. Thanks to block based data
transfer provided by Onedata large files stored on legacy storage systems
can be efficiently accessed from the cloud. The approach has been initially evaluated in a multi-cloud deployment scenario, where a large data
collection stored on legacy storage system located in a super-computing
center is processed on a commercial cloud.

Keywords: virtual filesystem · hybrid cloud · distributed data
management · legacy application · legacy storage · data-intensive
application

1 Introduction

As demand for computational power provided by scientific data centers and
usage of data-intensive applications grows, researchers and institutions are faced
with well known problem of either expanding their on-premise infrastructure
or adopting a more modern and flexing approach of moving part of data and
computation to the cloud.

With respect to scaling-out scientific applications outside of the premise of a
single data center, existing solutions provide satisfactory functionality to form a
hybrid or multi-cloud solutions that seamlessly extend the computing resources
of a data center, but the problem of data movement specific for data-intensive
applications remains. Most existing solutions require users to manually prestage

R. Wyrzykowski et al. (Eds.): PPAM 2022, LNCS 13826, pp. 305–317, 2023.
https://doi.org/10.1007/978-3-031-30442-2_23

data close to the computational resources, and then stage out the data back to the data center for long term storage, which results in poor user experience and suboptimal bandwidth usage. Furthermore, at the multi-institutional and multi-national levels, data access and data sharing become very complicated due to heterogeneous storage technologies, issues with policies as well as provenance and reproducibility of the results.

Many existing data-intensive applications require transparent access to large, file-based data collections. Some representative use cases from this category include satellite image processing, bioinformatics and genome processing or high energy physics. Such applications usually assume the on-premise access to a high-performance network file system available on each computing node. These legacy requirements make it difficult to execute the data-intensive applications on cloud or multi-cloud infrastructures. Users have to either abandon transition to the cloud or rewrite their applications to adapt to cloud-specific object-based storage solutions and suffer vendor lock-in. Moreover, the redesign of how the application accesses the data still leaves the user with the problem of file-based data collections being stored on-premise data management systems, that usually do not allow for easy data transfer to the cloud.

In this paper, we present our solution which enables easy migration of legacy data-intensive applications to multi-cloud infrastructures by providing global and transparent access to legacy data-sets in such environments. We realize our solution by combining the global multi-cloud data access functionality of One-data with legacy data-set access provided by Data Indexing Subsystem (DIS). The introduction of techniques and methods for guaranteeing continuous consistency and optimizations for handling the indexing of large legacy data-sets is the novelty of this paper.

The paper is organized as follows. Section 2 discusses the problem statement and related work in the area of distributed file systems and hybrid-cloud support. Section 3 presents our solution: the indexing subsystem for integration of pre-existing data collections on legacy storage including with its design and implementation. Section 4 describes in more detail Onedata data management system and its integration with our solution for supporting multi-cloud applications. Section 5 provides evaluation of the solution with performance results. Finally Sect. 6 concludes the paper.

2   Problem Statement and Related Work

To address the problem of running legacy data-intensive applications on multi-cloud infrastructures, a data management system which can solve the following issues is necessary:

- Global, transparent access to data in multi-cloud environments – in order to easily scale out of private cloud, applications need a transparent data access solution, enabling the users to simply deploy the application in the public cloud, and let the application access the data as if it was available locally,

- Support for legacy applications – the applications assume they can access the data as if it was available over a local file system (POSIX [10]) on virtual machines or containers in the cloud, while cloud providers only provide object-storage or a local network file system,
- Vendor lock-in with respect to data access – the applications cannot be easily moved between different cloud providers due to incompatible data access and management interfaces,
- Simultaneous access to the same data over different protocols – complex applications, composed of multiple components, some legacy relying on file system based data access, and some novel, already adapted to object storages such as S3 [1], need to access the same data, spanning different clouds, using different types of protocols, which is not possible with existing solutions,
- Scalability – cloud storage, in particular from smaller and more affordable providers, often lacks scalability characteristics required by some of the large scale data processing applications,
- High-throughput and low latency – applications running in multi-cloud deployments, still require high throughput and low latency data access, however existing solutions often require cumbersome prestaging of data, which introduces large latency and complicates application logic,
- Security and access control - per file, or per data set fine grained access control on the individual user as well as organization level with ability to share data and collaborate on data across multiple clouds,
- Legacy data collections support – exposing legacy data via a data management system without the necessity of making a copy of the data collection.

An example general overview of existing data management systems can be found in [13]. Few solutions exist which support transparent access to legacy data collections and storage systems for automatic application scaling to the cloud [4]. Most existing solutions are commercial and prone to vendor lock-in, requiring the users to adapt their applications to specific vendor APIs. AWS Storage Gateway [3], is a hybrid cloud data management framework, allowing access to on-premises data sets from the Amazon cloud infrastructure and including easy integration with other Amazon cloud data services such as S3 and Glacier. Another example is IBM Spectrum Scale [2], which is a software-defined scalable parallel filesystem providing a comprehensive set of storage services, built on top of the GPFS [7] filesystem. Both these solutions are commercially proven, however they are very expensive and require the users to commit to vendor specific interfaces.

In the area of non-commercial solutions one example is iRODS [6] which can be also used to achieve distributed data access. However, it does not implement location transparency of the stored data, i.e., the files must be manually moved/copied between iRODS zones. Several high-performance parallel filesystems exist, such as Ceph [11], GlusterFS [8], NFS [9], unfortunately they do not scale outside of a single Data center. Onedata [12] is an open-source, global high-performance, transparent data management system, that unifies data access across globally distributed infrastructures and multiple types of underlying storages and perform computations on data using applications relying on POSIX compliant data access.

Having evaluated multiple data management systems, the Onedata system seems to fulfill the most crucial of the above requirements connected with global, multi-cloud and transparent data access. Hence it has been chosen as a software solution to assist with solving a problem of performing computation on legacy data-sets on multi-cloud infrastructures.

3   Data Indexing Subsystem

Data Indexing Subsystem (DIS) is our solution for unlocking legacy data-sets, stored on legacy storage systems and with help of Onedata exposing them to multi-cloud environments. It is designed to scan a designated location on a storage system, index a data-set and expose it to Onedata, which in turn can expose the data-set as a cloud resource. DIS allows Onedata and a legacy storage system, that originally managed a data-set, to operate on a data-set at the same time. To create DIS the main two challenges were addressed: 1) large number of files in a legacy data-sets, 2) possible mutability of a legacy data-set by processes controlled or governed by Onedata and legacy storage system.

The main assumption is that DIS is based on data-sets metadata management and its organization. Indexing of existing data-sets can be performed only by scanning data-sets that are to be synchronized and creating metadata for the data, without replicating until necessary, i.e. requested a user. Periodic scans can be enabled to ensure continued consistency of the indexed data-set.

3.1   Policies and Options

The solution exposes a generic mechanism, which allows for defining various policies (algorithms) for scanning data. The supported policies include:

- *One-time data scan* - after the first scan no future changes on the legacy storage (new files, modified files, removed files) are detected. The indexing procedure is time and resource consuming as it creates metadata in the database for each indexed file.
- *Continuous scanning* - indexing needs to be repeated automatically, i.e. the files on the legacy storage can be added, removed or modified by users or computational jobs.

Furthermore, the following options can be configured to further control the data indexing process:

- *Maximum depth* - maximum directory depth the scanner should follow for consecutive updates,
- *Scan interval* - the time period between consecutive scans of the filesystem changes,
- *Write-once* - determines that if a file was created on the legacy storage, it will not be modified, allowing for optimized filesystem scanning. There is no need to compare files metadata that exist in DIS with those on storage,

– *Delete-enabled* - enable or disable detection of deleted files. Detection of created or modified files on the legacy storage requires checking whether each file visible on storage has associated metadata in DIS and whether the metadata differs from those on storage. Detection of files deleted on the legacy storage requires checking whether each file on storage has a corresponding metadata representation in DIS. That results in higher number of operations that must be performed to complete the scan.

The above policies and options allow to customize the scan process, in terms of the load generated on a legacy storage by DIS in order to versatilely perform metadata gathering, management and organization.

3.2 Data Consistency

DIS consists of a metadata database and a pool of Erlang processes that are responsible for creating, updating, and deleting metadata in response to the detection of changes in the data-sets on the legacy storage system. Due to DIS integration with Onedata, Onedata informs DIS about changes made to a data-set managed by DIS. On the other hand, DIS makes Onedata aware of changes that take place directly on the legacy storage system.

Conflict Resolution. From the perspective of global, transparent data access DIS is responsible for detection and resolution of conflicts between modifications of data-sets via Onedata and data-sets modifications done directly on the legacy storage system (see Fig. 1.)

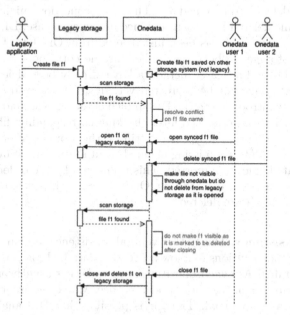

Fig. 1. Data Index Subsystem (red) working with Onedata to ensure data consistency. (Color figure online)

File name conflict resolution is an integral part of Onedata, as files belonging to the same data-set can be created and modified by multiple users in parallel. Information about this change is distributed with a small delay due to eventual consistency that is inherit to Onedata. Due to this delay the problem of file name conflicts is resolved by using dynamic suffixes which are concatenated to conflicting file names. This solution is also used by DIS to resolve file name conflicts between Onedata and legacy storage system.

A race condition can occur when deleting an already opened file from Onedata, and – at the same time – scanning a legacy storage system. In Onedata, similarly to POSIX, a file may be deleted only when it is not used (open) by any user. When a user deletes a file that is already open, its metadata representation is deleted from Onedata and therefore the file is not visible to others. However, the file on the storage system is still available to users and applications that opened this file before deletion of the metadata. To prevent DIS from re-indexing the file, it is tagged with metadata, thus allowing for its later deletion.

Another issue (not depicted in Fig. 1) is a possible race condition between deleting not an open file from Onedata and importing it back from the legacy storage system. As it was mentioned in Sect. 3.1 DIS scans the legacy data-set and checks each file, whether its corresponding metadata exists in Onedata and whether they are up to date. That way, DIS decides whether metadata of scanned files should be created, updated, or deleted in Onedata.

Listing files on storage and synchronizing them to Onedata is not an atomic operation. Therefore, it is possible that DIS finds the file on storage and before it synchronizes it, the file might be completely deleted from Onedata. Deleted completely means that first, the file is deleted from the storage, and then, its metadata are deleted from Onedata. This race condition might result in re-importing the file deleted by user from Onedata. In such case, DIS must be able to distinguish the file that has been just deleted from Onedata, from the newly created file on storage. In both cases, there are no corresponding file metadata in Onedata as in the first case, metadata have already been deleted and in the second, metadata have not been created yet. In order to avoid such problems, double-check was introduced to the DIS implementation: a second call to storage to fetch file attributes, performed after checking corresponding file metadata in Onedata. Let's notice that if the file is still on the storage, after checking that corresponding metadata are missing in Onedata, it means that it must be a newly created file that should be imported. This is ensured by the order of operations performed when the file is deleted from Onedata. First, it is deleted from storage and then its metadata are deleted.

Eventual Consistency. Due to the eventual consistency used in Onedata, there is a need for further solutions to allow processing data by legacy applications and Onedata in parallel. As synchronization of metadata is asynchronous, different metadata describing a file can not appear at once. Moreover, order of appearance of this metadata is not fixed. Thus, it is possible that DIS analyzes the file's metadata having only a part of metadata changes as a result of some action on the file. For this reason, DIS creates additional metadata during the scan that cannot be modified by any other Onedata mechanism. Thanks to this metadata, DIS is able to assess whether the inconsistency is due to asynchronous broadcast of changes or due to the file/metadata corruption. DIS responds appropriately by delaying the file processing until the missing metadata is fully synchronized.

DIS can detect file changes that occur between scans. DIS evaluates if the file changes were made by Onedata or by applications external to Onedata. In the second case, it is needed to invalidate the copies of file blocks replicated to other clouds. DIS analyzes the file timestamps on the legacy storage system and in its own metadata database, invalidating the corresponding copies when required.

The above considerations show our original approach of using known mechanisms related to the handling of parallel modification of a file by Onedata and applications external to Onedata. Analyzing a file during its synchronization is an expensive operation in terms of CPU. Therefore, our approach allows for limiting the number of analyzed files, which is presented in the next chapter.

3.3   DIS Optimizations

In order to decrease the number of operations performed when continuous synchronization is enabled, two optimizations have been introduced. Both of them allow to prune file system tree that is processed during the scan.

Timestamp-Based optimization. The first optimization relies on the fact, that the modification time of a directory is changed if and only if a child file is created/deleted in the directory. The algorithm checks the directory modification time and compares with it the value from the previous scan to verify whether the directory is to be scanned.

Hash-Based Optimization. The second optimization allows to determine whether any children metadata of the scanned directory has been changed since the previous scan without comparing the metadata from the database with those on storage for each file. To achieve this, the scanning algorithm divides each directory into batches, then it computes and saves hash values for each batch separately. In the next scan, the previous and current hash values are compared to verify modifications of the file system.

Both optimizations together with *delete-enable* and *write-once* options reduce the number of operations needed to perform the scan.

DIS also introduces API that allows manual file registration. If an external file change tracking mechanism is available, one can opt out of periodic legacy storage scans and take advantage of notifications for newly created files. In this case, after the first scan for importing files, DIS is limited to handling notifications and the resulting conflicts and race conditions. It is true that such integration requires work from the administrators (preparation of the script calling API), but it allows to reduce the resource consumption.

4   Exposing Legacy Data Collections with Onedata

Onedata data management system provides transparent access to data stored on the distributed storage resources, which can be managed by multiple storage providers. Due to its eventual consistency [14], Onedata provides highly scalable solution [12] even in high performance computing scenarios with large data throughput. The Onedata system is composed of three elements:

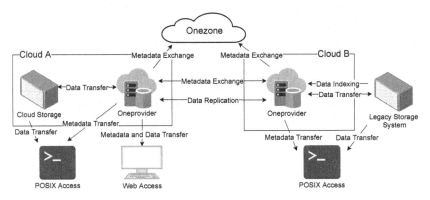

Fig. 2. An exemplary use case of the DIS as a part of Oneprovider, for exposing legacy data collections stored on Legacy Storage Systems to Onedata, thus making it available for access and processing from any Onedata-enabled cloud.

- *Onezone* - the main point of access for users allowing single-sign on login mechanism for all providers who granted the user access to their resources. Based on the Onezone authentication and authorization decisions, Oneprovider instances control user data access operations.
- *Oneprovider* - storage providers that connect to Onezone to form a storage federations, based on heterogeneous storage backends, while still providing to users unified, transparent data access.
- *Oneclient* - a command line client provides a POSIX interface to files allowing batch jobs to process data as in it was available locally.

Due to the features of Onedata it is easy to create a hybrid-cloud or multi-cloud architecture with transparent access to data as illustrated in Fig. 2. To expose legacy data-sets we devised DIS as a subsystem of Oneprovider. With DIS the data-set is indexed by Oneprovider, deployed on Cloud B, and after propagating its metadata to Onezone, the data-set becomes globally accessible via Onedata. From the data-set point of view Oneprovider connected to a legacy storage system becomes a source Oneprovider as it posses the original replica of the data-set. Users can then use tools provided by Onedata to process and modify the data-set and any change done to the data-set via Onedata is reflected on a legacy storage system (see right side of Fig. 2).

  To efficiently process data from a legacy storage system on an external cloud, we deploy another instance of Oneprovider - on Cloud A - and connect it to a cloud storage system that acts as a cache for replicated data. When accessing the data, missing data blocks are transparently replicated between Oneproviders.

More Oneproviders can be deployed on clouds where we want to process data thus creating a network of caching Oneproviders. The data is replicated between them depending on which Oneprovider stores a needed replica. Users then can leverage Oneclient, that exposes the data-set via POSIX filesystem abstraction and perform computation on a data-set as in it was present locally. The on-the-fly replication process fetches any missing blocks needed by the computation.

5 Evaluation

To evaluate the propose solution first we show the performance aspect of DIS, then we focus on the aspect of global data access to legacy data collections.

5.1 DIS Performance

For very large data collections the time before a new file is detected can be significant. However, files already indexed by DIS are immediately visible via Onedata filesystem and available to any application that uses Onedata for data access. This is thanks to the eventual consistency metadata propagation algorithm build into Onedata. In order to perform the evaluation of DIS, we started with a small data-set test followed by a larger test showing the DIS performance.

Table 1. DIS Performance

Set	1	2	3	4
Number of files (number of directories)	10k(2)	30k (303)	125k (1273)	800k(83)
Time of 1st scan (import) [s]	35.1	61.7	254.7	3178.9
Time of next scan [s]	16.1	22.8	119.9	2985.6
Time of scan with optimizations [s]	0.5	15.9	75.0	60.9

Table 1 presents the indexing times of 4 file sets of increasing size: 10,000, 30,000, 125,000 and 800,000 files respectively. The number of directories where the files are located is given in brackets. The rows represent the following times:

- Time of the first scan - the most time-consuming operation as the system creates metadata documents in the database for each new detected file,
- Time of a consecutive scan without optimizations - for each file the system performs all checks (modified, added, deleted),
- Time of a consecutive scan with both optimizations (*timestamp-based* and *hash-based*) with options *write-once* disabled and *delete-enabled*.

The results show that time of scan with optimizations depends on both the number of files and the directory structure. Table 2 presents the scan times on the 800,000 files (Set 4 in Table 1) depending on different combinations of settings *write-once* and *delete-enabled*. The former setting determines whether file modifications are acceptable, while the latter – whether file deletions are anticipated. From the results we can see the more restrictive settings result in shorter scan times. The second column ("Time of next scan") shows the time of a consecutive scan without any optimizations (which can be considered here a worst-case scenario), the third column shows the scan time with optimizations and no changes in the filesystem (considered as the most economical, preservative case) and the last column shows the scan time with optimizations active and 1 file added on the storage.

Table 2. Time of Set 4 scan with DIS different configurations

DIS configuration		Time of next scan [s]	Time of scan with optimizations [s]	
write-once	*delete-enabled*		no files changed	1 file created
true	false	1184.6	42.9	50.7
true	true	2155.5	51.0	60.3
false	true	2985.6	60.9	68.7

The results presented in Tables 1 and 2 show how fast we can enable operating on existing, legacy data sets with the Onedata system keeping possibility for their modifications performed independently on legacy storage.

5.2 Transparent Global Data Access

To show the global access to data, we deploy Onedata on two cloud infrastructures: the first at ACK Cyfronet AGH in Krakow, the second – on Google Cloud Site in Paris. The legacy storage located in Krakow connects to Onedata deployed there and DIS indexes the whole data-set.

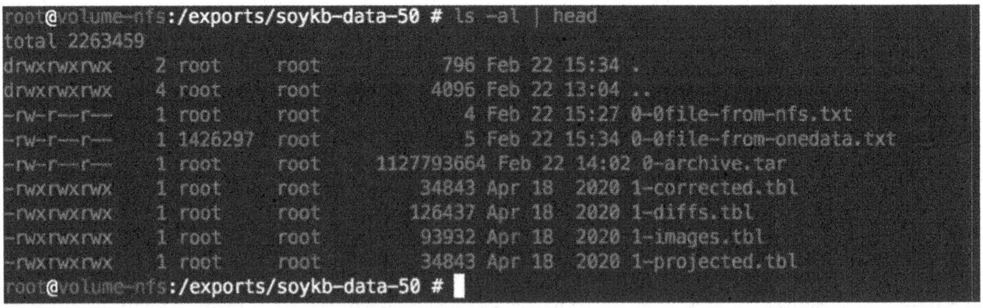

Fig. 3. Legacy data accessible via POSIX filesystem

Upon completion of the indexing process the data can be accessed via Onedata installation in Krakow or in Paris. The POSIX client can be used to list the files and access them regardless of the physical location of files, see Fig. 3. The list operation does not require data transfer as it only presents metadata

Fig. 4. Partial distribution of blocks of a file between Onedata installations

of the files, when opening a file a actually data transfer between Onedata and POSIX client is started.

When accessing data via Onedata installation in Paris, data is transparently partially replicated from Onedata installation in Krakow to Paris location. Since Onedata supports block based replication, when accessing some portions of the file only requested blocks are transferred, as it can be observed on Fig. 4. The transferred blocks are a partial replica and yield significant benefits with regards to time needed to access requested blocks from the second location.

6   Conclusions

In this paper, we have presented a solution for exposing preexisting large data collections stored on legacy storage systems to multi-cloud environments. Thanks to our solution - Data Indexing Subsystem integrated with the Onedata data management system - applications running on cloud environments can access legacy data-sets provided by many independent service providers. Due to the fact, that DIS gathers and organizes metadata of indexed files, there is no redundant data-sets replication. Data-sets are replicated between clouds only when they are read in another cloud and the replication is limited to the data fragments read by the user/application. Our solution differs significantly form existing sync and share solutions like Dropbox, Owncloud, or Seafile as it does not require synchronization of file blocks. It focuses on metadata management and synchronization, postponing any data transfer to the moment when the data transfer it's actually required.

Periodic action of re-indexing of already indexed data-set is a source of intensive process, hence DIS provides multiple policies, options, and methods of optimization of the indexing process. All of them allow for limiting the size of re-indexed data-set significantly, hence lowering the cost of continuous of the changes. The DIS notification API of newly created files, allows for deep integration with legacy storage systems by allowing for manual registration of metadata of files. This makes it possible to perform periodic re-indexing very rarely, only to detect files for which the notification was lost or another error occurred.

Due to the highly customize nature of DIS, the assessment of its cost should be case based. The presented tests show the upper time limits (first scan, then full scan without optimization) along with exemplary optimizations.

The presented evaluation shows the indexing times of storage resources containing data-sets during the metadata indexing processes for different data-sets and various DIS configurations. The longest time is the time of the first indexing when metadata must be created for each file/directory from the data-sets attached to Onedata. The cost of subsequent indexing varies considerably and depends not only on the size and structure of the data-sets but also on the DIS settings and on the number files added/deleted between indexing runs. In some cases, the reduction in the time of subsequent indexing is significant.

Thanks to integration with Onedata, the legacy data can be accessed globally from multi-cloud environments. Easy and transparent access to data proved to be especially attractive for distributed scientific workflows. The workflow management systems is able to use Onedata and DIS API to achieve a fine grained control over exposure of specific parts of large data-sets (see [5]).

Acknowledgements. This scientific work is co-financed in part by an international project and by the program of the Minister of Science and Higher Education entitled "PMW" in the years 2020–2023; contract No. 5145/H2020/2020/2; contract No. 5193/H2020/2021/22 and by The National Centre for Research and Development under the program entitled ERA-NET CO-FUND ICT-AGRI-FOOD, contract No. ICTA-GRIFOOD/I/FINDR/ 02/2022. JK and RGS are grateful for support from the subvention of Polish Ministry of Education and Science assigned to AGH University of Science and Technology.

References

1. Amazon: Amazon s3 developer guide. Technical Report, Amazon (2010). http://aws.amazon.com/documentation/s3/
2. Haustein, N., Christ, A.: IBM SpectrumScale. automation of storage services. https://www.ibm.com/support/pages/system/files/inline-files/Spectrum_Scale_Automation_v1.6.pdf
3. Kalavade, A.: AWS storage gateway in 2019. https://aws.amazon.com/blogs/storage/aws-storage-gateway-in-2019/. Accessed 3 Feb 2020
4. Linthicum, D.S.: Emerging hybrid cloud patterns. IEEE Cloud Comput. **3**(1), 88–91 (2016). https://doi.org/10.1109/MCC.2016.22
5. Orzechowski, M., Baliś, B., Słota, R.G., Kitowski, J.: Reproducibility of computational experiments on Kubernetes-managed container clouds with HyperFlow. In: Krzhizhanovskaya, V.V., et al. (eds.) ICCS 2020. LNCS, vol. 12137, pp. 220–233. Springer, Cham (2020). https://doi.org/10.1007/978-3-030-50371-0_16
6. Röblitz, T.: Towards implementing virtual data infrastructures - a case study with iRODS. Comput. Sci. (AGH) **13**(4), 21–34 (2012)
7. Schmuck, F.B., Haskin, R.L.: GPFS: a shared-disk file system for large computing clusters. In: D.D.E. Long (ed.) FAST, pp. 231–244. USENIX (2002)
8. Selvaganesan, M., Liazudeen, M.A.: An insight about glusterfs and its enforcement techniques. In: ICCCRI, pp. 120–127. IEEE Computer Society (2016)
9. Shepler, S., et al.: NFS version 4 Protocol. RFC 3010 (Proposed Standard) (2000)
10. The IEEE and the open group: the open group base specifications issue 6 - IEEE Std 1003.1, 2004 Edition. IEEE, New York, NY, USA (2004)

11. Weil, S.A., Brandt, S.A., Miller, E.L., Long, D.D.E., Maltzahn, C.: Ceph: a scalable, high-performance distributed file system. In: Bershad, B.N., Mogul, J.C. (eds.) OSDI, pp. 307–320. USENIX Association (2006)
12. Wrzeszcz, M., Łukasz Dutka, Słota, R.G., Kitowski, J.: New approach to global data access in computational infrastructures. Future Gener. Comput. Syst. **125**, 575–589 (2021). https://doi.org/10.1016/j.future.2021.06.054
13. Wrzeszcz, M., Kitowski, J., Słota, R.G.: Towards trasparent data access with context awareness. Comput. Sci. **19**(2), 201–221 (2018). https://doi.org/10.7494/csci.2018.19.2.2844
14. Wrzeszcz, M., et al.: Consistency models for global scalable data access services. In: Wyrzykowski, R., Dongarra, J., Deelman, E., Karczewski, K. (eds.) PPAM 2017. LNCS, vol. 10777, pp. 471–480. Springer, Cham (2018). https://doi.org/10.1007/978-3-319-78024-5_41

Applications of Parallel and Distributed Computing

MD-Bench: A Generic Proxy-App Toolbox for State-of-the-Art Molecular Dynamics Algorithms

Rafael Ravedutti Lucio Machado[✉], Jan Eitzinger, Harald Köstler, and Gerhard Wellein

Erlangen National High Performance Computing Center (NHR@FAU), Friedrich -Alexander -Universität Erlangen-Nürnberg (FAU), Erlangen, Germany
`rafaelravedutti@gmail.com`

Abstract. Proxy-apps, or mini-apps, are simple self-contained benchmark codes with performance-relevant kernels extracted from real applications. Initially used to facilitate software-hardware co-design, they are a crucial ingredient for serious performance engineering, especially when dealing with large-scale production codes. MD-Bench is a new proxy-app in the area of classical short-range molecular dynamics. In contrast to existing proxy-apps in MD (e.g. miniMD and coMD) it does not resemble a single application code, but implements state-of-the art algorithms from multiple applications (currently LAMMPS and GROMACS). The MD-Bench source code is understandable, extensible and suited for teaching, benchmarking and researching MD algorithms. Primary design goals are transparency and simplicity, a developer is able to tinker with the source code down to the assembly level. This paper introduces MD-Bench, explains its design and structure, covers implemented optimization variants, and illustrates its usage on three examples.

Keywords: proxy-app · molecular dynamics · performance analysis

1 Introduction and Motivation

Molecular dynamics (MD) simulations are used in countless research efforts to assist the investigation and experimentation of systems at atomic level. Both their system size and timescale are crucially limited by computing power, therefore they must be designed with performance in mind. Several strategies to speedup such simulations exist, examples are Linked Cells, Verlet List and MxN kernels from GROMACS [11,12]. These improve the performance by exploiting either domain-knowledge or hardware features like SIMD capabilities and GPU accelerators. MD application codes can achieve a large fraction of the theoretical peak floating point performance and are therefore among the few application classes that can make use of the available compute power of modern processor architectures. Also, cases scientists are interested in are frequently strong scaling throughput problems, a single run only exhibits limited parallelism but

R. Wyrzykowski et al. (Eds.): PPAM 2022, LNCS 13826, pp. 321–332, 2023.
https://doi.org/10.1007/978-3-031-30442-2_24

thousands of similar jobs need to be executed. This fact combined with arithmetic compute power limitation makes an optimal hardware-aware implementation a critical requirement. MD is used in many areas of scientific computing like material science, engineering, natural science and life sciences.

Proxy-apps are stripped down versions of real applications, ideally they are self-contained, easy to build and bundled with a validated test case, which can be a single stubbed performance-critical kernel or a full self-contained small version of an application. Historically proxy-apps assisted in porting efforts or hardware-software co-design studies. Today they are a common ingredient of any serious performance engineering effort of large-scale application codes, especially with multiple parties involved. Typically proxy-apps resemble a single application code, e.g., miniMD [3] mimics the performance of LAMMPS [2,10]. A proxy-app can be used for teaching purposes and as a starting point for performance oriented research in a specific application domain.

To investigate the performance of MD applications, we developed MD-Bench — a standalone proxy-app toolbox implemented in C99 that comprises the most essential MD steps to calculate trajectories in an atomic-scale system. MD-Bench contributes clean reference implementations of state-of-the-art MD optimization schemes. As a result, and in contrast to existing MD proxy-apps, MD-Bench is not limited to represent one MD application but aims to cover all relevant contributions. MD-Bench is intended to facilitate and encourage performance related research for classical MD algorithms. Its applications are low-level code analysis and performance investigation via fine-grained profiling of hardware resources utilized by MD runtime-intensive kernels.

This paper is structured as follows: In Sect. 2 we present related work on proxy-apps for MD simulations, pointing out the differences compared to MD-Bench. In Sect. 3 we explain the basic theory for MD simulations. In Sect. 4 we list and discuss current features offered in MD-Bench, besides its employment on benchmarking, performance analysis and teaching activities. In Sect. 5 we present cases with analysis studies and results to illustrate how MD-Bench can be used. Finally Sect. 6 presents the conclusion and outlook, and a discussion of future work.

2   Related Work

There already exist multiple proxy-apps to investigate performance and portability for MD applications. One of the better known examples is Mantevo miniMD, which contains C++ code extracted from LAMMPS and provides a homogeneous copper lattice test case in which the short-range forces can be calculated with Lennard-Jones (LJ) or embedded atom method (EAM) potentials. It was used to investigate the performance of single instruction, multiple data (SIMD) vectorization on the most internal loops of the neighbor-lists building and force calculation steps [9], as well as to evaluate the portability of MD kernels through the Kokkos framework, thus executing most of the code on GPU instead of only the pair force and neighbor-lists. Outcomes from miniMD in LAMMPS include better SIMD parallelism usage on code generated by compilers and most efficient use of GPU by avoiding data transfers at all time-steps of the simulation.

ExMatEx coMD is another proxy-app from the material science domain that focuses on co-design to evaluate the performance of new architectures and programming models. Besides allowing users to extend and/or re-implement the code as required, the co-design principle also permits to evaluate the performance when switching strategies, for example using Linked-Cells for force calculations instead of Verlet Lists.

ExaMiniMD is an improved and extended version of miniMD with enhanced modularity that also uses Kokkos for portability. Its main components such as force calculation, communication and neighbor-list construction are derived classes that access their functionality through virtual functions.

In previous work we developed tinyMD [8], a proxy-app (also based on miniMD) created to evaluate the portability of MD applications with the AnyDSL framework. tinyMD uses higher-order functions to abstract device iteration loops, data layouts and communication strategies, providing a domain-specific library to implement pair-wise interaction kernels that execute efficiently on multi-CPU and multi-GPU targets. Its scope is beyond MD applications, since it can be used to simulate any kind of particle simulation that relies on short-range force calculation such as the discrete element method (DEM).

Beyond proxy-apps, performance-engineering of MD can be achieved via auto-tuning by either running simulations as a black-box for finding optimal system and hardware specific simulation parameters [4] or by providing programming interfaces that dynamically tune the application at run-time by selecting the best optimization strategies and data layouts [5].

MD-Bench differs from available offerings because it was primarily developed to enable an in-depth analysis of software-hardware interaction. With that in mind, MD-Bench provides a stubbed variant to evaluate the force calculation at different levels of the memory hierarchy, as well as a gather benchmark that mimics the memory operations used in those kernels, thus allowing investigation of the memory transfers without side-effects from arithmetic operations. In contrast to other proxy-apps MD-Bench contains optimized algorithms from multiple MD applications and allows to compare those using the same test cases. Apart from standard Verlet Lists algorithms it contains state-of-the-art optimization strategies as, e.g., the GROMACS MxN kernels, which attain higher data level parallelism in modern architectures by using a more SIMD-friendly data layout and up to now are not yet available as part of a simple proxy-app. Although the significant majority of MD-Bench code is implemented in C, it also relies on SIMD intrinsics and assembly code kernels allowing low-level tweaking of the code without interference from a compiler.

3   Background and Theory

Fundamentally, atom trajectories in classical MD systems are computed by integrating Newton's second law equation (Eq. 1) after computing the forces, which are described by the negative gradient of the potential of interest. Equation 2 shows how to compute each interaction for the LJ potential, with x_{ij} being the distance vector between atoms i and j, ϵ being the width of the potential well, and σ specifying at which distance the potential is 0.

$$F = m\dot{v} = ma \tag{1}$$

$$F_2^{LJ}(x_i, x_j) = 24\epsilon \left(\frac{\sigma}{x_{ij}}\right)^6 \left[2\left(\frac{\sigma}{x_{ij}}\right)^6 - 1\right] \frac{x_{ij}}{|x_{ij}|^2} \tag{2}$$

To optimize the computation of short-range potentials, only atom pairs within a cutoff radius may be considered because contributions become negligible at long-range interactions. Hence, a Verlet List (see Fig. 1(a)) can be regularly created for each atom to track neighbor candidates within a specific radius r, which is the cutoff radius plus a small value (verlet buffer).

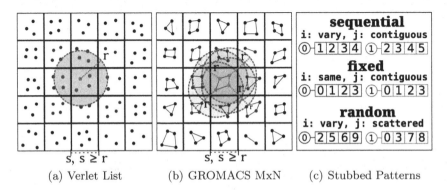

(a) Verlet List   (b) GROMACS MxN   (c) Stubbed Patterns

Fig. 1. (a, b) Pair list creation for the red atom (cluster) in Verlet List (GROMACS MxN), blue atoms (clusters) are evaluated and the ones within the green circle with radius r are added to the pair list. Cell size s must be greater or equal than r. (c) 4-length neighbor-lists for atoms 0 (purple) and 1 (orange) in Stubbed Case patterns. (Color figure online)

4   MD-Bench Features

Figure 2 depicts MD-Bench[1,2] features. To facilitate experimentation with a range of settings that influence performance, a robust build system with various configurations from the compiler and flags to whether atom types should be explicitly stored and loaded from memory is available. Due to its modularity, the build system permits to replace kernels at the assembly level. Particularly, we maintain simplified C versions of each kernel with an eye toward low-level code analysis and tweaking, which is hardly achievable on production MD applications due to the massive code base size and extensive employment of advanced

[1] https://github.com/RRZE-HPC/MD-Bench.
[2] MD-Bench is open source and available under LGPL3 License.

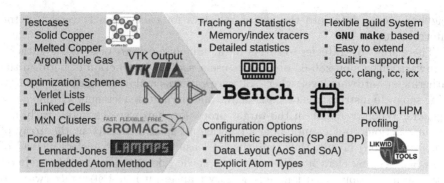

Fig. 2. Overview about MD-Bench Features

programming language techniques, which brings in substantial complexity and makes an analysis more difficult. Apart from that, kernels are instrumented with LIKWID [13] markers to allow fine-grained profiling of kernels using hardware performance monitoring (HPM) counters.

4.1 Optimization Schemes

Verlet Neighbor-Lists. The most common optimization scheme used in MD applications to compute short-range forces is arguably the Verlet List algorithm. It consists of building a neighbor-list for each atom in the simulation, where the elements are other atoms that lie within a cutoff radius that is higher or equal than the force cutoff radius. Thus, forces are computed for each atom by traversing their neighbor-list and accumulating forces for neighbors which distance is smaller than the cutoff (see Algorithm 1).

Algorithm 1. Force calculation

```
for i ← 1 to Nlocal do                                          ▷ Number of local atoms
    f ← 0                                    ▷ Partial forces (required for parallelism)
    for k ← 1 to Nneighs[i] do                       ▷ Number of neighbors for atom i
        j ← neighbors[i, k]                               ▷ k-th neighbor of atom i
        d ← calculate_distance(i, j)
        if d ≤ cutoff_radius then                             ▷ Force cutoff check
            f ← f + calculate_force(d)             ▷ Depends on the potential used
        end if
    end for
    force[i] ← force[i] + f                                   ▷ Accumulate forces
end for
```

The algorithm contains two major drawbacks with respect to SIMD parallelism: (a) irregular access pattern, since neighbor atoms are scattered across memory and (b) no reuse of neighbor data (positions) across atom iterations. The consequence for them is the requirement of a gather operation to load the neighbor atoms data into the vector registers for each atom traversed in the outermost loop.

There are two strategies to gather data, namely *hardware* or *software* gathers. Hardware gathers on x86-64 processors use a *vgather* instruction to perform the gathering at hardware level, where software gathers emulate the gather operation using separate instructions to load, shuffle and permutate elements within vector registers. When available in the target processor, hardware gathers clearly use less instructions, but cannot take advantage of spatial locality in the array of structures (AoS) layout, thus requiring at least three data transfers instead of one when keeping elements aligned to the cache line size. Due to this trade-off between instruction execution and memory transfer, it is not straightforward to determine the best strategy, as it will depend on the target processor.

To avoid the costs of gathering data and enhance data reuse, a different data layout is necessary. Therefore, we also introduce the GROMACS MxN optimization scheme in MD-Bench, which is currently not present in any of the existing MD proxy-apps. Despite its SIMD-friendly data layout, it introduces extra computations because interactions are evaluated per clusters instead of per atom, thus the trade-off between extra computations and overhead for SIMD parallelism must also be assessed.

For all kernel variants available, MD-Bench contains their half neighbor-lists counterpart, which take advantage of Newton's Third Law to compute only half of the pair interactions, thus decreasing the amount of partial forces to calculate. Despite the clear benefit of having less operations, this strategy harms parallelism because it introduces race conditions for the neighbor atoms because forces are stored back to memory in the innermost loop. Also, gather and scatter operations are needed for the forces of the neighbor atoms, which not only takes effect in the instruction execution cost but also increases memory traffic.

MxN Cluster Algorithm. To address the lack of data reuse and necessity of costly gather operations, the MxN algorithm introduced in GROMACS clusters atoms in groups of $max(M, N)$ elements (see Fig. 1(b) for $M = 4, N = 4$ example). Thus, tailored kernels with SIMD intrinsics are implemented to compute interactions of MxN atoms. Positions for atoms in the same cluster are contiguously stored in an array of structures of arrays (AoSoA) fashion, and can be loaded without a gather operation. In this algorithm, M parametrizes the reusability of data as atoms in the same i-cluster contains the same pair lists, and therefore a single load of a j-cluster of size N is enough to compute the interaction among all pairs of atoms. Since two kernel variants for the force calculation are present (namely **4xN** and **2xNN**), then N is optimally chosen as either the SIMD width of the target processor or half of it. Since kernels must be kept simple and bidirectional mapping between i-clusters and j-clusters is needed, M is either $\frac{N}{2}$, N or $2N$. Note that when a cluster size is less than $max(M, N)$, it is filled in with atoms placed in the infinity to fail the cutoff checking. Also, different atoms in paired clusters may not be within the cutoff radius. Hence, choosing large values for M and N can significantly grow the amount of pairs interactions to compute, wasting resources and injuring performance.

4.2   Benchmark Test Cases

Short-range force kernels for LJ and EAM potentials are available, with Copper face-centered cubic (FCC) lattice and Noble gases (pure argon) setups to embrace both material modeling and bio-sciences simulation fields. Setups are provided by providing atoms positions (and velocities in some cases) in a Protein Data Bank (PDB), Gromos87 or LAMMPS dump file.

4.3   Tools

Detailed Statistics Mode. To collect extended runtime information for the simulation, a detailed statistics mode can be enabled. It introduces various statistics counters in the force kernels in order to display relevant performance metrics such as cycles per SIMD iterations (processor frequency must be fixed), average cutoff conditions that fail/succeed and useful read data volumes.

Memory Traces and Gather-Bench. The gather benchmark is a standalone benchmark code for x86-64 CPUs (currently) that mimics the data movement (both operations and transfers) from MD kernels in order to evaluate the "cost of gather" from distinct architectures. It currently gathers data in the following patterns: (a) simple 1D arrays with fixed stride, to evaluate single gather instruction in the target CPU, (b) array of 3D vectors with fixed stride, to evaluate MD gathers with regular data accesses and (c) array of 3D vectors using trace files from MD-Bench *INDEX_ TRACER* option, to evaluate MD gathers with irregular data accesses. The benchmark exploits the memory hierarchy by adjusting the data volume to fit into a different cache level in successive executions, and yields a performance metric based on the number of cache lines touched. There are options to determine the floating point precision and include padding to assure alignment to the cache line size.

Stubbed Force Calculation. To execute MD kernels in a steady-state and understand their performance characteristics, we established a synthetical stubbed case where the number of neighbors per atom remain fixed and the data access pattern can be predicted. Figure 1(c) depicts examples for data access patterns available (namely sequential, fixed and random), indicating whether neighbor-lists vary or are the same across different atoms in the outermost loops (i) and if atoms in the lists (j) are contiguous or scattered over memory. It addresses both irregular data accesses and variations in the inner-most loop size, thus providing a stable benchmark that can isolate effects caused by distinct reasons like memory latency and overhead for filling in the CPU instruction pipeline.

5   Examples

For this work experiments, we made use of the following processor architectures:

Intel Cascade Lake: Intel(R) Xeon(R) Gold 6248 CPU at 2.50 GHz, with two 20-cores sockets, two threads per core (hyper-threading enabled). Individual 32KB L1 and 1024KB L2 caches for each core, and 28 MB of shared L3 cache for each socket, with one memory domain per socket.

Intel Ice Lake: Intel(R) Xeon(R) Platinum 8360Y CPU at 2.40 GHz, with 36-cores per chip. Individual 80KB L1 per core (32 instructions + 48 data), 512KB L2 caches for each core, and 54 MB of shared L3 cache per chip.

We used LIKWID (V5.2) to fix the CPU frequency, pin tasks to specific cores, enable/disable prefetchers and make use of HPM counters.

5.1   Assembly Analysis

This example illustrates how MD-Bench allows to evaluate the optimizations performed by compilers at the instruction code level to pinpoint possible improvements in the compiler generated code. In the AVX512 generated code from the Intel compiler (ICC) 2020.06.23, we notice *lea* and *mov* instructions before gathering the data (see Listing 1.1). Removing such instructions does not change the semantics of the code because the destination registers of the *mov* operations are not read afterwards, so we can exclude them to improve performance. For the Copper FCC lattice case with 200 time-steps, the runtime on Cascade Lake for the force calculation is about 4.43 s without these instructions and about 4.81 with them, leading to a 8% speedup.

```
1    ; ymm3 <- neighs [k] * 3
2    vmovdqu ymm3, [r13+rbx*4]
3    vpaddd ymm4, ymm3, ymm3
4    vpaddd ymm3, ymm3, ymm4
5    mov r10d, [r13+rbx*4]  ; neighs [k]
6    mov r9d, [4+13+rbx*4]  ; neighs [k+1]
7    lea r10d, [r10+r10*2]  ; neighs [k] * 3
8    lea r9d, [r9+r9*2]  ; neighs [k+1] * 3
9    ... ; Same for k+2, k+3,...k+7
10   vgatherdpd zmm4{k1}, [16+rdi+ymm3*8]
11   vgatherdpd zmm17{k2}, [8+rdi+ymm3*8]
12   vgatherdpd zmm18{k3}, [rdi+ymm3*8]
```

```
1    vrcp14pd zmm24, zmm25
2    vcmppd   k2, zmm25, zmm14, 1
3    vfpclasspd k0, zmm24, 30
4    kmovw    edi, k2
5    knotw .k1, k0
6    vmovaps zmm17, zmm25
7    and     r10d, edi
8    vfnmadd213pd zmm17, zmm24, ...
9    kmovw    k3, r10d
10   vmulpd zmm18, zmm17, zmm17
11   vfmadd213pd zmm24{k1}, zmm17, zmm24
12   vfmadd213pd zmm24{k1}, zmm18, zmm24
```

Listing 1.1. LEA and MOV instructions.   **Listing 1.2.** Correction instructions.

Further instructions are also included to perform corrections after computing the reciprocal (see Listing 1.2), which are not present in kernels with explicit SIMD intrinsics (like MxN kernels). Their usefulness is arguable because other factors can change the results at this precision, like the order for partial forces calculation that varies significantly across different optimization and parallelization strategies. Table 1 shows performance, temperature and pressure for the Verlet Lists algorithm with and without such instructions, as well as for the MxN algorithm. Without them, we can perceive a performance improvement of about 11% in the force calculation runtime. In terms of accuracy, not only the differences for temperature and pressure are small, but even smaller than when comparing to the MxN algorithm.

5.2   Investigate Memory Latency Contributions

An important assumption for performance engineering of streaming kernels is their non-significant latency contribution due to regular data access pattern,

Table 1. Temperatures, pressures and runtimes for Verlet with/without corrections (+C/-C) and MxN. Quantities are unitless and reflect lj style from LAMMPS.

Algorithm	Temperature	Pressure	Time(s)
Verlet+C	7.961495×10^{-1}	6.721043×10^{-1}	4.78
Verlet-C	7.961635×10^{-1}	6.721161×10^{-1}	4.27
MxN	7.961966×10^{-1}	6.721441×10^{-1}	3.13

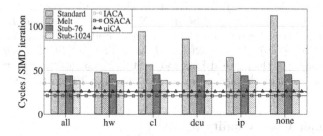

Fig. 3. Cycles per SIMD iterations on Standard, Melting and Stubbed setups with different prefetchers enabled, together with predictions from static analyzers.

which is trivially foreseeable by cache prefetchers. On a first thought, MD simulations are expected to have significant latency impact due to their memory access characteristics, and MD-Bench can assist on measuring such impact via its stubbed sequential case. Nonetheless, when executing them against standard copper lattice and melting cases, we observed that such impact is minor. Furthermore, we also compare measurements in Cascade Lake from our stubbed version with kernel throughput predictions under ideal conditions from IACA [6] (for Skylake-X micro-architecture), OSACA [7] and uiCA [1] static code analyzers.

Figure 3 depicts cycles per SIMD iteration for mentioned cases with distinct prefetcher settings, together with IACA, OSACA and uiCA predictions. For the stubbed case, the impact for disabling prefetchers is negligible as expected, and two versions with different number of neighbors per atom (76 and 1024) are shown to evaluate the overhead contribution from control flow divergence. With unsteadier memory accesses, the average cycles grows by 2.1 (4%) in standard case and 1.3 (3%) in melting case with all prefetchers, a similar behavior with only the hardware prefetcher enabled, which makes it the most effective one. From 76 to 1024 neighbors per atom, the number of cycles decreases by about 5.8 (15%), hence control flow divergence contribution is higher than latency contribution. Predictions from OSACA and uiCA are too optimistic with only 55% and 68% of best execution, respectively, where IACA prediction matches 92%. IACA reports stalled backend allocation in the CPU due to frontend bubbles, but a frontend model is not present in OSACA. Frontend stalls therefore contribute significantly to kernel throughput, and based on IACA results our stubbed case is close to optimal execution.

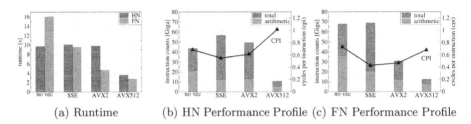

(a) Runtime   (b) HN Performance Profile (c) FN Performance Profile

Fig. 4. Runtime (subfigure (a)), and HPM counter profiling results (Half neighbor-list HN subfigure (b) and full neighbor-list FN subfigure (c)) for the Lennard-Jones copper lattice testcase. Results are shown using compiler flags to enforce no SIMD vectorization, SSE (16b), AVX2 (32b), and AVX512 (64b) SIMD vectorization. In subfigures (b) and (c) the stacked bars show total and arithmetic instruction counts on the left y-axis, the black lines cycles per instruction (CPI) on the right y-axis.

5.3   Compiler Code Quality Study

In this example the Verlet List algorithm with half neighbor-lists (HN) and full neighbor-lists (FN) is benchmarked and profiled to analyze how well these are suited for vectorization and to explain the observed runtimes in more detail. AoS data layout was used with double precision floating point arithmetic. Please note that HN in MD-Bench currently does not implement the Ghost Newton optimization, hence its benefits are not accounted for. This study was performed on the Intel Ice Lake node using the Intel compiler (ICC) 2021.4.0. The force field kernel was compiled for several target SIMD instruction sets and without vectorization using the `-no-vec` option. The compiler requires a `#pragma omp simd` to vectorize the HN variant. The binaries were benchmarked with Turbo mode enabled, all executions were performed in the same cluster node with the same frequency, which was endorsed via HPM measurements.

Figure 4(a) shows the runtime for the standard Copper lattice test case. Without vectorization, the HN variant is as expected faster by almost a factor of two. When using wider SIMD units, FN shows almost linear speed-up and is faster than HN for all SIMD widths. HN gets slower for SSE, stagnates for AVX2, and then improves by a large step with AVX512 but still being 23% slower than FN. For instruction throughput bound codes, the best case uses least instructions combined with optimal pipelined and superscalar execution, improving instruction-level parallelism (ILP in the processor hardware used. Both aspects can be directly measured using HPM counters. Figure 4(b) and Fig. 4(c) show instruction counts and cycles per instruction (CPI) measurements for all HN and FN variants. For HN with SSE it can be seen that the arithmetic instruction count is almost half due to using the SSE 16b registers. Still, the compiler does not manage to reduce the overall instruction count. 29.6% more instructions are required to get the operands into the SIMD registers. The additional instruction work is partially compensated by an improved CPI resulting in only 3.7%

worse runtime. An explanation for this improved CPI is that the register/register SIMD instructions on Intel processors are executed on different scheduler ports than the arithmetic instructions and therefore can be executed out-of-order. The compiler refused to employ 32b arithmetic SIMD instructions in the AVX2 variant, the instruction count was still decreased and the runtime slightly improved. The enhanced capabilities of the AVX512 instruction set extension enables the compiler to generate a version with just 25% of the instruction count of the no-vec variant. The runtime advantage is smaller because this instruction mix is executed with a significantly worse CPI of 1.01. It is still impressive that a code that was impossible to vectorize efficiently with the previous SIMD instruction set extensions now shows an instruction count reduction of a factor of four (out of the optimal eight).

For FN the compiler manages to reduce the arithmetic instruction count with every wider SIMD unit. The overall instruction count increased slighly for SSE, but then is just 45% for AVX2 and 18% for AVX512 compared to the no-vec variant. This underscores that the FN version is very well suited for SIMD vectorization. This kind of study gives interesting insights and is easy to perform. Apart from comparing algorithmic variants it can be applied to different processor architectures focusing on the CPI metric or different compilers focusing on instruction counts. While this type of study can also be done on other proxy-apps or application it is especially easy in MD-Bench, because all kernels are already instrumented for LIKWID.

6   Conclusion and Outlook

This paper introduced MD-Bench, a proxy-app toolbox for performance research of MD algorithms. It facilitates and encourages performance related research and provides clean implementations of state-of-the-art MD optimization schemes such as Verlet List and GROMACS MxN. We list and describe the most important MD-Bench features and its differences to other offerings, highlighting its usage on low-level code analysis and investigation of performance implications through profiling with HPM. Further, we support our statements on the applicability of MD-Bench by providing three use case examples that expose interesting insights concerning the performance of short-range classical MD kernels.

MD-Bench is mature and usable, but there are still multiple open points. We want to consider more MD applications as, e.g., NAMD. MD-Bench is currently a CPU-only application with a few OpenMP parallel loops. A competitive distributed memory parallelization based on MPI is one of the next work packages. Another sorely missing part are implementations and specific optimization schemes for GPU accelerators. Work on supporting GPUs has already started but is in an early stage. We hope to encourage others with this paper to participate and contribute to the development of MD-Bench. A project like MD-Bench is an ongoing effort keeping track with recent developments and supporting novel hardware architectures.

Acknowledgements. The authors gratefully acknowledge the scientific support and HPC resources provided by the Erlangen National High Performance Computing Center (NHR@FAU) of the Friedrich-Alexander-Universität Erlangen-Nürnberg (FAU). NHR funding is provided by federal and Bavarian state authorities. NHR@FAU hardware is partially funded by the German Research Foundation (DFG) - 440719683.

References

1. Abel, A., Reineke, J.: A parametric microarchitecture model for accurate basic block throughput prediction on recent intel CPUs. In: ICS 2022. pp. 1–12 (June 2022)
2. Brown, W.M., Kohlmeyer, A., Plimpton, S.J., Tharrington, A.N.: Implementing molecular dynamics on hybrid high performance computers - particle-particle particle-mesh. Computer Physics Communications **183**(3), 449–459 (2012)
3. Edwards, H.C., Trott, C.R.: Kokkos: Enabling performance portability across manycore architectures. In: 2013 Extreme Scaling Workshop (xsw 2013). pp. 18–24 (Aug 2013)
4. Gecht, M., Siggel, M., Linke, M., Hummer, G., Köfinger, J.: Mdbenchmark: A toolkit to optimize the performance of molecular dynamics simulations. The Journal of Chemical Physics 153(14), 144105 (2020), https://doi.org/10.1063/5.0019045
5. Gratl, F.A., Seckler, S., Tchipev, N., Bungartz, H.J., Neumann, P.: Autopas: Autotuning for particle simulations. In: 2019 IEEE IPDPSW. pp. 748–757 (2019)
6. Intel: Intel architecture code analyzer (Aug 2019), https://www.intel.com/content/www/us/en/developer/articles/tool/architecture-code-analyzer.html
7. Laukemann, J., Hammer, J., Hofmann, J., Hager, G., Wellein, G.: Automated instruction stream throughput prediction for intel and amd microarchitectures. In: 2018 IEEE/ACM PMBS. pp. 121–131 (2018)
8. Machado, R.R.L., Schmitt, J., Eibl, S., Eitzinger, J., Leißa, R., Hack, S., Pérard-Gayot, A., Membarth, R., Köstler, H.: tinymd: Mapping molecular dynamics simulations to heterogeneous hardware using partial evaluation. Journal of Computational Science **54**, 101425 (2021)
9. Pennycook, S.J., Hughes, C.J., Smelyanskiy, M., Jarvis, S.: Exploring simd for molecular dynamics, using intel® xeon® processors and intel® xeon phi coprocessors. In: 2013 IEEE 27th IPDPS. pp. 1085–1097 (2013)
10. Plimpton, S.: Fast parallel algorithms for short-range molecular dynamics. Journal of Computational Physics **117**(1), 1–19 (1995)
11. Páll, S., Hess, B.: A flexible algorithm for calculating pair interactions on simd architectures. Computer Physics Communications **184**(12), 2641–2650 (2013)
12. van der Spoel, D., Lindahl, E., Hess, B., Groenhof, G., Mark, A.E., Berendsen, H.J.C.: GROMACS: fast, flexible, and free. Journal of Computational Chemistry **26**(16), 1701–1718 (2005)
13. Treibig, J., Hager, G., Wellein, G.: Likwid: A lightweight performance-oriented tool suite for x86 multicore environments. In: Proceedings of PSTI2010, the First International Workshop on Parallel Software Tools and Tool Infrastructures. San Diego CA (2010)

Breaking Down the Parallel Performance of GROMACS, a High-Performance Molecular Dynamics Software

Måns I. Andersson$^{(\boxtimes)}$ (ID), Natarajan Arul Murugan, Artur Podobas, and Stefano Markidis

KTH Royal Institute of Technology, Stockholm, Sweden
`mansande@kth.se`

Abstract. GROMACS is one of the most widely used HPC software packages using the Molecular Dynamics (MD) simulation technique. In this work, we quantify GROMACS parallel performance using different configurations, HPC systems, and FFT libraries (FFTW, Intel MKL FFT, and FFT PACK). We break down the cost of each GROMACS computational phase and identify non-scalable stages, such as MPI communication during the 3D FFT computation when using a large number of processes. We show that the Particle-Mesh Ewald phase and the 3D FFT calculation significantly impact the GROMACS performance. Finally, we discuss performance opportunities with a particular interest in developing GROMACS for the FFT calculations.

Keywords: Molecular Dynamics · Particle-Mesh Ewald Calculations · Fast-Fourier Transform

1 Introduction

Molecular Dynamics (MD) [8] is the use of computer simulations to study the physical system particle dynamics and interactions. Today, this technique is widely used in different scientific domains, such as biochemistry and material science, among many others. In particular, the MD software landscape is dominated by a number of well known HPC codes, including GROMACS [18], NAMD [14], and CHARMM [4].

In this work, we investigate the GROMACS parallel performance. GRO-MACS originated in the early 1990s s at the University of Groningen [2] and has since then been developed and maintained as a community effort. It supports an open-source policy and, among its many strengths, can be executed on a large number of systems, including small (personal) laptops all the way to large high-performance computers (HPC) [1]. Furthermore, GROMACS supports both general-purpose processors (CPUs) as well as Graphics Processing Units (GPUs) [12]. However, despite the continuous improvement in hardware technologies, GROMACS (and other MD frameworks) are still challenged - from the computational point of view - to simulate critical biological processes such

R. Wyrzykowski et al. (Eds.): PPAM 2022, LNCS 13826, pp. 333–345, 2023.
https://doi.org/10.1007/978-3-031-30442-2_25

as protein folding, conformational transition in bio-molecules (such as R to T transition in Hemoglobin), bacterial and viral infections [3,5]. These simulations require the usage of supercomputers and accelerators. Needless to say, GRO-MACS is constantly developed and extended to improve its parallel efficiency as well as algorithmic improvements [13] to facilitate the study of larger and more complex molecular simulations.

This paper seeks to understand the GROMACS parallel performance and identify optimization possibilities. For this reason, we run GROMACS on two state-of-the-art HPC systems, analyze their results, and identify key performance-limiting characteristics. In short, our contributions are:

1. A quantitative and systematic performance evaluation of GROMACS on two HPC systems.
2. We study the impact of different GROMACS phases' implementations, varying the number of processes. We quantify their different impact on the overall GROMACS performance and analyze their respective performance-degrading contribution. For a different number of processes, we identify various optimization opportunities.
3. We quantify the performance impact of using various FFT libraries.

2 Background

MD simulations mimic the dynamics of molecules by numerically solving the equation of particles' motion using Verlet or leap-frog algorithms. To determine each particle's new position and velocities, we need to calculate the force acting on each particle. Examples of such forces are the van der Walls and the Coulombic forces. While the cost of particle position and velocity calculations scale with the number of particles under study, a naïve algorithm for the calculation of the forces requires calculating the contribution to the force for each pair of particles present in the system, making the computation scaling as the square of the number of particles present in the system. To decrease the computational complexity of force calculations, modern MD algorithms divide the interactions between the molecules into short-range interactions, such as the ones from van der Waals interactions, and long-range interactions, such as electrostatic interactions. For instance, van der Waals forces are short-range in nature and decay with distance rapidly. Short-range interactions are only computed for the neighboring particles within a cut-off distance, usually 15–20 Å for many applications. The force contribution from particles farther than the cut-off distance is neglected, effectively reducing the interaction of one particle to the closest particles only. However, the electrostatic interactions are long-range in nature, and farther particles contribute to its calculations, still requiring $O(N^2)$ calculations.

Modern MD codes, such as GROMACS, use the Particle-Mesh Ewald (PME) method to solve this problem. The basic strategy of the PME technique is to discretize the simulation domain in a uniform computational grid and calculate the charge density for each grid point, for instance, using interpolation functions. After the charge density on the grid points is known, the Poisson Equation

$\nabla^2 \Phi = -\rho/\epsilon_0$ is solved on the grid for the electrostatic potential Φ and the electric field (still on the grid points) is calculated from it as $E = -\nabla\Phi$. The electric field information on the grid is transferred to the particle by using again interpolation functions. The PME method use FFT to solve the Poisson equation for electrostatic potential on the grid: we transform first the charge density information to the spectral space, we solve the Poisson equation in the spectral space as an algebraic equation (multiplication in spectral space), and then apply an inverse FFT to calculate the potential in the real-space. The PME method also accounts for force contributions arising from periodic infinite systems, such as the typical systems studied with MD, by working in the spectral spaces. In the PME method, 1D FFT (and the inverse 1D FFT) requires $O(N_g \log N_g)$, where N_g is the number of grid points. We first use a 3D FFT on a real data input (the charge density) to calculate the electrostatic potential. After the convolution, we apply a 3D FFT to move the potential to the physical space.

GROMACS divides the calculations at different parallelization levels, ranging from MPI to OpenMP, CUDA, and CPU vector instructions. At a high level, **GROMACS uses a pipelined parallelism** with two main phases: the Particle-Particle (PM) and PME calculations. GROMACS allows dividing the MPI processes into PME processes dedicated only to PME and PP phase responsible for all the other calculations, such as computing the particle dynamics and short-range interactions. The two phases can run in parallel and typically on different kinds of resources, such as different nodes, cores, or devices. To finish a GROMACS computational cycle, the PME phase needs to be completed. This synchronization might introduce a delay in the simulation (causing an idle time on the PP processes) and load imbalance if the PP and PME phases are not finishing at the same time. Naturally, the number of PP and PME MPI processes impacts the load balance and the performance. In GROMACS, the choice of the number of processes dedicated to PME and PP calculations can be set by using the command line (via -npme option) or can be set by GROMACS in preparation for a simulation by an auto-tuning tool: gmx tune_pme (which is not to be confused with the PME tuning done at run-time). GROMACS allocates 1:3 or 1:2 ranks for the PME and PP computations based on the domain if left unspecified by the user. In this study, we set the ratio of PME to PP equal to 1:3.

The GROMACS PME performance largely depends on six major components [15]. If we focus on PME calculations, we identify the six major phases as:

1. **Redistribution of positions and forces (X/F).** This phase redistributes atoms, parameters, and coordinates before each 3D FFT calculation.
2. **Spread.** Using interpolation functions (often called window functions), such as p-th order b-spline, the charges of the particles are distributed on the uniform grid.
3. **1D FFT calculations.** The distributed forward and backward 3D FFT is done with a GROMACS specific 1D or 2D FFT factorization. Currently, GROMACS allows the use of three different FFT libraries when calculating

the FFT on CPU, namely FFTW3 [6], FFTMKL, FFTPACK [17] for the PME computation.

4. **3D FFT communication.** These costs relate to parallel communication performed during the transpose operations during the 3D FFT operations. In GROMACS, this is achieved either by a `MPI_Alltoall` or by FFTW transpose operation if the FFTW's 3D library is used on a single node. When the 3D FFT size in the domain x-direction is evenly divisible by the number of PME ranks, a 2D decomposition is used, which requires less communication than a 1D decomposition.

5. **Solution of the Electric Field.** In this step, we perform the calculation of the electrostatic force by differentiating the electrostatic energy.

6. **Gather.** The potential (force or energy) is evaluated at the target particles with the same interpolation functions as in the spreading step.

7. **Leonard-Jones.** Leonard-Jones is a commonly used potential. It is not used in this paper because it is not possible to run this step on GPU systems at the moment.

3   Related Work

Given the importance of GROMACS for MD studies, there is a history of benchmarking the throughput of GROMACS. Ref. [7] discusses optimal GROMACS configuration for a given problem on a given cluster. An additional performance and benchmark analysis on the SuperMUC supercomputer is Ref. [11]. Ref. [13] presents the future of GROMACS development and discusses the limitations of performance due to PME's limited scaling. As the PME and FFT limit the strong scalability, new algorithmic advancements, such as the use of the Fast Multipole Method (FMM) for MD [19] are pursued.

4   Methodology

This work quantifies GROMACS parallel performance using different configurations, HPC systems, and FFT libraries (FFTW, Intel MKL FFT, and FFT PACK). We break down the cost of each GROMACS computational phase and identify non-scalable stages. The performance evaluation uses test cases that are similar to production runs. To better explain the scaling of the different components, we turn load balancing and PME tuning off. We evaluate the impact of the PME calculations and associated FFTs using two basic configurations, presented in Table 1. The first system, simulating Lysozyme in water, is a relatively small benchmark system in terms of grid points and the number of particles: the 3D grid consists of $44 \times 44 \times 44$, and there are 35,000 atoms. Instead, the second configuration represents a simulation of the Spike protein. In this case, the grid points are $108 \times 144 \times 144$, and the number of atoms is 850,000. The number of particles is 35,000 and 0.85 million approximately for the two configurations. In particular, the viral Spike protein studied here is involved in the interaction with the host cell receptor called hACE-2 and is responsible for the first phase of viral infection and is one of the potential viral targets for developing Covid-19 therapeutics.

Table 1. Specifications for the use cases

MD system	Lysozyme in water	Spike protein: ACE-2
# atoms	35 000	0.85 M
Time step [fs]	0.002	0.002
Domain size [nm]	7 ×7 ×7	17 ×21 ×23
Cut-off radii [nm]	1	1
PME grid [nm]	0.16	0.16
PME interpolation order	4	4
Steps (Beskow)	5 000	5 000
(Tetralith)	100 000	100 000

To characterize the performance of FFT libraries on a large scale, we evaluate the CPU code on two systems. For CPU evaluations, we use a system called "Beskow" and one called "Tetralith" with CPU FFT libraries (FFTW, MKL, and FFTPACK). In addition to two supercomputers, we evaluate the GROMACS performance on GPUs; we use a cluster called "Kebnekaise" and a workstation called "NJ" with cuFFT. We note that the PP and PME phases are highly intertwined on GPU, and a clear separation of the phases is challenging (for this reason, we limit the study on GPU to the total performance). We summarize the configurations of the systems in Table 2.

Table 2. The hardware architecture of our evaluation platforms.

Name	CPU	RAM	GPU	Compiler Env.
Beskow	2x Intel Xeon E5-2698v3	64 GB	-	GCC 10.3, Intel 19.1, HT on, OpenMPI
Tetralith	2x Intel Xeon Gold 6130	96 GB	-	GCC 7, HT off,
Kebnekaise	2x Intel Xeon Gold 6132	192 GB	2 x NVIDIA V100	GNU 10.3, CUDA 11.3
	2x Intel Xeon E5-2690v4	128 GB	2, 4 x NVIDIA K80	
NJ	AMD EPYC 7302P		2 x NVIDIA A100	GNU, CUDA 11.3

All simulations were performed with GROMACS 2021.3. We compile GROMACS using the optimal settings, as advised in the user guide. We build FFTW from the source. In particular, we specify to use single-precision compute. We also enable vectorization by specifying `GMX_SIMD=AVX2_256` on Beskow and `GMX_SIMD=AVX_512` on Tetralith. We use the GNU compiler collections on all platforms combined with CUDA when GPU is used. MKL's FFT was compiled with the Intel compiler.

The figures of merit we use in this paper are the total execution time and nanoseconds (ns) per day. This last metric is how many nanoseconds can be simulated within a day of the simulation and represents the total GROMACS throughput. Each simulation is performed ten times on Beskow and five times on Tetralith, showing a high standard deviation. The figures consist of the mean (median) of these simulations. The simulation parameters are: `-notunepme -dlb no` and for the GPU `-notunepme -dlb no -nb gpu -update -gpu`.

Furthermore, to minimize the effects of congestion and impact from the network topology (explained in detail in [16]), every job evaluates all FFT libraries with the same node configuration. This is not done for the Tetralith simulations. On both Beskow and Tetralith, we run with two OpenMP threads per MPI rank, and on Beskow, hyperthreading is turned on by default.

5   Results

As the first step of our study, we analyze the GROMACS parallel performance. Figure 1 shows a tracing of a GROMACS run instrumented with Score-P [9] and visualized with the Vampir tool [10]. In this run, four processes (with thread numbers 5, 11, 17 and 23) are dedicated to the PME calculations, while there are 20 PP processes. Within the PME processes, the all-to-all communication is reduced to only four processes decreasing the communication cost for the transposition in the 3D FFT. It is important to note that the PP processes wait for the PME processes to finish in this run, and the PME calculations dominate the computational time step. We can also observe that the PME ranks are severely imbalanced as the 1D FFT calculations (blue) in rank 17 is much slower than the corresponding calculations in rank 5 and 11.

We investigate the total impact of PME calculations on the GROMACS' total execution time. Figure 2 shows the fraction of simulation time spent in the PME calculations with respect to the PP time and the total time, varying the total number of cores per GROMACS simulation.

The left panel presents the strong scaling results for the Lysozyme simulations (small-size problem). In this case, the simulation scales up to 256 cores then we observe an increase in the simulation time for 512 cores. In this case, more than 90% of the simulation is spent on MPI communication. We note that the switch from a PP-dominated to PME-dominated simulations appears around 128 cores. In fact, PP scales well beyond 512 cores. There is a significant imbalance between PP and PME. This imbalance can be seen by inspecting the difference between the slowest PP and PME and the total time. The right panel of Fig. 2 presents the results for the Spike strong scaling test. In this case, we observe strong scaling up to 2,048 cores. The simulation is bound by PP up to 256 cores and limited by PME beyond that. We note that PP keeps scaling like in the Lyso case.

After identifying PME as the main obstacle to strong scalability, we analyze which parts of the PME calculations show performance bottleneck and are amenable to performance optimization. Figure 3 presents a breakdown of the different phases during the PME calculations on the Beskow system with FFTW (the right panel shows the percentage to ease the comparison).

From an analysis of the plots, we note that when a small number of cores are dedicated to PME calculation, the PME spread and gather operations accounts

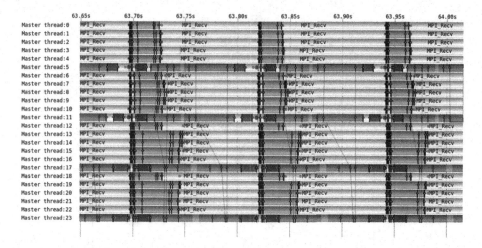

Fig. 1. Tracing of a GROMACS run with 24 processes using ScoreP and Vampir tools. Four processes (three visible) complete the PME calculations in this run, while twenty processes quickly carry out the PP calculations. The PP processes wait for the PME processes to finish. We can also see a significant load imbalance between the PME ranks. The dark red is `MPI_Alltoall` (Color figure online) for FFT communication. All other MPI calls are light red. The green color represents the general compute, dark green is gather, blue is 1D FFT, purple is spread, and turquoise is the convolution calculation.

for most of the time. On the contrary, for a larger number of cores, e.g., more than 256 PME cores, the communication for the 3D FFT (parallel transpose) and PME redistribution time dominate the PME calculation and, therefore, the whole simulation time. These two PME phases are responsible for losing scalability at large numbers of the core. Spread and Gather also level out at high core counts but at a lower total cost. At peak performance of the PME calculation, 50% of the time is spent on 3D FFT calculation, and most of that is communication.

An interesting question for GROMACS users is what performance improvement can be achieved by changing the FFT library and what is the best performing one in GROMACS. We compare the results for three PME phases (3D-FFT communication, PME 3D-FFT, and PME redistribution X/F) for different 1D FFT libraries. The results are shown in Fig. 4.

As expected, we do not observe any significant performance change in the communication cost as GROMACS handles the communication, and it remains the same regardless of the library in use. Yet, we notice a difference in individual FFT performance. While for a small number of core counts, FFTW and MKL perform equally well, for a more significant number of cores, the FFT, built with GNU compilers, provides the best performance on Beskow. We also notice that the 3D FFT communication and redistribution measurements are noisy. We also note that the different clusters perform significantly differently: the Tetralith

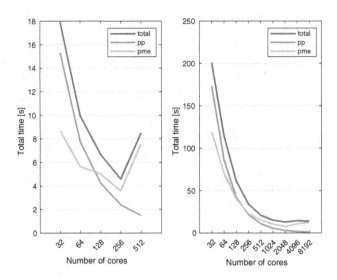

Fig. 2. The fraction of time for PME, PP, and execution time on the Beskow system varying the total number of cores, to the left the Lysozyme system and to the right the Spike system. 1/4 of the cores are dedicated to the PME calculations. In this case, we use FFTW as the FFT library. Due to a lack of complete overlap and synchronization costs, the total execution is longer than each component phase duration.

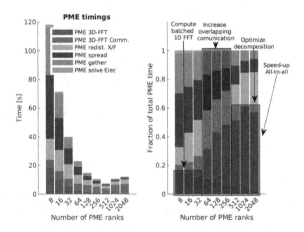

Fig. 3. The left panel shows the strong scaling results for the different parts of PME for the Spike test case. The right panel present the PME time as a fraction of its components. The experiment was performed on Beskow, and the optimization phases are highlighted.

results communication results show a significant performance variability in Fig. 4. We also note that MKL is slightly faster than FFTW.

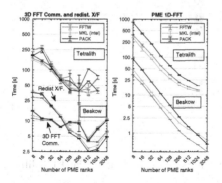

Fig. 4. To the left: Strong scaling for the parts of PME with worst scaling on CPU for Spike on Beskow and Tetralith. To the right: The strong scaling of the FFT calculation. Note that the time (y-axis) does not align between plots.

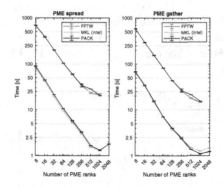

Fig. 5. Strong scaling of the Gather (left) and Spread (right), top three lines are from Tetralith bottom three lines are from Beskow. The simulation uses 4th order interpolation.

We present the strong scaling behavior of the interpolation steps in Fig. 5. We notice that the scaling stops at approximately 512 cores for these parts, similar to the FFT communication and redistribution. However, it only displays a reduced performance variability after scaling breaks down compared with the parallel transpose and redistribution. We note that the gather and spread phases make up only 20% of the total PME calculation after they have stopped scaling.

The total performance of the PME calculations, varying FFT libraries, can be seen in Fig. 6. It shows the diminishing effects of the 1D FFT compute and

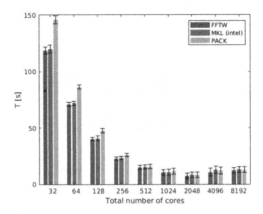

Fig. 6. The total time for PME depending of the FFT library on Beskow with the Spike case.

the increasing performance variability coming from the communication with an increased number of cores. It is clear that FFTW and MKL are better choices than FFTPACK and are always motivated choices.

Finally, we analyze the performance of GROMACS PME on GPUs and present the results in Fig. 7. The GPU performance for the Lysozyme test case out-perform the CPU configurations significantly: PME on GPU and bonded calculations on CPU resulted in a throughput of approximately 640 ns/day compared with close to 380 ns/day for 128 CPU cores with FFTW.

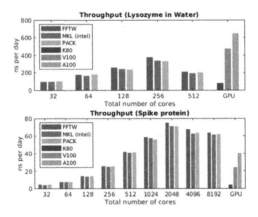

Fig. 7. The total throughput for the different FFT libraries on Beskow (CPU), NJ (Nvidia A100 GPU) and Kebnekaise (Nvidia K80 and V100 GPU).

We observe a slight advantage in using FFTW as the FFT library with a total throughput increase of 10% compared with the other libraries for the small Lysozyme system. In the Spike test case, GROMACS runs on the Nvidia A100 perform comparably to 512 CPU cores on Beskow (46 ns/day) and a bit better than 512 cores on Tetralith (36 ns/day).

6   Discussion and Conclusion

In this paper, we presented an evaluation of GROMACS parallel performance. We conclude that the performance of PME is highly correlated with the parallel transpose and the redist functions. Redist is dependent on the domain decomposition of the PP part of the simulation, and therefore their performance is problem specific. The 3D FFT size can be varied to more accurately solve the Electrostatics or to balance the load. These two are also the parts of the PME calculation with the most variance between runs. We identified three main factors in the GROMACS PME that can be improved. Firstly, there are many classes of problems, such as embarrassingly parallel ensemble jobs or parameter searching jobs, where many simulations can be distributed on many nodes with one job running on a single node. Improving 1D FFT performance for a single node can make noticeable overall performance in such ensemble simulations. Using FFTW or MKL instead of the backup library is advised; FFTW performs twice that of PACK in the spike problem. For the future, a possible further optimization technique is to use batched 1D FFTs parallelized with SIMD vector instructions. Secondly, within the most scalable range, we can see that the cost associated with the interpolation steps and the transpose are similar in size. We would suggest an overlap between the communication needed from Spread-Gather and the parallel transpose. Since the GROMACS CPU code does not depend on an external 3D FFT library, it might be possible to incorporate the interpolation steps and therefore limit the need for communication. Finally, we have the transpose-dominated range – the Achilles' heel of the method.

Acknowledgments. Financial support was provided by the SeRC Exascale Simulation Software Initiative (SESSI) and the DEEP-SEA project. The DEEP-SEA project has received funding from the European Union's Horizon 2020/EuroHPC research and innovation program under grant agreement No 955606. National VR contribution from Sweden matches the EuroHPC funding. The computations of this work were enabled by resources provided by the Swedish National Infrastructure for Computing (SNIC) at HPC2N, partially funded by the Swedish Research Council through grant agreement no. 2018-05973.

References

1. Abraham, M., et al.: GROMACS: high performance molecular simulations through multi-level parallelism from laptops to supercomputers. SoftwareX **1**, 19–25 (2015). https://doi.org/10.1016/j.softx.2015.06.001
2. Berendsen, H.J., van der Spoel, D., van Drunen, R.: GROMACS: a message-passing parallel molecular dynamics implementation. Comput. Phys. Commun. **91**(1–3), 43–56 (1995). https://doi.org/10.1016/0010-4655(95)00042-E
3. Borhani, D.W., Shaw, D.E.: The future of molecular dynamics simulations in drug discovery. J. Comput. Aided Mol. Des. **26**(1), 15–26 (2012). https://doi.org/10.1007/s10822-011-9517-y
4. Brooks, B.R., al.: Charmm: the biomolecular simulation program. J. Comput. chem. **30**(10), 1545–1614 (2009). https://doi.org/10.1002/jcc.21287
5. Elber, R.: Long-timescale simulation methods. Curr. Opin. Struct. Biol. **15**(2), 151–156 (2005). https://doi.org/10.1016/j.sbi.2005.02.004
6. Frigo, M., Johnson, S.G.: The design and implementation of FFTW3. Proc. IEEE **93**(2), 216–231 (2005). https://doi.org/10.1109/JPROC.2004.840301, special issue on "Program Generation, Optimization, and Platform Adaptation"
7. Gruber, C.C., Pleiss, J.: Systematic benchmarking of large molecular dynamics simulations employing GROMACS on massive multiprocessing facilities. J. Comput. Chem. **32**(4), 600–606 (2011). https://doi.org/10.1002/jcc.21645
8. Karplus, M., McCammon, J.A.: Molecular dynamics simulations of biomolecules. Nat. Struct. Biol. **9**(9), 646–652 (2002). https://doi.org/10.1038/nsb0902-646
9. Knüpfer, A., et al.: Score-p: a joint performance measurement run-time infrastructure for periscope, scalasca, TAU, and vampir. In: Brunst, H., Muller, M., Nagel, W., Resch, M. (eds.) Tools for High Performance Computing 2011, pp. 79–91. Springer, Berlin (2012). https://doi.org/10.1007/978-3-642-31476-6_7
10. Knüpfer, A., et al.: The vampir performance analysis tool-set. In: Tools for High Performance Computing, pp. 139–155. Springer, Berlin (2008). https://doi.org/10.1007/978-3-540-68564-7_9
11. Kutzner, C., Apostolov, R., Hess, B., Grubmuller, H.: Scaling of the GROMACS 4.6 molecular dynamics code on superMUC. Adv. Parallel Comput. **25**, 722–727 (2014). https://doi.org/10.3233/978-1-61499-381-0-722
12. Kutzner, C., Páll, S., Fechner, M., Esztermann, A., de Groot, B.L., Grubmuller, H.: More bang for your buck: Improved use of GPU nodes for GROMACS 2018. J. Comput. Chem. **40**(27), 2418–2431 (2019). https://doi.org/10.1002/jcc.26011
13. Páll, S., Abraham, M.J., Kutzner, C., Hess, B., Lindahl, E.: Tackling Exascale software challenges in molecular dynamics simulations with GROMACS. In: Markidis, S., Laure, E. (eds.) EASC 2014. LNCS, vol. 8759, pp. 3–27. Springer, Cham (2015). https://doi.org/10.1007/978-3-319-15976-8_1
14. Phillips, J.C., et al.: Scalable molecular dynamics with NAMD. J. Comput. Chem. **26**(16), 1781–1802 (2005). https://doi.org/10.1002/jcc.20289
15. Shamshirgar, D.S., Hess, B., Tornberg, A.K.: A comparison of the spectral EWALD and smooth particle mesh EWALD methods in GROMACS. arXiv preprint arXiv:1712.04718 (2017). 10.48550/arXiv.1712.04718
16. Smith, S.A., Cromey, C.E., Lowenthal, D.K., Domke, J., Jain, N., Thiagarajan, J.J., Bhatele, A.: Mitigating inter-job interference using adaptive flow-aware routing. In: SC 2018: International Conference for High Performance Computing, Networking, Storage and Analysis (2018). https://doi.org/10.1109/SC.2018.00030

17. Swarztrauber, P.N.: Vectorizing the FFTs. In: Rodrigue, G. (ed.) Parallel Computations, pp. 51–83. Academic Press (1982). https://doi.org/10.1016/B978-0-12-592101-5.50007-5
18. Van Der Spoel, D., Lindahl, E., Hess, B., Groenhof, G., Mark, A.E., Berendsen, H.J.: Gromacs: fast, flexible, and free. J. Comput. Chem. **26**(16), 1701–1718 (2005). https://doi.org/10.1002/jcc.20291
19. Yokota, R., Barba, L.A.: A tuned and scalable fast multipole method as a preeminent algorithm for exascale systems. Int. J. High Perform. Comput. Appl. **26**(4), 337–346 (2012). https://doi.org/10.1177/1094342011429952

GPU-Based Molecular Dynamics
of Turbulent Liquid Flows with OpenMM

Daniil Pavlov[1,2]([✉])[iD], Daniil Kolotinskii[1,2][iD], and Vladimir Stegailov[1,2,3][iD]

[1] Joint Institute for High Temperatures of RAS, Moscow, Russian Federation
[2] Moscow Institute of Physics and Technology (National Research University),
Dolgoprudny, Russian Federation
pavlov.dg@phystech.edu
[3] National Research University Higher School of Economics, Moscow, Russian
Federation

Abstract. In this paper we describe the computational framework for
GPU-based molecular dynamics of turbulent flows. The framework is
based on the open-source molecular dynamics library OpenMM. The
implementation of a special type of open boundary conditions is presented together with a generic case of a turbulent flow of Lennard-
Jones liquid. We compare the computational efficiency of OpenMM with
another popular MD library LAMMPS and other legacy MD programs
used for studying turbulence.

Keywords: Molecular dynamics · Liquid flows · GPU computing ·
OpenMM · LAMMPS · KOKKOS · Performance portability

1 Introduction

Classical molecular dynamics (MD) simulation method is a key research tool in
many areas of science and engineering. The first attempts to use MD to study
microscopic details of turbulent flows date back to the late 1980s (e.g. see [28]).
Nowadays MD is one of the major consumers of supercomputer resources worldwide. The development of MD tools that enable ultra-long MD trajectories and
extreme MD system sizes is one of the important vectors of development for high
performance computing methods [33]. Shortly after the Nvidia CUDA technology had been introduced in 2007, hybrid MD algorithms appeared and showed
their promising performance. Currently, GPU-accelerated hardware provides the
most efficient and affordable way of doing MD studies [18,20,21,32] and makes
various applied MD studies feasible.

The emergence of parallel distributed memory supercomputing systems stim-
ulated the development of parallel algorithms for MD calculations. Among others, LAMMPS [34] and GROMACS [5] are two MD packages that have developed into complex simulation packages and are widely used nowadays. Since the
emergence of general-purpose computing on graphics processing units (GPGPU),
both packages have been supplemented with GPU offloading capabilities [3,6–8].
Newer MD libraries like HOOMD [4,12] and OpenMM [9,11] use GPU-oriented

R. Wyrzykowski et al. (Eds.): PPAM 2022, LNCS 13826, pp. 346–358, 2023.
https://doi.org/10.1007/978-3-031-30442-2_26

MD algorithms that are designed in a way that keeps the amount of CPU-GPU communication to an absolute minimum.

In this work, we describe our OpenMM based framework based for modelling turbulent flows. We propose a novel implementation of open boundary conditions, demonstrate a working OpenMM based implementation of such boundary conditions and compare the performance of OpenMM and the KOKKOS GPU backend of LAMMPS for very large system sizes.

2 Related Work

With the rise of supercomputing capabilities in 2000s, molecular dynamics calculations at extreme length scales were considered in LANL as a tool that is able to complement Navier-Stokes-based continuum fluid-simulation methods [17]. A special MD package ls1 mardyn focused on extreme length scales is under development [33] and used for the corresponding multiscale simulations [14,15].

The paper of E. R. Smith provided a detailed description of MD modelling of a turbulent flow [30] with the details about computational efficiency of the MD algorithm deployed using the SGI Altix ICE 8200 EX supercomputer with manycore CPUs and Infiniband interconnect. Below, we compare the data of [30] with our results for modern GPUs.

The coupling between CFD and MD algorithms is under active development: for example, Grinberg et al. discuss the coupling of Navier-Stokes equations with particle-based models [13,26], Smith et al. described such a coupling for OpenFOAM and LAMMPS [31].

3 Software: OpenMM as a Flexible MD Framework

As a part of this work, we implemented a new kind of boundary conditions using the OpenMM library.

OpenMM [11] is an open source toolkit for molecular dynamics. With its main focus being computational biology, it still performs remarkably well on other systems. This is achieved because unlike the high-level OpenMM Application Layer Python API [24], which is built around domain-specific constructs such as force fields, residue chains and topologies, OpenMM Library Level C++/Python API [25] is completely divorced from such constructs and provides a lower-level access to the underlying structures that can be used in a broader range of applications.

OpenMM supports four platforms: Reference, CPU, CUDA, OpenCL. There's also an ongoing effort [16] to add HIP to the list. Both CUDA and OpenCL are GPU-oriented platforms, and they provide the best performance. The underlying algorithms that are used in these platforms are almost identical, with most of the code having been merged into a meta-platform called Common Compute. Here, we focus on the CUDA platform, implying that OpenCL and HIP operate in mostly the same way.

When parallelizing over a big amount of processing units, there are three wide classes of approaches [27]: atom-decomposition, force-decomposition and domain-decomposition. For distributing workload *inside* a GPU, OpenMM uses a force-decomposition-like algorithm [10]: for N atoms, the N × N force matrix is divided into 'tiles' of size 32×32. Then, only the tiles that might contain non-zero forces are marked as 'interacting' based on comparing the tiles' coordinate bounds. Then, the list of interacting tiles is traversed to calculate forces and energy. Once the tiles' bounds change to a point that new interactions might appear, the list of interacting tiles is rebuilt.

There are a few important quirks of this algorithm that must be accounted for: first, due to the SIMT architecture of GPU execution, it does not matter whether there's only one pair of atoms interacting within a tile or all atoms are interacting with the other, the tile will take the same time to compute in either case. This suggests that the amount of interacting tiles should be brought to a minimum: either most atoms should interact within a tile, or none. Such an effect is achieved by making atoms 'spatially coherent': when atoms within a tile all lie close to each other, there are more interactions per tile and therefore fewer tiles. To achieve the 'spatial coherence', every 250 steps atoms are reordered along a Hilbert curve [22]. This does not eliminate the inherent possibility that there might still be tiles with only a few interactions, so the tiles that still are not "dense" are not processed as a whole, but split into individual atoms that are processed separately.

The second important quirk of this algorithm is its complexity: traversing an N × N force matrix has the complexity of $\mathcal{O}(N^2)$. This means that this algorithm is not infinitely scalable: at some point the rapidly increasing cost of finding interacting tiles would outweigh the benefits of being able to simulate bigger systems. The question is how soon. Current limitations restrict the use of OpenMM to systems with about $10^7 - 10^8$ atoms.

In this work we also compare the OpenMM performance with the LAMMPS backend based on KOKKOS. KOKKOS [35] is an open-source performance portability parallel programming library. With LAMMPS being a go-to tool for molecular dynamics in materials science, and KOKKOS being the highest performance LAMMPS backend so far, it is only reasonable to use it as a baseline when measuring performance of other packages.

4   Constant Temperature Open Boundary Conditions

When running MD simulations, it is impossible to simulate a macroscopic system due to its enormous amount of particles. So it is common practice to simulate a small system as a part of the whole by putting it in periodic boundary conditions (PBC). This approach imitates an isotropic, uniform system, acting under the assumption that the system looks the same everywhere. However, this is not the case for stationary flows: whenever viscosity is present, there is a pressure gradient that counteracts this viscosity. The presence of the pressure gradient introduces anisotropicity and makes the simple PBC unfit for this purpose. This problem can be addressed in a number of ways: for example, by introducing moving walls to create Couette flow [30], or by reintroducing particles that left the cell with a reset velocity [28]. In this paper, we expand upon the latter method. The Open Boundary Conditions (OBC) that we introduce are a special kind of boundary conditions that resembles PBC, but resets particles' velocities whenever they cross a z-axis boundary.

For simplicity, we assume that all particles in the system are the same, with a mass of m, and that the system is an ideal gas. Let us consider the Boltzmann equation:

$$\frac{\partial f(\mathbf{r}, \mathbf{v}, t)}{\partial t} + \mathbf{v} \cdot \frac{\partial f(\mathbf{r}, \mathbf{v}, t)}{\partial \mathbf{r}} + \frac{\mathbf{F}_{\text{ext}}}{m} \cdot \frac{\partial f(\mathbf{r}, \mathbf{v}, t)}{\partial \mathbf{v}} = \left.\frac{\partial f}{\partial t}\right|_{\text{coll}}.$$

We wish to create a stationary flow by using some sort of boundary conditions. Since the flow is stationary, the desired density function $f_{\text{obc}}(\mathbf{r}, \mathbf{v})$ does not depend on time. Also, there are no external forces, therefore $\mathbf{F}_{\text{ext}} = 0$. The right-hand side of the equation represents the collision term. Since we assume that the gas is ideal, the collision term represents only the interactions with OBC. The analytical form $s(\mathbf{r}, \mathbf{v})$ of this term shall dictate the exact behavior of OBC:

$$s(\mathbf{r}, \mathbf{v}) = \mathbf{v} \frac{\partial}{\partial \mathbf{r}} f_{\text{obc}}(\mathbf{r}, \mathbf{v}).$$

Say the left-side boundary is situated at plane $z = z_1$. Particles to the left of the boundary are not simulated directly, but their impact must be somehow approximated. We can outline two kinds of impact that these particles make: first, they interact with particles on the right side, and second, the left and the right side exchange particles. The former impact is sufficiently approximated by PBC in both isotropic and anisotropic systems. The latter one, however, is not: in the case with stationary fluid flow, it is impossible to maintain the pressure gradient with just PBC. The solution we propose is to make OBC emit particles into the right side of the left-side boundary, instead of them naturally coming from the left side. For this, we want to remove all particles with $z < z_1$ and $v_z > 0$ from the initial distribution $f(\mathbf{v})$, while preserving it where $z > z_1$.

$$f_1(\mathbf{r}, \mathbf{v}) = \begin{cases} 0, z < z_1, v_z > 0 \\ f(\mathbf{v}), z < z_1, v_z < 0 \\ f(\mathbf{v}), z > z_1 \end{cases}$$

In other words, we just multiply the initial distribution by some $a_1(z, v_z)$:

$$f_1(\mathbf{r}, \mathbf{v}) = a_1(z, v_z) f(\mathbf{v}) = (\theta(v_z) \theta(z - z_1) + \theta(-v_z)) f(\mathbf{v}).$$

By analogy, for the right-side boundary we can define $a_2(z, v_z)$:

$$f_2(\mathbf{r}, \mathbf{v}) = a_2(z, v_z) f(\mathbf{v}) = (\theta(-v_z) \theta(z_2 - z) + \theta(v_z)) f(\mathbf{v}).$$

By multiplying initial distribution $f(\mathbf{v})$ by both $a_1(z, v_z)$ and $a_2(z, v_z)$, we will get a sector $z_1 < z < z_2$ where all particles that come inside are emitted by OBC:

$$f_{\text{obc}}(\mathbf{r}, \mathbf{v}) = a_1(z, v_z) a_2(z, v_z) f(\mathbf{v}),$$

$$s(\mathbf{r}, \mathbf{v}) = \mathbf{v} \cdot \frac{\partial}{\partial \mathbf{r}} f_{\text{obc}}(\mathbf{r}, \mathbf{v}) = \mathbf{v} \cdot \frac{\partial}{\partial \mathbf{r}} \left(a_1(z, v_z) a_2(z, v_z) f(\mathbf{v}) \right).$$

It is worth noting that $a_1(z, v_z) \frac{\partial}{\partial z} a_2(z, v_z) = \frac{\partial}{\partial z} a_2(z, v_z)$ and $a_2(z, v_z) \frac{\partial}{\partial z} a_1(z, v_z) = \frac{\partial}{\partial z} a_1(z, v_z)$ for any z, v_z, when $z_1 < z_2$.
Then, finally,

$$s(\mathbf{r}, \mathbf{v}) = a(z, v_z) f(\mathbf{v}) = (v_z \theta(v_z) \delta(z - z_1) + v_z \theta(-v_z) \delta(z - z_2)) f(\mathbf{v}).$$

The resulting distribution $f_{\text{obc}}(\mathbf{r}, \mathbf{v})$ fully matches $f(\mathbf{v})$ in the $z_1 < z < z_2$ sector that we're modelling. In other words, if we're working *inside the aforementioned sector*, there is no observable difference whether a system follows the $f_{\text{obc}}(\mathbf{r}, \mathbf{v})$ distribution or the $f(\mathbf{v})$ distribution.

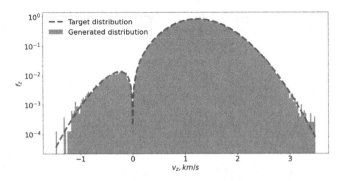

Fig. 1. The distribution generated by our OBC implementation for $v_{\text{flow}} = 1000$ m/s, $T = 2000$ K, $m = 55.845$.

5   Open Boundary Conditions Implementation

The nature of the collision term $a(z, v_z) f(\mathbf{v}) = s(\mathbf{r}, \mathbf{v}) = \left. \frac{\partial f_{\text{obc}}}{\partial t} \right|_{\text{coll}}$ dictates how often, on which side and with what velocity particles are emitted. Our implementation does not change the amount of particles in the system, it only resets their velocities when they hit the periodic border, effectively re-emitting them from an appropriate side with an appropriate velocity, according to the distribution. There is an emergent property that since the flow is stationary, the amount of particles that leave the sector $z_1 < z < z_2$ equals the amount that is emitted. It eliminates the need to change the amount of particles over the course of the simulation.

Once a particle crosses the border, the first thing that needs to be computed is which side it should be re-emitted on (the possibility of the particle being re-emitted is one of the distinguishing traits of our approach; it wasn't accounted for in [28]):

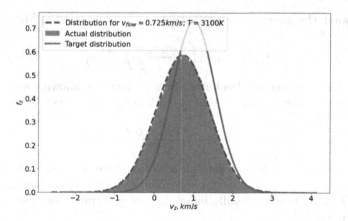

Fig. 2. The speed distribution for a liquid system of Lennard-Jones particles after $\tau = 2$ ns relaxation in OBC, $T = 2000$ K, $m = 55.845$, $v_{flow} = 1000$ m/s. The resulting distribution does not match the desired distribution. Such an effect can be attributed to the fact that the premise that the system is an ideal gas does not hold anymore, therefore causing a shift.

$$p_{\text{left}} = \frac{\iint s(\mathbf{r}, \mathbf{v}) dxdydv\big|_{z=z_1}}{\iint s(\mathbf{r}, \mathbf{v}) d\mathbf{r}d\mathbf{v}} =$$

$$= \frac{\int_{-\infty}^{+\infty} a(z_1, v_z) f_z(v_z) dv_z}{\int_{-\infty}^{+\infty} \int_{-\infty}^{+\infty} a(z, v_z) f_z(v_z) dv_z dz} =$$

$$= \frac{\int_0^{+\infty} v_z f_z(v_z)\, dv_z}{\int_0^{+\infty} v_z f_z(v_z)\, dv_z - \int_{-\infty}^0 v_z f_z(v_z)\, dv_z},$$

$$p_{\text{right}} = 1 - p_{\text{left}}.$$

It's worth noticing that the above formula is agnostic to whether the particle left the cell upstream or downstream.

From now on, let's assume that the particle is emitted from the left side. The new velocities on x and y need only be picked from $f_x(x)$ and $f_y(y)$ distributions (which are just Maxwell distributions in our case). The v_z can be inferred from the following equation, where $\xi_0 \in (0, 1)$ is a uniformly-distributed random number:

$$F(v_z) = \iint s(\mathbf{r}, \mathbf{v}') dxdydv'\bigg|_{z=z_1, v_z' < v_z} = \int_0^{v_z} v_z' f_z(v_z')\, dv_z',$$

$$\xi_0 F(\infty) = F(v_z).$$

Now, we want the underlying distribution $f(\mathbf{v})$ to be a shifted Maxwell distribution:

$$f_z(v_z) \propto \exp\left(-\frac{m(v_z - v_{\text{flow}})^2}{2kT}\right).$$

Then $F(v_z)$ can be computed in terms of error functions, allowing us to solve the equation numerically. We use Newton's method to find the root of the equation:

$$v_{i+1} = v_i - \frac{F(v_i) - \xi_0 F(\infty)}{F'(v_i)}.$$

In our case, the $F(v)$ is a monotonic function with a single inflection point on $(0, +\infty)$, and $F'(0) = F'(+\infty) = 0$. Therefore the best starting point for Newton's method to avoid oscillation and guarantee convergence would be that inflection point:

$$v_0 = -\frac{1}{2}\left(v_{\text{flow}} - \sqrt{v_{\text{flow}}^2 + \frac{4kT}{m}}\right).$$

The illustration of the implementation is shown on Fig. 1 and Fig. 2. The lack of the exact correspondence between the model parameters of the equilibrium values of temperature and flow velocity is due to the non-ideal character of the Lennard-Jones model. This discrepancy does not disqualify the algorithm but requires its preliminary calibration.

Fig. 3. $40 \times 80 \times 1$ grid of vorticity for a small system with an cylindrical obstacle in the middle ($N = 425651$, $T = 2000$ K, $v_{\text{flow}} = 1000$ m/s, $a = 0.0645$ nm, $m = 55.845$, $N_{U(\mathbf{r})} = 6$); the vorticity units are ps^{-1}; the velocity error is $\sigma_{\langle v_x \rangle} \approx 47 \frac{m}{s}$; the vorticity error is $\sigma_\omega = 2\frac{\sigma_{\langle v_x \rangle}}{a N_{U(\mathbf{r})}} \approx 0.14$ ps^{-1}.

6   Grid Aggregation

When processing trajectory data from simulations, it is not always feasible to process it on per-particle basis, and some kind aggregation is necessary. Here, we calculate average velocities on a grid of $N_{\text{cells}} = N_x \times N_y \times N_z$ cells.

One of the principal metrics in analyzing fluid flows is vorticity:

$$\omega = \nabla \times \mathbf{v} = \begin{pmatrix} \partial_x \\ \partial_y \\ \partial_z \end{pmatrix} \times \begin{pmatrix} v_x \\ v_y \\ v_z \end{pmatrix}.$$

Then, by abuse of notation, we can derive a numerical approximation of vorticity for our grid:

$$\omega(\mathbf{r}) = \frac{1}{N_{U(\mathbf{r})}} \sum_{\Delta \mathbf{r} \in U(\mathbf{r})} \left(\begin{pmatrix} 1/\Delta r_x \\ 1/\Delta r_y \\ 1/\Delta r_z \end{pmatrix} \times (\langle \mathbf{v} \rangle (\mathbf{r} + \Delta \mathbf{r}) - \langle \mathbf{v} \rangle (\mathbf{r})) \right).$$

Here, $U(r)$ is a set of neighboring grid cells. One important part is to exclude the terms where $\Delta r_i = 0$ from the average to avoid infinite results.

However, the images obtained using this approximation can be noisy. Indeed, it is not always correct to assume that it is possible to measure a continuous field of values on an atomic level. Next step is quantifying errors of values obtained from averaging on grid cells.

The single-axis Maxwell velocity distribution is:

$$f_x(v_x) = \sqrt{\frac{m}{2\pi kT}} \exp\left(-\frac{m(v_x - \langle v_x \rangle)^2}{2kT} \right),$$

and if there is N particles in total spread over cells with a side of a, then the standard error of velocity, averaged over one cell is

$$\sigma_{\langle v_x \rangle} = \sqrt{\frac{\sigma_{v_x}^2}{N/N_{\text{cells}}}} = \sqrt{\frac{N_{\text{cells}}}{N} \cdot \frac{kT}{m}} = \sqrt{\frac{1}{a^3} \cdot \frac{kT}{\rho}} = \sqrt{\frac{kT}{m_{\text{cell}}}}.$$

When approximating the error of vorticity, the following approximation might be useful:

$$\langle v \rangle (r + \Delta r) - \langle v \rangle (r) \approx \omega a N_{U(\mathbf{r})}.$$

Now, the error of vorticity is:

$$\sigma_\omega = \omega \epsilon_\omega = \omega \cdot \epsilon_{\overline{v}(r+\Delta r) - \overline{v}(r)} = \omega \cdot \frac{2\sigma_{\overline{v_x}}}{|\overline{\mathbf{v}}(r + \Delta r) - \overline{\mathbf{v}}(r)|} \approx 2\frac{\sigma_{\overline{v_x}}}{a N_{U(\mathbf{r})}} = 2\frac{\sqrt{kT}}{a^{5/2} N_{U(\mathbf{r})} \sqrt{\rho}}.$$

An illustration is presented on Fig. 3.

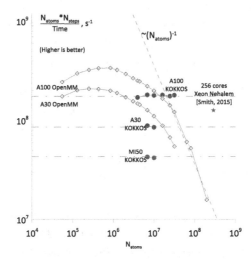

Fig. 4. Benchmark results for the Lennard-Jones liquid. The performance of MD calculations is shown as $N_{atoms}N_{step}$ per unit of wall-clock time. Results for A100, A30 and MI50 GPUs are presented. The rhombs show the data for OpenMM, the circles show the data for KOKKOS backend of LAMMPS. The performance of 256 Intel Xeon Nehalem cores used by Smith [30] for a 300 million atom simulation is shown as a star.

7   Performance Analysis

The analysis presented in this work is based on the data obtained on 3 models of GPUs: Nvidia A100 in the cHARISMa supercomputer [19] and Nvidia A30 and AMD MI50 in the Desmos supercomputer [29] (see Table 1).

Table 1. The specifications of the GPUs considered in this work.

	AMD MI50	Nvidia A30	Nvidia A100
Memory size	32 GB	24 GB	80 GB
Memory bandwidth	1 TB/s	0.9 TB/s	2 TB/s
FP32 performance	13.3 TFLOPS	10.3 TFLOPS	19.5 TFLOPS
FP64 performance	6.6 TFLOPS	5.2 TFLOPS	9.7 TFLOPS

Both libraries were built in the "Release" mode. Precision was set to mixed in OpenMM, and to double in LAMMPS/KOKKOS (due to the fact that the mixed precison is not supported by KOKKOS). The runtimes used were: cuda-11.7 for A100, nvhpc-21.9 for A30, rocm-5.0.0 for MI50. OpenMM was not benchmarked on MI50 because its HIP implementation is still highly experimental.

Currently, the master branch of OpenMM uses 32-bit counters for storing tile indices. This makes it impossible to correctly run systems bigger than ~ 30

million atoms. However, in this work, a patch has been developed to change the counters to 64-bit. This allowed benchmarking bigger systems.

The benchmarks were carried out for a Lennard-Jones system with $\sim 10^2$ neighbors per atom (Argon fluid at $T = 1500$ K, initial configuration is an FCC lattice with $a = 5.376$ Å and $r_{\text{cutoff}} = 13$ Å). Since the best achievable algorithmic complexity of molecular dynamics is $\mathcal{O}(N_{\text{atoms}} * N_{\text{steps}})$, we use $\frac{N_{\text{atoms}} * N_{\text{steps}}}{\text{Time}}$ as a performance metric. Then we can say that a library "scales well" if this performance metric remains at the same level as the amount of atoms grows, and that a library '"scales poorly" if this performance metric drops. Time measurements were taken for $N_{\text{steps}} = 50000$ for small systems, gradually decreasing to $N_{\text{steps}} = 250$ for the biggest systems.

Comparison of KOKKOS performance on MI50, A30 and A100 shows that the difference between A100 and A30 is about 2x and can be explained by about 2x lower peak performance and 2x lower memory bandwidth of A30. However, there is practically no difference between A30 and MI50 in terms of peak performance and memory bandwidth. That is why their performance difference should be attributed to the lack of hardware support of fp64 atomic operations in MI50 (KOKKOS relies heavily on atomic operations).

OpenMM results for A100 show its superiority over KOKKOS for system sizes up to 10 million particles. For larger system sizes the $\mathcal{O}(N^2)$ becomes the dominating factor in OpenMM's performance, whereas KOKKOS' algorithmic complexity is $\mathcal{O}(N)$, allowing it to surpass OpenMM at high values of N.

For the sake of comparison it is instructive to list the performance features of the SGI Altix ICE 8200 EX supercomputer partition used in [30]: 256 Xeon Nehalem cores correspond to 64 4-core Xeon Nehalem CPUs that give in aggregation 2 TB/s of memory bandwidth and 3 TFlops/sec DP. Figure 4 shows that the performance point based on the data from [30] corresponds qualitatively well to the performance of the KOKKOS backend of LAMMPS/KOKKOS on A30 and A100 GPUs (the MD model with the Lennard-Jones potential is a memory bound problem [23]).

An important difference between OpenMM and LAMMPS/KOKKOS is in the memory consumption. OpenMM allows calculations with 300 million atoms in one GPU with 80 GB of memory. Under similar conditions LAMMPS/KOKKOS allows only 40 million atoms due to a difference in how neighbor lists are stored.

For really large models LAMMPS/KOKKOS gives the best performance scalability without any efficiency degradation for large N. There are MPI parallelization capabilities in LAMMPS/KOKKOS (that lies beyond the analysis of this paper). Using LAMMPS/KOKKOS on a multi-GPU system, one can make effective MD calculations for very large models. Adaptation of the OBC method proposed in this work to LAMMPS/KOKKOS is an ongoing effort.

To summarize, OpenMM is best at efficiently (both in terms of memory and CPU time) calculating MD trajectories for systems of small and medium sizes ($\lesssim 10^7$) on a single GPU, whereas LAMMPS/KOKKOS is better at handling extra large systems and employing MPI to distribute the both CPU and memory workload across multiple GPUs.

8   Conclusions

In this work we described a computational framework that allows computationally effective modelling of turbulent flows. The framework is based on the OpenMM MD engine. Comparison with LAMMPS/KOKKOS shows more efficient memory usage by OpenMM (nearly 300 million atoms fit into one GPU with 80 GB of memory). However, the neighbor list updates in OpenMM result in the $\mathcal{O}(N^2)$ scaling that significantly affects the performance for large system sizes. The open boundary conditions algorithm has been implemented in OpenMM that allows one to control the flow speed and the flow temperature. Source code for OBC [1] and the patch for big systems in OpenMM [2] are publicly available on GitHub.

Acknowledgment. This research was supported in part through computational resources of the Supercomputer Centre of JIHT RAS and HPC facilities at HSE University. The study was supported by the Russian Science Foundation (project no. 20-71-10127).

References

1. https://github.com/dann239/openmm/tree/open-boundary
2. https://github.com/openmm/openmm/pull/3577
3. Abraham, M., et al.: GROMACS: high performance molecular simulations through multi-level parallelism from laptops to supercomputers. SoftwareX **1–2**, 19–25 (2015). https://doi.org/10.1016/j.softx.2015.06.001
4. Anderson, J.A., Lorenz, C.D., Travesset, A.: General purpose molecular dynamics simulations fully implemented on graphics processing units. J. Comput. Phys. **227**(10), 5342–5359 (2008). https://doi.org/10.1016/j.jcp.2008.01.047
5. Berendsen, H., van der Spoel, D., van Drunen, R.: GROMACS: a message-passing parallel molecular dynamics implementation. Comput. Phys. Commun. **91**(1), 43–56 (1995). https://doi.org/10.1016/0010-4655(95)00042-E
6. Brown, W.M., Kohlmeyer, A., Plimpton, S.J., Tharrington, A.N.: Implementing molecular dynamics on hybrid high performance computers – Particle-particle particle-mesh. Comput. Phys. Commun. **183**(3), 449–459 (2012). https://doi.org/10.1016/j.cpc.2011.10.012
7. Brown, W.M., Wang, P., Plimpton, S.J., Tharrington, A.N.: Implementing molecular dynamics on hybrid high performance computers – short range forces. Comput. Phys. Commun. **182**(4), 898–911 (2011). https://doi.org/10.1016/j.cpc.2010.12.021
8. Brown, W.M., Yamada, M.: Implementing molecular dynamics on hybrid high performance computers-three-body potentials. Comput. Phys. Commun. **184**(12), 2785–2793 (2013). https://doi.org/10.1016/j.cpc.2013.08.002
9. Eastman, P., et al.: OpenMM 4: a reusable, extensible, hardware independent library for high performance molecular simulation. J. Chem. Theory Comput. **9**(1), 461–469 (2013). https://doi.org/10.1021/ct300857j
10. Eastman, P., Pande, V.S.: Efficient nonbonded interactions for molecular dynamics on a graphics processing unit. J. Comput. Chem. **31**, 1268–1272 (2009). https://doi.org/10.1002/jcc.21413

11. Eastman, P., et al.:OpenMM 7: rapid development of high performance algorithms for molecular dynamics. PLOS Comput. Biol. **13**, 1–17 (2017). https://doi.org/10.1371/journal.pcbi.1005659

12. Glaser, J., et al.: Strong scaling of general-purpose molecular dynamics simulations on GPUs. Comput. Phys. Commun. **192**, 97–107 (2015). https://doi.org/10.1016/j.cpc.2015.02.028

13. Grinberg, L., et al.: A new computational paradigm in multiscale simulations: Application to brain blood flow. In: Proceedings of 2011 International Conference for High Performance Computing, Networking, Storage and Analysis, pp. 1–5 (2011)

14. Hitz, T., Heinen, M., Vrabec, J., Munz, C.D.: Comparison of macro-and microscopic solutions of the riemann problem I. supercritical shock tube and expansion into vacuum. J. Comput. Phys. **402**, 109077 (2020)

15. Hitz, T., Jöns, S., Heinen, M., Vrabec, J., Munz, C.D.: Comparison of macro-and microscopic solutions of the riemann problem II. two-phase shock tube. J. Comput Phys **429**, 110027 (2021)

16. Johar, A.: Final HIP Platform implementation for AMD GPUs on ROCm 3338 (2021). https://github.com/openmm/openmm/pull/3338

17. Kadau, K., Barber, J.L., Germann, T.C., Holian, B.L., Alder, B.J.: Atomistic methods in fluid simulation. Philos. Trans. R. Soc. A Math. Phys. Eng. Sci. **368**(1916), 1547–1560 (2010)

18. Kondratyuk, N., Nikolskiy, V., Pavlov, D., Stegailov, V.: GPU-accelerated molecular dynamics: State-of-art software performance and porting from nvidia CUDA to AMD HIP. The International Journal of High Performance Computing Applications **35**(4), 312–324 (2021). https://doi.org/10.1177/10943420211008288

19. Kostenetskiy, P., Chulkevich, R., Kozyrev, V.: HPC resources of the Higher School of Economics. J. Phys. Conf. Ser. **1740**, 012050. IOP Publishing (2021)

20. Kutzner, C., Páll, S., Fechner, M., Esztermann, A., de Groot, B.L., Grubmüller, H.: Best bang for your buck: GPU nodes for GROMACS biomolecular simulations. J. Comput. Chem. **36**(26), 1990–2008 (2015)

21. Kutzner, C., Páll, S., Fechner, M., Esztermann, A., de Groot, B.L., Grubmüller, H.: More bang for your buck: Improved use of GPU nodes for GROMACS 2018. J. Comput. Chem. **40**(27), 2418–2431 (2019)

22. Moon, B., Jagadish, H., Faloutsos, C., Saltz, J.: Analysis of the clustering properties of the Hilbert space-filling curve. IEEE Trans. Knowl. Data Eng. **13**(1), 124–141 (2001). https://doi.org/10.1109/69.908985

23. Nikolskiy, V.P., Stegailov, V.V., Vecher, V.S.: Efficiency of the Tegra K1 and X1 systems-on-chip for classical molecular dynamics. In: 2016 International Conference on High Performance Computing & Simulation (HPCS), pp. 682–689. IEEE (2016)

24. OpenMM team: OpenMM application layer python API http://docs.openmm.org/latest/api-python/app.html

25. OpenMM team: OpenMM library level C++/Python API http://docs.openmm.org/development/api-c++/

26. Perdikaris, P., Grinberg, L., Karniadakis, G.E.: Multiscale modeling and simulation of brain blood flow. Phys. Fluids **28**(2), 021304 (2016)

27. Plimpton, S.: Fast parallel algorithms for short-range molecular dynamics. J. Comput. Phys. **117**(1), 1–19 (1995). https://doi.org/10.1006/jcph.1995.1039

28. Rapaport, D.C., Clementi, E.: Eddy formation in obstructed fluid flow: A molecular-dynamics study. Phys. Rev. Lett. **57**, 695–698 (1986). https://doi.org/10.1103/PhysRevLett.57.695

29. Shamsutdinov, A., et al.: Performance of supercomputers based on Angara inter-connect and novel AMD CPUs/GPUs. In: Balandin, D., Barkalov, K., Gergel, V., Meyerov, I. (eds.) MMST 2020. CCIS, vol. 1413, pp. 401–416. Springer, Cham (2021). https://doi.org/10.1007/978-3-030-78759-2_33

30. Smith, E.: A molecular dynamics simulation of the turbulent Couette minimal flow unit. Phys. Fluids **27**(11), 115105 (2015)

31. Smith, E., Trevelyan, D., Ramos-Fernandez, E., Sufian, A., O'Sullivan, C., Dini, D.: CPL library – a minimal framework for coupled particle and continuum simulation. Comput. Phys. Commun. **250**, 107068 (2020)

32. Stegailov, M., et al.: Angara interconnect makes GPU-based Desmos supercom-puter an efficient tool for molecular dynamics calculations. Int. J. High Perform. Comput. Appl. **33**(3), 507–521 (2019). https://doi.org/10.1177/1094342019826667

33. Tchipev, N., et al.: Twetris: twenty trillion-atom simulation. Int. J. High Perf. Comp. Appl. **0**(0), 1094342018819741 (2019). https://doi.org/10.1177/1094342018819741

34. Thompson, A.P. et al.: LAMMPS – a flexible simulation tool for particle-based materials modeling at the atomic, meso, and continuum scales. Comput. Phys. Commun. **271**, 108171 (2022)

35. Trott, C.R., et al.: Kokkos 3: programming model extensions for the exascale era. IEEE Trans. Parallel Distrib. Syst. **33**(4), 805–817 (2022). https://doi.org/10.1109/TPDS.2021.3097283

A Novel Parallel Approach for Modeling the Dynamics of Aerodynamically Interacting Particles in Turbulent Flows

Ahmad Ababaei[1]([✉])(iD), Antoine Michel[1](iD), and Bogdan Rosa[1,2](iD)

[1] Institute of Meteorology and Water Management – National Research Institute, Podleśna 61, 01-673 Warsaw, Poland
`ahmad.ababaei@imgw.pl`
[2] Department of Applied Mathematics, Warsaw University of Life Sciences, Nowoursynowska 159, 02-776 Warsaw, Poland

Abstract. In this paper, the computational performance of a novel parallel code for simulating collision–coalescence of aerodynamically interacting droplets in turbulent flows is examined. Modeling such systems is essential for the quantitative description of processes relevant to precipitation formation. This knowledge, in turn, is crucial to develop more realistic parameterizations in numerical weather forecasting systems. The code is based on the standard Eulerian–Lagrangian approach. Direct numerical simulations (DNS) to solve the homogeneous isotropic turbulence are combined with analytical solutions of the Stokes flow to account for aerodynamic interaction (AI) among particles. Also, short-range interaction, the so-called lubrication forces, between particles is incorporated into the algorithm to improve the AI representation. The cubic computational domain is decomposed into smaller subdomains where calculations are handled by different processes. The Message Passing Interface (MPI) library is employed to transfer particle and flow data. This hybrid DNS (HDNS) algorithm enables tracking millions of interacting droplets in turbulent flows simulated on high-resolution meshes. The performance is evaluated by measuring the wall-clock time of major numerical operations. The results compare the time for treating AI, measured separately for long- and short-range forces, with the time required for the other particle operations as well as the time to advance the turbulent flow field. The effects of the number and size of the particles, the range of AI, and the number of processors are examined.

Keywords: Parallel computing · Particle-laden turbulence · Aerodynamic interaction · Lubrication force

1 Introduction

Particle-laden turbulent flows are present in a large number of industrial and natural processes such as fuel combustion, dispersion of pollution by air, or

Supported by National Science Centre of Poland.

R. Wyrzykowski et al. (Eds.): PPAM 2022, LNCS 13826, pp. 359–370, 2023.
https://doi.org/10.1007/978-3-031-30442-2_27

sediment transport in water. In clouds, turbulence is the main cause of collision–coalescence of rain drops within the radii range 10–60 μm. This results in droplets growing and eventually initiates rainfall.

Simulating microphysical processes in clouds entails enormous computational costs due to the wide range of length and time scales associated with turbulent flows and the consideration of aerodynamic interactions among a large number of particles. Thanks to development of modern high-performance computing techniques, such simulations are feasible within a reasonable time. The standard approach to model cloud processes is based on an Eulerian–Lagrangian description. It employs the direct numerical simulations (DNS) for simulating the turbulent flow. Droplet tracking is carried out by integrating their individual trajectories [1]. DNS handles the evolution of the turbulent field resolving all scales of the flow down to the smallest (i.e. Kolmogorov) ones. The locations of the droplets in the domain are updated at every time step, and therefore the numerical cost is proportional to the number of particles in the domain.

Aerodynamic interaction among the particles can be accounted for via "superposing" the disturbance velocity fields induced around every single particle due to its motion in a viscous medium [2]. This results in a very large system of equations for three components of disturbance velocities at the location of every particle generated by its neighboring particles [3]. Consequently, solving such a large system substantially adds to the computational cost of simulations [4]. In the literature, the combination of DNS for the background turbulent field and this analytical representation of interaction is known as hybrid DNS. HDNS by itself, however, is unable to capture short-range viscous forces, known as lubrication interactions, acting on particles [2]. Once the distance between particles is comparable to their average radii, superposition of their disturbances does not yield the accurate force, because the superposition method is based on the solution to the Stokes flow around a single sphere. Thus, the representation of aerodynamic interaction can be improved by utilizing HDNS [3] for distant particles together with exact analytical solutions [5] for particles in proximity.

The physics of this model has already been investigated [6], but a quantitative evaluation of the computational aspects remains to be addressed. Furthermore, it has been shown that without lubrication effects simulation time increases with the number of droplets in the domain [4], but it is expected that considering lubrication reduces this time. This is because for the particles in proximity short-range interaction is considered, thereby excluding such pairs from the matrix of disturbances for AI. As a result, a smaller matrix needs to be inverted which is less demanding. In addition, the size of the distance below (over) which the lubrication effect (superposed disturbances) would be considered is another key factor affecting computation time. Moreover, it is important to address the scalability of this implementation with the number of CPU cores. Additionally, we want to check the feasibility and evaluate the cost of simulations with higher resolution meshes and larger liquid water contents (LWC). The aim of this study is to assess all these aspects of the model by making use of data from numerical simulations.

2 Methodology

In order to precisely represent the momentum transfer from the background turbulent air to the particles, the smallest scales (i.e. Kolmogorov) of the flow need to be fully resolved [1]. (The transfer of momentum from the particles to the flow is negligible due to the small mass loading of water droplets in clouds.) This is achievable via direct numerical simulations of the flow. However, due to the computational cost of DNS, such simulations are limited to small Reynolds numbers ($\approx 10^2$) that correspond to small domain sizes (≈ 10 cm) not typical for atmospheric clouds. To simulate larger domains, higher resolutions of DNS are required, which are only possible by conducting massively parallel simulations on supercomputers. To date, the most complex DNS simulations of homogeneous isotropic turbulent flows have been performed using meshes with 8192^3 and 12288^3 grid nodes, yielding the Reynolds numbers $R_\lambda = 650$ and 1300, respectively [7,8]. The second challenge of large-scale simulations is the need for tracking a substantial number of droplets. It is noteworthy that when the size of a cubic domain in each spatial direction is doubled, an eight-fold increase in the number droplets is necessary for keeping the same liquid water content. Tracking a considerable number of aerodynamically interacting droplets can increase the cost of the simulations by at least one order of magnitude (see Fig. 9 in [4]).

These challenges are addressed by a two-dimensional decomposition of the cubic domain that assigns the operations in each subdomain to a CPU core [6]. The governing equations for modeling the turbulent flow, i.e. Navier–Stokes (N–S) and continuity, are as follows:

$$\frac{\partial U}{\partial t} = U \times \omega - \nabla \left(\frac{P}{\rho} + \frac{U^2}{2} \right) + \nu \nabla^2 U + f, \tag{1}$$

$$\nabla \cdot U = 0, \tag{2}$$

where $U(x, t)$ and $\omega(x, t)$ are vectors of velocity and vorticity of the flow, respectively. $P(x, t)$ is the pressure field, and ρ and ν denote the density and kinematic viscosity of air, respectively. $f(x, t)$ is the external body force acting on the fluid to maintain the turbulent flow. The equations are discretized on a grid of size N^3 and solved by the pseudo-spectral method [1]. The required three-dimensional fast Fourier transforms (FFTs) need access to the data from all of the subdomains. Therefore, global data transfer is necessary to advance the turbulent flow.

After introducing the droplets into the domain at random locations, their motion is tracked by integrating the equations of motion as follows:

$$\frac{dV^{(k)}}{dt} = -\frac{V^{(k)} - \left(U^{(k)} + u^{(k)} \right)}{\tau_p^{(k)}}, \tag{3}$$

$$\frac{dY^{(k)}}{dt} = V^{(k)}, \tag{4}$$

in which $V^{(k)}$ and $Y^{(k)}$ are the velocity and location of droplet k, where $k = 1, \ldots, N_{\mathrm{part}}$. To simplify the notation, $U^{(k)} \equiv U(Y^{(k)}, t)$ is the background flow velocity $U(x, t)$ interpolated at the location k-th droplet. Also, $u^{(k)}$ is the disturbance velocity sensed at the location of k-th droplet resulting from the interaction with the neighboring droplets. In addition, $\tau_{\mathrm{p}}^{(k)} = 2\rho_{\mathrm{p}}\left(a_{\mathrm{p}}^{(k)}\right)^2/9\mu$ is the Stokes inertial relaxation time of droplet k, with ρ_{p} and μ being the water density and dynamic viscosity of air, respectively.

Figure 1 presents the order in which the algorithm performs computations. Three major tasks related to the evolution of the flow, particles, and computing AIs are marked using different colors. The particle tasks are carried out locally within each subdomain and data exchange is conducted between neighboring subdomains. The main particle tasks unrelated to handling AI include solving their equations of motion, interpolation of the turbulent flow at droplet locations, transferring particle data to a neighboring subdomain when they cross subdomain or domain boundaries (i.e. imposing periodicities), and collecting particle statistics such as collision kinematics (average relative velocity and distribution) as well as dynamics (collision rate), root mean square in velocity fluctuations, etc.

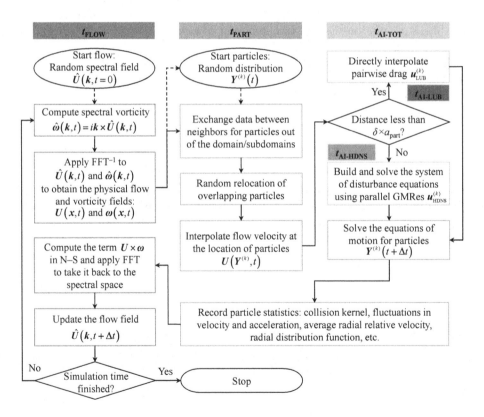

Fig. 1. Schematic diagram of the simulation algorithm. The colors mark time measurements related to the flow, particles, and AIs.

Also, two major opertations are needed to compute particle aerodynamic interaction, including generation and solving the system of equations that yields AI
among the particles and the calculation of lubrication forces from analytical
solutions. The total disturbance in Eq. (3) is the sum of these two components,
i.e. $\boldsymbol{u}^{(k)} = \boldsymbol{u}_{\mathrm{HDNS}}^{(k)} + \boldsymbol{u}_{\mathrm{LUB}}^{(k)}$.

Figure 2 shows a group of interacting particles. There are two spherical
regions that define different approaches to represent aerodynamic interactions.
(i) For particles closer than δa, exact analytical solutions [5] are employed to
accurately represent the lubrication forces. Generally, the normal and tangential viscous forces are functions of separation distance and radii ratio, which is
unity in this study as all the particles in the domain are of the same size. These
solutions are in forms of infinite series and hence it is extremely time-consuming
to calculate forces for every interacting pair at every time step. Instead, in the
current implementation the forces are tabulated as functions of separation distance at the beginning of the simulation and for every instance the forces are
interpolated from the tables. (ii) For particles interacting from a larger distance,
$\delta a < r \le 50a$, the superposition (HDNS) approach is used [2,3]. The Stokes
disturbances of all neighboring particles are superposed at the location of every
particle, building a system of linear equations, i.e. Eq. 6 in [3]. A parallel preconditioned solver based on the generalized minimal residual (GMRes) method
is used to efficiently solve this system [9]. For most of the cases analyzed here,
short-range interactions [5] are considered when the minimum distance between
the surfaces is less than or equal to their mean radius, i.e. $\delta = 3$. This is the characteristic distance below which the superposition method loses its accuracy (see
Fig. 1 in [6]). For particles that are considerably distant, $r > 50a$, aerodynamic
interaction is negligible (see Sect. 4.2 in [3]). The effects of gravity are entirely

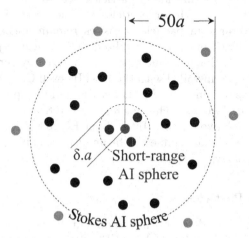

Fig. 2. The two spherical regions scanned around every particle (red) for neighboring
particles interacting from short (blue) and long (black) distances (Color figure online)

neglected and in all simulations only non-settling particles are considered. The rest of the details regarding the methodology used in this study are available in [6].

3 Parallel Performance

To analyze the performance of this implementation, a series of tests have been performed. The computational cost has been estimated for various values of the following parameters: the number of particles N_{part}, their radius a_{part}, the size of the normalized distance in which lubrication is considered δ, and the number of CPU cores utilized to simulate the same system n_{cores}. The results are presented in terms of three major operations in the code: (i) the time to evolve the turbulent flow field t_{FLOW}, (ii) the time for all particle operations discussed above except for their aerodynamic interaction t_{PART}, and (iii) the time to assess their aerodynamic interaction $t_{\text{AI-TOT}}$ which is the sum of times for their long-range drag forces from the superposition method $t_{\text{AI-HDNS}}$ and their short-range lubrication interactions from analytical solutions $t_{\text{AI-LUB}}$. Each task includes calculations and communications. For the performance analysis here, the wall-clock times of these two operations are summed up. The first step preceding performance tests is to generate a turbulent particle-free flow field. Beginning from a random field, the flow is evolved to a fully developed homogeneous isotropic turbulence that will be used for simulations with different settings (N_{part}, a_{part}, etc.). This stage lasts five eddy turnover times, where one eddy turnover time corresponds roughly the time scale of the largest eddies in the domain. The particles are then added to the domain at random locations and each case is run for five particle response times. This relaxation time reduces the effect of initial random distribution of particles (see Sect. 3.4 in [3]). (This time, however, might not be enough for particles to reach a statistically stationary stage where the averages in particle statistics remain unchanged over time.) Data collection is carried out over five subsequent particle response times.

The performance of this implementation is analyzed by running the tests on Okeanos supercomputer installed with the Intel Haswell Cray XC40 architecture at the Interdisciplinary Centre for Mathematical and Computational Modelling (ICM), University of Warsaw. The machine has 1084 nodes, each containing 128 GB of RAM and two 12-core Intel Xeon E5-2690 processors running at 2.6 GHz. All system nodes are connected by an ultra-scalable Cray Aries network with Dragonfly topology.

3.1 Number of Particles

The number of particles (droplets) in the domain is the main factor contributing to all the tasks related to particles. In Fig. 3(a), the average wall-clock time of the selected operations per single time step is displayed as a function of the number of particles for $N_{\text{part}} = \{0.5, 1, 2, 4, 8, 16, 32\} \times 10^5$. Thus, for this range of N_{part}, the average number per cell, i.e. $N_{\text{part}}/64^3$, would roughly be

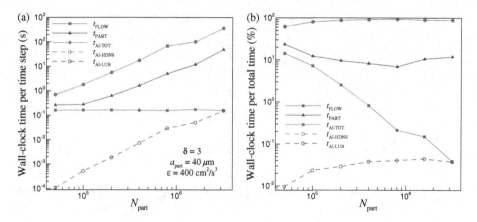

Fig. 3. Wall-clock time (a) per time step and (b) per total simulation time of different tasks as a function of the number of particles

0.2 to 12 particles. The droplets were of the same size 40 mum for which the inertial response time of the particles τ_p is roughly equal to the Kolmogorov time scale of the flow τ_K, leading to the Stokes number unity where $St = \tau_p/\tau_K$. Therefore, the particles are strongly affected by the smallest scales of the flow. It is noteworthy that having a greater number of particles in the domain enlarges the liquid water content, thus changing the phyisics of the system. Still, only the performance of the model is being investigated here. The time for all particle operations, e.g. evaluation of lubrication forces, increases with N_{part}. For the settings considered here, the calculation of long-range AI by solving large systems of linear equations from HDNS is the most time-consuming task. Conversely, the computation of the short-range lubrication forces is several orders of magnitude faster than all the other tasks because, to maximize efficiency, the values are precomputed and interpolated as needed. For long-range AI, the size of the system of equations generated is $3N_{\mathrm{part}}$, yielding a net disturbance at the location of every particle along every spatial direction. Solving such a large system requires much more computational work comparing to evaluation of short-range AI forces, which basically reduces to a simple 1D interpolation scheme.

Integrating the equations of motion of particles, interpolating fluid velocity at particle locations, and post-processing (collision detection and computing other collision statistics including radial relative velocity and radial distribution functions) take less time, approximately one order of magnitude, than all operations related to AI. The total time for numerical operations handling particle dynamics can be compared with the time required to simulate the turbulent flow. The time needed to model the particle-free flow is the same in each considered case. As shown, computing AI forces can be one ($N_{\mathrm{part}} = 10^5$) to three ($N_{\mathrm{part}} = 3.2 \times 10^6$) orders of magnitude more time-consuming than evolving the turbulent flow field at 64^3 resolution considered here. However, at larger resolutions, e.g. 512^3 or 1024^3, advancing the flow field is a significantly more complex

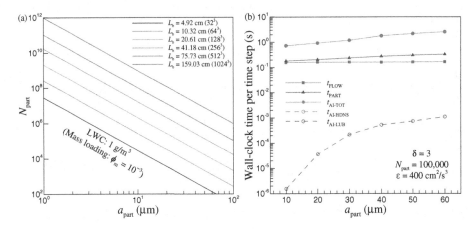

Fig. 4. Variation in the (a) number of particles, and (b) wall-clock time per time step for different operations with the size of particles

operation which can be (depending on LWC) more demanding than all particle tasks (see Fig. 4 in [4]).

In order to provide a relative comparison between different cases, their percentage of the total time is presented in Fig. 3(b). There is a reduction in the shares of flow and particle wall-clock time with N_{part} because computing AI via both HDNS and lubrication forces takes a larger fraction of the total simulation time. For instance, in simulation with $N_{part} = 5 \times 10^4$ AI takes 60% of the total time whereas for $N_{part} = 3.2 \times 10^6$ the contribution rises to 90%.

3.2 Size of the Particles

The liquid water content in the domain depends on the size and number of droplets. Figure 4(a) shows the relationship between the number of equal-size droplets and their radius for a system with a fixed LWC of $1 \, \text{g/m}^3$ in cubic boxes of six different lengths (L_b). These lengths are *chosen* to match DNS flow parameters (Kolmogorov scales) in Table 1 of [10] obtained on grids of different resolutions (N^3). The number of particles grows exponentially by decreasing their radii or expanding size of the box.

The effect of radii of the particles on the performance of the model is presented in Fig. 4(b). A large enhancement (y–axis is in logarithmic scale) is seen for the total wall-clock time of the AI operation. A substantial contribution to this enhancement comes from the increase in the time needed to compute long-range interacting forces, while computing short-range lubrication forces has a minor influence on the increase in wall-clock time for AIs. Although having larger particles in the domain affects their dynamics, the increase in computation time for both AI tasks is largely due to the expansion of the volume that is scanned around every particle to account for the influence of its disturbance on the neighboring particles (Fig. 2). That is, the larger the particle, the larger the size $(50a)$ of the scanned volume for potential AI with other particles, and hence, the higher the possibility of finding such particles. Also, clustering in the distribution of particles is another factor that affects the time to compute the AI. Smaller particles are less willing to accumulate owing to their low inertia that is insufficient to deviate from the streamlines of the flow. On the other hand, larger particles with higher inertia tend to cluster, thereby increasing the number of AIs.

Similar to AI, particle tasks show a slight enhancement with particle radius. Data exchange is the main factor contributing to this increase in time. In order to conduct several particle operations – e.g. detection and relocation of particles that overlap, recording collision statistics, and computing aerodynamic interaction – near the boundaries of every subdomain, data of the particles within a thin region of all neighboring subdomains have to be added to every subdomain. The size of this "halo" region depends on the size of the particles. Thus, larger particles need a thicker halo region which encompasses a larger number of particles, and hence requires a greater number of calculations and communications.

3.3 Size of the Short-Range Interaction Region

So far, the results were presented for a fixed size of the region in which lubrication forces are considered: $\delta = 3$. There are two reasons for this particular choice. Firstly, the accuracy in the superposition method (HDNS) begins to decline for pairs separated at normalized distances $\delta \leq 3$ (see Fig. 1 in [6]). For such pairs short-range lubrication forces can be obtained from the analytical solutions to the Stokes flow around *two* spherical particles [5]. Secondly, since two-sphere

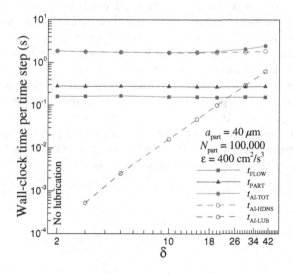

Fig. 5. Variation in wall-clock time of different operations per time step with the size of lubrication region

analytical solutions are limited to pair-wise interactions, increasing the size of lubrication region, i.e. a larger δ, results in losing the effect of many-body interaction among particles, which is taken into account by superposing perturbation induced by all neighboring particles [2,3]. Therefore, $\delta = 3$ is a choice in between that considers the effects of both lubrication forces and many-body interaction.

Figure 5 shows the wall-clock time required by each operation as a function of the size of lubrication region. When $\delta = 2$, there is no lubrication region and AI is entirely handled by HDNS (i.e. $t_{AI\text{-}LUB} = 0$). As the size of lubrication region changes from one particle radius ($\delta = 3$) to forty particle radii ($\delta = 42$), the time to calculate lubrication forces increases by three orders of magnitude. As a result, the total AI time (i.e. $t_{AI\text{-}TOT} = 0$) grows, too. The rest of the tasks do not depend on the size of lubrication region.

3.4   Number of CPU Cores

Several tests have been performed to check how each task scales with the number of computational cores utilized: $n_{cores} = 2^n$ for $n = 6, \ldots, 10$. The results are demonstrated in Fig. 6 for three systems simulated on grids of sizes 64^3, 128^3, and 256^3 with the same liquid water content $10\,g/m^3$. The range of y–axis is identical on all three panels to facilitate comparisons. Panels (a)–(c) illustrate the increase in execution time for all tasks as the domain is enlarged. In general, computing long-range aerodynamic interactions is the most time-consuming operation. This is caused by the necessity to track a large number of particles owing to the high LWC (assumed for the systems simulated here). A large fraction of this time is due to HDNS, whereas interpolation of lubrication forces takes several orders of magnitude less time. The time to advance the flow is shorter than the time to evaluate AIs, but longer than that for particle operations (velocity interpolation, recording collision statistics, etc.). Another finding is the improvement in scalability at higher resolutions. At 64^3, the three major tasks – i.e. AIs, flow, and particles – do not show a better performance with the number of CPU cores employed. Wall-clock times of the flow and particle operations even begin to increase when more than 256 cores are used. Scalability slightly improves at the higher resolution 128^3 displaying a logarithmic decrease in computation time, again, until $n_{cores} = 256$. However, using a larger number of cores does not lead to a lower wall-clock time for advancing the flow and particle operations. The best performance is observed at the resolution 256^3 showing a logarithmically decreasing time with the number of processors used.

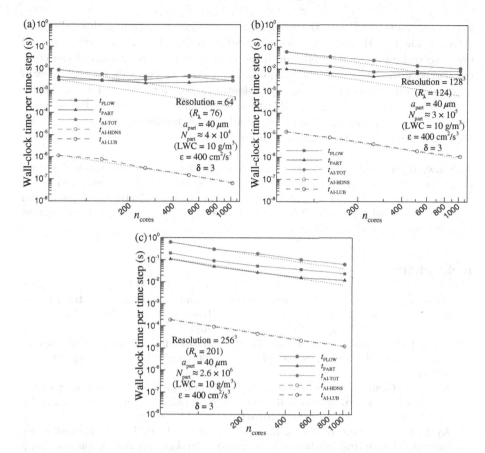

Fig. 6. Wall-clock time per time step of different operations as a function of the number of CPU cores for three systems with the same LWC $10\,\text{g/m}^3$ and turbulent flows at resolutions: (a) 64^3, (b) 128^3, and (c) 256^3 (dotted lines: slope $= -1$)

4   Conclusions

This study addresses the parallel performance of a novel implementation for tracking inertial particles in turbulent flows. This code serves for modeling cloud processes and examining the role of turbulence on the droplet collision rate. The main innovation of this implementation lies in the representation of aerodynamic interactions (both short- and long-range) between the droplets. The computational performance was assessed based on a number of testing simulations by measuring the time required to conduct individual operations. The focus was on computation time for aerodynamic interaction and lubrication forces, and the results were directly compared with the time required for the other tasks related to droplet tracking and computing collision statistics as well as the time to advance the turbulent flow field. The factors examined here were the number and size of the particles in the domain, the size of the region in which lubrication effects are considered, and the number of processors to simulate three different systems. The first three factors increased computation time. It has been observed that the scalability of the code improves with increasing resolution of the computational grid. This is an encouraging perspective to run simulations on even larger computational meshes, or equivalently larger Reynolds numbers. Therefore, the approach makes it possible to conduct simulations in conditions more similar to those in realistic clouds. This leads to the development of more realistic parameterizations for weather forecasting models.

Acknowledgements. We wish to thank the financial support of the National Science Centre of Poland under the grant 2018/30/Q/ST8/00341. Also, we are grateful for the computational resources provided by the Interdisciplinary Centre for Mathematical and Computational Modelling (ICM) at the University of Warsaw, Poland, under grant numbers GA73-14 and G87-1145.

References

1. Wang, L.-P., Maxey., M. R.: Settling velocity and concentration distribution of heavy particles in homogeneous isotropic turbulence. J. Fluid Mech. **256**, 27–68 (1993). https://doi.org/10.1017/S0022112093002708
2. Wang, L.-P., Ayala, O., Grabowski, W. W.: Improved formulations of the superposition method. J. Atmosp. Sci. **62**(4), 1255–1266 (2005). https://doi.org/10.1175/JAS3397.1
3. Ayala, O., Grabowski W.W., Wang, L.-P.: A hybrid approach for simulating turbulent collisions of hydrodynamically-interacting particles. J. Comput. Phys. **225**(1), 51–73 (2007). https://doi.org/10.1016/j.jcp.2006.11.016
4. Ayala, O., Parishani, H., Chen, L., Rosa, B., Wang, L.-P.: DNS of hydrodynamically interacting droplets in turbulent clouds: Parallel implementation and scalability analysis using 2D domain decomposition. Comput. Phys. Commun. **185**(12), 3269–3290 (2014). https://doi.org/10.1016/j.cpc.2014.09.005
5. Jeffrey, D.J., Onishi, Y.: Calculation of the resistance and mobility functions for two unequal rigid spheres in low-Reynolds-number flow. J. Fluid Mech. **139**, 261–290 (1984). https://doi.org/10.1017/S0022112084000355
6. Ababaei, A., Rosa, B., Pozorski, J., Wang, L.-P.: On the effect of lubrication forces on the collision statistics of cloud droplets in homogeneous isotropic turbulence. J. Fluid Mech. **918** (2021). https://doi.org/10.1017/jfm.2021.229
7. Buaria, D., Pumir, A., Bodenschatz, E., Yeung, P.K.: Extreme velocity gradients in turbulent flows. New J. Phys. **21**(4), 043004 (2019). https://doi.org/10.1088/1367-2630/ab0756
8. Buaria, D., Bodenschatz, E., Pumir, A.: Vortex stretching and enstrophy production in high Reynolds number turbulence. Phys. Rev. Fluids **5**(10), 104602 (2020). https://doi.org/10.1103/PhysRevFluids.5.104602
9. Torres, C. E., Parishani, H., Ayala, O., Rossi, L.F., Wang, L.-P.: Analysis and parallel implementation of a forced N-body problem. J. Comput. Phys. **245**, 235–258 (2013). https://doi.org/10.1016/j.jcp.2013.03.008
10. Rosa, B., Parishani, H., Ayala, O., Grabowski, W.W., Wang, L.-P.: Kinematic and dynamic collision statistics of cloud droplets from high-resolution simulations. New J. Phys. **15**(4), 045032 (2013). https://doi.org/10.1088/1367-2630/15/4/045032

Reliable Energy Measurement on Heterogeneous Systems–on–Chip Based Environments

Alberto Cabrera[ID], Pavel Nichita[ID], Sergio Afonso[ID], Francisco Almeida[ID], and Vicente Blanco[✉][ID]

HPC Group of Universidad de La Laguna, Escuela Superior de Ingeniería y Tecnología., 38270 San Cristóbal de La Laguna, Tenerife, Spain
{acabrerp,pnichita,safonsof,falmeida,vblanco}@ull.es

Abstract. The proper evaluation of System–on–Chip architectures and Single Board Computers, requires from scientists and developers to acquire reliable data from their performance and energy consumption. The performance analysis becomes a hard task due to the high variations in the systems that change dynamically even during the execution, caused by limited power budgets or temperature constraints among others, and producing very different results from one execution to the other. An extra added obstacle in energy analysis arises with the difficulty to obtain the measurements due to the lack of both a unified measurement standard and appropriate sensors to gather them. Attaining a benchmarking process to produce reliable and reproducible data results constitutes a difficult problem to solve and an extremely necessary task. As a consequence, unified solutions that simplify the process and reduce the number of issues to tackle during the computational experiments are of great beneficial to the scientific community. We enumerate several factors that hinder proper metric gathering and propose the use of a unified benchmarking framework to simplify energy measurements to address and hide the toughest aspects. Finally, to validate our proposal, we present a performance and energy evaluation to illustrate the enhance of the quality of measurements obtained where the reliability and reproducibility are improved. A mini-cluster collecting a set of heterogeneous devices running computer fluid dynamics kernels have been used as the testbed.

Keywords: Multiprocessor SoC · Energy Efficiency · Reliable Benchmarking · Reproducibility

1 Introduction

In the last decade, System–on–Chip (SoC) based platforms have grown significantly. Embedded systems deal with low power complex environments involving energy–aware computer architectures [3]. At the same time mobile devices have become ubiquitous at personal and professional environments. While CPUs and

R. Wyrzykowski et al. (Eds.): PPAM 2022, LNCS 13826, pp. 371–382, 2023.
https://doi.org/10.1007/978-3-031-30442-2_28

SoCs are microchips of a slightly similar area, the amount of features a SoC comprises is much richer and heterogeneous, introducing inherent difficulties for an efficient use of these devices. Both scientists and developers require to attain reliable data results to properly evaluate them. Additionally, power and energy efficiencies have also become a primary concern in SoCs design. In one hand, mobile devices need to operate providing good performance for as long as possible [8]. On the other hand, the shrinking of components has improved circuit density, and power budgets have dropped exponentially due to the existence of the *utilization wall*, heavily affecting modern hardware design [20]. Proper measurement of performance and energy consumption in SoCs is key to design the software applications that will be run in them.

Gathering data and resource usage is key to properly optimize any system. The usual cycle of experimentation starts by designing and implement a benchmark for applications. Then experiments are launched and after the results are gathered, data is analyzed to extract conclusions. If any flaw or optimization opportunity is found, then hardware or software is redesigned and this process is repeated.

SoC architectures add complexity to benchmarking due to their unique set of characteristics, where thermal management, Dynamic Voltage and Frequency Scaling (DVFS), and thermal design power have been identified as a problem to performance evaluation [15]. The reproducibility of data results in computational analysis is a well–known problem of experimental research in computer science [21], constantly challenging the scientific community to find better methodologies for experimentation [14]. Also, any experiment designed for SoCs has to be aware of the noise induced by the aforementioned issues or the attained results may lead to false conclusions [1].

On the other hand, energy measurements involve a set of challenges already known in some scientific fields, such as High Performance Computing [2], where there has been efforts towards achieving standards to obtain this metric. Similarly, the absence of energy metric gathering standards in SoCs presents an additional challenge. While vendors may integrate a direct mean to gather energy measurements from sensors, such as the now obsolete Odroid-XU3, it is often required to rely on external meters that have their own limitations, i.e., coarse grained measurements or asynchronous measurements between the external device and the application. Finally, the lack of standardization also increments the complexity of our benchmarks.

Since the release of the first Raspberry Pi model in February 2012, the Single Board Computer (SBC) market has seen a flurry of different models being released. Most of them have an ARM architecture from different semiconductor manufacturers, while a few have an x86/amd64 architecture. Their low power paired with their performance has attracted the interest in HPC communities, where multiple analyses have been made [7,11,22] since SBCs are seen as a way to solve the huge energy usage problem that current HPC centers have [6].

This work presents a methodology to reliably benchmark energy consumption in a highly heterogeneous SoC environment using SBCs, so that the computational results may be reproducible. Measurements performed following our methodology is used to analyze the energetic impact of a target Java application in a chosen architecture and reliably detect optimization opportunities. Also, data results could be used to detect performance and energetic anomalies and develop power models of said architectures. To illustrate and justify our proposal we perform multiple experiments and discuss the issues addressed at each step of the methodology. We enumerate the main contributions of this work:

- We implement a Java interface for a standard energy measurement library to unify energy measurement and tackle different SoC architectures, using an already validated external measurement device. This increases the homogeneity of our setup and hides fine details for each target architecture.
- We implement a measurement methodology to increment measurement precision, reduce external noise and greatly increase experimental reproducibility for energy metrics by tackling thermal management, the cpu governor, operative system scheduling issues and processor affinity.
- We validate our proposal using the Java version of the NAS Parallel Benchmarks [4] (NPB) to experiment in a SoC board using a Linux operative system, and compare it to a traditional benchmarking methodology.

We analyzed the results obtained by executing various NPB kernels and observed how the variability of the gathered metrics was reduced significantly. Using this methodology for benchmarking, we can accurately perform optimizations in our benchmarks and ensure that improvements are caused by our modifications and not due to external factors. Moreover, with more accurate measurements, we would be able to develop more accurate energy consumption and performance models.

The rest of the paper is structured as follows: Sect. 2, related work in the field is discussed and analyzed; Sect. 3 describes the solution to reliably measure energy consumption in SBCs, an evaluation and validation of the proposed methodology is presented in Sect. 4 and finally, Sect. 5 concludes our work.

2   Related Work

Several authors have introduced significant advances in the process for the measurement and analysis of energy usage in SoCs. They have run over some of the aforementioned problems associated to SoCs in this contexts. Some solutions have been fixed but in general the problem of analysis and modeling of energy in SoCs still remains open.

Núñez-Yáñez et al. [18] describes a methodology for power modeling and energy estimation in complex SoCs based on developing statistical power models for the system components. The obtained results show the effects of different hardware configurations on power and energy for a given application and how system level energy consumption analysis can help the design team to make informed architectural trade-offs during the design process. They focus on the interaction of the application processor and the memory subsystem in terms of energy analysis. However, they do not consider the effect of dynamic and frequency scaling what would introduce a high variation on the measurements and presumably in the models. Models based on physical information of the development platform, Performance Monitoring Unit (PMU) events and CPU state information are presented in [17]. These models present a very high accuracy to predict the average power between different CPU energy levels under simulated scenarios, and also consider DVFS and advanced scheduling strategies. However important deviations and inaccuracies may arise under real production processes. The models need to be recalibrated since new PMU or different CPU states could be considered in the architecture provided for new devices.

Milosevic et al. [10, 16] introduces an environment for automated power measurements of programs running on a mobile development platform, mPowerProfile. The environment relies on minimally invasive instrumentation of a mobile platform using a shunt resistor on the power line and an inexpensive data acquisition system (DAQ) for sampling the voltage at the shunt resistor. Energy consumption when transferring data with and without compression is analyzed in Linux and Android. It worth to mention the high resolution and accuracy presented, the setup allows collection of up to 200,000 samples per second of power supply current. Our work uses also external power meters to perform measurements but we are less intrusive, we also try to go deeper in the reproducibility of the computational results.

An ESL-tool (Electronic System Level) power estimation methodology supporting black box models been presented in [19], it uses ARM Cortex-A9 for reference. The method is based on automatic tracing of the transactions of the Virtual Platform (VP). In an even simpler mode, only the processor activity is traced via the instruction fetch port showing for the VP a timing error of 9% compared to the reference system. The power estimation error is only about 5% on average for fixed-frequency power models. Because the ARM Cortex-A9 processor is a rather complex RISC processor, it is expected that similar levels of accuracy can be achieved for most RISC processors.

As stated, there are multiple ways of collecting energy data: external power meters, models based on PMUs and CPU states or estimation methodologies based on ESL. Our work with SBCs reveals significant variations in energy measurements appear during experimentation. Reproducibility is a key factor in these studies and we propose a unified solution that address this problem.

3   Reliable Energy Benchmarking

Ideally, the experimental codes developed to benchmark any target architecture should be portable and independent, for both the hardware (SBCs) and the measurement devices. We propose to assemble a software solution to simplify the programming challenges associated with the development experimental benchmarks, to prevent errors associated with erroneous metric gathering, and to deal with external factors affecting our applications. Traditionally ignored for CPUs, SoC architectures require special attention to finite power budgets, temperature

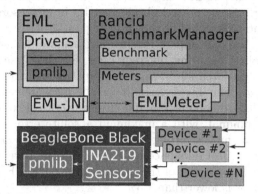

| Matrix | Avg. Energy (J) | |
Size	Eml C	Eml Java
200	0.571	0.752
300	1.916	1.892
400	5.989	5.912
500	9.668	9.702
	Error (%)	Error
200	24.07	0.181
300	-1.27	-0.024
400	-1.30	-0.077
500	0.35	0.034

(a) Experimental setup interconnection diagram.   (b) EML C and JNI comparative

Fig. 1. EML JNI Evaluation and interconnection

limits and, due to the lack of active cooling, temperature dissipation problems. Also, in big.LITTLE architectures two different types of processor clusters are available, usually powerful and efficient cores. The operative system scheduler moves continuously processes between each group to optimize the energy consumption of the system. If unaddressed, the less computationally intense sections from our benchmark could be scheduled in efficient cores altering our final results. Thus benchmark developers have many additional issues to tackle for precise testing.

3.1   EML Java Native Interface

We propose a Java interface for energy measurement as an extension of our previous work, EML [9]. EML was developed to unify multiple energy measurement devices, external and internal meters, and provide homogeneous measurement metrics using a single interface. The objective of *EML-JNI* is to keep a unified interface for measurement while maintaining all the already existing features, such as auto–discovery of measurement devices or nested measurements. This library covers most of the needs to perform the experimentation as it tackles the complexity of having multiple measurement interfaces that are accessed through different Application Programming Interfaces, while also managing the differences between instant power measurements and accumulated energy consumption. The result is a library with a very low code intrusion that hides many of the measurement details to the user.

To obtain the measurements, we make use of the AccelPowerCape [13], a BeagleBone Black combined with the Accelpower module [12], which uses INA219 sensors to attain current, voltage and wattage. The Accelpower module uses a modified version of `pmlib` library [5], a server daemon specifically created to monitor energy consumption. `pmlib` is run in the BeagleBone Black, which is then, accessed by the EML `pmlib` driver. This driver is a client library developed to communicate with the `pmlib` server and obtain metrics from sensors selected by the user at runtime, interconnected as shown in Fig. 1a.

In the Table appearing in Fig. 1b, we compare the measurements obtained executing a simple matrix multiplication using different sizes, for the C and Java versions of EML. The code is executed 30 times for each matrix size, from 200 to 500, which is then averaged. The Java overhead for the measurement section is negligible as the JNI calls are done before and after our critical code has been executed, thus error is minimal, with a maximum absolute error of 0.181 J. The average error is high for smallest problem size, 24.07%, as the code consumes little energy, and that 0.181 J of difference between each code is very high, but could also be caused by the precision of the measurement device. For the remaining sizes, the relative error is lower than 1.3%.

To minimize overhead in SoCs, removing all the non–essential operations from the evaluated hardware is a key factor. Therefore, we also implemented a remote variant of the EML driver to remove all intrusion caused by the EML workflow in our hardware. Servers such as `pmlib` continuously poll power or energy metrics and delegates data management and synchronization to the end–user. The remote EML solution is a server based driver, but follows the workflow of all EML drivers and serves stop–watch like operations for energy measurement. Thus, switching from a local EML–JNI interface to remote measurements is hidden from the experimental code. Moreover, in the presented case, as energy metrics have to be gathered using `pmlib` the network access is unavoidable. Hence moving all network usage in our benchmarks outside of the critical measurement zone is the best option.

3.2   Reliable Benchmarking

Rancid [1] is a flexible benchmarking framework designed in Java to reduce the programming efforts required to address all issues that add potential noise to our measurements in Android devices. While SBCs are the target architecture, many of the issues that affect Android devices also add noise to metric measurement in SoCs, such as bad temperature dissipation, process priority and process affinity. Benchmarks also have to be error–free, so implementing all the operations for each benchmark is not only impractical, but prone to error. Moreover, techniques to reduce the variability of benchmarks should be designed to be independent from the specific hardware they are being developed for.

Rancid is designed as a modular and extensible framework. To avoid scenarios that potentially add noise to our experimentation, it includes techniques to provide control over CPU frequencies, temperature monitorization, and process priority and affinity. The framework also provides measurement classes to define a set of desired metrics to evaluate in a running benchmark. In Fig. 2, all the main components of the Rancid framework are illustrated. The *Benchmark-Manager* is able to execute all the *Benchmarks* defined by users, were multiple metrics are gathered through the *Meter* interface. Once the benchmark process is finished, data can be analyzed within the Java program or can be exported to be processed at a later time.

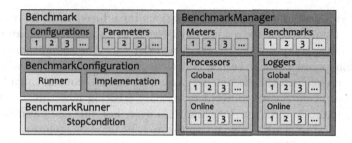

Fig. 2. Main components of the Rancid framework.

To include energy consumption as a possible metric to evaluate benchmarks, we developed the *EMLMeter* class, extending the provided interface *Meter*. *EMLMeter* uses the previously presented *EML-JNI* interface and interconnecting to the measurement devices as shown in Fig. 1a. To implement a new Meter, only three functions require an implementation: *EMLMeter.start()*, *EMLMeter.stop()* and *EMLMeter.stoperror()*. The similarities with *EML-JNI* made the implementation trivial, with a small addition to stop the energy measurement and discard the value on *EMLMeter.stoperror()*, a function necessary to reset a benchmark run that has failed.

To develop a set of benchmarks, users are required to extend the *BenchmarkImplementation* class with the target code. Users can override methods to execute before and after each designed benchmark (*PreBenchmark()* and *PostBenchmark()*) to reconfigure the system into a desired state, and outside of the measurement section (*PreRun* and *PostRun*), so that users deal with initialization and finalization operations required by test codes. To finalize the configuration, users have to specify a set of inputs for each *Benchmark*, and a *StopCondition*, that may be a simple condition based on a fixed number of runs or a complex condition to achieve a specific objective through experimentation.

In our *Rancid BenchmarkManager*, we incorporated the *EMLMeter* implementation to connect through the *EML-JNI* interface to the `pmlib` driver and read energy consumption metrics from the BeagleBone Black. Finally, before and after executing any of our *Benchmarks*, all the techniques developed to reduce potential noise within our experiments are implemented, including selecting the performance cpu governor, forcing thread pinning in the powerful cores, controlling the temperature of the device with cooldown operations and setting the *StopCondition* to meet carefully selected error criteria.

4 Experimentation

We evaluate our methodology by executing multiple instances of the NAS Parallel Benchmarks (NPB) kernels, Block Tri–diagonal solver (BT), Integer Sort (IS), and Multi-Grid on a sequence of meshes (MG), in their Java 3.0.0 version. These are three of multiple computational kernels derived from computational fluid dynamics (CFD) applications designed to help evaluate the performance of parallel supercomputers. The modifications introduced to these benchmarks are the strictly necessary to execute our benchmarks using Rancid, and to measure the critical computational code designed by its original authors after the initialization phase of each kernel. Moreover, as NPB kernel codes are introduced within our *BenchmarkImplementation*, we have to control thread creation in the initialization phase, to avoid repeatedly creating new threads that keep running indefinitely until our benchmark is over. For this computational experience, we opted to study a single size for each benchmark, referred as *class* by the NPB authors. The selected sizes for each kernel are BT W (a grid size of $24 \times 24 \times 24$, executed 200 iterations with a time step of 0.0008), IS B (an array of 2^{25} keys) and MG A (grid size of 256^3 elements executed 4 iterations). In this section we will compare two evaluations for each benchmark: a standard approach, where results are obtained by executing a given benchmark for fixed amount of iterations; and a reliable managed approach, where we introduce all of viable techniques to improve the quality of the executed benchmarks.

The target architecture is a Hikey960 development ARM 64 platform, comprised of a *Huawei Kirin 960* SoC, with a Cortex A7 @ 2.36 GHz and a Cortex A53 @ 1.8 GHz, and has 6 GB, LPDDR4X@1866 MHz of DRAM. Is has installed a *Debian* 9 kernel version 4.9. For compiling and executing the NPB, we used *Java* openjdk 1.8.0_272.

In the benchmark we denote as standard, the experimental codes are executed for fixed number of 300 repetitions. The reliable approach introduces a more complex stop condition. We calculate the target error of the energy consumption metric for the last *window* iterations and stop when the calculations are inferior to a definite threshold. In our case, the objective error was set at 5% within the last 50 repetitions for the total energy consumption metric e. The error at the i-th iteration is calculated as follows:

$$Err_i = \frac{\sqrt{\mathrm{Var}\left([e_{i-window}, e_{i-window+1}, \cdots, e_i]\right)}}{\frac{\sum_{j=i-window}^{i} e_i}{n}} \tag{1}$$

Thus, the stop condition is defined as $Err_i <= 0.05 \land i > 50$. To avoid infinite experimentation if error does not converge, a fixed amount of iterations is also set as an alternative stop condition. The reliable version also includes mechanisms to control the temperature of the devices to avoid performance degradation, ensures that threads are assigned to the powerful cores if a big.LITTLE architecture is detected, and gives our process real time priority. Finally, warm up operations are included beforehand to increase the frequency of the processor.

Figures 3a and 3b illustrate the measurement irregularities that are caused by the issues detected in SoCs, using the HiKey960. While every algorithm presents a different behaviour, a reliable benchmarking methodology is mandatory to ensure that different executions of the same benchmarks achieve similar results. Figure 3a illustrates one scenario where execution time is completely stable, yet energy readings vary through four different states during the benchmarking procedure. On the other hand, the situation presented in Fig. 3b illustrates a situation where the thermal design power is reached. In this second case, temperature,

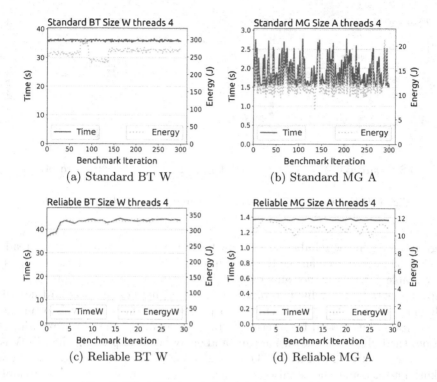

Fig. 3. Hikey960 detailed benchmark measurements

governor, and frequency issues affect the final results in the standard benchmarking procedure. In Figs. 3c and 3d, we apply the proposed reliable benchmarking methodology to reduce the noise from external sources, yielding in more stable results.

Our computational experience is condensed in Fig. 4. These bar plots illustrate the median execution time and the energy consumption of the BT W, IS B and MG A, and their interquartile range (IQR). Each group of bars portrays the result of the benchmark execution for 1, 2, 3 or 4 threads. Within each group, the first 2 bars represent the execution time, using the standard approach and our reliable proposal, respectively. The third and fourth bar represent the energy consumption measurements, following the same pattern. Be aware that the Y axis does not start at 0 in Figs. 4a and 4b. In each case, our objective is to minimize the IQR in order to improve the precision of our benchmarking methodology, reduce external noise, and increase the reproducibility of our experimentation, i.e., a smaller the IQR in these Figures is better.

Figure 4a illustrates the results obtained by executing the BT W kernel. In this first case, we are tackling the scenario presented in Fig. 3a. The standard benchmarking procedure is clearly worse in the serial execution, as its IQR is notably higher than the reliable version in both execution time and energy measurements. The parallel versions of the benchmark, from 2 to 4 threads, are

380   A. Cabrera et al.

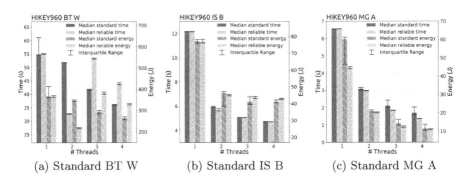

(a) Standard BT W   (b) Standard IS B   (c) Standard MG A

Fig. 4. HiKey960 NPB benchmark measurements, standard v. reliable.

slightly better in the reliable case except for the execution time using 4 threads. In Figs. 3a and 3c, we can see this case in detail. The execution time is already very stable for this kernel and its variability is very small to appreciate any improvements by the reliable procedure. However, neither the standard nor the reliable version of the kernel is able to portrait the different levels of energy consumption introduced by external factors. Using our proposal for experimentation, the IQR for the execution time and energy consumption in the BT W is, on average, 1.394 s and 14.46 J (3.03% and 4.56%) better respectively. Without taking into account the serial case, which is very favorable for us, the reliable benchmarking attains a slightly worse IQR for execution time, 0.484 s compared to the 0.289 s from the standard version (0.42% worse). Still, for energy consumption the reliable benchmark IQR, 7.60 J, is better compared to the standard benchmark IQR, 18.78 J (1.56% improvement).

In Fig. 4b, we observe the behavior for the IS B kernel. This kernel is more stable than the BT, and we observe how the execution time variation for the standard (0.020 s) and the reliable (0.035 s) procedure is negligible. The IQR is 0.015 s (0.22%) better for the standard procedure. For energy consumption however, we observe great variability, specially for the 2 threaded case. On average, IQR is improved by 3.063J (5.96%) when using our benchmarking proposal.

Finally, Fig. 4c depicts the last case, the MG A kernel. This kernel produces very irregular measurements using the standard benchmarking, as shown in Fig. 3b, since it is heavy both computationally and in memory usage. Hence, the results obtained through the reliable methodology have a significantly lower IQR, specially for the 3 and 4 threaded cases, where all the components of the device are used, except for the GPU. The standard time IQRs are, on average, 0.179 s and 5.616 J for execution time and energy consumption respectively, while the reliable methodology IQRs are 0.007 s and 0.777 J (5.11% and 17.41% improvement).

Overall we can observe how the IQRs are equal or better in this computational experience using our methodology. In some cases, as presented in the BT W, the median of the measurement for the reliable benchmarking methodology is different to the standard benchmarking. Still, the variability of the results is reduced and the IQR is lower overall. On the other hand, algorithms with great variability such as the MG are greatly improved, specially for energy consumption measurements.

5 Conclusion

New factors introduced in SoCs have been proven to heavily affect algorithm performance due to their limited power, temperature constraints or lack of active cooling. Reliable benchmarking is a mandatory tool to improve the performance and the energy consumption of computational systems. In order to apply optimization techniques in any procedure, metrics have to be accurate. Any variability may hide performance variations, be it improvement or losses, thus increasing the difficulty of comparing optimization techniques. In this work we propose a reliable methodology to benchmark SoCs and reduce the variability for time and energy consumption measurements. To do so, we have implemented a Java native interface for EML and extended Rancid to make use of energy measurements. Using Rancid, we designed a computational experience to evaluate multiple NPB kernels. These experiments indicate that our proposal reduces the variability of the final benchmark results, which we can then use to evaluate algorithms and optimization techniques accurately.

Acknowledgments. This work has been supported by the Spanish Ministry of Science and Innovation with the PID2019-107228RB-I00 project, and Contract FPU16/00942; by the Government of the Canary Islands, with the project ProID2021010012 and the grant TESIS2017010134, which is co-financed by the Ministry of Economy, Industry, Commerce and Knowledge of Canary Islands and the European Social Funds (ESF), operative program integrated of Canary Islands 2014–2020 Strategy Aim 3, Priority Topic 74(85%); and the Spanish network CAPAP-H.

References

1. Afonso, S., Almeida, F.: Rancid: reliable benchmarking on android platforms. IEEE Access **8**, 143342–143358 (2020)
2. Almeida, F., Arteaga, J., Blanco, V., Cabrera, A.: Energy measurement tools for ultrascale computing: a survey. Supercomput. Front. Innov. **2**(2), 64–76 (2015)
3. Andrae, A.S., Edler, T.: On global electricity usage of communication technology: trends to 2030. Challenges **6**(1), 117–157 (2015)
4. Bailey, D., Harris, T., Saphir, W., Van Der Wijngaart, R., Woo, A., Yarrow, M.: The NAS parallel benchmarks 2.0. Technical Report, Technical Report NAS-95-020, NASA Ames Research Center (1995)
5. Barrachina, S., Barreda, M., Catalán, S., Dolz, M.F., Fabregat, G., Mayo, R., Quintana-Ortí, E.: An integrated framework for power-performance analysis of parallel scientific workloads. In: Energy pp. 114–119 (2013)
6. Bergman, K., Borkar, S., Campbell, D., Carlson, W., et al.: ExaScale computing study: technology challenges in achieving exascale systems peter Kogge, Editor & Study Lead (2008)

7. Bez, J.L., Bernart, E.E., dos Santos, F.F., Schnorr, L.M., Navaux, P.O.A.: Performance and energy efficiency analysis of HPC physics simulation applications in a cluster of ARM processors. Concurrency Comput. Pract. Experience **29**(22), e4014 (2017)

8. Borkar, S., Chien, A.A.: The future of microprocessors. Commun. ACM **54**(5), 67–77 (2011)

9. Cabrera, A., Almeida, F., Arteaga, J., Blanco, V.: Measuring energy consumption using EML (energy measurement library). Comput. Sci.-Res. Dev. **30**(2), 135–143 (2015)

10. Dzhagaryan, A., Milenkovic, A., Milosevic, M., Jovanov, E.: An environment for automated measuring of energy consumed by android mobile devices. In: Ahrens, A., Benavente-Peces, C. (eds.) Proceedings of the 6th International Joint Conference on Pervasive and Embedded Computing and Communication Systems (PECCS 2016), Lisbon, Portugal, 25–27 July 2016, pp. 28–39. SciTePress (2016)

11. Göddeke, D., et al.: Energy efficiency vs. performance of the numerical solution of PDEs: an application study on a low-power arm-based cluster. J. Comput. Phys. **237**, 132–150 (2013)

12. González Rincón, J.D.: Sistema basado en open source hardware para la monitorización del consumo de un computador (2015)

13. Group of architecture and technology of computing systems (ArTeCS) of the Complutense University of Madrid: AccelPowerCape reference Page. https://artecs. dacya.ucm.es/tools/accelpowercape/ Accessed 17 Feb 2021

14. Hunold, S., Träff, J.L.: On the state and importance of reproducible experimental research in parallel computing (2013)

15. Kim, J.M., Kim, Y.G., Chung, S.W.: Stabilizing CPU frequency and voltage for temperature-aware DVFS in mobile devices. IEEE Trans. Comput. **64**(1), 286–292 (2015)

16. Milosevic, M., Dzhagaryan, A., Jovanov, E., Milenkovic, A.: An environment for automated power measurements on mobile computing platforms. In: Saad, A. (ed.) ACM Southeast Regional Conference 2013, ACM SE'13, Savannah, GA, USA, 4–6 April 2013. pp. 19:1–19:6. ACM (2013)

17. Nikov, K., Núñez-Yáñez, J.L.: Intra and inter-core power modelling for single-ISA heterogeneous processors. Int. J. Embed. Syst. **12**(3), 324–340 (2020)

18. Núñez-Yáñez, J.L., Lore, G.: Enabling accurate modeling of power and energy consumption in an arm-based system-on-chip. Microprocess. Microsyst. **37**(3), 319–332 (2013)

19. Schürmans, S., Onnebrink, G., Leupers, R., Ascheid, G., Chen, X.: Frequency-aware ESL power estimation for ARM cortex-a9 using a black box processor model. ACM Trans. Embed. Comput. Syst. **16**(1), 26:1–26:26 (2016)

20. Venkatesh, G., et al.: Conservation cores: reducing the energy of mature computations. ACM Sigplan Not. **45**(3), 205–218 (2010)

21. Vitek, J., Kalibera, T.: R3: repeatability, reproducibility and rigor. SIGPLAN Not. **47**(4a), 30–36 (2012)

22. Yokoyama, D., Schulze, B., Borges, F., Mc Evoy, G.: The survey on ARM processors for HPC. J. Supercomput. **75**(10), 7003–7036 (2019). https://doi.org/10. 1007/s11227-019-02911-9

Distributed Objective Function Evaluation for Optimization of Radiation Therapy Treatment Plans

Felix Liu[1,2][(✉)] [iD], Måns I. Andersson[1] [iD], Albin Fredriksson[2],
and Stefano Markidis[1]

[1] KTH Royal Institute of Technology, Stockholm, Sweden
`felixliu@kth.se`
[2] RaySearch Laboratories, Stockholm, Sweden

Abstract. The modern workflow for radiation therapy treatment planning involves mathematical optimization to determine optimal treatment machine parameters for each patient case. The optimization problems can be computationally expensive, requiring iterative optimization algorithms to solve. In this work, we investigate a method for distributing the calculation of objective functions and gradients for radiation therapy optimization problems across computational nodes. We test our approach on the TROTS dataset— which consists of optimization problems from real clinical patient cases—using the IPOPT optimization solver in a leader/follower type approach for parallelization. We show that our approach can utilize multiple computational nodes efficiently, with a speedup of approximately 2-3.5 times compared to the serial version.

Keywords: Optimization · Radiation Therapy · Distributed Computing

1 Introduction

Radiation therapy is one of the most common forms of cancer treatment today. Before a patient undergoes treatment, the control parameters for the treatment machine, such as the dose rate and the shape of the aperture through which to irradiate the patient, must be determined. This process is known as *treatment planning*. Ultimately, the goal of the treatment is to deliver sufficient dose to the tumor to kill cancerous cells, while sparing surrounding healthy tissue.

In modern radiation treatment planning, mathematical optimization is used to determine parameters for the treatment machine (often a linear- or particle accelerator). The planning process typically begins after a CT (Computed Tomography) scan of the patient has been imported into a *treatment planning system* (TPS), a software product designed for radiation treatment planning. Contours of important structures such as risk organs and the tumor—the regions-of-interest (ROIs)—in the patient are drawn on the CT. Optimization functions

R. Wyrzykowski et al. (Eds.): PPAM 2022, LNCS 13826, pp. 383–395, 2023.
https://doi.org/10.1007/978-3-031-30442-2_29

in the form of objectives and constraints corresponding to desirable qualities of the dose delivered to the ROIs are defined, yielding a mathematical optimization problem. The optimization problem is then solved numerically, and, if needed, the process is repeated in a trial-and-error fashion where the optimization functions and possible importance weights are changed until a high-quality plan is achieved.

The treatment planning process is time-consuming, in part because the optimization problem is computationally demanding. Efficient algorithms for solving the problem is crucial, both for efficiency at the clinics and for the quality of the resulting treatment plans. Due to the high computational demand, utilizing HPC resources such as accelerators or distributed computing clusters is an important step.

In this work, we propose a method for distributing the computation of objective function, constraints and gradients—in many cases an important computational bottleneck—across multiple computational nodes. We show the effectiveness of our approach by utilizing the IPOPT solver [9], a general software library for nonlinear optimization, together with our method for distributing optimization function evaluations across nodes, on optimization problems from radiation therapy. We study problems from the TROTS dataset, an open dataset with data for optimization problems from real patients treated for cancers in the head-and-neck region. We provide an implementation to calculate function values and gradients using input data from TROTS in a distributed fashion and show that our approach can produce solutions of high quality while being able to effectively utilize distributed computing resources, with approximately a 2-3x speedup compared to the single node version.

2   Background and Related Work

We consider treatment planning for high-energy photons using the treatment technique *volumetric modulated arc therapy* (VMAT) [7], where the gantry head of the treatment machine is continuously rotated around the patient during the treatment. The optimization variables in our problems are *beamlet weights*, which are intensity values for the delivered beams in the plane in front of the gantry. From the beamlet weights, the actual treatment machine settings required to deliver such an intensity profile at each beam angle can be determined and a deliverable plan can be created.

2.1   TROTS Dataset

The TROTS dataset [2] consists of data for patients with cancers in the head-and-neck region, liver or prostate. The dataset contains objective functions and constraints for the dose in each ROI of the patient, which form the nonlinear optimization problem to be solved. Furthermore, *dose influence matrices* are

Table 1. The different types of optimization functions used in the TROTS dataset problems we have used. In the following $f(x)$ denotes an optimization function, $d_i(x)$ is the dose in voxel i of a given ROI, and $\hat{d}$ denotes a desired dose level.

Name	$f(x)$	Comment
LTCP:	$\frac{1}{n}\sum_{i=1}^{n} e^{-\alpha(d_i(x)-\hat{d})}$	where $\alpha \in \mathbb{R}$ is a parameter
min/max dose:	$g(d(x))$	g is min/max function
Mean dose	$\frac{1}{n}\sum_{i=1}^{n} d_i(x)$	
Generalized mean:	$\left(\frac{1}{n}\sum_{i=1}^{n} d_i(x)^a\right)^{\frac{1}{a}}$	$a \in \mathbb{R}$ is a parameter
Quadratic:	$\frac{1}{2}x^T A x + b^T x + c$	A is a matrix, b, c are constant vectors

provided for each ROI separately. The dose influence matrix gives the relation between the optimization variables, beamlet weights, and the resulting dose in the ROI. In previous work, the TROTS dataset has for instance been used to evaluate the performance of optimization solvers tailored for radiation therapy [1].

We note that having separate dose matrices for each ROI is not ubiquitous in radiation therapy optimization, it is also possible to provide a single dose matrix covering the entire relevant part of the patient volume and to extract the doses for each ROI from the total dose. Since there is only a single dose matrix in this case, distributing the computation becomes more complicated, in which case it may be more natural to look to GPU accelerators instead, see for instance the work in [6].

For our experiments, we use the same optimization functions as provided in TROTS, with the exception of the min and max dose constraints, which we substitute with quadratic penalties of the form:

$$f(x) = \frac{1}{n}\sum_{i=1}^{n}(g(d_i(x) - \hat{d}, 0))^2$$

where g again is either min or max.

The dependence between the dose $d(x)$ for a given ROI and the optimization variables x is linear. To calculate the dose for a given ROI and value of x, we simply multiply x by the dose influence matrix A for that ROI: $d(x) = Ax$. The TROTS dataset provides one dose influence matrix for each ROI, which is stored as a sparse matrix.

The optimization problem for a TROTS case is then specified using a weighted sum of the objectives, shown in Table 1 on the different ROIs, together with the constraints on ROIs in the following form:

$$\min_{x} \quad \sum_{i=1}^{n} w_i f_i(x)$$
$$\text{s.t.} \quad g_i(x) \leq 0$$
$$x \geq 0$$

Here, $f_i(x)$ are the objectives for the different ROIs, with w_i being their corresponding weight and $g_i(x)$ are the constraint functions on the doses in the ROIs. Typically, very strict requirements on some dose function in a particular ROI may be specified as a hard constraint, instead of as a term in the objective function.

2.2   Dose Influence Matrices

Since all the optimization functions used in the optimization problems are functions of dose in the different regions of interest in the patient, dose calculation is an important computational kernel. The dose calculation in our case is a sparse matrix-vector product, $d = Ax$, with the dose influence matrices A being provided by the TROTS dataset. Note also that in the case of TROTS, the dose influence matrices are given for each ROI separately, instead of for the patient volume as a whole.

The size of the dose influence matrix varies quite significantly between the ROIs, meaning that the computational time needed to compute the optimization function for the different ROIs varies significantly. A histogram of the number of non-zero values in the different dose influence matrices (there are approximately 40 in total) is shown in Fig. 1a. We see that the number of non-zeros varies significantly, with some matrices having approximately 5000 non-zero elements, while others have closer to 10 million.

2.3   Radiatiation Therapy Plan Quality

The ultimate goal when solving optimization problems in radiation therapy treatment planning is to create treatment plans of high quality. To this end, the mathematical optimization problem can be seen as a proxy, providing a way to produce plans with desirable dose characteristics. Considering this, the quality of the resulting plan should not only be evaluated based on how accurately the optimization problem was solved, but also using other dose-based metrics which may reflect plan quality more accurately.

One common method for evaluating and comparing treatment plans is using dose-volume histograms (DVH) [4]. DVHs are defined using the so called volume-at-dose metric. For a given ROI with n voxels (with identical sizes), discretized dose $d \in \mathcal{R}^n$ and dose level $\hat{d}$, the volume-at-dose $V_{\hat{d}}(d)$ is defined as:

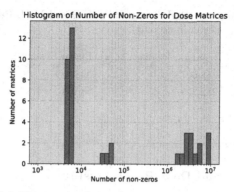

(a) Histogram of the distribution of the number of non-zeros for the dose influence matrices in the Head-and-Neck problem 01 from the TROTS dataset.

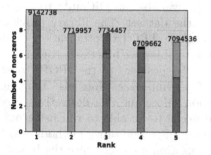

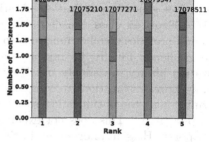

(b) Greedy distribution of the dose influence matrices for objective functions.

(c) Greedy distribution of the dose influence matrices for constraints.

Fig. 1. Distribution of the dose influence matrices using the greedy algorithms on six ranks (one rank reserved for IPOPT). The histogram of the distribution of non-zeros of the dose matrices is shown on top. The bottom figure shows the distribution of dose matrices produced by our greedy heuristic with MPI ranks on the x-axis and corresponding colored bars being the sizes of the dose matrices assigned to that rank. The total size of all dose matrices for each ranks is shown above each bar.

$$V_{\hat{d}}(d) = \frac{\sum_{i=1}^{n} \mathbb{1}(d_i \geq \hat{d})}{n},$$

where $\mathbb{1}$ is the indicator function. Informally, the volume-at-dose gives the proportion of the ROI volume receiving a dose of at least $\hat{d}$. A DVH for a given ROI is a plot showing $V_{\hat{d}}$ as a function of different dose levels $\hat{d}$, and can be used to visually compare dose distributions from different plans.

Table 2. Timings comparing IPOPT using MUMPS and MKL Pardiso. All times are wall-clock times and measured in seconds.

Setup	Function Evaluation (s)	Linear System Sol. (s)	Total Time (s)
IPOPT w. MUMPS	248.607	598.884	891.163
IPOPT w. MKL Pardiso	212.223	58.951	279.399

3   Methodology

3.1   Serial Version and Data Preprocessing

While the TROTS dataset provides the data required to specify the optimization problems for each of its patient cases, it does not provide the code to compute the objective functions, constraints or gradients, or code to interface the data to optimization libraries. To be able to interface the problem to the IPOPT solver, we have developed a C++ library (which is available on Github[1]) to enable the use of general optimization libraries on the dataset. The library provides a TROTSProblem class, which represents a single TROTS optimization problem and provides member functions to compute objective functions, constraints and gradients. Finally, to interface the TROTS problem to the IPOPT optimization library, we simply use IPOPT's C++ interface. Note also that our library provides functions to compute function values and first-derivatives only, meaning that the optimization solver used needs to be able to run using only first-derviatives. This does not exclude the use of second-order methods which incorporate Hessian information in the optimization however, since the Hessian can be approximated using quasi-Newton methods [3], which are supported in IPOPT.

IPOPT supports the use of multiple different linear solvers to solve the linear systems arising internally from its optimization algorithm. In general, one can expect that the overall performance of the optimization solver depends on the choice of linear solver. Initially, we tried IPOPT using the linear solvers MUMPS, and MKL Pardiso (a part of Intel MKL), since those packages are freely available. We used IPOPT's internal timers to compare the two linear solvers, and the results are summarized in Table 2. The optimization was run for a total of 3000 iterations.

As seen in Table 2, we get significantly better performance when using the MKL Pardiso linear solver, compared to MUMPS. Thus we use the MKL Pardiso solver for the remainder of this work.

When using IPOPT with MKL Pardiso, we see that the computational time becomes dominated by the function evaluations, taking approximately 76% of the total wall clock time in optimization. This part is thus a natural candidate for parallelization to further improve performance.

---

[1] https://github.com/felliu/Optimization-Benchmarks.

3.2 Parallelization

As mentioned in the previous section, function evaluation is a significant computational bottleneck in the optimization. This part thus becomes a natural target
for parallelization, which can be achieved by distributing terms of the objective function and constraints between computational nodes. Indeed, that is the
approach we use in this work.

We use MPI to distribute the computation, where MPI rank 0 (the leader)
holds the IPOPT instance (which does not natively support MPI), and the
remaining ranks compute objective function and constraints in parallel when
requested by rank 0. The parallelization works such that each MPI process is
assigned a set of terms of the objective function and constraints for which it is
responsible for computing values. When rank 0 requires new function values, it
broadcasts the current values of the optimization variables to all other processes,
which then computes the function and gradient values for which it is responsible, before MPI collectives are used to aggregate the result to rank 0, which can
then proceed with the next iteration in the optimization algorithm. A conceptual
overview of the parallelization method is shown in Fig. 2.

Listing 1.1 shows the code for the function handling the dispatching of function evaluations to the different MPI ranks which is the key in enabling the use
of a distributed method for computing function values with an MPI-unaware
optimization solver. At startup, when initialization is finished, all ranks, except
rank 0, call the `compute_vals_mpi` function and wait at the `MPI_Barrier`. When
the optimization solver requires new function and constraint values to continue,
it calls `compute_vals_mpi`, thus releasing the barrier and allowing all ranks to
compute the required values in parallel.

Considering the uneven distribution in sizes of the dose matrices, as seen
in Fig. 1a, a way to balance the workload between processes is required. When
calculating objectives and constraints, the most computationally expensive part
is the sparse matrix-vector product for the dose. Thus, we use the number of
non-zeros in the dose influence matrices for each term to balance the workload
between processors.

The problem of distributing the terms of the objectives and constraints as
evenly as possible is an instance of the *multi-way number partitioning problem*
[8], where one seeks a partitioning of a multiset of integers into k partitions, such
that the discrepancy between the sizes of the partitions is minimal. This problem
is NP-complete, making heuristic algorithms attractive choices. A simple greedy
heuristic is to sort the numbers in descending order, then, in order, assign the
numbers to the partition with the smallest sum at that point. On average, one
would expect this to give a partitioning with a discrepancy on the order of the
smallest number [8]. Considering the difference in size between the smallest and
largest dose influence matrices (again, see Fig. 1a), we expect the greedy heuristic
to work well enough in our case. Thus, our method of distributing terms of the
objectives and constraints is as follows:

```
1    double compute_vals_mpi(bool calc_obj, const double* x, double* cons_vals,
2                            bool calc_grad, double* grad,
3                            LocalData& local_data,
4                            std::optional<ConsDistributionData> distrib_data,
5                            bool done) {
6        while (true) {
7            //"Task-pool", wait here until rank 0 is requesting function
                 values to be computed
8            MPI_Barrier(MPI_COMM_WORLD);
9
10           //Check if rank 0 is signalling that the optimization is done
11           int done_flag = static_cast<int>(done);
12           MPI_Bcast(&done_flag, 1, MPI_INT, 0, MPI_COMM_WORLD);
13           if (done_flag)
14               return 0.0;
15
16           int rank;
17           MPI_Comm_rank(MPI_COMM_WORLD, &rank);
18           double obj_val = 0.0;
19
20           //Are we calculating objectives or constraints?
21           int calc_obj_flag = static_cast<int>(calc_obj);
22           MPI_Bcast(&calc_obj, 1, MPI_INT, 0, MPI_COMM_WORLD);
23           if (calc_obj) {
24               obj_val = compute_obj_vals_mpi(x, calc_grad, grad, local_data);
25           } else {
26               compute_cons_vals_mpi(x, cons_vals, calc_grad,grad, local_data,
                     distrib_data);
27           }
28
29           //Rank 0 returns to the optimization solver
30           //to continue to the next iteration / step
31           if (rank == 0)
32               return obj_val;
33       }
34   }
```

Listing 1.1. "Task-pool", function handling dispatching of function evaluations to different ranks. All ranks but 0 wait in the barrier at line 7 until rank 0 requests new function values to be computed.

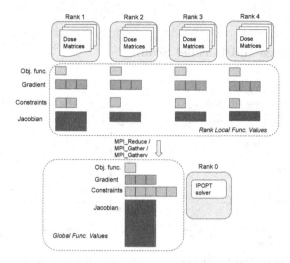

Fig. 2. Illustration of the parallelization method used. Rank 0 holds the optimization solver and the global values for objective functions, constraints and gradients. The different terms and values are spread across the ranks, which compute local values that are aggregated back to Rank 0 using MPI collectives.

1. Sort the terms in descending order based on number of non-zeros in the corresponding dose matrix
2. Go through the terms in order, assigning each term to the processor with the smallest total number of non-zeros.

An example of a resulting distribution of matrices for the case with six total MPI ranks (recalling that one rank is reserved for the optimization solver) is shown in Fig. 1.

3.3 Experimental Setup

The performance experiments in this study are carried out on following systems:

- **Dardel** is an HPE Cray EX supercomputer at PDC in Stockholm, Sweden. We use the `main` partition on Dardel where each node has two AMD EPYC 7742 CPUs.
- **Kebnekaise** is a supercomputer at HPC2N in Umeå, Sweden. Again we use the `Compute` partition of the cluster where each node has a single Intel Xeon E5-2690v4 CPU, 128 GB of RAM.

We compile our codes using GCC 11.2.0 on both systems. We refer to the Github repository of the code for the dependencies required to build our library. For MPI, we use Cray MPICH 8.1.11 on Dardel and OpenMPI 4.1.1 on Kebnekaise.

4   Results

4.1   Performance and Parallel Scaling

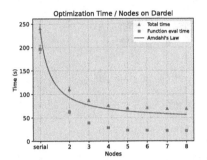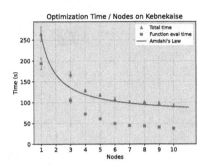

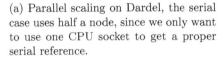

(a) Parallel scaling on Dardel, the serial case uses half a node, since we only want to use one CPU socket to get a proper serial reference.

(b) Parallel scaling on Kebnekaise. The 2 node case is omitted, since there is no parallelism in that case due to the optimization solver occupying one full node.

Fig. 3. Scaling tests on Dardel and Kebnekaise

We begin by assessing the performance and parallel scaling of our code on two supercomputing clusters. Figure 3 shows the total run time of the optimizer depending on the number of nodes. In all cases, the optimization was run for 3000 iterations, and repeated five times with the average times and standard deviations (vertical red lines) shown. All times were measured using IPOPT's internal timers, using the `print_timing_statistics` option. The upper data points (triangles) show the total execution time of the optimization. The lower data points (squares) show the portion of time in function evaluations only. The solid red line shows the theoretically possible time as predicted by Amdahl's law, where the serial portion is the time spent in IPOPT.

4.2   Plan Quality

To verify that our approach produces treatment plans of high quality, we compare DVH curves (see Sect. 2.3) from our plans with the reference solution provided from TROTS. Figure 4 shows DVH curves from our parallel implementation (solid lines) compared to a reference plan provided by TROTS (dashed lines) on the first VMAT Head-and-Neck case. While a complete discourse on evaluating plans based on DVH curves is out of scope for this paper, we can see that the DVH curves between our solution and the reference are quite similar. A general guideline for treatment plans is that the planning target volume (PTV), which encompasses the tumor, should receive a sufficiently high uniform dose, while organs at risk should receive as little dose as possible.

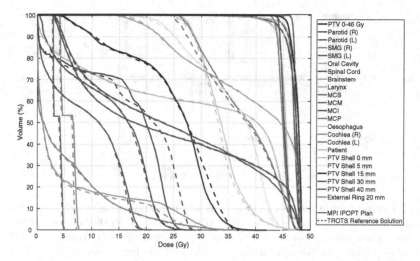

Fig. 4. DVH comparison between our plan, computed using IPOPT and 3 nodes on Dardel, and a reference plan from the TROTS dataset. The DVH curves from our plan are shown in solid lines and the reference plan is the dashed line. This plot was created using a slightly modified version of Matlab scripts provided by the TROTS authors[5].

4.3 Performance Analysis and Execution Tracing

To further understand the performance of our code, we traced our applications using Score-P [5]. We traced for a total of 100 iterations using 6 MPI ranks on the Dardel system, and the trace for a few iterations can be seen in Fig. 5, which shows the tracing for a few iterations but zoomed in at different scales. The red bars show the idle time in MPI_Barrier for each rank, the green bars in rank 0 is the time rank 0 spends in the IPOPT optimization solver. The cyan bars in the other ranks is the time computing the sparse matrix-vector products to evaluate function values, and the brown bars come from time spent in function evaluations outside the matrix-vector products.

From the tracing in Fig. 5 we see that our load balancing scheme works reasonably well, with the amount of time spent in the different ranks when computing function values being similar. There is some imbalance, especially when looking at rank 5, which appears to be caused by the function value evaluation from the dose. On closer investigation the function type causing the long evaluation times is the generalized mean, for which we use the C++ standard library function std::pow to compute the powers, which may be quite expensive. From the tracing we can also see the limitation in scaling imposed by the serial IPOPT solver, where the other MPI ranks are idle.

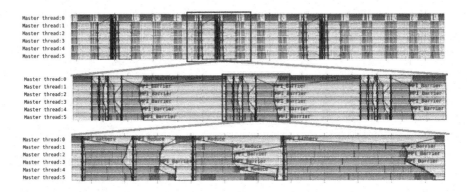

Fig. 5. Tracing from a number of iterations of the optimization. Rank 0 handles the optimization solver (green is time spent in IPOPT) while the other ranks do the function evaluations where cyan is sparse linear algebra operations (to compute the dose), red is time waiting for the optimization solver, and the brown is computing function values from the dose. In the second panel we zoom in and show three evaluations. In the third panel the different stages of the objective function evaluation are clearly distinguishable. (Color figure online)

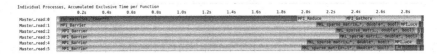

Fig. 6. The accumulated exclusive time per function. The optimization solver is found on rank 0 and, green represents compute. The color scheme is the same as in Fig. 5 (Color figure online)

Figure 6 shows the accumulated time spent in different functions for the MPI ranks, with each row representing one MPI rank. The length of each bar shows the proportion of time spent in the corresponding function call. We see that the load balancing between the ranks is decent, but with some room for improvement.

5 Discussion and Conclusion

We have developed a parallel code for solving optimization problems from the TROTS dataset for radiation therapy treatment planning, capable of utilizing multi-node computational clusters for evaluating objective functions, constraints and their gradients. We show that our code can produce treatment plans of high quality while utilizing high-performance computing clusters effectively. Our approach distributes the function evaluations at each iteration across computational nodes, while using the state of the art single-node optimization solver IPOPT to compute the next iteration. We show that our approach can improve solution times by a factor of around 3.5 when compared to the serial time on a traditional supercomputer. While the possible parallel scaling is limited by the serial portion coming from the optimization solver, computational efficiency is often crucial for real clinics, and improvements in optimization times and time-to-solution are valued highly.

Acknowledgements. The computations were enabled by resources provided by the Swedish National Infrastructure for Computing (SNIC) at High Performance Computing Center North (HPC2N) and PDC Center for High Performance Computing, partially funded by the Swedish Research Council through grant agreement no. 2018-05973.

References

1. Breedveld, S., van den Berg, B., Heijmen, B.: An interior-point implementation developed and tuned for radiation therapy treatment planning. Computational Optimization and Applications **68**(2), 209–242 (2017). https://doi.org/10.1007/s10589-017-9919-4
2. Breedveld, S., Heijmen, B.: Data for trots-the radiotherapy optimisation test set. Data in brief **12**, 143–149 (2017). https://doi.org/10.1016/j.dib.2017.03.037
3. Dennis, J.E., Jr., Moré, J.J.: Quasi-newton methods, motivation and theory. SIAM review **19**(1), 46–89 (1977). https://doi.org/10.1137/1019005
4. Drzymala, R., Mohan, R., Brewster, L., Chu, J., Goitein, M., Harms, W., Urie, M.: Dose-volume histograms. International Journal of Radiation Oncology* Biology* Physics 21(1), 71–78 (1991). https://doi.org/10.1016/0360-3016(91)90168-4
5. Knüpfer, A., Rössel, C., Biersdorff, S., Diethelm, K., Eschweiler, D., Geimer, M., Gerndt, M., Lorenz, D., Malony, A., Nagel, W.E., et al.: Score-p: A joint performance measurement run-time infrastructure for periscope, scalasca, tau, and vampir. In: Tools for High Performance Computing 2011, pp. 79–91. Springer (2012). https://doi.org/10.1007/978-3-642-31476-6_7
6. Liu, F., Jansson, N., Podobas, A., Fredriksson, A., Markidis, S.: Accelerating radiation therapy dose calculation with nvidia gpus. In: 2021 IEEE International Parallel and Distributed Processing Symposium Workshops (IPDPSW). pp. 449–458. IEEE (2021). https://doi.org/10.1109/IPDPSW52791.2021.00076
7. Otto, K.: Volumetric modulated arc therapy: Imrt in a single gantry arc. Medical physics **35**(1), 310–317 (2008). https://doi.org/10.1118/1.2818738
8. Schreiber, E.L., Korf, R.E., Moffitt, M.D.: Optimal multi-way number partitioning. Journal of the ACM (JACM) **65**(4), 1–61 (2018). https://doi.org/10.1145/3184400
9. Wächter, A., Biegler, L.T.: On the implementation of an interior-point filter line-search algorithm for large-scale nonlinear programming. Mathematical programming **106**(1), 25–57 (2006). https://doi.org/10.1007/s10107-004-0559-y

Soft Computing with Applications

GPU4SNN: GPU-Based Acceleration for Spiking Neural Network Simulations

Nitin Satpute$^{(\boxtimes)}$, Anna Hambitzer, Saeed Aljaberi, and Najwa Aaraj

Cryptography Research Centre, Technology Innovation Institute, 9639, Masdar City, Abu Dhabi, UAE
{nitin.satpute,anna.hambitzer,saeed.aljaberi,najwa.aaraj}@tii.ae
https://www.tii.ae/

Abstract. Spiking Neural Networks (SNNs) are the most common and widely used artificial neural network models in bio-inspired computing. However, SNN simulation requires high computational resources. Therefore, multiple state-of-the-art (SOTA) algorithms explore parallel hardware based implementations for SNN simulation, such as the use of Graphics Processing Units (GPUs). However, we recognize inefficiencies in the utilization of hardware resources in the current SOTA implementations for SNN simulation, namely, the Neuron (N)-, Synapse (S)-, and Action Potential (AP)-algorithm. This work proposes and implements two novel algorithms on an NVIDIA Ampere A100 GPU: The Active Block (AB)- and Single Kernel Launch (SKL)-algorithm. The proposed algorithms consider the available computational resources on both, the Central Processing Unit (CPU) and GPU, leading to a balanced workload for SNN simulation. Our SKL-algorithm is able to remove the CPU bottleneck completely. The average speedups obtained by the best of the proposed algorithms are factors of $0.83\times$, $1.36\times$ and $1.55\times$ in comparison to the SOTA algorithms for firing modes 0, 1 and 2 respectively. The maximum speedups obtained are factors of $1.9\times$, $2.1\times$ and $2.1\times$ for modes 0, 1 and 2 respectively.

Keywords: SNNs · GPUs · Dynamic Parallelism · Grid-stride Loop · Parallelization Algorithms

1 Introduction

The brain has inspired many researchers due to its energy efficiency, accuracy and robustness. The field of neuromorphic computing aims to mimic the underlying neurological processes. Spiking Neural Networks (SNNs) are the most widely used neural network model in the neuromorphic research community [23].

Researchers from deep learning community are exploring bio-inspired Artificial Neural Networks (ANNs) [10]. ANNs are known for their ability to recognize patterns in images (e.g. [20]) or time-series data (e.g. [26]), and solve complex problems like navigating autonomous vehicles or –in combination with reinforcement learning– mastering the game of Go [29]. SNNs can be seen as the new, 3rd

R. Wyrzykowski et al. (Eds.): PPAM 2022, LNCS 13826, pp. 399–413, 2023.
https://doi.org/10.1007/978-3-031-30442-2_30

generation of ANNs [14] and can, in principle, be used for the same applications. One motivation to develop the "traditional" ANNs to a new generation is the surprising fact that ANNs are "easy to fool" [17], e.g. an adversarial image can be engineered in a way that, for example, a human can still easily recognize a stop-sign, however, the ANN will now identify the same sign as a speed-limit. SNNs may hold the promise of greater inherent robustness to such manipulations [9]. An additional motivation for the investigation of SNNs as per Roy et al. [28] is that the human brain accomplishes extremely complex tasks with a tiny energy budget when compared to traditional ANNs. Currently under investigation are memristor-based hardware [9], Intel Loihi [7], SpiNNaker [13], and IBM TrueNorth [8].

However, SNN computations are challenging in contrast to ANN computations, since they involve the timing information of spikes and internal neuron dynamics [23]. On the other hand, SNN training is an ongoing field of study [25,32]. ANNs have already benefited massively from the utilization of Graphics Processing Units (GPUs) by using the Compute Unified Device Architecture (CUDA) programming framework. The most common modelling tools, PyTorch [27] and TensorFlow [1] readily provide a high-level CUDA interface for Deep Neural Networks (DNNs).

Another research field with interest in the efficient simulation of biologically plausible neural networks is computational neuroscience. The size and complexity of biological networks by far exceeds the one of current artificial neural networks [4]. It is recognized that the analysis of biological and ANN have developed largely independent in the past [32], though facing a set of similar challenges [4] and future synergies are expected [35]. To handle the additional requirements of SNNs simulation in the neuromorphic research community, several hardware and software frameworks have been developed, such as NEURON [6], NEST [11], NeMo [12], NCS6 [18], CARLsim [5], GeNN [33], Spike [2], BRIAN2 [30], PyNN [3] and NeuronGPU [15]. The frameworks differ in the level of detail with which they model neural functions. In terms of utilizing parallel hardware, BRIAN2 [30] supports multithreaded parallel computations, while NEURON [6] and NEST [11] support distributed simulations on computer clusters with NVIDIA GPUs using CUDA and Message Passing Interface (MPI).

At the core of simulators lie detailed algorithms which differ in their parallelization approach on NVIDIA GPUs. In such approaches, the number of parallel threads depends on either the number of neurons (Neuron (N)-algorithm), or synapses (Synapse (S)-algorithm) or action potentials (Action Potential (AP)-algorithm) [23]. The N-, S- and AP-algorithms have their own limitations when implemented on NVIDIA GPUs. The N-algorithm is compute-intensive, since the time-complexity of the N-algorithm is proportional to the number of synapses. The S-algorithm is resource-intensive with high GPU resource requirements, since the space-complexity is proportional to the number of neurons and synapses. Both N- and S- algorithms require Central Processing Unit (CPU) intervention which may result in the so-called *CPU bottleneck*. The AP-algorithm aims to overcome limitations of the N- and S-algorithms by using the Dynamic

Parallelism (DP) [23]. However, the AP-algorithm is resource-intensive for a large number of spikes. There is only a limited amount of studies of the scaling of SNNs simulation time with the number of spikes [23].

All the above-mentioned challenges motivate an efficient use of CPU-GPU resources for improving the performance of SNN simulation. The objective of this paper is to optimize parallelization approaches for SNN simulation. We propose two novel algorithms for NVIDIA GPUs using CUDA. The overall contributions of our work are as follows:

- We recognize that the scheduling and allocation of tasks on the GPU in existing SNN simulation algorithms limit the performance.
- We propose two new parallelization algorithms [Single Kernel Launch (SKL) and Active Block (AB)] and evaluate them against the state-of-the-art (SOTA) approaches. For the evaluation, we use the same network (a pulse-coupled network of Izhikevich neurons) as in the SOTA work [23] across a wide range of modes, neuron and synapses values.
    • SKL-algorithm: The CPU bottleneck is completely avoided. Iterative kernel calling is shifted to the GPU, resulting in a single kernel call from the CPU.
    • AB-algorithm: An efficient GPU utilization based on available processing blocks for computations and communications has led to a significant speedup.
- The average speedups obtained by the best of the proposed algorithms are factors of 0.83×, 1.36× and 1.55× in comparison to the SOTA algorithms with maximum speedups of 1.9×, 2.1× and 2.1× for firing modes 0, 1 and 2 respectively.

The rest of this paper is organized as follows. Section 2 provides background information on SNN simulation, the used neuronal model, and the grid-stride loop. Section 3 introduces the SOTA and the proposed algorithms for the SNN simulation on heterogeneous CPU-GPU platforms. Sections 4 and 5 explain the evaluation methodology and present the detailed experimental results and discussions. Finally, we conclude the paper in Sect. 6.

2   Background

In this section, we first discuss the general flow in an SNN simulation (Sect. 2.1). In particular, we use the popular Izhikevich neuron model, introduced in Sect. 2.2. The network dynamics and modes are discussed in Sect. 2.3. We conclude the section by giving the necessary background knowledge on the grid-stride loop in Sect. 2.4.

2.1   General Flow of SNN Simulation

SNN simulation involves the propagation of spikes through a network of neurons and synapses. An SNN simulation starts with input signals in the time domain (called spikes) applied to the neurons of the input layer. The state of each neuron is defined by its membrane potential value. The spike at the input layer causes an input current, which in turn results in a change of the neuron membrane potential. If the neuron membrane potential crosses a certain threshold, the neuron "fires" and the spike is propagated to the neurons of the subsequent layer in the next time stamp through synapses. Consequently, the membrane potential values of the neurons in the subsequent layer are updated and the spike is propagated again and so on. This process of spike propagation is recursive or iterative depending upon the implementation. In the recursive spike propagation model, only activated neurons take part in the computation, while in the iterative spike propagation model, the state of all neurons at all time steps is considered.

The implementation of the SNN simulation on the CUDA level involves the invocation of two main kernels. The first kernel is an update kernel, given by Pseudo-code 1, for updating the state variables of an individual neuron and the spike list if the potential crosses the threshold value.

Algorithm 1. Update Kernel

1: start a thread for each neuron i:
2:      update state variables $v_i(t_{n+1})$, $u_i(t_{n+1})$ using eqs. (1) to (3)
3:      **if** $v_i(t_{n+1}) > v_\theta$ **then**
| add i to the spike list:
4: synchronize all threads:

The second kernel is propagating the spikes to postsynaptic neurons as given by Pseudo-code 2.

Algorithm 2. Propagate Spike Kernel

1: start a thread for each synapse from i to j:
2:      **if** *presynaptic neuron i spikes* **then**
| update $I_j(t_{n+1})$ by eq. (4) using an atomic operation:
3: synchronize threads to proceed to the next time step:

In each of the approaches presented in Sect. 3, these two kernels are executed in each iteration of the SNN simulation. Typically, the CPU invokes a parent kernel on the GPU and both kernels, corresponding to Pseudo-codes 1 and 2, are executed on the GPU. The resulting data is transferred back to the CPU and a new iteration starts.

2.2   Izhikevich Neuron Model

There are a number of neuron models that are currently being used in SNN simulations. These models range in complexity, biological plausibility, and computational efficiency. In this work we simulate a pulse-coupled Izhikevich neural network as it has been used to benchmark the SOTA AP algorithm by Kasap and Opstal [23], as well as the GeNN SNN simulator [34].

The Izhikevich neuron model [21] is a reduced-order model of the Hodgkin-Huxley model [19], which is obtained by means of bifurcation theory. The Izhikevich model sacrifices the biological plausibility of the Hodgkin-Huxley model, but retains its functionality. In this way the Izhikevich model is less complex and more efficient to simulate in comparison to Hodgkin-Huxley model [22][1]. Furthermore, it possesses the capacity to describe more complex neuronal behaviors (spiking patterns), which make it more attractive than Leaky-integrate-and-fire neuron models [21].

The Izhikevich model is a 2-dimensional system consisting of the states u and v, which are the membrane potential and its recovery variable, respectively. Their instantaneous rate of change obey the following set of ordinary differential equations:

$$v' = 0.04v^2 + 5v + 140 - u + I \tag{1}$$

$$u' = a(bv - u) \tag{2}$$

$$\text{if } v \geq 30\,\text{mV, then} \begin{cases} v \leftarrow c \\ u \leftarrow u + d \end{cases} \tag{3}$$

where the prime $'$ represents the derivative with respect to time, a, b, c and d are dimensionless parameters that are chosen to fine-tune the desired neuronal behavior (spiking, bursting, etc.), and I is the current. A spike is propagated if the neuron membrane potential crosses the threshold value of 30 mV given by Eq. (3)- if it accumulates the necessary amount of inputs. The value of v resets to resting value c and the value of u increases by recovery reset d when the neuron fires the spike. In our system the injected current I is modeled as

$$I_j(t_{n+1}) = g_{exc,inh} \cdot q_j(t_n) + w_s \sum_i^S S_{ij}\delta_i(t_n) \tag{4}$$

where S_{ij} is the connectivity matrix element from presynaptic neuron i to neuron j, and w_s is a fixed synaptic scaling factor that depends on the total number of synapses in the network. The δ_i variable is equal to 1 if neuron i spikes at time t_n, i.e. $\delta_i(t_n) = 1$ and $\delta_i(t_n) = o$ otherwise.

Neurons are classified to be either *excitatory* or *inhibitory*, and their ratio is conventionally chosen as 4:1 in the network, inspired by the mammalian cortex [21,23]. If a neuron is excitatory or inhibitory is defined by its connection strength: The connection strengths S_{ij} to an excitatory (or inhibitory) neuron are chosen randomly from a uniform distribution on [0, 0.5] ([−1, 0]) [23]. The input current I_j for neuron j from Eq. (4) consists of the sum of the stochastic input current q_j scaled by an excitatory or inhibitory conductance $g_{exc,inh}$ and the synaptic currents received from its active presynaptic neurons [23].

---

[1] However, there have been a number of studies that rigorously analyze the performance aspects of the different models that suggest otherwise. The interested reader is referred to [31] and references therein.

2.3 Network Dynamics and Modes

The network dynamics are determined by the values of the input conductance values $g_{exc,inh}$ in Eq. (4), resulting in different firing regimes or *modes* of the network as presented in Table 1. The definition is identical to the one used by Kasap and van Opstal in [23].

Table 1. Definition of the *quiet, balanced* and *irregular* firing modes based on the chosen excitatory or inhibitory conductance values $g_{exc,inh}$.

mode index	mode name	g_{exc}	g_{inh}
0	*quiet*	2.5	1.0
1	*balanced*	5.0	2.0
2	*irregular*	7.5	3.0

The processing of the propagation of each spike through the network requires a certain amount of hardware resources. The *balanced* and *irregular* networks generate a large number of spikes, which makes their simulation computationally challenging compared to mode 0, i.e. *quiet* networks.

2.4 Grid-Stride Loop

GPUs, in general, support dynamic (or random) scheduling of the tasks based on the available hardware resources. This dynamic scheduling mode will assign a loop iteration to an available thread [16].

It allows a more balanced execution time across threads, but incurs a higher processing overhead as it requires the thread (or a block of threads) to wait after each task(s) to receive the next iteration(s) to execute. The default scheduling policy on the GPU, is generalized for the varying execution times for different workloads and does not favor tasks that have similar execution time [16].

An alternative scheduling, the grid-stride loop is illustrated in Fig. 1. The grid-stride loop [24] avoids inefficiencies in terms of idle time on the hardware by preallocating the loop iterations to each thread in the following way: The grid-stride loop uses a static schedule that assigns loop iterations to threads for execution [24]. In a 4-thread application with 8000 loops, static scheduling will assign loops 0 to 1999 to thread ID 0, loops 2000 to 3999 to thread ID 1, loops 4000 to 5999 to thread ID 2 and lastly loops 6000 to 7999 to thread ID 3 [16]. This scheduling policy favors tasks that have similar execution time which is suitable for the special case of spike propagation. Further, GPU resources are freed as in the grid-stride loop the block processing is CPU-orchestrated in the sense of a static pre-allocation.

Depending on the parallelized task static pre-allocation in the grid-stride loop demonstrates advantages over the random block processing, for example a speedup factor of 1.4x in [16].

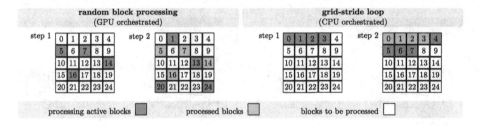

Fig. 1. Illustrated are two processing methods for computational blocks of threads. In our example, the GPU can process four blocks in parallel at a time. In the random block processing (left hand side) the GPU-resource manager handles the workload allocation. In contrast, in the grid-stride loop (right hand side) the CPU organizes the workload, freeing resources on the GPU.

3   SNN Simulation Algorithms

In this section, we discuss the SOTA (N-, S- and AP- [23]) algorithms and propose the AB- and SKL-algorithm. The implementation of the AB- and SKL-algorithm and comparison to the SOTA (AP, N, S) are made available as open access in the following GitHub repository: GPU4SNN.

The number of neurons $\mathcal{N}$ and synapses $\mathcal{S}$ in the SNN determine the required processing blocks on the GPU. However, the algorithms differ in their scheduling and allocation tactics of the processing blocks, as well as their CPU-GPU communication pattern. Figure 2 shows a simplified overview and each algorithm is discussed in the following.

N-algorithm. In the N-algorithm, the spike kernel is implemented by invoking $\mathcal{N}$ threads in parallel, as detailed in [23]. The heterogeneous implementation of the N-algorithm using CPU-GPU platforms is shown in Fig. 2. The algorithm implementation requires repeated GPU kernel calling from the CPU. Each iteration involves two kernel calls (Update Kernel and Propagate Spike Kernel) from the host CPU. The N-algorithm starts with $\mathcal{N}$ parallel threads simultaneously. Each thread operates $\mathcal{S}$ times repeatedly. Hence, the computational overhead for each thread is a factor of $\mathcal{S}$ and therefore increases with the number of synapses. The potential problem with the N-algorithm is the underutilization of the GPU resources due to launching of only $\mathcal{N}$ threads.

S-algorithm. In the N-algorithm, $\mathcal{N}$ threads are invoked in parallel and each of them iterates $\mathcal{S}$ times. In the S-algorithm [23], however, $\mathcal{N} \times \mathcal{S}$ threads are invoked in parallel and each of them iterates one time. The $\mathcal{N} \times \mathcal{S}$ threads might create a hardware resource constraint in terms of space on the GPU. Therefore, it is said to have an increased *space-complexity*. The N-algorithm, however, needs $\mathcal{S}$ iterations, each of which due to its time-consumption might lead to an increased *time-complexity*.

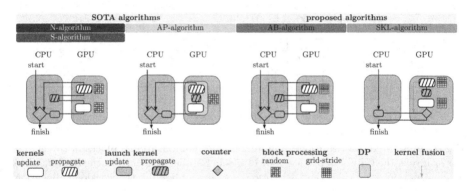

Fig. 2. Simplified communication patterns between CPU and GPU for SNN simulation with the SOTA algorithms (left hand side) and proposed algorithms (right hand side). At the core of the proposed algorithms lies a grid-stride loop, which is shown schematically in Fig. 1.

In all algorithms the same **kernels** as described in Sect. 2.4 are used. The **kernel launch** can be handled by the CPU or GPU. A **counter** tracks the iteration of the SNN simulation. **Block processing** can take place in a random or grid-stride loop fashion as described in Sect. 2.4. Particular CUDA methods are **DP** (dynamic parallelism) used by the AP-algorithm and **kernel fusion** used by the SKL-algorithm.

The $\mathcal{N} \times \mathcal{S}$ threads in the S-algorithm are combined together to form blocks of threads. The GPU resource manager randomly allocates the blocks of threads as illustrated in Fig. 1. Due to this random allocation of tasks on the GPU, the hardware resources are likely to be used inefficiently.

AP-algorithm. The AP-algorithm exploits the DP using CUDA on an NVIDIA GPU [23]. As shown in Fig. 2, in the AP-algorithm, the CPU invokes one parent kernel on the GPU with $\mathcal{N}$ threads. Given a spike from each of the $\mathcal{N}$ neurons, the respective thread will launch a child kernel with $\mathcal{S}$ threads of its own. Since launching of the child kernel depends on the presence of a spike, caused by the potential crossing of a threshold value, this algorithm is called the Action Potential algorithm. The space complexity of the AP-algorithm increases with the number of spikes.

AB-algorithm. The communication pattern of the AB-algorithm is similar to the N- or S-algorithm, as shown in Fig. 2. The main difference in the communication pattern of AB-algorithm between CPU and GPU in comparison to the N- and S-algorithm is as follows: In the AB-algorithm, the CPU is used to place the optimized workload on the GPU instead of immediately placing the total workload of the respective iteration, as was done in the case of the N- and S-algorithm. Therefore, hardware resources are used in a more balanced way. The time consuming random resource allocation and scheduling used in the N- and S-algorithm are thereby avoided to gain possible performance improvements.

SKL-algorithm. There are circumstances under which the AB-algorithm might not be the optimal choice, such as: *i)* If there is already a high workload present on the CPU, or *ii)* if the data transfers between CPU and GPU are costly. For these circumstances, we propose the SKL-algorithm. The SKL-algorithm is shown schematically in Fig. 2. The CPU launches one kernel only on the GPU. The initialization and computations of the grid-stride loop are handled by the GPU. Since all kernels are directly invoked on the GPU, the SKL-algorithm completely avoids a possible CPU bottleneck. However, it adds an extra step consisting of inter-block GPU synchronization after each stage, i.e. update and spike (*kernel fusion*).

In brief, each of the proposed algorithms first calculate the availability of the hardware resources in terms of the computational thread blocks. Later on, the proposed algorithms distribute the workload (i.e. loop iterations) of the simulation equally to each thread block using grid-stride loop on the GPU. The CPU is not only distributing the workload equally on the GPU by calling an application program interface using CUDA but also accumulating the total number of spikes obtained from the simulation for evaluating the accuracy of the simulation. The GPU simultaneously update the neurons mapped onto the threads and propagate the spikes while the accumulation of the spikes continues on the CPU. We named the proposed approaches the way they are implemented on the GPU (i.e. Active Block(AB) and Single Kernel Launch(SKL)) as opposed to the way described in terms of SNN terminologies i.e. Neuron(N), Synapses(S), and Active Potential(AP) [23].

4   Performance Evaluation

SNN simulators need to perform well on a wide range of possible neural networks: from relatively small ones with only a few number of neurons and synapses to extensively large ones. Additionally, the number of spikes may change in a quiet (0), balanced (1), or irregular (2) mode (defined in Table 1), and for how many time steps (or iterations) the simulation is performed. To ensure optimal performance under the above mentioned conditions, the scaling of the underlying parallelization algorithm needs to be favorable.

Here, the three SOTA parallelization algorithms (AP, N, S) are compared to the proposed ones (AB, SKL) in terms of their total simulation time under scaling of the number of neurons and synapses for 2000 iterations for modes 0, 1, and 2. We vary the number of neurons N by more than two orders of magnitude: in eight steps on a logarithmic scale from $N = 10^3, \ldots, 2.5 \cdot 10^5$. Similarly, we vary the number of synapses S in seven steps from $S = 2^7, \ldots, 2^{13}$ ($128, \ldots, 8192$).

We evaluate all scenarios by the total time each algorithm requires for the simulation. Figure 3 visualizes the winning algorithm with the shortest total simulation time for each neuron-synapses number pair. Overall, we see significant speedup factors of the proposed algorithms (AB, SKL) for larger spiking neural networks with a larger number of neurons in modes 1 and 2. The AP algorithm performs well in the low-spiking regime (mode 0).

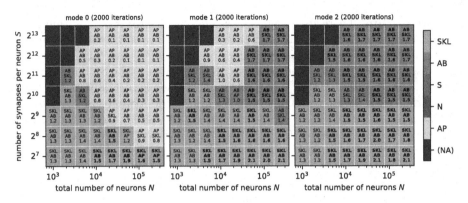

Fig. 3. Shown is the winning algorithm with the smallest total simulation time t for firing modes 0, 1, and 2 when the total number of neurons ($N = 10^3 \ldots 2.5 \cdot 10^5$) and synapses per neuron ($S = 2^7 \ldots 2^{13}$) are changed. The *two names* of the algorithms in each rectangle indicate the top two approaches with smallest simulation times, i.e. the winning algorithms, which can be SOTA and/or proposed algorithm(s). The *number* in the rectangle represents the speedup obtained by the best of the proposed algorithms over the best of the SOTA ones (i.e. $t_{\text{best SOTA}}/t_{\text{best prop.}}$). Therefore, factors > 1 show speedup obtained by the proposed algorithms over the SOTA ones. The average speedups obtained by the best of the proposed algorithms are factors of 0.83×, 1.36× and 1.55× in comparison to the SOTA algorithms with maximum speedups of 1.9×, 2.1× and 2.1× for firing modes 0, 1 and 2 respectively. Bold font highlights speedup factors above or equal to 1.5, i.e. the speedup is larger than 50% compared to the best current SOTA algorithm.

In our case the total number of neurons N is equal to the number of pre-synaptic neurons, as well as the number of post-synaptic neurons. In region "(NA)", no simulation is possible because the number of synapses per pre-synaptic neuron S is larger than the total number of post-synaptic neurons N.

To discuss the scaling behavior of each algorithm in more detail, we perform following analysis: Fig. 4 shows the absolute values for the elapsed times of each algorithm for a horizontal cut (scaling with the number of neurons) and a vertical cut (scaling with the number of synapses) through Fig. 3. We evaluate the total number of spikes ("unsigned int") obtained from each algorithm to evaluate the accuracy of the simulation. We use single precision (32-bit) float variables from CUDA for representing the state variables of neurons. We follow the same state variables (introduced in Sect. 2.2) and precision as mentioned in SOTA approaches [23]. We note the following scaling behaviors:

The **N algorithm's** scaling behavior is compatible with our expectation: The GPU is likely to have enough (N) threads. Therefore, the N algorithm scales favorably with an increasing number of neurons (see left-hand side of Fig. 4). However, as each thread has to operate S times in the N algorithm, its time complexity increases with S (see right-hand side of Fig. 4).

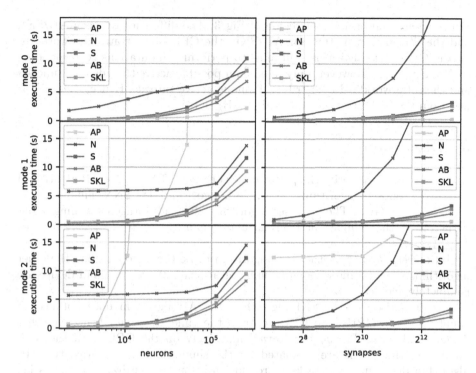

Fig. 4. Shown are the total simulation times for each algorithm when the *(left)* number of neurons is scaled ($S = 2^{10}$, $N = 10^3 \ldots 2.5 \cdot 10^5$), and *(right)* the number of synapses is scaled ($N \approx 10^4$, $S = 2^7 \ldots 2^{13}$) in modes 0, 1, and 2 *(from top to bottom)* of Fig. 3.

The **S algorithm** shows a more favorable scaling with the number of synapses than the N algorithm. The S algorithm aims to launch $N \times S$ threads in parallel. Each thread only operates one time. The GPU may not provide enough space (space complexity), and the random allocation will consume GPU resources.

The **AP algorithm** launches N threads. Given a spike of a neuron, the respective thread will launch a child kernel with S threads of its own. Therefore the space complexity is expected to increase with the number of spikes. Therefore the AP algorithm performs excellent under the conditions of low spike count. However, in the higher firing modes with higher spike count (left-hand side of Fig. 4) the launching of child kernels per spike can become costly and the total simulation time diverges.

The **AB and SKL algorithm** show a favorable scaling of the total simulation time under both, the number of neurons or synapses in Fig. 4. AB and SKL algorithm's scaling with the number of synapses is comparable to the one of the S algorithm and therefore favorable. In contrast to the S algorithm, though, the two proposed algorithms show a more favorable scaling under an increasing neuron number. This favorable scaling explains why the proposed algorithms win in the higher neuron number region of Fig. 3. The difference between AB/SKL and the S algorithm is that for AB/SKL, the CPU orchestrates the workload on the GPU. The algorithm still aims to perform computations corresponding to $N \times S$ threads. However, only maximum possible active threads are launched and the total workload is distributed among active threads. Hence, the GPU is free from the orchestration workload in AB/SKL.

5 Discussion

In this paper, we quantify the performance of the SOTA (S-, N-, AP-algorithm) and two proposed algorithms (AB-, SKL-algorithm) for SNN simulation on A100 NVIDIA GPU. The proposed algorithms show advantageous scaling under variation of the number of neurons and synapses ($N = 10^3, \ldots, 2.5 \cdot 10^5$, $S = 2^7, \ldots, 2^{13}$).

Intuitively, we expect the SKL-algorithm to be the fastest among the other algorithms since all intermediate communications between host and device are completely avoided.

In comparison to the SKL-algorithm, the AB-algorithm does not need a counter on the GPU. The CPU controls the time steps and hence launches *Update* and *Spike Propagation kernel* iteratively on the GPU until the total number of time steps are evaluated for the simulation. In this way, the AB-algorithm distributes the tasks more efficiently on the hardware resources i.e. CPU and GPU, resulting in a significant speedup and maintaining the accuracy in terms of the total number of spikes.

Two possible drawbacks of the SKL-algorithm could be the following: First, since all intermediate communication is avoided, the SKL-algorithm cannot store the temporal variation of an SNN since the data is transferred in the last iteration. Especially in the context of neuroscience the time dynamics and evolution of membrane potentials and spikes in an SNN might be important. In such a case, the limitation of intermediate communication in the SKL-algorithm limits its applications. A possible future solution could be to modify the SKL-algorithm to provide flexibility to send the data after a certain number of iterations instead of the last iteration. Another solution is to always use the proposed AB-algorithm: In the N-S configurations where the SKL-algorithm is the winner in terms of total execution time, the runner-up in the vast majority of the cases is the proposed AB-algorithm (see Fig. 3). A second disadvantage may be memory limitation. The SKL-algorithm assumes the input data as well as intermediate results will be available in the GPU memory for all the iterations. If the device memory is not large enough then its better to utilize the AB-algorithm to pipeline computations and communications. If the device memory does not entirely fit the input data and/or neural network model, then the data and/or model will be evaluated in phases. This multi-phase mode will involve the CPU intervention to load the GPU memory when the evaluation of the previous phase of the data and/or model is finished. Such a mode requires iterative kernel launching, which can be implemented by the AB-algorithm but not by the SKL-algorithm.

6   Conclusion

In this paper, we propose and evaluate two novel GPU-based algorithms (SKL and AB) for SNN simulation with a grid-stride loop as their core element. Iterative invocations of a GPU kernel from the host CPU involve time consuming tasks and the corresponding complexity increases with an increase in the number of iterations. The SKL-algorithm avoids iterative kernel calling from the host CPU. In this way, the CPU bottleneck is completely avoided and iterative calling of a kernel is shifted to the GPU resulting in a single kernel call from the CPU.

An efficient heterogeneous CPU-GPU utilization using the AB-algorithm has also provided significant speedup while maintaining the SNN accuracy in terms of the total number of spikes. The average speedups obtained by the best of the proposed algorithms are factors of $0.83\times$, $1.36\times$ and $1.55\times$ in comparison to the SOTA algorithms with maximum speedups of $1.9\times$, $2.1\times$ and $2.1\times$ for firing modes 0, 1 and 2 respectively.

References

1. Abadi, M., et al.: Tensorflow: a system for large-scale machine learning. In: 12th {USENIX} Symposium on Operating Systems Design and Implementation ({OSDI} 2016), pp. 265–283 (2016)
2. Ahmad, N., Isbister, J.B., Smithe, T.S.C., Stringer, S.M.: Spike: a GPU optimised spiking neural network simulator. bioRxiv, p. 461160 (2018)
3. Balaji, A., et al.: PyCARL: a PyNN interface for hardware-software co-simulation of spiking neural network. arXiv preprint arXiv:2003.09696 (2020)
4. Barrett, D.G., Morcos, A.S., Macke, J.H.: Analyzing biological and artificial neural networks: challenges with opportunities for synergy? Curr. Opin. Neurobiol. **55**, 55–64 (2019). https://doi.org/10.1016/j.conb.2019.01.007. Machine Learning, Big Data, and Neuroscience
5. Beyeler, M., Carlson, K.D., Chou, T.S., Dutt, N., Krichmar, J.L.: Carlsim 3: a user-friendly and highly optimized library for the creation of neurobiologically detailed spiking neural networks. In: 2015 International Joint Conference on Neural Networks (IJCNN), pp. 1–8 (2015). https://doi.org/10.1109/IJCNN.2015.7280424
6. Carnevale, N.T., Hines, M.L.: The NEURON Book. Cambridge University Press, Cambridge (2006). https://doi.org/10.1017/CBO9780511541612
7. Davies, M., et al.: Loihi: a neuromorphic manycore processor with on-chip learning. IEEE Micro **38**(1), 82–99 (2018). https://doi.org/10.1109/MM.2018.112130359
8. DeBole, M.V., et al.: Truenorth: accelerating from zero to 64 million neurons in 10 years. Computer **52**(5), 20–29 (2019). https://doi.org/10.1109/MC.2019.2903009
9. Demin, V., et al.: Necessary conditions for STDP-based pattern recognition learning in a memristive spiking neural network. Neural Netw. **134**, 64–75 (2021). https://doi.org/10.1016/j.neunet.2020.11.005
10. Diamant, E.: Designing artificial cognitive architectures: brain inspired or biologically inspired? Procedia Comput. Sci. **145**, 153–157 (2018)
11. Eppler, J., Helias, M., Muller, E., Diesmann, M., Gewaltig, M.O.: Pynest: a convenient interface to the nest simulator. Front. Neuroinform. **2**, 12 (2008). https://doi.org/10.3389/neuro.11.012.2008

12. Fidjeland, A.K., Shanahan, M.P.: Accelerated simulation of spiking neural networks using GPUs. In: The 2010 International Joint Conference on Neural Networks (IJCNN), pp. 1–8. IEEE (2010)

13. Furber, S.B., Galluppi, F., Temple, S., Plana, L.A.: The spinnaker project. Proc. IEEE **102**(5), 652–665 (2014)

14. Ghosh-Dastidar, S., Adeli, H.: Third Generation Neural Networks: Spiking Neural Networks. In: Yu, W., Sanchez, E.N. (eds.) Advances in Computational Intelligence, vol. 61, pp. 167–178. Springer, Heidelberg (2009). https://doi.org/10.1007/978-3-642-03156-4_17

15. Golosio, B., Tiddia, G., De Luca, C., Pastorelli, E., Simula, F., Paolucci, P.S.: Fast simulations of highly-connected spiking cortical models using GPUs. Front. Comput. Neurosci. **15**, 13 (2021). https://doi.org/10.3389/fncom.2021.627620

16. Gupta, K., Stuart, J.A., Owens, J.D.: A study of persistent threads style GPU programming for GPGPU workloads. In: 2012 Innovative Parallel Computing (InPar), pp. 1–14 (2012). https://doi.org/10.1109/InPar.2012.6339596

17. Heaven, D.: Why deep-learning AIs are so easy to fool. Nature **574**(7777), 163–166 (2019). https://doi.org/10.1038/d41586-019-03013-5

18. Hoang, R.V., Tanna, D., Jayet Bray, L.C., Dascalu, S.M., Harris, F.C., Jr.: A novel CPU/GPU simulation environment for large-scale biologically realistic neural modeling. Front. Neuroinform. **7**, 19 (2013)

19. Hodgkin, A.L., Huxley, A.F.: A quantitative description of membrane current and its application to conduction and excitation in nerve. J. Physiol. **117**(4), 500 (1952)

20. Hu, J., Shen, L., Sun, G.: Squeeze-and-excitation networks. In: 2018 IEEE/CVF Conference on Computer Vision and Pattern Recognition, pp. 7132–7141 (2018). https://doi.org/10.1109/CVPR.2018.00745

21. Izhikevich, E.M.: Simple model of spiking neurons. IEEE Trans. Neural Networks **14**(6), 1569–1572 (2003). https://doi.org/10.1109/TNN.2003.820440

22. Izhikevich, E.M.: Which model to use for cortical spiking neurons? IEEE Trans. Neural Networks **15**(5), 1063–1070 (2004)

23. Kasap, B., van Opstal, A.J.: Dynamic parallelism for synaptic updating in GPU-accelerated spiking neural network simulations. Neurocomputing **302**, 55–65 (2018)

24. Mark, H.: CUDA Pro Tip: Write Flexible Kernels with Grid-Stride Loops. online (2013)

25. Neftci, E.O., Mostafa, H., Zenke, F.: Surrogate gradient learning in spiking neural networks: bringing the power of gradient-based optimization to spiking neural networks. IEEE Signal Process. Mag. **36**(6), 51–63 (2019)

26. Oreshkin, B.N., Carpov, D., Chapados, N., Bengio, Y.: N-beats: neural basis expansion analysis for interpretable time series forecasting. In: International Conference on Learning Representations (2020)

27. Paszke, A., et al.: Automatic differentiation in pytorch. Openreview (2017)

28. Roy, K., Jaiswal, A., Panda, P.: Towards spike-based machine intelligence with neuromorphic computing. Nature **575**(7784), 607–617 (2019)

29. Schrittwieser, J., et al.: Mastering Atari, Go, chess and shogi by planning with a learned model. Nature **588**(7839), 604–609 (2020). https://doi.org/10.1038/s41586-020-03051-4

30. Stimberg, M., Brette, R., Goodman, D.F.: Brian 2, an intuitive and efficient neural simulator. eLife **8**, e47314 (2019). https://doi.org/10.7554/eLife.47314

31. Valadez-Godínez, S., Sossa, H., Santiago-Montero, R.: On the accuracy and computational cost of spiking neuron implementation. Neural Netw. **122**, 196–217 (2020)

32. Woźniak, S., Pantazi, A., Bohnstingl, T., Eleftheriou, E.: Deep learning incorporating biologically inspired neural dynamics and in-memory computing. Nat. Mach. Intell. **2**(6), 325–336 (2020). https://doi.org/10.1038/s42256-020-0187-0

33. Yavuz, E., Turner, J., Nowotny, T.: GeNN: a code generation framework for accelerated brain simulations. Sci. Rep. **6**(1), 1–14 (2016)

34. Yavuz, E., Turner, J., Nowotny, T.: GeNN: a code generation framework for accelerated brain simulations. Nat. Sci. Rep. **6**(Jan), 1–14 (2016). https://doi.org/10.1038/srep18854

35. Zenke, F., et al.: Visualizing a joint future of neuroscience and neuromorphic engineering. Neuron **109**(4), 571–575 (2021)

Ant System Inspired Heuristic Optimization of UAVs Deployment for k-Coverage Problem

Krzysztof Trojanowski[ID], Artur Mikitiuk[ID], and Jakub Grzeszczak[✉][ID]

Cardinal Stefan Wyszyński University in Warsaw, Wóycickiego 1/3,
01-938 Warsaw, Poland
{k.trojanowski,a.mikitiuk,jakub.grzeszczak}@uksw.edu.pl

Abstract. When ad-hoc connectivity for a group of ground users has to be delivered, one can use a network of Unmanned Aerial Vehicles (UAV) equipped with Mobile Base Stations (MBS). In this research, we minimize the number of UAVs by effectively deploying UAVs over the zone where users are located. The proposed model divides zone into sectors of different areas and shapes depending on users' location and the ranges of MBSs. Deployment of UAVs in sectors is optimized by a method inspired by the Ant System approach and extended by a new problem-specific heuristic. We propose a new set of benchmark problems, called SCP2, for simulations. Simulation results show the algorithm's efficiency and reveal the most beneficial values of the algorithm's parameters.

Keywords: Unmanned Aerial Vehicles · Ant Systems · k-Coverage Problem

1 Introduction

A network of Unmanned Aerial Vehicles (UAV) equipped with Mobile Base Stations (MBS) can provide communication services for ground users in the case of disaster or festive areas management, military operations, or any other scenarios where ad-hoc connectivity is needed. The performance of the MBSs service depends on the locations of users and UAVs; thus, it can be a subject of optimization. In this research, we focus on minimizing the number of UAVs when establishing new connectivity for a group of users in a given zone. The number is minimized by the effective deployment of UAVs over the zone.

In our research, the optimization problem is stationary; that is, ground users represent, for example, routers placed in crucial locations which deliver WLAN service to the surrounding receivers. Hence, ground users can be regarded as immobile and previously known to the UAV swarm, so the swarm does not have to adapt over time to the changing positions of users.

Numerous publications address different variants of the problem of deploying UAVs for optimal wireless coverage. In [5], the authors present a method minimizing the number of MBs covering a set of immobile ground terminals with known

R. Wyrzykowski et al. (Eds.): PPAM 2022, LNCS 13826, pp. 414–428, 2023.
https://doi.org/10.1007/978-3-031-30442-2_31

locations on the horizontal plane. The method applies a spiral algorithm building its solution by placing the MBSs sequentially until the total coverage is satisfied. In [2], the authors use K-means clustering and a stable marriage approach to partition users into clusters and find 2-D coordinates of UAVs first. Then, the third coordinate, altitude, is optimized using search space-constrained exhaustive search and particle swarm optimization (PSO). In [8], the authors also use 3-D coordinates to represent UAVs' locations. The proposed method finds optimal deployment of UAVs iteratively invoking a clustering algorithm K-means and one of the population heuristics: Particle Swarm Optimization, Genetic Algorithm, or Artificial Bees Colony. In [6], the authors propose a problem-specific heuristic optimization method working on a discrete representation of a UAV location, where nodes of a square grid of $L \times L$ are considered for discrete locations. In [1], UAVs ensure connectivity for the people uniformly and randomly distributed over the area in previously unknown locations. The authors assume that the number of UAVs may be insufficient to cover the entire area, and initially, some users may not be in range. Hence, to achieve higher coverage, UAVs have to move over time. Such a network of UAVs offers intermittent coverage to the users. Therefore, its primary aim is to receive messages from users and route them to neighbor UAVs closer to the gateway or the gateway in range. The approach maximizes average people-to-drone connected time and the percentage of people in the communication range of UAVs for two cases: without and with mobility of UAVs. In [11], the authors maximize users' coverage probability using particle swarm optimization to find optimal locations of UAVs in 3-D space. A particle in a swarm represents coordinates for an entire group of N UAVs, which is a real-valued vector of $3N$ dimensions. In [10], the aim is to maximize the number of users covered by the net of UAVs without losing network connectivity in urban disaster scenarios where the area consists of streets, parks, and buildings. Users move randomly, and UAVs deploy over the area using the tactical movement generation rules based on the Jaccard distance and artificial intelligence algorithms. In [4], the authors notice that due to the limited maximum distance of UAVs flight, the emergency network should consist of mobile base stations and terrestrial, portable base stations, and solve the problem of optimal deployment for the network consisting of base stations of two types.

We propose a model where the zone is divided into sectors of different areas and shapes depending on users' location and non-uniformly distributed inside the given zone and the range of MBSs. We do not need to find precise coordinates of UAV locations because any location within a sector has the same impact on the connectivity coverage. One or multiple UAVs can occupy every single sector. In this model, the deployment of a minimal number of UAVs represents a combinatorial problem. Due to its complexity, we apply a heuristic optimization method inspired by the Ant System approach but extended by a new problem-specific heuristic aimed at generating a single solution. The proposed zone model defines a new structure of a pheromone matrix and new rules of the pheromone deployment. For experimental verification, we created a set of benchmark problems and conducted experiments to show the algorithm's efficiency and reveal the most beneficial values of the algorithm's parameters.

The paper consists of five sections. The wireless communication system, its model, its hypergraph representation, and optimization criteria are described in Sect. 2. Section 3 presents an Ant System-inspired approach to optimize the deployment of UAVs. The experimental part of the research is described in Sect. 4. Section 5 concludes the paper.

2 The Optimization Problem

We optimize the number of UAVs equipped with base stations and their locations to provide connectivity for n immobile ground users in the given zone. We assume that all UAVs and MBSs have the same functionality and parameters. Moreover, a third-party entity provides connectivity to the UAVs, so their distances have no meaning for the network functionality. There are also some other simplifications in our model of the problem. The model lacks radio resource management, interference management, channel estimation, prediction, or energy efficiency. We also assume that all UAVs fly at the same altitude, offering the best compromise between flight safety and productivity. Due to the homogeneity of MBSs transmitters, the round areas with satisfying connectivity offered by MBSs have the same size. In formal terms, we consider a set of n immobile ground users $V = \{v_1, \ldots, v_n\}$, and a set of p MBSs $M = \{m_1, \ldots, m_p\}$. The connectivity radius of each MBS is r. We want to ensure a k-coverage for each user in V, that is

$$\forall v \in V \; \exists \mathbf{c} \in [M]^k \text{ such that } \forall m \in \mathbf{c} \; dist(v, m) \leq r, \tag{1}$$

where $\mathbf{c}$ indicates the set of k MBSs covering the ground user v, $[M]^k$ is the set of all the subsets of M with exactly k elements, and $dist(v, m)$ denotes the distance between the ground user v and the MBS m. Our optimization goal is to minimize the number of MBSs p.

For a continuous 2-D representation of the ground users' and MBSs' coordinates, the problem can be formulated as the Geometric Disk Cover (GDC) problem [9]. In GDC, we minimize the number of disks of a given radius covering a set of immobile ground users, which is an NP-hard problem. When we use a discrete model, where the area is a grid of small rectangular cells, the problem of the effective deployment of UAVs can be similar to generating an overview image. Cells of the observation areas represent regions of ground users' locations. For this model, the problem of minimizing the number of UAVs can be formulated as ILP (integer linear programming) problem [7].

2.1 The Model of a Wireless Communication System

The communication system has to ensure a k-coverage for each user, which means that each user requires at least k MBSs available in its connectivity range. Our goal is to minimize the number of UAVs by optimizing their locations.

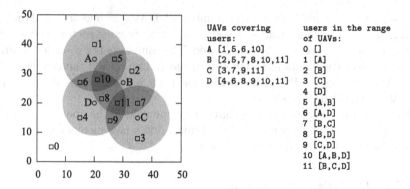

Fig. 1. Example of an operating wireless network with four users: A, B, C and D (circles) and 12 UAVs: 0, 1, 2, ..., 11 (squares)—on the left, and lists of UAVs covering users and users in the range of UAVs—on the right

Figure 1 depicts an example deployment of 12 UAVs over the four users. Gray circles around users have a radius equal to the connectivity radius of MBSs carried by UAVs. Thus, locating MBS wherever in the circle guarantees connectivity to the user in the circle's center.

The circles divide the zone into sectors. Each sector represents a different set of users, which we can cover by MBS service. The shades of gray of the sectors represent the number of covered users; the darker sector, the more users. In the example, the UAVs are placed alone in each sector. For example, UAV no. 10 hovers in the sector where its MBS covers users A, B, and D. MBS of UAV no. 11 covers users B, C, and D. MBS of UAV no. 5—users A and B. And so on. The sector of UAV no. 0 is white, which means there are no users in its range. The precise coordinates of a UAV location have no meaning as long as it remains entirely in the respective sector.

2.2   Hypergraph Representation of the System

The example presented in Fig. 1 can be modeled as a hypergraph $H = (V, E)$ where V is a set of nodes (ground users), and E is a set of non-empty subsets of V (sectors of the zone) called hyperedges. There are four nodes and 11 hyperedges in this example. Let us label the hyperedges according to the UAVs' IDs and nodes according to the users. For example, the hyperedge no. 10 connects nodes A, B, and D. The hyperedge no. 11—nodes B, C, and D. The hyperedge no. 5— nodes A and B. And so on.

2.3   Representation of Solution

A solution **s** represents a set of UAVs assigned to the zone sectors, where each sector may contain zero, one, or more UAVs. In particular, the sector may have no UAV assigned when UAVs from other sectors deliver connectivity. On the other side, there is no limit to the number of UAVs in one sector. Formally, $\mathbf{s} = \{e_i, e_j, \ldots, e_q\}$ where values $e_i, e_j, \ldots, e_q$ identify zone sectors (hyperedges in the hypergraph) where UAVs are located. The solution $\mathbf{s}$ is a so-called *multiset*. That is, some of the values in $\mathbf{s}$ may appear more than once if there is more than one UAV in the sector. When the sector identifier is absent in $\mathbf{s}$, it means that no UAV is needed in this sector.

Since multiple elements in $\mathbf{s}$ can have the same values, the operator $\cup$ applied in, for example, the expression $\mathbf{s} \cup \{e\}$ always adds a new element e to $\mathbf{s}$ even if an element with such value already exists in $\mathbf{s}$.

2.4   The Optimization Criteria

The optimization aims to minimize the number of UAVs over the zone while ensuring all ground users' connectivity parameters. Thus, the value of a solution is proportional to the number of UAVs in the network. Moreover, we want to avoid UAV overcrowding in sectors. Therefore, when we have two solutions containing the same number of UAVs, we also consider the diversity of the UAVs' distribution over sectors. The fewer UAVs occupying the same sectors, the better. As such, the fitness function f is evaluated simply as Eq. 2, but a secondary function (Eq. 3) can be used to pick between two similar in-length solutions.

$$f(\mathbf{s}) = len(\mathbf{s}) \tag{2}$$

$$f(\mathbf{s}) = len(\mathbf{s})/set(\mathbf{s}) \tag{3}$$

where $len(\cdot)$ returns the number of the hyperedge IDs in the solution, that is, the number of UAVs in the network, and $set(\cdot)$—the number of unique hyperedge IDs in $\mathbf{s}$. When the assignment of UAVs to hyperedges is unique, that is, each UAV occupies a different sector, the penalty component $len(\mathbf{s})/set(\mathbf{s})$ equals one. Otherwise, it is greater than one and rises as the uniqueness falls.

The fulfillment of sufficient connectivity conditions depends on the number of UAVs in the user vicinity. Every user needs access to at least k MBSs simultaneously. Otherwise, the solution is unfeasible. Therefore, we call this a k-coverage problem. For the example given in Fig. 1, k can be equal at most four because users A and C have four MBSs in their ranges, the lowest level of coverage among all users. Hence, the proposed deployment of UAVs can also represent a feasible solution for the k-coverage problem where $k = 1, 2, 3, 4$. One can notice that for $k = 4$, the deployment is feasible but not optimal because there exist deployments of fewer UAVs also delivering connectivity for $k = 4$.

3   The Optimization Method

For the aim of optimization, we apply an iterative heuristic approach inspired by the Ant Systems. Ant Systems have two main distinguishing characteristics which separate them from other heuristics, e.g., evolutionary or swarm approaches. First is a pheromone matrix containing trails left by artificial ants when they create new solutions. The other is that ants are not representatives of solutions improved over subsequent iterations. Construction of solutions with respect to already deployed pheromone trails is the only job for ants. It is important to stress that ants are not information transmitters between iterations; the only information transferred is the pheromone information.

Typically, an ant constructs a solution by a sequence of probabilistic decisions. Every decision extends a partial solution by adding a new component to the solution until a complete solution is derived. The sequence of decisions can be viewed as a path through a corresponding decision graph, so ants find paths through the graph that correspond to reasonable solutions. Ants that have found reasonable solutions can mark the edges of the corresponding path in the graph with an artificial pheromone. This pheromone guides ants in the next iteration. The paths can improve in subsequent iterations due to the pheromone indicating beneficial decisions of ants.

In our problem model, a solution represents an assignment of UAVs to the hyperedges of the hypergraph. Therefore, we update the pheromone trail in the hyperedges contributing to the solution, and the update is inversely proportional to the solution's length. To ensure that the pheromone from older iterations does not influence the following iterations for too long, some percentage of the pheromone evaporates during an update step. Algorithm 1 presents the generic scheme of the Ant System.

Algorithm 1

1: Initialize pheromone values
2: **repeat**
3:     **for all** ant$_k$ **do**
4:         construct k-th solution   ▷ 1. ants find their paths
5:     **for all** pheromone values **do**
6:         decrease the value by a certain percentage   ▷ 2. evaporation
7:     **for all** pheromone trails contributing to solutions **do**
8:         increase the value   ▷ 3. intensification: ants pheromone is laid
9: **until** termination condition met

3.1   The Problem–Specific Step: Generation of a Solution

Each ant constructs one solution. The constructing method is a heuristic using problem-specific knowledge about the hypergraph representation of the system. The hypergraph H, elite set of hyperedges e_{elit}, and the required coverage level k are the input of the method.

The set e_{elit} consists of hyperedges having a large number of nodes since they are regarded as the most efficient for covering. For each $v \in V$, we do the following two steps: For all hyperedges containing v, we calculate their cardinality, which is the number of vertices in the hyperedge. Then, all the hyperedges having the highest cardinality become $\mathbf{e}_{\text{elit}}$ members. The pseudocode of the method generating $\mathbf{e}_{\text{elit}}$ is presented in Algorithm 2.

Algorithm 2

1: **function** GENERATEELITESET(H)
2:                 ▷ Input: hypergraph H ▷ Output: elite set of hyperedges $\mathbf{e}_{\text{elit}}$

3:    $\mathbf{e}_{\text{elit}} \leftarrow \emptyset$ ▷ create an empty elite set of hyperedges $\mathbf{e}_{\text{elit}}$
4:    **for all** $v \in V$ **do**
5:        $mc_v \leftarrow \max_{e|v \in e}(\mathbf{card}(e))$ ▷ find the max cardinality of e among e
      containing v
6:        $\mathbf{e}_{\text{elit}} \leftarrow \mathbf{e}_{\text{elit}} \cup \{e|(v \in e) \wedge (\mathbf{card}(e) = mc_v)\}$
7:    **return** $\mathbf{e}_{\text{elit}}$

The complexity of the for loop in this algorithm is $O(d_v)$, where d_v is the degree of vertex v, that is, the number of hyperedges v belongs to. The whole algorithm has complexity $O(n * d_{\max})$, where $d_{\max}$ is the maximum vertex degree in the hypergraph.

The method generating a solution $\mathbf{s}$ consists of five steps. The pseudocode of this method is presented in Algorithm 3. Please note, that the solution $\mathbf{s}$ is a multiset of hyperedge identifiers representing respective locations of UAVs (one identifier represents location of one UAV), whereas $\mathbf{e}_{\text{elit}}$ and $\mathbf{e}_{\text{init}}$ are regular sets of hyperedges.

#1 Stochastic selection of an initial set of hyperedges $\mathbf{e}_{\text{init}}$ among the hyperedges in $\mathbf{e}_{\text{elit}}$. The chances of being selected as a candidate to $\mathbf{e}_{\text{init}}$ depend on the pheromone trails. However, the candidate is omitted when its recruitment does not extend the set of covered nodes. The selection stops as soon as no nodes remain uncovered. The complexity of this step is $O(|\mathbf{e}_{\text{elit}}| * c_{\text{emax}})$ where c_{emax} is the maximal cardinality of a hyperedge in $\mathbf{e}_{\text{elit}}$.

#2 Sequential deployment of UAVs in $\mathbf{e}_{\text{init}}$. For each of these hyperedges, we try to deploy new UAVs. We assign as many new UAVs as necessary to guarantee the requested level k of coverage for all the nodes joined by this hyperedge. We process hyperedges in the same order as they were put into $\mathbf{e}_{\text{init}}$ in Step #1. The UAV assignment is asynchronous. It means that the coverage of nodes by UAVs already assigned is considered when adding the next ones. For $|\mathbf{e}_{\text{init}}| * c_{\text{imax}}$ nodes, where c_{imax} is the maximal cardinality of a hyperedge in $\mathbf{e}_{\text{init}}$, we have to verify whether these nodes have k-coverage by the UAVs already declared in $\mathbf{s}$. It takes $O(k * |\mathbf{e}_{\text{init}}|)$ operations. When the coverage is insufficient, we add additional UAVs to $\mathbf{s}$, which takes $O(k)$ operations. Thus, the complexity of this step is $O(k * |\mathbf{e}_{\text{init}}|^2 * c_{\text{imax}}))$.

#3 Dispersion of UAVs over the hyperedges in their neighborhood. All generated UAVs are shifted to a random adjacent hyperedge. We consider a hyperedge to be adjacent if it connects all but one of the nodes connected to a previous one. If no such hyperedges exist, the UAV is removed from the solution. In

---

Algorithm 3

1: **function** BUILDANEWSOLUTION(H, e_{elit}, k)
2:         ▷ Input: hypergraph H, elite set of hyperedges e_{elit}, k ▷ Output: s

3:    $V' \leftarrow V$ ▷ create a set of uncovered nodes V'
4:    $e_{init} \leftarrow \emptyset$ ▷ create an empty initial set of hyperedges e_{init}
5:    s $\leftarrow \emptyset$ ▷ create an empty solution s

6:    **repeat**   ▷ Step #1: ——————— select hyperedges to the initial set
7:        randomize $e \in e_{elit}$ ▷ select randomly w.r.t. pheromone trail levels
8:        **if** $\{V' \cap e\} \neq \emptyset$ **then**   ▷ if any node in e remains uncovered
9:            $e_{elit} \leftarrow e_{elit} \setminus \{e\}$ ▷ e is removed from e_{elit}
10:            $e_{init} \leftarrow e_{init} \cup \{e\}$ ▷ e is added to e_{init}
11:            $V' = V' \setminus e$ ▷ all the nodes connected by e are removed from V'
12:    **until** $V' = \emptyset$

13:    **for all** $e \in e_{init}$ **do** ▷ Step #2: —— build a preliminary version of the solution
14:        **for all** $v \in e$ **do**   ▷ for all the nodes connected by e
15:            **if** v has l-coverage by the UAVs already declared in s, where $l < k$ **then**
16:                add $(k - l)$ UAVs to the hyperedge e in s

17:    **for all** $e \in$ s **do** ▷ Step #3: —— disperse UAVs to their neighbour hyperedges
18:        **if** $\mathcal{N}(e) \neq \emptyset$ **then**
19:            **while** there exist identifier e in s **do**
20:                randomize $e' \in \mathcal{N}(e)$ ▷ select randomly one of the neighbours
21:                replace e by e' in s   ▷ move one UAV from the hyperedge e to e'
22:            remove all identifiers e from s   ▷ remove UAVs from the hyperedge e

23:    **for all** $e \in e_{init}$ **do**   ▷ Step #4: ——————— repeat #2 to fix the solution
24:        **for all** $v \in e$ **do**   ▷ for all nodes joined by the hyperedge e
25:            **if** v has l-coverage by the UAVs already declared in s, where $l < k$ **then**
26:                add $(k - l)$ UAVs to the hyperedge e in s

27:                          ▷ Step #5: — remove redundant UAVs from the solution
28:    divide hyperedges present in s into groups w.r.t. the number of joined nodes
29:    label groups: $\{g^1(s), g^2(s), \ldots, g^m(s)\}$ according to the number of joined nodes
30:    **for** $i \leftarrow 1$ to m **do**   ▷ start with groups of hyperedges joining least nodes
31:        **for all** $e \in g^i(s)$ **do**   ▷ take the hyperedges in $g^i(s)$ in a random order
32:            **while** all $v \in e$ have coverage higher than k **do**
33:                remove identifier e from s   ▷ remove one redundant UAV

34:    **return** s   ▷ Finish: ——————— return the obtained solution s

---

this step, the inner loop (while) requires $O(k * |e_{init}|)$ iterations and every iteration has cost $O(1)$. The outer loop (for) also requires $O(k * |e_{init}|)$ iterations. Therefore, the complexity of this step is $O(k^2 * |e_{init}|^2)$.

#4 Fixing the deployment of UAVs. Modifications introduced in Step #3 can make the solution unfeasible. Thus, we repeat Step #2 in this step to make the solution feasible again. The complexity of this step is the same as in Step #2, i.e. $O(k * |\mathbf{e}_{\text{init}}|^2 * c_{\text{imax}})$.

#5 Removal of redundant UAVs. After Step #4, some UAVs can be redundant (the requested coverage level for all the nodes remains satisfied even without these UAVs). Therefore, we analyze groups of hyperedges regarding their cardinality, starting from one. Within each group, and in random order, we verify if the lack of any UAVs makes the solution unfeasible. If it does not, the redundant UAVs are removed from the hyperedge. Dividing hyperedges into groups has the complexity $O(k*|\mathbf{e}_{\text{init}}|)$. In the nested for loop, the while loop is invoked $k * |\mathbf{e}_{\text{init}}|$ times. A single while loop invocation is $O(c_{\text{emax}})$. Thus, the complexity of this step is $O(k * |\mathbf{e}_{\text{init}}| * c_{\text{emax}})$.

The whole Algorithm 3 has the complexity $O(|\mathbf{e}_{\text{elit}}|*c_{\text{emax}})+O(k*|\mathbf{e}_{\text{init}}|^2*c_{\text{imax}})+O(k^2 * |\mathbf{e}_{\text{init}}|^2) + O(k * |\mathbf{e}_{\text{init}}| * c_{\text{emax}})$. Since $|\mathbf{e}_{\text{init}}| \leq |\mathbf{e}_{\text{elit}}|$ and $c_{\text{imax}} \leq c_{\text{emax}}$, we can assess this complexity as $O(k * |\mathbf{e}_{\text{elit}}|^2 * (k + c_{\text{emax}}))$.

3.2   The Main Loop

The algorithm starts with the generation of the hypergraph $H = (V, E)$ from the input data with the area size and locations of the ground users. Then, the function GENERATEELITESET generates the set $\mathbf{e}_{\text{elit}}$. Next, we create a pheromone vector P of size $|\mathbf{e}_{\text{elit}}|$. For each of the hyperedges in $\mathbf{e}_{\text{elit}}$, the initial pheromone level in P equals the number of ants used by the algorithm.

Next, the main loop starts. The main loop of the algorithm corresponds to the one presented in Algorithm 1. In the beginning for each ant, we generate a new solution of UAVs deployment using the function BUILDANEWSOLUTION with arguments: H, $\mathbf{e}_{\text{elit}}$, and the requested level of coverage k. We then evaluate each new solution as the inverse of its length. Next, evaporation arises. Pheromone values for all hyperedges in $\mathbf{e}_{\text{elit}}$ are reduced by a fixed proportion ρ according to the formula: $P_e = (1 - \rho)P_e$. Finally, we update the pheromone trails. For each of the solutions, we want to reward those hyperedges whose membership in $\mathbf{e}_{\text{init}}$ gave a feasible solution. However, the reward value δ is inverse proportional to the solution length and equal to the solution score. Therefore, the new pheromone level for a hyperedge e is calculated according to the formula $P_e = P_e + \delta_e$. The coefficient δ_e is the sum of scores of those solutions, where e was a member of $\mathbf{e}_{\text{init}}$ and has assigned at least one UAV.

The main loop ends when the stopping condition is met, and then the best-found solution is returned.

4 Experiments

4.1 Benchmark

We evaluated the algorithm experimentally on the benchmark set of test cases called SCP2 [3]. The set consists of six classes of problems that differ in the number of ground users and their locations. Nodes of a rectangular grid over the square zone of size one unit define possible users' locations. There are two densities of grids with grid cell dimensions s_{grid} equal 0.04 by 0.04 or 0.02 by 0.02 units (676 or 2601 nodes in the zone, respectively). In every case, the number of users is smaller than the number of nodes: 100, 200, or 500. The users' locations are selected randomly among the nodes. However, we additionally shift the final user location from the node coordinates toward a random direction by a random distance smaller than 1.5 of s_{grid}. Two grids with different cell dimensions and three sizes of the ground users' set eventually give six classes of users' distribution. For every class, we generated 50 instances based on different locations of users on the grid and directions and distances of shifts.

The zone is divided into sectors as presented in the example Fig. 1. The MBS signal power defines the radius of circles around users, which we arbitrarily set to 0.05 units. Locations of sectors define the structure of hypergraphs obtained for each problem instance according to the rules described in Sect. 2.2. On average, hypergraphs representing problem instances in the two classes with 100 users have around 18.6 (with a range of 9 to 25) connected components for $s_{grid} = 0.02$ and 20 (13 to 27) for $s_{grid} = 0.04$. For the problem instances from the two classes with 200 users, we got the average of about 3.9 (from 1 to 10) connected components for $s_{grid} = 0.02$ and 3 (from 1 to 6) for $s_{grid} = 0.04$. When the number of users equals 500, the hypergraph always consists of one connected component. The decreasing number of connected components is not surprising because more intersections between users' surrounding areas occur when the number of users grows.

The last parameter of the problem is the minimum coverage level k, equal to 1, 2, 5, or 10. Eventually, we get a benchmark consisting of 24 classes of problems: six classes of users' distribution over the zone by four levels of the minimum coverage k.

4.2 Plan of Experiments

The algorithm has three parameters: the number of ants n_{ants}, evaporation coefficient ρ, and stopping condition parameter, that is, the maximum number of fitness function calls max_{nffc}. In the preliminary experiments, we observed that satisfying results were obtained for $\rho = 0.1$ and $n_{ants} = 10$. We set $max_{nffc} = 2000$, so an experiment takes 200 iterations. In the presented experiments, the coefficient ρ is also the subject of experimental tuning and varies from 0.1 to 0.5.

The experiments are divided into two groups. In the first group, we performed experiments with $\rho = 0.1$ for all 24 classes (six classes of SCP2 by four values of k). In the second group, we selected the two classes of problems that proved to be the most demanding in the first group of experiments: $s_{\text{grid}} \in \{0.02, 0.04\}$ for 500 ground users and $k = 10$. For these classes, we observed optimization progress for five different values of $\rho \in \{0.1, 0.2, 0.3, 0.4, 0.5\}$.

We repeated experiments 32 times for every problem instance, excluded the best and worst results and calculated the mean number of UAVs for the remaining ones.

4.3 The Results

Figure 2 shows the results of our experiments with the benchmark described in Sect. 4.1. As the diversity level of UAVs' deployment serves only as a tie-breaker between two similar in-length solutions, our analysis concerns only the average number of UAVs for each class of the problem.

For smaller numbers of users in the area, which resulted in hypergraphs with plenty of connected components of smaller size, the proposed algorithm found itself near the optimal solution almost instantly. Even for the highest considered coverage of 10, it could not further improve the results after about a fifth of the given computational time. When the user population grows, the complexity of the corresponding hypergraph increases. Then our method needed much more time to stop improving.

Interestingly, the algorithm reached the suboptimal solutions after similar numbers of iterations regardless of the desired coverage level k. For classes of 100 users (Fig. 2a, 2d, 2g, 2j) this method reached the suboptimal solution within fewer than 10 iterations, barely improving for up until iteration 30. Classes with 200 users (Fig. 2b, 2e, 2h, 2k) showed steady improvement for about 70 iterations (700 evaluations), but further improvement stopped after about 100 iterations.

The most challenging classes of 500 users (Fig. 2c, 2f, 2i, 2l) almost doubled the time required to find suboptimal solutions, reaching as far as 150 iterations of varied improvement. The pace of this improvement also shows the ability of the algorithm's transition between different local optima, which initially slowed down the search for the best solution.

The results of the second group of experiments with different evaporation rates are presented in Fig. 3. One can see that a higher evaporation rate could significantly hasten the search process at the cost of a noticeable but relatively small tradeoff in the quality of the found solution.

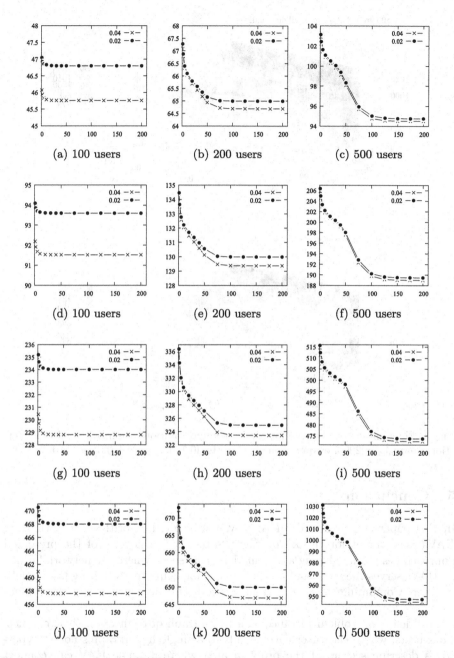

Fig. 2. Mean numbers of UAVs for the best-found solutions For two densities of grids: with grid cell dimensions s_{grid} equal 0.04 by 0.04 and 0.02 by 0.02 units. For $k = 1$: (a), (b), and (c), $k = 2$: (d), (e), and (f), $k = 5$: (g), (h), and (i), and $k = 10$: (j), (k), and (l); X-axis represents the iteration number; $max_{nffc} = 2000$

500 ground users, grid cell dim.: 0.02

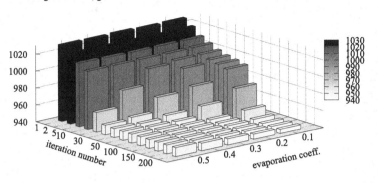

500 ground users, grid cell dim.: 0.04

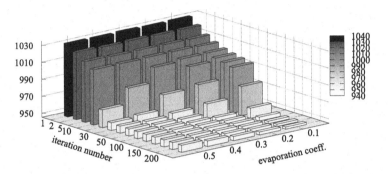

Fig. 3. Mean numbers of UAVs for the best-found solutions observed in selected iterations; $max_{\text{nffc}} = 2000$; evaporation coefficients: $[0.1, 0.2, 0.3, 0.4, 0.5]$, $k = 10$

5   Conclusions

In this paper, we proposed an Ant System-inspired algorithm for optimizing UAVs deployment for the k-Coverage Problem. The novelty of the presented approach lies in introducing a new model of the space where the network formed by UAVs serves the users and a problem-specific heuristic exploiting the model's features. Combining the Ant System method and the heuristic is also an innovative element.

We define a problem instance as a hypergraph of connections between network users, where each user corresponds to a single hypergraph's node. Hyperedges describe sectors of the problem area where a single UAV can connect simultaneously to a given set of users. The shape of each sector is defined by user positions and the range of a carried MBS.

We use the model-specific characteristics of the problem to construct an input space for the Ant System step of the algorithm and build new solutions using a proposed heuristic.

A generated solution is represented as a variable-length array of hyperedges, which can be translated to UAV positions within the problem area. We use the feedback loop of the algorithm to find a subset of the hyperedges that results in the shortest solutions while avoiding overcrowding within each sector. Among solutions of a given length, the one with the lowest average UAV count per sector within the solution is considered the best.

We tested our algorithm using three pairs of classes from the presented dataset. The number of nodes in each problem instance differed for each pair, and classes within pairs had different deployment characteristics. For each class, we repeated tests for four values of the required coverage level for a solution k—1, 2, 5, and 10.

The experiments' results correlate with some of the benchmark problem properties and reflect the expected behavior of the Ant System-based approaches. The density of the created hypergraph is closely related to the problem parameters and directly affects the time required to obtain good results. Similarly, choosing between different evaporation rates can hasten the search but at a slight cost to the quality of the obtained solutions.

References

1. Guinand, F., Guérin, F., Łubniewski, P.: Allowing people to communicate after a disaster using FANETs. In: Krief, F., Aniss, H., Mendiboure, L., Chaumette, S., Berbineau, M. (eds.) Communication Technologies for Vehicles. LNCCN, vol. 12574, pp. 181–193. Springer, Cham (2020). https://doi.org/10.1007/978-3-030-66030-7_16
2. Hydher, H., Jayakody, D.N.K., Hemachandra, K.T., Samarasinghe, T.: Intelligent UAV deployment for a disaster-resilient wireless network. Sensors 20(21), 6140 (2020). https://doi.org/10.3390/s20216140
3. Grzeszczak, J., Mikitiuk, A., Trojanowski, K.: Station Coverage Problem 2 (SCP2) dataset (2022). https://jaga.blog.uksw.edu.pl/scp2/. Accessed 25 Apr 2022
4. Košmerl, J., Vilhar, A.: Base stations placement optimization in wireless networks for emergency communications. In: 2014 IEEE International Conference on Communications Workshops (ICC), pp. 200–205 (2014). https://doi.org/10.1109/ICCW.2014.6881196
5. Lyu, J., Zeng, Y., Zhang, R., Lim, T.J.: Placement optimization of UAV-mounted mobile base stations. IEEE Commun. Lett. 21(3), 604–607 (2017). https://doi.org/10.1109/LCOMM.2016.2633248
6. Masroor, R., Naeem, M., Ejaz, W.: Efficient deployment of UAVs for disaster management: a multi-criterion optimization approach. Comput. Commun. 177, 185–194 (2021). https://doi.org/10.1016/j.comcom.2021.07.006
7. Quaritsch, M., Kruggl, K., Wischounig-Strucl, D., Bhattacharya, S., Shah, M., Rinner, B.: Networked UAVs as aerial sensor network for disaster management applications. e & i Elektrotechnik und Informationstechnik 127(3), 56–63 (2010). https://doi.org/10.1007/s00502-010-0717-2
8. Sawalmeh, A., Othman, N.S., Liu, G., Khreishah, A., Alenezi, A., Alanazi, A.: Power-efficient wireless coverage using minimum number of UAVs. Sensors 22(1), 223 (2021). https://doi.org/10.3390/s22010223

9. Srinivas, A., Zussman, G., Modiano, E.: Construction and maintenance of wireless mobile backbone networks. IEEE/ACM Trans. Netw. **17**(1), 239–252 (2009). https://doi.org/10.1109/TNET.2009.2012474

10. Sánchez-García, J., García-Campos, J.M., Toral, S.L., Reina, D.G., Barrero, F.: An intelligent strategy for tactical movements of UAVs in disaster scenarios. Int. J. Distrib. Sens. Netw. **12**(3), 8132812 (2016). https://doi.org/10.1155/2016/8132812

11. Yuheng, Z., Liyan, Z., Chunpeng, L.: 3-D deployment optimization of UAVs based on particle swarm algorithm. In: 2019 IEEE 19th International Conference on Communication Technology (ICCT). IEEE, October 2019. https://doi.org/10.1109/icct46805.2019.8947140

Dataset Related Experimental Investigation of Chess Position Evaluation Using a Deep Neural Network

Dawid Wieczerzak and Paweł Czarnul[(✉)] [ID]

Faculty of Electronics, Telecommunications and Informatics,
Gdańsk University of Technology, Narutowicza 11/12, 80-233 Gdańsk, Poland
dawwiecz@pg.edu.pl, pczarnul@eti.pg.edu.pl

Abstract. The idea of training Artificial Neural Networks to evaluate chess positions has been widely explored in the last ten years. In this paper we investigated dataset impact on chess position evaluation. We created two datasets with over 1.6 million unique chess positions each. In one of those we also included randomly generated positions resulting from consideration of potentially unpredictable chess moves. Each position was evaluated by the Stockfish engine. Afterwards, we created a multi class evaluation model using Multilayer Perceptron. Solution to the evaluation problem was tested with three different data labeling methods and three different board representations. We show that the accuracy for the model trained for the dataset without randomly generated positions is higher than for the model with such positions, for all data representations and 3, 5 and 11 evaluation classes.

Keywords: chess position evaluation · deep neural network · model evaluation · accuracy

1 Introduction

Artificial Neural Networks (ANNs) have become models able to predict or estimate otherwise unknown values for various applications, based on prior training using big data sets. Convolutional Neural Networks (CNNs) are widely used for recognition of patterns, that can be of interest in many applications. One of these could be an attempt to evaluate game positions based on their visual representation, for example in chess [15]. There are several interesting factors including the quality of evaluation versus the number of classes we might want to assign to as well as versus training and validation data sets, especially regarding their size and coverage. In the context of chess, several other uses of neural networks were proposed in the literature such as: determination of the optimum number of moves towards winning an endgame assuming optimum play of the other side (for some characteristics of a board position as input) [16]; using a CNN as a piece selector that determines which chess piece should be moved followed by a move selector to determine which move to make [12]; generation of

R. Wyrzykowski et al. (Eds.): PPAM 2022, LNCS 13826, pp. 429–440, 2023.
https://doi.org/10.1007/978-3-031-30442-2_32

natural-language commentary [4]. It should also be noted that high performance computing systems are important in the chess context as well, either for fast training of models or for running algorithms in parallel [5,10,17].

In this paper, we focused on training a deep neural network for numerical evaluation of chess positions indicating advantage of either the white or black player, based on a set of positions previously evaluated by the Stockfish chess engine[1]. Rather than focusing on tuning a particular neural network model, we adopted a model from the literature [15] and subsequently aimed at performing investigation on how using data sets of various scope (in terms of consideration of moves of various quality) impacts performance of a trained deep neural network model. Additionally, we investigated to what extent the number of classes as well as data representation in the model impacts accuracy of the final model.

2   Related Work

In paper [15] authors experimented with training ANNs for the purpose of evaluating chess positions. They used the Fics Games Database to generate around 3000000 chess positions which were evaluated by Stockfish. They created various datasets with various numbers of labels referring to position evaluation such as: 3 for dataset 1, 15 for dataset 2 and 20 for dataset 3 and normalized evaluation of [0,1] for dataset 4. For particular datasets, authors tested tuned Multilayer Perceptrons (MLPs) versus CNNs showing benefits of the former for the task achieving high test accuracies of 96.07%, 93.41% and 68.33% for datasets 1, 2 and 3 respectively for bitmap representation (distinguishes presence of particular chess pieces) which were higher than for an algebraic representation (distinguishes values of particular chess pieces - pawns 1, bishops and knights 3, rooks 5, queens 9 and kings 10) by approx. 2–5%. Finally, the authors mentioned that the trained ANN reached an Elo of approximately 2000 on the chess24.com server. It should be noted that an example of works that focus on obtaining positional values of the chess pieces for particular positions is [20] in which authors used neural networks for that and an evolutionary algorithm for adjustment which resulted in increasing the ranking of their chess engine from ranking 1745 to 2178.

Another paper on playing chess with limited look-ahead is [11]. The author used a large number of board positions – 20 million samples where boards extracted from publicly available databases were extended in such a way that for some positions random legal moves were made and positions evaluated using Stockfish 11. The author tested a classifier for labeling positions with winning for white, black and draw based on evaluation of cp ≤ -150, $-150 \leq ... \leq 150$ and 150 respectively. A deep neural network with 5 layers, 25% dropout, Adam optimizer and categorical cross entropy, ReLU activation and softmax obtaining approximately 87% testing accuracy.

A different way of chess position assessment and incorporation into a chess playing engine was proposed in [6]. Specifically, they designed and implemented

---

[1] https://stockfishchess.org/.

a solution that learned to compare chess positions. They used the CCRL dataset (www.computerchess.org.uk/ccrl) with 640000 chess games, out of which white won 221695 games and black won 164387 games – only games that ended with a win were of interest. Firstly, they trained a deep belief network (DBN) called pos2vec that converted a position into a vector. Then, they created a network called DeepChess in which two copies of pos2vec were stacked side by side for position comparison and they trained fully connected layers on top of those for comparison. The authors reported both training and validation accuracies at the very high level of 98%. Subsequently, they conducted play experiments against Falcon for which the evaluation function was 4 times faster than that of the developed solution. Given that DeepChess performed on par, given 4 times more time outperformed Falcon. It also showed 70 more Elo strength than Crafty.

Another work in which the author attempted evaluation of chess positions using a CNN network is presented in [19], versus Stockfish evaluations. The author used the April 2019 https://database.lichess.org database out of which training data was generated from the first 100000 games when white was to move. Finally, 310690 samples were generated with numerical evaluations between -255 and $+255$ (boundary values for checkmates), forced checkmate $+/-127$ and normal evaluation capped onto the $[-63,63]$ range. The author used a model with four 2D convolutional layers: the first three with kernel size 3 by 3, the last: 2 by 2. The number of filters were 8, 16, 32 and 64 respectively, with ReLU-activation. 60% of the data set was used for training, 20% for validation and 20% for testing. Final loss and MAE for the test data set were 863.48 and 12.18 respectively. At the same time it was concluded that the model is not able to recognize combinations and tactics and a more complex model shall be tried for improved results. However, whether such can be obtained has to be investigated.

In work [9] the author used a CNN to predict the winning side for positions of a game that ended with a particular result (win for white or black). The model, in the implementation, included layers: Mocha.AsyncHDF5DataLayer, Mocha.ConvolutionLayer, Mocha.PoolingLayer, Mocha.ConvolutionLayer, Mocha.InnerProductLayer, Mocha.DropoutLayer, Mocha.InnerProductLayer, Mocha.BinaryCrossEntropyLossLayer. The data set used for training included games played by opponents with ranking 2000 or higher downloaded from FICS games database[2], finished with checkmates. Data representation used 6 channels corresponding to the boards storing $\{-1, 0, 1\}$ information concerning particular piece types. Finally, obtained validation and test accuracies were 73.5% and 71.8% respectively.

An interesting idea of chess position evaluation was introduced in [12]. Instead of providing numerical board evaluation authors proposed a method for predicting a probability distribution over the grid for pieces to move. For each chess piece they trained a separate model based on a CNN. This approach allowed to predict situations such as escape when a piece is under attack or the king needs to move. The results show that this evaluation method performs significantly better for pieces with local movement (pawn, knight, king). The authors also noticed

---

[2] https://www.ficsgames.org/download.html.

that a downside of this approach was that highly specific move combinations between nets were not learned. A newer model [13] proposed by other authors based on a similar architecture and board representation showed evaluation as a single numerical value. The output was passed through a mini-max algorithm to determine the best move. A chess engine based on this model showed simple tactics such as sacrificing a piece or forks. In 100 games against the Stockfish engine the system was able to win 3% and draw 2% of games.

In paper [14] authors, motivated by the fact that chess engines can beat even top human players, they assessed the quality of play of many human players, even from various generations, using the Stockfish engine as a quality benchmark. Specifically, score of each move by a human player was compared versus a chess engine move which allowed to compute average error, whether the human player selected first, second etc. engine's preference etc. Out of the world championship (WCC) players, best were Carlsen and Caruana with errors 0.0674 and 0.0709 respectively. Best move percentage winners were Gelfand and Kramnik with 59.9% and 59.2% respectively and average numbers of blunders per WCC were best for Caruana (1.0) and Carlsen (1.3). Work [2] provides selected results of large-scale analysis of chess games with chess engines – authors gathered and analyzed 4.78 million unique games publicly available on some Web repositories. They provided information on Elo distribution, Elo differences between players, plys per game depending on player's Elo differences, percentage of win for white player depending on Elo, first moves depending on game date.

3   Data Used for Experiments

We used the Lichess Elite Database [1] that includes a collection of lichess.org games from https://database.lichess.org/ that was filtered to include only games played by players with 2400+ ranking against players with 2200+ ranking, without bullet games.

3.1   Data Preparation

Games were downloaded in the PNG format and each position of the games was saved in a database in the FEN format. For selected tests, the original set of positions was also augmented with randomly generated positions in the following way. For each of the positions acquired from the database from Lichess.org 3 moves were generated randomly from all legal moves. This way for each position, 3 potentially unpredictable moves were generated. In some positions, because of checks or specific situations, the number of legal moves was smaller than 3. Such positions were skipped for new position generation. Repeating positions were removed from both the original as well as randomly generated position sets. Afterwards, counts of the two sets were equalized. This way, we acquired two sets with over 1.6 million unique positions each – later marked as no rand and rand respectively. The reason for considering the rand dataset was our aim of additional testing the solution with a presumably more diverse data set including board positions potentially reached by weaker players.

Afterwards Stockfish was used to label all positions from previously mentioned sets. Labels generated by Stockfish contained board evaluations expressed as centipawns (cp). Value of 100 cp corresponds to a difference of one pawn and this metric shows a current difference in strategic and material strength between players. As an example, when the evaluation is $+100$ cp it means that the moving side has a potential advantage of one pawn. Evaluations of all positions were stored from the point of view of white regardless of the player to move. We also scaled the evaluations by dividing them by 100 and thus obtaining what we call a value in scaled centipawns (scp). For our evaluations we used Stockfish 13 with a depth of 28.

3.2   Board Representation

Positions processed in the previous step were converted into a vector representation making it usable as an input for neural networks. We used a bitboard representation which turns each position in FEN format into binary vector with total length of 768 bits. This method of transforming chess position into a vector was used in some previous works [6,11,15]. Another similar bitboard approach has been used in many chess position analyses based on CNNs [12,15,19].

We also introduced modifications into the bitboard representation which gives us two additional representations. In total we tested 3 board representations: bitboard representation, algebraic representation, piece value representation.

A bitboard vector consists of 12 chessboards linked with one another that form a 64-bit position vector. Each of the boards, which are considered as a feature, stores position of a given piece (type). The first 6 features represent positions of the white player pieces while the other 6 of their opponent – black. Pieces are represented in the following order: pawns, knights, bishops, rooks, queen, king. A piece position inside each 64 bit vector is represented as 1 when it belongs to the player who should move or -1 when it belongs to the opposite player. The total length of the vector is 768 because it stacks 64 bit features for 12 different pieces.

The algebraic representation is an extension of the binary one. We introduced this modification in order to see what the effect of differentiating chess pieces on position evaluation will be. Beside presence of particular pieces it also considers different pieces by assigning them following integer numbers starting from 1. In this method pawns are represented as 1, knights as 2, bishops as 3, rooks as 4, queens as 5 and kings as 6. Similarly to the previously described method, opposite player's side is represented by negative numbers.

In the last representation piece strength and its potential value were taken into account. We used a common assignment of point values which is 1 for pawns, 3 for knights and bishops, 5 for rooks and 9 for queens. Because of its non exchangeable nature the king is not considered in most evaluation systems. In this piece value representation we decided to assign 10 points to the king.

It stemmed from the important strategic role of the piece, also considered in
[20]. Point values replaced binary presence of each piece and negative values to
distinguish moves of opposite sides have also been used. We shall note that this
piece strength representation corresponds to the one called algebraic in [15], as
described in Sect. 2.

3.3 Data Labeling

For classification of positions using games with previously added Stockfish evaluations we followed the approach from [15] experimenting with different numbers
of classes and data representations. We created three labeling methods for the
classification task.

Method 1: In this method each of the positions was assigned to one of three
classes: Winning, Losing or Draw. Labels were assigned according to scaled cen-
tipawn evaluations with the following conditions: positions were considered as
Winning when its *scp* evaluation was greater than 1.5, losing when its *scp* was
lower than −1.5 and draw when *scp* was between those two values.

Method 2: This method extends *Method 1* by dividing both the Winning and
Losing classes into two separate classes for a total of 5 different labels including
Draw. The division was done in such a way that the first Winning label contains
positions with *scp* between 1.5 and 4.5 and the second Winning label contains
positions with *scp* greater than 4.5. The same has been done for labels in the
Losing class where division point was set to −4.5 *scp*. Labeling conditions for
Draw class remained the same as in *Method 1*.

Method 3: In this method even more labels were created. All classes including
Draw have been extended by creating new labels as follows: In Winning class,
with 2 starting from 1.5 *scp*, four new labels were created so that the last labeling window contains positions with evaluations greater than 7.5 *scp*. Labels in
the Losing class were assigned in the same way. If scp decreases by 2 starting
from −1.5 *scp*, a new label was created. Draw class, which originally contained
positions with its *scp* between −1.5 and 1.5, was divided into equal intervals
each of them 1 *scp* wide. This method creates 11 different labels in total: four
labels in Winning class, four labels in Loosing class and 3 Draw labels.

4   Test Methods

In this section we describe data analysis methods concerning the data described
in Sect. 3. We present an ANN architecture used for testing different inputs in
detail, subsequently we discuss the experiments and the training process of the
model.

4.1 Neural Network Architecture

In order to address classification tasks we created a 3 hidden layer MPL based
on the architecture and hyper parameters proposed in [15]. Similarly to the originally proposed classifier, hidden layers consisted of 1048, 500 and 50 hidden

units. Each of 3 hidden layers has been activated by the Rectified Linear Unit (ReLU) activation function. Due to targeting classification tasks the final output layer has been connected to Softmax activation. Furthermore, in order to achieve better model generalization Batch Normalization and Dropout regularization were applied to all hidden layers of the network. We set the probability of Dropout to 0.2 as recommended in [18].

4.2 Experiment

As a result of our experiments we wanted to assess the impact of different chess board representations on classification performance. In order to do that, we divided the experiment into three steps corresponding to different board representations proposed in the previous section. For each board representation three different classification tasks were tested. We used three previously mentioned labeling methods: *Method 1*, *Method 2* and *Method 3* respectively. As input data firstly we used the dataset without random positions and then the dataset extended with randomly generated positions.

This test configuration gives us 2x3 separate network training cases in each experimental step.

4.3 Training Method

We have split each relevant data set into training, validation and test sets in proportion of 8:1:1. In each training the *Adam* algorithm was used as an optimizer and it was initialized with the following parameters: $lr = 0.001$, $\beta_1 = 0.9$, $\beta_2 = 0.99$, $\epsilon = 1e - 8$. We trained the networks with *minibatches* of 128 samples and *categorical cross entropy* as a loss function. The whole training was stopped after the validation loss has not improved by at least 0.00001 within the last 100 epochs. For each epoch we measured the following metrics: accuracy, precision, recall, f1 [8].

In all experiments we used Tensorflow and Python 3.8 as a programming base running on computers with Intel i7-7700 CPU, 32GiB RAM and GeForce GTX 1070.

5   Results

In Figs. 1, 2 and 3 we summarize results of training after the stop condition has been met for each given configuration i.e. 3, 5 and 11 classes respectively. There are six configurations in total i.e. for the algebraic, bitboard and piece strength data representations, each for the no rand and rand data set. For each configuration we present validation accuracy and f1 metrics.

In order to see the progress of training, as an example for the 5 class configuration and the best bitboard representation, in Fig. 4 we show how validation accuracy and f1 scores change over 135 epochs.

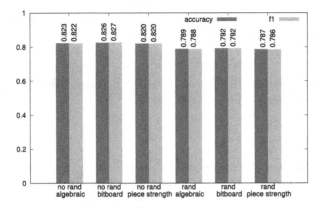

Fig. 1. validation accuracy and f1 metrics, 3 classes

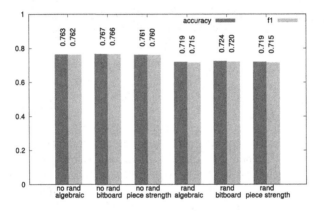

Fig. 2. validation accuracy and f1 metrics, 5 classes

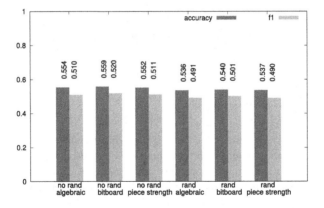

Fig. 3. validation accuracy and f1 metrics, 11 classes

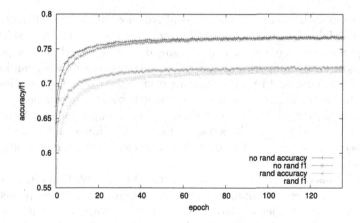

Fig. 4. validation accuracy and f1 metrics, 5 classes, bitboard representation

Following these tests, for the best representation (bitboard) in Table 1 we provide final precision and recall values for the three cases (3, 5 and 11 classes) for the two data sets. Finally, in Table 2 we included accuracy values computed for the test dataset and the bitboard representation.

Table 1. Precision and recall values for various configurations, bitboard representation, validation

Number of classes	Data without random pos.		Data with random pos.	
	precision	recall	precision	recall
3	0.83205	0.82112	0.80039	0.78325
5	0.79523	0.73922	0.76249	0.68148
11	0.69183	0.41733	0.69250	0.39315

Table 2. Test accuracy for various configurations, bitboard representation

Number of classes	Data without random pos.	Data with random pos.
3	0.82528	0.79158
5	0.76727	0.72316
11	0.55795	0.53964

6 Discussion

Based on the presented results, we can conclude the following:

1. For all tests with 3, 5 and 11 classes, configurations with data without random positions yield slightly but visibly better accuracy and f1 score values than corresponding configurations trained using data with added random positions.
2. For almost each configuration and either data without or with random positions, the order of data representations from best to worst accuracies is generally: bitboard, algebraic and piece strength with bitboard being the best one for all the cases. For 5 and 11 classes piece strength and algebraic configurations resulted in virtually same results, with minimal differences.
3. As expected, we see a visible drop in accuracies as the number of classes is increased.
4. Taking into account results for the best tested representation bitboard we see that with an increasing number of classes, differences between precision and recall values for particular data sets are increasing and are visibly larger for the data set with random positions. Additionally, while for 11 classes precision values for the two data sets are very close, there is a visible difference of approximately 0.024 for recall values.

We shall note that, based on our experiment and particular data sets, the accuracy/f1/precision/recall scores for the rand data set, presumably a more diverse one, turned out to be worse than for the no rand data set. On the other hand, while we did not focus on ultimate improvement of the model per se and rather focused on comparison per various data sets in these experiments, we shall note that accuracy values obtained in [15] for 3 classes were higher. Further investigation could be performed on if and how this could be related to the different training data sets and/or Stockfish settings used for evaluation, in both cases, etc. In [15] for the other data sets (for larger numbers of classes) a different MLP structure was used.

7   Summary and Future Work

In the paper we investigated accuracy, precision/recall and f1 metrics for training an artificial model for evaluation of chess positions – for two data sets: one – with games by 2400+ players playing against 2200+ ranking players and another – the same one augmented with randomly generated positions by making random moves from already known positions. We tested three different data representations such as bitboard, algebraic and with consideration of piece strength values – results showed that there were measurable albeit very small differences with best results for the bitboard version. We investigated assignment of numerical evaluations into 3, 5 and 11 classes. We found out that the dataset with randomly generated positions (that intuitively corresponds to positions that could also be reached by weaker players) resulted in test accuracy scores smaller than that of the data set with positions obtained by stronger players. This suggests that in this particular case it is more difficult to obtain high accuracies for a data set with presumably more diverse positions. On the other hand, based on that, in the future, it would be an interesting research task to investigate whether it can be generalized and how using even more restricted data sets affects network performance metrics. This might refer to certain phases of the game played by very good players, e.g. endgames, with possibly even selected sets of pieces on the board. Another interesting topic would be training the models with consideration of a training data set extended with similar positions [7] to those originally in the dataset. Furthermore, a test on whether the observations from this paper would also be applicable to more fine-tuned models would be of interest.

References

1. Lichess elite database. https://database.nikonoel.fr/
2. Acher, M., Esnault, F.: Large-scale analysis of chess games with chess engines: A preliminary report. CoRR abs/1607.04186 (2016). http://arxiv.org/abs/1607.04186
3. Baldi, P., Sadowski, P.J.: Understanding dropout. In: Advances in Neural Information Processing Systems, vol. 26 (2013)
4. Butner, C.: Chesscoach is a neural network-based chess engine capable of natural-language commentary (2021). https://pythonrepo.com/repo/chrisbutner-ChessCoach-python-natural-language-processing
5. Czarnul, P.: Benchmarking parallel chess search in Stockfish on intel Xeon and intel Xeon phi processors. In: Shi, Y., et al. (eds.) ICCS 2018. LNCS, vol. 10862, pp. 457–464. Springer, Cham (2018). https://doi.org/10.1007/978-3-319-93713-7_40
6. David, O.E., Netanyahu, N.S., Wolf, L.: DeepChess: end-to-end deep neural network for automatic learning in chess. In: Villa, A.E.P., Masulli, P., Pons Rivero, A.J. (eds.) ICANN 2016. LNCS, vol. 9887, pp. 88–96. Springer, Cham (2016). https://doi.org/10.1007/978-3-319-44781-0_11
7. Ganguly, D., Leveling, J., Jones, G.J.: Retrieval of similar chess positions. In: Proceedings of the 37th International ACM SIGIR Conference on Research & Development in Information Retrieval, SIGIR 2014, pp. 687–696. Association for Computing Machinery, New York, NY, USA (2014). https://doi.org/10.1145/2600428.2609605
8. Goodfellow, I., Bengio, Y., Courville, A.: Deep Learning. MIT Press, Cambridge (2016). http://www.deeplearningbook.org
9. Int8: Chess position evaluation with convolutional neural network in Julia (2016). https://int8.io/chess-position-evaluation-with-convolutional-neural-networks-in-julia/
10. Jouppi, N.P., et al.: A domain-specific supercomputer for training deep neural networks. Commun. ACM **63**(7), 67–78 (2020). https://doi.org/10.1145/3360307
11. Maesumi, A.: Playing chess with limited look ahead. CoRR abs/2007.02130 (2020). https://arxiv.org/abs/2007.02130
12. Oshri, B., Khandwala, N.: Predicting moves in chess using convolutional neural networks (2016)
13. Panchal, H., Mishra, S., Shrivastava, V.: Chess moves prediction using deep learning neural networks. In: 2021 International Conference on Advances in Computing and Communications (ICACC), pp. 1–6. IEEE (2021)
14. Romero, O., Cuenca, J.F., Parra, L., Lloret, J.: Computer analysis of world chess championship players. In: ICSEA: The Fourteenth International Conference on Software Engineering Advances, pp. 200–205 (2019). ISBN: 978-1-61208-752-8

15. Sabatelli., M., Bidoia., F., Codreanu., V., Wiering., M.: Learning to evaluate chess positions with deep neural networks and limited lookahead. In: Proceedings of the 7th International Conference on Pattern Recognition Applications and Methods - ICPRAM, pp. 276–283. INSTICC, SciTePress (2018). https://doi.org/10.5220/0006535502760283

16. Samadi, M., Azimifar, Z., Jahromi, M.Z.: Learning: an effective approach in endgame chess board evaluation. In: Sixth International Conference on Machine Learning and Applications (ICMLA 2007), pp. 464–469 (2007). https://doi.org/10.1109/ICMLA.2007.48

17. Silver, D., et al.: A general reinforcement learning algorithm that masters chess, shogi, and go through self-play. Science **362**(6419), 1140–1144 (2018). https://doi.org/10.1126/science.aar6404

18. Srivastava, N., Hinton, G., Krizhevsky, A., Sutskever, I., Salakhutdinov, R.: Dropout: a simple way to prevent neural networks from overfitting. J. Mach. Learn. Res. **15**(1), 1929–1958 (2014)

19. Vikstrom, J.: Training a convolutional neural network to evaluate chess positions. KTH Royal Institute of Technology, School of Electrical Engineering and Computer Science, Stockholm, Sweden (2019)

20. Vázquez-Fernández, E., Coello Coello, C.A., Sagols Troncoso, F.D.: Assessing the positional values of chess pieces by tuning neural networks' weights with an evolutionary algorithm. In: World Automation Congress 2012, pp. 1–6 (2012)

Using AI-based Edge Processing in Monitoring the Pedestrian Crossing

Łukasz Karbowiak$^{(\boxtimes)}$ ⓘ and Mariusz Kubanek ⓘ

Czestochowa University of Technology, Dabrowskiego 69,
42 -201 Czestochowa, Poland
{lukasz.karbowiak,mariusz.kubanek}@icis.pcz.pl

Abstract. In edge processing, data collection devices are used to pre-filter data. As a result, only data of interest will be written to memory. This approach significantly reduces the amount of transferred data. Various algorithms, such as background segmentation or artificial intelligence (AI) techniques based on various neural networks, can be used to detect data of interest. This paper uses an AI-based technique in the edge processing environment to perform the learning process with a chosen neural network. The environment containing Nvidia Jetson Xavier NX is employed to train the MobileNetV3 network dedicated to detecting objects of interest like people or vehicles while monitoring the pedestrian crossing. The network consists of the initial fully connected convolution layer with 32 filters, followed by 19 residual bottleneck layers. This paper also proposes a learning process that uses the collected data after manual validation and significantly improves accuracy over the original network.

Keywords: artificial intelligence · edge computing · convolutional neural networks · pedestrian crossing

1 Introduction

Edge processing assumes pre-processing data on an edge device as close to sensors as possible. Such an approach is becoming an eminent trend because it offers significant business benefits. First, if the input data are pre-filtered on edge, the customer only pays for the data that are useful to him. Secondly, it enhances security and helps the correct transmission of data between different countries, taking into account the various legal regulations. Security is enhanced by using distributed data storage spread across multiple devices with their own security layers. Another advantage is reducing network bandwidth requirements. Due to transferring only relevant data, their amount is significantly reduced relative to raw data.

In this work, edge processing is applied to data from pedestrian crossings [1–3]. Two cases are considered: (i) with fixed cameras (e.g., city surveillance) and (ii) mobile cameras, e.g., mounted in cars. The analysis makes it possible to create a system that warns of unusual situations within the pedestrian crossing. Among such situations is a pedestrian and a vehicle in the lanes simultaneously.

R. Wyrzykowski et al. (Eds.): PPAM 2022, LNCS 13826, pp. 441–450, 2023.
https://doi.org/10.1007/978-3-031-30442-2_33

The material of the paper is organized in the following way. The experimental environment is presented in Sect. 2, while the case with stationary and mobile cameras are discussed in Sect. 3 and Sect. 4, respectively. Section 5 concludes the paper.

2   Experimental Environment

The workflow for the two cases considered in this paper is presented in Fig. 1. The workflow starts with retrieving data from a camera, either a stationary one that monitors the pedestrian crossing or a mobile camera mounted on a moving car. The second step involves transferring the data thus obtained to a pre-trained neural network. The selection of the neural network is made through an in-depth analysis and testing. The neural network analyzes the received image and performs labeling. Then our software checks whether the labels correspond to the image of interest for the analysis. If yes, the image is saved to memory in the folder corresponding to a label. If not, the image is dropped. The next steps are responsible for training the neural network in the learning process. Step 3 is performed after a sufficiently large amount of data has been collected. The data have to be manually verified because sometimes the pre-trained network performs labeling incorrectly. Corrections at this step are very important and cannot be overlooked, as this significantly affects the accuracy of detection performed by the neural network after the learning process. The final step 4 involves swapping the initial neural network that analyzes the camera images (in step 1) with the new one obtained through the learning process. Such swapping allows a better accuracy of detection. The learning process can also increase the number of detected objects. This is the case with mobile cameras.

The Nvidia Jetson Xavier NX [24] device is used for edge processing. The required computing power is provided by 384 GPU CUDA cores and 48 Tensor cores. In addition, a 6-core ARM CPU is included in this device with 8GB

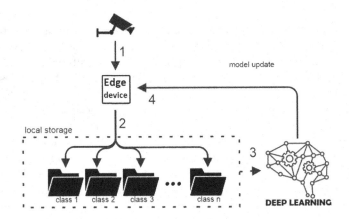

Fig. 1. Workflow for the experimental environment

of DRAM memory, providing a bandwidth of 51.2 GB/s. Two cameras collect images - one dedicated to Raspberry Pi, connected via the CSI interface, and the second is the LifeCam Studio camera from Microsoft. The second camera has a resolution of 1280×720 and is connected via a USB port.

3   Case with Stationary Cameras

3.1   Data Collecting

Collecting data for stationary cameras involves taking a frame from a stationary surveillance camera. The frame is passed to a pre-trained neural network. For fixed cameras, this is the MobileNetV3 network [5]. After analyzing data in the frame, this network returns the class to which the data can be assigned. During data collection, the relevant information embraces the situations in which the frame contains: a car, a pedestrian, both of them, and an empty pedestrian crossing. The classes should consider different weather and lighting conditions, as they should encompass the diversity of the scene to the best possible extent.

3.2   Network Training and Detection

For fixed cameras, the learning process is performed after obtaining about 2,000 patterns. Learning is based on the MobileNetV3 network, and the final network return classes in the range: person, car, both of them, empty. For the first class of person, exemplary training data are shown in Fig. 2. Among these data are examples with one person as well as with a group of pedestrians.

Training data for the class of car (Fig. 3) include samples containing different models, colors, and types of cars located at different positions in the image. Another class, both, corresponds to samples (Fig. 4) with a mixture of single or several vehicles and a single pedestrian or a group of pedestrians. Training data for the last class, empty, contain static images (Fig. 5) of an empty pedestrian crossing.

All samples are collected under different weather conditions. In addition, samples are acquired at different times, resulting in varying lighting conditions, which also positively affects the effectiveness of detecting the defined classes.

The learning process is performed using full scenes from the above-defined classes. The accuracy of the newly created model is 98.6% for all classes, using data for the studied pedestrian crossing (Fig. 6). This high accuracy of the model

Fig. 2. Training data for the class person

Fig. 3. Training data for the class car

Fig. 4. Training data for the class both

is due to a sufficient amount of learning data for this case. The fixed camera and the study of a single pedestrian crossing minimize the variability of background [25]. Variable weather conditions are not an issue for this network model as the learning process uses data collected at different hours and with different weather.

4   Mobile Cameras

4.1   Analysis of Different Neural Network

In the case of mobile cameras, the choice of the final neural network is made experimentally. We decided to analyze publicly available solutions and refine the one that would achieve the best results, namely, the best accuracy of detecting vehicles and pedestrians with a high frame per second (FPS) ratio.

The approach using a Convolutional Neural Network (CNN) is discussed first. Image recognition and classification with CNNs are used to detect objects, recognize faces, etc. The proposed improvement involves [4] automatically optimizing the feature representation for the detection task and regularizing the neural network. The accuracy of the Support Vector Machine (SVM) classifier using the features learned by the CNN is equivalent to the accuracy of the CNN, confirming the importance of automatically optimized features. However, the computational demand of the CNN classifier is more than an order of magnitude lower than that of the SVM, irrespective of the type of features used.

Fig. 5. Training data for class empty

Fig. 6. Results of detection corresponding to various situations

The next group relates to Region-based CNNs (R-CNNs), namely, pure R-CNN, Fast R-CNN, and Faster R-CNN. Region-based CNNs first generate region proposals used then to locate objects within the input image. Girshick et al. [6,7] proposed extracting 2,000 region proposals from images and processing them. The disadvantage of such a solution is the high computing cost of processing a large number of region proposals. This disadvantage makes it practically impossible to process data in real time since processing a single image takes a few to tens of seconds. In addition, the quality of the candidate region proposals cannot be improved. Based on this knowledge, a modified approach was introduced in works [8,9]. The resulting Fast R-CNN and Faster-CNN methods do not require determining a large number of region proposals that significantly reduce the computing cost.

The analysis of the Faster R-CNN method for pedestrian detection was performed in paper [10]. The study showed the effectiveness of this method. Another proposal [11] to improve the Faster R-CNN method focuses on improving the quality of the network and using the K-means cluster analysis. In particular, the Faster R-CNN method can detect people from a drone [12]. By incorporating feature fusion and context analysis, a new FCF R-CNN algorithm was developed [13]. The proposed algorithm gives better results for pedestrians that are small in size and obscured, and it is also robust for difficult scenes.

In 2015, Redmon et al. proposed the first single-stage detector YOLO [14]. The first version achieved a reduced detection accuracy relative to the two-stage detector but allowed significantly increasing detection speed. High speed and accuracy are crucial for pedestrians and unusual situations on the road. The next versions of the YOLO network were introduced to improve the detection quality. Among them is the YOLOv2 network [15,18]. The improvement provided by this network begins with a modification of the DataNet53 model, in which feature creation is strengthened. In addition, three inceptive depth convolution modules are added and integrated at different levels. All these changes lead to a more comprehensive characterization of the object in the image. The next version is the YOLOv3 network [16,19] that applies the HOG (histogram of oriented gradients) method to implement pre-processing. This method makes it possible to highlight pedestrian contour features, especially small pedestrian target features, and reduce the implication of background information for detection results.

Further improvements were provided by the YOLOv4 [20] network based on implementing a modified detection model. The proposed model combines a new type of SPP (spatial pyramid pooling) network and K-means clustering algorithm with the YOLOv4 model for easier feature extraction. In addition, the Mish activation function is applied to the neck of the detection model, replacing the Leaky ReLU activation function to improve detection accuracy.

Another solution to improve pedestrian detection accuracy is an updated version of MobileNet [21] combined with SSD (Single Shot MultiBox Detector) [22,23]. This method provides four components that are important for pedestrian detection: feature extraction, deformation, occlusion handling, and classification. The proposed solution allows the coordination of the components to increase their strength with fewer parameters.

In the analysis of the capabilities of each neural network (Tab. 1), the two parameters that are most relevant to the analysis of pedestrian crossings were taken into account - the efficiency (accuracy) of detection of pedestrians and vehicles, and the speed of the network, i.e., the number of analyzed frames per second (FPS). The last parameter is crucial for real-time data analysis for monitoring the pedestrian crossing. The best results for pedestrian recognition are achieved by YOLOv4, YOLOv3 and MobileNetv3. For car recognition, high accuracy and speed are provided by ResNet50 and ResNet101, but YOLOv4 gives the best results. At the same time, MobileNetv3 seems to be a suitable network for less powerful edge devices, another being YOLOv4. As a result, we finally select MobileNetv3 for static cameras and YOLOv4 for mobile cameras.

4.2   Data Collecting

Collecting learning data for mobile cameras is similar to that for fixed cameras. In our study, we use records from cameras placed in cars, and YOLOv4 [17] is applied as the pre-trained neural network. As in the previous case, all data have to be manually verified and prepared for the learning process.

4.3   Network Training and Detection Results

The learning process for the YOLOv4 network is different from the process used in the previous case. To learn the model, it is required to define the position of all objects of interest within the current scene. To improve the quality of monitoring pedestrian crossings and detecting objects, the model is extended to include new classes: pedestrian crossing, pedestrian crossing signs, and traffic

Table 1. Comparison of the various neural networks based on the accuracy of detecting pedestrians and cars, as well the parameter FPS (frames per second)

Name	Pedestrian (%)	Car (%)	FPS
VGG16	72,89	83.51	18
ResNet50	73.05	88.74	25
ResNet101	74.19	89.13	22
Fast RCNN	68.4	74.64	23
Faster RCNN	70.4	77.42	56
YOLO	57.9	59.98	25
YOLOv2	76.8	62.76	36
YOLOv3	78.12	79.31	31
YOLOv4	82.30	93.39	61
MobileNetv3	76.17	86.65	73

lights. The LabelImg tool [26] is used for labeling (Fig. 7), which allows us to improve the labeling process significantly. The tool automatically loads images, allowing us to define the classes to be labeled on scenes, and after defining all objects of the scene, a file containing information about classes, objects, and their location is automatically generated. Based on data available in all files containing the description of the scene, a single file is generated where data are stored in the format required for the learning process.

Fig. 7. Example of using LabelImg tool for label scenes

For mobile monitoring of pedestrian crossings, an additional functionality has been added to warn of a person in a close proximity. The algorithm is based on the knowledge of objects detected by the network, and the distance between them. The algorithm uses several distance values calculated on successively captured frames. When the algorithm determines that a pedestrian is, or is about to be, at a pedestrian crossing, the appropriate warning is displayed.

Fig. 8. Example results for the trained model

Fig. 9. Scene with algorithm attention information

The accuracy of the model refers to two criteria. The first is the accuracy of object detection, which is 97.4% (see Fig. 8). The second is the accuracy of the pedestrian warning algorithm equal to 82.9% (see Fig. 9). The reason for such a low value is discussed in the next subsection.

4.4 Accuracy Analysis

Accuracy analysis concerns two aspects. The first one is labeling pedestrian crossings correctly. None of the analyzed networks did this by default, so our network is trained based on the collected recordings. After the learning process with the YOLOv4 network, an average accuracy of 97.4% is achieved. The second aspect concerns the new functionality - warning of dangerous situations at pedestrian crossings. Here the final accuracy is influenced by the accuracy of detecting pedestrians and vehicles and the accuracy of detecting pedestrian crossings. When the system correctly receives data about all these objects, it becomes possible to identify a real danger at the pedestrian crossing correctly. For this reason, the average accuracy of this solution is 82.9%.

5 Conclusions

This paper presents the application of various neural networks in monitoring pedestrian crossings with fixed and mobile cameras. In the case of fixed cameras, the study shows a high efficiency of correct detection using the trained MobileNetV3 network. This is due to a relatively static background for the image of exactly the same area. At the same time, such a learned neural network model only works for the pedestrian crossing used in the learning process. In future work, we will replace the current neural network with the network applied for mobile cameras.

The solution for mobile cameras based on the YOLOv4 network achieves good results for the detection of all classes, including the newly created ones. Future works will focus on improving the accuracy of the algorithm that warns drivers of dangerous situations.

References

1. Tian, D., Han, Y., Wang, B., Guan, T., Wei, W.,: A Review of Intelligent Driving Pedestrian Detection Based on Deep Learning. Comput. Intell. Neurosci. article ID 5410049 (2021)
2. Gauerhof, L., Hawkins, R., Picardi, C., Paterson, C., Hagiwara, Y., Habli, I.: Assuring the safety of machine learning for pedestrian detection at crossings. In: Casimiro, A., Ortmeier, F., Bitsch, F., Ferreira, P. (eds.) SAFECOMP 2020. LNCS, vol. 12234, pp. 197–212. Springer, Cham (2020). https://doi.org/10.1007/978-3-030-54549-9_13
3. Zhang, S., Abdel-Aty, M.: Real-time pedestrian conflict prediction model at the signal cycle level using machine learning models. IEEE Open J. Intell. Transp. Syst. **3**, 176–186 (2022)
4. Szarvas, M., Yoshizawa, A., Yamamoto, M., Ogata, J.,: Pedestrian detection with convolutional neural networks. In: IEEE Proceedings. Intelligent Vehicles Symposium, pp. 224–229 (2005)
5. Andrew H., et al.: Searching for MobileNetV3. arXiv:1905.02244 (2019)
6. Girshick, R., Donahue, J., Darrell, T., Malik, J.,: Rich Feature Hierarchies for Accurate Object Detection and Semantic Segmentation. In: 2014 IEEE Conference Computer Vision and Pattern Recognition, pp. 580–587 (2014)
7. R-CNN, Fast R-CNN, Faster R-CNN, YOLO - Object Detection Algorithms https://towardsdatascience.com/r-cnn-fast-r-cnn-faster-r-cnn-yolo-object-detection-algorithms-36d53571365e (October 22, 2022)
8. Dong, P., Wang, W.: Better region proposals for pedestrian detection with R-CNN. In: 2016 Visual Communications and Image Processing (VCIP), pp. 1–4 (2016)
9. Dollár, P., Appel, R., Belongie, S., Perona, P.: Fast feature pyramids for object detection. IEEE Trans. Pattern Anal. Mach. Intell. **36**(8) 1532–1545 (2014)
10. Zhang, L., Lin, L., Liang, X., He, K.: Is faster R-CNN doing well for pedestrian detection? In: Leibe, B., Matas, J., Sebe, N., Welling, M. (eds.) ECCV 2016. LNCS, vol. 9906, pp. 443–457. Springer, Cham (2016). https://doi.org/10.1007/978-3-319-46475-6_28
11. Zhang, H., Du, Y., Ning, S., Zhang, Y., Yang, S., Du, C.: Pedestrian Detection Method Based on Faster R-CNN. In: 13th International Conference Computational Intelligence and Security, pp. 427–430 (2017)
12. Hung, G.L. et al.: Faster R-CNN deep learning model for pedestrian detection from drone images. SN Comput. Sci. **1**(116), 427–430 (2020)
13. Zhai, S., Dong, S., Shang, D., Wang, S.: An improved faster r-cnn pedestrian detection algorithm based on feature fusion and context analysis. IEEE Access **8**, 138117–138128 (2020)

14. Redmon, J., Divvala, S., Girshick R., Farhadi, A.: You Only Look Once: Unified, Real-Time Object Detection. In: 2016 IEEE Conference Computer Vision and Pattern Recognition, pp. 779–788 (2016)
15. Redmon, J., Farhadi, A.: YOLO9000: Better, Faster, Stronger. arXiv:1612.08242 (2016)
16. Redmon, J., Farhadi, A.: YOLOv3: An Incremental Improvement, arXiv:1804.02767 (2018)
17. Bochkovskiy, A., Chien-Yao W., Hong-Yuan M.: YOLOv4: Optimal Speed and Accuracy of Object Detection. arXiv:2004.10934 (2020)
18. Panigrahi, S., Raju, U.S.: InceptionDepth-wiseYOLOv2: improved implementation of YOLO framework for pedestrian detection. Int. J. Multimed. Inform. Retrieval 11(12), 409–430 (2022)
19. Ao L., Xiuxiang G., Chengming Q.: Pedestrian detection based on improved YOLOv3 algorithm. In: ICSEE 2021: Intelligent Life System Modelling, Image Processing and Analysis, pp. 221-231 (2021)
20. Boyuan, W., Muqing, W.: Study on Pedestrian Detection Based on an Improved YOLOv4 Algorithm. In: IEEE 6th Int. Conf. Computer and Communications, pp. 1198–1202 (2020)
21. Howard, A.G. et al.: MobileNets: Efficient Convolutional Neural Networks for Mobile Vision Applications. arXiv:1704.04861 (2017)
22. Liu, W., et al.: SSD: single shot multibox detector. In: Leibe, B., Matas, J., Sebe, N., Welling, M. (eds.) ECCV 2016. LNCS, vol. 9905, pp. 21–37. Springer, Cham (2016). https://doi.org/10.1007/978-3-319-46448-0_2
23. Murthy, C.B., Hashmi, M.F., Keskar, A.G.: Optimized MobileNet + SSD: a real-time pedestrian detection on a low-end edge device. Int. J. Multimed. Inform. Retrieval. 10(8), 1–14 (2021)
24. Nvidia Xavier NX. https://www.nvidia.com/en-us/autonomous-machines/embedded-systems/jetson-xavier-nx/ (2022)
25. Karbowiak, L., Bobulski, J.: Background segmentation in difficult weather conditions. PeerJ Comput. Sci. article 8, e962 (2022)
26. LabelImg tool. https://github.com/heartexlabs/labelImg (2022)

Special Session on Parallel EVD/SVD and its Application in Matrix Computations

Automatic Code Selection for the Dense Symmetric Generalized Eigenvalue Problem Using ATMathCoreLib

Masato Kobayashi[1], Shuhei Kudo[1], Takeo Hoshi[2], and Yusaku Yamamoto[1(✉)]

[1] The University of Electro -Communications, Tokyo 182-8585, Japan
`yusaku.yamamoto@uec.ac.jp`
[2] Tottori University, Tottori 680-8552, Japan

Abstract. Solution of the symmetric definite generalized eigenvalue problem (GEP) $A\mathbf{x} = \lambda B\mathbf{x}$ lies at the heart of many scientific computations like electronic structure calculations. The standard algorithm for this problem consists of two parts, namely, reduction of the GEP to the symmetric eigenvalue problem (SEP) and the solution of the SEP. Several algorithms and codes exist for both of these parts, and their execution times differ considerably depending on the input matrix size and the computational environment. So, there is a strong need to choose the best combination of codes automatically given these conditions. In this paper, we propose such a methodology based on ATMathCoreLib, which is a library to assist automatic performance tuning. Numerical experiments using performance data on the K computer, Fujitsu FX10 and SGI Altix show that our methodology is robust and can choose the fastest codes even in the presence of large fluctuations in the execution time.

Keywords: automatic code selection · automatic performance tuning · ATMathCoreLib · generalized eigenvalue problem · parallel computing · ScaLAPACK · ELPA · EigenExa · performance prediction

1 Introduction

Suppose that there are M computer programs that can perform a given task. Their functions are all equivalent, but their execution times may be different and may vary depending on the input problem size, the computing environment and random factors such as influence from other programs running on the same machine. Suppose also that we want to perform the task N $(\geq M)$ times using the same computing environment, using different inputs of the same size, and minimize the total execution time. If we have no prior knowledge on the execution time of each program, a possible strategy is to use each of the M programs once for the first M executions, choose the fastest one, and use it for the remaining $N - M$ executions. But the execution time may fluctuate due to random factors and therefore the estimations from the first M executions may not be accurate. Then, what is the best strategy?

© The Author(s), under exclusive license to Springer Nature Switzerland AG 2023
R. Wyrzykowski et al. (Eds.): PPAM 2022, LNCS 13826, pp. 453–463, 2023.
https://doi.org/10.1007/978-3-031-30442-2_34

More specifically, let the execution time of the mth program be denoted by $T(m, \mathbf{n}, \mathbf{p}, \mathbf{z})$, where $\mathbf{n}$, $\mathbf{p}$ are parameters that specify the input problem size and the computing environment, respectively, and $\mathbf{z}$ denotes the random factor. Note that $\mathbf{n}$, $\mathbf{p}$ and $\mathbf{z}$ are in general vector variables. For example, in the case of eigenvalue computation, $\mathbf{n}$ consists of the matrix size and the number of eigenvalues to be computed. The parameter $\mathbf{p}$ might consist of integers specifying the target machine and the number of processors to be used. Then, our objective is to choose the sequence $m_1, m_2, \ldots, m_N$ $(1 \leq m_i \leq M)$ judiciously to minimize the expected value $\mathbb{E}[\sum_{i=1}^{N} T(m_i, \mathbf{n}, \mathbf{p}, \mathbf{z}_i)]$, given $\mathbf{n}$, $\mathbf{p}$ and some assumptions on the probability distribution of $\{\mathbf{z}_i\}$. Note that m_i may depend on the already measured execution times, $\{T(m_j, \mathbf{n}, \mathbf{p}, \mathbf{z}_j)\}_{j=1}^{i-1}$. This problem is known as *online automatic tuning* [1].

There are two criteria in choosing $m_1, m_2, \ldots, m_N$. On one hand, we need to estimate the mean execution time $\mathbb{E}[T(m, \mathbf{n}, \mathbf{p}, \mathbf{z})]$ for each m accurately to find the fastest program. In general, the accuracy is improved as the number of measurement for each m is increased. On the other hand, we want to exploit the knowledge obtained by previous measurements as much as possible, by maximizing the use of the program estimated to be the fastest. These two objectives are conflicting, so there is a tradeoff between *exploration* and *exploitation*.

To solve this problem, Suda developed ATMathCoreLib [2], which is a library to assist online automatic tuning. It constructs a statistical execution time model for each of the M programs and chooses the one to be executed next time by considering the tradeoff between exploration and exploitation. After execution, it receives the actual execution time and updates the model using Bayes' rule. This process is repeated N times. In this way, the total execution time is minimized in the sense of expected value.

In this paper, we apply ATMathCoreLib to automatic code selection for the dense symmetric generalized eigenvalue problem (GEP) $A\mathbf{x} = \lambda B\mathbf{x}$, where $A, B \in \mathbb{R}^{n \times n}$ are symmetric and B is positive definite. For this problem, the standard procedure is to transform it to the standard symmetric eigenvalue problem and then solve the latter [3]. There are several algorithms both for the first and second parts and several implementations exist, such as ScaLAPACK [4], ELPA [5,6] and EigenExa [7,8]. Which one is the fastest depends on the problem size n and the computational environment. Since the dense symmetric GEP lies at the heart of many scientific computations and it requires long computing time, it is desirable to be able to choose the best code for a given condition automatically. As computing environments, we consider the K computer, Fujitsu FX10 and SGI Altix. In our experiments, we add artificial noise corresponding to $\mathbf{z}$ to measured data given in [9] and study if ATMathCoreLib can find the optimal code for each case even in the presence of noise.

The rest of this paper is structured as follows. In Sect. 2, we detail the operation of ATMathCoreLib. Section 3 explains algorithms for the dense symmetric GEP and their implementations. In Sect. 4, we apply ATMathCoreLib to the dense symmetric GEP and give experimental results in several computing environments. Finally, Sect. 5 gives some conclusion.

2   Operation of ATMathCoreLib

The operation of ATMathCoreLib is illustrated in Fig. 1 [10]. Here, we assume that there is a master program that executes one of the M equivalent codes depending on the code selection parameter k. The master program also measures the execution time of the code. ATMathCoreLib works interactively with this master program. At the ith iteration ($1 \leq i \leq N$), it selects the code to be executed in such a way that the expected value of the total execution time is minimized. To achieve this, it uses its internal execution time model, which holds the estimates of the mean and variance of the execution time of each code. A code is more likely to be selected if its mean is smaller (faster code) or its variance is larger (meaning that the model for the code is not yet accurate enough). This corresponds to choosing the code to be executed by considering the tradeoff between exploration and exploitation. Then it passes the code number k_i to the master program. The master program receives it, executes the k_i-th code, measures its execution time, and passes it to ATMathCoreLib. Then, ATMathCoreLib uses it to update its internal model. This process is repeated for $i = 1, 2, \ldots, N$.

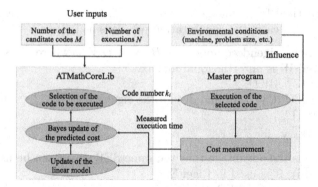

Fig. 1. Operation of ATMathCoreLib.

Actually, the model update process in ATMathCoreLib is more intricate; it consists of two steps called update of the coefficients of the linear model and Bayes update. But we do not go into details here. Readers interested in mathematical foundations of ATMathCoreLib should consult [1, 2].

3   Algorithms for the Dense Symmetric GEP and Their Implementations

Here, we consider computing all the eigenvalues and eigenvectors of a dense symmetric GEP $Ax = \lambda Bx$. The standard procedure to solve this problem consists of the following two parts:

1. Reduction of the GEP to a standard symmetric eigenvalue problem (SEP).
2. Solution of the SEP.

There are several algorithms for both of them. For the first part, the standard method is to use the Cholesky decomposition of B. In that case, the whole computation proceeds as follows:

(i) Compute the Cholesky decomposition $B = LL^\top$.
(ii) $C \equiv L^{-1}AL^{-\top}$.
(iii) Solve the SEP $C\mathbf{y} = \lambda\mathbf{y}$ and obtain the eigenvalues $\{\lambda_j\}_{j=1}^n$ and the eigenvectors $\{\mathbf{y}_j\}_{j=1}^n$.
(iv) $\mathbf{x}_j \equiv L^{-\top}\mathbf{y}_j$ for $j = 1, 2, \ldots, n$.

Here, steps (i), (ii) and (iv) correspond to part 1 and step (iii) corresponds to part 2 above. There are two options in computing steps (ii) and (iv). The first one is to use forward and backward substitutions to multiply L^{-1} or $L^{-\top}$. This approach is adopted by ScaLAPACK. The second one is to compute the inverse matrix L^{-1} explicitly and compute steps (ii) and (iv) by matrix multiplications. This approach has the advantage that the number of forward and backward substitutions, which have limited parallelism, is minimized and is adopted by ELPA.

Another method for reducing the GEP to SEP is to use the eigendecomposition of B. In this case, the computation proceeds as follows.

(i) Compute the eigendecomposition $B = WDW^\top$, where D is a diagonal matrix and W is an orthogonal matrix.
(ii) $C \equiv D^{-\frac{1}{2}}W^\top AWD^{-\frac{1}{2}}$.
(iii) Solve the SEP $C\mathbf{y} = \lambda\mathbf{y}$ and obtain the eigenvalues $\{\lambda_j\}_{j=1}^n$ and the eigenvectors $\{\mathbf{y}_j\}_{j=1}^n$.
(iv) $\mathbf{x}_j = D^{\frac{1}{2}}W^\top\mathbf{y}_j$ for $j = 1, 2, \ldots, n$.

This method has the advantage that the same SEP solver can be used both for steps (i) and (iii). It is used in EigenExa.

In the solution of the SEP, the matrix C is transformed to an intermediate symmetric tridiagonal matrix T or a penta-diagonal matrix P by orthogonal transformations, the eigenvalues and eigenvectors of T or P are computed, and the eigenvectors are transformed to those of C by back-transformation. There are several approaches to achieve this, as listed below.

(A) C is transformed directly to a symmetric tridiagonal matrix T by the Householder method. The eigenvalues and eigenvectors of T are computed by standard methods like the QR algorithm, the divide-and-conquer algorithm, or the MR^3 (Multiple Relatively Robust Representations) algorithm.
(B) C is first transformed to a symmetric band matrix S and then to a symmetric tridiagonal matrix T. The eigenvalues and eigenvectors of T are computed by the standard methods.
(C) C is transformed directly to a symmetric penta-diagonal matrix P. The eigenvalues and eigenvectors of P are computed by a specially designed divide-and-conquer method.

Approach (A) is a conventional one and is adopted by ScaLAPACK. In ELPA and EigenExa, there are also routines using this approach. We denote them as ELPA1 and EIGS, respectively. While this approach is the most efficient in terms of computational work, it has disadvantages that many inter-processor communications are incurred in the tridiagonalization step and that matrix-vector multiplications (DGEMV [11]) used in the tridiagonalization cannot use cache memory effectively. In contrast, approach (B) requires less inter-processor communications. Also, since most of the computations in the tridiagonalization can be done in the form of matrix-matrix multiplications (DGEMM [12]), cache memory can be used effectively. This approach is used by one of ELPA's routine, which we call ELPA2. Approach (C) is an intermediate approach between (A) and (B) and is used in one of the routines in EigenExa. We call this EIGX.

In summary, there are three routines we can use for reducing the GEP to SEP, namely, those from ScaLAPACK, ELPA and EigenExa. Also, there are five routines to solve the SEP, namely, ScaLAPACK, ELPA1, ELPA2, EIGS and EIGX. While ScaLAPACK, ELPA and EigenExa have different matrix storage formats and data distribution schemes, there is a middleware called EigenKernel [13] that allows the user to freely combine routines from these libraries, by providing automatic data conversion and re-distribution functions. Using EigenKernel, we can evaluate the performance of various combinations and choose the fastest one for a given matrix size and computational environment.

4   Automatic Code Selection for the Dense Symmetric GEP Using ATMathCoreLib

Now we apply ATMathCoreLib to automatic code selection for the dense symmetric GEP and evaluate its performance. To this end, we use execution time data on three distributed-memory parallel computers, namely, the K computer, Fujitsu FX10 and SGI Altix ICE 8400EX, given in [9]. We add artificial random noise to these data and study if ATMathCoreLib can choose the optimal combination in the presence of error.

Among $3 \times 5 = 15$ possible combinations of the algorithms for reduction to the SEP and solution of the SEP, 8 promising combinations (workflows) are chosen as candidates in [9]. They are shown in Table 1. The specifications of the parallel computers are listed in Table 2. The size of test matrices is $n = 90,000$ and $n = 430,080$. They are matrices from the ELSES matrix library, which is a collection of matrix data from electronic structure calculations.

From the many test cases reported in [9], we picked up three cases for our evaluation: the problem of $n = 430,080$ on the K computer, $n = 90,000$ on SGI Altix and Fujitsu FX10. The number of nodes used is $p = 10,000$ and 256 for the K computer and SGI Altix, respectively. For Fujitsu FX10, p is either 1,024 or 1,369, depending on the workflow. This is because some library puts restrictions on the number of nodes that can be used. The total execution times for the three cases are shown in Table 3. Here, workflow D' is the same as workflow D except

Table 1. Combinations of the algorithms used in [9].

Workflow	Solution of SEP	Reduction to SEP
A	ScaLAPACK	ScaLAPACK
B	EIGX	ScaLAPACK
C	ScaLAPACK	ELPA
D	ELPA2	ELPA
E	ELPA1	ELPA
F	EIGS	ELPA
G	EIGX	ELPA
H	EIGX	EigenExa

Table 2. Specifications of the parallel computers.

Name	CPU	Clock	# of cores	Byte/Flop
K computer	SPARC 64 VIIIfx	2.0 GHz	8	0.5
Fujitsu FX10	SPARC64 IXfx	1.848 GHz	16	0.36
SGI Altix ICE 8400EX	Intel Xeon X5570	2.93 GHz	8	0.68

that it does not use SSE-optimized routines in the ELPA2 solver. For each case, the workflow with the shortest execution time is marked with bold letters.

In our numerical experiments, we operated ATMathCoreLib by using these data as inputs, instead of actually executing the GEP solver each time. More specifically, at the ith execution ($1 \leq i \leq N$), if the workflow selected by ATMathCoreLib was k_i, we picked up the execution time of the k_i-th workflow from Table 3, added random noise to it, and input it to ATMathCoreLib. As random noise, we used a random variable following normal distribution with mean zero and standard deviation equal to 10%, 20%, or 40% of the corresponding execution time. The number of total executions was set to $N = 100$ for all cases.

The results of automatic code selection is illustrated in Figs. 2 through 7. Figures 2, 4 and 6 show the execution time for each iteration, while Figs. 3, 5 and 7 show the workflows selected by ATMathCoreLib for each iteration. As can be seen from the latter graphs, ATMathCoreLib tries various workflows at the beginning, but gradually narrows down the candidates to one or two, finally chooses the one it considers the fastest and then continues executing only that one. In all the cases given here, the workflow finally chosen by ATMathCoreLib was actually the fastest one, even if the noise level was as high as 40%. Thus we can conclude that automatic code selection using ATMathCoreLib is quite robust against fluctuations in the execution time. These final choices show that ELPA is the fastest for reduction to the SEP in all three cases. For solution of the SEP, EIGX was the fastest for the $n = 430,080/K$ and $n = 90,000/Altix$ cases, while EIGS was the fastest for the $n = 90,000/FX10$ case.

Table 3. Execution time of each workflow for three cases (taken from [9]).

Matrix size/Machine	Workflow	Total execution time (sec)
$n = 430,080$/K	A	11,634
($p = 10,000$)	B	8,953
	C	5,415
	D	4,242
	E	2,990
	F	2,809
	G	**2,734**
	H	3,595
$n = 90,000$/Altix	A	1,985
($p = 256$)	B	1,883
	C	1,538
	D	1,621
	D'	2,621
	E	1,558
	F	1,670
	G	**1,453**
	H	2,612
$n = 90,000$/FX10	A	1,248 ($p = 1,369$)
($p = 1,024/1,369$)	B	691 ($p = 1,024$)
	C	835 ($p = 1,369$)
	D	339 ($p = 1,024$)
	E	262 ($p = 1,024$)
	F	**250** ($p = 1,369$)
	G	314 ($p = 1,024$)
	H	484 ($p = 1,369$)

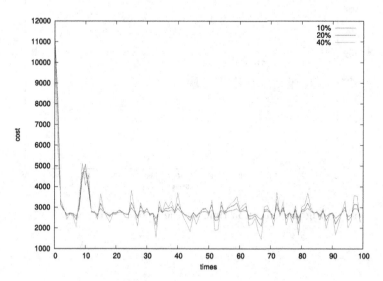

Fig. 2. Execution time for the 430,080/K case.

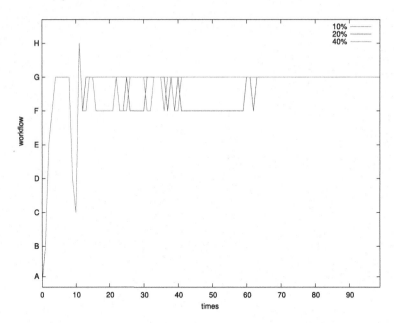

Fig. 3. Workflows selected by ATMathCoreLib in the 430,080/K case.

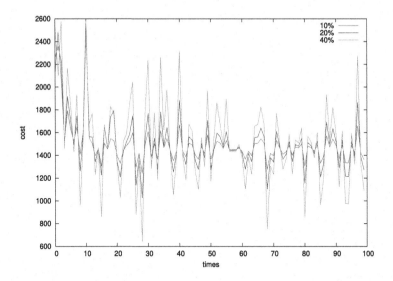

Fig. 4. Execution time for the 90,000/Altix case.

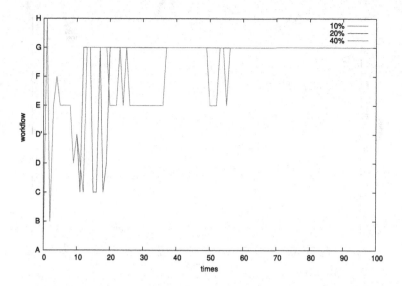

Fig. 5. Workflows selected by ATMathCoreLib in the 90,000/Altix case.

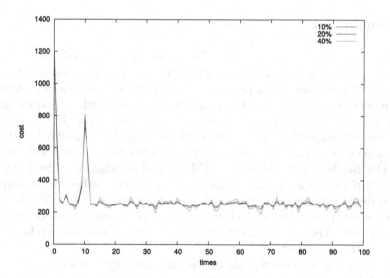

Fig. 6. Execution time for the 90,000/FX10 case.

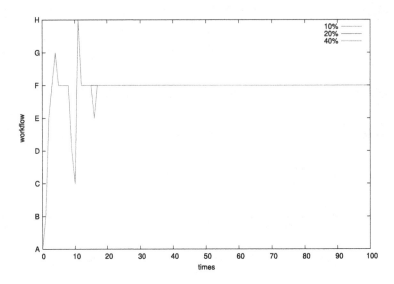

Fig. 7. Workflows selected by ATMathCoreLib in the 90,000/FX10 case.

5 Conclusion

In this paper, we proposed a strategy for automatic code selection for the dense symmetric generalized eigenvalue problem. We consider the situation where N GEPs of the same size are to be solved sequentially in the same computational environment and there are multiple GEP solvers available whose performance we do not know in advance. Then, our objective is to choose the GEP solver to try for each execution judiciously, by taking into account the tradeoff between exploration and exploitation, and minimize the expected value of the total execution time. This can be realized by using ATMathCoreLib, which is a library to assist automatic performance tuning. Numerical experiments using the performance data on the K computer, Fujitsu FX10 and SGI Altix show that ATMathCore-Lib can actually find the best solver even if there are large fluctuations in the execution time. Thus we can conclude that our method provides a robust means for automatic code selection.

Our future work includes applying this methodology to other matrix computations and extending it to optimization of parameters in solvers.

Acknowledgements. The authors thank the anonymous reviewers for valuable comments that helped us to improve the presentation of this paper. The present study is supported in part by the Ministry of Education, Science, Sports and Culture, Grant-in-Aid for Scientific Research Nos. 19KK0255 and 22KK19772.

References

1. Naono, K., Teranishi, K., Cavazos, J., Suda, R. (Eds.): Software Automatic Tuning: From Concepts to the State-of-the-Art Results, Springer, 2010. https://doi.org/10.1007/978-1-4419-6935-4

2. Suda, R.: ATMathCoreLib: mathematical core library for automatic tuning (in Japanese), IPSJ SIG Technical Report, Vol. 2011-HPC-129, No. 14, pp. 1–12 (2011)

3. Golub, G.H., Van Loan, C.F.: Matrix Computations, 4th edn. Johns Hopkins University Press, Baltimore (2012)

4. Blackford, L.S., et al.: ScaLAPACK Users' Guide, SIAM. Philadelphia (1997). https://doi.org/10.1137/1.9780898719642

5. Auckenthaler, T., et al.: Parallel solution of partial symmetric eigenvalue problems from electronic structure calculations. Parallel Comput. **37**(12), 783–794 (2011). https://doi.org/10.1016/j.parco.2011.05.002

6. Marek, A., et al.: The ELPA library - scalable parallel eigenvalue solutions for electronic structure theory and computational science. J. Phys.: Condens. Matter **26**, 213201 (2014). https://doi.org/10.1088/0953-8984/26/21/213201

7. Imamura, T., Yamada, S., Yoshida, M.: Development of a high performance eigensolver on a peta-scale next-generation supercomputer system. Prog. Nucl. Sci. Technol. **2**, 643–650 (2011). https://doi.org/10.15669/pnst.2.643

8. Imamura, T., Hirota, Y., Fukaya, T., Yamada, S., Machida, M.: EigenExa: high performance dense eigensolver, present and future, 8th International Workshop on Parallel Matrix Algorithms and Applications (PMAA14), Lugano, Switzerland, 2014. http://www.aics.riken.jp/labs/lpnctrt/index_e.html

9. Imachi, H., Hoshi, T.: Hybrid numerical solvers for massively parallel eigenvalue computation and their benchmark with electronic structure calculation. J. Inform. Process. **24**(1), 164–172 (2016). https://doi.org/10.2197/ipsjjip.24.164

10. Nagashima, S., Fukaya, T., Yamamoto, Y.: On constructing cost models for online automatic tuning using. ATMathCoreLib, In: Proceedings of IEEE MCSoC 2016, IEEE Press (2016). https://doi.org/10.1109/MCSoC.2016.52

11. Dongarra, J., Du Croz, J., Hammarling, S., Hanson, R.J.: An extended set of fortran basic linear algebra subprograms. ACM Trans. Math. Softw. **14**(1), 1–17 (1988). https://doi.org/10.1145/42288.42291

12. Dongarra, J.J., Du Croz, J., Hammarling, S., Hanson, R.J.: Algorithm 656: an extended set of basic linear algebra subprograms: Model implementation and test programs. ACM Trans. Math. Softw. **14**(1), 18–32 (1988). https://doi.org/10.1145/42288.42292

13. Tanaka, K., et al.: EigenKernel. Jpn. J. Ind. Appl. Math. **36**(2), 719–742 (2019). https://doi.org/10.1007/s13160-019-00361-7

14. http://www.elses.jp/matrix/

On Relative Accuracy of the One-Sided Block-Jacobi SVD Algorithm

Gabriel Okša[(✉)] and Martin Bečka

Institute of Mathematics, Slovak Academy of Sciences, Bratislava, Slovak Republic
{Gabriel.Oksa,Martin.Becka}@savba.sk

Abstract. We are interested in the relative accuracy of computed singular values in the serial real one-sided block-Jacobi SVD algorithm with dynamic ordering using approximate weights, and in the orthogonality of computed left and right singular vectors. Test matrices are of the form $A = BD$, where B is a random matrix with a prescribed condition number $\kappa(B)$ and D is diagonal with given $\kappa(D)$. We compare the relative accuracy of singular values as well as the orthogonality of left and right singular vectors computed by the Jacobi SVD algorithm with results computed using the SVD algorithm based on the matrix bi-diagonalization. When B is well-conditioned, the one-sided block-Jacobi algorithm inherits a high relative accuracy from its element-wise counterpart over a wide range of condition numbers $\kappa(A)$.

Keywords: singular value decomposition · one-sided block-Jacobi algorithm · preconditioning · dynamic ordering · relative accuracy

1 Introduction

In general, as a consequence of the Hoffman–Wielandt theorem [8], the algorithms for the singular value decomposition (SVD) based on the bi-diagonalization of matrix $A \in \mathbb{R}^{m \times n}$, $m \geq n$, only compute its singular values $\sigma_i(A)$ with an *absolute* accuracy:

$$|\hat{\sigma}_i(A) - \sigma_i(A)| \leq \sigma_{\max}(A)\, O(\varepsilon_M), \ 1 \leq i \leq n,$$

where $\hat{\sigma}_i(A)$ is the ith computed singular value, $\sigma_{\max}(A)$ is the maximal singular value of A, ε_M is the machine precision and the term $O(\varepsilon_M)$ includes the perturbation of A caused by its updates during computation. This means that the smallest singular values may be computed with a small relative accuracy. In contrast, the element-wise one-sided Jacobi SVD algorithm with the column-cyclic ordering and the preconditioning based on the QR decomposition (QRD) of A can achieve a high *relative* accuracy for all singular values, i.e.,

$$\frac{|\hat{\sigma}_i(A) - \sigma_i(A)|}{\sigma_i(A)} \leq O(\varepsilon_M) \min_S \kappa(AS), \ 1 \leq i \leq n, \tag{1}$$

R. Wyrzykowski et al. (Eds.): PPAM 2022, LNCS 13826, pp. 464–475, 2023.
https://doi.org/10.1007/978-3-031-30442-2_35

where S is a diagonal regular matrix that scales the columns of A. If $\kappa(AS) \ll \kappa(A)$ for some S, all singular values will be computed with high relative accuracy [6]. As shown in [9], a diagonal scaling by reciprocal Euclidean norms of columns of A (i.e., AS has all columns of unit norm) is nearly optimal.

Hence, for matrices of the form $A = BD$, where D is diagonal and B is random with columns of unit norm and a prescribed 2-norm condition number $\kappa(B)$, the relative error is mainly governed by $\kappa(B)$. This theoretical result was confirmed for the element-wise one-sided Jacobi SVD algorithm with column-cyclic ordering and preconditioning based on the QRD of A in [7] by numerical tests for small values of $\kappa(B)$ and a wide range of values of $\kappa(D)$. Here we test and analyze the relative accuracy of the one-sided block-Jacobi SVD algorithm (OSBJA) with dynamic ordering using approximate weights (see [1,2]) and compare it with the relative accuracy of the SVD algorithm based on the matrix bi-diagonalization (BIDSVDA). The same form of matrix A, $A = BD$, was adopted as in [7] with prescribed values of $\kappa(B)$ and $\kappa(D)$. Although both algorithms were serial, the conclusions also apply for their parallel versions.

2 One-Sided Block-Jacobi Algorithm with Preconditioning

The OSBJA is listed below as Algorithm 1 (see [3] for details of preconditioning).

Algorithm 1. *The OSBJA with Preconditioning and Dynamic Ordering*

Input: ℓ, $A = (A_1, A_2, \ldots A_\ell)$, each block column is $m \times n/\ell$
$bsw = \ell(\ell - 1)/2$
Compute the Gram matrix: $B = A^T A$
$[W, \Lambda] = \mathrm{EVD}(B)$
$A = AW$
Set: $V = W$
Compute the weights w_{rs}
Choose the pair (i, j) of block columns with the maximum weight $maxw$
$iter = 0$
while $(maxw \geq (2n/\ell)\,\varepsilon_\mathrm{M})$ and $(iter < 10\,bsw)$ **do**
    $iter = iter + 1$
    $G_{ij} = [A_i, A_j]$
    $[X_{ij}, \Sigma_{ij}] = \mathrm{SVD}(G_{ij})$
    $(A_i, A_j) = (A_i, A_j) * X_{ij}$
    $(V_i, V_j) = (V_i, V_j) * X_{ij}$
    Update the weights w_{rs}
    Choose the pair of block columns (i, j) with the maximum weight $maxw$
end while
$\sigma_r = \|A(:, r)\|_2$ (the Euclidean norm of the rth column of A, $1 \leq r \leq n$)
$U = A\,\mathrm{diag}(\sigma_r^{-1})$ (left singular vectors of A)
end

Its detailed description together with the analysis of its implementation in finite arithmetic can be found in [2,3]. Briefly, using the blocking factor ℓ, the input matrix is divided into ℓ block columns $(A_1, A_2, \ldots A_\ell)$, where each block column is of size $m \times n/\ell$. The variable bsw is the value of *block sweep*. Recall that in any cyclic ordering a block sweep is the number of consecutive iteration steps during which each off-diagonal block is zeroed exactly once. Although the dynamic ordering does not have such a property, it is useful to introduce this notion for a comparison of performance of the OSBJA with dynamic ordering with any Jacobi SVD algorithm based on a cyclic block ordering.

For any r, $1 \leq r \leq \ell$, let $\tilde{A}_r$ be normalized block column A_r where each column has the unit Euclidean norm. Taking any $\tilde{A}_s$, define the vector c_s as

$$c_s \equiv \frac{\tilde{A}_s \, e}{\|e\|_2}, \quad e = (1, 1, \ldots, 1)^T$$

as the *representative* vector of subspace span(A_s). Then the approximate weight w_{rs}, $r < s$, is defined as

$$w_{rs} \equiv \|\tilde{A}_r^T c_s\|_2 = \frac{\|\tilde{A}_r^T \tilde{A}_s \, e\|_2}{\|e\|_2}.$$

When the columns of blocks A_r and A_s are mutually orthogonal, $w_{rs} = 0$. A large, positive value of w_{rs} corresponds to highly mutually inclined block columns.

Inside the OSBJA, the SVD of each G_{ij} of size $m \times 2n/\ell$ was computed starting with its QRD, and then using the classical element-wise two-sided SVD algorithm on its square upper triangular factor R_{ij} of order $2n/\ell$. Recall the meaning of 'classical': The off-diagonal element with maximal modulus was zeroed in each iteration step. For these inner iterations, the following stopping criterion at inner iteration step k was used:

$$\|\text{off}(R_{ij}^{(k)})\|_F < \|R_{ij}\|_F \, \varepsilon_M \quad \text{or} \quad \max_{p \neq q} |R_{ij}^{(k)}(p,q)| < \sqrt{\frac{2}{n(n-1)}} \, \|R_{ij}\|_F \, \varepsilon_M, \quad (2)$$

where $\|R_{ij}\|_F$ and $\|\text{off}(R_{ij}^{(k)})\|_F$ is the Frobenius norm of R_{ij} and off-diagonal Frobenius norm of $R_{ij}^{(k)}$, respectively. Note that no Gram matrix was computed for the inner SVD.

3   Test Matrices

As mentioned above, the square test matrices of order n were of the form $A = BD$. A matrix B of order n was random with a prescribed $\kappa(B)$ and a decreasing geometric sequence of singular values lying in the interval $[\kappa(B)^{-1}, 1]$:

$$\sigma_i(B) = [\kappa(B)]^{-(i-1)/(n-1)}, \ 1 \leq i \leq n. \quad (3)$$

A matrix B was constructed as follows (see [7]). First, two random orthogonal matrices Q_1, Q_2 distributed uniformly according to the Haar measure were generated. If $\tilde{\Sigma}$ is diagonal with prescribed singular values from (3), then $C = Q_1 \tilde{\Sigma} Q_2$

was created. Second, for the matrix $C^T C$ there always exists an orhogonal Q_3 such that the diagonal entries of $Q_3^T (C^T C) Q_3$ are all equal to $\text{Trace}(C^T C)/n$ (see [4]). Then the matrix $B = CQ_3$ has all columns of the same Euclidean norm and singular values from (3).

A matrix D was diagonal with a prescribed $\kappa(D)$ and a decreasing arithmetic sequence of singular values on main diagonal:

$$\sigma_i(D) = 1 - \frac{i-1}{n-1}[1 - \kappa(D)^{-1}], \ 1 \le i \le n, \tag{4}$$

i.e., they lay in the interval $[\kappa(D)^{-1}, 1]$.

Since all columns of B had the same norm, the *scaling* of columns of A was controlled mainly by a diagonal matrix D. Furthermore, each test matrix A belonged to one *class* described by a pair $(\kappa(B), \kappa(D))$. Various values of $\kappa(B)$ and $\kappa(D)$ enabled to construct matrices A with a wide range of condition numbers $\kappa(A)$. Moreover, for a given class one could construct several independent random matrices A as to get some insight into the statistical behavior of that class.

Note that singular values $\sigma_i(A)$ were *not* simple functions of $\sigma_i(B)$ and $\sigma_i(D)$. However, it can be easily proved that $\kappa(A) \le \kappa(B)\kappa(D)$. Also the distribution of singular values A could not be deduced from distributions in B and D–except when $D = I$ and $\sigma_i(A) = \sigma_i(B)$ for all i.

Now suppose that for a given matrix A of order n its SVD, $A = U\Sigma V^T$, was computed by two algorithms: the OSBJA with dynamic ordering using approximate weights (see Algorithm 1) and some BIDSVDA (e.g., the routine svd in MATLAB). Denote the results computed in the OSBJA by a lower index 'jc', whereas those computed using the second algorithm by a lower index 'bd'. Further assume that the singular values at the end of computation are ordered in the same way (e.g., non-increasingly) in both cases. Finally, we needed 'exact' singular values for each matrix A, which were denoted by $\sigma_{i,\text{ex}}(A)$ and ordered in the same way. Note that the 'exact' singular values were computed using the variable precision arithmetic (vpa) with 32 decimal digits in MATLAB, while all other computations were performed in double precision. Then the relative accuracy of both SVD algorithms was measured by following three parameters (the results computed in double precision are denoted by a hat):

1. Maximal relative error in computed singular values:

$$\eta_{\text{jc}} = \max_{1 \le i \le n} \frac{|\hat{\sigma}_{i,\text{jc}}(A) - \sigma_{i,\text{ex}}(A)|}{\sigma_{i,\text{ex}}(A)}, \quad \eta_{\text{bd}} = \max_{1 \le i \le n} \frac{|\hat{\sigma}_{i,\text{bd}}(A) - \sigma_{i,\text{ex}}(A)|}{\sigma_{i,\text{ex}}(A)}. \tag{5}$$

2. Orthogonality of the computed left singular vectors:

$$\omega_{\text{jc}} = \|\hat{U}_{\text{jc}}^T \hat{U}_{\text{jc}} - I_n\|_{\text{F}}, \quad \omega_{\text{bd}} = \|\hat{U}_{\text{bd}}^T \hat{U}_{\text{bd}} - I_n\|_{\text{F}}. \tag{6}$$

3. Orthogonality of the computed right singular vectors:

$$\tau_{\text{jc}} = \|\hat{V}_{\text{jc}}^T \hat{V}_{\text{jc}} - I_n\|_{\text{F}}, \quad \tau_{\text{bd}} = \|\hat{V}_{\text{bd}}^T \hat{V}_{\text{bd}} - I_n\|_{\text{F}}. \tag{7}$$

4   Implementation in MATLAB

Algorithm 1 was implemented in MATLAB, v. 2020b, together with the creation of test matrices. Condition numbers $\kappa(B)$ were taken from the set $\mathcal{Z}_B = \{10^j, \, 1 \leq j \leq 4\}$, whereas those of $\kappa(D)$ from the set $\mathcal{Z}_B = \{10^j, \, 0 \leq j \leq 7\}$. For each class $(\kappa(B), \kappa(D))$, $nmat = 5$ random matrices $A = BD$ were constructed. For this purpose, the MATLAB function $B = $ gallery('randcolu', svB) was used where svB is the vector of singular values of matrix B. Note that before calling this function the singular values of B were properly scaled: The sum of their squares was equal to the number of matrix columns n. Then all columns of B had the unit Euclidean norm. Given $\kappa(D)$, the construction of diagonal matrix D was straightforward. In the experiment, square matrices of order $n = 500$ and blocking factor $\ell = 10$ were used.

Matrices $A = BD$ were created using three embedded cycles. The outermost cycle, $I = 1 : |\mathcal{Z}_B|$, where $|\mathcal{Z}_B|$ is the number of elements in the set $\mathcal{Z}_B$, computed a vector of singular values of B for given $\kappa(B)$ (see (3)). Similarly, the second cycle, $J = 1 : |\mathcal{Z}_D|$, computed a vector of singular values of D for given $\kappa(D)$ (see (4)). Finally, the innermost cycle, $K = 1 : nmat$, computed matrices B, D and $A = BD$.

The eigenvector matrix W of the Gram matrix $A^T A$, used for the preconditioning in the OSBJA, was computed using the MATLAB function eig(A' * A), where $A' = A^T$.

Matrices AW and A then entered the OSBJA and the MATLAB function svd, respectively, to compute the SVD of A using two different algorithms. The innermost loop (for index K) was repeated $nmat$ times, each time with a new random matrix B (but with the same $\kappa(B)$) and the same matrix D. Hence, together $|\mathcal{Z}_B| \times |\mathcal{Z}_D| \times nmat = 160$ matrices were analyzed. For each matrix, its global index $globind$ was computed as follows:

$$globind = (I - 1) \times |\mathcal{Z}_D| \times nmat + (J - 1) \times nmat + K.$$

Note that for a given (constant) $\kappa(B)$ there were $8 \times 5 = 40$ matrices when going through all values of $\kappa(D)$ and $nmat$.

Almost all computations were performed in double precision with $\varepsilon_M \approx 2.22 \times 10^{-16}$. However, for the computation of 'exact' singular values of A, the MATLAB function svd with 32 decimal digit accuracy was used: svd(vpa(A, 32)). Subsequently, the 'exact' singular values were rounded to double precision and served as the reference values for the computation of maximal relative errors η_{jc} and η_{bd} in (5).

5   Discussion of Numerical Results

We start with the estimated values of $\kappa(A)$ that are depicted in Fig. 1. As can be seen, the values of $\kappa(A)$ range from the very well-conditioned matrices with $\kappa(A) = 10$ for the class $(10, 1)$ (here A has the same singular values as B) up to very ill-conditioned ones with $\kappa(A) \approx 10^{10}$ for the class $(10^4, 10^7)$. In each class,

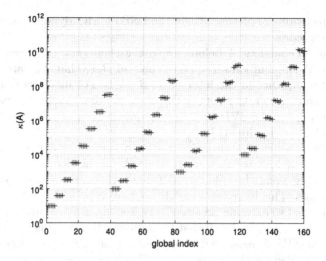

Fig. 1. Estimated values of $\kappa(A)$

all $nmat = 5$ random matrices have practically the same condition number. The increase of $\kappa(A)$ with global index is organized into 4 groups of 40 matrices, where each group corresponds to constant $\kappa(B)$ and variable $\kappa(D)$.

For a given class $(\kappa(B), \kappa(D))$, the maximal number of outer iterations needed for the convergence of the OSBJA is provided in Table 1. Note that for each class the *minimal* number of outer iterations was about 2-3 iterations less that the maximal one when going through $nmat = 5$ random matrices. In this sense, the OSBJA was very consistent.

Table 1. Maximal number of outer iterations in the OSBJA

$\kappa(B)\backslash\kappa(D)$	1	10	10^2	10^3	10^4	10^5	10^6	10^7
10	0	1	8	9	9	9	9	9
10^2	11	16	17	19	19	19	19	19
10^3	28	31	31	30	31	31	32	32
10^4	35	37	37	37	37	37	37	41

Several interesting observations can be made by analyzing Fig. 1 and Table 1. The number of iterations clearly depends on $\kappa(B)$, and is practically constant for given $\kappa(B)$ and increasing $\kappa(D)$. This means that for matrices $A = BD$ the column-scaling of B by diagonal D is not important for the convergence of the OSBJA. It is well-known that the element-wise Jacobi algorithm with column-cyclic ordering 'sees' through the column scaling of A (compare with (1)), and its high relative accuracy is the consequence of this property. Our experiments show that this feature is present also in the OSBJA with dynamic ordering using approximate weights.

Note that all matrices A belonging to the class $(\kappa(B), 1)$ (first column in Table 1) have all singular values equal to those of B, so that they are distributed as a geometric sequence in the interval $[\kappa(B)^{-1}, 1]$. For matrices from the class $(10, 1)$ there were *no* iterations of the OSBJA needed; a simple application of the preconditioning gave the SVD of A with required accuracy. In other words, all computed weights were already less than $2n\varepsilon_M/\ell \approx 2.22 \times 10^{-14}$ at the beginning of the OSBJA. Very similar situation can be observed for matrices in the class $(10, 10)$ where only one iteration of the OSBJA was needed.

When moving along the columns of Table 1, the number of iterations in the OSBJA increases. This increase is clearly controlled by $\kappa(B)$ and is very consistent if one forgets two extreme classes of very well-conditioned matrices discussed in the previous paragraph. Recall that according to the analysis in [3] the quality of preconditioner W decreases with increasing value of $\kappa(A)$, so that more outer iterations are needed for the convergence. This is confirmed by increasing numbers of iterations in any fixed column of Table 1 whereby $\kappa(A)$ also increases. However, it is *not* confirmed by an approximately *constant* number of iterations along any fixed row of Table 1, where $\kappa(A)$ also increases (compare with Fig. 1). To explain this observation one needs more information about the MATLAB EVD function `eig`, namely, what algorithm is used for the EVD of a symmetric Gram matrix $A^T A$ in the factored form. Note that in our experiment the Gram matrix had a special structure $DB^T BD$ with $10^2 \leq \kappa(B^T B) \leq 10^8$. Hence, a well- or ill-conditioned 'core' matrix $B^T B$ had its rows and columns scaled by the same diagonal matrix D. It is possible that these properties enable to compute such W that AW is close to range(U) *regardless* of $\kappa(D)$.

It is interesting to note, that the OSBJA converged in *less than one block sweep* for all matrices A with a huge range of $\kappa(A)$ covering 10 orders of magnitude (in our case, $bsw = 45$ outer iterations). This is an excellent result, especially w.r.t. the element-wise Jacobi SVD algorithm with some cyclic ordering, which usually requires 5–8 sweeps for convergence. It also explains why the parallel OSBJA with dynamic ordering is comparable in speed with some parallel SVD algorithms based on bi-diagonalization–see [5].

The comparison of achieved relative accuracy in computing singular values and orthogonality of computed left and right singular vectors for the OSBJA and BIDSVDA is provided in Fig. 2.

The final maximal weight for the OSBJA is depicted on Fig. 2a, where the thick horizontal line denotes the convergence tolerance $2n\varepsilon_M/\ell \approx 2.22 \times 10^{-14}$. Clearly, all maximal weights are located below that horizontal line, some of them substantially below.

Figure 2b contains a comparison of achieved relative accuracy in computed singular values between the OSBJA and BIDSVDA. For the first two values of $\kappa(B) = 10$ and 10^2 (global indices in the interval $[1, 80]$), the OSBJA computes all singular values of A with the relative accuracy of 10^{-15}, while the BIDSVDA can be more than 2 orders of magnitude worse. The first jump in η_{jc} comes

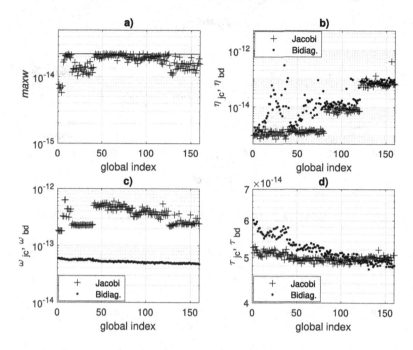

Fig. 2. Relative accuracy of the OSBJA and BIDSVDA

with $\kappa(B) = 10^3$ (global indices in $[81, 120]$), the second one with $\kappa(B) = 10^4$ (global indices in $[121, 160]$). Each jump in η_{jc} means a loss of one decimal digit of relative accuracy. While for $\kappa(B) = 10^3$ the OSBJA has still a better relative accuracy than the BIDSVDA, this is not true for $\kappa(B) = 10^4$ where the OSBJA can achieve even *lower* relative accuracy than the BIDSVDA. All these results confirm the upper bound in (1) (note that in our notation $AS = B$). In other words, if $B = AS$ is ill-conditioned, the OSBJA may loose its property to compute all singular values with high relative accuracy.

More insight into the loss of relative accuracy in the OSBJA is enabled by Fig. 3. Its upper part repeats (albeit with better resolution) Fig. 2b. Additionally, the lower part depicts the index of that singular value of A at which η_{jc} was achieved. As can be clearly seen, for well-conditioned B with $10 \leq \kappa(B) \leq 10^2$ (global indices in $[1, 80]$), the index of η_{jc} is distributed almost randomly and the maximal relative error is sometimes achieved for maximal singular value of A with index 1 (recall that the singular values are ordered non-increasingly). However, the situation changes substantially for $10^3 \leq \kappa(B) \leq 10^4$ (global indices in $[81, 160]$), where the index of η_{jc} is limited to the interval $[400, 500]$, i.e., to the smallest singular values of A. This observation can be, at least partially, explained as follows. Recall that matrices B have geometrically distributed singular values in the interval $[(\kappa(B)^{-1}, 1]$, which means that for large values of $\kappa(B)$ they form tight clusters in the vicinity of $\sigma_n(B) = \sigma_{\min}(B)$. Although these clusters are modified by arithmetically distributed singular values of D,

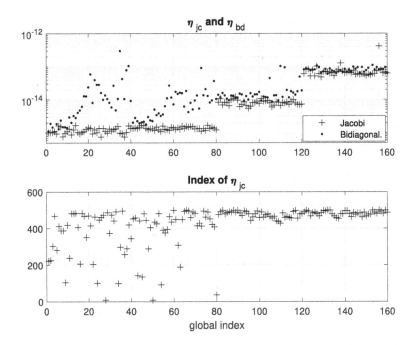

Fig. 3. Maximal relative error in computed singular values and the index of maximal relative error for the OSBJA

they may be dispersed only partially, and even new tight clusters can be formed. Additionally, for very ill-conditioned matrices A with $\kappa(A) > 10^8$ (see Fig. 1), $\sigma_{\min}(A)$ can be tiny, say, of order 10^{-9}. Apparently, for both algorithms it is then difficult to compute members of tight clusters and/or tiny singular values with high relative accuracy.

Figure 2c contains the comparison of the loss of orthogonality of computed left singular vectors by both algorithms. As can be seen, for the BIDSVDA the parameter $\omega_{\mathrm{bd}} \approx 5 \times 10^{-14}$ for all matrices, whereas for the OSBJA ω_{jc} varies in the interval $[2 \times 10^{-13}, 6 \times 10^{-13}]$ and is about one order of magnitude larger. In our experience, the level of orthogonality of left singular vectors computed by the OSBJA cannot be improved easily. Recall that at the end of the OSBJA the Euclidean norms of columns of the iterated matrix A are singular values of A, and after scaling of the ith column by $(\hat{\sigma}_i(A))^{-1}$ one obtains the ith column of $\hat{U}_{\mathrm{jc}}$. In each outer iteration step, two block columns of A are updated by an orthogonal transformation X_{ij}, which is the accumulation of the Givens rotations in the inner SVD of G_{ij} (see Algorithm 1). Hence, an accumulation of rounding errors in the computation of X_{ij}, an inaccuracy of X_{ij} due to the stopping criterion in the inner SVD as well as an inexact update of two block columns (A_i, A_j) may result in the loss of orthogonality of computed left singular vectors.

Finally, Fig. 2d depicts the loss of orthogonality of computed right singular vectors. Note that in Algorithm 1 these vectors are updated by the same accumulated orthogonal matrix X_{ij} as the iterated matrix A, but initially $\hat{V}_{jc} = W$, where W is the preconditioner, i.e., the matrix of eigenvectors of $A^T A$. Hence, the orthogonality of final $\hat{V}_{jc}$ critically depends on the orthogonality of computed W (see the analysis in [3]). As can be observed, one has $\tau_{jc} \approx 5 \times 10^{-14}$ for all matrices, which is about one order of magnitude better than ω_{jc} in Fig. 2c.

However, for very ill-conditioned matrices with $\kappa(A) > 10^8$ (see Fig. 1, global indices in [140, 160]) the preconditioner W looses its orthogonality, so that τ_{jc} starts to increase. Our numerical experiment was extended with $\kappa(B) = 10^5$ and all 8 values of $\kappa(D)$ used above, so that additional 40 matrices were processed with $\kappa(A) \in [10^5, 10^{11}]$ and global indices in [161, 200]. In Fig. 4, the loss of orthogonality of computed right singular vectors is depicted. As can be observed, τ_{jc} may almost double for matrices in classes $(10^4, \kappa(D))$ with $\kappa(D) > 10^2$ (global indices in [176, 200]).

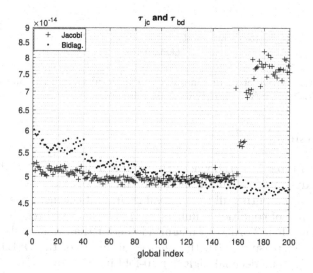

Fig. 4. Loss of orthogonality of right singular vectors in extended experiment

If the preconditioner W looses its orthogonality, the SVD of the preconditioned AW may be a severe perturbation of that of A. This conclusion is confirmed by Fig. 5. Besides an additional jump in η_{jc} for matrices with $\kappa(B) = 10^5$ (global indices in [161, 200]) one can observe another significant increase of η_{jc} by 2 orders of magnitude for some matrices in the classes $(10^5, 10^6)$ and $(10^5, 10^7)$ (global indices in [191, 200]). It seems that for a very ill-conditioned A, the computation of a 'sufficiently' orthogonal W by eig($A'*A$) in MATLAB has its limits in double precision. One possible explanation may be the presence of tight clusters of eigenvalues of the Gram matrix $A^T A$ (which are the squares of singular values of A) that cause an ill-conditioning of the corresponding eigenvectors.

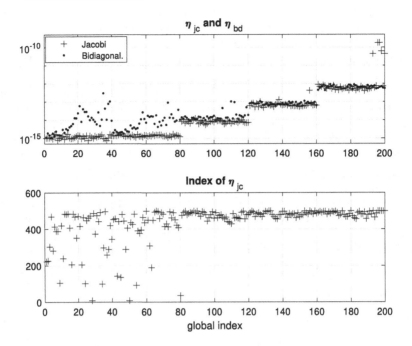

Fig. 5. Maximal relative error in computed singular values and the index of maximal relative error for the OSBJA in extended experiment

6   Conclusions

For matrices of type $A = BD$, where B is well-conditioned and D diagonal, the OSBJA with dynamic ordering using approximate weights inherits a high relative accuracy in computing all singular values from its element-wise counterpart over a wide range of condition numbers $\kappa(A)$. The achieved relative accuracy is sometimes more than 2 orders of magnitude better than that of the BIDSVDA. However, with increasing $\kappa(B)$, the relative accuracy of the OSBJA decreases by approximately one decimal digit per 10-fold increase of $\kappa(B)$.

The use of the orthogonal eigenvector matrix W of the Gram matrix $A^T A$ as a preconditioner gives fast convergence of the OSBJA for almost all matrices A, but it has its limits for huge values of $\kappa(A^T A)$. Another open issue is the problem of achieving a better orthogonality of computed left singular vectors $\hat{U}_{\mathrm{jc}}$ by an iterative orthogonalization of the columns of A.

Acknowledgment. Authors were supported by the VEGA grant no. 2/0015/20.

References

1. Bečka, M., Okša, G., Vajteršic, M.: New dynamic orderings for the parallel one-sided block-Jacobi SVD algorithm. Parallel Proc. Lett. Ser. **25**, 1–19 (2015). https://doi.org/10.1142/S0129626415500036

2. Bečka, M., Okša, G., Vidličková, E.: New preconditioning for the one-sided block-Jacobi SVD algorithm. In: Wyrzykowski, R., et al. PPAM17, Springer Nature. LNCS, vol. 10777, pp. 590–599. Springer, Cham (2018). https://doi.org/10.1007/978-3-310-78024-5_51

3. Bečka, M., Okša, G.: Preconditioned Jacobi SVD algorithm outperforms PDGESVD. In: Wyrzykowski, R., et al. (Eds.) PPAM19, Springer Nature. LNCS, vol. 12043, pp. 555–566. Springer, Cham (2020). https://doi.org/10.1007/978-3-030-43229-4_47

4. Davies, P.I., Higham, N.J.: Numerically stable generation of correlation matrices and their factors. BIT Numer. Math. Ser. **40**, 640–651 (2000). https://doi.org/10.1023/A:1022384216930

5. Dongarra, J., et al.: The singular value decomposition: anatomy of optimizing an algorithm for extreme scale. SIAM Rev. Ser. **60**, 808–865 (2018). https://doi.org/10.1137/17M1117732

6. Drmač, Z., Veselić, K.: New fast and accurate Jacobi SVD algorithm: I. SIAM J. Matrix Anal. Appl. Ser. **29**, 1322–1342 (2008). https://doi.org/10.1137/050639193

7. Drmač, Z., Veselić, K.: New fast and accurate Jacobi SVD algorithm: II. SIAM J. Matrix Anal. Appl. Ser. **29**, 1343–1362 (2008). https://doi.org/10.1137/05063920X

8. Hoffman, A.J., Wielandt, H.W.: The variation of the spectrum of a normal matrix. Duke Math. J. Ser. **20**, 37–39 (1953). https://doi.org/10.1215/S0012-7094-53-02004-3

9. van der Sluis, A.: Condition numbers and equilibration of matrices. Numer. Math. Ser. **14**, 14–23 (1969). https://doi.org/10.1007/BF02165096

Author Index

R. Wyrzykowski et al. (Eds.): PPAM 2022, LNCS 13826, pp. 477–480, 2023.
https://doi.org/10.1007/978-3-031-30442-2

Printed in the United States
by Baker & Taylor Publisher Services

Printed in the United States
by Baker & Taylor Publisher Services